THE PROVINCIAL STATE IN CANADA

THE PROVINCIAL STATE IN CANADA

Politics in the Provinces and Territories

EDITED BY
KEITH BROWNSEY & MICHAEL HOWLETT

Canadian Cataloguing in Publication Data

Main entry under title:
The provincial state in Canada: politics in the provinces and territories

Includes bibliographical references and index.
ISBN 1-55111-368-6

1. Provincial governments – Canada.* 2. Canada – Politics and government – 20th century.
I. Brownsey, Keith, 1955- II. Howlett, Michael, 1955- .

JL198.P772 2000 971.06 C00-932736-3

BROADVIEW PRESS LTD.,
is an independent, international publishing house, incorporated in 1985.

NORTH AMERICA
P.O. Box 1243,
Peterborough, Ontario,
Canada K9J 7H5

3576 California Road,
Orchard Park, NY 14127

Tel: (705) 743-8990;
Fax: (705) 743-8353
customerservice@broadviewpress.com
www.broadviewpress.com

AUSTRALIA
St. Clair Press,
P.O. Box 287, Rozelle, NSW 2039
Tel: (02) 818-1942; Fax: (02) 418-1923

UNITED KINGDOM
Turpin Distribution Services Ltd.,
Blackhorse Rd, Letchworth,
Hertfordshire SG6 1HN
Tel: (1462) 672555;
Fax: (1462) 480947
turpin@rsc.org

Broadview Press gratefully acknowledges the financial support of the Book Publishing Industry Development Program, Ministry of Canadian Heritage, Government of Canada.

Cover Design by Black Eye Design, Inc.
Interior pages designed by Liz Broes, Black Eye Design, Inc.

PRINTED IN CANADA

For Philip, Duncan, and Sophia; Alex and Anna

CONTENTS

ACKNOWLEDGEMENTS

We cannot begin to thank the many individuals who have helped in this project. Our greatest debt is to the contributors for their patience and forbearance in seeing this edition through to publication and in making necessary—sometimes frustrating—additions to their chapters as provincial election after provincial election was called during the run-up to publication. We would also like to thank Ed Black and Alan Cairns for their groundbreaking work on the politics and government of Canada's provinces, and Don Blake and Norman Ruff for awakening in us an interest in provincial political life.

Several individuals deserve special mention. At Simon Fraser University useful comments and advice were received at various stages in the the project from Rebecca Raglon, Paddy Smith, Alex Netherton, David Laycock, Jim Bickerton, and the many students who used draft chapters in course work. At Mount Royal College we would like to thank Bruce Foster and Duane Bratt for their useful and insightful comments on various chapters. Kathryn Brownsey proofread the manuscript and did more than her share of child-rearing duty. Philip, Duncan, and Sophia Brownsey and Alex and Anna Howlett provided moral support and encouragement throughout the project.

At Broadview Press we would like to thank both Michael Harrison and Don LePan for taking on this project at an advanced stage of development. Barbara Conolly and Betsy Struthers are the true makers of this book. Their efforts are greatly appreciated.

LIST OF TABLES

1 INTRODUCTION

The Provincial State in Canada

KEITH BROWNSEY AND MICHAEL HOWLETT

One of the enduring myths of Canadian political life is that John A. Macdonald and the other Fathers of Confederation believed the provinces would wither away. Macdonald and his colleagues argued that the British North America Act gave the important powers to the federal government and that the provinces would become no more than municipal governments providing a few insignificant services to individuals and communities within their boundaries.[1] But Macdonald was wrong. The provinces have become much more than municipal governments. Not only have the powers assigned to them in the original Confederation agreement become increasingly important, the very fact that they are separate political entities has given them the institutional and political legitimacy to seek further powers and support from the national government, the judiciary, and their own constituents.[2]

One of the most neglected areas in the study of Canadian history and politics is the development of the provincial state. While there has been much written over the past several decades about province building and "the state" in Canada, little effort has been made to understand the similarities and differences in the political life of Canada's provinces and territories. Although there are a number of studies that examine particular policies in the provinces—from comparisons of environmental regulation to economic development strategies to social services and social assistance programs—there has been surprisingly little effort made to understand the similarities and peculiarities of the politics and governments of Canada's provinces and territories.

Over the last few years there have been a number of studies focusing on "state." There is debate over the autonomous state, the state in capitalist society, the Canadian state, and the globalization and convergence of the world state system. The literature is extensive; it encompasses a wide ideological range from Weber/Hintze concepts of the rational and autonomous state to crude instrumental Marxist notions of the state as captive of the bourgeoisie. What the literature on Canada's provinces neglects is the question of whether Canadian provinces and territories are "states" in the same sense as the better-known nation states of the world system.

States, as Rueschemeyer and Evans claim, are sets of organizations that have the ability to make binding decisions for people and organizations located within a territory. They are a mix of social tensions, class struggles, and external influences that define their territory and frame their policy communities.[3] They are, moreover, able to implement these decisions by force if necessary.[4] In this sense Canada's provinces and territories qualify as states. Not only are they constitutionally empowered to make binding decisions on their residents, they are shaped and defined by the very constitutional arrangements that give them their authority as much as they are by their internal class structures and external economic relations.[5]

Canada's provinces and territories share a number of ideological and institutional features which have created a system of interaction and discourse in Canada that helps to hold the country together. But this is only one part of the federal-provincial dialectic. Faced with specific problems—the collapse of the forestry industry or the preservation of a distinct linguistic and cultural community—the provinces have responded in ways that constitute variations on the common Canadian theme. Although there is an increasing literature on the politics of individual provinces, there have been surprisingly few overviews of provincial and territorial politics in Canada. As well, these collections have focused on the themes of political culture and electoral analysis or have been descriptive histories. None has attempted an overview of provincial politics in Canada within the broadly defined intellectual tradition of political economy. The essays in this volume provide very different insights into provincial political life than previous collections, and while there are thematic differences they may all be regarded as belonging to that tradition of political economy.[6]

Historically Canada's provinces have been characterized by their distinctiveness and, at the same time, by a multiplicity of national and regional centres and subcentres, both political and economic, which has led to a convergence[7] in policies and programs. These characteristics can be categorized as follows. First, the political and economic centres in Canada have always claimed some autonomy from each other: Montreal from Toronto, Calgary from Vancouver. Second, each of these centres could support its claim by a certain amount of political, economic, or cultural power. Third, there have developed within Canada secondary centres that have some degree of autonomy and claim a certain amount of regional influence. Examples of these secondary centres are Saint John, St. John's, Quebec City, and Victoria.

These general characteristics combine with such factors as the structure of the predominant elites and certain political-geographical conditions to generate in Canada a very high degree of cross-cutting social, political, and economic orientations. This heterogeneity within Canadian society is evident in the number of political, economic, and social divisions that are re-enacted in the language of national political life. For example, the divisions between Quebec and the Rest of Canada, between the Atlantic region and the Prairie West, between British Columbia and Ontario, and between the North and the South are obvious but relevant manifestations of these various orientations. It is these divisions that explain some of the distinctive characteristics of government and politics in Canada's provinces and territories.

Out of these qualities of provincial life have developed two historical patterns. First, there has been a continuous connection between the construction of regional and national centres and the process of building economic, cultural and political institutions. Institution building in the provinces and territories has been essential to what various authors have described as "province-building." The strength of provincial governments has been judged according to their capacity to construct institutions such as a provincial bureaucracy, provide a diversified economic structure, and maintain social harmony. Second, there has also been competition between different groups or elites within the provinces over access to and control of these local centres of power. It is this competition for control of provincial institutions that has led to confrontation between the different elements of provincial society over the proper role and purpose of provincial and territorial government. In other words, different interests within provincial societies have had differing ideological visions of the purpose and content of provincial and territorial government.

There is another dimension to these traditional political and ideological battles in Canada: that is, provincial and territorial political life has turned not only on local issues of government intervention in the market place and the legitimacy of the welfare state, but also on such larger trans-provincial tensions as those between strong provinces and strong central governments, or between centralization and decentralization of Canadian federalism.[8]

Associated with the institutions of Canadian provincial and territorial life has been the development of unique patterns of change. These patterns are characterized by a predisposition of elites aligned with the federal government to be transmitters of economic, political, and social innovations. There has also been a tendency on the part of provincial and territorial elites to establish close relations with a broader social stratum than the elites of the central government and hence with the movements of protest and reform. Finally, there is an accompanying predisposition for provincial and territorial elites and groups to develop institutions away and apart from the central or national government.

While Canadian provinces share many of the characteristics of other sub-national units in federal states they have also tended to develop specific institutional profiles of their own. The most common problem for the provinces has been, and remains, the maintenance of a general standard of economic and socio-cultural development which is at more or less the same level as that prevailing in the most prosperous areas. Because of attempts to maintain such a standard, certain problems occur. As a number of social scientists have pointed out in a variety of contexts, small internal markets such as those found in the provinces and territories are not—with a few exceptions—large enough to obtain sufficient economies of scale necessary for autarchous development.

The politics of Canada's provinces and territories, therefore, has been shaped very frequently by the various responses of their governments to rapidly changing economic circumstances. The economies of the provinces and territories are neither large enough nor diversified enough to produce all that the province needs nor to consume all that it produces. The result is that provinces have tended to specialize for external markets. This specialization is based on geographic location, resources, social structure, and cultural traditions. Quebec, for example, has, with the help of the federal government, attempted to specialize in aerospace, pharmaceuticals and other technology-intensive goods and services in order to offset a reliance on declining industries such as low-wage textile and footwear manufacturing and resource exploitation. Because of their particular resource endowments other provinces have tended to specialize in particular goods such as grain, fish products, oil and natural gas, automobiles, and forest products. This specialization has been further reinforced by "the pressures of a liberal international economy."[9] Yet unlike a number of small European states, the provinces and territories have not been able to make the necessary economic adjustments to the new globalized economy without political, economic, and social dislocations, such as those experienced in the Atlantic provinces since the 1970s, British Columbia in the mid 1980s and again in the late 1990s, and Ontario and Alberta in the 1990s.

Whatever the response to changing economic conditions, specialization has created a dependency upon, and a sensitivity to, changes in international markets. As Saskatchewan's grain farmers have understood for generations, a province or territory cannot directly influence the demand for its products. Nevertheless, different provinces and territories have developed different strategies for coping with these problems. Alberta, for example, tried in the 1970s and 1980s to lessen its dependence on oil and natural gas through generous incentive programs and loan guarantees to technology-based industry, pulp and paper mills and, more recently, agribusiness. The failure of these projects left the province in a precarious fiscal situation that reminded many of the fiscal and economic troubles of the 1930s. Under the neo-conservative regime of Mike Harris, Ontario has attempted to deal with its fiscal and economic crisis through tax cuts and program reduction and elimination. Instead of policies and programs designed to promote economic flexibility and political stability, the Ontario government, like its predecessors, has relied on crisis management and the free market with little thought or money given to long-range solutions. Yet every province and territory in Canada appears to have converged on spending cuts, program elimination, privatization, and deregulation as necessary steps in coping with economies increasingly vulnerable to a liberalized international trading regime.

These problems are present not only in the economic life of the provinces and territories but also in the areas of cultural, technological, social, and political life. In the field of technology one of the major problems is how various scientific discoveries with economic promise can be exploited when the necessary investment in facilities and personnel is not forthcoming in Canada from either private or public sources. The small scientific communities in the provinces and territories face a problem of maintaining their autonomy and distinctiveness from either transnational corporations or the larger and better funded scientific communities in the United States, Western Europe, and Asia. In the area of education the provinces and territories are under enormous international pressure to bring their educational systems into line with those in Japan and the European Community as well as other nations.[10] As trade barriers continue to crumble in Canada—not only in external markets but internally as well—provincial societies are finding it increasingly necessary to standardize their educational systems with those in their competitors' jurisdictions. In order to compete in the globalized economy, a trained and flexible work force, as Robert Reich argues, is increasingly necessary.[11] But this standardization may endanger the distinctive cultural identities of provincial and territorial societies. Instead of accepting the more universal reforms of their economic competitors, provinces and territories may emphasize their own traditions, history, and internal problems. In terms of culture, each province and territory is faced with the issue of how to absorb the flood of cultural "goods and services" from the United States and elsewhere and still maintain its own identity.

Nevertheless, the types of specialization open to Canada's provinces and territories and the nature of their economic circumstances may change over time. One of the problems they have encountered is a reliance on a single international market. Any downward shift in the demand for the product(s) they produce leads to both economic and social problems that are destructive of provincial and territorial society. The classic Canadian example of this is Saskatchewan's dependence on the production of grain and oil seeds. Since 1900 Saskatchewan has adapted to a particular type of international market and pattern of trade. With powerful ministers in Ottawa the province had been able to focus the national government's attention on its needs in the international and domestic setting. But once grain prices begin to decline—as they first did in the 1920s and again in the 1980s—there is little that either the provincial or federal government can do for Saskatchewan's farmers. The province did not and does not have enough flexibility to change. The problems of economic flexibility faced by Saskatchewan confront all of Canada's other provinces and territories.

In one way or another all of the essays in this volume speak to the questions of the preservation of distinct cultures and traditions amidst the exigencies of the international marketplace—what may be referred to as the issue of divergence and convergence in the age of global capital. Each of the chapters examines the development of a provincial state in Canada and the efforts of provincial governments to respond to rapidly changing political and economic circumstances. While the ten provinces and three territories have sought different solutions to these questions they are remarkably similar in their methods. Governments of both the left and the right have cut spending and programs in order to balance their budgets and reduce debt and many have lowered taxes in order to preserve and foster economic growth. This process has seen a convergence of policy across the country.

The provincial state is seen as an integral part of economic and social development in all of Canada's provinces and territories. Each of the authors makes connections between the rise of provincial and territorial governments and various social and economic policies. Despite claims to the contrary, provinces and territories have not been passive bystanders willing to act simply as rule makers and umpires. As the chapters indicate, in the contemporary era they have aggressively adopted policies of privatization, deregulation, and spending cuts in order to deal with a range of social and economic forces produced by free trade and global markets.

In spite of the apparent convergence of many policies, the essays attempt to situate the actions of each provincial and territorial government within its political and social context. Several of the authors describe the provincial (and territorial) state as an independent actor, but they never forget the context within which those actors operate. Although territorial and provincial governments are not viewed simply as instruments in the hands of a particular social class, it is this cultural, historical, and social context that gives each territory and province its unique character.

CHAPTER BY CHAPTER OVERVIEW

While each chapter takes into account the varied political, social, historical, cultural, and economic circumstances of the various provinces, they also reveal the similarities that exist between and among otherwise disparate jurisdictions. Valerie Summers in her chapter, "Between a Rock and a Hard Place: Regime Change in Newfoundland," and James Bickerton in "Nova Scotia: The Political Economy of Regime Change," for example, write of the dependency of the Atlantic region on the political and economic institutions of central Canada. Bickerton argues that decentralization of power from Ottawa to the provinces brings increased economic hardship and political instability for Nova Scotia, while Summers claims that the continuing devolution of responsibility to the provinces and the decline in federal fiscal transfers creates even greater problem for Newfoundland's political and economic stability.

In a similar vein, David Milne in his overview of the development of political life in Prince Edward Island, "Politics in a Beleaguered Garden," describes the continuous struggle of the provincial government to reflect and maintain a rural, agricultural life in Canada's smallest province. While Milne focuses on the sustaining myth of a traditional agricultural society, Hugh Mellon in his overview of politics in New Brunswick, "The Challenge of New Brunswick Politics," describes the modernizing efforts of the Liberal government of Frank McKenna to deal with dwindling federal transfers, the decline of traditional resource industries, and the impact of North American free trade and global markets. Mellon suggests that although he is often praised for his innovations, judgement must be reserved on whether or not McKenna's efforts to deal with these problems have been successful.

Alex Netherton in his study of the evolution of Manitoba politics also focuses on the nature of change in the dominant provincial ideological paradigm. No provincial government, he argues, can ignore the impact of globalization and its impact on political life. The era of Keynesian intervention is over and has been replaced by a greater reliance on the free market. Fiscal austerity, privatization, and deregulation now dominate the political agenda. A similar pattern of transition is the focus of Ken Rasmussen in "Saskatchewan: From Entrepreneurial State to Embedded State." Rasmussen describes the transition from an era of state capitalism to an the era of globalization. He argues that "globalization, budget deficits, and reductions in federal transfers have simultaneously reduced the autonomy of the Saskatchewan state as an independent actor, but at the same time forced it to act decisively with regard to local interests in the name of restructuring." As in the other chapters, Rasmussen discusses the efforts by the provincial government to find an optimum set of social, economic, and political arrangements to help ease the pains of regional and global integration.

Peter J. Smith focuses on the changes in Alberta society since World War II and their impact on provincial politics and policy. He argues that certain elements of the capitalist class—the transnational corporations and the private-sector middle class—have influenced government policy in their favour with the promise of further economic development. But Smith claims that Albertans have witnessed a change from the politics of plenty in the 1970s to the politics of scarcity and conflict due to declining revenues from the oil and gas sector. In effect, Alberta has become "a province just like all the others." With declining resources the provincial government has continued to favour economic development over social programs. What is new in the most recent period is that the province has abandoned its earlier program of direct state intervention and loan guarantees, in favour of privatization, deregulation, and cutbacks in social programs.

On a different note, in "The Northwest Territories: Old and New: Class Politics on the Northern Frontier," Peter Clancy examines the evolution of a hunter-gatherer society into a modern administrative state. He argues that the particular social patterns of northern life and ethnicity have influenced the development of an unique type of politics in the Northwest Territories that reflects the mode of production found in the region. The class structure that appears to dominate politics in the Northwest Territories is moreover complicated by a strong ethnic overlay that sees First Nations concentrated at the margins of the wage labour market.

This perspective complements both Graham White and Jack Hicks in their discussion of the new territory of Nunavut and Floyd McCormick in his description of the politics of the Yukon. Hicks and White examine the reasons for the creation of Nunavut—the first government in recent Canadian history to be dominated by a First Nation—and the complex set of social and political relations emerging in this new entity. Similarly, McCormick argues that recent land claims settlements in the Yukon will have an enormous influence on the future political life of this territory.

There are also interesting similarities and contrasts revealed in the chapters on Quebec and Ontario. The rise of the Quebec state stands in sharp contrast to the laissez-faire, free-market approach to state intervention in Ontario. From the beginning of Quebec's Quiet Revolution in the 1960s, Quebec and Ontario have taken divergent paths. The Quebec state, Luc Bernier argues, developed a comprehensive strategy for economic development that saw the development of regular consultation between business, labour and government. Bernier notes that institutional changes to concentrate capital and develop provincial industry have been underway since the early 1960s with such projects as the nationalization of electrical power in Quebec and the establishment of the caisse de dépôt.

On the other hand, successive Ontario governments have sought only to maintain a favourable environment for investment. While the Liberal government of David Peterson and its successor New Democrats led by Bob Rae promised to begin a process of economic planning and enhanced state intervention, Greg Albo and Robert McDermid argue that the election of the Progressive Conservatives under Mike Harris in June 1995 signalled a return to free-market solutions and an end to provincial efforts at progressive income redistribution and economic planning. Even Quebec under Lucien Bouchard has adopted many of the prescriptions of his neo-conservative colleagues across the country, such as restructuring of program delivery, cuts to spending, and deregulation. This change in direction for the Quebec state may signal a closer alignment of economic and fiscal policy between it and the other provinces. Interestingly, however, this may well occur without closer political ties. In fact, competition for investment and markets may lessen the ties among the provinces and regions and exacerbate an already precarious national constitutional situation.

The exception to the convergence of provincial policies and politics is British Columbia. As Howlett and Brownsey argue, in the 1980s the government of British Columbia curtailed various social programs and made substantial cuts in the civil service while spending billions of dollars on a world's fair and the development of the province's northeast coal fields. The New Democratic party government of Glen Clark continued the interventionist tradition of his "free market" predecessors with subsidies and loan guarantees to several corporations in the resource sector, as well as continued deficit budgeting and an active industrial policy promoting hi-tech ventures such as fast catamaran ferry construction. The authors argue that British Columbia's particular class configurations account for this anomaly among Canada's provinces, although it too is likely to change course in the very near future.

The final chapter, "Comparative Provincial Politics: A Review," provides an overview of the various approaches and themes in the study of Canada's provinces and territories. Here Christopher Dunn again asserts that the provinces are becoming increasingly similar and emphasizes the theme of convergence and divergence.

The following chapters present a variety of issues and approaches. New ideas and different ways of understanding the provincial state have been used. Yet despite their differences they all seek to expand the intellectual tradition of Canadian political economy. The willingness to try novel approaches to explain political life in Canada's provinces and territories makes these essays distinctive and contributes to their ability to shed light on the continued development of Canada's increasingly important sub-national actors.

NOTES

1 Donald Creighton, *The Road to Confederation. The Emergence of Canada*: 1863–1867 (Toronto: MacMillan, 1964), 164–65.

2 Alan C. Cairns, "The Governments and Societies of Canadian Federalism," *Canadian Journal of Political Science X* (December 1977): 695–734.

3 Otto Hintze, "The Formation Of States And Constitutional Development: A Study In History And Politics," *The Historical Essays of Otto Hintze*, ed. and trans. Felix Gilbert (New York: Oxford University Press, 1975), 159–61.

4 Dietrich Rueschemeyer and Peter B. Evans, "The State and Economic Transformation: Toward an Analysis of the Conditions Underlying Effective Intervention," *Bringing the State Back In*, eds. Peter B. Evans, Dietrich Rueschemeyer, and Theda Skocpol (New York: Cambridge University Press, 1985), 46–47.

5 Alan C. Cairns, "The Governments and Societies of Canadian Federalism," 695–725.

6 The four best known collections or overviews of provincial politics in Canada are: David J. Bellamy, Jon H. Pammet, and Donald C. Rowat eds., *The Provincial Political Systems. Comparative Essays* (Agincourt, ON: Methuen, 1976); David Elkins and Richard Simeon, eds., *Small Worlds: Provinces and Parties in Canadian Political Life* (Agincourt: Methuen, 1980); Martin Robin ed., *Canada's Provincial Politics* (Scarborough: Prentice Hall Canada, 1978); and Rand Dyck, *Provincial Politics in Canada* 2nd ed. (Scarborough: Prentice Hall Canada, 1991).

7 For an overview of the concept of convergence see Colin Bennett, "Review Article: What is Policy Convergence and What Causes It?" *British Journal of Political Science* 21 (1991): 215–33.

8 Christopher Dunn, "Do Canadian Provinces Have Too Much Power?" (Paper delivered at the Annual Meeting of the Canadian Political Science Association, Victoria, British Columbia, May 1990).

9 Peter J. Katzenstein, *Small States in World Markets. Industrial Policy In Europe* (Ithaca, NY: Cornell University Press, 1985), 10.

10 Charles Frank, "Management school's U.S. accreditation in danger," *Calgary Herald*, 23 March 1998, B1; and Jeffrey Simpson, "The counter-revolution Canada needs to get in step with the world," *Globe and Mail*, 2 January 1992, A14.

11 See Robert B. Reich, *The Work Of Nations* (New York: Alfred A. Knopf, 1991), especially Parts Two and Three.

2 NEWFOUNDLAND

Between a Rock and a Hard Place: Regime Change in Newfoundland

VALERIE A. SUMMERS

INTRODUCTION: A POLITICAL ECONOMY OF VOLATILITY

It is now just over fifty years since Newfoundland entered the Canadian federation. While 1949 was a watershed year in Newfoundland's political history, this date signifies but one of many major changes in Newfoundland's political institutions. Newfoundland has had a five-hundred-year economic history, originally tied to the European fishery, and an indigenous democratic political history dating from 1832 with the introduction of representative government. This democratic political tradition was interrupted by a fifteen-year colonial and authoritarian political hiatus under the Commission of Government which preceded democratic union with Canada in 1949. Newfoundland's social formation since joining Confederation has also been characterized by marked changes in the rules of the game of politics—or regime change—and by a continual focus on natural resource development to provide for economic growth.

At the end of the century, the Newfoundland economy is as precarious as it was at the turn of the nineteenth century, and Newfoundlanders find themselves, after fifty years of Canadian citizenship, still residents of the poorest province in Canada. The safety net of social citizenship is under attack from the right, at the same time that Canada itself is undergoing a prolonged constitutional crisis with the threat of Quebec secession, an event that would leave Newfoundland among the most vulnerable of the Canadian provinces. Another regime change appears inevitable, whether it involves devolutionary adjustments in Canadian federalism, or a more thoroughgoing regime change brought about by Quebec sovereignty.

RESOURCE POLITICS AND REGIME CHANGE

Resource politics in Newfoundland is inextricably tied to changes of political regime. In a resource economy like Newfoundland's, changes in the rules of the political game are made at least partially as a result of the actions of resource capitalists and other resource actors. Regimes change because the underlying dynamics of the political system propel such transformations. The dynamics in Newfoundland's case include internal dualism and external dependency.[1] External dependency resulted from a heavy reliance on foreign direct investment in the resource sector after the turn of the twentieth century. Internal dualism was created by the way in which resources, capital, and culture were spatially dispersed within Newfoundland. St. John's and the Avalon Peninsula constituted a commercial and mercantile core, while rural Newfoundland, for the most part, was a hinterland to be exploited. Commodity producers in the fisheries and miners, loggers, and paper workers were not integrated in any meaningful sense into the small and relatively wealthy urban core.

Changes in the political regime were created through the way in which governmental and non-governmental resource actors, through their resource development interactions, tactics, strategies and goals, created and transformed the political environment. While the dualistic nature of the Newfoundland economy and society is evident during most of Newfoundland political history, fundamental transformations of the political regime sometimes entailed the creation of fragile and temporary coalitions of urban and rural class fractions. The most fundamental of Newfoundland's twentieth-century regime changes occurred in 1949, and the two referenda leading up to that transformation reflected the province's underlying political dualism. However, after Confederation Smallwood was able to consolidate the political power of the Confederates and retain a twenty-two-year hold on the reins of power. The provincial election of 1971 heralded another regime change. The PCs under Frank Moores experienced their first success in urban areas and, later, in the 1972 election, consolidated that breakthrough in rural Newfoundland. The Wells election in 1988 constituted another change of regime. The different policies of the new government in federal-provincial relations, particularly as revealed in Wells's vision of Newfoundland in Confederation, which received much publicity during the Meech Lake debate, left earlier views of a decentralized Canada with expanded resource development powers for Newfoundland, in abeyance. Since the failure of the Meech Lake Accord, the Charlottetown Referendum, and the perilously close referendum in Quebec on sovereignty, nationalists within Newfoundland have been contemplating the place of Newfoundland in a Canada without the province of Quebec.

POLITICS IN PRE-CONFEDERATION NEWFOUNDLAND

Newfoundland politics did not begin with federation in 1949. There were several important changes of regime in the nineteenth century associated with the establishment of liberal democratic politics. Newfoundland moved from a colonial dependency of Britain to representative government in 1832 and responsible government in 1855. In the interim there were also minor adjustments in legislative–executive relations, the most interesting of which was the Amalgamated Assembly of 1842.[2] These changes did not take place independently of the social and economic basis of politics. Dependency on Britain, political and economic, in the nineteenth century resulted in a distorted social formation such that class, culture, and region reinforced great inequalities in the quality of life, in terms of both life opportunities and conditions. External dependency on Britain and, later, Canada created a culture that was very hostile to fundamental change; nevertheless the system did change, sometimes in reactionary ways.

Newfoundland's economy has always been export-led. With World War I, however, came a dramatic change in the structure of the economy. Canada replaced Britain as the principal source of imports and fish became a secondary export earner. By the 1930s minerals and paper were higher export earners than fish. Though less important overall, fish remained crucial for the local economy. Until the 1930s fish was the principal source of income and the fisheries were the principal source of employment for a large proportion of the population. Domestic commodity production involving fishing families, both dependent and independent,[3] struggled through economic crises. The liberal democratic regime which had been put in place in the nineteenth century collapsed in the 1930s due to the poor performance of the export economy and what was, in reality, a moderate public debt. Unfortunately the debt was to British and Canadian bondholders who were unwilling to refinance without stringent controls over the political process. The five major Canadian banks had formed a syndicate to deal with Newfoundland's fiscal crisis and demanded that interest charges on the debt be the first priority of the Newfoundland government at a time when the weight of the international depression was felt by virtually every citizen of Newfoundland, whether merchant, resource capitalist, fisher, or miner. The outcome of this political and economic crisis was a change of regime from the liberal democratic politics of Responsible Government to the authoritarianism of the Commission of Government.

The Commission of Government (1934–48) was an appointed, non-democratic government. The major portfolios were filled by British Commissioners and the government has been described as a "dictatorship of the bureaucracy."[4] The government was composed of a Governor and a commission of six who together performed legislative and executive functions. Political parties and the legislative assembly of the old regime ceased to exist. This government was accountable not to the people of Newfoundland but to the Dominions Office in Britain and, through the Undersecretary of State for Dominion Affairs, to the British Parliament in which Newfoundlanders had no representation. As Newfoundland was not a paramount concern of British MPs, the Commission of Government was really responsible to the bureaucracy at Whitehall. Politics continued, of course, but it was conducted in a shroud of secrecy and red tape quite unlike the often tumultuous openness of the regime which preceded it.[5]

Although the regime was not overtly coercive there was a patent concern on the part of the Commissioners for social control. Despite its benign veneer the regime was resisted by Newfoundlanders. Dissatisfaction with the government began shortly after its installation. Police reports indicate that by the winter of 1937 there were demonstrations against the Commission and books and pamphlets resisting the regime were circulated. By the early 1940s calls for constitutional change abounded in the press. In general these news reports were very critical of the Commission regime and called for more representation by Newfoundlanders in their government. The authoritarian Commission of Government monitored the press, kept tabs on the police, created the Rangers, a new police force for outport Newfoundland, and also used magistrates as conduits for information. By 1945 it was clear that Britain could not continue to govern Newfoundland with even a minimal degree of legitimacy. Newfoundland and Canada were part of the British colonial state, and the British state, wishing to divest itself of Newfoundland, made overtures to Canada.[6]

Despite the behind-the-scenes diplomatic manoeuvring which preceded the regime change of 1949, it was a transition which was accomplished through democratic means involving the Newfoundland population in a National Convention and two passionately contested referenda. The National Convention and the referenda brought the fundamental cleavages of Newfoundland society into the open political arena. While Newfoundlanders overwhelmingly rejected a return to Commission of Government for even a five-year period they were severely divided along class and regional lines as to their preferred constitutional future. The British government clearly favoured confederation with Canada and had overruled the recommendation of the popularly elected National Convention that this option not be placed on the ballot. As a result of the British Dominions Office decision, Newfoundlanders were presented with three options on the first referendum ballot: the continuation of Commission of Government for a further period of five years; the re-establishment of responsible government as it existed in 1933; and confederation with Canada. Political leadership mobilized the population around these last two options. The principal leaders were Joseph R. Smallwood and Gordon Bradley for confederation and Peter Cashin for responsible government. Smallwood and Cashin were well matched in their oratorical and propaganda skills and the ensuing campaign was passionate and often bitter. Two referenda were necessary, as neither option secured a majority on the first referendum. In fact the most popular option on the first ballot was the re-establishment of responsible government The campaign was marked by strident nationalism, religious divisions, and class cleavages.

Smallwood, portraying himself as the spokesman for Newfoundland's "toiling masses," ardently put forward confederation and the Canadian welfare state as the panacea for Newfoundland's economic woes and inequitable class system. Smallwood was scathing in his attack on St. John's merchants and the viciousness of the dependent Newfoundland staple economy for ordinary people. As S.J.R. Noel aptly notes:

> That the vision of the new messiah was not of socialism as such but of union with Canada governed by the Liberal party of Mackenzie King was an odd touch, but it did not alter his message: confederation would mean new dignity for the 'little man' or in a vivid phrase coined by another Confederate, William Keough, for the "lost forgotten fisherman off the bill of Cape St. George."[7]

Smallwood promised that confederation and the policies of the Newfoundland Liberal Party would transform the Newfoundland economy from a semi-feudal fishing economy to a modern industrialized one. Newfoundland fishermen were told that one day they could "burn their boats" and live in comfort in the new industrial Newfoundland, an industrialization promoted by government policy to develop and attract resource capital in the non-fish sector and in secondary manufacturing. Newfoundland in federal Canada would be "brought kicking and screaming into the twentieth century." If the provincial state had a role to play in attracting investment and restructuring the economy, the federal role was immediately important in raising incomes through unemployment insurance, old age pensions, and mothers' allowances. Confederation in 1949 brought with it a change of political regime and a fundamental transformation of the Newfoundland economy and society that in turn propelled later political transformations.

SMALLWOOD AND INDUSTRIALIZATION: 1949-1959

Smallwood's newly created Liberal Party was the natural inheritor of the confederate campaign. Shortly after the second referendum, Smallwood made an appearance at the national Liberal convention in Toronto and declared himself a Liberal.[8] He was sworn in as Premier of Newfoundland on April 1, 1949; on April 28 the founding convention of the Liberal Party of Newfoundland opened, and on May 27 the first provincial election was held.[9] The alignment of the party system originated in the results of the referenda campaigns. Smallwood portrayed the Conservatives as founded on anti-confederation sentiments and won 22 of the 28 seats in the House of Assembly. The Conservatives won only five seats and these were on the Avalon Peninsula, which had supported the re-establishment of responsible government in the referenda campaigns. Federal election results mirrored Smallwood's political power and throughout the 1950s Smallwood delivered to Ottawa five of the seven federal seats. In return "Uncle Ottawa" channelled programs and patronage back to the province through Smallwood.

Smallwood made economic development the first priority of the new government and accordingly took on this portfolio himself. He made Alfred Valdmanis, a Latvian economist with dubious credentials, his key advisor at a salary exceeding that of any other public servant. Smallwood, like many Newfoundland prime ministers before him, sought to diversify the Newfoundland economy away from a reliance on the fisheries through a program of rapid government-induced industrialization. Newfoundland's $45-million surplus, which had been accumulated thanks to the parsimony of the Commission of Government, would be used first to kick-start and then to bail out a number of ill-conceived industrial and manufacturing ventures. Scorning the conservatism of Newfoundland capital, Smallwood and Valdmanis crisscrossed Europe in search of new industries for the province. Within months many new enterprises were started in Newfoundland including industries to manufacture cement, gypsum wallboard, hardwood products, textiles, rubber goods, heavy machinery, batteries, boots and shoes, chocolates, leather goods, and gloves.[10] Fifteen enterprises began operation between 1952 and 1956. Of these only three were successful.[11] The reasons for failure were various, but included the high cost of bringing raw materials into Newfoundland for processing, an inexperienced or unskilled labour force for these specialized industries, obsolescent equipment, poor management, and inadequate control by government over the disposition of the taxpayers' money.[12] By the mid-1950s Newfoundland's surplus of cash had been spent with virtually no permanent jobs or economic benefits to show for it. Smallwood then turned his attention to large-scale resource development which would be financed largely through foreign direct investment.

The first initiative in the matter of large-scale resource development was the formation of the Newfoundland and Labrador Corporation (NALCO, a Crown corporation with a million dollars in capital and rights to explore and develop large tracts of Crown land. A million dollars was an inadequate amount of money for the task of resource development and Smallwood soon turned to the private sector for more. NALCO was sold to Canadian Javelin, under the control of John C. Doyle, for a nominal amount. The Newfoundland government guaranteed a $16.5 million bond issue for the construction of a railway to Lake Wabush,[13] and Canadian Javelin then entered into an American-dominated consortium to develop the iron ore mines at Wabush.

The other mineral development in Labrador was undertaken by the Iron Ore Company of Canada (IOCC). IOCC, which was 77-per-cent American owned and 17-per-cent Canadian owned,[14] built the town of Schefferville in Quebec to service its Newfoundland mine. Unfortunately, the royalty and tax structures for both of these Labrador mining concerns had been established during the Commission of Government regime and were very generous to the companies.[15] Despite large-scale resource developments such as these there was only a modest increase in employment levels and most of the increase was attributable to a demand for unskilled labour in construction.[16] Subsequent economic and political decisions further impeded the contribution of minerals to the growth of the Newfoundland economy. The decision to ship Labrador ore from Sept-Iles, Quebec, for example, created a north-south transportation and communication axis that diverted many of the benefits from Newfoundland to Quebec. As a result of pressure from the government of Quebec, the pelletizing plant for Labrador ore was located in Pointe Noire, Quebec.[17]

Smallwood's political rhetoric on development took the form of superlatives: Newfoundland was to have the biggest, the best, and the most modern economy of all of the Canadian provinces. To this end Smallwood courted international financiers to put in place his twentieth-century resource and industrial mega-projects. Two of these stand out as bittersweet legacies of the Smallwood regime in the last decade of the century. They are the huge hydro-electric facility at Churchill Falls and the oil refinery at Come by Chance. The former was, at the time, the largest building project in Canadian history. It was built on time and stayed within budget but, unfortunately for Newfoundland, the cost of the development was a long-term supply contract with Hydro-Québec which resulted in the loss of economic rent to the province from what could have been a resource bonanza. The latter project at Come by Chance is remembered as one of the largest bankruptcies in Canadian history.

The Churchill Falls hydro-electric development was undertaken by BRINCO, which was formed by twenty companies at Smallwood's initiative. Among the principals were the de Rothschilds banking interests of England. A number of Canadian companies were also involved in the engineering and design of Churchill Falls. As was the case with the Labrador mining development, the chief beneficiary of the Churchill Falls project was the province of Quebec. Apart from the construction jobs, which were shared with Quebec workers, the economic benefits of this huge Canadian development to Newfoundland were minimal. In many ways Labrador became a resource hinterland of Quebec, not Newfoundland, despite the 1927 decision of the Judicial Committee of the Privy Council (JCPC) which had settled the boundary dispute in Newfoundland's favour.

In order for the development of Churchill Falls to be possible, markets had to be secured for the electricity that was to be produced. The largest potential market was in the United States, and after lengthy discussions, first with Premier Lesage and later with Premier Johnson of Quebec, it became clear that the government of Quebec would not permit the construction of transmission lines across Quebec to deliver power to the American market. Instead Newfoundland would have to sell the power at the Labrador boundary to Hydro-Québec which would in turn market the power. An extraordinarily long-term contract for the sale of Churchill Falls power to Hydro-Québec was negotiated. The agreement set a fixed price which was to decline over a quarter of a century, remain at a low level for a further 15 years, and then be renewable at the buyer's option at the same low price.[18] With the explosion in world energy prices in the 1970s, Quebec reaped windfall profits while Newfoundland, lacking an escalator clause in the agreement, lost out on considerable economic rent. To further exacerbate matters, in the early stages of the development Newfoundland lost one dollar of equalization payments from Ottawa for every dollar in revenue collected from Churchill Falls.[19]

Smallwood's development policy was two-pronged. On the one hand industrial development would be nurtured by the provincial state, and provincial infrastructure in roads, schools, hospitals, and electrification would be undertaken to further enhance development possibilities and at the same time improve the quality of life of the people.[20] Part of this strategy involved a provincially-sponsored program of rural resettlement. Smallwood claimed that modern services could not be economically provided to every cove and inlet scattered along Newfoundland's coastline. To provide modern amenities and to create new industrial communities, a growth-pole strategy for Newfoundland's development was endorsed amid much controversy in rural Newfoundland. People were resettled to these new communities from their isolated villages which, though harsh in terms of amenities, had been economically viable in their reliance on the inshore fishery. In many cases people were moved to new communities that lacked the industrial base necessary to support the employment of the expanding population.

Over twenty years the cumulative impact of Smallwood's development policy, particularly policies aimed at creating a more educated population, was to create a more sophisticated Newfoundland electorate, which became less attuned to Smallwood's previously charismatic style of governing and, as one major project after another failed, more cynical of his vision of the new industrial Newfoundland. By the late 1960s, Smallwood's previously invincible political machine was in trouble.

REGIME CHANGE: SMALLWOOD TO MOORES

Smallwood's policies toward organized labour, particularly in the forest sector, had by the late 1950s brought him into conflict with Ottawa. In his youth Smallwood had been associated with the trade union movement and socialist causes. However, ten years in power as the often demagogic premier of Newfoundland had dampened his sympathy for organized labour, particularly if its leadership challenged his grip on the Newfoundland electorate. In 1959 he crushed the International Woodworkers of America (IWA), which had organized loggers in Newfoundland. During a labour dispute involving the pulp and paper companies, Smallwood took the side of management. He enacted punitive labour legislation of general applicability and decertified the IWA, a union that had been supported by an overwhelming majority of the Newfoundland loggers. In doing so, he received criticism and condemnation from just about every progressive force in the country. Smallwood's intervention in the labour dispute brought him into open political conflict with Prime Minister Diefenbaker and Liberal opposition leader Lester Pearson. Diefenbaker's cabinet, after a lengthy meeting, refused to send the RCMP reinforcements that Smallwood had requested. In the House of Commons Diefenbaker stated that Smallwood had "greatly aggravated" the situation in the labour dispute by his intervention.[21] Lester Pearson shortly after indicated that the policy of the federal Liberals was based "on the right of free collective bargaining through unions chosen by the workers themselves."[22]

During the IWA strike, Smallwood waged a public relations campaign against organized labour and the Diefenbaker government which relied on appeals to emotionalism, particularism, and, indeed, fear. While the IWA situation was still on the political agenda, Smallwood fought another battle with Ottawa over the fiscal terms of Newfoundland's place in the federation. The focus of debate was Term 29 of Newfoundland's Terms of Union with Canada. In anticipation of a review of Newfoundland's fiscal situation, Smallwood appointed his own Royal Commission, which recommended that Newfoundland receive an annual grant of $15 million. The federal Royal Commission, the McNair Commission, recommended a sliding scale of payments which would reach $8 million per year and be paid in perpetuity. Diefenbaker's "final and irrevocable" decision was that the $8 million be paid only until 1962. The stage was thus set for another federal-provincial conflict. The issue was not settled until 1963 when the federal Liberals regained power and agreed to pay the $8 million in perpetuity. Throughout the Pearson years, Smallwood's relations with Ottawa were cordial. This was in no small part attributable to the role played in Ottawa by Jack Pickersgill, Newfoundland's representative in the federal cabinet. As a result of Pickersgill's influence between 1963 and 1967, Newfoundland became Ottawa's favourite province.[23]

The electoral results for the federal Liberals were consistently high throughout the 1960s until 1968 when the Progressive Conservatives garnered 53 per cent of the popular vote.[24] By the mid-1960s, Smallwood's economic strategy was unravelled by critical opposition forces. The opposition came from all fronts both within and outside the Liberal Party. John Crosbie and Clyde Wells bolted from Smallwood's cabinet for a number of reasons: criticism of Smallwood's relationship with John Shaheen over the Come By Chance oil refinery deal, the general industrial development policy, and Smallwood's dictatorial style of cabinet government. Opposition also came from a rejuvenated PC party but had a broad societal base. Smallwood's patronage-ridden style of leadership had become a non-starter in the modern capitalist society that Smallwood policies had themselves nurtured. The diffusion of modern technology, particularly communications, had created a society less impressed with the grandeur of Smallwood's modernization program and more in tune with a post-industrial "small is beautiful" model of development.

Resettlement policies, which were supported federally and provincially by the state, were subject to a thoroughgoing criticism that entailed opposition to the established development policy. While Overton claims that this critique was primarily motivated by "rural romanticism" on the part of the new urban middle class,[25] the dissatisfaction with the disappearance of Newfoundland's rural culture represented an alliance of class fractions that cut across regions within the province. The provincial electoral results of both 1971 and 1972 indicate that the Progressive Conservatives gathered support in rural and urban areas. Although Matthews attributes the PC vote in 1971 and 1972 to "urbanism,"[26] the urban St. John's vote for the

Progressive Conservatives had been present since Confederation. Frank Moores himself came from an old "outport" merchant family, a traditional Newfoundland upper-class family. The working class, which was also now primarily urban, was disenchanted with the regressive labour policies of the Smallwood regime.

Rural Newfoundland, meanwhile, had been ravaged by the rural resettlement program. Coupled with this, there was a partly state-induced decline in the fishery, and labour strife in this sector as well. The Newfoundland Fish, Food and Allied Workers had recently organized under the leadership of Richard Cashin. On the one hand, there remained the vestiges of an isolated fishing economy largely based on the inshore fishery and, on the other, a more modern industrial and service urban economy had emerged. In 1971 the PCs won support in urban centres and those towns with the least direct dependency on the fishery.[27] Of the 22 urban districts, the PCs won 15, the Liberals won 6, and the New Labrador party won 1.[28] Overall, the result of the 1971 election necessitated recounts in several districts. The outcome after recounts was 20 seats for the Liberals, 21 for the PCs and 1 for the New Labrador Party. In January 1972 Smallwood resigned and Frank Moores took over as Premier. In the 1972 election, the change of regime was consolidated with the election of 33 PCs to the provincial legislature.

The Smallwood years had seen many changes in Newfoundland society. Provincial infrastructure in roads, schools, and hospitals was much improved. Urbanization and the decline of the inshore fishery resulted in the transformation of an isolated rural economy into a more industrial and service-based economy. One interpretation of the change of regime in 1971-1972 is that Smallwood's modernization policies had created the societal basis for a change of regime. Two decades of Newfoundland's existence within the Canadian federal political system and the social and economic policies which accompanied federation had resulted in the coming of age of a new middle class skeptical of the misguided industrial development policies and political corruption of the Smallwood years. It was the younger, more urban, and better educated Newfoundlanders who ultimately rejected Smallwood's vision for their province. Whether Smallwood's policies had resulted in the social mobilization of a large segment of the population who were willing to be re-socialized into more modern political attitudes is a moot point,[29] but it was certainly the more urban and educated who rejected Smallwood in 1971. The 1972 election saw the consolidation of the PCs' ascendant power in rural Newfoundland as well. In the 1972 election the PCs won 14 of the 20 rural districts.[30]

MOORES AND ADMINISTRATIVE REFORM

The Moores administration from 1972 to 1979 was preoccupied with the reform of the provincial bureaucracy, the managed phase-out of some of Smallwood's megaprojects and a program of rural development to revitalize rural Newfoundland after the misguided growth-pole strategy which underlay the rural resettlement program of the 1960s. The election slogan had been "the time has come," and indeed Newfoundland was ready for a change of political style and policy after the twenty-two-year Smallwood reign.

Moores pursued administrative reform on various fronts. Shortly after he came to power, a White Paper on reform of the administrative branch of government was released. The model adopted was typical of administrative reform in Canada in the 1970s. Cabinet committees were created and supported by a secretariat, and the Treasury Board was strengthened. All of this was to ensure a more complete discussion of complex issues and provide for policy integration.[31] These procedures were in marked contrast to the personalized politics of the Smallwood years.

The other area of major reform was the electoral system. Historically, the electoral system had been based on the equal representation of the major religious denominations in Newfoundland. An important effect of this way of dealing with the religious cleavage was the under-representation of urban areas. The over-represented rural areas had traditionally supported Smallwood's Liberals. Moores, with an urban support base, was eager to right this wrong. As a result of an election promise, the 1973 *Electoral Boundaries Delimitation Act* was proclaimed. Under this legislation the House of Assembly was increased to 51 members and all constituencies had to be within 2,500 of the 10,000 average number of people per district. Other reform initiatives included a restructuring of the Liquor Commission, the passage of a *Public Tendering Act*, the creation of a Rural Development Agency, and the establishment of Newfoundland and Labrador Hydro and the Newfoundland and Labrador Development Corporation.

There were also important developments in resource politics during the Moores regime. In 1974 the government purchased the Churchill Falls (Labrador) Corporation from BRINCO. Negotiations on the purchase or nationalization of BRINCO began between the government and company executives a few weeks after a Toronto investment firm, Burns Bros. and Denton, recommended that the Newfoundland government take over BRINCO by making a cash offer of $6.75 per share to all shareholders. The Moores government mulled over the report and was assured by the Bank of Nova Scotia that funds would be forthcoming for the transaction. Trading in BRINCO shares was suspended as the government of Newfoundland indicated its intention to make an offer for the shares. This move was designed to open negotiations with the company. The negotiations centred on two points: the desire by BRINCO to maintain its corporate identity and the price of the shares. The company was willing to give up its water rights but wished to retain its other interests and argued that the offered price per share was too low because the shareholders had foregone dividends during the construction phase in the expectation of large dividends later. This argument was made despite the fact that the government's offer was $1.50 above the trading value of the shares.[32]

The Newfoundland government increased its offer for the shares to $7.07 but maintained that BRINCO was "not divisible." The company counter-offered that the water rights and the Churchill Falls operation would be sold for $164 million and that dissatisfied shareholders would be offered the $7.07 per share. Shortly after, Frank Moores introduced expropriation legislation into the Newfoundland House of Assembly. In announcing the government's decision, Moores noted that "the resources of Newfoundland are the property of our people. It follows that control over these resources must rest with the people's government."[33]

This move by the Progressive Conservative government should not be interpreted as support for a policy of nationalization. The introduction of expropriation legislation was merely a tactic to show the company what the government could do. In fact, while Moores was introducing the legislation, John Crosbie informed the company that there was still room for agreement.[34] The company's principals flew to St. John's and, shortly after, Premier Moores announced that an amicable settlement had been reached. BRINCO was in fact divisible—the Churchill Falls company and the water rights in Labrador were sold to the government for $164 million, and all shareholders could sell back their shares to the company for $7.07. This deal was carried through by the government in order to increase its manoeuvrability in re-negotiating the power contract with Hydro-Québec and in developing the Lower Churchill. While the purchase of the Churchill Falls (Labrador) Corporation may in some ways have increased the capability of the provincial state, the cost of buying the company contributed to the accumulating deficit of the government of Newfoundland.

While the Moores government represented a fundamental change from the Smallwood regime, the transformation in politics which occurred in 1971-72 was not as fundamental as Newfoundland's pre-confederation changes of political regime. Politics since 1949 have been conducted under the framework of a federal liberal democratic political regime. One interpretation of the change of government was that it brought to power a new middle class created in the early federal period as a result of provincial and federal development policies. Though there is some truth in this assertion, it is also true that a politically significant middle class had existed in

Newfoundland since the nineteenth century.[35] There is no doubt, however, that there was a flowering of Newfoundland culture during the 1970s.[36] Part of this awakening was a nationalist spirit that was more inclined to favour Newfoundland autonomy from foreign investors and, in the extreme, political independence from Canada itself. But it should also not be forgotten that urban middle class St. John's had not supported confederation with Canada in the referenda of 1948. The Moores victory in 1972 made possible a political agenda headed by nationalist programs supported in urban Newfoundland, an agenda which Smallwood, shut out electorally from the St. John's area, had spurned.

Smallwood was so chagrined by the unrelenting critique of his policies by the Moores government that he decided to re-enter the political fray in 1975. First, in 1974 Smallwood challenged Ed Roberts's leadership of the Liberal Party and lost, and then he formed a new party, Liberal Reform, to contest the 1975 election. The effect of Smallwood's Liberal Reform party's entry into the 1975 election was to split the Liberal vote and deny Roberts's Liberals a victory. Liberal Reform won 13 per cent of the vote while contesting only 28 seats, the Liberals won 37 per cent of the vote, while Moores continued in power with 30 seats and 45 per cent of the vote.

Moores remained premier for three more years. His final term was marked by a moderate improvement in the provincial economy attributable to the 1977 Canadian declaration of a two-hundred-mile zone for the Atlantic fishery, and the increasing activities of multinational oil companies in the exploration for oil and gas offshore Newfoundland. Immediately following the declaration of the two-hundred-mile limit, there was a boom in the fishery in rural Newfoundland and St. John's experienced an upturn in the real estate market and general economic prosperity from the oil boom. At this time, A. Brian Peckford made his debut on the political scene as Moores's aggressive minister of Mines and Energy. Peckford won political kudos for taking on the oil companies and the federal government in demanding that the companies take out provincial exploration permits for offshore activity. When Moores resigned as premier, Peckford defeated the old guard of the PC party and handily won the leadership and the subsequent provincial election on the issue of ownership and control of resources.

PECKFORD AND RESOURCE POLITICS

The Peckford years were characterized by intense federal–provincial conflict over resource ownership and control. Three resource issues headed the agenda: ownership and control of offshore oil and gas, fisheries management, and hydro development. Peckford pursued these issues with such zeal that he became known as "the bad boy of Confederation." In all these areas he argued for a decentralization of Canadian federalism and Newfoundland autonomy from Ottawa in the development of Newfoundland's rich resource endowment so that Newfoundlanders would not have to continue as second-class Canadians continually going to Ottawa "cap in hand." His political rhetoric stressed a pride in Newfoundland and was accompanied by a call for increased powers for the provincial state.[37] In the interests of Newfoundland autonomy and indigenous development, Peckford sought a redefinition of the Canadian federal state. Changes in the Canadian political regime through constitutional politics were advocated so that Newfoundland could be an equal partner in Confederation and so that "have-not would be no more."

The most antagonistic conflict with Ottawa occurred over offshore oil and gas jurisdiction. During the Trudeau years, relations were acrimonious and bitter on this and other issues. Trudeau, in the "restoration period" of 1980 to 1984, took a strong centralist line with the provinces which collided with the policy objectives of the government of Newfoundland. Newfoundland, unlike the other Atlantic provinces, was more in tune with the positions of advocates of decentralized federalism such as Quebec, Alberta, and to some extent Saskatchewan.[38] Newfoundland argued that, to deal with dependency and deprivation, it was essential that the province control its major resources in oil, hydro, and fish. Ottawa claimed to have jurisdiction over offshore oil development; the fisheries were managed primarily from Ottawa; and Quebec was reaping the major benefits from Labrador power. To deal with these problems, Peckford advocated various re-definitions of the federal division of powers so that Newfoundland, stealing a phrase from the Quiet Revolution in Quebec, could be "master of its own house."

The Newfoundland case for ownership and control of the offshore was based on its interpretation of Newfoundland's pre-confederation constitutional status. The Newfoundland government attempted to set itself apart from the other provinces and, particularly, argued that the province be exempt from the 1969 British Columbia offshore reference in which the Supreme Court of Canada had decided in favour of the federal government. The Newfoundland case for offshore oil jurisdiction centred on its claim that rights in international law to the Newfoundland continental shelf had accrued to the government of Newfoundland prior to Confederation and that these rights were maintained by the province upon union with Canada. As part of this argument the Newfoundland government claimed that the Commission of Government period prior to Confederation entailed no effective loss of sovereignty in international law and that Newfoundland did not give up its rights to the continental shelf in the Terms of Union. Newfoundland claimed that it had entered Canada as a sovereign nation state in international law with a status similar to Canada itself under the Statute of Westminster. The Supreme Court of Canada disagreed with the Newfoundland argument. On March 8, 1984 the Court decided that Canada had the right to explore and exploit the resources of the continental shelf off Newfoundland because any continental shelf rights available in 1949 would have been acquired by the United Kingdom, not Newfoundland. The Court ruled that even if Newfoundland had continental shelf rights prior to union with Canada, they would have passed to Canada by virtue of the Terms of Union and that in any event international law did not recognize continental shelf rights prior to 1949.[39]

After the defeat of the Newfoundland case for jurisdiction of the offshore in the courts, the emphasis shifted to the political arena. Fortuitously for Newfoundland, Brian Mulroney, then leader of the opposition, was gearing up for the 1984 federal election and offered Newfoundland a deal on the offshore. Ownership would be set aside and equal participation in management was a key principle, one which later underlay the Atlantic Accord. Brian Peckford campaigned vigorously for Brian Mulroney in the September federal election and Newfoundland returned four PCs to the House of Commons. Peckford, throughout the federal–provincial conflict, had preferred a political resolution of the offshore dispute and claimed that Newfoundland was forced into the court by the intransigence of the federal Liberal government.

Ironically for Peckford, by the time the promise of the Atlantic Accord was realized in an agreement with the oil companies on offshore development in 1988, the Newfoundland electorate had become very cynical of the potential of Hibernia to contribute to Newfoundland's development. This skepticism was based in part on the declining international price for crude oil which did not bode well for Hibernia's expensive product and also in part on the costly commitments undertaken by both governments to get development started. For cynics in Newfoundland and elsewhere in Canada, Hibernia was generally viewed as one of the most costly regional development projects in Canadian history and one of the biggest gambles in Newfoundland history.

On other fronts the Peckford resource development policies were also thwarted. Despite numerous attempts to renegotiate the Upper Churchill hydro contract, no progress was made. As was the case with jurisdiction over the offshore, the province attempted court challenges to attain a more equitable arrangement on this resource. The strategy was to attempt to recall the water rights to Churchill Falls under the *Water Rights Reversion Act* and thus to force a renegotiation of the deal with Hydro-Québec. The Supreme Court, however, ruled that this legislation would be a "colourable" attempt to interfere with the contract with Hydro-Québec and was thus *ultra vires* the legislature of Newfoundland. Earlier, the Court of Appeal of Newfoundland had decided that the *Water Rights Reversion Act* was within the ambit of property and civil rights powers of the province and therefore *intra vires*. The decision of the Supreme Court exhausted the province's legal powers of redress.[40]

The other major Newfoundland resource was the fishery, and throughout the 1980s this industry was in crisis. In fact, two separate crises characterized the decade: the first was a rapid corporate expansion in an era of skyrocketing interest rates while the second, and more recent, was a depletion of fish stocks due to federal mismanagement and foreign over-fishing. The response of the state to the first crisis was the appointment of the Kirby task force on the Atlantic fisheries and the subsequent corporate re-structuring of the industry. The task force and the corporate bailout that followed were "intent on providing a brighter and more certain future for the corporate sector—all at a direct cost to independent fishermen, small fish processors, and many fisheries dependent coastal communities."[41] With the creation of the super-company, FPI, came plant closures and poor catches for inshore fishermen which were partially blamed on over-allocation to the offshore fleet. In the late 1980s and early 1990s, however, the major problem was the depletion of the stocks themselves. In this context, the most vexatious question for Newfoundland was foreign over-fishing. In 1988-89, Ottawa announced reductions in allowable fish catches in an attempt to rebuild the stocks. This resulted in massive lay-offs of fishermen, plant closures, and increased discord with European and other foreign fleets, and it further exacerbated tensions between the Newfoundland inshore and offshore sectors.

In the fisheries, as in the other resource sectors of petroleum and hydro, Peckford unsuccessfully attempted to use constitutional politics to enhance Newfoundland's resource development autonomy. For the fisheries, Newfoundland under Peckford proposed a split concurrency of constitutional powers. In the constitutional talks of the period, this proposal did not garner sufficient provincial support and was, in particular, opposed by Nova Scotia. Therefore the federal government supported the status quo on fisheries jurisdiction.[42] One of the principal reasons that Peckford supported the Meech Lake Accord was that the Accord, if ratified, would have made possible a discussion of fisheries jurisdiction in a future constitutional conference.

Peckford, tired of doing battle with Ottawa and coming under increasing criticism within Newfoundland, announced his decision to retire from politics in 1989. The actual impetus for Peckford's decline in popularity was the Sprung Greenhouse affair which involved the induction of large sums of provincial money to grow cucumbers hydroponically in Mount Pearl. Crop failures, poor management, and government oversight resulted in the failure of this industrialization project on a magnitude that rivalled Smallwood's early industrialization schemes in the 1950s. A leadership convention in March chose Tom Rideout, the fisheries minister, as the new Tory leader, and within months a general election was called.

NEWFOUNDLAND AT THE MILLENNIUM: THE PROSPECTS FOR REGIME CHANGE

The potential for regime change in contemporary Newfoundland comes from two sources: the indigenous cleavages of the Newfoundland social formation and the external federal system. Both of these dynamics were reflected in Clyde Wells's Liberals' electoral victory in 1989. In that election the Liberals broke through the traditional Tory urban strongholds. While the Liberals under Smallwood had been mostly shut out of St. John's, the Liberals captured all but one of the seven St. John's seats in the 1989 provincial election. From 1985 to 1989 the Liberals increased their share of the popular vote within the city from 25 to 45 per cent.[43] In the St. John's urban region, which includes an additional 6 districts, the Liberal vote went from 26 to 40 per cent.[44] The PCs retained their 1985 rural vote but lost heavily in urban areas. Historically the Liberals had fared better with fishermen,[45] those with lower educational levels, and Protestants.[46] The 1989 vote, however, suggests that the Liberals made inroads into the new urban middle class and among Catholics.

In the early years of the Wells administration, the major issues were the Meech Lake Accord, economic recovery, and cutbacks. Meech Lake was not an issue in the 1989 provincial election but soon became one as the ratification deadline approached. For Wells and, in his view, for Newfoundland, the Accord represented a potentially threatening decentralization of the Canadian federation. Wells, unlike Peckford, maintained that the last thing Newfoundland needed was more legislative powers. Wells saw Newfoundland best served by a strong central government capable of initiating and carrying through national regional development policies in a federation which maintained the fundamental equality of the provinces. What Newfoundland needed was not greater autonomy but a stronger voice in such national institutions as the Senate. His was an "intra-state" vision of Canadian federalism, not the more centrifugal "inter-state" view advocated by Peckford. Newfoundlanders, jaded by the seeming futility of the Peckford vision and inured to federal–provincial conflict, rallied around Wells.

In attempting to deal with the public debt through massive cutbacks in social services and public-sector wage freezes, Wells incurred the wrath of organized labour in the province. Labour responded with the "Clyde Lied" campaign, which referred to broken electoral promises, broken collective agreements on wages, and, unfortunately for Wells, suggested a criticism of how Meech Lake was handled by the Premier in the dying days of the Accord. St. John's, as the hometown of most public-sector employees, was particularly hard hit by the public-sector wage freeze. The economy faltered under the weight of the recession, the failure of Hibernia construction to give the anticipated boost to the local economy, and the unpopular fiscal policies of the provincial government.

Shortly after the failure of the Meech Lake Accord, constitutional politics were again on Wells's provincial agenda with negotiations for the Charlottetown Agreement and the following constitutional referendum. Although Wells supported the Agreement, Newfoundlanders were somewhat indifferent to the Charlottetown deal. The greatest number on referendum day, October 26, 1992 were in fact those not voting.[47] Despite this, Newfoundland was one of the few provinces to support an accord which was overwhelmingly rejected by Canadians despite being supported by the preponderance of Canadian political elites.[48] With the defeat of the Charlottetown agreement Wells turned his attention away from the national stage of constitutional change. Having won the 1993 provincial election he now focussed on economic and educational reform with the intention of bringing about major transformations in the political regime from the inside. In both of these initiatives Wells was to be a pivotal yet transitional actor.

The reform of the staple fishing economy was vital after 40,000 fishers and plant workers were laid off in the cod moratorium. Canadian and foreign over-fishing, federal quota mismanagement,[49] and inappropriate harvesting techniques for a delicate ecosystem had resulted in the depletion of the fish stocks, long the economic lifeline of rural Newfoundland. While federal adjustment and temporary income support programs were devised, the long-term prospects for a generation of Newfoundlanders and the rural communities they support appear bleak. As always in Newfoundland's vulnerable fishing economy the panacea has been seen as diversification away from the fishery into other resource sectors, most recently into high-tech knowledge-based industries and tourism. This new thrust appeared in Wells's Strategic Economic Plan, which was prepared by the Economic

Recovery Commission (ERC), initiated by Wells and headed by Memorial University sociologist Douglas House.

Educational reform was tied to the decline of fiscal resources to run the province's inefficient denominational school system and the need for highly skilled graduates for the new economy. Premier Wells, acting on the advice of the Williams Royal Commission, introduced a referendum as a device to break the two-hundred-year power of the established churches in education. After many consultations with the churches the referendum of September 1995 provided a slim majority in favour of reforming the denominational school system. This referendum resulted in the amendment of Term 17 of Newfoundland's Terms of Union with Canada while at the same time providing some rights to churches in the education of children. Though opposed by the church hierarchy, the 1995 amendment to the Terms of Union was Premier Wells's compromise solution to education inefficiency.[50] The compromise proved itself to be unworkable as conflict escalated over the designation of schools as uni-denominational or inter-denominational.

After Wells's final constitutional initiative in the Term 17 referendum and amendment, and after a decade in politics, he announced his intention to step down as premier. He was replaced as Liberal leader and premier by Brian Tobin, the federal minister of fisheries and oceans. Tobin came to international prominence in the foreign over-fishing conflict with the European Union and had become a hero in Newfoundland with the arrest of the Spanish trawler, the *Estai*. In the 1996 general election Tobin swept the province with over 60 per cent of the vote. The slogan of the Liberals was "For a Brighter Tomorrow."

In August 1997 Premier Tobin announced another referendum on educational reform for early September. This time the referendum question provided clearly for an end to church control in the education system and in effect for public schools for Newfoundland. This time an overwhelming 73 per cent voted "yes" to reform.[51] The House of Assembly and the Parliament of Canada ratified the amendment.

Tobin's tomorrow did in fact look brighter after nickel was discovered at Voisey's Bay in 1994. The Voisey's Bay nickel deposit was discovered by Newfoundland geologists Al Chislett and Chris Verbiski. The exploration was financed by Diamond Field Resources, which in August 1996 sold its interest in the project to INCO Limited. INCO now holds claims covering 2,059 square kilometres in Labrador.[52] Voisey's Bay is potentially one of the most important and profitable nickel properties in the world; when in full production it is expected to have an annual yield of 270 million pounds of nickel, 200 million pounds of copper, and 7 million pounds of cobalt.[53]

Tobin promised that INCO would build a mine, mill, and refinery in Newfoundland and Labrador.

While Voisey's Bay has the promise of a resource bonanza, its development is deeply enmeshed in aboriginal politics, partisan politics, and intergovernmental relations. Aboriginal land claims and benefits have yet to be negotiated, as has a royalty regime with the company. In the meantime aboriginal peoples have successfully won an injunction to stop construction of a road and airstrip until environmental assessments have been completed. INCO threatened a capital strike. Faced with declining world prices for nickel, INCO proposed a slowdown in the development of Voisey's Bay, particularly in the construction of a new mill and refinery. The company indicated its intention to mill the Labrador ore at its facility in Sudbury, Ontario, a plan that has received support from Ontario's Mike Harris Tory government.

The discovery also spawned a new political party. Al Chislett, the co-founder of the Voisey's Bay nickel deposit, created the Newfoundland and Labrador Party. The party was launched in the fall of 1997 with a populist and nationalist base and is committed to accept donations from members only, not corporations or unions. Its platform calls for resource development with solid benefits for Newfoundland in terms of rentals, royalties, and secondary processing.

With this new party still in an embryonic organizational stage, Tobin called a provincial election for February 9, 1999, nearly two years before his mandate ran out. With the promise of Voisey's Bay threatened by INCO's intention to mill the ore in Ontario, Tobin portrayed the company (and the Harris government in Ontario) as the latest villain and asked Newfoundlanders for a renewed mandate to ensure that the benefits of Voisey's Bay remained in Newfoundland. In what was, by Newfoundland standards, a quiet affair, the Liberals were easily returned to power with 32 seats to 14 seats for the PCs and 2 for the NDP. The Newfoundland and Labrador party was shut out.

CONCLUSION

The "politics of hope"[54] springs eternal among political and economic elites in beleaguered Newfoundland. While Newfoundlanders under Brian Tobin voted for a better tomorrow, the grinding realities of dependency are manifested in a closed fishery, cuts to federal transfers, hospital closures, and out-migration that threatens the survival of communities. During the late 1970s and 1980s, sentiments for Newfoundland separatism ran high. Various provincial and national surveys reveal a strong attachment to Newfoundland as a political entity, a prior loyalty to Newfoundland, not Canada, and nascent separatist sentiments.[55] There is in Newfoundland an emergent ethnicity which could be mobilized into an independence movement.[56] Peckford successfully managed to co-opt this perspective in the 1980s with arguments for Newfoundland control over resources within a decentralized federation. As constitutional politics heats up in a Canadian attempt to meet Quebec's demands for change, there will also be a re-examination of the Newfoundland soul, Newfoundland's place in the union, and Newfoundland's potential outside of Canada. Ties to Newfoundland as a cultural and political entity run deep in a society where regime change is frequently contemplated as a way out of dependency and generalized economic woes.

NOTES

1 Valerie A. Summers, "The Politics of Underdevelopment: Resource Policy and Regime Change in Newfoundland" (Ph.D. dissertation, Carleton University, 1987).

2 Gertrude Gunn, *The Political History of Newfoundland, 1832-1864* (Toronto: University of Toronto Press, 1966).

3 For a discussion of dependent and independent commodity production see Wallace Clement, *The Struggle to Organize* (Toronto: McClelland and Stewart, 1986).

4 Thomas Lodge, *Dictatorship in Newfoundland* (London: Cassal and Company, 1939).

5 S.J.R. Noel, *Politics in Newfoundland* (Toronto: University of Toronto Press, 1971).

6 See David Mackenzie, *Inside the Atlantic Triangle: Canada and the Entrance of Newfoundland into Confederation 1939-1949* (Toronto: University of Toronto Press, 1986), and Valerie A. Summers, "The Politics of Underdevelopment."

7 S.J.R. Noel, *Politics in Newfoundland*, 252.

8 Richard Gywn, *Smallwood: The Unlikely Revolutionary* (Toronto, McClelland and Stewart, 1968), 116.

9 Peter Neary, "Party Politics in Newfoundland, 1949-71: A Survey and Analysis," *Newfoundland in the Nineteenth and Twentieth Centuries*, ed. James Hiller and Peter Neary (Toronto: University of Toronto Press, 1980), 205-06.

10 Economic Council of Canada, *Newfoundland: From Dependency to Self Reliance* (Hull: Minister of Supply and Services Canada, 1980), 6.

11 Report of the Royal Commission on Employment and Unemployment, *Building on Our Strengths* (St. John's: Office of the Queen's Printer, 1986), 47.

12 Economic Council of Canada, *Newfoundland: From Dependency to Self Reliance*, 7.

13 Frederick W. Rowe, *The Smallwood Era* (Toronto: McGraw-Hill Ryerson, 1985), 21.

14 Report of the Royal Commission on Employment and Unemployment, *Building on Our Strengths*, 48.

15 Summers, "The Politics of Underdevelopment," Chap. 7.

16 Report of the Royal Commission on Employment and Unemployment, *Building on Our Strengths*, 46.

17 Economic Council of Canada, *Newfoundland: From Dependency to Self Reliance*, 8.

18 Economic Council of Canada, *Newfoundland: From Dependency to Self Reliance*, 9.

19 Philip Smith, *BRINCO: The Story of Churchill Falls* (Toronto: McClelland and Stewart, 1975), 362.

20 Ralph Matthews, *The Creation of Regional Dependency* (Toronto: University of Toronto Press, 1983), *passim*.

21 Gwyn, *Smallwood*, 217-18.

22 Gwyn, *Smallwood*, 219.

23 Susan McCorquodale, "Newfoundland: Plus Ca Change, Plus C'est la Même Chose," *Canadian Provincial Politics*, ed. Martin Robin (Scarborough: Prentice Hall Canada, 1978), 149.

24 Neary, "Party Politics in Newfoundland," 238.

25 James Overton, "Towards a Critical Analysis of Neo-Nationalism in Newfoundland," *Underdevelopment and Social Movements in Atlantic Canada,* ed. Robert J. Brym and R. James Sacouman (Toronto: New Hogtown Press, 1979), 239.

26 Ralph Matthews, "Perspectives on Recent Newfoundland Politics," *Journal of Canadian Studies* (May 1974): 24.

27 Matthews, "Perspectives," 24-25.

28 Matthews, "Perspectives," 25.

29 Mark Graesser and Michael Wallack, "Social Mobilization and Voting in Newfoundland," paper presented to the Atlantic Provinces Political Studies Association, Wolfville, Nova Scotia (1976), *passim.*

30 Matthews, "Perspectives," 27.

31 McCorquodale, "Newfoundland," 165.

32 For a detailed discussion of the BRINCO purchase see Smith, *BRINCO*, 371-78.

33 Quoted by Smith, *BRINCO*, 375.

34 Smith, *BRINCO*, 376.

35 Summers, "The Politics of Underdevelopment," Chap. 4.

36 Overton, "Towards a Critical Analysis of Neo-Nationalism in Newfoundland," *passim.*

37 Robert Paine, *Ayatollahs and Turkey Trots: Political Rhetoric in the New Newfoundland* (St. John's: Breakwater Press, 1981).

38 Bruce G. Pollard, "Newfoundland: Resisting Dependency," *Canada: The State of the Federation 1985*, ed. Peter Leslie (Kingston: Institute of Intergovernmental Affairs, 1986).

39 Pollard, "Newfoundland: Resisting Dependency," 95.

40 Douglas M. Brown, "Sea-Change in Newfoundland: From Peckford to Wells," *Canada: The State of the Federation 1990*, ed. Ronald L. Watts and Douglas M. Brown (Kingston: Institute of Intergovernmental Affairs, 1990), 214.

41 Gene Barrett and Anthony Davis, "Floundering in Troubled Waters: The Political Economy of the Atlantic Fishery and the Task Force on Atlantic Fisheries," *Journal of Canadian Studies*, (Summer 1984): 134.

42 Brown, "Sea Change in Newfoundland: From Peckford to Wells," 208-09.

43 Mark W. Graesser, "The 1989 Newfoundland Provincial Election: A Case of Partisan Realignment?," paper presented to the Canadian Political Science Association, Queen's University, Kingston (1991), 4.

44 Graesser, "The 1989 Newfoundland Provincial Election," 4.

45 Parzival Copes, "The Fishermen's Vote in Newfoundland," *Canadian Journal of Political Science* 3 (1970): 579-604.

46 Graesser and Wallack, "Social Mobilization and Voting in Newfoundland," 12-13.

47 Elections Canada, 1992.

48 Valerie A. Summers, *Regime Change in a Resource Economy: The Politics of Underdevelopment in Newfoundland Since 1825* (St. John's: Breakwater, 1994), 197-98.

49 Susan McCorquodale, "The Fisheries Crisis in Newfoundland," *Canada: The State of the Federation 1994*, ed. Douglas M. Brown and Janet Hiebert (Kingston: Institute of Intergovernmental Affairs, 1995), 85.

50 Mark W. Graesser, "Education Reform in Newfoundland, 1990-1995: The Impact of Constitutional Restraints and Referendum Politics," paper delivered to the Canadian Political Science Association, Memorial University, Newfoundland (June 1997).

51 *Evening Telegram*, 3 September 1997, 3.

52 INCO *Annual Report 1996*, 16-17.

53 INCO *Annual Report 1996*, 17

54 James Overton, "The Politics of Hope in Newfoundland in Two Depressions," *Journal of Newfoundland Studies* 9:1 (1993).

55 See, for example, Michael Ornstein, Michael Stevenson, and A. Paul Williams, "Region, Class and Political Culture in Canada," *Canadian Journal of Political Science* 13 (1980): 227-71; and Mark Graesser, "The Newfoundland 1982 Election Study," paper, Memorial University of Newfoundland (1982).

56 Harry H. Hiller, "Dependence and Independence: Emergent Nationalism in Newfoundland," *Ethnic and Racial Studies* 10 (July 1987): 265.

3 NOVA SCOTIA

The Political Economy of Regime Change

JAMES BICKERTON

Historically, traditionalism and provincialism have gone hand-in-hand in Nova Scotia, for generations forming the core of the province's political culture. This was the general conclusion reached by J. Murray Beck and other political scientists who studied the province's political system. Tradition, they asserted, would always hold sway over innovation or radical change.[1] This understanding of the province's political character has been dealt a number of setbacks since the early 1980s, including updated political culture studies,[2] methodological and analytical critiques,[3] as well as some electoral "firsts" for the region (the first elected woman party leader in Canada and the first party leader to be chosen by party members in a televote).[4] But it is the federal and provincial election results of 1997 and 1998 that constitute the most dramatic evidence that Nova Scotia politics is not what it once was.

In this chapter I will argue that these changes and others, taken together, constitute a form of *regime change* in the province, understood most clearly in the context of the ramifications for the province of broader changes in the political, economic and fiscal environment. In particular, the political and fiscal arrangements which set the terms and parameters for Nova Scotia's relationship with Canada have come under considerable stress, due primarily to the gradual dissolution of the postwar political economy. This changing economic-fiscal context has triggered political responses and policy changes that have undermined the basis for "traditional politics" in Nova Scotia and encouraged the emergence of new structures and techniques of governance, rooted in a provincial political economy that has been significantly altered.

NOVA SCOTIA IN CONFEDERATION

The economic fate of Nova Scotia within Confederation has been well documented. Having built a prosperous pre-Confederation economy based on fishing, lumbering, agriculture, shipbuilding and sea-going trade, Nova Scotia's merchant capitalists were induced in the last two decades of the nineteenth century to invest their wealth in the creation and expansion of various heavy and light industries behind the tariff walls of John A. Macdonald's national policy. A wave of industrial consolidation beginning in the 1890s under the aegis of central Canadian syndicates was followed by a process of centralization that moved or closed down many Maritime branch plants. Other Nova Scotia firms were driven out of business by the elimination of regional transportation subsidies which followed the government re-structuring of Canada's overbuilt and bankrupted railroads in 1917. During a brief period in the 1920s, about half of all manufacturing employment in Nova Scotia was eliminated, at a time when provincial resource industries were also in decline or suffering a loss of traditional markets. The cumulative effect on the province was economically devastating: deindustrialization, disinvestment, economic contraction, and mass outmigration. While the resource sector gradually recovered from this setback, Nova Scotia was effectively transformed from a fully participating region in Canada's early industrialization to a peripheral, fragmented, resource-based economy. Such an economy could not provide Nova Scotians with either the quality or range of employment and income opportunities that were available in proximate American states or in central and western Canada.[5]

While World War II brought considerable economic benefits to Nova Scotia (as wars always have), these proved to be temporary, in no small measure because of investment and production decisions taken by the national government that consistently favoured central Canadian production sites for new or expanded industries.[6] As a result, a postwar slump pushed the province and its neighbours back into their by-now familiar position, trailing the rest of the nation in employment and income levels.[7] While Newfoundland's entry into Confederation in 1949 added to the political clout of the region, it didn't affect a well-established regional division of labour that already had relegated the Maritime provinces to the margins of the national economy. By the time the economic stimulus provided by the Korean conflict (1949-53) had ended, the structural weaknesses of Nova Scotia's economy had become clear, and demands resumed for federal intervention to do something about the structural inequalities from which the whole Atlantic region suffered. But the Keynesian economic management role assumed by the federal government in the postwar era, with its highly centralist bias, offered no prescriptions for any particular regional distribution of economic activity, and state managers in Ottawa resisted the notion that Canada needed a regional policy to address chronic regional disparities in economic growth.[8]

It would not be until the late 1960s that the combined effects of political competition, economic buoyancy, and Quebec's "Quiet Revolution" led to the completion of the welfare state in Canada, including more or less full equalization for the poorer provinces in 1967 and a proactive Department of Regional Economic Expansion (DREE) in 1969. In combination with an expanded and enriched unemployment insurance program in 1971, federal spending became a central pillar in the economy of Nova Scotia and the whole Atlantic region, underwriting the development of modern provincial public sectors, as well as social and economic infrastructure. Incomes in seasonal industries such as forestry and the fishery were stabilized by unemployment insurance payments and federal make-work programs. Federal-provincial economic development agreements provided federal funds for discretionary spending on economic development. At the extreme, Cape Breton Island—now referred to in Nova Scotia's tourism campaigns as "Nova Scotia's masterpiece"—was transformed into what one parliamentary critic called a "socialist island" through the creation of the federal government-owned Cape Breton Development Corporation (Devco) and provincially-owned Sydney Steel Corporation (Sysco). For two decades or more after their creation in 1966-67, the trials and tribulations of these Crown Corporations occupied a prominent place in Nova Scotia politics and provincial economic strategy; indeed, three decades later, a final resolution of their long-term future had yet to be determined. Coal and steel, economic development, and Nova Scotia politics have been so intimately intertwined that examining the history of one inevitably draws in the others.

ECONOMIC DEVELOPMENT AND NOVA SCOTIA POLITICS

The coal and steel industry, at the foundation of Nova Scotia's industrial growth between 1880 and 1914, is also at the heart of the province's later economic problems. Like the forest industry in British Columbia or the auto industry in Ontario, its historic importance to the Nova Scotia economy over the first six decades of this century can hardly be overstated: in 1960 it still employed one in five Nova Scotians. Consolidated at the end of World War I into Canada's largest single industrial enterprise (Besco—the British Empire Steel and Coal Corporation), Besco's corporate managers attempted to increase the company's profitability through Draconian cuts in miners' wages, triggering prolonged labour struggles, near-starvation conditions in mining towns, and military occupation of the Cape Breton coalfields. By the late 1920s, the longest-serving provincial administration in Canadian history (44 years of uninterrupted Liberal government under Premiers Fielding, Murray, and Armstrong) had been defeated, a royal commission had reported its findings on what to do about the Nova Scotia coal industry, and Besco had been replaced by a new, less "iron-fisted" industrial syndicate (Dosco—Dominion Steel and Coal Corporation).

The industrial strife of the 1920s was only the beginning of the problems of the Nova Scotia coal and steel industry. The coal industry was linked to domestic demand for coal as a fuel and to local demand from the steel industry; as coal was replaced by oil in the 1950s, and as the market for the steel industry's primary product (rails) stagnated and contracted, the whole industrial complex teetered into crisis. New foreign owners in the late 1950s did nothing to reverse the decline. The urgent and increasingly desperate entreaties of the Nova Scotia government to the new corporate owners were ignored, as vitally important reinvestment to modernize Dosco's operations was put off in favour of squeezing operations for any remaining profits and milking the federal government for subsidies. In 1966 Dosco's British owners announced the complete closure of coal operations in Nova Scotia, triggering the appointment of another royal commission; a year later Dosco made a similar closure announcement for steel production. During Canada's centennial year celebrations, at the height of the greatest prosperity the country had ever known—when unemployment was low, wages were rising, national social programs were being implemented, and Canadian optimism knew no bounds—Nova Scotia was faced with an economic and social crisis of major proportions.[9]

Since the destruction of much of Nova Scotia's secondary manufacturing sector in the 1920s, the province had exhibited a poorly integrated dual economy based on rural resource industries on the one hand, and coal and steel towns on the other. By the mid-1950s, little had changed: provincial Liberals under Premier Angus L. Macdonald (1933-40; 1945-54) and federal Liberals under Prime Ministers King and St. Laurent (1935-57) were both quite conservative political regimes averse to direct government involvement in the economy. Macdonald's repeated calls for federal action to aid and compensate Nova Scotia and its neighbours for the ill-effects on the region of national policies had little discernible impact on the federal government. This was not allowed to interfere, however, with a high level of integration and cooperation between federal and provincial Liberals in Nova Scotia, a relationship cemented by entrenched patronage practices and a seemingly unending string of electoral successes.[10]

In 1956-57, close to a quarter-century of Liberal dominance over Nova Scotia politics came to an end, to be succeeded by a new political dynasty at the provincial level and a new approach to the province's economic problems. In 1956, Progressive Conservative Robert Stanfield defeated the incumbent Liberals led by Premier Henry Hicks (the near-legendary, Gaelic-speaking "Angus L" having died two years earlier). There were no substantive differences of note between the two parties in this election, on either issues or approach; nor, in fact, had there ever been. As Murray Beck points out in his two-volume history of Nova Scotia politics and government, the provincial party system historically was characterized by the notable absence of clear-cut party philosophies. Both major parties tended to be pragmatic and generally supportive of business. This historical reality, Beck argues, accentuated the role of political leadership and party organization in Nova Scotia politics, commodities over which the provincial Liberals had a distinct advantage between the 1880s and 1950s.[11] Dalton Camp offered the same assessment with regard to the 1956 election: the distinction between one party and another came down to differences in political leadership, "the quality of the chieftain." Stanfield possessed the necessary qualities for this role: an "anti-politician" with a rather patrician demeanor and a strong sense of "noblesse oblige," he exuded honesty, sincerity, and integrity.[12] His election as Premier was a reaffirmation of the important position of political leadership and party organization in a system of party competition largely devoid of meaningful philosophical or ideological differences; in other words, a confirmation of the dominance of traditional, small "c" conservative politics.

In another sense, however, the Stanfield government did represent an important departure from previous administrations. It clearly brought a new activism and spirit of interventionism to government in Nova Scotia, especially with regard to the problem of economic development. This was made easier by the unexpected defeat of the federal Liberals by John Diefenbaker's Conservatives in 1957. With a more activist provincial administration and a federal government more sympathetic to the plight of the smaller, poorer provinces, a spate of new regional development initiatives were launched aimed at reducing Canada's chronic regional disparities. The Stanfield government introduced a number of innovations, including Industrial Estates Ltd. (IEL), a government-funded agency that offered a range of incentives to attract new industries, a Voluntary Economic Planning Board, and a Labour-Management Study Committee. These initiatives, which drew on British, French, and Scandinavian experiences, were an attempt to alter the industrial structure of the province, as well as its social and business culture.[13]

The record of government initiatives during the Stanfield period is mixed. Stanfield himself left to assume the role of national leader of the Progressive Conservatives in 1967, while optimism about his government's efforts was still high and their ultimate impact still unknown. In retrospect there were a few enduring successes and some spectacular failures. Clearly, a small province with very limited technical and bureaucratic capacities was bound to make misjudgements and miscalculations when dealing with multinational corporations and business entrepreneurs "shopping around" their footloose industries. On the other hand, public investments were often made in ventures based on cutting-edge technologies of the day (e.g., colour television production or components of the nuclear energy industry) whose growth prospects were thought to be excellent; that they turned out not to be so was unfortunate for Nova Scotia, but hardly predictable at the time. Moreover, when the government of Nova Scotia was joined after 1968 in this "buffalo hunt" approach to bagging industries by federal government agencies such as the Department of Regional Economic Expansion (DREE), the latter's record of success was not much better.[14]

As noted, the provincial government's economic strategy of government-induced diversification through incentives for secondary manufacturing enterprises to locate in Nova Scotia suffered a major setback with the Dosco crisis of 1966-67. The new businesses the province was so intently pursuing were always meant to be a supplement to the province's heavy industrial sector. This diversification was made urgent by two major mine disasters followed by permanent mine closures on mainland Nova Scotia (Springhill and Pictou county, in 1957-58). Then, just when the Stanfield government appeared to be making some headway in its efforts to replace lost mining jobs with new industries, these efforts were made to seem trivial by the looming prospect of the total shutdown of Cape Breton's integrated coal and steel industry. That such an eventuality was staved off by the federal decision to take over ownership and management of the mines, and by the province's own takeover of Dosco's Sydney steel operations, is only half the story. The crisis effectively diverted both the province's attentions and its limited resources toward stabilizing, maintaining, and modernizing the steel industry; the federal government, for its part, was reluctantly drawn into this effort in addition to its own mandate to wind down the coal industry while simultaneously diversifying the local (Cape Breton) economy. Thirty years (and hundreds of millions of dollars) later, the coal and steel industries in Cape Breton would still be in operation, but with 7,000 fewer workers, while government-directed diversification efforts over this period proved to be largely futile.

The mounting problems associated with economic development issues faced by Stanfield's successor as premier, G.I. Smith,[15] produced a narrow opposition victory in the election of 1970, and for the next eight years Liberal Gerald Regan served as premier. In retrospect, this period was the high point of federal largesse in the cause of regional development, which added to the inflow of federal dollars associated with other statutory programs (equalization, social program transfers, unemployment insurance). This flow of federal monies clearly helped buoy Liberal political fortunes through the 1970s. Politically, however, the Regan government failed to follow through with badly-needed reforms (many of which were recommended in a 1974 provincial royal commission);[16] more to the point, none of the fundamentals of the province's economic predicament was altered. Plans for a new steel mill to be financed by an international consortium fell through as steel markets softened in the mid-1970s, a projected industrial boom for the deep-harbour Strait of Canso area never materialized, and the far-off promise of offshore oil (Regan held a news conference to display a vial of crude oil dredged up from the seabed) was not sufficient to win the Liberals a third mandate. With economic growth stagnant, unemployment rising, and the cost of electricity soaring, the Liberals lost in 1978 to the John Buchanan-led Conservatives, beginning fifteen years of uninterrupted Tory government (most of them under Buchanan).[17] After his provincial loss, Regan moved on to the federal arena, winning election for the riding of Halifax and serving as a federal cabinet minister in Pierre Trudeau's last government between 1980 and 1984.[18]

John Buchanan's years as premier (1978-90) have become notable for the subsequent revelations that patronage and partisan bias was pervasive in the operations of his government. In 1981 and again in 1984, he used the prospect of offshore oil and gas (and the lavish federal subsidies for offshore exploration associated with the National Energy Program) to fuel his re-election campaigns, with great success. (He also knew how to ride coat-tails, scheduling the 1984 provincial election in the wake of the huge federal victory for the Conservatives that year.) A charming, folksy political personality who exuded optimism and excelled at the art of glad-handing and political campaigning, Buchanan was a politician of the old school, generally fighting elections not on issues, but on personality and "leadership." He also knew how to "wrap himself in the tartan" and appeal to Nova Scotians' sense of pride and tradition.[19]

Economic development policy during the Buchanan era was a schizophrenic affair. On the one hand, there was a growing recognition on the part of provincial bureaucrats that the province had to increase its autonomy in this area by doing its own analysis and developing its own coordinated strategy; on the other hand, federal economic strategy and the availability of federal dollars continued to determine provincial priorities. During the early 1980s, proposed energy megaprojects in Atlantic Canada generated tremendous development hype. The federal government was offering generous incentives for oil companies to drill offshore, and government and private sector reports were projecting that relative to the size of the economies involved, the Atlantic region would lead the nation in major capital projects between 1983 and 1995 in terms of capital investment and jobs created.[20] In light of these projections and the willingness of the federal Liberal government to subsidize exploration and development costs, the Buchanan government enthusiastically attached itself to the megaproject strategy. While negotiations between Ottawa and Newfoundland over ownership of the offshore seabed dragged on, Nova Scotia rushed to "get the jump" on its neighbour in attracting exploration activity and energy-related businesses.[21] Rising energy costs and the megaproject strategy also promised new life for Devco. It began to look as if "King Coal" might make a comeback, and the notion of totally scrapping coal-mining was replaced by grandiose plans to develop Cape Breton's still untapped storehouse of expensive undersea coal reserves and to foster the creation of other coal-related energy industries (such as coal liquefaction and synthetic fuels).[22]

For a time, then, swollen energy prices and the development hype surrounding energy-related industries seemed to promise an economic boom for Nova Scotia, creating in its wake a wave of optimism that floated the Buchanan Tories to two easy election victories (1981, 1984).[23] By the mid-1980s, however, collapsing oil prices and an international recession burst the energy bubble, the mega-project strategy, and the development dreams and schemes of the Nova Scotia government. A more sobering reality quickly set in: the offshore bonanza faded and Devco and Sysco's debts mounted. In 1984, a moratorium was placed on Devco's expansion plans; the same year a disastrous fire killed one miner and threw another 1200 out of work, as the corporation was forced to permanently seal one of its mines.[24] With Cape Breton's economic situation deteriorating noticeably, it was clear that after almost 20 years of activity, Devco had failed in its mission to put the island's economy on a stable footing. At Sysco the situation was no better, as provincial and federal bureaucrats and politicians haggled over a modernization plan while losses piled up. The Buchanan government publicly voiced its solidarity with the position of the union and local politicians (that any modernization should maximize employment at the plant), even though independent studies (both its own and a federal study) were recommending a smaller, less expensive operation. As the sad litany of political gamesmanship and bureaucratic vetoes continued to stall decision-making, employment at the mill steadily dropped through the 1980s. Unglamorous and forlorn, Sysco was not, nor perhaps had it ever been, a major element in either government's economic development strategy.[25]

In the late 1980s and early 1990s, the Buchanan government with federal cooperation took two steps that held out the promise of some long-term future for the province's beleaguered steel and coal industries. It reached a modernization agreement with the federal government that promised economic viability for the steel industry by introducing new technology and dramatically downsizing steel operations to a "mini-mill" employing only 700 workers. Negotiations were subsequently undertaken with several potential private-sector buyers, with the province promising to be out of the steel industry, one way or another, by 1998.[26] Two provincial elections (1998 and 1999) delayed matters, but by summer 2000 it appeared that the still unsold Sysco would cease operations, and its assets sold to the highest bidder.

With regard to coal, the province proceeded with its conversion program to burn coal rather than oil in its electrical generators, and built a new $450-million thermal generation plant at Point Aconi in Cape Breton, utilizing an innovative coal slurry process to reduce the acid rain-producing emissions of Cape Breton's sulphurous coal. Construction proceeded after environmentalists were unsuccessful in convincing the federal government to initiate a full-scale environmental assessment of the project. In the 1900s, however, the coal industry (like steel) suffered setbacks and further employment declines. In 1999, the Government of Canada announced that it would be "winding up" Devco, closing one mine and selling the other. Its less-than-generous compensation package to the miners was bitterly denounced and contested, resulting in an arbitration ruling that significantly improved pension and severance benefits.[27] Nonetheless, the negative impact of the closure on the local economy was projected to be very substantial, at the end of a decade during which Cape Breton Island's population share, employment levels, labour force participation rates, and earned income per capita had all fallen in relation to provincial figures.[28] During the twentieth century, coal and steel constituted a central pillar of the Nova Scotia economy; in the twenty-first century, if present at all, they are destined to be no more than a minor component.

One other Buchanan-era initiative on the economic development front is worth noting here because it is suggestive of the price that organized labour in Nova Scotia was forced to pay in order to facilitate corporate expansion in the province (and the jobs that go along with it). In December, 1979, the Buchanan government passed the so-called "Michelin Bill" through the legislature, incurring the wrath of organized labour and bringing an end to the province's Joint Labour-Management Study Committee, a Stanfield-era experiment in labour-business cooperation. The bill (which prevented labour from organizing Michelin's operations in Nova Scotia one plant at a time, the normal practice elsewhere) was clearly anti-union and directly served the interests of the Michelin Tire Corporation. The government was rewarded with a third Michelin Tire plant in the province, subsequently located in a predominantly agricultural area with no history of industrial unionism. Michelin is now the largest single private-sector employer in Nova Scotia.[29]

DEPENDENCY AND POLITICAL TRADITIONALISM

Viewed from an end-of-century perspective, it seems clear that the fiscal component of Nova Scotia's relationship with Canada in the second half of the twentieth century was a growing annual fiscal transfer to the province for equalization and social programs, a regionalized unemployment insurance system that became an important component of the annual income of seasonal workers, a series of bilateral federal-provincial economic development agreements for infrastructure and modernization, and substantial direct federal spending in the province through such departments as Fisheries and Oceans, Defence, Energy, Public Works, and Transportation. Clearly federal transfers have benefitted Nova Scotia, and especially the province's capital region (metropolitan Halifax), which was transformed by the expansion of its government, defence, health, and education sectors. At the same time, disparities *within* Nova Scotia increased as other parts of the province were denied the economic stability and relative prosperity enjoyed by the capital region. Moreover, the structure of the province's private sector remained substantially unaltered.

A provincial economy so dependent on transfers and federal spending of one sort or another is not driven by its own internal dynamism, but by the economic vitality of other regions and the fiscal resources this provides to the national government for redistribution. In economic and fiscal terms, Nova Scotia was a policy-taker, a passive recipient of what the economic and political system had to offer, forced to work within and exploit when possible an "opportunity structure" that was determined largely by external actors, either economic or political. This dependent political economy had its corollary in the character of Nova Scotia's political regime and its associated political culture milieu. Vertically-integrated patron-client relations were central to the politics of the province. This system, extending from the local to the national level, operated through elite-organized friendship networks that processed rewards for client loyalty and service through an integrated party system. Politics were intensely partisan, elitist, and leader-dominated, but partisanship for many if not most, it could be argued, has been a matter of *political entrepreneurism* as much as *partisan loyalty*. So long as "times were hard" and earning a sufficient livelihood strictly on the basis of what the private sector offered proved difficult, the rewards (both material and status-related) proffered by the political system remained an attractive inducement to citizen participation in the game of partisan politics.[30]

The development of the Canadian welfare state did reduce the scope of traditional patronage politics by making many decisions about "who got what" non-discretionary and therefore not open to manipulation for partisan purposes. Universal social programs are the clearest case in point. But in the context of continuing provincial economic weakness, insecurity, and dependence, government spending and transfers of all sorts provided the material basis for *quasi*-traditional political regimes, with bureaucratic clientelism and transfer dependency overlaying more traditional forms of patronage politics. So the role of elite networks and political "fixers" in the modern era did not disappear (indeed, in some ways they were aggrandized). Local and provincial elites continued to cultivate the federal connection as the most likely and accessible source of resources, especially for economic development purposes. This privileged certain elites and modes of social and political organization, while inhibiting the emergence of others. The general effect on the composition and character of the province's elite was noted by historian T.W. Acheson:

> Another side effect of the federal intervention was the creation of a new bourgeoisie elite composed of professional civil servants, medical doctors and academics who joined the lawyer-politician-businessman leadership of the community and gave it a distinctly professional flavour. Indeed, with its emphasis on place and sinecures, and the patron-client relationship which the monopolistic hierarchies of provincial governments and institutions of higher learning encouraged, Maritime society began to more closely resemble an eighteenth- than a nineteenth-century society.... It was a captive elite largely dependent for opportunity, position, and status on federal resources and ultimately subject to the will of the federal government. Most important, it was an elite with no resource base, one incapable of generating anything more than services ... producers of primary or secondary goods played little role in its ranks.[31]

The continuing importance enjoyed by *vertically-integrated* political and bureaucratic mechanisms as the main means of acquiring or leveraging an inflow of resources discouraged the formation of strong *horizontal* linkages at the local and regional level, as well as cooperative, solidaristic and community strategies of coping with and overcoming economic and social problems. Localities and provinces tended to turn to the federal benefactor rather than to each other; political and bureaucratic elites gained sustenance and status in the role of "go-betweens" or lynchpins in the transfer system. Municipalities were encouraged to engage in competitive fund- and project-seeking strategies, exploiting whatever vertical political links existed in order to do so. The overall long-term effect of this orientation on regional and local solidarity and cooperation was corrosive. Cooperation and trust were undermined, while entrepreneurial parasitism, elite dominance, and federal bureaucratic paternalism were encouraged. Conversely, popular participation and community involvement were discouraged. The privileging of vertical over horizontal relations thus contributed to the fragmentation of local community politics and to the historic withering of once vibrant regional social movements such as the cooperative movement.

This history of dependency and regional policy failures provided fertile ground for "desperation development" schemes and a long line of development boondoggles in the province and region.[32] A small, leader-dominated provincial state like Nova Scotia, with limited bureaucratic expertise at its disposal and operating within the context of past development failures or a simple "strategy vacuum," was highly vulnerable to the schemes of "lone wolf" entrepreneurs and the job-creating promises of footloose industries. The seemingly inevitable failure of such ventures, usually involving a significant loss of public funds, took its toll on public confidence and reinforced federal paternalism towards the provincial government. In the modern history of Nova Scotia, governmental ineffectiveness, quasi-traditional politics, a disaffected political culture, and failed development schemes became part of an interwoven pattern in the province's social and political fabric, interlocking elements of a dependency-traditionalism syndrome that eventually created amongst Nova Scotians themselves an increasing restiveness and dissatisfaction.

NOVA SCOTIA POLITICS IN THE 1990s

With the underlying regional political economy changing radically in the 1980s, political regimes in Atlantic Canada also began to assume a different character. In New Brunswick and Nova Scotia in particular, quintessential old-time politicians who practised elitist, leader-oriented politics were replaced by governments with radically reformist programs. In Nova Scotia, the mounting deficits of the Buchanan regime were threatening the province's fiscal stability. At the same time, political scandals were breaking out all around the Premier, whose media-coined nickname of "Teflon John" was beginning to wear very thin. One of these "scandals" affected not only the Buchanan government, but the whole Nova Scotia justice system.

This was the Marshall Inquiry, an investigation into the false conviction for murder and 11-year incarceration of Donald Marshall, a Mi'kmaq Indian. The Inquiry revealed incompetence, systemic racism, and cover-ups that involved the judiciary, police, and successive provincial governments. A more personally damning scandal was the testimony of a former deputy minister of Government Services that Buchanan had repeatedly interfered in government operations to the benefit of his friends.[33]

After twelve years as premier, and with his political legitimacy draining away, Buchanan in 1990 retreated to the safety of the Canadian Senate, courtesy of his political ally Brian Mulroney. Out of the rubble of "Buchananism," an almost diametrically opposite politician emerged who was determined to pursue a reform agenda aimed at revamping Nova Scotia's political system. Former industry minister Donald Cameron, premier from 1991-93, injected a large dose of straight-laced probity and frugality into a system plagued by deeply-rooted corruption and budgetary laxity. He pledged himself to breaking up the patronage networks and mechanisms which underlay Nova Scotia politics and set about to do so with a series of reforms to election financing laws, electoral boundaries, the Human Rights Act, judicial appointments, the method of tendering government contracts, privatization of Crown Corporations and contracting-out of government services. In the process, he slashed 300 government jobs and broke existing collective agreements in order to freeze the wages of all public-sector employees.[34]

Having spent two years reining in government spending, while shaking up the provincial bureaucracy and his own party's patronage practices, Cameron went to the polls in 1993. However, besides the weight of 15 years of Conservative government, Cameron had his own personal burden to carry: his involvement in the Westray Mine Affair. On May 9, 1992, 26 miners died when they were trapped underground by a coal dust explosion triggered by a methane gas fire. Blame was attributed to negligence on the part of provincial mine inspectors as well as the mine operator, Curragh Inc. of Toronto. Cameron, for his part, had been instrumental in securing provincial and federal loans for the mine.[35] Tainted by this disaster, and unable to shake the public's desire to be rid of the Tories (in both their federal and provincial incarnations), Cameron lost the 1993 election in a landslide to the Liberals; he immediately resigned his own seat and the party leadership, and soon thereafter accepted a federal appointment as Canadian Consul-General in Boston.[36]

The provincial Liberal government elected in May, 1993 was led by John Savage, a physician-politician who has the distinction of being the first party leader in Canada elected to his position in a universal membership vote by telephone. The Savage government followed up Donald Cameron's reforms with a full plate of its own: further reforms to party patronage practices, health care, education, municipalities, social services, as well as the financing and organization of universities. It also sought to privatize a long list of public ventures, including school and highway construction. Such widespread and fundamental reforms—popular or not with Nova Scotians—make it difficult to envisage any return to the syndrome of quasi-traditional politics in Nova Scotia.

The overriding priority of the Savage Liberals—to the seeming exclusion of all other considerations—was to eliminate the province's large and increasingly burdensome deficit, an undertaking with profound implications for government programs given the profligacy of the Buchanan years and the drastic cuts in transfers being initiated by a new federal Liberal government, also elected in 1993. Orchestrating this attack on the deficit was the province's new finance minister, Bernie Boudreau. He introduced a succession of provincial budgets that featured tax increases (breaking a Liberal election promise), public-sector salary rollbacks and freezes, deep cuts in spending on health and education, forced municipal amalgamations, modest tax breaks for business, and the building of two gambling casinos that were touted as cash-cows for the province.[37] Restructuring of the health care and education systems was also undertaken, but with the main emphasis on achieving savings for the government. This was particularly the case with health care reform, the blueprint for which promised a system that would be more effective, comprehensive and democratic; in reality, the imperative of deficit reduction left health reform in a shambles, as well as the political career of Health Minister Ron Stewart (who eventually resigned both his cabinet post and his seat).[38]

By 1997, both the provincial and federal Liberals were highly unpopular with Nova Scotians. Voters took a particular dislike to Premier John Savage, who came across to many people as cold and arrogant. Hobbled by this public image, internal challenges to his leadership from disaffected Liberals, and growing public anger over cuts to public services (especially health), Savage announced his intention to resign as premier and party leader. During the race to replace him, a federal election campaign took place, with shocking results for the Liberals, who had won every Nova Scotia seat in 1993. On June 2, 1997, every one of these Liberals went down to defeat, including the high-profile Minister of Health and Welfare, Dave Dingwall. Even more surprising was the performance of the NDP, which achieved an historic breakthrough by winning 6 of the 11 provincial seats. This can be attributed partly to affection for federal NDP leader Alexa McDonough, who struggled through 15 years in the Nova Scotia legislature as leader of an always-tiny NDP caucus. Clearly, however, this was also a protest vote against the drastic cuts in social program funding carried out by Liberal governments at both levels.[39] In the aftermath of this federal debacle in Nova Scotia, provincial Liberals were presented with a leadership choice that featured two Cape Bretoners, Finance Minister Bernie Boudreau and long-time federal MP Russell MacLellan. Burdened by his close association with the same unpopular policies for which the federal Liberals so recently had been punished, Boudreau lost the leadership to MacLellan, then announced his own retirement from politics. Two years later Boudreau re-emerged as a Chrétien-appointed senator and Nova Scotia representative in the federal cabinet, charged with restoring Liberal political fortunes in the province.

The change of provincial leadership to the seemingly more affable and approachable MacLellan seemed to temporarily buoy Liberal electoral prospects. Leading in public opinion polls, MacLellan called the election for March 24 1998, *before* his government was scheduled to bring down a promised balanced budget. An ill-prepared Liberal Party, surprised by its leader's election call, stumbled through a one-note campaign that attempted to focus exclusively on the economic dividends that were expected to flow from five years of fiscal restraint. Pressed to make some response to concerns about the health-care system, MacLellan added to his campaign the plank of some additional health-care spending. But this poorly conceived "front-runner" strategy soon was felled by poor execution (in particular MacLellan's poor performance in a televised leaders' debate) and by the opposition parties' comparatively strong campaigns. Robert Chisholm, Alexa McDonough's successor as leader of the provincial New Democrats, and John Hamm, who took over the reins of the Progressive Conservatives after Donald Cameron's abrupt departure, ridiculed MacLellan for running a "Where's Waldo" campaign and attacked his government's policies, especially on health care, the issue which dominated the campaign. The outcome was a dead heat in both seats and votes for the Liberals and New Democrats (19 seats and 35 per cent of the vote apiece), with the Tories finishing a strong third (14 seats on 30 per cent of the vote).[40]

The election result suggests a profound change in the pattern of party competition in Nova Scotia. The New Democrats became a major political force and the dominant party in metropolitan Halifax. Even in rural areas of the province, previously a "dead-zone" for the NDP, the party was able to win two seats while finishing second in 10 others. Conservative support provincially, restricted to rural areas of mainland Nova Scotia, mirrored that of the federal party. Overall, the election results of 1997-98 revealed three distinct zones of party competition in the province: metropolitan Halifax (NDP and Liberals), Cape Breton (Liberals and NDP), and mainland Nova Scotia (predominantly Tory). Facing a "hung Parliament," MacLellan's hold on power in the spring of 1998 was precarious indeed; also unclear was the general policy direction likely to emerge from the political and legislative manoeuvring engaged in by all three parties.

The precariousness of the Liberals' hold on power was brought home in the early summer of 1999 when the government tried to introduce a deficit budget. Having stated publicly that his party would vote against a deficit budget, provincial Conservative leader John Hamm made good on his promise and, along with the NDP, brought down the government. Premier MacLellan went on the offensive in the campaign leading up to the July 27 election, claiming the campaign was an unnecessary expense brought on the province by power-hungry opposition leaders.[41] Both opposition leaders, however, argued that the Liberals were a spent political force and had to be removed from office. While the Liberals and the NDP traded slurs and attacked each other's policies and records, the Conservatives traded on the popularity and probity of their country doctor leader and emerged from the election as the new government, taking 29 seats to the NDP's 12 and the Liberals' 11.[42]

The 1999 results reinforced the changes to the provincial electoral landscape that had emerged from the 1998 election. Although it failed to win the government, the NDP assumed the role of official opposition, only the second time in provincial history that a party other than the Liberals or Conservatives had been able to fill that position. Premier John Hamm and his Progressive Conservative government are assured of a four-year term of office, but the party's position atop the political heap in Nova Scotia is somewhat precarious. Although rewarded by the electoral system with a majority of seats, the Tory party took less than 40 per cent of the popular vote and benefitted from the almost exact division of the remaining 60 per cent between the NDP and the Liberals. Each of those latter parties lost only five per cent of its 1998 vote, just enough to push the Conservatives to a solid majority in a three-way contest.

A REGIONAL RESPONSE TO FISCAL RESTRAINT AND CONSTITUTIONAL CRISIS?

By the early 1980s, the impact of the trend toward globalization and the worsening fiscal crisis of the welfare state began to be felt in earnest in Canada. Technological change, the internationalization of capital and production, and the ongoing removal of barriers to trade had led to intensified international competition, especially in mass production industries. Under such pressures, serious cracks began to appear in Canada's postwar political economy. This continued apace through the 1980s, as government deficits remained stubbornly high and the pace of economic and technological change increased.[43]

Following the 1988 federal election, which gave Brian Mulroney's Conservatives their second consecutive majority, a succession of federal budgets were introduced aimed at reducing the federal deficit through tax increases and spending cuts. Transfers to the provinces for health and education were frozen at 1989-90 levels, while the growth of transfers to the richer provinces for social services was capped at a time when numerous plant shut-downs had swelled the ranks of the unemployed and those dependent upon welfare, especially in Ontario. In response to these federal cuts, provincial governments, preoccupied with their own rising deficits, reduced their own spending and public-sector employment and repeatedly warned their citizens to moderate their demands and learn to expect *less* from government in the future.

These developments constituted a "double-whammy" for the fiscal situation of provinces such as Nova Scotia. Direct cuts in program spending had their greatest impact where government spending was most central to the economy. At the same time, stalled national economic growth in the early 1990s, and particularly the serious loss of jobs in Ontario, resulted in reduced equalization payments to the poorer provinces. Adding to Nova Scotia's fiscal difficulties were the problems faced by its rural resource industries. The ecological crisis in the fishery and the supply-and-demand problems of regional pulp and paper producers cast serious doubt on their future as pillars of the province's private sector economy.

These changes in the fiscal and economic context provoked a fundamental re-thinking of political and administrative assumptions and economic development strategies in Nova Scotia. The almost continual constitutional discussions and negotiations between 1985 and 1992 also contributed to this re-examination of government roles, responsibilities, and relations. Both the Meech Lake and Charlottetown Accords proposed limits on the federal spending power and some further decentralization of powers to the provinces. The presumed alternative, especially in the period between the failure of Meech Lake and the Charlottetown Accord, was the likelihood of a sovereign Quebec, with unpredictable and worrisome consequences for the remaining federation, especially for the Atlantic Provinces. The defeat of the Charlottetown Accord in 1992 temporarily removed constitutional reform from the public agenda, but the near-defeat of federalist forces in the 1995 Quebec Referendum renewed political uncertainties about the future shape and direction of the Canadian federation.

Perhaps the most dramatic response from within the Atlantic region to this harsher fiscal and political environment was the idea of further economic integration of the three Maritime or four Atlantic provinces. The goal was to significantly strengthen horizontal linkages amongst economic and political actors in the region, primarily as a means of compensating for the weakening protections and benefits of vertically-integrated federal-provincial relations. A more horizontally-integrated and coordinated approach to procurement, regulation, and provision of services was expected to provide benefits in terms of cost savings for government, as well as economic advantages in the form of a more competitive and capable private sector. A long-term squeeze on federal transfers to the provinces dictated the first concern; globalization and a declining government capacity to shelter uncompetitive private sectors the second.

Resort to the idea of regional integration should be understood within the context of a long tradition in the region of responding to economic and political crises (or other types of external challenge) by promoting the idea of greater internal unity. Maritime Union was the topic of a regional conference in 1864, before it was dropped in favour of Confederation. Then in the early part of the twentieth century, Maritime Union was promoted by regional business and professional groups as a logical development that was in accordance with the progressive spirit of the age. Again in the 1960s, at the height of the Quiet Revolution in Quebec, the three Maritime premiers commissioned a study on Maritime Union (the Deutsch Report), which urged them to move toward full political union as an important step in solving the economic and social ills of the region.

Twenty years after the release of the Deutsch Report, a new study carried out at the behest of the Council of Maritime Premiers made three key recommendations: removal of all interprovincial trade barriers in the region, a Maritime Savings Development Fund similar to Quebec's Caisse de dépôt, and a trade promotion strategy to increase the level of exports from the Maritime region by 50 per cent in five years. The aim was to allow the region to escape its "have-not" status within Canada by the year 2000.[44] Even before the tabling of the report, Premier McKenna of New Brunswick was promoting the idea of Maritime Economic Union, a regional common market without any internal barriers to doing business. Given the extent to which Canadian provinces had over the years moved to protect their own provincial businesses, McKenna's proposal was more radical than might appear at first blush. More than just a call for removing internal trade barriers, McKenna was suggesting a closer integration of the strategic objectives of the three Maritime provinces on such issues as health care, energy, transportation, tourism and economic development. His initiative was applauded by regional business associations and supported by both governing and opposition parties in the three provinces.[45]

Nor was support for the new integration initiative merely rhetorical. At the 78th session of the Council of Maritime Premiers held on October 10, 1990, the three premiers agreed that their governments, facing the prospect of continuing declines in federal transfers, would have to increase their cooperative activity, leading to rationalization of the three provincial economies.[46] In June, 1991, at a forum of Maritime cabinets, it was decided to take action on a number of regulations and restrictive practices recognized as barriers or restrictions on the free movement of people, goods, capital, and services within the region. There was also agreement on government procurement and joint purchasing, as well as a decision to create a Maritime Securities Commission and to develop a regional agricultural strategy.[47] In total, work was initiated on 30 policy issues, an immense broadening of the Maritime cooperative effort.[48]

What distinguishes this latest push toward regional integration from earlier initiatives of this sort, especially that which led up to and followed the Deutsch Report? In the years following the latter, federal transfers rose steadily, and bilateral federal-provincial agreements formed the basis for provincial economic development plans and initiatives. The strength of provincialism in the Atlantic region seemed to grow in positive association with an increase in federal transfers and federal government involvement in the economic development field: expanding federal intervention had as its corollary an expansive provincialism, especially when viewed from the perspective of regional affairs. This was reinforced by the political culture and techniques of governance that characterized Maritime politics. Particularly in the case of Nova Scotia, movement toward further regional integration was inconceivable as long as an extensive provincial patronage system remained intact. The mechanisms of patronage require a significant measure of political discretion over government spending, especially the awarding of contracts, and over government appointments. In this sense, the end of "Buchananism" in Nova Scotia—and Buchanan's replacement as premier with reformers determined to overturn his political legacy—removed a significant barrier to further regional integration.[49]

Provincialism in the 1970s and 1980s was also strengthened by development strategies that were based on provincially-owned natural resources. These strategies neither required nor envisaged extensive regional cooperation; indeed, the latter often seemed to run directly contrary to provincial interests in the further development of their own resource base. In contrast, the new economy seems to demand a greater degree of horizontal integration and cooperation. Unlike economic activity linked to natural resources, knowledge- and information-based industries rely on a highly-educated and highly-skilled workforce, and upon high-quality transportation and communication infrastructures. Unlike natural resources, highly-trained people are a flexible, mobile and shareable resource, dictating at the very least a regional resource rather than distinct provincial ones. Cooperation on education, labour standards and relations, health and social services, and so on, becomes a logical next step for governments wishing to develop and exploit this common human resource pool. Moreover, to the extent that knowledge industries tend to be urban-centred, and only a limited number of such centres within the region is possible, provinces are encouraged to widen and improve inter-urban linkages and specialization.

Still, it must be recognized that throughout the 1990s Nova Scotia and neighbouring New Brunswick continued to compete with one another to attract various "high-tech" or information-age industries (such as Call Centres), showering subsidies and benefits on these corporations in the process. And in other ways regional cooperation associated with the integration initiative was stalled. Changes of government, the conflicting pressures on governing politicians exerted by different political contexts and political cycles, and the inevitable bureaucratic brick walls took their toll. Sustained political must be present amongst all partners in any multi-government, multi-year initiative of this sort to overcome the tremendous inertia exerted by existing bureaucratic structures and myriad differences in policies, programs, and procedures. These will tend to multiply if not consciously catalogued and rolled back.[50] Moreover, any provincial hedging or retrenchment with regard to already established areas of regional cooperation—such as Nova Scotia's decisions (later overturned) to pull out of a regional police training program and a regional lottery—can quickly lead to retaliatory actions by other provinces and the rapid unravelling of earlier cooperative efforts.[51]

A key development in Nova Scotia's economic prospect at the beginning of the twenty-first century is Mobil Oil's $3-billion Sable Gas Project. Given the go-ahead in late 1997 and in operation two years later, the Sable project marks the beginning of a major new industry for the province. However, the overall impact of this new industry is still a matter of speculation.[52] Moreover, initial optimism about the benefits of the project was somewhat tempered by severe criticism of the deal struck by the Nova Scotia government with the Sable Gas consortium, one which featured a royalty structure and industrial benefits package that was significantly less generous than that which Newfoundland secured for its offshore oil industry (Hibernia and ancillary developments).[53] The prospect of further offshore oil and gas development also had the unfortunate effect of reviving "province-first" and "beggar-thy-neighbour" attitudes within the region. This emerged between Nova Scotia and New Brunswick during negotiations over the question of who would get Sable gas and at what price, and between Nova Scotia and Newfoundland over the issue of the offshore boundary between the two provinces and ownership of the potentially rich sub-sea gas and oil deposits that may lie there.[54] However, the first dispute was quickly settled and the second has gone to federal arbitration. The decades-old promise of offshore bounty appears to be on the cusp of realization.

CONCLUSION

Whether or not a full and effective integration of the economies and policies of Maritime or Atlantic region governments is an attainable ideal is an open question. While the integration initiative is a significant indicator of the fiscal, economic and political pressures on the region and its provincial governments (one which helps to explain why political regimes in the region, and particularly Nova Scotia, have been mutating), there is no guarantee that it can be sustained, nor whether it ultimately will reduce regional dependence on Ottawa. If the integration effort revives and deepens, the region may benefit from more coherent governmental approaches to the region's economic, social, and environmental problems. But will such measures be enough to significantly enhance Nova Scotia's capacity to respond to external pressures and competitive challenges such that its future economic prospects and performance will be dramatically better than its past?

The transition to an information-based, global economy presents both dangers and opportunities for disadvantaged or dependent regions within advanced industrial societies, including Nova Scotia and its neighbours. As the political, economic and technological parameters of production change, so does the opportunity structure for previously disadvantaged or under-industrialized regions. What previously had been considered economic weaknesses now have the potential to be converted into strengths. Within the new order, a fuller development of the considerable human and physical resources of Nova Scotia and the broader Maritime region may be possible. The regional integration initiative represents one response to these changing economic and political circumstances. Yet it is likely to be an effective response only if it forms part of a more comprehensive, interrelated set of policies and strategies, involving every level of government, and in cooperation with business and labour.

In this connection, a warning should be offered concerning the danger of formally devolving substantial new powers to all provinces as part of a reconstructed Canadian federalism. It is sometimes argued that greater *jurisdictional autonomy* for "have-less" provinces is necessary if chronic transfer dependence is ever to be overcome. But leaving poorer provinces unaided to deal with the new development challenges they face would be a cure worse than the disease. The desirability of regional integration does not equate with the desirability of any major decentralization of powers and responsibilities to the regions. This would undermine both the quality and scope of the social programs that undergird the new economy; it would weaken, perhaps fatally, a strong *national* sentiment and identity; it would leave a more autonomous Maritime region with a somewhat hollow freedom of action on economic and social matters, deprived as it would be of the stabilizing influence of national social programs and other forms of federal assistance. While regime change and further regional integration may alter the political and economic parameters for provincial development, for the foreseeable future the fate of Nova Scotia and its Maritime neighbours will continue to be tied to that of the rest of Canada.

NOTES

1 J. Murray Beck, "The Party System in Nova Scotia: Tradition and Conservatism," *Canadian Provincial Politics*, ed. Martin Robin (Scarborough: Prentice Hall, 1972), 168-97; D.J. Bellamy, "The Atlantic Provinces," *The Provincial Political Systems: Comparative Essays*, ed. D.J. Bellamy, J.H. Pammett, and D.C. Rowat (Toronto: Methuen, 1976), 3-18; J.M. Beck, "An Atlantic Region Political Culture: A Chimera," *Eastern and Western Perspectives*, ed. D.J. Bercuson and P.A. Buckner (Toronto: University of Toronto Press, 1981), 147-68; Agar Adamson and Ian Stewart, "Party Politics in the Mysterious East," *Party Politics in Canada*, 5th ed., ed. H.G. Thorburn (Scarborough: Prentice Hall, 1985), 319-33.

2 M.D. Ornstein, H.M. Stevenson, and A.P. Williams, "Region, Class and Political Culture in Canada," *Canadian Journal of Political Science* 13:2 (1980): 227-72; M.D. Ornstein, "Regionalism and Canadian Political Ideology," *Regionalism in Canada*, ed. R.J. Brym (Richmond Hill: Irwin, 1986) 47-88.

3 Robert Young, "Teaching and Research in Maritime Politics: Old Stereotypes and New Directions," *Teaching Maritime Studies*, ed. P.A. Buckner (Fredericton: Acadiensis Press, 1986), 153-73; David Milne, "Challenging Constitutional Dependency: A Revisionist View of Atlantic Canada," *The Constitutional Futures of the Prairie and Atlantic Regions of Canada*, ed. J.N. McCrorie and M.L. MacDonald (Regina: Canadian Plains Research Centre, 1992), 308-17; James Bickerton, "Creating Atlantic Canada: Culture, Policy and Regionalism," *Canadian Politics: An Introduction to the Discipline*, ed. Alain G. Gagnon and James P. Bickerton (Peterborough: Broadview Press, 1990), 325-44.

4 Alexa McDonough became the first woman party leader in Canada when she took over leadership of the Nova Scotia New Democrats in 1980; John Savage became the first party leader elected in a universal membership telephone vote when he was chosen by Nova Scotia Liberals in 1992.

5 T.W. Acheson, "The National Policy and the Industrialization of the Maritimes," *Acadiensis* 1 (Spring, 1972): 2-28; E.R. Forbes, *The Maritime Rights Movement 1919-1927* (Montreal: McGill-Queen's, 1979).

6 E.R. Forbes, "Consolidating Disparity: The Maritimes and the Industrialization of Canada During the Second World War," *Acadiensis* 15:2 (1986): 2-27.

7 A.C. Parks, *The Economy of the Atlantic Provinces 1940-1958* (Halifax: Atlantic Provinces Economic Council, 1960), 76.

8 James Bickerton, *Nova Scotia, Ottawa and the Politics of Regional Development* (Toronto: University of Toronto Press, 1990), Chap. 4.

9 Bickerton, *Nova Scotia*, 195-203.

10 Bickerton, *Nova Scotia*, 121, 124-32.

11 J. Murray Beck, *The Government of Nova Scotia* (Toronto: University of Toronto Press, 1957), 158-70.

12 Dalton Camp, *Gentlemen, Players and Politicians* (Toronto: McClelland and Stewart, 1970), 212-13.

13 Bickerton, *Nova Scotia*, 144-54.

14 Bickerton, *Nova Scotia*, 207-28.

15 In 1967, Stanfield contested and won the national leadership of the Progressive Conservative Party, replacing John Diefenbaker in that role. He lost three elections to Pierre Trudeau (the 1972 election by a mere two seats), and resigned as leader in 1976.

16 This was the Graham Royal Commission on Education, Public Services and Provincial-Municipal Relations.

17 The 1978 election also marked a high point for the New Democratic Party in Nova Scotia politics, with the party taking four seats, all in the coal and steel towns of Cape Breton. Within two years, however, the party would be riven with internal conflict: the resignation of its leader, Jeremy Akerman, and his replacement with Alexa McDonough; the expulsion of renegade MLA Paul MacEwan; and the subsequent loss of the party's Cape Breton base. In a strange twist, MacEwan was elected as a Liberal in 1993 and made Speaker of the Nova Scotia legislature.

18 Regan was defeated in the 1984 Conservative landslide. More than a decade later, the former premier and federal cabinet minister became the subject of a lengthy and high profile criminal trial involving numerous sexual assault charges spanning a period between 1956 and 1978.

19 See Peter Kavanaugh, *John Buchanan: The Art of Political Survival* (Halifax: Formac, 1989).

20 The Atlantic Provinces Economic Council reported that $35 billion worth of major projects were on stream for the Atlantic region, with oil and gas contributing 80 per cent of this total. *Globe and Mail*, "APEC reports $35 billion worth of projects for region," 9 May 1984.

21 *Globe and Mail*, "Doing Business in Nova Scotia," 8 March 1982; *Citizen* (Ottawa), "Battling Brian a fading hero in Newfoundland," 26 February 1983.

22 The projected investment being considered was huge: $330 million to open the first new mine; $2 billion to bring three new mines into production by 1993. DEVCO, *13th Annual Report*, 1981; *Globe and Mail*, 18 October 1981, B18.

23 Simultaneously, another key industry, the province's fishery, was saved from financial collapse by a corporate reorganization plan put together by both levels of government. This led to a renewed fishing effort so intensive that it would soon precipitate a major collapse of Atlantic groundfish stocks, requiring further massive government intervention in the form of the TAGS program.

24 Devco, *Annual Report*, 1982; *Report on Business Magazine*, July-August 1985, 68; *Citizen* (Ottawa), 7 November 1983, 5; *Atlantic Insight*, September 1984, 47.

25 *Chronicle-Herald* (Halifax), 10 November 1982; 9 April 1985; 16 May 1985; 15 June 1985; 24 July 1985.

26 In May 1998, the government of Nova Scotia was in the final stages of formalizing a sale agreement with a Mexican steelmaker, Grupo Acerero Del Norte. The agreement-in-principle requires Sysco's new owners to invest a substantial sum to expand and diversify operations at the mill. Dale Madill, "Sale of Sysco done deal by July, MacDonald says," *Chronicle-Herald* (Halifax) 1 May 1998.

27 Kevin Cox, "Coal miners get $50-million boost," *Globe and Mail* 3 June 2000, A17.

28 Gardner Pinfold Consulting Economists, *Economic Impact of the Devco Closure*, report prepared for Local 26, United Mine Workers, September 1999.

29 K. Antoft, "Harnessing Confrontation: A Review of the Labour-Management Study Committee, 1962-1979," *Social Science Monograph Series, Volume 4: Labour and Atlantic Canada* (Fredericton: University of New Brunswick, 1981), 113-14.

30 This argument is made in greater detail in James Bickerton, "The Party System and Centre-Periphery Relations: The Case of the Maritimes," *Canadian Parties in Transition*, ed. A.G. Gagnon and A.B. Tanguay (Scarborough: Nelson, 1989), 496-514.

31 T.W. Acheson, "The Maritimes and 'Empire Canada'" *Canada and the Burden of Unity*, ed. David Jay Bercuson (Toronto: MacMillan of Canada, 1977), 104-05.

32 For some examples, see Philip Mathias, *Forced Growth* (Toronto: James, Lewis and Samuel, 1971).

33 Rand Dyck, *Provincial Politics in Canada*, 3rd ed. (Scarborough: Prentice Hall, 1996), 153-54.

34 Dyck, 155.

35 For one rendering of the Westray Mine Affair, see Shaun Comish, *The Westray Tragedy: A Miner's Story* (Halifax: Fernwood, 1993).

36 Comish, 155-56.

37 Comish, 156-58.

38 See James Bickerton, "Health Care Reform in Nova Scotia: Redesigning Democracy?", paper presented to the annual meeting of the Canadian Political Science Association, Brock University, St. Catherines, Ontario (2-4 June 1996).

39 See Alan Whitehorn, "Alexa McDonough and Atlantic Breakthrough for the New Democratic Party," *The Canadian General Election of 1997*, ed. Alan Frizzell and Jon Pammett (North York, ON: Dundurn Press, 1997).

40 Six weeks after the election, one of the 19 newly-minted NDP MLAS, under investigation by the provincial law society, resigned from the caucus. He decided to sit as an Independent pending the outcome of the investigation.

41 See Kevin Cox, "MacLellan takes the Offensive on Campaign Trail," *Globe and Mail*, 19 June 1999, A7.

42 See Kevin Cox, "Nova Scotia Tories Win Majority: Premier-Elect Hamm Sweeps Liberals Aside," *Globe and Mail*, 28 July 1999, A1.

43 According to David Harvey, this new "flexible regime of accumulation ... is marked by a direct confrontation with the rigidities of Fordism. It rests on flexibility with respect to labour processes, labour markets, products, and patterns of consumption. It is characterized by the emergence of entirely new sectors of production, new ways of providing financial services, new markets, and, above all, greatly intensified rates of commercial, technological and organizational innovation. It has entrained rapid shifts in the patterning of uneven development, both between sectors and between geographic regions, giving rise to a vast surge in so-called 'service sector' employment as well as to entirely new industrial ensembles in hitherto underdeveloped regions. It has also entailed a new round of what I shall call 'time-space compression' in the capitalist world—the time horizons of both public and private decision-making have shrunk, while satellite communication and declining transport costs have made it increasingly possible to spread these decisions immediately over an ever-wider and variegated space.... Flexible accumulation appears to imply relatively high levels of structural unemployment, rapid destruction and reconstruction of skills, modest (if any) gains in real wages, the roll-back of trade union power ... [and] the apparent move away from regular employment towards increasing reliance upon part-time, temporary or sub-contracted work arrangements." David Harvey, *The Condition of Postmodernity* (Oxford: Basil Blackwell, 1989), 149-50.

44 Charles McMillan, *Standing Up to the Future: The Maritimes in the 1990s*, Report to the Council of Maritime Premiers (Halifax: Council of Maritime Premiers, December 1989).

45 Canadian Press, "McKenna pushes Maritime Coalition," *Chronicle-Herald* (Halifax), 12 September 1990, A2; Tom McCoag, "N.B. Tory Leader backs Maritime economic union," *Chronicle-Herald*, 16 October 1990, C2; Brian Ward, "MacLean, P.E.I. premier discuss cooperation plan," *Chronicle-Herald*, 10 January 1991, C12.

46 Council of Maritime Premiers, *Press Release*, 78th session, 30 October 1990.

47 A full list of what was agreed to follows: a Maritime Securities Commission to be established in 1992; removal of provincial protection for makers of paint, culverts and guardrails; the Maritime Procurement Agreement was expanded to include more services and to include the purchases of electrical utilities and liquor boards; electrical utilities were directed to study joint planning of supply systems; for the first time some joint purchasing was agreed to (e.g., fire hose); barriers to commercial trucking are to be removed; bus service disruptions at the N.S.-N.B. border are to end; a strategic plan for agriculture is to be developed; a regional environmental accord is to be negotiated; and provincial loans for construction of fishing boats are to be tenable at any boatyard in the region. Conference of Maritime Premiers, "Highlights of Second Session," 31 May 1991.

48 Conference of Atlantic Premiers. "Highlights of Second Session," 31 May 1991. Since the first forum of Maritime cabinets, Newfoundland has agreed to join the Maritime Procurement Agreement.

49 The arguments made by the premiers for economic union reveal both their fiscal concerns and the economic assumptions underlying their support for regional integration. Integration, they argued, would result in "significant savings to the taxpayer and equally important greater improvement in the economic capabilities of producers in the four Atlantic provinces." It would also create "a more entrepreneurial society" and "competitive business."

50 Michael Tutton, "Bureaucratic brick walls stifle Maritime economic union," *Chronicle-Herald* (Halifax), 8 August 1995.

51 Steve Proctor, "Agricultural college caught in crossfire," *Chronicle-Herald* (Halifax), 9 May 1998.

52 Judy Myrden, "Sable gas, at last," *Chronicle-Herald* (Halifax), 28 October 1997.

53 Parker Barss Donham, "Parker's Column," *Sunday Daily News* (Halifax), 14 December 1997.

54 Judy Myrden, "Premiers to discuss oil feud," *Chronicle-Herald* (Halifax), 4 May 1998. Such disputes are all too reminiscent of the provincialism which marked the demise of regional cooperation on energy strategy in 1980, associated with the demise of the Maritime Energy Corporation. Though the federal government offered to make a sizeable financial contribution toward the creation of a regional energy corporation that would fund and develop energy megaprojects, this approach was repudiated by the Buchanan government shortly after it took office in 1978. Instead the province decided to pursue development of its own energy sources (especially coal and offshore oil/gas reserves). *Chronicle-Herald*, 20 December 1978; *Maclean's*, 6 October 1980, 38.

4 NEW BRUNSWICK

The Challenge of New Brunswick Politics

HUGH MELLON

Compared to most other Canadian jurisdictions New Brunswick is rather small, having an official population in 1996 of 738,133.[1] Travel times from most parts of the province to the capital city, Fredericton, usually span a couple of hours. The province sends ten members to the House of Commons and would be considered over-represented by strict representation-by-population equations. There are 55 Members of the provincial Legislative Assembly for only 525,132 registered voters.[2] New Brunswickers are a people used to having access to their politicians and this expectation of availability extends all the way to the premier. A rough and ready sense of egalitarianism exists among the general population. Politicians deemed to have lost touch with the "folks" back home can be candidates for a rude awakening at election time.

The small scale of political life generates a preoccupation with the position of the premier. Reliance upon the premier to represent New Brunswick to the nation is coupled with the small scale of governing machinery, allowing the holder of this office extensive influence and power. This is in keeping with the other Atlantic provinces. As Adamson and Stewart point out, "Leaders dominated their parties, not only during election campaigns, but also in party programs, in the legislature and when in office, in defining government policy."[3] Premiers are expected to be aware of developments throughout their province, and their personalities and abilities are the focus of party appeals and popular commentary.

Interest in politics is high for a number of fundamental reasons. Perennial economic weakness presents an ongoing challenge for the entire province. Premiers and leading cabinet ministers are expected to deal with economic promotion and to champion provincial causes in federal–provincial forums. Despite the province's significant economic problems, there are wealthy commercial interests, the best known of which are those associated with the Irving and McCain family empires. A common strain of popular debate is whether or not the provincial government is doing too much or too little for these wealthy interests. Governments are also expected to keep close tabs on federal-provincial transfers and emerging trends in equalization payments which form a significant percentage of provincial revenues.

Another cause for preoccupation with politics is the ever-present interplay of linguistic and cultural relations between the province's sizable francophone population and its anglophone majority. Among Canada's provinces, New Brunswick's linguistic profile most closely matches that of the country as a whole and the province's official bilingualism is constitutionally entrenched. Over the past decades successive governments have worked to improve relations among linguistic groups, and this concern has produced considerable cooperation and empathy. However, issues such as education or intra-provincial disparities (the largely anglophone south and south-west has generally been better off than the largely francophone north and north-east) always carry with them underlying political tensions.

This combination of small-scale leadership preoccupation and keen interest in political topics produces an interesting brand of politics. Patronage, once a defining characteristic of New Brunswick politics, has ebbed with bureaucratization, bilingual administration, and modernization. Its influence remains, though, and partisan traditions are still strong in some areas. Premiers must vigilantly monitor local allegiances and party organization, but they are simultaneously expected to foster modern commercial development and to represent the province to outsiders.

Defining the province's links to the broader Canadian community has also presented an interesting political challenge for provincial leaders. From Canada's earliest days, the nature of New Brunswick's inter-provincial and federal-provincial linkages has been a contentious issue. As Robert Finbow asserts, "The Atlantic provinces were reluctant participants in Canadian confederation."[4] Anti-confederates were prominent in the Maritimes in 1867 and the reluctance of a sizable part of the population to embrace Confederation was partially addressed by railway construction and federal government assistance. These amenities, however, were scant comfort as the regional economy suffered dislocation and relative decline compared to central Canada. This decline generated continual questions about the value of Confederation and the worth of Ottawa's commitment to the "national interest." Periodically, protest movements arose, but the general pattern of decline accompanied by public skepticism about federal government policies and assistance persisted.

One of these protest movements was the "Maritime Rights" agitation in the years following World War I, which involved New Brunswick in disputes over rail rates, regional representation in Ottawa, federal-provincial relations, and Maritime development.[5] Another period marked by regional efforts to recast regional relations with Ottawa came in the 1950s. This time New Brunswick, under Conservative premier Hugh John Flemming, took the lead in mounting the regional campaign against Ottawa's unwillingness to promote regional development through favourable fiscal and program policies.[6]

Despite the discontent, success in these and other instances of protest proved elusive. Economic vulnerability, and the weakness of a small population without a new flow of either investment or settlers, forced New Brunswick politicians to accommodate themselves to the prevailing federal government mood. This produced an interesting collection of political adaptations. New Brunswick governments of whatever partisan stripe have had to maintain close working relations with regional ministers appointed by successive federal governments.[7] As well, the province's reliance on fiscal transfers gave the federal government considerable influence over provincial political life.

Provincial governments in the Atlantic region generally have displayed differing degrees of willingness to accede to federal plans. New Brunswick, however, usually adopted a pattern of cooperative federal-provincial relations, where collegial relations with Ottawa were cultivated. This accommodation extended to cautious support for federal efforts to promote Maritime integration after the end of World War II. New Brunswick has done as much, if not more, than its Atlantic counterparts to support regional institutions such as the Council of Maritime Premiers and other efforts to foster regional cooperation. Provincial identities remain strong, however, and integration remains a tough sell.[8] The cultivation of a close relationship with Ottawa extended even into the constitutional realm. It was former New Brunswick premier Richard Hatfield who, along with Ontario's Bill Davis, supported Pierre Trudeau's efforts to reform the Constitution without substantial provincial consent and, after a slow start, Frank McKenna proved to be one of the strongest supporters of the Meech Lake and Charlottetown Accords. Successive New Brunswick governments have often joined the federal government in promoting national bilingualism and la Francophonie.

BACKGROUND: LIFE PRE-1960

Through the course of his life the late Professor W.S. MacNutt of the University of New Brunswick was widely regarded as one of the province's foremost historians. In his landmark *New Brunswick—A History: 1784-1867*, he offered these concluding observations on the nature of New Brunswick politics to the time of Confederation: "Men were virile but institutions were puny. Such a country, not so blessed by nature as other parts of British North America, required art and strong management, but, in the nature of things, these were denied."[9] Within this short quotation one finds reference to at least three important points that also characterize the 1867-1960 years: political and economic weakness, the general lack of strong management within the ranks of government, and an unreflective expectation that men and their activities defined the public life of the provincial community. One should also add that these men were largely anglophones. Each of these considerations merits elaboration.

A sense of political and economic weakness has been a central feature of the provincial political culture for decades, if not centuries. New Brunswick was created in 1784 amid the settlement of Loyalists displaced from the former southern colonies. From the outset, life in the colony was difficult. MacNutt reports that in the fall of 1784, "Reports of impending starvation were coming from the outlying settlements, and Carleton [the first governor] had to take emergency measures to supplement the stock of provisions in the royal stores."[10] During the course of subsequent decades, the timber trade became a cornerstone of the colony's economy. By the early 1860s things appeared to be going relatively well. Trade with the United States was bolstered by the Reciprocity Treaty of 1854 and the increased demand for foodstuffs and other products resulting from the U.S. Civil War.

However, things were soon to change dramatically. Pressure from Great Britain and the Canadas pushed the notion of uniting the British North American colonies to the forefront. Meanwhile, the winding down of the Civil War coupled with the U.S. government's decision to terminate the reciprocity treaty altered the nature of New Brunswick-U.S. relations. With Great Britain opting for union, and U.S. markets less available, the Confederation option gained strength. The British North America Act ultimately promised an intercolonial railway, but Confederation never became the enthusiastic choice of New Brunswickers. Hugh Thorburn characterized the province's response this way: "New Brunswick entered the new federation with the resignation of a sick man going to a quack, after he had tried everything else."[11]

The nineteenth century had within it the golden days of wood, wind, and water when the ports of the Maritime provinces were integrated within the global shipping patterns of the British Empire. With the passing of this economic order, iron, steel, and railroads came to prevail. In the early decades of this century other localities grew in importance. Writing of the period between the turn of the century and the early 1920s, E.R. Forbes points out that "the new industrial growth tended to follow a linear pattern from Saint John eastward through Moncton, Amherst, Truro, and the towns of Pictou and Cape Breton counties."[12]

For New Brunswick and the Maritimes, conditions continued to prove difficult. The combined impact of freight rate increases and the loss of regional control over the operations of the Intercolonial Railway dramatically altered the ability of regional firms to compete.[13] This was accompanied by the concentration of capital in central Canada and explosive growth in western Canada. As a result of these forces the economic and political position of the Maritimes was undermined. Large-scale emigration from the region reflected the lack of local opportunities.

Regional feelings of despair were exacerbated by the region's declining share of seats in the House of Commons: "The reductions in federal representation which followed each census from 1891 to 1921 reminded Maritimers of their region's decline and usually produced fresh efforts to reverse that process."[14] These efforts, generally speaking, proved to be almost completely unsuccessful. The most significant of the efforts was the Maritime Rights movement that gripped the region through much of the 1920s. Central to the movement was the argument that the Canadian government had failed to live up to what was felt by many Maritimers to have been implied commitments accompanying the British North America Act provisions relating to the building of the Intercolonial Railway to the Maritimes. These implied commitments related to the use of the Intercolonial "as an instrument of regional and national development."[15] Instead, the management and operation of the Intercolonial had been brought under the CNR's control and freight rates rose. Ultimately the Maritime Rights agitation led to a federal royal commission into regional grievances. Maritime hopes soon fell victim, however, to Mackenzie King's preference for strategic delay and the placating of other more electorally lucrative interests.[16] The King government's political manipulation of the issue prevailed and within the region cynicism came to dominate. Such feelings were intensified by the ensuing years of depression and global conflict.

New Brunswick and the Maritimes generally did not share in the postwar prosperity of other parts of Canada. There is vigorous ongoing debate about the reasons for this. Various observers have pointed to such factors as an apparent bias against Maritime industry in the federal government's wartime procurement efforts,[17] or the lack of activist provincial leadership willing, during the 1940s, to move beyond political and economic patterns built up around "the traditional channels of a patronage system rooted mainly in the primary-sector clientele networks."[18] Whatever the case, economic conditions remained far behind those in central Canada.

For New Brunswick the provincial political economic situation was bleak by the early 1950s. Provincial creditors tightened their reins on the McNair government (Liberal, 1940-52) and appointed an outside financial adviser to review governmental transactions and issue reports on the province's creditworthiness.[19] Over the course of the ensuing decade the governments sought greater levels of federal government financial assistance. The Diefenbaker government was sensitive to such aspirations but was itself constrained by uncertain leadership and recessionary conditions.

The provincial economy remained generally weak through the 1950s. Electric power production was a high priority sector under the Hugh John Flemming government[20] (Progressive Conservative, 1952-60), but other opportunities seemed to hold limited potential. A noteworthy exception to the general pessimism was the emerging empire of industrialist K.C. Irving. Irving investments encompassed a variety of economic sectors including shipping, forestry, newspapers, hardware retailing, and energy; Irving Oil, for example, by 1952 "controlled 23 different companies and had assets of nearly $30 million."[21] Over 4000 New Brunswickers were employed by Irving interests in that same year.[22]

Despite the strong growth exhibited by the Irving interests, economic and political weakness was a continuing feature of New Brunswick life. Consigned to the position of supplicant within Confederation, successive provincial leaders urged Ottawa to recognize the grievances of the Maritimes relating to transportation policy, national government insensitivity, and transfer payments. The difficulties faced by New Brunswick and Maritime leaders in attempting to persuade the rest of Canada of the historic legitimacy of these grievances were a source of continuous disappointment. New Brunswick's economic disparity with the rest of Canada remained a critical issue. Feelings of being Canada's "poor relations" permeated provincial society.

The New Brunswick of 1960 was a poor, predominantly rural province. Its 1961 population[23] was 597,936, of which 319,923 were categorized as "rural," living in locales of less than 1000 people. Relatively small, closely knit communities were the backbone of provincial society. Restricted economic prospects led many anglophone New Brunswickers to emigrate. The province's Acadian population was much less affected by emigration.[24] New Brunswick emigrants flowed both south and west in search of opportunities. It was this reality that Henry Veltmeyer was referring to in his depiction of the Maritimes as a pool of reserve labour for the national economy.[25]

The second important point to be drawn from MacNutt's comments is the early lack of attention to the quality of management in provincial government and political circles. Politics was seen as the localized competition of celebrated individuals who were loosely bound in government or opposition by party ties. Rivalries were intense and patronage networks became important political instruments. They communicated electoral information, popular satisfaction or discontent, and means for requesting and allocating jobs, funds, and appointed offices.

Reliance upon patronage was the response of a society with limited job or economic opportunities outside the public sector. Civil service jobs were regarded highly in light of the pervasive lack of employment alternatives and their generally non-seasonal character. In an era of limited government where a large number of civil service positions required little in the way of formal professional or academic requirements, there were few constraints on the distribution of a broad range of positions according to partisan affiliation. This system thrived for generations not only because of the economic limitations, but also because of the entrenched character of the province's party system that both sustained, and was sustained by, widespread reliance upon patronage. Party networks not only distributed rewards, but also collected campaign funds, recruited poll workers, and spread the party message. In the absence of third parties, public-sector unionization, and job guarantees, and with a "shift from a regional economy dominated by local business proprietors to a national, or even a continental one, controlled from head offices"[26] outside the province, patronage networks were not threatened. As these factors began to appear, cracks began to deepen in the structure of the patronage system.

Historically, public service was not widely perceived as a career profession for talented people seeking to promote societal change. Partisan identifications were deeply ingrained and there were few expectations that government would promote policy innovations. There were noteworthy exceptions, though. In 1918 New Brunswick was the first government within the British Empire to establish a formal Department of Health. Under its first minister, the Hon. Dr. William F. Roberts, it tackled the spread of infant mortality and venereal disease. Programs to vaccinate against smallpox, gather vital statistics, and check on food distribution outlets were begun.[27]

More common than innovation and the building of expertise was the installation of party supporters into civil service[28] positions and the removal of their opponents' people. Elections where the opposition forces succeeded in overthrowing a government were often followed by purges of the civil service. Over the course of the mid-twentieth century, changes in government became less dramatic. The McNair government passed a Civil Service

Act in 1943. A Civil Service Commission was created and in 1948 the first full-time commission chairperson was installed.[29] These steps were indicative of the gradual emergence of changing attitudes. In 1952, when Hugh John Flemming and the Progressive Conservatives defeated McNair and company, the only deputy minister who left was "one who had reached retirement age."[30] This partisan restraint was far less evident, however, in the case of recruitment to lower level positions requiring limited formal skills or training.

This reduction in partisan decision-making and appointments was most evident in the case of the provincial power commission, the New Brunswick Electric Power Commission. The commission was an atypical branch of government, though. By the 1950s, power generation had been targeted by the provincial government as a growth sector of the economy. The Commission's Executive came to enjoy considerable autonomy due to the specialized nature of power generation and the single-profession domination of commission ranks by engineers. These factors, coupled with the priority attached by Premier Flemming to hydro-electric power production,[31] made the New Brunswick Electric Power Commission (NBEPC) an "elite" branch of the government. Traditionally, politicians supervised the NBEPC very closely, gearing its activities to partisan needs and directing its spending through localized channels of patronage. But in the quest for economic growth, the public utility was seen as an essential tool, and the organization was newly oriented towards the efficient provision of electricity for industry.[32] With their operational autonomy came freedom from patronage controls and the application of performance criteria based upon the assumptions of the professional engineers leading the organization.

While the Civil Service Act constrained wholesale firings, doubts remained as to the overall quality of the public service.[33] Some have, in fact, argued that the Act simply allowed both sides to hire partisans and produce a bloated civil service.[34] Few of New Brunswick's political leaders over the decades accorded real importance to improved government administration. As a result, the provincial political structures were becoming inadequate and outdated. A clear example of this was the county-based local government system. New Brunswick had in the 1950s and early 1960s "much the same local institutions it acquired during the second half of the last century."[35] Public attitudes were shifting and the financial disparities between the counties, and between New Brunswick and other parts of Canada, were becoming visible to all with the growth of television and the availability of other sources of information. Public support for increased provincial involvement in local affairs increased as proponents saw in it the possibility of improved service standards. The Report of the provincial Royal Commission on the Financing of Schools in New Brunswick, which was issued in 1955, disclosed that their public hearings revealed "a somewhat general opinion that the problem of school financing had reached the stage where it overrode purely local interest."[36] Despite public opinion and the mounting evidence of structural problems, governments continued to rely on incremental adjustments.

The final set of points to be abstracted from MacNutt's comments relate to participation in public life. For generations women, francophones, and others worked to achieve greater access to the levers of power. Their efforts faced difficult obstacles. Women faced cultural and political barriers. Their struggle involved long years of striving to be heard. Evidence of interest in political issues on the part of women had been clearly visible for decades. Women utilized church and community groups as well as petitions to the Legislative Assembly[37] long before 1900. However, the voice of women was banned from legislative office and was largely absent from the corridors of actual political power.

The right to vote had long been restricted to property-owning men. The barrier against other men was gradually breached, but votes for women remained out of reach. Groups of concerned women joined forces. For example, in March/April 1894 a Women's Enfranchisement Association was formed in Saint John. Association efforts were directed towards a wide range of public issues. These included education, facilities for juvenile offenders, support for immigrants, and health care.[38] Obtaining the right to vote was a central focus, for it would carry with it political clout: "The WEA petitioned the Legislature in 1894, 1899, 1901, 1905, 1908, 1909, 1912, and finally in 1917. Little wonder then that when the vote was finally granted in 1919, without the companion right of being able to sit in the Legislature, there were few hosannas."[39] It was not until the year 1934 that women were able to run for office; the first female MLA was elected in 1967.

Acadians also faced difficulties in their efforts to break into the ranks of political influence and power. Among the difficulties were religious and linguistic prejudice, poverty, and limited educational opportunities. Their numbers were sizable (in the late 1850s, for example, francophones constituted about one quarter of the province's population),[40] but opportunities were limited. The relative absence of Acadians from elite circles continued for decades. It was not, for example, until 1870 that the first Acadian "was admitted to the Bar of New Brunswick."[41] Arthur Doyle asserts that in the immediate years after Confederation "their influence in provincial affairs, though expanding, was still token."[42] Their Roman Catholic religious beliefs were also publicly attacked. The slogan of the victorious party leader in the 1874 provincial campaign was "Vote for the Queen against the Pope."[43]

Three major factors helped bring Acadians into the mainstream. These were the forging of compromises to overcome hostilities associated with schooling questions, the "Acadian Renaissance" of the 1880s, and the twentieth-century battles over conscription. Through all this the Acadians showed themselves to be a close-knit community concerned about being recognized both by their fellow New Brunswickers, and by *les Québécois* as a proud people with a rich culture. Evidence of this can be seen in decisions taken during the Renaissance era to ensure that Acadians would have their own feast day (la Fête de l'Assomption, August 15, not la Fête Saint-Jean Baptiste, June 24), national flag,[44] and hymn.

Politically, the Acadians came to find their own electoral home with the Liberals. Despite having found a solid base within one of the major parties, Acadians found their path within the provincial public service was much slower. In his examination of conditions during the mid-1960s, Thorburn uncovered a striking pattern in provincial public-sector salaries:

> Persons of French ethnic origin tend to receive lower salaries than those of British and other ethnic origins. Over 30 per cent of the civil servants of French origin receive salaries below $3000 per year compared to 22 per cent of the British ethnic group and 21 per cent of the others.[45]

There were a number of coincident factors that necessitate caution when using this data, however. Many of the francophones involved had less formal schooling and had been with the public service for less than five years. Thorburn's data do point to two key barriers: low educational attainment and the English-speaking character of Fredericton, the provincial capital. In fact, there was a broad constellation of structural obstacles. The Acadian areas of New Brunswick, the north and east, were poor even by provincial standards. Counties in Acadian areas were unable to provide levels of service commensurate with those elsewhere in New Brunswick or Canada as a whole. Using education expenditures by county in 1960 as an example, Ralph Krueger found that "Only one county in New Brunswick was spending as much per student as the Canadian average, and nine of the fifteen counties were spending only 60 per cent or less of the Canadian average."[46] Many of the low-spending counties were those of the Acadian regions. Thus a lack of educational advantages coupled with linguistic obstacles combined to limit career opportunities and horizons in both the public and private sectors.

Life remained difficult for many Acadians. The best efforts of local communities, county governments, and the Roman Catholic Church led to provision of health care, educational, and social welfare services, but these still fell short of those elsewhere. Massive structural changes were needed. One political change of note came on October 11, 1958, when Louis Robichaud emerged victorious over six other candidates for the provincial Liberal leadership. Robichaud was, at the time, only thirty-three. His selection represented a change for more than age reasons, though. The only other Acadian to lead a major provincial party had been Peter Veniot (Liberal, 1923-25), who assumed the premiership in 1923. His achievement had been "the culmination of a forty-year career as a political activist."[47] His years of service notwithstanding, Veniot's government was soundly defeated at the next provincial election, winning only eleven of forty-eight seats.[48] Robichaud, on the other hand, went on to victory in his first election as leader and remained as premier for a decade.

The political life of New Brunswick up to approximately 1960 was marked by three overarching themes: political and economic difficulties marked by scepticism about their place in the Canadian Confederation, a patronage-oriented system of managing public business, and the existence of informal and formal barriers of access to the ranks of the politically powerful.

THE OLD SCHOOL: PATRONAGE EVERYWHERE

For many, the first acquaintance with literature depicting political life in New Brunswick likely came through passages such as the following from Thorburn and Fitzpatrick:

> Politics at the provincial level is largely a battle of the ins versus the outs for patronage plums.[49]
>
> To the rest of the country, politics here may appear insupportably rustic; to the people of New Brunswick their style is preferable to the mass media politics that merchandise candidates like so much soap powder. But the electoral system and the Assembly are still in need of reform, great families run the political affairs of some areas, non-issue-oriented politicians and a substantial patronage system prevail. Yet the people prefer their political system the way it is.[50]

While such descriptions point to an undeniable reality—the existence of widespread reliance upon patronage—both comments ultimately obscure more than they illuminate. No matter how partisan and parochial a society may be, all politics cannot be subsumed under the simple "ins versus outs" model. Such a model overlooks the potential importance of economic, cultural, and/or religious factors. In the case of New Brunswick, Thorburn's basic approach underestimates the importance of developments like the Maritime Rights movement. Furthermore, it fails to capture the full range of government-business relationships. Patronage networks were undoubtedly strong, but as the examples of the unionist movement during World War I and the range of public submissions to those planning for post-World War II reconstruction[51] illustrate, there were many New Brunswickers capable of envisioning other political arrangements.

Fitzpatrick's comments are even more questionable. Perhaps the most obvious problem is the lack of evidence to support the assertions regarding citizen attitudes. Neither the work of Simeon and Elkins,[52] nor that of Ornstein, Stevenson, and Williams,[53] confirms Fitzpatrick's view of provincial citizens as happy, issue-avoiding, self-satisfied rustics. Simeon and Elkins found cynicism and alienation[54] while Ornstein and his collaborators suggest that class interests prevail over regional viewpoints in terms of public attitudes.

What is striking about patronage-oriented accounts of provincial politics is their narrow sense of what constitutes political life: campaigns and elections. Issues such as the evolution of the provincial power commission, the political economy of the forestry, or the ability of the province to make its voice heard nationally are generally not given sufficient attention, and instead emphasis is placed on election campaigns and the distribution of spoils. In fairness, it must be acknowledged that authors such as Thorburn and Fitzpatrick had a very limited secondary literature to draw upon. Yet that does not excuse their narrow frame of reference or their limited definitions of what constituted New Brunswick politics.

The other critical problem is that both Thorburn and Fitzpatrick devote too little attention to the inter-relationship between patronage and available economic opportunities. Instead, patronage is viewed as a socio-cultural characteristic derived solely from past experiences and attitudinal preferences. Patronage should instead be understood as a response from a society with limited job or economic opportunities outside the public sector. Civil service jobs were highly regarded in light of the pervasive lack of employment alternatives and their generally non-seasonal character. This condition of limited economic expectations and dependence upon the decisions of the politically and economically influential becomes entrenched over the course of decades if not centuries. From the colony's earliest years through the rise in the early nineteenth century of powerful timber barons, New Brunswick's citizens have had to cope with limited expectations and opportunities.[55] Economic pressures produced an environment where the main alternatives for many were patronage and clientelism, or emigration.

The other point to be made in this regard is that over the course of the postwar era important changes were underway which led to a decline in the widespread reliance upon patronage. Government programs provided people with funds by virtue of meeting common, non-partisan prerequisites—age, numbers of children, income levels, etc. Transformation of the labour market and the gradual shrinking of unskilled labour positions also weakened the hold of patronage. Professionalism, technological development, and the increased entry of extra-provincial firms into the New Brunswick market[56] all contributed to the erosion of patronage. As these factors were coupled with the rising expectations of government fostered in the postwar era internationally, the existing system of patronage networks grew less appropriate as either a guide to government organization, or an allocation method for public-sector goods and services.

This is not to say that patronage ever completely disappeared—far from it. Rather, the argument is that this sort of literature not only overemphasizes the patronage dimension of public life, it also pays insufficient attention to the relationship of patronage to social and economic conditions. This needs to be asserted here, for otherwise the events of the years from 1960 onward can be approached with a misleading sense of the provincial political culture. The assumption that New Brunswickers were simply temperamentally suited to patronage has yet to be substantiated. Thorburn's dismissal of provincial politics as a parochial struggle between "ins and outs" is based on an unnecessarily limited sense of the political. Consideration of the events of subsequent decades gives proof that New Brunswick's citizens and political leaders could produce a more exciting and sophisticated political scene.

THE ROBICHAUD/HATFIELD ERA: 1960-1987

Under the leadership of Louis Robichaud, the Liberal Party upset the government of Hugh John Flemming. By the time he left office Robichaud was known for much more than being the first Acadian to lead a provincial party to electoral victory. The centrepiece of his government's legislative record was his "Equal Opportunity" program, a complete redesigning of the allocation of responsibilities between the provincial and local levels of government. The county structure was disbanded and the province assumed authority for delivery of education, health care, social services, and local law enforcement. As Della Stanley has pointed out, New Brunswick, unlike other provinces, moved decisively to implement comprehensive revision of the provincial-local relationship: "New Brunswick in its boldness set the example. Subsequent social reforms in Ontario, Manitoba, Nova Scotia, and

Prince Edward Island in the areas of health, education, justice and municipal structure and taxation were reminiscent of Robichaud's program."[57] Others adopted change on a piecemeal basis while "New Brunswick had attempted a massive far-reaching reform of social conditions."[58]

During the Robichaud years there were also other noteworthy innovations. Examples include the passage of official languages legislation, the granting of collective bargaining rights to provincial public servants, reform of liquor regulations, and the adoption of medicare. In New Brunswick, the 1960s was a decade of widespread centralization and modernization. Corresponding adjustments were required in the ranks of the public service. The government was able to gather together some very talented public servants, some of whom had served Saskatchewan's CCF government before Ross Thatcher's Liberal victory in 1964. More emphasis came to be placed on the selection of senior public servants according to administrative talent and professional skills rather than longevity or partisan compatibility. While the public service gained strength the government had to depend upon royal commissions and special reports or studies for sources of new ideas. The best example was the Royal Commission on Finance and Municipal Taxation headed by Edward Byrne.[59] This commission's report laid out the blueprint for the Equal Opportunity effort.

As premier, Robichaud was very receptive to proposals for reform. This coupled with his vigorous leadership style led to the actual implementation of many of the proposals generated by the commissions and studies. Norman Ruff reports that Robichaud "displayed an unusual willingness to use his authority to effect what were regarded as necessary steps to meet the urgent economic and social needs of the province and to persist in his policies in the face of formidable political opposition."[60] Harley d'Entremont concurs by declaring that Robichaud's contribution to Equal Opportunity and the achievement of major reforms "can hardly be over-stated."[61]

Ruff's reminder that New Brunswick's social and economic difficulties be considered is a useful one. Before Equal Opportunity there had been wide intraprovincial variations in service levels. Stagnant governing structures were, if anything, serving to worsen the existing levels of deprivation. The Equal Opportunity program was a creative response to a "system grown sclerotic throughout."[62] It stressed provincial government service delivery and individual entitlement. The results were a reduction of the intraprovincial competition for new revenue sources and the detrimental bidding wars for new businesses. Also, there were savings resulting from the dismantling of the decaying county system. This streamlining made the province better able to utilize effectively the increased federal government transfers made available during the 1960s. However, as with most things in New Brunswick, Equal Opportunity had to endure linguistic bitterness.

Narrow-minded individuals regarded it as the product of an Acadian leader catering to his cultural community. Nevertheless, Robichaud and his supporters triumphed in the pivotal 1967 election. While they were to lose office to Richard Hatfield and the Progressive Conservatives three years later, by then the reform package was settling into place.

Richard Hatfield represented something of an anomaly in the history of New Brunswick politics. Born into a Tory family from an area long considered a Conservative bastion, Hatfield was an intriguing combination of both old and new elements of the provincial Progressive Conservative Party and of provincial society generally. He possessed a personal worldliness and an appreciation of francophone concerns that helped him see beyond parochialism and traditional practices. Occasionally, as in the ill-fated effort to launch the Bricklin automobile, or his government's "on-again, off-again" approach to the kindergarten issue, these skills seemed to desert him. However, in the case of many other matters—such as the retention of Equal Opportunity, the eventual proclamation of all sections of Robichaud's bilingualism legislation, his government's belated conversion to the need for a comprehensive revision of the provincial regulatory regime for party and political financing, or the promotion of structural reform within government[63]—his openness and vision proved beneficial. Hatfield's career showed him to be both a fascinating public figure as well as a shrewd survivor of the political wars. While his later years in office (1983 onward) were caught up in his efforts to retain the premiership despite personal difficulties, widespread public dissatisfaction, and intraparty feuding, there is much in his overall record that merits serious study. Hatfield was New Brunswick's longest serving premier. His time in office was an important one, encompassing the 1970s and much of the 1980s.[64]

After assuming office Hatfield and his cabinet did not move to uproot the Robichaud initiatives. On a variety of issues Hatfield helped manoeuvre his party away from its traditional roots. The New Brunswick Progressive Conservatives had long received much of their support from anglophone Protestants. As Richard Starr notes, for example, "Flemming's governments of the 1950s had included a few Francophones, but a decade later the Tory caucus had not a single Acadian member."[65] Hatfield, meanwhile, was committed to making his party and government more receptive to Acadian concerns. While the medium- and longer-term success of these efforts is now proving to have been limited, Hatfield did endeavour to broaden his party's appeal to the francophone population. After elaborating upon the important points of similarity between the Robichaud and Hatfield governments, our attention will return to current political divisions born of language issues.

These divisions and the recent electoral advances of the Confederation of Regions Party (to be discussed momentarily) suggest that anti-bilingualism forces remain a potent provincial force. In recognition of Hatfield's receptiveness, not only to the aspirations of both linguistic communities, but also to the governing improvements of the Robichaud years, Della Stanley asserts:

> In some ways, it seemed as though Hatfield was the successor Robichaud wanted for he could take the best of the Liberal administration's legislation and policies and integrate them into Conservative programmes without being hampered by the ethnic, religious and socialist accusations and insults which had come to mar Robichaud's image and handicap his government.[66]

With these observations Stanley has drawn our attention away from the sterile retelling of political legends about the quaint character of politics in the Maritimes.[67] Rather than emphasizing short-term or partisan differences, my focus moves to the important elements of continuity which were features of provincial politics for roughly a quarter of a century. It is worth examining these key elements and speculating on their implications in light of the current political scene. Much could be said about the interrelationships and similarities in "legislation and policies" between the Robichaud and Hatfield years in government. I refer here to three key strategic themes shared by the Robichaud and Hatfield governments: pragmatic co-operation with the federal government, sensitivity and support for Acadian aspirations, and encouragement of reformed policy-making structures.

Both Robichaud and Hatfield preferred to develop co-operative, non-confrontational relations with the federal government. Sensitive to the ability of a strong central government to allocate resources throughout the country, New Brunswick's leaders were sceptical of a further decentralized and divided federation. Central to the federal-provincial outlooks of Robichaud and Hatfield was encouragement of increased federal government support for regional development and linguistic accommodation. Financial reliance upon federal coffers and the region's chronically uncertain economic prospects have contributed to "the pragmatic approach that Atlantic provinces have taken to federal-provincial relations."[68] A main feature of this pragmatism was the careful development of close, personal contact with senior federal government figures, particularly those from a premier's home province. Robichaud and Hatfield worked hard at this. Of relations between Robichaud and Prime Minister Pearson, "There was no doubt that Pearson admired the fiery Acadian leader and that he was prepared to consider the projects he recommended; and Robichaud was never one to be shy when it came to asking favours."[69] Hatfield was also active in such relationships. Herman Bakvis reports that "Romeo LeBlanc, throughout his career as [a Trudeau government] minister, was in close contact with Richard Hatfield."[70]

It is significant that Hatfield, unlike his Maritime contemporaries, opted to join Ontario premier William Davis in supporting Pierre Trudeau's patriation efforts. This support came at a time when all the other eight premiers had banded together to form the "Gang of Eight." Hatfield personally was a strong supporter of the then proposed charter of rights and of federal protection for linguistic minorities. However, these were not the constitutional package's only benefits from his perspective. Hatfield had lobbied for inclusion within the package of provisions guaranteeing federal actions to redress regional disparities. Such efforts were met with federal government acceptance and New Brunswick lined up with Ottawa. Section 36 of the *Canada Act, 1982*, dealing with "Equalization and Regional Disparities" is in large measure the result of New Brunswick labours.

The province's sizable Acadian minority adds an extra dimension to dealings with Ottawa. Through the 1960s and 1970s the federal government promoted increased sensitivity to francophone aspirations within not only federal government, but also those governments of provinces with sizable numbers of French speakers. Prime Minister Pearson's appointment of the Royal Commission on Bilingualism and Biculturalism was a landmark event. During the course of their work, Commission co-chair André Laurendeau recalled his impressions of Robichaud this way. Robichaud, he noted in his diary, "strikes me as very Acadian, in every sense of the word: very loyal, and always ready to make the compromises that are judged necessary."[71] Pearson and Trudeau found allies in both Robichaud and Hatfield in the promotion of official bilingualism. Each persevered despite periodic outbursts from segments of the province's anglophones.

After the 1986 census, Statistics Canada reported that "As a percentage of the total population, New Brunswick had the largest French-speaking minority. This proportion was about 31 percent and has remained stable since 1971."[72] This minority community has a long and rich history. However, linguistic divisions have long constituted the province's fundamental cleavage. Aside from being an Acadian premier, Robichaud's other primary contribution to the upgrading of opportunities and horizons for provincial Francophones was his government's passage of Bill 73: An Act Respecting the Official Languages of New Brunswick. Then Opposition leader Hatfield strongly endorsed the bill; as premier he was, in fact, to oversee its eventual complete proclamation. During the Hatfield years two other extremely important steps were taken to recognize the concerns of the Acadian population. Assimilation pressures continued to generate anxiety within the Francophone community. Under Hatfield's leadership New Brunswick's official bilingualism was entrenched in the *Canada Act, 1982* (sections 16(2), 17(2), 18(2), 19(2), and 20(2)). This came on the heels of legislation passed in the provincial legislature in 1981 that recognized the existence of English and French communities within New Brunswick. Hatfield explained the need for such legislation as the necessary acknowledgement of two official linguistic communities which merited respect and support.[73]

Unfortunately Hatfield's ability to navigate the province's linguistic divide evaporated in the mid-1980s. His inattention to government affairs in the aftermath of the 1982 election and the uncertain judgement that marred his leadership over the entire 1982-87 period diminished some of his earlier achievements. Bitter debate emerged over a provincial government-commissioned investigation into the operation of the languages legislation.[74] Subsequent public hearings became a recipe for tension, controversy, and recriminations. Initially debate centred around calls for dual language units within government structures.[75] However, widespread economic weakness and the rise of a provincial Confederation of Regions Party anxious to cut back on official bilingualism made the political atmosphere extremely heated.

Facing both unrest within his own party and personal difficulties,[76] Hatfield proved unable to master the situation. His apparent inability to grasp the implications of the growing polarization of the 1980s was one of his most critical failings. However, the failings and division of these years should not eclipse the sensitive leadership on language matters displayed over the first twelve years of his premiership. Those years saw him build upon the steps taken by Louis Robichaud on the road to bilingualism and appreciation of Francophone concerns. Later years brought quarrelling and unrest, but not repeal of the legislative achievements.

The third of the common priorities was a willingness to experiment with policy-making structures. As the sway of patronage eroded and government became more activist, structural adjustments were required. Over the 1960s, 1970s, and 1980s New Brunswick's political leadership oversaw the cultivation of a small but capable public service. A number of senior contemporary public servants will indeed privately suggest, if asked, that the province possesses the most competent public service in the Maritimes.

While Premier Robichaud helped direct the complete re-creation of provincial-local government relations, the provincial government was in the process of being refashioned so as to enable it to participate in the resolution of a wider range of public issues. Organizational improvements and adjustments had to take place to accommodate this. New structures such as the Office of the Economic Adviser[77] and that of the Provincial Ombudsman[78] were created. Late in the 1960s public servants obtained the right to unionize and engage in collective bargaining. This contributed to the fostering of a bureaucratic ethic at the same time as it built barriers to partisan-oriented job firings.

Given the extent of the transformations begun during the Robichaud period, it is noteworthy that major structural adjustment was also an early priority of Richard Hatfield as premier. One of the major priorities of the early Hatfield years was the development of a system of cabinet committees that co-ordinated policy initiatives and that structured formal decision-making channels.[79] The committee system was complemented by the creation of a cabinet secretariat that provided support to the premier and other cabinet members. These and other structural reforms helped build the infrastructure to handle the new demands being placed on government. Decision-making structures were also revised and new avenues of access to the corridors of political influence were created. One measure that helped to achieve this was the appointment of an Advisory Council on the Status of Women. Creation of the Advisory Council emphasized the premier's interest in women's issues, and provided those actively interested in such issues with a government organization dedicated to dealing with their concerns.

Another measure that helped to increase political access was the introduction of single-member constituencies. When Hatfield and his government took office they inherited a system of electoral districts based largely upon large multi-member county constituencies. Breaking these up into single-member districts gave explicit voice to all corners of the province. Hatfield's interest in revised governing structures extended beyond the boundaries of New Brunswick. He of all Maritime premiers at the time was most supportive of expanding regional co-operation in the aftermath of the 1970 report of the Maritime Union study.[80] This co-operation led to joint structures such as the Council of Maritime Premiers.

As I close off this section of the chapter several points deserve reiteration. The governments of both Robichaud and Hatfield displayed some truly significant similarities. Taken together they bequeathed subsequent provincial leaders a heritage of modern, progressive reforms. Appreciating the significance of this legacy helps us understand the challenges faced by the McKenna government. In the limited confines of a chapter there always remain things unsaid. What has been included here reflects the major themes that characterized the governments through the years. This should serve to provide the context for more recent times and events. It is to these that we will turn momentarily. However, first a word should be said about two factors that have shaped the province's political economy and government-business relations: the Irving empire and federal government transfer payments and regional development incentives.

The Irving empire has continued to grow and expand over the years. When all is said and done, their name is behind at least 300 companies, with assets of nearly $7 billion. In 1990, *Fortune* magazine ranked the Irvings as the tenth-richest family in the world.[81] Given their massive wealth, Irving interests cast a long shadow in New Brunswick. Irving dominance in fields such as forestry and media industries has become a recognized feature of the political landscape. Some, like Maurice Mandale of the Atlantic Provinces Economic Council, regard Irving influence over the province as "unique in the industrialized world. You are unlikely to find one family wielding this much power anywhere outside of the Third World."[82] Charting the actual impact of the Irvings upon provincial life and politics is difficult, but Russell Hunt and Robert Campbell attempted this task in *K.C. Irving—The Art of the Industrialist.*[83]

In asking how New Brunswick's fate might have been different in the absence of K.C. Irving, they concluded that there are no easy answers:

> Such questions can probably never be answered definitely. But if you accept that the dinosaur has been the most important single element in the history of New Brunswick in the middle of this century, there can't be much doubt that New Brunswick—and eastern Canada as a whole—would be a vastly different place if the dinosaur had never existed. Nor can it be seriously disputed that the dinosaur's control of the media—whether directly or indirectly through influences—has been central to its control of the province and therefore to its own growth.[84]

Hunt and Campbell are alert to the role played by the Irving media investments. The provincial media is not widely noted for its investigative search into Irving corporate behaviour.

In the end, it is difficult to make easy generalizations about the sway of Irving influence. Taken together, the Irving legacy is a complex one about which debates will continue into the future. Irving companies have contributed to the pollution of the Saint John River and the local area. In this they were not, however, alone. Also, the Irvings over the years have not developed a reputation for public-spirited generosity: "For decades, he [K.C. Irving] refused to allow United Way contributions to be taken off employee paycheques."[85] Yet the Irving interests have shown a long-term commitment to the provincial economy. As large-scale employers in a small and peripheral economy they naturally have become major players on the provincial stage. They have squared off against the federal government over issues such as their dominance of the provincial communication media, and have emerged successful. Still, the Irving empire has suffered defeats. The most notable were those inflicted during the Robichaud years. For example, Noranda, not the Irving interests, was ultimately given the go-ahead to develop the Brunswick Mining mineral deposits near Bathurst.[86] Despite criticism from the Irvings over the Equal Opportunity program and despite the flamboyant campaigning of Progressive Conservative leader J.C. "Charlie" Van Horne, Robichaud and the Liberal forces won a clear victory in the 1967 provincial election.[87]

Another topic that can stir up heated discussion in New Brunswick is the attitude of the federal government towards the Maritimes. There have existed over the years an extensive array of federal government transfers and regional incentive grants that have helped the provincial economy. These funds have helped fill provincial coffers and assisted commercial enterprises. Furthermore, they have in various ways facilitated provincial policy innovation and the reform of government structures. Robichaud's efforts to implement the Equal Opportunity Program were made easier by the federal funds made available under the new Canada Assistance Plan.[88] Savoie argues that the General Development Agreement Process sponsored by the former Department of Regional Economic Expansion contributed to increased bureaucratic planning and a centralization of power to the premier and cabinet.[89] This centralization helped "provide a focal point to respond to federal initiatives."[90]

In the mid-1980s, the Mulroney government revamped the structures of regional development promotion and the Atlantic Canada Opportunity Agency (ACOA) was created. ACOA was one of a number of regionally-based development agencies set up for various parts of Canada. Designing a federal government organization whose mandate is restricted to the Atlantic provinces was a response to accusations that the then-existing Department of Regional Industrial Expansion was "overly bureaucratic" and primarily interested in Ontario and Quebec.[91]

Indeed, federal incentive grants of various sorts have been helpful to many New Brunswick businesses. While such grants remain a feature of federal government policy towards the Atlantic area, recent years have seen increased federal concentration on promotion of entrepreneurship and enterprise values.

FRANK MCKENNA AND THE GOVERNING OF NEW BRUNSWICK

Frank McKenna became premier of New Brunswick in the fall of 1987 when his Liberal team shut out Richard Hatfield and the Progressive Conservatives. Re-elected in 1991 and 1995, his governments came to dominate political life in the province. At the time of his departure from office he stood as one of the country's longest-serving premiers. Recognition came his way for a range of policy initiatives. Development of information technology and investment promotion were high government priorities. The rhetoric of self-sufficiency was articulated as a government vision. Budgetary restraint and intensive program reform became embedded in the provincial vocabulary. And McKenna generally remained on good terms with the federal government: aside from early opposition to the Meech Lake Accord, the McKenna government kept close ties with the governments of both Brian Mulroney and Jean Chrétien, unlike many other provincial administrations. This was facilitated through McKenna's support of trade liberalization and his willingness to re-think the role of government generally. The political record reveals a premier who was a tireless campaigner, a determined agent of change, and a hard-headed politician sensitive to events and trends far beyond provincial borders. In the words of a 1995 *Globe and Mail* editorial, "His particular mix of fiscal parsimony and hard-sell boosterism may not be your cup of tea, but you'll have to acknowledge that Mr. McKenna is stalwart and square."[92]

McKenna's electoral prowess is unquestioned. In 1995, the veteran premier led his party to the third in their string of convincing electoral triumphs. After serving as the government for approximately eight years, the victorious Liberals still went on to receive 51.6 per cent of the popular vote.[93] Meanwhile, the modestly resurgent Progressive Conservatives obtained only 30.9 per cent and a handful of seats. The New Democrats took 9.6 per cent of the vote and only one seat.

But while the McKenna juggernaut remained formidable, all was not well in New Brunswick. Despite McKenna's high-profile commitment to computers and the information highway, some commentators suggest that the results may have been less than imagined. Intra-provincial disparities are pronounced, and resource-extraction industries still serve as the provincial economic foundation. Prolonged fiscal restraint and elite public service re-invention have been accomplished without much sense of popular participation. McKenna was a politician capable of blunt determination, but often little interested in free-wheeling consultation and open public participation. His governing style tended toward the mildly autocratic. Citizen anxiety over service reductions, particularly in the health-care field, percolated away just below the surface. Meanwhile, the uncertainties associated with future federal transfers offered portents of continued restraint.

Coming to grips with the overall McKenna record means assessing the electoral outcomes along with reference to provincial socio-economic conditions and New Brunswick's relationship with the federal government. Taken together, a complex picture emerges and the analytical challenge expands.

FRANK MCKENNA AND THE AGENDA OF MODERNIZATION

McKenna endeavoured to change the image of New Brunswick held by both outsiders and citizens. In order to get a handle on external views of the province, McKenna retained the New York-based image consultants Lippincott and Margulies Inc., a firm whose client list included Coca-Cola Co.[94] Their work convinced the government that prevailing attitudes toward the province were negative. Without serious public relations efforts and the crafting of sophisticated appeals, business executives were unlikely even to consider New Brunswick as an investment centre. Despite the magnitude of that promotional challenge, perhaps an even larger one awaited in terms of citizen attitudes. Studies of the provincial political culture have often emphasized tradition, patronage, deference to elites, and considerable disaffection.[95] McKenna, instead, offered a vision of self-reliance, competitiveness, high technology, educational promotion, and self-sufficiency. These virtues were presented as alternatives to reliance on federal transfers and other federal support. In a speech to Toronto's Empire Club in 1990, McKenna declared,

> ...we in New Brunswick have no hesitation in saying we are Canadians first and New Brunswickers second. We are proud of it. We believe in Canada.
>
> There was a time when it may have been said that New Brunswickers felt this way because they were so heavily dependent on the rest of Canada for financial support. That may have been true at one time. It is not true today. I come here today as an equal, not as a supplicant.[96]

McKenna continually asserted that New Brunswickers needed to adapt to the tough realities of modern global economic and technological competition. This entailed adaptation to change and acceptance of global horizons. The New Brunswick government, therefore, supported the free trade deal with the United States, and McKenna participated in multiple trade missions attempting to drum up trade and investment. Central to his message was the suitability of New Brunswick as a commercial location. It has a bilingual workforce, proximity to New England, Quebec, and Atlantic Canada, a commitment to modern information technology, a highly regarded telecommunications provider in NB Tel, and a government attentive to business concerns. McKenna was such an aggressive salesperson that his actions raised the hackles of others. British Columbia and Manitoba officials questioned New Brunswick's tactics. For example, the British Columbia government accused New Brunswick of violating inter-provincial understandings by luring jobs away from that province through offers of tax and financial blandishments. Given that 900 United Parcel Service jobs were at issue, the stakes were high.[97]

The conception of government offered by McKenna involved managing efficiently, educating competently, and dealing with business sensitively. A practising disciple of the "new public administration" (NPM), McKenna adapted easily to the model of voters as customers and governments as service catalysts and facilitators rather than bureaucratic service providers. The NPM school of thought reflects the influence of those seeking to make governments more flexible and entrepreneurial. It calls for reduction in the size of government, replacement of rigid bureaucracies by "a more client-focused, service-oriented system,"[98] and a re-examination of the instruments of government action to reflect the limits of what governments can actually do effectively.[99] For his part, McKenna urged a turning away from past acceptance of government largesse and patronage. Illustrations of his approach can be seen in his enthusiasm for information technology and his implementation of government reforms allied to expenditure restraint and balanced budgets.

Under his leadership New Brunswick engaged in a broad-based set of initiatives designed to encourage modern information technology and computerization. McKenna embraced the notion of the information highway and was a national leader in the use of computerization as a means of disseminating government information. Traditional reliance upon resource extraction had not produced widespread prosperity, and global competition was intensifying. McKenna searched for a competitive edge for the province and "hit upon the information technology sector as one that could flourish in even the remotest corner of the continent and that might well be attracted by the province's low labor and land costs as well as its bilingual workforce."[100]

Service delivery was transformed in fields such as education and health care. School curricula reflected a push toward computer capability and proficiency. Various initiatives in the area of health care were also undertaken. One was a two-year trial where nurses utilize a diagnostic computer program to offer medical advice and assistance: "More than 300 medical conditions are listed in the sophisticated computer program used by Tele-

Care. Whatever the illness, if questions about it can be answered over the phone, the patient may be saved a long wait in emergency for treatment that can safely be provided by the family doctor the next day."[101] Trials such as this prepared the way for innovations such as the Children's TeleHealth Network sponsored by the Moncton City Hospital. "The network is a high performance, PC-based video conferencing system with medical imaging (X-ray) capability and high speed data networking. It connects sites for all aspects of paediatric care...."[102] NB Tel planned early and well for technological developments and has installed modern equipment such as digital switches and fibre optic cable, "giving New Brunswickers an array of services unknown in other provinces."[103] In September 1996 the province unveiled its "Get Connected" program whereby citizens received rebates of up to $250 on provincial sales taxes relating to purchases of "Internet-ready" computers. As part of the program NB Tel offered three months of free Internet access, the Royal Bank added low-cost loans, and computer retailers were expected to offer discounts to boost sales.[104] McKenna declared: "If we don't create a base of prepared workers, we are going to lose some of the thousands of jobs that are ready to go in this industry."[105] Meanwhile, recent events show the provincial telephone utility branching out into other service markets. In March 1998, NB Tel applied to the Canadian Radio-television and Telecommunications Commission (CRTC) to become the first "Canadian telephone company to permanently enter the cable television business."[106]

Probably the best known result of the information technology drive was the fostering of a thriving provincial "call centre" industry. Call centres are locations where firms concentrate telephones, computers, and staff to handle consumer and business requests related to product and/or service information. Based on the available high-quality technology, a pool of bilingual employees, and supportive government regulations,[107] numerous call centres sprung up. Among the various companies involved are the Royal Bank, Xerox Canada, HFS Canada, Purolator Courier Ltd., and United Parcel Service Canada.

Another highly publicized McKenna priority was the re-design of government services and expenditure restraint. Major areas of government operation have been extensively evaluated with an eye to improvements in efficiency and reduction in layers of government. Claire Morris, Secretary to the Cabinet, reported that "in recent years, New Brunswick has moved towards selective reviews of key areas which have initiated reform in a number of major program areas."[108] School and hospital boards have been rationalized, with school boards declining in number from 42 to 18 and hospital boards going from 51 to 8. Services have been centralized and rationalized. Health care serves as a particular example as McKenna's government was among the national leaders in terms of cost reduction efforts. The province established an extensive relationship with a major consulting firm, Andersen Consulting, to improve operations and find savings in the welfare system. Another aspect of government reform has been involvement with Nova Scotia and Newfoundland in a deal with the federal government to harmonize provincial sales taxes with the federal GST[109] This produced reformulation of the list of taxable items and federal financial assistance for the change-over.

McKenna and his finance ministers showed determination in dealing with the provincial debt. Bear in mind that they did this amid a time of ongoing federal restraint in many fields of activity including health and social spending. Poorer provinces are very conscious of the equalization payments they receive under Canada's equalization arrangements. In the case of New Brunswick these payments have been sizable; in 1996-97 they stood at $903.7 million (the 1995-96 figure was $902.5 million).[110] Overall, however, the share of New Brunswick's budgetary revenues made up by federal transfers of all sorts dropped from around 40 per cent to approximately 35 per cent.[111] The province implemented increases in taxes and fees, but most of the emphasis was on expenditure cuts. Legislation mandating balanced budgets on total account, both operating and capital, became the order of the day. In the 1996-97 budget, Finance Minister Edmond Blanchard asserted, "We have turned the corner and in 1995-1996 will have reduced net debt as a result of budgetary actions for the first time since 1979-80.... This year (1995-1996) we will make a direct payment on our debt. At $75.9 million, this will be one of the largest payments made on provincial debt in the country."[112] This type of progress caught the attention of bond-rating agencies. The Canadian Bond Rating Service elevated their view of the province's long-term debt from negative to stable in 1995 and in 1996 upgraded the evaluation to positive.[113] Standard and Poor's cited New Brunswick's "exemplary track record with respect to controlling expenditures,"[114] and accorded it double A-minus credit rating.

NEW BRUNSWICK AND SELF-SUFFICIENCY: INSPIRATIONAL RHETORIC OR POLITICAL SLOGAN

The McKenna years involved extensive efforts at promotion and upgrading. However, there is also another side to events over the past decade, a somewhat less captivating image. There is considerable evidence of continued economic difficulty and ongoing heavy reliance on the federal government. The pay-out from the information highway innovations may take longer than expected. Intra-provincial disparities are deep and significant. Unemployment and struggle continue to characterize life for many.

Restigouche County, a large area in New Brunswick's North Shore, for example, is a chronically disadvantaged portion of the province. According to Statistics Canada the official unemployment rate for Restigouche County in March 1997 was 19.3 per cent. Resource industries such as pulp and paper remain the economic foundation in the region. Public-sector jobs and hospital and health-care work have been in a significant decline. In April 1997 the Liberal government announced a $1.5-million job creation fund designated to aid small business and create employment and committed "that the Premier and his senior economic ministers would visit Restigouche County on a weekly basis for the next three months to oversee the job-creation effort."[115]

These conditions were not atypical of smaller centres across the province. Health care and the accompanying work had been regionally centralized while pressure had been exercised to close smaller schools in light of ongoing enrolment declines.[116] Work on the fixed link to Prince Edward Island had wound down. The province-wide unemployment rate in March 1997 stood at 13.6 per cent, several points above the national average. This came on top of a provincial labour force participation rate that is traditionally below the Canadian average.[117] Employment prospects for those who were struggling to make ends meet remained limited. William J. Milne, an economist at the University of New Brunswick, suggested that "over time, a greater proportion of able New Brunswickers are becoming unemployed or are going on social assistance, and they remain on assistance for longer periods of time."[118] Intra-provincial disparities have intensified, as call centre work and other new commercial activity is largely in southern New Brunswick, particularly Moncton and Saint John. Federal and provincial government job cuts have affected even these localities, but with some new jobs have been being created. Hence disparity between the south and the more resource dependent north has become even more evident.

Despite the apparent cause for optimism over the call centres and the planned technological development, a word of caution needs to be voiced.

Call centre work is potentially highly footloose as the investors search for low-cost alternatives. The pressures to operate with low costs and overheads keep wages and benefits low. As the level of skill required to do the work is limited, the chances for advancement are few. New Brunswick's Federation of Labour has serious reservations about call centre-based development strategies.[119] In one of the most thoughtful assessments available of New Brunswick's foray into call centres and the information highway, Jonathan Rose offered this assessment: "For all its high technology, New Brunswick is still basically a province dependent upon its primary resources. The information highway and call-centres are merely first steps towards diversifying the economy."[120] Given the large and pervasive presence of the Irving and McCain corporate empires, the dominance of primary and secondary industry should not be surprising. However, this fact has often been overlooked amid the excitement over new technology and the capability of the provincial telephone company.

THE CONTEMPORARY ERA

A dramatic advantage for the McKenna Liberals was the internal discord that plagued the provincial Progressive Conservatives, the traditional alternative governing party in New Brunswick. Former PC premier Hatfield hung on to the leadership long after his stature began to wane among the citizenry. Party networks atrophied and discord overcame Hatfield's successor as party leader. The party was further weakened by linguistic division as a portion of the anglophone community engaged in a brief dalliance with the Confederation of Regions (COR) party and its antipathy to francophone concerns. COR lacked the ability to formulate a coherent organization and soon broke up in a laughable series of factional disputes. Even as COR engaged in a confusing and unimpressive exercise of self-destruction, the Conservatives were unable to rebound successfully. In the last provincial election, Bernard Valcourt, a former Mulroney-era minister, led the PC charge. The result was largely ineffective, and McKenna's most capable political opponent was the NDP leader, Elizabeth Weir. Weir represents an urban Saint John seat, but has experienced difficulty in electing other New Democrats. Valcourt's leadership was publicly challenged by a significant portion of his party colleagues in early 1997, leading to his resignation as party leader. A spirited leadership race ensued and in October 1997 thirty-two-year-old Bernard Lord won the leader's post. Lord had run unsuccessfully for a seat in the 1995 provincial election. In 1998, Lord won the by-election in a Moncton riding that had been considered a Liberal stronghold.

While the opposition parties struggled to re-build, the Liberals began the search for a replacement leader. The leadership convention was held in early May 1998. While Finance Minister Edmond Blanchard was perceived to be the early front-runner, he dropped out of the contest in mid-January citing health difficulties.[121] Fellow cabinet minister Camille Thériault triumphed.

Following his victory Thériault opted to distance himself from elements of the restructuring and restraints of his predecessor. However, a number of factors foreshadowed the eventual defeat of the Liberals. Lord's victory in the by-election led to a re-invigorated legislative opposition. Some of McKenna's most popular ministers, like Health Minister Russ King, announced their retirement. The provincial utility, NB Power, struggled with debt, public criticism, and concern over the future of its nuclear power plant. Meanwhile, NB Tel entered into talks with other telecommunications firms in Atlantic Canada about a possible merger. Through these and other complications, Thériault was less able than McKenna to win public trust and act authoritatively.

The New Brunswick provincial election of June 7, 1999 produced an amazing transformation. Despite leading opinion polls at the outset of the campaign, the Liberals found themselves reduced to 10 seats out of 55 (the total number of seats had been reduced during the McKenna years). Bernard Lord, whose previous political achievements had been in university politics, led the Progressive Conservatives to victory with 44 seats. The remaining seat was retained by Elizabeth Weir, the New Democratic Party leader, in the Saint John area.

Lord participated in a well-organized campaign marked by expansive promises, expert support from Progressive Conservative professionals, and the collapse of the Confederation of Regions Party. Among the promises were removal of highway tolls, significant tax cuts, employment of additional nurses and teacher assistants, reduction in provincial communications officers, more open review of public appointments, an increase in the provincial minimum wage, an extra million dollars for school supplies, added protection for schools with small enrolments, and recruitment of more physicians. Campaign assistance came from such party professionals as John Laschinger and David McLaughlin, both long active in Conservative campaigns across Canada. For their part the Liberals ran a lacklustre campaign marked by passivity in the face of dwindling support. Without McKenna's strong hand and the presence of certain experienced ministers, they drifted. Thériault faltered, pausing occasionally either to refer to the demands of office and past Liberal achievements or to engage in a limited bidding war with the ascendant Lord. Neither proved effective or well conducted.

Drawing a message from the election results involves pointing first to the absence of McKenna and then to other factors—a search for change, resistance to continued public sector restraint, a provincial trend toward youthful and dynamic leaders, and decay in the Liberal organization. Promises of perks and eased fiscal discipline sounded appealing for many, and the Progressive Conservatives effectively welded together assorted groups, each of whom had acquired some grievance with the McKenna-era reforms. While some outside commentators have sought to link Lord's victory to national trends toward tax reduction and more limited government, the accuracy of this inference is undercut by the accompanying campaign promises, few of which received serious costing out amid the campaign. Lord promised to listen, to decentralize decision-making, and to open up purse strings. In his preference for promises and spending commitments and his reluctance to provide specifics on paying for expanded spending commitments amid provincial economic weakness, Lord ran a politically strong campaign. Whether his leadership will prove effective and beneficial over the long run remains unknown.

CONCLUDING OBSERVATIONS

Four common traditions of New Brunswick public life warrant note in the synthesis of this account: one, the continued ability of a premier to dominate the provincial political landscape; two, the centrality of economic weakness to the priorities of governments and their agendas; three, the continued high-level support for the province's bilingual character and its formal recognition; and four, the continuing effort to upgrade provincial administration.

Postwar New Brunswick politics represents a cautious, complex move towards what is generally considered progressive reform and modern bureaucratization. Past reliance on patronage and tightly-knit partisan networks has been greatly reduced. New Brunswick governments now have professional, albeit small, bureaucracies offering programs and services at levels comparable to elsewhere in Canada. This has been a massive transformation.

Major questions remain. In particular, the province's contemporary political economy merits further study. Investigations into government-business relations in forestry and transportation needs to be done. Evaluation of the impact of the province's active Conservation Council and environmental movement could tell us much. There are also important studies to be performed in the field of social change and political culture. Fresh looks at topics such as rates of linguistic assimilation and urban-rural tensions would be valuable.

NOTES

1 Chart accompanying Alanna Mitchell, "It's Official: Quebec Falls Below 25% of Population," *Globe and Mail* 16 April 1997, sec. A.

2 *Report of the Chief Electoral Officer—Thirty-third General Election September 11, 1995* (New Brunswick, 1995), 31.

3 Agar Adamson and Ian Stewart, "Party Politics in the Not So Mysterious East," *Party Politics in Canada*, 7th ed., ed. Hugh G. Thorburn (Scarborough: Prentice Hall, 1996), 523.

4 Robert Finbow, "Atlantic Canada: Forgotten Periphery in an Endangered Confederation?," *Beyond Quebec: Taking Stock of Canada*, ed. Kenneth McRoberts (Montreal: McGill-Queen's, 1995), 62.

5 See, for example, Ernest R. Forbes, *Maritime Rights: The Maritime Rights Movement, 1919-1927—A Study in Canadian Regionalism* (Montreal: McGill-Queen's, 1979).

6 Margaret Conrad, "The Politics of Place: Regionalism and Community in Atlantic Canada Canada," *The Constitutional Future of the Prairie and Atlantic Regions of Canada*, eds. James N. McCroirie and Martha L. MacDonald (Regina: Canadian Plains Research Center, 1992), 29.

7 For an illuminating depiction of the regional minister phenomenon see Herman Bakvis, *Regional Ministers: Power and Influence in the Canadian Cabinet* (Toronto: University of Toronto, 1991).

8 Stephen Tomblin, *Ottawa and the Outer Provinces: The Challenge of Regional Integration in Canada* (Toronto: Lorimer, 1995).

9 W.S. MacNutt, *New Brunswick—A History: 1784-1867* (Toronto: MacMillan, 1984), 460.

10 MacNutt, 53.

11 Hugh G. Thorburn, *Politics in New Brunswick* (Toronto: University of Toronto Press, 1961), 180.

12 E.R. Forbes, *Maritime Rights: The Maritime Rights Movement, 1919-1927* (Montreal: McGill-Queen's University Press, 1979), 4.

13 E.R. Forbes, "Misguided Symmetry: The Destruction of Regional Transportation Policy for the Maritimes," *Essays on the 20th Century Maritimes—Challenging the Regional Stereotype* (Fredericton: Acadiensis, 1989), 114-35.

14 Forbes, *Maritime Rights*, 13.

15 Forbes, "Misguided Symmetry," 134.

16 Forbes, "Misguided Symmetry," 170.

17 E.R. Forbes, "Consolidating Disparity: The Maritimes and the Industrialization of Canada during the Second World War," *Essays*, 172-99.

18 R.A. Young, "'and the people will sink into despair': Reconstruction in New Brunswick, 1942-52," *Canadian Historical Review* 69:2 (June 1988): 127.

19 Young, "'and the people...,'" 165.

20 R.A. Young, "Planning for Power: The New Brunswick Electric Power Commission in the 1950s," *Acadiensis*, 12:1 (Autumn 1982): 73-99.

21 John Demont, *Citizen Irving: K.C. Irving and His Legacy* (Toronto: Doubleday, 1991), 49.

22 Demont, 49.

23 See "Table 14. Population by Sex for Counties and Census Divisions, Rural Farms, Rural Non-Farm and Urban Size Groups, 1961—New Brunswick," 14-2 and 14-3, *1961 Census of Canada*: Series 1:1 Population Rural and Urban Distribution, Bulletin 1:1-7 (8-2-1963).

24 Thorburn, *Politics*, 16.

25 H. Veltmeyer, "The Capitalist Underdevelopment of Atlantic Canada," *Underdevelopment and Social Movements in Atlantic Canada*, ed. Brym and Sacouman (Toronto: New Hogtown Press, 1979), 19.

26 Thorburn, *Politics*, 182.

27 Arthur T. Doyle, *Front Benches and Back Rooms* (Toronto: GreenTree, 1976), 182-84.

28 See, for example, Doyle, 142.

29 See J.D. Love, "The Merit Principle in the Provincial Governments of Atlantic Canada," *Canadian Public Administration* 31:3 (Fall 1988): 342-45; and Thorburn, *Politics*, 159-60.

30 Thorburn, *Politics*, 160.

31 Young, "Planning for Power," 79-80, 99.

32 Young, "Planning for Power," 73.

33 Rand Dyck, *Provincial Politics in Canada* (Scarborough: Prentice Hall, 1986), 145.

34 Dyck, 145.

35 *Report of the Royal Commission on Finance and Municipal Taxation in New Brunswick* (Fredericton: Queen's Printer, 1963), 56.

36 *Report of the Royal Commission on the Financing of Schools in New Brunswick* (Fredericton: Queen's Printer, 1955), 2.

37 Gail G. Campbell, "Disenfranchised but not Quiescent: Women Petitioners in New Brunswick in the Mid-19th Century," *Acadiensis,* 18:2 (September 1989): 22-54.

38 Janet Toole, "Remarkable Women of Saint John ... How They Won the Vote, *Atlantic Advocate* (October 1989): 27.

39 Toole, 27.

40 MacNutt, 366-67.

41 Della M. Stanley, *A Man for Two Peoples: Pierre Amand Landry* (Fredericton: 1988), 22.

42 Doyle, 13.

43 E.A. Aunger, *In Search of Political Stability* (Montreal: McGill-Queen's University Press, 1981), 110.

44 For an interesting account of the origins of the Acadian flag see Perry Biddiscombe, "Le Tricolore et l'étoile: The Origins of the Acadian National Flag, 1867-1912," *Acadiensis* 20:1 (Autumn 1990): 120-47.

45 Hugh G. Thorburn, "Ethnic Participation and Language use in the Public Service of New Brunswick" (unpublished study prepared for the Royal Commission on Bilingualism and Biculturalism, February 1966), 166.

46 Ralph Krueger, "The Provincial-Municipal Government Revolution on New Brunswick," *Canadian Public Administration* 13:1 (Spring 1970): 62.

47 Doyle, 225.

48 Doyle, 255.

49 Thorburn, *Politics*, 163.

50 P.J. Fitzpatrick, "New Brunswick—The Politics of Pragmatism," *Canadian Provincial Politics*, 2nd ed., ed. Martin Robin (Scarborough: Prentice Hall, 1978), 135.

51 Young, "'and the people...,'" 137-44.

52 Richard Simeon and David Elkins, "Regional Political Cultures in Canada," *Canadian Journal of Political Science* 7:7 (September 1974): 397-437.

53 Michael D. Ornstein, H. Michael Stevenson, and A. Paul Williams, "Region, Class and Political Culture in Canada," *Canadian Journal of Political Science* 13:2 (June 1980): 227-71.

54 Simeon and Elkins, 409-12.

55 See, for example, Graeme Wynn, *Timber Colony: A Historical Geography of Early Nineteenth-Century New Brunswick* (Toronto: University of Toronto Press, 1981), 152.

56 R.A. Young, "Non-Development on the Periphery: The Case of New Brunswick Multiplex," (paper presented at the Annual Meeting of the Atlantic Provinces Political Science Association, Antigonish, Nova Scotia, 18-20 October 1984), 1.

57 Stanley, *Louis Robichaud*, 227.

58 Stanley, *Louis Robichaud*, 227.

59 See n. 35.

60 Norman J. Ruff, "Administrative Reform and Development: A Study of Administrative Adaptation to Provincial Government Development Goals and the Re-Organization of Provincial and Local Government in New Brunswick, 1963-67" (Ph.D. diss., McGill University, 1972), 197.

61 Harley Louis d'Entremont, "Provincial Restructuring of Municipal Government: A Comparative Analysis of New Brunswick and Nova Scotia" (Ph.D. diss., University of Western Ontario, 1985), 265.

62 R.A. Young, "Remembering Equal Opportunity: Clearing the Undergrowth in New Brunswick," *Canadian Public Administration* 30:1 (Spring 1987): 89.

63 Paul C. Leger, "The Cabinet System of Policy-Making and Resource Allocation in the Government of New Brunswick," *Canadian Public Administration* 26:1 (Spring 1987): 16-35.

64 Richard Starr, *Richard Hatfield: The Seventeen Year Saga* (Halifax: Formac, 1987).

65 Starr, 25.

66 Stanley, *Louis Robichaud*, 227.

67 See Agar Adamson and Ian Stewart, "Party Politics in the Mysterious East," *Party Politics in Canada*, 5th ed., ed. Hugh Thorburn (Scarborough: Prentice Hall, 1985), 319-33.

68 See Donald J. Savoie, "The Atlantic Region: The Politics of Dependency," *Perspectives on Canadian Federalism*, ed. R.D. Olling and M.W. Westmacott (Scarborough: Prentice Hall, 1988), 298.

69 Stanley, *Louis Robichaud*, 112.

70 Herman Bakvis, *Regional Ministers: Power and Influence in the Canadian Cabinet* (Toronto: University of Toronto Press, 1991), 297.

71 André Laurendeau, *The Diary of André Laurendeau* (Toronto: Lorimer, 1991), 41.

72 Statistics Canada, *Population and Dwelling Characteristics—Language: Part 2: The Nation* (Ottawa, 1989, Cab No. 93-103), Highlights, vii.

73 For an extensive treatment of this and a comparison with Northern Ireland, see Augner, *In Search of Political Stability*.

74 Task Force on Official Languages, *Towards Equality of Official Languages in New Brunswick* (Fredericton: Cabinet Secretariat Official Languages Branch, 1982).

75 Task Force on Official Languages, 416.

76 Starr, *Richard Hatfield*, 176-237.

77 Anthony Careless, *Initiatives and Response: The Adaptation of Canadian Federalism to Regional Economic Development* (Montreal: McGill-Queen's University Press, 1977), 111.

78 Stanley, *Louis Robichaud*, 166-67.

79 Leger, "The Cabinet Committee," 16-35.

80 *Report on Maritime Union Commissioned by the Governments of Nova Scotia, New Brunswick and Prince Edward Island* (Fredericton: Maritime Union Study, 1970).

81 DeMont, 4.

82 DeMont, 5.

83 Russell Hunt and Robert Campbell, *K.C. Irving: The Age of the Industrialist* (Toronto: McClelland and Stewart, 1973).

84 Hunt and Campbell, 189-90.

85 DeMont, 60.

86 DeMont, 78-88.

87 See DeMont, 90-92; and Stanley, 167-75.

88 Dyck, 154.

89 Donald J. Savoie, *Federal-Provincial Collaboration: The Canada-New Brunswick General Development Agreement* (Montreal: IPAC, 1981), 143-45.

90 Savoie, *Federal-Provincial Collaboration*, 144.

91 Donald J. Savoie, "ACOA: Something Old, Something New, Something Borrowed, Something Blue," *How Ottawa Spends, 1989-90*, ed. Katherine Graham (Ottawa: Carleton University Press, 1991), 142.

92 Editorial, "Mr. McKenna's Hat Trick," *Globe and Mail*, 12 September 1995, sec. A.

93 *Report of the Chief Electoral Officer*, 30.

94 Merle MacIsaac, "Faith, Hope and Hold the Charity," *Canadian Business* (December 1992): 72.

95 For a helpful summation of work on this issue see Rand Dyck, *Provincial Politics in Canada: Towards the Turn of the Century*, 3d ed. (Scarborough: Prentice Hall, 1996), 176-77.

96 Hon. Frank McKenna, *Speech for Delivery to Empire Club*, Toronto, Ontario, 21 February 1990, 2.

97 New Brunswick rejected B.C. efforts to refer the matter to an interprovincial trade tribunal. "N.B. Says No," *Globe and Mail*, 12 September 1996, sec. B.

98 Leslie A. Pal, *Beyond Policy Analysis: Public Issue Management in Turbulent Times* (Toronto: Nelson, 1997), 56.

99 This depiction is drawn from Pal, 56. For further material on these themes and related debates useful reference may be made to Peter Aucoin, *The New Public Management: Canada in Comparative Perspective* (Montreal: Institute for Research on Public Policy, 1995) and to F. Leslie Seidle, *Rethinking the Delivery of Public Services to Citizens* (Montreal: Institute for Research on Public Policy, 1995).

100 Brian Bergman, "McKenna Calls It Quits," *Maclean's*, 20 October 1997, 14.

101 Jane Coutts, "New Brunswick Tries Out Telephone Triage," *Globe and Mail*, 28 July 1995, sec. A.

102 *Hospital News* (January 1998), 4.

103 Jonathan W. Rose, "The Selling of New Brunswick: Fibre Optics or Optical Illusion," *Canada: The State of the Federation 1995*, ed. Douglas M. Brown and Jonathan W. Rose (Kingston: Queen's Institute of Intergovernmental Relations, 1995), 175.

104 Don Richardson, "Get Connected Programme May Take Years to Bear Fruit," *Telegraph Journal*, 4 September 1996, sec. A.

105 Richardson, see n. 104.

106 Lawrence Surtees, "NB Tel Cable Bid Hearing Set," *Globe and Mail*, 24 January 1998, sec. B.

107 See Rose, 182, where he points out, "Reforms to the Workers Compensation Act removing stress as a legitimate claim have provided further incentives to businesses. By re-classifying call-centre employees, McKenna has reduced the amount of money paid by firms to Workers' Compensation. In New Brunswick, companies pay only 22 cents for every $100 of payroll." This is far less than rates prevailing in Ontario.

108 Claire Morris, "An Overview of Programme Review in New Brunswick," *Hard Choices Or No Choices: Assessing Programme Review*, ed. Amelita Armit and Jacques Bourgault (Toronto: Canadian Public Administration with the cooperation of the Great Plains Research Center, 1994), 73.

109 Hugh Mellon, "The Complexity and Competitiveness of Fiscal Federalism: Blending the GST with Provincial Sales Taxes," *Challenges to Canadian Federalism*, ed. Martin Westmacott and Hugh Mellon (Scarborough: Prentice Hall Canada, 1998), 164-68.

110 Figures were provided by the N.B. Finance Department via e-mail on 8 December 1997.

111 Province of New Brunswick, Budget 1997-1998, 15.

112 Province of New Brunswick, Budget 1996-1997, 10.

113 Campbell Morrison, "Bond Firm Boosts N.B.'s Credit Rating," *Telegraph Journal*, 13 April 1996, sec. B.

114 Quoted from "Standard and Poor's Confirms N.B.'s Credit Rating," *Telegraph Journal*, 30 April 1996, sec. B.

115 Don Richardson, "'This is Just a Start,'" *Telegraph Journal*, 8 April 1997, sec. A.

116 See, for example, Alan White, "Enrolment Drops Doom 30 N.B. Schools," *Telegraph Journal*, 26 March 1997, sec. A.

117 Statistics Canada, "Statistical Summary," *Canadian Economic Observer* (Ottawa: March 1997), Table 40—Provincial Labour Force Estimates.

118 William J. Milne, *The McKenna Miracle: Myth or Reality* (Toronto: University of Toronto, 1996), 66.

119 See, for example, the sentiments expressed by Bob Hickes, the Federation President reported in John Wishart, "Moncton's Miracle," *The Times-Transcript*, 2/3 September 1995, sec. F.

120 Rose, 182.

121 Giselle Goguen, "Blanchard Bows Out," *Saint John Telegraph Journal*, 19 January 1998, sec. A.

5 PRINCE EDWARD ISLAND

Politics in a Beleaguered Garden

DAVID A. MILNE

They came out by the tens of thousands to celebrate the opening of Confederation Bridge. Joggers, walkers, and hawkers swarmed this, the world's largest free-standing structure of its kind, spanning thirteen kilometres of ocean that is the Northumberland Strait. They had come, they said, not only to experience this engineering marvel first hand, but also to witness "history in the making." A unique and fateful moment in the Island's history, to be sure, May 30, 1997 symbolized for these revellers economic promise and prosperity, while for so many thousands of others it marked the end of an island.

Islanders had been debating the depth and meaning of this rupture of identity for a decade or more. In their last official voice on the subject of a fixed link to the mainland in January 1988, Islanders had appeared to give the project their approval, though the 59-per-cent vote could scarcely be called a commanding one. The issue drove deep fissures in Islanders' collective unconscious, challenging their sense of themselves, their past, and their future. Later the same year, Islanders turned out to vote decisively, if in vain, against free trade in the federal election. In both cases, however, change relentlessly altered the face of Canada and Prince Edward Island. The logic of integration, it seemed, was inexorable. Yet there was a familiar paradox in all of this. Just as larger economic forces of change appeared ready to overtake and dismantle local ways of life, there appeared in Prince Edward Island, as frequently elsewhere, evidence of renewed and assertive localism.

These themes have haunted the modern politics of Prince Edward Island since World War II. How to control and fashion modernization so that it sustains and supports rather than undermines the Island community? How to achieve sustainability and self-reliance amidst the erosions of a larger national and international political economy? In effect, this had been the perennial question of dependency arising from Prince Edward Island's entire history, whether as a colony of France and Britain, or later as the smallest and most vulnerable member of the Canadian federation. But it is only in the modern era, where the scale and threat of change is so massive, that this struggle has taken on a unique existential urgency. The battle has been fought on a host of fronts. The issues have ranged from the future and shape of *island* land, agriculture, and economy, island schools, island tourism, and island community to, most starkly with the fixed link to the mainland, the very geographical identity of Prince Edward Island as *island* or peninsula.

At the rhetorical level at least, it is easy to see the stake that Islanders have had in picturing themselves as a unique people living on a small, beautiful, protected, territorially distinct place. Immortalized in the nostalgic work of Lucy Maud Montgomery, and subsequently popularized in stage and worldwide television productions, Prince Edward Island has come to be seen by both insiders and outsiders as a romantic, bucolic refuge from metropolitan stress and sprawl. As I have argued elsewhere:

> At the centre of the question of identity—of the 'Island way of life'—has rested a garden myth, which organized for Islanders an ideal picture of themselves as an independent agricultural people protected from the world in an unspoiled pastoral setting. Some elements of this idyllic metaphor—the geographical isolation, the presence of farming families working a rich soil, and, not least, the magnificent, tamed quality of the Island landscape—were always strong enough to make the garden myth compelling and realistic.[1]

Of course, as noted above, the Island's long history of dependency hardly squares with this quasi-Jeffersonian imagery. Nor does the Island's current political economy and demography fit the image now. Yet the rhetoric lives on. Indeed, that would appear to be the central paradox of Island politics: the more that change has caught up with the province and proceeded to dismantle the "Island way of life," the more stubbornly do Islanders (and sentimental outsiders) resist dissolution in the name of the past. It is in this ironic commitment to a traditional economy and values amidst modernization that Islanders demonstrate their distinctiveness from the residents of most other provinces.

THE LAND, AGRICULTURE, AND THE PASTORAL IDEAL

Just as the land question has dominated the historical imagination of Islanders—the story of a people fending off rent collectors and wresting control of their lands from absentee landlords—the idea of an independent, rural, and prosperous Prince Edward Island has been a constant preoccupation of Island politicians. With the possible exception of Alexander B. Campbell's early years (1966-71), Island politicians have returned again and again to this vision. No premier ever expressed this noble pastoral image as poetically as Walter Shaw (1959-66), but it was a mandatory metaphor for thinking about the Island and for charting its future.[2] This picture of the Island was already threatened in the days of Walter Jones (1943-53), but his truculent defence of rural interests and values was a lot closer to reality than was the later, pointedly nostalgic "rural renaissance" rhetoric of Premier J. Angus MacLean (1979-81) or of Premier Pat Binns (1996-). In between these leaders' celebration of the myth lies an erosion of the traditional farm economy and community life.

An awareness of this crisis underlies the postwar period and shapes the policies of every administration. Although Jones boasted in his 1948 "state of P.E.I." address that he knew "of no area anywhere that provides as good a chance to make a good living as Prince Edward Island," he had already admitted three years earlier that "nearly forty percent [of his people] were forced to leave the province in their productive years."[3] Nor were such facts startling to Islanders. Agriculture had long been a precarious business; those engaged in farming as an occupation had declined steadily from a high of over 21,000 in 1901, to 18,306 in 1931, to 16,661 in 1941, and to 12,943 in 1951.[4] The decline in the number of bona fide farmers in the next four decades would, however, accelerate at an even more alarming rate.

Farmer Jones (as the premier liked to be called) recognized the menacing trend away from the land and set out to reverse it. Drawing on his background as a former student of scientific farming and one-time lecturer at the Virginia Institute in Hampton, Jones set up a modern agricultural laboratory, a pathological service for livestock and poultry, and an extensive soil-analysis program. He formed a government-owned company to operate a cold-storage plant, and even invested in a 400-ton ship to transport Island produce to markets in Newfoundland. While urging Islanders to undertake more processing of agricultural products at home, he lectured the federal government concerning its dismal support for agriculture in eastern Canada and for its bias towards the industrial areas of the nation.

His electioneering tactics, from the 1943 election onward, were so blatantly pro-farmer that they prompted the Conservative *Guardian* to deplore his appeal to "class warfare in this Province." The editors argued that those "who seek to set class against class and cater to narrow sectional prejudice as the Liberal organ [*Patriot*] is doing in this case, deserve nothing but condemnation." This criticism did not deter Jones from virtually equating the interests of Prince Edward Island with the rural farm interest on every available occasion, and the strategy secured him the farm vote every time. As befits a former Progressive turned Liberal, Jones told delegates to the Maritime Board of Trade in 1949 that "the heart of the province was in its rural districts and that the cities were only a place where people can meet and do their business. If the farmers all go foolish like the people in the towns," observed Farmer Jones, "good-bye Prince Edward Island."[5]

If other classes had any doubts about the seriousness of Jones's remarks, they had only to remember the Canada Packers strike of 1947. Over a six-month period following the strike vote of the local on September 11, Island meatpacking workers watched Jones's government take possession of the factory, operate it with scab labour, declare the strike itself illegal, and finally outlaw unions affiliated with national or international labour organizations (or any other unions objectionable to the government). Cabinet minister Horace Wright advised the workers that "anything that affects the farmer adversely affects every class of citizen" and therefore "the Government must protect the farmers' interests." The premier noted that a lowly paid and respectful labour force was essential to bringing new industry to the Island and that "if union men don't like to pitch in like the big majority of our people here ... then I say let them go somewhere else."

This high-handed defence of Prince Edward Island as an agricultural community of primary producers was coloured not only by a suspicion of unions but also by rabid anti-communism. The anti-labour measure had been taken, according to Horace Wright, "to keep communism out of this province." He went on to declare that "a communist agent from Toronto had been in the province until after the bill was passed—hoping that he would be able to take over."[6]

In the December election of 1947, called during the off-season to accommodate farmers' busy schedules and only weeks after the strike had ended, the anti-labour measures helped Jones not only win the election but increase his popular vote standing.[7] As the opposition to Jones mounted nationally, even the Liberal *Patriot* condemned him, and the Federation of Agriculture later formally opposed his union-busting. Although Jones was forced to repeal the measures in 1949, the entire incident revealed the darker side of life in the garden. It would not be the last time Island governments reacted to outside threats with clumsy legal repression. Nor would it be the last time non-farmers were relegated to second-class status.

Even Premier Jones's best efforts, however, failed to come to grips with the vicious pattern of declining farm income, farm vacancies, and the outmigration of able young people from the countryside. Rural electrification was a principal strategy to help stem this tide. The policy was begun in Jones's administration, but it formed the centre of Premier Alex Matheson's efforts from 1953 to 1959. It was expected not only to ease working life on the farm by making labour-saving devices available, but also to equalize social opportunities and entertainment as compared with the towns. The irony is that while the provision of television and other media probably did close the gap with the towns, and the expansive road-building made distances easy to surmount with the automobile, these developments contributed mightily to the breakdown of local community life.

After Matheson's electoral victory in 1955, Islanders began to witness firmer attempts to put in place an industrial strategy consistent with the Island's agricultural character. The obvious answer was industry that could absorb, process, and market Island products while not disturbing the agreed-upon character of Island life. A fish-processing plant in Souris, a new cannery in Bedeque, a chicken-processing plant in Charlottetown—these were seen to be the appropriate industrial building blocks in an economy of farmers and fishermen.[8] The whole strategy hinged upon the success of government-assisted private firms. Government was bold enough even at this early stage to engage the services of a director of marketing to enhance the prospects for improved income for the Island's primary producers.

And yet the alarm over a "farm crisis" was being taken up again in 1957 in the speeches of the new Conservative leader Walter Shaw, who, following the Diefenbaker sweep at the federal level, laid claim to provincial office in the election of 1959. In attacking the crisis with a new comprehensiveness, Shaw ironically gave birth to a new planning industry whose values and usefulness in a farm province were openly debated a decade later. Although his speech and personal style never forewarned Islanders of the managerial revolution that he was to introduce—leading most to mistake him as a spokesman for an older order—Shaw in fact brought to government the confidence of the rational planner and civil servant. Unfortunately, his planning and bureaucratic interests quickly led him into dependence on outside consultants, so that in many respects he unwittingly laid the foundation for the 1969 Development Plan he was later to denounce so bitterly.

During his tenure the numbers of civil servants rose by almost 20 per cent, posts were classified and rationalized, and the beginnings of a professional bureaucracy were put into place.[9] Deliberate planning of the Island economy was undertaken in a new, comprehensive way. Surveys and studies by outside consultants, from Toronto to Colorado Springs, were mounted by government either separately or in conjunction with ARDA, the new federal development agency. In total the Shaw government had funded eight complete surveys and used scores of consultants before it engaged H.G. Acres of Toronto to pull all of the work together and propose a comprehensive plan in 1965.[10]

The initial move into a systematic politics of development was begun by Hartwell Daley of the *Journal Pioneer*, who later became Shaw's director of research. Inspired by a development program begun in Perry County, Indiana, and reported in the *New York Times* on May 8, 1960, Daley outlined improvements being sought in Perry County by planning groups in a number of sectors—agriculture, industry, education, health, and tourism—under the promising headline "Adventures in Progress." Later, as the new research director, Daley set in motion similar studies for Prince Edward Island and participated as executive director of a forty-five member Provincial Development Council that gave advice to a cabinet committee chaired by the premier. A series of pilot projects was initiated in different parts of the province to test the self-help principles of Perry County in Prince Edward Island. Although this planning process was said to be a grassroots movement—"little more than a return to basic democratic principles"[11]—even at this stage it is easy to see how precariously democracy and public participation were wedded to central bureaucratic planning.

The crisis in the farm sector, as in most other areas, was unfortunately treated as a "development problem ... basically, or at its beginnings at least, an adult education matter."[12] The government strategy of providing study courses in farming, arts and crafts, and other fields, while helpful in dealing with some marginal problems, failed to come to grips with the structural and external causes of Prince Edward Island's underdevelopment. Increasing poverty on the farms stemmed not from farmers' lack of technical or educational expertise, but from market forces and conditions over which isolated Island farmers had precious little control. The same simple stress on "education" and "technical sophistication" reappeared in the 1969 Development Plan. Yet in spite of increasing agricultural productivity during this period, farmers did not and could not receive the financial returns commensurate with their new success. Ironically, the emphasis on education and technical sophistication worsened the farmers' situation by encouraging even more dependency, with crop specialization, expensive machinery and fertilizers, high debt load, and more soil erosion.

Another part of the Island's economy was also about to undergo changes through a more deliberate application of industrial methods and marketing techniques. Tourism received a dramatic boost in status when Shaw created a separate government department in 1960. Studies and plans were immediately begun to exploit its economic potential, with none other than Dalton Camp and Associates of Toronto hired to provide the appropriate metropolitan leadership.

By November 1963, however, industrial development had begun to overshadow much of the Resources Development Program. In addition to the earlier Langley Fruit Packers plant in Montague, and Seabrook Farms Frozen Foods in New Annan, the Shaw government backed two new ventures for Georgetown: Gulf Garden Foods, a fish and vegetable processing plant, and Bathurst Marine, a New Brunswick shipbuilding firm. As well, an advertising program promoting the Island as an ideal industrial location was announced in the 1965 Throne speech and the first steps taken in 1966 to establish an industrial park. Although constrained by the link with agriculture, this policy of forced growth would soon entangle Islanders, as it had Canadians elsewhere, in the dismal politics of luring outside businesses with generous concessions and of providing outlays of public funds to keep them afloat.[13] It also seemed to be introducing an alternate vision of development on the Island, based more and more on the standard industrial model.

It is worth underlining as well that the idea of a causeway to the mainland was already being taken up in the 1960s as an important part of the Shaw administration's development plans, with preliminary land-based construction actually under way by the mid-sixties. A causeway, presented then (and later) as a panacea for the Island's problems, had by 1968 competed with Premier Campbell's Development Plan as a shared federal-provincial project and development symbol. Although the fixed link project was ultimately shelved in favour of the Development Plan, the megaproject reappeared as a policy option in the 1980s and ultimately came to fruition a decade later.

Meanwhile, even with the ongoing electrification program, life on the farm was not getting easier. Average farm income failed to keep pace with that in other occupations and increased costs for mechanization were adding to the financial strain. Shaw's government continued its educational program for farmers, and by 1965 was also offering marketing assistance, programs to enlarge farm operations, and other means of raising farm income. Despite the fact that all of these measures were moving Prince Edward Island further away from the reigning myth of a garden of independent yeomen, Shaw's rhetoric continued to hark back to it.[14] If agriculture was still the province's "bedrock" industry, then Islanders were on shaky ground. To the youthful leader of the opposition, Alex Campbell, it seemed obscurantist and romantic to dwell on the old days. Scorning Shaw and his associates as the "horse and buggy boys," he promised to bring to the Island fresh approaches and pragmatic reform.[15] In 1966 Islanders, doubtless noting the Liberal return to power in Ottawa, were now ready to give Campbell a chance.

For Premier Campbell, and especially for his minister of industry and commerce, Dr. John Maloney, the appeal of the garden myth was considerably reduced. Not only were they sufficiently immune to its spell to see its mawkish nostalgia and romanticism, but they were urbane enough to accept rather coolly the logical implications of the transformation overtaking Prince Edward Island. Imbued with reform zeal, they came not to bemoan the decline of the "Island way of life," but to accelerate it. Even if on close examination so many of the Liberal policies turned out to be retreads from Shaw's administration and earlier, there is an undeniable shift in attitude, language, and policy focus. Indeed, in terms of Island conventions, the Campbell men can only be described as revolutionaries.[16] The cornerstone of Campbell's administration, for example, was the Development Plan, a fifteen-year federal–provincial agreement intended to restructure and rationalize the Island economy and society. Although politicians had long declared that the incomes of farmers (or fishermen) had to be improved, no previous Island leader would have dared to declare that putting two-thirds of the remaining farmers off the land (or fishermen out of their boats) was an appropriate means of doing so.[17] Yet this was precisely the policy objective of the plan for the Island's primary industries.

While earlier politicians had directed their efforts towards stemming the tide of farmers leaving the land, the new administration argued that the resource could neither sustain nor be effectively managed by more than 2500 farmers. Through the Land Development Corporation, incentives were offered to direct less successful farmers into other work. Although many attributed this blatant attack on Island values to insensitive federal planners and politicians, it would be a mistake to write off the policy as a nefarious plot "from away." Instead, a new unsentimental Island elite with its own interests and program of change had come of age. The new leaders were middle-class and statist and they cared much less about the past.[18]

In industrial policy, the new Liberals built on the work of their predecessors, although again with far more aggressiveness and a different emphasis. Creating a host of new agencies, such as Industrial Enterprises Incorporated, the Market Development Centre, and, not least, the new Department of Development, industrial promotion was accelerated far beyond the efforts of Matheson and Shaw. By 1979, at least 23 new companies had been set up in the industrial parks in West Royalty, Parkdale, and Summerside, most of which had little or no relation to agriculture and the fisheries. Clothing and ski manufacturing, metal parts fabrication, chemical industries, all indicated a commitment to a small-scale business sector no longer based on the Island's natural resources. All of these initiatives, as might be expected, provoked a disquieting response from many Islanders.

Within two years of the signing of the plan in 1969, farmers were registering their opposition to these unprecedented policies. Although now split into competing farm organizations, the older Federation of Agriculture and the newly formed National Farmers Union, farmers shared a concern for the future of the family farm and the place of agriculture in Island society. The National Farmers Union showed its disgruntlement in August 1971 with a tractor blockade of the Trans-Canada Highway. The premier's reaction was a good indication of how far events had moved from the days of Farmer Jones: "The role of government today is to protect the whole public against the excessive demands of special interest groups."[19] Campbell had managed to reduce farmers from the privileged status they had always enjoyed to that of one interest group among others.

However much Campbell's statement accurately reflected the government's thinking, it was politically an impossible posture. Campbell rapidly discovered that, with legislative representation heavily in favour of rural areas, no one could so flout Island values. Within a year he was announcing a revision of the plan's agricultural objectives to make room for the "family farm" and "community values." The conversion was so adeptly handled that in an article in the *Canadian Magazine* a cartoon depicted Campbell as the Island's veritable Jolly Green Giant towering over the lush green Garden of the Gulf.[20]

The new posture did not fool the Brothers and Sisters of Cornelius Howatt, a group of sympathizers of the nineteenth-century foe of Confederation for whom they named their society, spearheaded by historians David Weale and Harry Baglole. In several satirical sallies during the Island's 1973 Centennial festivities, they warned Islanders of government threats to the family farm heritage and eulogized the past as the Island's golden age. With wit and humour, they prepared the ideological ground for a decade-long battle with the plan.

With Campbell's rhetorical support for the "family farm" came other signs of a would-be ideological conversion. While industrial incentives continued at full speed, the premier spoke increasingly in his speeches of the limits of technology and the drawbacks of an industrial style of life. The virtues of Prince Edward Island's rural landscape and values, the beauty of its small-scale institutions and society, and the promise of an ecological future sensibly built on renewable energy sources began to replace the earlier bureaucratic talk of development objectives and targets. Gone was the dashing young prince of planning elected in the sixties. Here was a sobered leader preaching a new conserver mentality closer to traditional Island values. With the exception of the establishment of the high-profile Institute of Man and Resources in 1975 and the energy experiments at the Ark, there was very little new to go on, and Campbell spent the remainder of the decade carrying out the basic Development Plan strategy with whatever modest adjustments political life made necessary.[21]

The opposition to the Campbell government mounted on a number of fronts, especially as the public became more aware of the plan's failure to achieve its objectives. The erosion of Island communities, caused in part by school consolidation, coupled with the obvious crisis in agriculture, made Islanders intensely receptive to the calls for "rural renaissance" from the reassuring grandfatherly voice of Angus MacLean, the new Conservative leader. The April 1978 election appeared to seal the Liberals' fate: with 17 seats in a 32-member House, Premier Campbell eluded the unattractive prospects of stalemate in the Assembly and possible electoral defeat by retiring to take up a position as a Supreme Court justice. Bennett Campbell, former minister of education, was left to lead the party. The election of the Conservatives on April 23, 1979 signalled a return to Islanders' roots and to the politics of nostalgia.[22]

It would be difficult to imagine a more appropriate leader for re-awakening Islanders to their traditional values than Premier MacLean. Himself a farmer, former minister of fisheries in the Diefenbaker government, and Member of Parliament from Malpeque through all the Trudeau-Campbell years, he brought to the office a healthy scepticism concerning Liberal state planning and a deep reverence for the Island's rural and community values. Assisted by his speechwriter David Weale, one-time founder of the Brothers and Sisters of Cornelius Howatt, MacLean masterfully exploited the real and mythical qualities of the Island's golden age, accenting at every point conservative virtues of moderation, conservation, stability, respect, self-reliance, humility, community, and the sanctity of the family farm.

The Conservatives' nostalgia under premier MacLean and his successor James Lee (1981-86) was abruptly tested in 1981 by the request of the Irving interests at Cavendish Farms to add six thousand acres of farmland to their existing holding of three thousand acres. The government responded to this challenge to family farming with a new Lands Protection Bill in 1982. It restricted corporate holdings of Island farmland to three thousand acres and individual holdings to one thousand acres. Rowing yet further against the corporate trend, the government announced a new Small Farm Program, schemes to increase individual land ownership, marketing, stabilization assistance, and so on. Even a charter property rights provision in the *Constitution Act* 1982 was unanimously opposed in the Island legislature in 1983 because it might be used to challenge P.E.I.'s land measures and hence imperil "the Island way of life." As Premier Lee declared on that occasion: "Control and management of the land by Islanders, through their provincial legislature, is essential to the province's economic and social well-being."[23] Similarly, when confronted with threats to the future of country stores by modern shopping mall expansion, for example, the Conservatives first declared an interim ban on shopping malls in May 1979, and then adopted amendments to the Planning Act in 1981 that vainly sought to sharply limit such expansion. The arrival of Wal-Mart and many other mega-stores on the Island some two decades later, however, indicated that this was ultimately a forlorn strategy.

As well, the MacLean government distanced itself from the old Liberal policy of purchasing nuclear power from Point Lepreau, New Brunswick, when it abrogated that agreement in 1981 and sought access to cheaper electrical energy through an intergovernmental agreement on electrical energy. In industrial policy there was a noticeable shift back toward a strategy focusing on the Island's indigenous resources; nonetheless, the policy welcomed the application of advanced technology to bolster the Island's natural resources, in programs such as lobster and fish farming. The arrival of the new Atlantic Veterinary College at the University of Prince Edward Island in 1982 was welcomed too for bringing in new technology that would strengthen agriculture and the fisheries in aquaculture research.

The continuing pre-eminence of agriculture was apparent in the swift government reaction to the proposed closure of the Canada Packers meat-packing facility in 1982 and the hefty financial support offered for a new kill and chill plant in Sherwood in 1984. The company was offered a sweetheart deal to continue to act as managers and part owners of the new facility, while farmers increased production of hogs by 20 per cent to meet the new plant schedule.[24] As in the past, the rescue of powerful agricultural interests, however, came at the expense of unionized labour. As part of the package, former Canada Packers workers were forced to accept a $2.25 per hour cut on threat of government stripping them of benefits and union affiliation. The whole incident was eerily reminiscent of anti-union farmer power under Premier Jones decades earlier. As Jim Macdonald, business agent for the union, complained: "It was just like holding a gun to our head. We had no choice."[25]

Hence, the defence of the small farmers' interests could cut across class lines: both labour and agribusiness could find themselves legislatively contained by the pre-eminence of this ideology and set of interests. It was much the same with the succeeding Ghiz and Binns governments. Under the Ghiz Liberals, the Lands Protection Act was further tightened in 1988 to require government approval for non-resident and corporate purchases of land exceeding five acres. Moreover, in another tussle with Irving interests in 1990, the Liberal government pressured Mary Jean Irving, P.E.I. resident and granddaughter of K.C. Irving, to dispose promptly of 2000 of the 4800 acres of land she had purchased in West Prince.[26] The Binns government has certainly been no less stringent.

Potato dealers received a similar lesson when the Ghiz government adopted the 1987 Driscoll Report recommending that producers gain stronger control over the industry through a producer-controlled Marketing Commission and a dealership of their own to counteract monopolistic practices in the domestic market.[27] Even Gemini Foods of Toronto was acquired to provide producers with "a window on the industry." Producers were protected too in a proposed "right to farm" bill introduced in 1988 amending certain sections of the *Environment Protection Act* to limit producers' liability for nuisance from noise and odours connected with their operations and to channel complaints through a non-judicial route. In all of these ways, the old pre-eminence of the farm interest is again in evidence.

Even Litton Industries was to learn with some surprise that Islanders meant what they said when they declared that only "appropriate technology and manufacturing" should be encouraged in the Garden of the Gulf. On December 11, 1985, Premier Lee joined the Litton president in announcing that a new anti-missile radar system would be built in Charlottetown if Litton was successful in its bid for a federal grant for that purpose. However, he had not counted on the groundswell of opposition from Islanders who felt the government had in this case betrayed its own mandate of promoting "appropriate" manufacturing compatible with Island values and norms. Clearly, a war industry fitted uncomfortably into the dominant "Anne of Green Gables" motif. Other Islanders opposed the meagre company commitments to the province for the financial outlays being sought from taxpayers. The newly elected Liberal Ghiz government gave expression to this anger, after failing to negotiate better terms with Litton following the provincial election on April 21, 1986: "Prince Edward Island," Ghiz thundered, "is *not* a banana republic."[28]

The June 1986 Throne speech declared the province "an agricultural community, [with] the family farm the pulse of our rural communities," and promised "an industrial strategy aimed at attracting secondary industry which can build on the economic activity generated by our primary resources. The strategy will be directed toward finding, and working with, industries which are compatible with the Island lifestyle and which are prepared to make a long-term commitment to the Island community." The same consensus continued throughout the Liberal years under premiers Ghiz and Callbeck (1993-96), and re-emerged again in the Tory legislative programme of government support for "small business" under Premier Binns (November 1996–). Adopting this strategy did not, of course, compromise the Island's receptiveness to high-value niche industries nor to calls for a stronger "knowledge economy," as was clear in the spring 1997 legislative programme of the Binns Tories, but it certainly put large corporations on notice concerning Islanders' preference for small business. Nothing quite underlined this bias more forcefully than the 1997 decision by the Binns government to turn down a request for a low-interest loan to the Irvings for a packaging plant in Borden, a move that promptly led the Irvings to transfer the plant to New Brunswick.

Revealing too was the Island battle against an inappropriate development in the field of tourism. By the early 1970s the Campbell government's tourist promotion policies were already beginning to run afoul of the garden myth. The marketing of tourism was being criticized for despoiling the Island countryside, for introducing tasteless metropolitan commercialism, for converting an independent people into a society of "panderers," and for dislodging the primacy of agriculture. In the witty pronouncements of the Brothers and Sisters of Cornelius Howatt or in the acerbic criticism of the late Marc Gallant, artistic custodian of the Island landscape, the government confronted a more sustained and intelligent ideological attack concerning the role of tourism than had ever been mounted before. This dissent had to await the maturing of Premier Shaw's initial policy initiatives in tourism from 1960. By Campbell's time, the Development Plan had given an explicit status to the tourist industry that simply could not be harmonized with the traditional model of the Island as a garden of independent yeomen.

At the root of the difficulty with development lay a basic contradiction between planners' rationality and objectives and Islanders' own deeply held values. This contradiction was recognized to some extent by planners, and accounts in part for both the initial secrecy surrounding the plan and the dismal experience with public participation. The planners' commitment to direct expenditure for tourism, especially for luxury resorts like Brudenell, naturally offended farmers and fishermen, just as the presence of "Kitten" waitresses at the resort's bar provoked a chorus of denunciation in letters to the Island newspapers in the summer of 1971. Another planner's commitment to extend tourism to the eastern part of Prince Edward Island with a new national park at East Point ran smack into residents' wishes to keep the land for traditional agricultural use. When the premier found himself, together with his officials, pitted against the local community, which was informed and supported by the Rural Development Council, the Social Action Commission, and the other sympathetic groups, he tore up the federal–provincial agreement in an open meeting on June 28, 1973. Although this ended the immediate park issue, public disquiet over the role of tourism continued.

Campbell's government had attempted to answer part of the concern, at least as it related to land use and ownership, with a 1972 measure to protect the Island landscape from the baneful effects of tourism. The amendment to the *Real Property Act* required cabinet consent for non-resident purchases of land exceeding either ten acres or five chains of shorefront.[29] The law found little support from the federal government, which unsuccessfully challenged its constitutionality in the courts. Despite some initial opposition by property owners, this amendment found a warm reception on Prince Edward Island. There had always been an underlying consensus that the land should not be alienated from its residents and that tourism should not disturb the primacy of agriculture.

Much the same consensus has sustained Islanders more recently in vigorous battles over inappropriate tourist developments, especially with the proposed wealthy Greenwich summer condominium complex planned for the St. Peters Bay area from the mid-1980s, and the unsightly cottage development project on Cousins Shore in 1990. Each of these development schemes encountered vigorous opposition from an ecological, economic, and aesthetic viewpoint. Indeed, the Cousins Shore controversy genuinely tested public support for maintenance of the Island's rural landscape: a campaign headed up by the late Marc Gallant solicited over $50,000 in public contributions toward the purchase of the land from the developers. Ultimately, the Ghiz government responded to these concerns with an eighteen-month moratorium on cottage development in coastal areas to allow time for a comprehensive study and public input on land development. The Greenwich development was blocked by a decision of the Land Use Commission which designated the area as "protected land" under the *Lands Protection Act*, a ruling subsequently supported by the Supreme Court of Prince Edward Island in October of 1990. Ultimately, and with much fanfare, it was announced that the beautiful coastal real estate near St. Peter's Bay would be integrated into the North Shore national park area.

Despite all of these skirmishes, the Island still looked to tourism as the second most important industry for bringing money to the provincial economy and the most important private-sector source of employment. It is not surprising, then, that government continues to pour millions into promotion and marketing, including new facilities at Brudenell and Mill River in Kings and Prince counties, to attract tourists to the less travelled parts of the province. Planners are also busy seeking ways to extend the tourist season into the shoulder months of June and September. In the 1990s, the development of premiere golf facilities like that at Crowbush in King's county, green tourism development with the "rails to trails" conversion of former railway lines, cultural tourism enhancement, the building of new cruise-ship docking facilities, and the improvement of air access to the Island have all figured in recent tourism policy aimed at enlarging and diversifying the Island's tourism product and clientele. The completion of Confederation Bridge in 1997 has, however, done more than all of these initiatives to increase the number of tourists. Yet the tourism industry, now boasting in excess of 1.5 million arrivals a year, is keenly aware that it operates within a strongly sensitized public framework, complete with strict regulations over appropriate signage and development.[30] And while some farmers continue to complain about the Island's extensive restrictions over market use of their land, in the end, this community defence of the Island way of life has most frequently outweighed the purely market dimensions of an otherwise petit bourgeois society.

It is worth stressing that this conserving arrangement of political forces has provided the basis for very progressive land use and protection policies. Indeed, by most standards, Prince Edward Island provides a strong base for asserting the public interest against the market and for the rational development of land. With a strong legislative framework, and powerful commissions such as the Land Use Commission to preside over conflicts, the Island might easily be called a planner's paradise. However, the relentless and intractable collision between private and public interests over land use and ownership, as the Royal Commission on Land Use itself recognized, is unlikely to disappear, no matter how powerful the public regulatory framework might be. But the political system has another face that, despite its promoters, is not always so enchanting.

THE SPORT OF POLITICS

Even attitudes about politics are caught up in the same communitarian romance.[31] Despite doleful admissions that politics in the garden had traditionally been tarnished by elitism, corruption, and intimidation, Islanders looked back on the feisty election contests "in the good old days" with unblushing admiration. The late Walter Shaw was an excellent spokesman for this sentimentalism. In his book, *Tell Me the Tales,* Shaw upbraids the present generation for its "milk and water" tactics and fondly recalls "the welter and strife of days gone by and the give-and-take of the 'knock 'em down and drag 'em out' elections."[32] While Islanders continue to enjoy their politics more than residents of any other province, Shaw's lament over the passing politics of yesteryear is nonetheless a commonplace theme. Some time ago Frank MacKinnon described the Islander's traditional stake in politics as either graft or entertainment,[33] and it is this loss in the entertainment value of politics with which Shaw's remarks are concerned. Against the spirited debate and rowdy partisanship of the older two-party meeting, today's managed one-party affairs are said to be dull spectacles: no gladiatorial contests these. But from such a sentimentalized view neither the corruption and shallowness of Prince Edward Island's older brand of politics nor the possible strengths of the new are likely to be seriously recognized. Ironically, this is all part of the Islander's attempt not to take his politics seriously.

Traditional Island politics, as depicted so colourfully by Marlene Clark or Wayne MacKinnon, often comes out looking at best like cynical comedy. Writers and readers, sharing the bias of politics as graft or entertainment, treat each other to outlandish tales of patronage and political buffoonery. Patronage in jobs became so serious, MacKinnon reminds us, that Premier Lee himself was charged by the federal minister of labour for this abuse under the *Unemployment Relief Act*.[34] We are told that the parties' bribery in 1966 drew from a bemused public this cynical epigram: "If it moves, pension it; if it doesn't, pave it."[35] For buffoonery we could hardly do better than recall Wayne MacKinnon's light-hearted treatment of Farmer Jones—especially the premier's "gift" to Fred Large who, in defiance of law and logic, held a seat in cabinet and legislature for three years without ever having to trouble himself to run in an election. "The Opposition leader ... didn't come to me with an offer from anyone to resign," clowned Jones. "None of our own members offered to and I didn't ask anyone. The only seat open was Fort Augustus, and we didn't suggest that he run there."[36] Party contests were similarly light-headed affairs, ignoring substance and playing up the virtues of local candidates before almost equal blocs of committed voters.[37] As Marlene Clark faithfully records, individual bribes of money, liquor, shoes, clothing, lawnmowers, and even bathrooms were commonplace, but even grander and more tantalizing bribes were frequent in party campaign promises. This treating game led Jim MacNeil in a post-1966 election issue of *Eastern Graphic* to quip: "The only real difference is that the bigger the bribe, the more easily the people accept it."

Most observers agree that much of this corruption has now abated.[38] However it is far from dead. For example, in March 1985, two PC party workers were fined for vote-buying in a by-election held in Fourth Kings the previous year.[39] Albert MacDonald's extensive 1979 study on this subject records a continuing number of incidents, but suggests that blatant treating "may gradually become a thing of the past ... as the change from a rural to a more urban society takes place."[40] MacDonald argues that the Island is moving very slowly from boss–follower politics (where patronage is dispensed by the boss or broker in return for his followers' or clients' votes), to civic culture politics (where bureaucrats increasingly are expected to take a larger view of the public interest). This complex transition was underway more than a decade ago as perhaps can best be seen in the contradictory practices of the MacLean government. On the one hand it made high moral appeals to the people for wise stewardship and community concern; on the other hand, there was a cynical reversion to boss–follower practices to ensure, as one cabinet minister put it, that after thirteen years of Liberal rule, "his people get their turn."[41]

When Premier Joseph Ghiz returned the Liberals to power in 1986, he promised to clean up patronage in Island politics but, despite his apparent sincerity on this issue, that promise turned out to be one he could not keep. Instead, shortly after assuming office, the government found itself the object of human rights complaints from disgruntled fired employees. The government lost some of these cases while others dragged on with protracted appeals and delays under two Liberal premiers, Ghiz and Catherine Callbeck. It took the arrival of the new Conservative government under Pat Binns in 1996 to see some of the cases of its former partisans settled. There was, however, not the slightest hint that the Binns government intended to forgo the politics of patronage. On the contrary, the Tories have defended the practice. In short, patronage is too deeply embedded in Island political culture to be easily rooted out.

The new *Civil Service Act* in April 1962 made an important contribution to improving standards of morality in Island political culture. By establishing a Civil Service Commission, a salary and classification system, and the rudiments of an administration based on the merit principle, Premier Shaw's government laid one of the chief foundations for an eventual shift away from the worst features of boss–follower politics. Two-thirds of government jobs were moved from direct partisan control and kept outside the spoils system. The new scientific planning style and development ambitions of government at this time forced politicians into recognizing the role of merit in modern government. Outside the planning circles, however, politicians operated within a public system where mores were changing much more slowly, and where loyalty and short-term interests lay with the older practices. It was not a comfortable world for Island politicians.

Bureaucratization undercut older patterns of politics in complex ways, but in no way more dramatically than with the members of the Legislative Assembly. In pre-bureaucratic days the local member dispensed or denied a formidable array of benefits in the district. These decisions were now mainly assumed and administered by the bureaucrats. Although the role of the MLA in securing benefits for constituents is still significant, it has moved considerably away from the days when he or she was a virtual social-welfare czar.[42]

The power of the political executive grew equally so that cabinets after 1960 dominated and directed the policy process. Whereas premiers in the past worked part-time hours while in office and held as many as four portfolios, after Shaw the office of premier demanded full-time attention. The professionalization of political life meant that the demands on cabinet ministers were relentless as well, even if the six- to eight-week legislative sessions seemed picayune by national standards. Some of this growth was a spin-off from federal-provincial relations: demands for conferences and planning in many areas of shared concern put tremendous pressure upon the rather limited administrative resources of the province.[43] The net effect of all this was to enhance even further the executive branch of government, particularly the Premier's Office, and to reduce the legislature increasingly to a rubber-stamp status. Hence, while the old party and legislature forms remained, real power was shifting upward.

Another of Shaw's measures removed the most venal anachronistic feature in Island politics: property encumbrances on voting. This too was a subject of much cynical entertainment on the Island, just the material for more colourful writing on the dubious charms of garden politics. The old electoral system both excluded citizens who did not hold $325 worth of land from running for office, and permitted voting by those who met district property qualifications in as many constituencies as they could make on election day. In principle, this permitted a man and his wife to vote up to 60 times. Moreover, there was no chief electoral officer, nor was an electors' list maintained. In these circumstances the tales of abuse that circulated about and among intimate neighbours in Anne of Green Gables land were many and legendary. Yet it was not until April 1963 that the Island finally rid itself of this relic from the pre-democratic past.

The same traditionalism also held up any meaningful electoral reform on the Island until legal challenges under the *Charter of Rights and Freedoms* (combined with the politics of restraint) forced the Legislature to redraw the Island's electoral map in 1994. Except for the addition of two seats for Queen's county in 1963, for example, the Island's legislature continued to divide the legislative seats equally by county; they also retained dual-member districts even though population densities in districts were low. There were also very large disparities in the size of electoral districts that could not, it turned out, be justified under the *Charter*. In 1994, after losing in the courts, the Callbeck government finally dropped equality of counties as a basis of representation, scrapped the dual-member system, and reduced the legislature from 32 seats to 27. This new map has so far resisted legal challenges, as it keeps disparities among constituencies to within a 25-percent deviation.

Since Islanders clung to a boss-follower system of politics that suited the province's rural and localized character while most other Canadians, at least west of the Maritimes, had rejected it, Islanders' high voting rates, stable patterns of partisanship, and electoral cynicism contrasted sharply with national norms. But as Island society began to change, pressures were brought to bear on boss-follower practices. Electoral reform, the development of bureaucratic power and standards, mass communications, a more educated public, and mobile residential and work patterns began to operate against the older political system. By the 1970s signs of change were appearing. Some constituencies that had virtually been the property of one party began to come unglued: long-time Liberal strongholds in Fourth Prince and Fourth Kings gave way to the Conservatives in 1978 and 1979. Evidence of split party voting began to mount: in First Kings in 1974 and 1979, Fourth and Fifth Kings in 1979, Third Queens in 1966, and in 1978, an all-time high of five split districts occurred. In the cities, the number of uncommitted voters (formerly a "heathen" condition) threatened to loosen the grip of custom. Certainly by the year 2000, Islanders had shown in dramatic fashion how bad electoral politics had really become. In the span of three elections, they had *twice* produced a legislature where government faced a single MLA as their sole opposition: first under the Liberals with Catherine Callbeck in 1993, and then in 2000 when the Tories, led by Pat Binns, swept to power.

During the 1980s the lie was also put to an old theory of Island political dependency: namely, that Islanders always vote provincially in conformity with the party in power federally. Indeed, the force of that unique tradition was analyzed and affirmed in an article by Ian Stewart in 1985, paradoxically at precisely the point when Islanders decisively turned against it.[44] The province rejected the Liberal party in 1982 when Trudeau was still firmly in power, and in 1986 and again in 1989, rejected the Island Tories when that party was ascendant in Ottawa under Brian Mulroney. Indeed, in the federal election of 1988, Islanders refused to elect a single Tory despite the continuing Conservative grip on power. In federal-provincial politics, too, there has also been no evident compliance of Island governments with Ottawa, particularly during the 1980s. Although Premier Ghiz was a prominent supporter of the Meech Lake Accord, he was a vociferous critic of the Conservative program of free trade with the United States. Premier MacLean, for his part, was a prominent member of the Gang of Eight that opposed Trudeau's unilateral patriation of the Constitution. Though all of these developments are now recognized as serious harbingers of change, they have not as yet been sufficiently influential to put a fundamentally new face on other parts of Island politics.

The traditional party system now seems less lively than it once was and presents Islanders by Canadian standards with a constricted range of political options, but there has been no significant departure from it. Although traditional partisanship has not precluded Islanders from surprising other Canadians by electing Canada's first female premier (Catherine Callbeck) or first premier from non-European extraction (Joe Ghiz), the island's size, rural character, patronage system, and habits have virtually shut out other party options. For example, only in the November 1996 provincial election, when NDP leader Herb Dickiesen won his seat in Prince County, did voters ever return a candidate from a party that was neither Liberal nor Conservative, though they reverted to tradition again by throwing out this single NDP representative in the landslide Tory election victory of April 17, 2000. With real ideological and party choices so restricted, citizens with substantial concerns over government policy have tended to create organizations outside the parties to advance their political objectives. This citizen-based movement, which mushroomed into prominence during the 1970s, points more reliably into the future politics of the Island than the apparently stable, monotonous picture suggested by Islanders' electoral behaviour.

While government had always received the views of established religious, agricultural, and business organizations—professional lobbying being an unnecessary oddity here—it had never before the 1970s confronted so many non-partisan, *ad hoc* community groups. The Development Plan first served as a focal point of discontent for citizens alarmed at its effects in agriculture, tourism, fisheries, education, and community development. The Brothers and Sisters of Cornelius Howatt, the Concerned Citizens for Education, the Civil Liberties Association, the National Farmers Union, The Social Action Commission, the volunteer Rural Development Council, the Voluntary Resource Council—the list goes on and on. These and other groups voiced the real political opposition during the 1970s, outmanoeuvring the opposition parties, using the electronic media to make their case to Islanders, and sometimes dealing directly in negotiations with the executive. While right-to-life and environmental groups, among others, have added new issues recently, it is clear that community groups now form a vital part of the structure of Island politics.

Ironically, in a small, highly politicized population so closely divided by party, these non-party groups, often led or supported by people from the university, the churches, and other autonomous public institutions, seem to be the only effective vehicles for developing sustained ideological alternatives to government planners and for actually harnessing public opinion around issues. As long as Island parties continue to hug the political centre, to invoke the same reigning platitudes, and to stress the personality factors of the local candidate or party leader, this extra-party opposition is likely to continue. The increasing breakdown of party allegiances in urban areas also suggests more reliance upon such tactics in the future.

If organized groups have become more and more the truly authentic sources of politics on the Island, it is the media that have made them so. By providing relatively open and effective access to Islanders on public issues, the media have given groups more public power and significance than they could otherwise enjoy. Indeed, so powerful has the fourth estate become that two premiers complained in interviews that the electronic media no longer report but make the news.[45] Initially served by exclusively Island-owned, vociferously partisan newspapers, most residents now read the comparatively neutral and stale prose from Conrad Black's newspapers, the *Guardian* and the *Journal Pioneer*. Passing from the pitfalls of newspapers as virtual party organs, Islanders fell prey to pedestrian papers whose highest vision was low cost and high profit. Thus, they were not compensated for a loss in partisanship and colour with modern advantages of professional scope and analysis. Fortunately, Islanders could also read the more critical *Eastern Graphic* and *Western Graphic*, small weeklies serving each end of the Island.

What constituted a more serious change in the media was the introduction of radio and television and especially of a local CBC. These invaded virtually every Islander's home, exposed Islanders to metropolitan standards, and even brought to local politics an unprecedented immediacy and critical exposure. Probably few developments have so permanently and subtly altered Island politics. By televising debates among the leaders of all parties, the media has brought back some of the virtues of the moribund two-party constituency meeting, even if the controlled format and sterile setting compare poorly with the old. The willingness of CBC television and radio to follow up and comment dispassionately on public issues, even if attacked by professional insiders and critics as unduly tame, superficial, or inconsistent, is nonetheless a revolutionary role for the Island media. Prior to 1960, live local news and public affairs hardly existed at all, unless reading the obituaries counts; now they command more broadcast time and vastly improved technical and research backup. For Island politicians unaccustomed to non-partisan public criticism, the entry of this new electronic instrument into public life has been deeply disturbing, not least because it cannot be controlled and defined within the traditional party system, as could the Island's earlier newspaper system. As for the public, the media slowly moved them further away from a constricted partisan domain of public opinion. In this sense, the new media are contributing significantly to the undermining of boss–follower politics. Regrettably, as rallies and marches are organized in the spring of the new millennium, these electronic media now appear to be under siege, not by local elites, but ironically by a distant CBC headquarters in Toronto with little comprehension of the profound importance of these instruments to the life of the province.

With bureaucratization and the growing professionalization of politics, all of this pointed to a transformed political environment, even if the party system and the concerns with Prince Edward Island as an agricultural garden appeared to suggest stability and continuity with the past. It is understandable that a society undergoing such a swift rate of social, economic, demographic, and technological change would seek to prolong its political forms and its mythical traditions. But the class and occupational revolution of Prince Edward Island over the last few decades cannot fail to make itself soon evident, so that reckoning with the Island's ancestral myths will then become unavoidable.

Statistics forewarn us of the virtual eradication of the small farmer from the P.E.I. landscape. Even though productivity and capital investment have grown steadily, farmers have been forced to desert the land at an average rate of two hundred for every year since World War II. The number of farms and the farm population were almost halved between 1971 and 1986. The attrition rate in farming continues to accelerate. This decline is typical throughout the Maritimes and is generating a new class of what one report calls the "rural dispossessed."[46] Many of these people are now added to unemployment rolls or occupy marginal positions in the new urban economy, often using this outside income to help sustain themselves in tenuous part-time farming.[47] The countryside is meanwhile filling up with rural non-farm residents, corporate farming is dangerously on the increase, and other occupational classes—professional, managerial, service, clerical—dominate the Island census.

This class transformation is already having a quiet but perceptible impact on the numbers of farmers in legislature and cabinet. In House membership, farmers have slipped from a position near or exceeding one-half of total members in the 1920-50 period to comprising, in the 1970s and 1980s, roughly one-quarter of the members. In the cabinet, their strength on average was halved between the 1940 and 1970 administrations. Their places have been taken by representatives from the professional, managerial, and service sectors. Recently, only premiers MacLean and Binns can still claim to carry on the premier-as-farmer ideal, while modern cabinets are drawn predominantly from the professional middle classes.

This change, of course, has not stilled nostalgic rhetoric but quickened it. Some of the most eloquent spokespeople are precisely the new professionals through whom Prince Edward Island's pastoral ideal of a land of independent yeomen is more consciously and conspicuously defined than ever. But even as the mythology of independence is advanced, growing commercial and corporate farming, together with an increased dependency on outside markets, reminds the Islanders of their actual distance from the garden myth.

THE ISLAND: GARDEN OR HINTERLAND?

On the critical side, the myth was least useful when it tended to reinforce Islanders' well-known insularity and to nurse illusions concerning Island autonomy in a romanticized past or future. For neither in its "Golden Age" nor since has the Island actually enjoyed autonomy. Its economic and political relations, either as a colonial appendage of the French or British Empires or as a relatively subordinate partner in Canadian Confederation, have never left it free to chart its own course. Despite the garden image of self-sufficiency, the Island was no island.

On the internal level, Island community has also encouraged a more sentimental view of Island social and political relationships. Neither Island historians nor the public are inclined to take internal class differences as seriously as they might. If the direction of Island development has not on the whole been regarded happily, the responsibility must in part be carried by a local elite rather blamed on outsiders such as absentee landlords or, in the case of the Development plan, the "feds." Not only did these elites approve the modernization program, but they have also been singly responsible for some of the darker moments in Island politics, including the drafting of legislation hostile to human rights.

One of the most notorious examples would be the fiasco over the *Public Gatherings Act* in 1970. Faced with the prospect of an unwanted rock festival, Alex Campbell's government prepared sweeping repressive measures to defend the Island community from an expected deluge of teenagers, raucous music, drugs, and doubtful morals. Hurriedly prepared and rushed through the legislature in an extraordinary twenty-four hours, with the consent of the opposition, this legislation empowered the attorney-general to prohibit in advance any public gathering "which in his opinion may contribute to the disruption of public order." In addition to howls of protest from young people, the legislation ran into serious local and national opposition. Though there was no question of the law's general acceptance by the Island public, the critics succeeded in pressuring the government to back down. The legislation was never proclaimed and was soon after quietly repealed.

The incident was in many respects reminiscent of the 1947 labour dispute. Each pointed to the use of extraordinarily heavy-handed measures to defend the Island from what were regarded as threats to the community. In each case, the principal danger was seen to come from external agents—people "from away." Each incident betrayed a state of siege mentality which directly accounted for the careless drafting of repressive legislation. After each measure was roundly denounced across the country and after the immediate passing of each crisis, second thoughts forced the removal of the offending statutes from the Island's books. For such knee-jerk insularity, the province earned from *Time* the unlovely epithet of "uptight little Island."[48]

Despite the garden imagery, there has been a demographic, class, and occupational revolution on Prince Edward Island over the past few decades. Life in the Island countryside has become transformed so fully that sentimental harking back to the age of the family farm will no longer do. Bureaucratic and executive government—in fact, the spawning of a state industry of full-time political and administrative professionals—has also taken political style and substance well beyond the antics and hoopla of Islanders' older party heritage. The new elite has a much deeper stake in the state's enterprise, and can easily find its interests at odds with primary producers. But for now, the interests of these classes prevail, though the new electoral weight of urban districts in the recast legislature may well undermine that dominance.

There are, of course, many changes afoot that will no doubt test the endurance of older patterns in the future direction of Prince Edward Island. While the Island economy continues to show impressive achievements in agricultural sales to Canada and abroad, in lobster and shellfish landings, including development of a successful aquaculture in mussels, and in some development of manufacturing and service industries,[49] the continuing problems of unemployment and outmigration remain. The development of more food processing on the Island, especially with the 1990 expansion of both McCain Foods and Cavendish Farms, now for the first time provides much more stability to the agricultural industry. In the public sector, there is the same pattern of tradition and change: new reductions in the size of government and of restraint on public-sector salaries, especially under Premier Callbeck in 1993-94, alongside the familiar rhythm of (admittedly declining) government transfers and ongoing federal initiatives ranging from Confederation Bridge to the establishment of the Department of Veterans Affairs in Charlottetown and the GST centre in Summerside.

Of course, there are many other imponderables in Prince Edward Island's future, not least the fate of Canada and of the Atlantic region in this country. There are also the effects of increasing economic integration of the Maritime region, a course that has won widespread bipartisan support. Important, too, is the new fixed crossing from Prince Edward Island to the mainland, carrying many large, unintended consequences. Any of these future changes may turn out to be decisive. But for Islanders, the question will always be the same: how can they accommodate all of this change without undoing their way of life? What could be more perennial?

NOTES

1 This theme appeared as the centrepiece of an earlier version of this article in "Politics in a Beleaguered Garden," in *The Garden Transformed: Prince Edward Island, 1945-1980* (Charlottetown: Ragweed Press, 1982).

2 Note, for example, the often-used designation of Prince Edward Island as a "million-acre farm."

3 Jones, "State of P.E.I. Address," Labour Day, 8 September 1948, as reported in the *Evening Patriot* the same day, and address to the Dominion-Provincial Conference, Ottawa, August 1945, reported in the Charlottetown *Guardian* 18 August 1945.

4 A.H. Clark, *Three Centuries and the Island* (Toronto: University of Toronto Press 1959) 131. See also Marc-Adélard Tremblay and Walter J. Anderson, eds., *Rural Canada in Transition* (Ottawa: Agricultural Economics Research Council of Canada 1968).

5 *Guardian*, 2 September 1943; *Evening Patriot*, 30 September 1949.

6 Wright, quoted in *Patriot*, 31 October 1947 and 20 February 1948; Jones, in *Patriot*, 30 October 1947.

7 All but the legislation banning affiliated unions was enacted prior to the election. The remaining measure was passed in March 1948.

8 The firms were respectively Usen Fisheries Ltd. in Souris, Campbell, and Burns in Central Bedeque, and Kinlock Poultry Farm Inc. of Charlottetown.

9 Although by the time of the Development Plan in 1969 the managerial capacity of the provincial government was still very much in doubt, an important start had been made under Shaw. With new federal funding the numbers of civil servants later jumped dramatically as part of the Development Plan agreement, and staff upgrading was stressed.

10 The Acres Study seemed to be needed, since according to the premier, the earlier studies "tell us things we already know" and are "long on diagnosis and very short on cures for our ills." *Journal Pioneer*, 14 August 1965.

11 Memorandum to Premier Shaw, March 1961.

12 Hartwell Daley, submission to the Special Senate Committee on Land Use, 5 April 1962.

13 See, for example, Philip Mathias, *Forced Growth: Five Studies of Government Involvement in the Development of Canada* (Toronto: James, Lewis and Samuel 1971). It was only a few years before the Georgetown projects turned belly-up with a consequent loss of millions of taxpayers' dollars.

14 Although both the federal and provincial Departments of Agriculture had been offering support and assistance to Island agriculture at least since 1901, the scale of intervention was now considerably stepped up. If the independent yeoman myth was compromised by the pre-1945 support, it was now even more flatly contradicted. Only the marginal subsistence farmer, who received virtually no government aid throughout the period, preserved the myth of independence, if not of prosperity.

15 Campbell, Prince Edward Island Legislative Assembly Debates, 18 March 1970, 249.

16 Speaking on the plan, Campbell realized that he had incorporated some "revolutionary ideas," in Prince Edward Island, Legislative Assembly Debates, 18 March 1969, 75.

17 Canada, Department of Regional Economic Expansion, Development Plan for P.E.I. (1969), 33. No specific target for numbers of fishermen was announced, though numbers were to be reduced; of the 6357 farming units in 1966, only a total of 2500 were regarded as viable for planning purposes. Liberal politicians have always sought to make a fine distinction between scientifically projecting 2500 farming units and advocating 2500 farming units as policy, but the argument is overdrawn, defensive, and artificial. The fact is that having targeted this number, it became the "normal," "scientific," and "inevitable" foundation of Liberal policy on which programs encouraging farmers out of agriculture were based. After all, whether a policy target is actively desired or merely conceded, as "inevitable" does not alter its character as policy.

18 The role of outside "experts" in this shift in values is, of course, important, especially from Premier Shaw onward. But the developing relationship between metropolitan advisers "from away" and a new full-time professional political elite on the Island is not accidental. Changes in the Island's class and occupational composition, as well as in the bureaucracy and in the political executive itself, account in part for this shift in ideas and interests. This argument is developed further in the rest of this paper.

19 Campbell, special radio broadcast, 20 August 1971, printed in the *Guardian* the next day.

20 Harry Bruce, "The Gardener of the Gulf," *Canadian Magazine*, 3 April 1976.

21 The Institute of Man and Resources was announced in January 1975 and the New Alchemy Institute's eco-house, dubbed the "Ark," was announced in March 1975. Despite national boosterism for the project, in July 1981 the government announced that the Ark was up for sale.

22 The election took place on 24 April 1978 and former Premier Campbell assumed his position on the bench on 1 December 1978. The election results gave the Conservatives 21 seats and the Liberals only 11.

23 *Canadian Annual Review 1983*, 288.

24 See details in David Milne and Ivan MacArthur, "Prince Edward Island," *Canadian Annual Review 1985*, 356.

25 *Financial Post*, 9 June 1984.

26 Suspicion over corporate holdings of land continued to spill over into the hearings of the Royal Commission on Land Use during these years, leading ultimately to the Commission recommendation in 1991 that the government investigate any person or corporation holding more than 750 acres of land.

27 See *Canadian Annual Review 1988* and subsequent reports for more information on this element of farmer power over the potato market.

28 Tracking of this reference is continuing.

29 As indicated earlier, the limit dropped to five acres in the amendments of 1988. It is also worth underlining that non-residents also found their interests curtailed when the Ghiz government imposed "double taxation" upon them in 1987.

30 For a careful treatment of this theme see Judith Adler, "Tourism and Pastoral," *The Garden*, 131-54. There have been occasional protests over government regulations on signs, however, most amusingly at Brackley in 1988 when a flashing sign reading "we'll go to any height to prove discrimination" was lifted 13 metres above the Millstream Dairy Bar.

31 For a treatment of several communitarian themes in social politics on the Island, including prohibition and school consolidation, see my earlier essay, "Politics in a Beleaguered Garden," *The Garden Transformed*, 52-57.

32 Shaw, *Tell Me the Tales* (Charlottetown: Square Deal Publications 1975) 115.

33 Frank MacKinnon, "Big Engine, Little Body: Prince Edward Island," *Canadian Provincial Politics: The party systems of the ten provinces*, ed. Martin Robin (Scarborough: Prentice Hall, 1978) 222-47.

34 Wayne MacKinnon, *Life of the Party* (Charlottetown: Liberal Party of Prince Edward Island, 1973) 80; Marlene Russell Clark, "Island Politics," *Canada's Smallest Province*, ed. Francis W.P. Bolger (Charlottetown: P.E.I. Centennial Commission 1973), 289-327.

35 Albert Francis MacDonald, "The Politics of Acquisition: A Study of Corruption in Prince Edward Island" (unpublished M.A. thesis, Queen's University, April 1979) 26.

36 MacKinnon, *Life of the Party*, 114-15.

37 "Between 1893 and 1963 over 37% of the 570 elected candidates received majorities of less than one hundred votes! Only three of the candidates received majorities of more than a thousand votes during this time. Also, the popular vote average over this period was 51.4% for the Liberals and 47.8% for the Conservatives. In the 1943 election, the Liberals won 20 of the 30 seats, yet given 100 votes to sprinkle about the same majority could have been produced for the Conservatives. The situation has not changed. In 1978 32 candidates had majorities of less than 50 votes while 13 candidates had majorities of less than 200 votes," MacDonald, "Politics of Acquisition," 23-24.

38 For a recent analysis of the possible decline of petty corruption on Prince Edward Island, see Ian Stewart, "On Faith Alone: Petty Electoral Corruption on Prince Edward Island," paper presented at the Atlantic Provinces Political Studies Association, Memorial University, St. John's, Newfoundland (October 1990).

39 The Island's electoral map is the most malapportioned in Canada and King's county, as the least populated—most overrepresented and economically backward—seems an obvious treating zone. See Stewart, "On Faith Alone," 12-13.

40 MacDonald, "Politics of Acquisition," 72. MacDonald's judgement here overlooks the plain connection between this kind of politics and urban life. Ward politics used to fit this model of treating just as much as rural politics did. However, his general argument that the practice is in decline is well taken.

41 Remarks in conversation with author. Similar views repeated by the minister in an interview with author's research assistant.

42 See J.E. Green, Brief to the Commission of Enquiry into Welfare Assistance, 1980.

43 In 1951 there were 351 provincial government employees on the Island, while in 1978 there were 3508—a growth of approximately 1000 per cent. MacDonald, "Politics of Acquisition," 62-63.

44 See Ian Stewart, "Friends at Court: Federalism and Provincial Elections on Prince Edward Island," *Canadian Journal of Political Science* (1986): 127-50.

45 The Hon. David MacDonald, former secretary of state, also regarded the CBC in 1978 and 1979 elections on the Island as virtually "a participant in the election process." Interview with author's assistant.

46 See *Rural Canada in Transition* 12.

47 A 1981 report was prepared on this sector of island agriculture for the MacLean government.

48 *Time* 97 (19 April 1971).

49 An interesting example here is the development of aerospace service industries in Slemon Park, the site of the former Summerside military base closed in 1992. Here, there has been considerable success over the past half dozen years in attracting companies doing service work on engines and interiors of small-scale commercial aircraft.

6 QUÉBEC

The Beleaguered State: Québec at the End of the 1990s

LUC BERNIER

Whether one prefers to call it "unique" or "distinct", the possibility that "country" could replace "province" or "society" after the adjective, makes Québec politics the most sensitive issue in Canadian political life. Although this issue cannot be neglected by the governments of the other provinces, following two to three decades of debate, an understandable fatigue currently overwhelms most specialists on the subject. Nevertheless, during the summer of 1997, attention was once again focused on Québec and the Constitution when the other nine provincial premiers decided to meet in Calgary to debate the state of the Canadian confederation in the wake of Québec's last referendum results. The premiers would have liked to avoid the entire constitutional issue on which, as recent history has shown, they can only lose votes.[1] However, the close nature of the October 30, 1995 referendum results meant they could not ignore it.

And, as long as there is no "satisficing"[2] solution to the Québec question—that is, no solution upon which Québécois can agree—the issue will continue to haunt Canadian politics. As I will show in this chapter, solutions to this problem are available, but the evolution of Canadian political life has made it difficult to reach an agreement. The political modernization of Québec over the last 40 years, as Guindon[3] has suggested, challenges the legitimacy of the Canadian federal system of government. Faced with the need to modernize Québec society, the provincial state has expanded into ever more areas of social life. In so doing it has continually come into conflict with the federal government and, as a result, the constitutional issue has continued to influence all the other issues with which the provincial state has grappled over recent decades.

To understand what has happened in Québec in recent years, and what could happen in the near future, requires a look at the eclectic forces involved in provincial political development since the early 1960s. It is difficult to single out one key factor from the many variables that continue to interact and shape provincial politics, such as urbanization, secularization, statism, the spread of mass education, the growth of mass communication networks, industrialization, changes in the social structure, and greater political participation.[4] And indeed, all these different elements have helped to reshape Québec society.

Nevertheless, Kenneth McRoberts[5] has suggested that we can limit our analysis by looking only at modernization, economic dependency, the cultural division of labour, the nature of class relations, the development of national consciousness, and the role played by Canadian federalism. Even the enumeration of these variables, however, is beyond the scope of this chapter. The purpose of this chapter is more modest: I focus on the role of the Québec state in relation to the evolution of Québec's society. The single most important social transformation in Québec over the last forty years has been the modernization of the state, and I analyze the impact the development of the state has had on Québec society and vice-versa. The reforms made after 1960—the "Quiet Revolution"—in the attempt to catch up with a changing social reality are discussed in the first section below. The political consequences of these reforms—notably the establishment, growth, and success of the Parti québécois—are set out in section two. As the final section suggests, the rhythm of change between state and society remains today, although the direction is much less clear than in earlier eras.

THE COMPONENTS OF THE QUIET REVOLUTION

In Québec, there is "before and after" 1960, just as there is "before and after" the British Conquest of 1760. There have been more changes in Québec in the decades since 1960 than at any previous time in Québec history post-1760. This period of accelerated political modernization was centred around the transformation of the provincial state. The resulting Quiet Revolution and rise of the Parti québécois have been the dominant political events of last 40 years.

A *state* can be defined as a collection on institutions, rules of behaviour, norms, roles, buildings, and archives with its own organizational culture and its own operating procedures. A state can be relatively autonomous in society, formulating policies not supported by particular interest groups, institutions, or social forces. It can sometimes lead the development of society, while at other times it can lag behind. In the 1950s, although Québec's society was evolving in a fashion similar to that of other parts of Canada and North America,[6] the development of its political structures was lagging behind. This led, eventually, to a period of tremendous change in which political practices and institutions caught up to, and surpassed, social developments.

At the time of the death of long-time Union nationale premier Maurice Duplessis in September 1959, Québec's political institutions in general, and state structures in particular, were out of step with social reality. While Québec had developed into an urban and industrial society, its political institutions were very similar to those of the previous century. Political development lagged far behind socioeconomic transformations. As Pierre Elliott Trudeau[7] argued in a long essay on the situation in the province in 1949, the dominant ideology lagged far behind social reality. Provincial leaders still promoted agricultural development, hostility toward capitalism and the retrenchment of Catholic social organizations, although the society was already highly urbanized and completely integrated in what is now known as the "global economy."

The changes in government and society associated with the Quiet Revolution were triggered by Duplessis's Union nationale successor as premier, Paul Sauvé, who implemented the first reforms before dying suddenly after only 100 days in power. In the subsequent election of 1960, the Liberals, under the leadership of Jean Lesage, accelerated the pace of transformation. Looking at the gap between the needs of modern Québec society and the limited capabilities of the antiquated provincial state, the Liberals increased their reformist efforts and ushered in the Quiet Revolution. Until the 1980s, successive Liberal, Union nationale, and Parti québécois governments continued to make incremental reforms along the same trajectory set out by Lesage. At that point, the 1980 referendum results, the 1982 recession, and a dominant ideological movement toward anti-statist neo-liberalism put an end to the Quiet Revolution.

Nationalism

The idiom "Quiet Revolution" encompasses three notions: the transformation of Québec nationalism, the transfer of powers from civil society to the state and the confrontation between the State and the traditional elites who dominated Québec.

The Quiet Revolution was first an ideological revolution. Nationalism, which until then had sought the preservation of an idyllic past—the contemplation of a rural life, a Catholic providential mission in North America—became less conservative.[8] Paul Sauvé summed up the new spirit in one word, *désormais*, which means "from now on." During the 1960 election, in Jean Lesage's words, the mood was, *"C'est le temps que ça change"* ("It is time for change"); during the 1962 election, it was *"L'ère du colonialisme économique est finie dans le Québec. Maintenant ou jamais, maîtres chez nous"*

("Economic colonialism is over in Québec. It's now or never—masters in our own house"). The buzzword was *rattrapage,* "catching up," with development elsewhere in Europe and North America.

State-Building

But how was *rattrapage* to be achieved? The second part of the transformations associated with the Quiet Revolution involved overhauling and reforming the fundamental institutional structure of the Québec state. In 1960, the state was seen by many people as the solution to the problem of continuing the modernization of Québec society and catching up with the rest of the western world. It was preferred by many because of how it fit with the new nationalism: of all social institutions which might bring about change, only the state could be entirely controlled by Québécois.

However, the necessity of transforming the Québec State in order to further social development was not obvious to everyone in Québec society. In fact, many groups in the population were suspicious of a political system they did not see as their own but rather as one imposed by British rulers over the previous two centuries.[9] The transformation of Québec nationalism proved very useful in giving legitimacy to the new, reformist, state. The transformation of the institutions of government could be sold as pragmatic to a leery population. The neglected provincial state could, it was argued, become the instrument of "liberation" for the French Canadian nation. Over the next two decades, the Québec government emerged as a mature and complex institution capable of governing in favour of provincial interests. From 1961 to the early 1980s, the administrative machinery developed rapidly, creating new government departments and over 100 agencies of all kinds. The number of employees in the public and parapublic sectors[10] increased rapidly until the early 1980s, subsequently grew at the same rate of growth as the general population in the late 1980s and early 1990s, and has gradually declined over the past few years.

One of the key reforms undertaken during the Quiet Revolution involved the sweeping review of the supervision and management of the growing number of public service employees through the implementation of merit-based hiring and career progression schemes. The *Civil Service Act*, assented to in August 1965, provided a framework for the work of public servants. The Act made provision for union recognition, collective bargaining, the granting to public servants of the right to strike, and guaranteed job security. The new regime marked the beginning of the development of the Québec system of public administration, an evolution which has since generated numerous, often acrimonious conflicts and, more recently, heated public debate on issues such as job security and downsizing.[11]

A contradiction of the Quiet Revolution was that it sprang into being under Jean Lesage. Lesage was anything but a reformist, but he did have the political wisdom to accept the reforms put forward by his high-profile ministers, including René Lévesque, Paul Gérin-Lajoie, Ernest Lapalme, and Eric Kierans. For six years, Lesage presided over transformations he could never have dreamed of the night he won the election in 1960. Under his Premiership, the Québec State became active in the economic sector with the nationalization of hydroelectric corporations and the creation of Hydro-Québec, now one of Canada's largest public enterprises. The *Caisse de dépôt et placement du Québec* (Québec Deposit and Investment Fund) was another important state-owned corporation, created in 1965 to administer government pension and insurance funds.

The legislation creating the Caisse was enacted as a result of the discussions surrounding the creation of the Canada Pension Plan in 1963-64. In the debates at the Legislative Assembly (now the National Assembly), Lesage predicted that the Caisse would become the most important and powerful economic instrument ever to exist in Québec, carefully managing pension money and stimulating Québec's economic development. The Caisse eventually emerged as the owner and manager of Canada's single largest stock portfolio. It now owns stock in most major Canadian companies and has a significant international portfolio. Although it has also raised concerns about the power of public-sector technocrats vis-à-vis those in the private sector,[12] because it redefined the nature of ownership in the economy, the Caisse de dépôt might eventually prove to have more impact than the much better known Hydro-Québec.

Confrontation with Traditional Elites

The third element of the Quiet Revolution was the battle the reformist state had with the dominant elites and the prevailing social institutions of the period: the Catholic Church over health and education matters, the English bourgeoisie based in Montreal and Toronto over the control of the economy, and the federal government over political affairs. In each of these domains, the provincial state brought about the major reforms: changes in education, the rise of a network of public enterprises already sketched, and the still-unfinished quest for more constitutional autonomy.

Usually, in the Western world, the status quo is defended by conservative institutions that are losing status, power, and privileges to different groups and organizations within the society. It is, then, the state that defends these interests. In Québec the reverse happened: modernization spurred the state to challenge conservative institutions. A significant qualitative change occurred in the wake of the Quiet Revolution: there was more direct intervention by the government in all sectors of society. Social regulation, which until then had been local, became the concern of the provincial government throughout the entire territory of the province. The government gradually supplanted civilian and religious institutions in order to offer health, social and education services.[13]

In education, there was a major redistribution of responsibilities after 1964, with the core of the system, the Department of Education, attempting to maintain a monopoly over the other parts of the system. The results have been impressive. In 1960, of 100 children who entered first grade, 70 went on to high school, 16 attended college, and 7 went as far as university. By 1983, of these 100, almost 100 entered high school, 52 went on to junior college (CEGEP), and 35 attended university. A similar expansion occurred in health and social services. The *Ministère de la Santé et des Services sociaux* (Ministry of Health and Social Services), now an enormous bureaucracy, was set up in 1970 to replace the Church and religious communities in this area. In previous years the Québec state had played only an indirect role in providing such services.

ASSESSING THE QUIET REVOLUTION

In summary, at the time of Maurice Duplessis's death in 1959, the extent of the government of Québec's intervention in the economy was negligible from both a quantitative and a qualitative standpoint. Provincial public servants were few in number, poorly trained, and badly paid. Hydro-Québec was a small company distributing electricity only in the Montréal area, Radio-Québec was nothing more than a legal fiction dating from 1944, and the Régie des alcools owed more to the Lacordaire leagues than to any conscious planning of government operations. Today, government corporations operate in the fields of energy, finance, industry, television, mining, transportation and forestry. They make up the most extensive network of government-owned corporations in the provinces.

In the 1960s government enterprises were regarded as the essential means of catching up with developments in the rest of the western world. The relative autonomy of the Québec government ensured that at least a portion of the province's economic growth would be directed by enterprises whose decision-making centres were not located in Toronto or New York, but in Québec. Public institutions are now well established for social and education services. But state-building in Québec has been shaped by a haphazard vision, has been influenced by the death of three premiers in office, the disproportionate power of a small group of influential civil servants, and by the necessity of successive governments to react to initiatives made by the federal government.[14] Reforms were implemented with their own logic, and had to be corrected frequently in order to compensate for their anarchical beginnings. Indeed, Québec government corporations have often served as the instruments of policies that were not yet devised.[15]

What exactly happened during the 1960s has been scrutinized from every possible angle. One persistent view posits that the Quiet Revolution did not in fact change Québec politics to any great extent. Daniel Latouche, for example, has argued that the sorts of changes which occurred during the 1960s were not much more extensive than those of the 1940s.[16] He has also noted that budgetary priorities set during the 1950s remained the same during the 1960s. For Latouche, the real shift in budgetary priorities occurred between 1945 and 1950, when expenditures on natural resources were de-emphasized in favour of increases in the fields of health and education. He argues that while there was a marked increase in the overall level of expenditures during the Lesage years, the distribution of these expenditures over various categories was not significantly different from that of previous years. McRoberts suggests, meanwhile, that the Quiet Revolution was not an instance of quantitative change but a qualitative one, the essence being transfer of power to the state.[17]

Simard, on the other hand, maintains that to understand what actually happened we have to look at the number of agencies created and who they were confronting.[18] He lists numerous organizations that were transformed or created: 23 departments, 55 consultative bodies, 9 administrative tribunals, 63 economic management institutions, the junior colleges (CEGEPS), the state university network, the social services institutions, and the state-owned enterprises. Given this large number of initiatives and their development in significant areas of social and economic life, Simard argues that state-building in the province was indeed very extensive and innovative. Young, Faucher, and Blais have summarized what happened in Québec as:

> 1. The attitude of the province toward the central government ... changed: Québec came to resist federal incursions more staunchly and increased demands pertaining to its own self-interest.
> 2. The province greatly increased its financial and human resources, both absolutely and relative to the central government.
> 3. The scope of provincial public policy widened enormously, and state intervention, especially in the economic realm, became deep and pervasive.
> 4. Provincial policy-making changed profoundly, becoming centralized, planned, and coherent.
> 5. The province became more strongly linked with the resource sectors.

6. Provincial state-building came into direct conflict with Canadian nation-building.[19]

As Young, *et al.*, point out, some, but not all, of this development occurred in other provinces, and the word "province-building" has been used to characterize the general expansion of all provincial states during this period.[20] Nevertheless, this process was best epitomized in Québec and underlines the special dynamics of the Québec situation. Since 1960, the Québec government has been more vocal than the other provincial governments in its desire to control its own destiny and has rapidly increased its capacity to govern in the interests of the provincial political economy.

THE RISE OF THE PARTI QUÉBÉCOIS: THE FIRST AND SECOND REFERENDUMS AND THEIR AFTERMATHS

One important question surrounding the reforms of the Quiet Revolution was whether they came too fast or too slow. Some observers have argued that Lesage's defeat in 1966 occurred because a significant segment of the population thought that the reforms were coming too quickly. On the other hand, the results of the election indicate that only a small fraction of the population actually switched parties. Did the reforms came too slowly? Some political violence did occur in Québec. But this violence was limited considering the amount and the speed of change compared to other countries.[21] And this violence disappeared when the Parti québécois became a legitimate political option in the early 1970s. The Union nationale government continued the reforms initiated during the first half of the 1960s after the 1966 election. And under the two short mandates of the Bourassa government from 1970 to 1976, the development of the Québec state was continually pursued.

One important consequence of the continued process of reform and the continual expansion of the capacity of the provincial state was the idea that more, and better, changes could be made if Québec was no longer a Canadian province but rather an independent country. For some, the capacity of Québec to continue its evolution and modernization was limited by its participation in the Canadian federation. For others, however, the predominant view was that Québec would continue to prosper only if it enjoyed the security afforded by staying within the Canadian union.

For many residents of the province, the modernizations of the last forty years have called into question the legitimacy of the Canadian state. The debate has been opened since the early days of the Quiet Revolution. The implications of virtually all of the different possible solutions have been studied at length by federal and provincial royal commissions, parliamentary inquiries, party task forces and others. What has been lacking is the window of opportunity required to link one solution to popular perceptions of the political problem which must be resolved.[22]

There were two new departures in Québec politics over the course of the 1960s. The first, concerning the re-organization and re-structuring of the state, has already been discussed. The second, a consequence of the first, was the creation of the Parti québécois (PQ). Until the PQ was formed, both major existing parties, the Liberals and the Union nationale, had nationalist wings. With the creation of the Parti québécois, the nationalist divide would be out in public between parties[23] rather than less visible within them. This would also mean that, if elected, one party could now decide to declare independence.

The Parti québécois has been a rather unique political party. At one point, it had between two and three hundred thousand members, making it both a political party and a potent social movement. It has always had a very large political program, a manifesto explaining a long list of policy positions. It remains a very difficult party to manage because of the militancy of many of its members. Party members do not hesitate to criticize the party president, even when he is premier of the province, if it is felt that the government is not complying strictly enough with the party program.

The Parti Québécois in Power

On November 15, 1976, René Lévesque and the PQ won the Québec election. Never before had so much emotion—hope on one side, fear on the other—been invested in a newly elected provincial government. Many were counting on a second Quiet Revolution, a second leap forward. In its first mandate the PQ completed reforms started in the 1960s in areas such as agricultural zoning, automobile insurance, and electoral and party financing reform.[24] The most important and controversial reform was the completion in 1977 of legislation concerning the language of work in Québec. Bill 101 was passed as a follow-up to Bill 22 of 1974. Basically, these laws stipulated that the language of work in Québec must be French, and required children of immigrants to attend French-language rather than English-language schools. Since then, amendments have limited some parts of the law.

Aside from the language bill, however, there were few other major changes after 1976. The Lévesque government had its hands full contending with a depressed economy, and because the PQ was already so securely in office with widespread popular support, the issue of Québec independence became less pressing.[25] It was partly due to the feeling that gains could be made within the federal framework that the PQ lost the constitutional referendum in 1980 by a 60-40 margin. Despite the referendum, or perhaps because of the lesson learned from it, the party enjoyed a decisive victory in the 1981 election. But that was the PQ's last great success of the period.

After the First Referendum

Sabatier has written that it takes between ten and twenty years to properly evaluate the implementation of any policy.[26] This is also true for the evaluation of institution-building. Many of the state agencies created in the 1960s took several years to achieve their full potential; others fell victim to the cutbacks of the 1980s before they had a chance to fulfil their mission. Before 1960, while the Québec state was still very small, Duplessis had a tight grip on every aspect of government operations. But today's premier, whose state is far more powerful and able to intervene in more sectors and activities than Duplessis could have imagined, has less control. This is because the more the responsibilities of a government increase, the more difficult it is to coordinate and control its various activities. Even during the Quiet Revolution, some problems were evident. But once started, the reforms proved impossible to stop. New programs were added endlessly to the previous ones, causing costs to spiral out of control. Moreover, because of federal-provincial competition, programs were frequently expanded.[27]

The expansion phase of the Québec public administration ended in the early 1980s. The 1981-82 recession marked a turning point in that it became apparent that the growth in the economy and in the population that had sustained the cost of programs could no longer be taken for granted. The crisis in public finances that followed was exacerbated by a handful of interrelated factors, such as globalization, a change in the ideology of governments, the alienation of the public with respect to governments and technological change.[28] Mention should also be made of an aging, increasingly educated population, and the proliferation of special-interest groups. Together, these factors changed the demand for the provision of government services. Major changes in the public administration resulted from the need to surmount the financial crisis and the problems facing the government. Initially, the solutions were strictly budgetary, although concerns about the quality and efficiency of services gradually came to the fore.

In 1985, the new Liberal government set up three committees to review the administrative machinery developed over the preceding 25 years. One committee, chaired by Paul Gobeil, submitted a report that noted the extensive sedimentation of programs and the advisability of abolishing a number of autonomous agencies, merging others or turning them over to the private sector. Another committee, chaired by MNA Reed Scowen, called for the streamlining of the regulations controlling the activities of society at a time when its expansion seemed impossible to curtail. A third committee, chaired by government minister Pierre Fortier, proposed the privatization of certain public enterprises according to certain "pragmatic" criteria.

While the Gobeil report did not initially result in significant changes in the Québec public administration, it was the first broad attempt to re-examine its scope and continues to serve as a key reference. It also offered the new Liberal government an opportunity to regain symbolical leadership over the administration after nine years in opposition. The deregulation proposed by the Scowen committee, in keeping with what was happening elsewhere in North America, has yet to produce the anticipated results. It is noteworthy, however, that former Bloc Québécois and now Parti québécois leader Lucien Bouchard deemed it necessary to announce the establishment of a "Secrétariat à la déréglementation" in the ministère du Conseil exécutif at a Summit Conference on the Economy and Employment in the fall of 1996, thus reiterating the positions expressed by his predecessors. Whether the Parti québécois or the Liberals are in power, similar problems and constraints force them to choose similar policy paths.

The Second Referendum[29]

The question of the extent of the legal powers Québec inherited at Confederation in 1867 has proven to be an endless source of debate. In general, the Canadian federal government was given the most significant powers, while provincial governments were given control over local affairs and the Imperial government in London retained control over international matters. The real benefit of Confederation for French Canada was the provision of a range of powers, limited but guaranteed, over its own affairs.[30] But until the 1960s, whether due to the presence of a too-conservative ideology or an absence of imaginative leaders, the Québec state remained backward, its powers never really exploited.

By the 1990s, however, Québec was at a crossroads. A more interventionist government could rejuvenate the large state apparatus, which has all the necessary expertise and skills to formulate and implement "national" policy. On the other hand, the state apparatus could be reduced to fulfil the more modest functions of another provincial state, for at this point, the monitoring, implementation, and modification of policies that had been started during the Quiet Revolution no longer require the current number of civil servants. The ambiguity of the current constitutional situation, however, makes it difficult for existing state institutions to function smoothly.

In 1995 a new Parti québécois government under Jacques Parizeau endorsed the national option and called a second provincial referendum, proposing negotiations with the rest of Canada on the terms of "sovereignty-association," or a new political arrangement for the northern half of the continent of North America. As the results of the 1995 referendum indicated, however, there was nothing close to a consensus among Québécois on this subject. The closeness of the referendum results—in which the "no" side won by a mere 50,000 votes in a 50.5 to 49.50-per-cent outcome—did not come merely from the popularity of leaders like Lucien Bouchard who supported the "yes" side. Rather, it was the result of a number of Québécois who wanted an important constitutional transformation than was the case in 1980. Asked if they preferred whatever they would get out of a "yes" vote or the status quo, there were many more people tempted by the adventure of a "yes" outcome in 1995 than there were in 1980. For anyone who believes that Canada should remain united, this should be worrying. The Parti québécois might win the next referendum simply because people want change—any change—rather than the endless debates over the merits of various alternatives that have been put forward over the last three decades.

A Léger and Léger poll published at the end of June 1997 indicates that what Québec wants is a new partnership with Canada. Also according to this poll, 40 per cent of the people in Québec who voted for the Conservatives in the last federal election are sovereigntists.[31] These numbers illustrate that if a third referendum were to be held in Québec at the present time, there is still only a narrow margin between a "yes" and a "no" victory. Everything depends on the "soft" nationalists who swing their vote from one side to the other depending upon the exact details of the proposal submitted to the public for consideration. There are important groups of voters in Québec who are strongly federalist or sovereigntist. Whatever the question asked, they are not likely to change their minds. In between are the "soft nationalists" who will make the difference if ever there is a third referendum. They could be tempted to vote to stay in Canada if someone gives them a good reason to do so since, for many, Québec can be a "distinct society" either within or outside Canada. A rephrased Meech Lake Accord, an offer a little more attractive than Charlottetown, something that is a little less than the Allaire report but still involves a lot of decentralization (as asked elsewhere in Canada) would appeal to these pivotal voters.

A new constitutional package—not radically different than the various packages discussed over the last decades—would do it. All of the different solutions available to solve the constitutional problem have been discussed at length in the province since the early 1960s. Independence options like "associated states" or "sovereignty" (with or without association) have all been examined, as have various permutations on renewed federalism such as those put forward by the provincial Liberal Party's Allaire report of 1991 or the failed Meech Lake and Charlottetown Accords. Various royal commissions, from the Laurendeau-Dunton inquiry into bilingualism and biculturalism in the 1960s, have dealt with these scenarios. What is lacking is not additional knowledge about what could be done but rather consensus within the province about which solution should be chosen.

THE 1998 ELECTION IN QUÉBEC: POPULATION 1, POLITICIANS 0

The November 30, 1998 Québec election was supposed to be the most interesting in some time. It was also seen as a critical election for the constitutional future of Canada. Less popular leaders had been replaced by two charismatic individuals at the head of the two major parties. Jean Charest had revived the hopes of the Liberals, and Lucien Bouchard of the PQ had been waiting for almost a year to call the election. Mario Dumont of the Action démocratique du Québec (ADQ) was hoping to elect a few members of his party to join him in opposition. The night the election was called the Liberals were a few percentage points ahead in the polls, but they needed a wider margin to win a majority of seats. On the opposite side, the PQ appeared in serious trouble in several ridings around Montreal where ministers would have to work hard to avoid defeat. ADQ support also seemed to be fading. The fact that the election was too close to call made it difficult for all three parties to attract new "star" candidates. One month later, none of the three leaders emerged from the contest with a decisive victory. While the Liberals won a plurality of the votes with 43.69 per cent, compared to the PQ's 42.7 per cent and the ADQ's 11.78, the Parti québécois would remain in power. On election night, Lucien Bouchard was obviously disappointed but had a majority government, having won 75 of the 125 seats in the National Assembly. A week before, the Parti québécois had dreamed of a landslide that had not materialized. Their percentage of the vote was less than the Liberals and exactly what the polls had indicated at the beginning of the campaign. Also disappointed, Mario Dumont remained the lone member of his party in the National Assembly even though he was the acknowledged winner of the mid-campaign leaders' debate. After a difficult campaign, Jean Charest had been able to rally Liberal support during the final week, and, in one of his first post-election announcements, he made it clear that he would be around for the next four years as opposition leader.

The results illustrate the aggregate wisdom of Québec voters. Most of all the election was an interesting lesson in democracy. Looking at the faces of the three leaders on election night, it was possible to believe that all of them had lost. And indeed, despite their charisma, new programs and new issues, the results were roughly the same as they had been in 1994 with Jacques Parizeau and Daniel Johnson Jr. This was not what either the Parti québécois or the Liberals had had in mind when they chose new leaders. The question remains: who won?

If aggregate results ever represented the wishes of the voters, this election is a textbook example. The Parti québécois was viewed as a skilled governing party. The party had the experience and could be trusted to protect Québec interests. At the same time their poor showing postponed another referendum despite a commitment to proceed with a vote when "winning conditions" prevailed. Simply put, the PQ was re-elected to govern, but not to hold a third referendum. As well, with Bouchard elected in his own right as premier, with 75 out of 125 seats, he was now in control of his party. Dumont and his Action Démocratique survived and gained some legitimacy, making gains at the expense of the two older parties. But the ADQ has a lot of work to do to become a serious alternative. For its part, the federal Liberal government managed to rid itself of Jean Charest who was far more of a threat to them in Ottawa than in Québec City. If he has the capacity to learn, Charest has four years to prepare to be premier and replace what will then be an aged Parti québécois. The two term limit that the Québécois have given their governments since 1960 should play in his favour.

The 1998 election was an interesting campaign to watch. Mario Dumont survived, able to navigate over the wave of discontent in the province. Lucien Bouchard proved a very astute politician coopting most of his main opponent's electoral platform. While the Parti québécois ran a very effective campaign, Jean Charest had a difficult time mixing his conservatism and liberalism together into a well-oiled electoral machine. The results also indicate that voters did not believe that Jean Charest was ready to be premier of Québec. It was not that his message failed to get through, but rather that he had almost nothing of substance to offer. His knowledge of his own party platform was poor and, although he managed to use the health-care issue to his advantage, he overplayed the constitutional question. Charest was the leader addressing the Constitution even when polls indicated that voters did not want to hear about it.

Winning a Québec election is no difficult task for a Liberal leader who understands the game and is cynical enough to play it. The English-speaking community and most of the ethnic groups concentrated in Montreal vote almost unanimously for the Liberals, since the Parti québécois leaders have never been able to win their trust. Except for temporary fringe parties such as the Equality Party, the Liberals can rely on almost forty safe seats. They have to convince the so-called "soft nationalists" who constitute most of the swing votes in Québec that on linguistic rights or economic development that they would not destroy what has been achieved since the early 1960s. As Robert Bourassa did through the 1980s, Liberal leaders have to be both federalists and nationalists. Doing so, they keep their votes in

Montreal but also make gains elsewhere in Québec where the French-speaking majority is more difficult to convince. Jean Charest now has time to learn this game.

SCENARIOS FOR THE NEAR FUTURE

The Constitution

Since the referendum, the constitutional issue has not evolved well. The idea of partition—which the experience of partitioned countries such as Ireland, Cyprus, Korea, and Viet Nam has illustrated is more a mirage than a practical possibility—has poisoned the debate in Québec. It could be argued that although secession is not yet prohibited by Canadian law (pending the outcome of a Supreme Court case now underway), an independent Québec could decide that it would not allow partition of some areas. This, of course, leaves the very real possibility of very real political violence. The idea has gained momentum since a federal minister from Québec, Stéphane Dion, decided to discuss the issue openly. This contrasts sharply with the conciliatory approach taken by the federal government during the Mulroney era.

It has yet to be proven that the current federal strategy will fare better than the previous one. The "hands-off" Chrétien government approach during the 1995 referendum was a disaster for the federalist side. One can well understand why the premiers of the remaining provinces do not want to leave the issue to the same "experts" in Ottawa who obviously have missed some important elements of Québec's evolution in recent years. Discontentment with the Chrétien government is also very apparent in Québec. It is difficult to analyze otherwise, given the fact that Québec returned 44 Bloc Québécois members to Parliament in the 1997 election. Other than being dissatisfied with the Chrétien government, the reasons to vote for the Bloc were scarce. After a lacklustre campaign, under a weak leader, and without an electoral platform, that the Bloc was able to keep so many seats should be the lesson to remember rather than emphasizing the ten seats that were lost. Still, it is likely that the Bloc will eventually disappear. In the meantime, however, the current Liberal majority of five seats could be very fragile and lead to an early, realigning election. In short, many possibilities are still open before a promised third Québec referendum is held.[32]

The Economy

Other issues also promise to affect the tenor and content of Québec politics in the near future. In the economic sector a significant fact is that, roughly, more than 80 per cent of Québec's exports now go to the United States. In this regard, the close international relations that Québec has developed with the French-speaking world are of limited economic interest.[33] Both the Premier of Québec and the Prime Minister have led groups of businessmen to Asia in an attempt to diversify economic relations and diminish the dependency of the economy on the American market. But still, Québec's economy relies more on the U.S. market than on interprovincial trade. One job out of three in the manufacturing sector now relies on a foreign market, especially the U.S. According to the data used by the provincial government, Québec exported close to $50-billion in 1996 while it imported only $40-billion. With the United States alone, Québec exported $40-billion and imported close to $20-billion. Among other things, these numbers help explain why free trade continues to be so popular among the Québec business community.

Another significant fact is that although the Canadian economy is growing rapidly, the Québec economy has been lagging behind. While Gross Domestic Product (GDP) grew for Canada as a whole at a rate of 4.7 per cent during the 1970s, 3.1 per cent during the 1980s and 1.3 per cent for 1990-1995, the same numbers for Québec were, respectively, 3.9, 2.4, and 1.1 per cent. Partially as a result, the unemployment rate in the province remains high: it has been around 11 to 12 per cent for most of the decade. Related indicators such as the length of time people remain unemployed (28 weeks in 1995) the percentage of people working part-time (17 per cent in 1995) also indicate that the provincial economy has deteriorated since the 1970s. It is difficult to believe that political factors have not negatively influenced Québec's economy, and vice versa.

The Deficit

Economic difficulties help to explain, in part, why it has taken so long for the provincial government to erase its deficit. When in 1997, Paul Martin, the federal Minister of Finance, stated that the federal deficit had been eliminated, Bernard Landry, his Québec counterpart, still plans to get rid of the deficit only by the year 2000. One of the things that make it more difficult to balance the budget is the increased globalization of Québec's economy. Moreover, Québec's fiscal policy has to be competitive with what is done in the other provinces, in particular Ontario and in the neighbouring American states. Whether or not some politicians in Québec are or pretend to be social democrats, they have to follow closely what has been done in Alberta or in Ontario. For example, for a population that is three million less than Ontario's, Québec spent $500-million more than Ontario on education in 1994, something that is difficult to sustain in the long term.[34]

What happened in Québec during the 1980s and 1990s can be explained in terms of normalization and fiscal austerity at a time when social problems became more complex. The welfare programs created two decades before became more expensive at the time when both economic and demographic growth slowed. More than 1.3 million people were living under the poverty line in Québec in the 1990s.[35] This leaves very little room for the government to manoeuvre. Social security costs 14 per cent of the budget, the debt also 14 per cent, and the departments of education, health, and employment together account for 65 per cent. This leaves very little to cut or to be spent elsewhere. One of the decisions that has been taken to balance the budget has been to reduce one of the symbols of Québec's uniqueness: its network of offices around the world. The government decided to maintain only six of the former 22 overseas offices.

The Size of Government

Institution-building is always complex. Because government is about crisis management, and because different policies simultaneously require constant attention, governments cannot always coordinate the activities of various agencies the way a rational decision-making body might be expected to. Moreover, priorities are not always clearly defined for government agencies, which means they must engage in a process of soul-searching just to understand what is expected of them. It is also difficult for governments simply to eliminate programs or agencies since entrenched constituencies tend to develop around them. Governments around the world are today caught in what has been called "the fiscal crisis of the State": the impossibility of raising any further taxes coupled with increased demands for government services and the maintenance of increasingly expensive government programs. However, the perception of government has changed: where it was once seen as the solution to problems, now it is often seen as the source of many of those problems. The reaction has been to push for reduction of the deficit, privatization, deregulation, more access to information, reduction of union rights, and increased accountability for civil servants.[36]

According to official Québec government statistics, 18 public agencies were established between 1867 and 1959, while 34 were created between 1960 and 1969. From 1970 to 1976, another 32 agencies were established, to which were added another 32 between 1977 and 1981, and another 32 up to the conclusion in 1985 of the Parti québécois government's mandate. Only five new agencies were created between 1986 and 1988, at a time when the size of government was first being seriously called into question. Since then, the number of government agencies has remained fairly stable; however, the number of agencies should decrease since the current Parti québécois government has clearly indicated its determination to reduce their number.

The differing levels of present-day involvement of the Québec state in education, health, and cultural affairs illustrates that the centralizing reforms initiated during the 1960s have not been uniformly successful. In the health sector, the government provides services directly to the population through Medicare, which was introduced in 1970-71 and is considered to be an efficient system. However, there is a well-publicized crisis in cost control. In education, school boards have been protected from central control by the Constitution. Efforts have been made to reduce their powers and to get rid of their sectarian aspects, but though the boards accommodate religious diversity, they have used the religious element to maintain their autonomy. In cultural affairs, centralization has failed because the relevant department has attracted relatively inefficient civil servants and created far too many autonomous agencies: 16 other departments and 17 agencies or governmental bodies are involved in the cultural sphere in the province.[37]

By September 1997, 204 agencies existed within the Québec state. The government is presently involved in an attempt to reduce their number,[38] and the number of public servants they employ. From 350,000 FTES (full-time equivalents or person years) in 1981-82, the overall number of employees rose to 379,000 FTES in 1992-93, of which 65,000 FTES were in the public service alone. In 1996-97, the total number of employees fell to 356,500 FTES and to 54,000 FTES in the public service. In 1997, 30,000 employees and 1900 managers accepted early retirement packages in an unprecedented effort to reduce government expenses in the long run. The capacity of the state to intervene in society has consequently been seriously diminished.

Demographics and Social Change

While governments in Québec have re-considered many elements of the post-Quiet Revolution Québec State, Québec society has continued to change and evolve. This is apparent in many realms of social life. Demographically, Québec, which used to have one of the highest birthrates in the Western world, now has one of the lowest. Social reality is also changing. Immigrants are now coming less from Europe and increasingly from all around the world. In 1969, about one immigrant out of three in Québec did not know either French or English upon his or her arrival in the province. It is now almost one in two. While a few tens of thousands of new immigrants come to Québec each year, people from Québec leave for other provinces. The result has been only a very slow increase in Québec's population.[39] One of the important political consequences of this is that the demographic importance of Québec within Canada is declining. The percentage that Québec represents within the Canadian population has fallen from almost 30 per cent in 1966 to one quarter three decades later. Among other things, this will have a direct impact on the number of seats Québec has in the House of Commons and on the "sentiment d'appartenance" Québécois have within Canada.

Another important area for social transformations has been the massive entry of women into the job market. In 1966, only one in three women was working outside of the home; by 1992 it was one in two. As well, unionization has gone down from 50 per cent of the workers in 1992 to 42 per cent in 1995. The number of work days lost to strikes has dropped even more, from over a million days lost in the 1980s to around half a million during the 1990s.[40]

A third social issue that also waits for a solution is the relationship of the Québec government to the aboriginal population of the province. In Québec, as elsewhere in Canada, how the relations with First Nations should be remodelled remains open for debate. The 1990 Oka crisis and its aftermath have illustrated how difficult it is to find a middle road with the Mohawk communities who do not easily accept the application of provincial laws in their communities. The creation and functioning of Mohawk peacekeepers to replace the Sûreté du Québec or the RCMP on their territory has been difficult. The Akwesasne reserve, at the corner of Ontario, Québec, and New York State, has been used for smuggling tobacco, alcohol and firearms over the St. Lawrence river without much control for many decades. Social problems such as drug abuse, violence, poverty are recurrent issues on some reserves and global solutions are presently not within easy reach.

CONCLUSION

The issues discussed in this chapter illustrate how difficult it is to predict the direction in which Québec's society is heading. Québec society and the Québec state have changed tremendously over the last forty years, but many of the reforms of the 1960s still need to be completed. For example, the secularization of the education system is not yet complete, although the recent decision of the federal government to approve a necessary constitutional amendment on the subject will end this saga. Because of budgetary cuts, what will survive of the health system is also unclear. On the other hand, the economic institutions created during the Quiet Revolution, such as Hydro-Québec and the Caisse de dépôt et placement, appear to be doing fine. Finally, the constitutional issue has yet to be solved. Perhaps the Meech Lake Accord could have solved the problem. Perhaps something built upon the 1997 Calgary declaration might do the trick. A deal in the waiting coming from beyond Québec's borders could offer a solution acceptable to the majority of the provincial population. If not, Québec could go its own way.

Is there a widening gap between Québec and the rest of Canada? The rise of the Reform and Alliance Parties outside the province is certainly not viewed in Québec as an invitation to become more integrated. Is Québec's stand in favour of free trade pushing it away from other provinces in which substantial portions of the population oppose increased continental and hemispheric integration?

In contemporary Québec politics, as elsewhere, problems exist and solutions are proposed. In Québec, however, both the problems and solutions can be traced to the continuing legacy of modernization, the state-building of the Quiet Revolution, and the subsequent statist transformation of the social life of the province. The present-day beleaguered provincial state owes as much to that legacy as it does to the legacy of its once proud forebearers.

NOTES

1 The premiers who supported the failed Meech Lake constitutional accord between 1987-1990 fared poorly in following elections. Some like Frank McKenna of New Brunswick were elected in part because they were opposed to the accord. The issue of the unpopularity of constitutional issues outside of Québec is very peculiar. Its peculiarity is even odder if you consider a recent Angus Reid poll that showed that Québec residents score highest on constitutional questions asked on typical recent citizenship exams. From Murray Campbell, "Canada, our home and...?" *Globe and Mail*, 1997, 1.

2 The word was invented by Herbert Simon to explain that when they decide, people do not maximize, but rather look for a solution that satisfies them for the time being. And in the late 1990s, this is exactly the kind of solution most Québécois want.

3 Hubert Guindon, "The Modernization of Québec and the Legitimacy of the Canadian State," *Modernization and the Canadian State*, ed. Daniel Glenday, Hubert Guindon, and Allan Torowetz (Toronto: Macmillan, 1978), 212-46.

4 See Guy Lachapelle, Gérald Bernier, Daniel Salée, and Luc Bernier, *The Québec Democracy: Structures, Processes and Policies* (Toronto: McGraw-Hill, Ryerson, 1993), in which we attempt to take into account all these factors.

5 Kenneth McRoberts, *Québec: Social Change and Political Crisis*, 3rd ed. (Toronto: McClelland and Stewart, 1993).

6 Daniel Salée, "Reposer la question du Québec? Notes critiques sur l'imagination sociologique," *Revue québécoise de science politique* 18 (1990): 83-106.

7 Pierre Elliott Trudeau, *The Asbestos Strike* (Toronto: James Lorimer, 1974).

8 Louis Balthazar, "La Dynamique du nationalisme au Québec," *L'état du Québec en devenir*, ed. Gérard Bergeron and Réjean Pelletier (Montréal: Boréal, 1980), 37-58.

9 Balthazar, 37-58.

10 Employees in the Québec public and parapublic sectors are remunerated through appropriations voted by the National Assembly and include the public service, the health and social services network, and the elementary and high schools in the education system.

11 Louis Borgeat, *La sécurité d'emploi dans le secteur public: essai* (Sainte-Foy: Presses de l'Université du Québec, 1996).

12 K.J. Huffman, J.W. Langford, and W.A.W. Neilson, "Public Enterprise and Federalism in Canada," *Intergovernmental Relations*, ed. Richard Simeon (Toronto: University of Toronto Press, 1985), 131-78.

13 Huffman, *et al.*, 131-78.

14 Luc Bernier, *De Paris à Washington: la politique internationale du Québec* (Sainte-Foy: Presses de l'Université du Québec, 1996).

15 Roland Parenteau, "Les sociétés d'état: autonomie ou intégration" (Montréal: HEC, 1980).

16 Daniel Latouche, "La Vraie Nature de la Révolution tranquille," *Canadian Journal of Political Science* 7 (1974): 525-36.

17 McRoberts, *Québec: Social Change and Political Crisis.*

18 Jean-Jacques Simard, "La Longue Marche des technocrates," *Recherches sociographiques* 18 (1977): 93-132.

19 R.A. Young, Philippe Faucher, and André Blais, "The concept of province-building: a critique," *Canadian Journal of Political Science* 17 (1984): 783-818.

20 Young, *et al.*, 818.

21 See Marc Laurendeau, *Les Québécois violents* (Montreal: Boreal, 1974). See also Ellen Kay Trimberger, *Revolutions From Above* (New Brunswick: Transaction, 1978) and Ted Robert Gurr, *Minorities at Risk: A Global View of Ethnopolitical Conflicts* (Washington, D.C.: Institute of Peace Press, 1993).

22 John W. Kingdon, *Agendas, Alternatives and Public Policies* (New York: Harper Collins, 1995).

23 Réjean Pelletier, *Partis politiques et société québécoise* (Montréal: Québec/Amériques, 1989).

24 Graham Fraser, *P.Q.: René Lévesque and the Parti Québécois in Power* (Toronto: Macmillan, 1984).

25 Fraser, *P.Q.*

26 Paul A. Sabatier, "Policy Change Over a Decade or More," *Policy Change and Learning: An Advocacy Coalition Approach*, ed. Paul A. Sabatier and H.C. Jenkins-Smith (Boulder: Westview, 1993), 13-39.

27 The problem of duplication of departments and services between the federal and provincial government has yet to be solved. In a study based on data from the federal government, Julien and Proulx have concluded that for Québec only hundreds of millions of dollars could be saved by eliminating duplication. Germain Julien and Marcel Proulx, "Le chevauchement des programmes fédéraux et provinciaux: un bilan," *Canadian Public Administration* 35 (1992): 402-20.

28 Rod Dobell and Luc Bernier, "Citizen-Centred Governance: Implications for Inter-Governmental Canada," *Alternative Service Delivery: Sharing Governance in Canada*, ed. Robin Ford and David Zussman (Toronto: KPMG/IAPC, 1997), 250-65.

29 Most of the numbers in this section, unless indicated otherwise, come from the data computed by Bellavance (see n. 33) in a document prepared over the summer of 1997. He used data from Statistique Canada and various Québec agencies among which is the Bureau de la Statistique du Québec. For a more historical perspective, see Simon Langlois, *La société québécoise en tendances, 1960-1990* (Québec: Institut québécois de recherche sur la culture, 1990).

30 A.I. Silver, *The French-Canadian Idea of Confederation*, (Toronto: University of Toronto Press, 1982).

31 See Michel Venne, "Le partenariat dans la peau: les Québécois en veulent et les souverainistes vont raffiner leur offre," *Le Devoir*, 22 June 1997, A-1. These numbers have been confirmed by a second study by André Blais, Elizabeth Gidengil, and Richard Nadeau, quoted by Venne.

32 The Reform Party campaign ads about the Québec origins of the other party leaders were not well received in Québec, whose population, of course, was not the expected target. Nevertheless, the immediate advantage sought by such manoeuvres could backfire.

33 Michel Bellavance, "Le contexte socio-économique de l'action gouvernementale, étude préparée pour le groupe de travail sur l'examen des organismes gouvernementaux," École nationale d'administration publique, juillet 1997.

34 Bellavance, "Le contexte socio-économique."

35 Bellavance, "Le contexte socio-économique."

36 William F. Averyt, "Québec's economic development policies, 1960-1987: between *étatisme* and Privatization," *American Review of Canadian Studies* 19 (1989): 159-75.

37 From a comparative analysis based on the various chapters of Yves Bélanger and Laurent Lepage, eds., *L'administration publique québécoise: évolutions sectorielles 1960-1985* (Sainte-Foy: Presses de l'Université du Québec, 1989).

38 Gouvernement du Québec, Groupe de travail sur l'examen des organismes gouvernementaux, *Rapport* (September 1997).

39 From Bellavance, 1997, table 2.15.

40 From Bellavance, 1997, table 1.29.

7 ONTARIO

Divided Province, Growing Protests: Ontario Moves Right

ROBERT MACDERMID AND GREG ALBO

The market triumphalism that has spread across the advanced capitalist countries since the early 1980s has found, after some delay, a secure presence in Canada's state institutions. Governments of varied political complexion, at both the national and sub-national levels, have either boldly trumpeted or quietly embraced neo-liberalism. The federal governments of Brian Mulroney and Jean Chrétien, for example, have steadily eroded social spending in the pursuit of flexible labour markets and free trade continentally and globally. Alberta's Tory government has been even more brazen in adopting the neo-liberal agenda, winning the hard hearts of *Globe and Mail* editorialists as a result. The rewards of this policy shift have been mixed at best. Government fiscal positions and corporate profits show improvement and all of Canada's regions have, in their own ways, tied their fortunes more closely to their adjacent American region—the "new" Atlantic economy, Cascadia, the Great Lakes Region and so on. However, labour markets across Canada still record high unemployment, after stagnating in the 1980s real per capita incomes have declined over the 1990s, and public infrastructure like universities and hospitals, the symbols of postwar Canadian reformism, are deteriorating from crippling funding cuts.

No jurisdiction in Canada has been able to insulate itself from the processes of economic restructuring and the political constraints it has imposed. But it has been—and continues to be—played out and contested in unique ways. Ontario has long been at the centre of Canadian politics, in economic space as well as geographically, as the most populous (about 40 per cent of Canada's total) and most industrialized (about half of Canada's manufacturing output) province. As the chief beneficiary of Canada's late industrialization under the National Policy, and home of the main manufacturing industries of the postwar boom, Ontario prosperity became synonymous with political conservatism and economic stability. Economic instability that no longer generated the same levels of high employment and prosperity was bound to lead to a hesitant and difficult process of political re-alignment.

Indeed, Ontario electoral politics has been torn asunder, dividing into two periods with an overlapping transitional phase. Beginning in 1945 and ending in 1971, the Progressive Conservative Party won eight majority governments in succession. As Table 7.1 indicates, that is a record only matched or surpassed by the Alberta Social Credit and Progressive Conservative administrations. When minority governments in 1943, 1975, 1977, and a final majority in 1981 are added to this record, the Conservative achievement of unbroken one-party rule surpasses all other periods in Canadian electoral history. For the entire postwar period up until 1985, Ontario knew only Tory premiers who seemed to metamorphose from George Drew (the dapper ex-colonel of assured conservative views) into Leslie Frost (the small town Lindsay lawyer who was everyone's favourite uncle) into John Robarts (the naval officer and lawyer from staunchly conservative London, the insurance capital of Ontario) into William Davis (the pipe-smoking lawyer from Brampton who was sometimes more inscrutable than the daily astrology column), in a kind of smooth succession of corporate CEOs.

From 1985 on, however, the Ontario electorate produced majority governments from three different parties in a row, beginning with a Liberal majority under David Peterson in 1987, ended by the Bob Rae NDP government in 1990, with it in turn replaced by the Mike Harris "Team" of Conservatives in 1995. Once again, Ontario voters had done what voters in no other Canadian jurisdiction had ever done: elect, in succession, majority governments from three different parties, a streak only broken with the re-

TABLE 7.1 **UNBROKEN CANADIAN POLITICAL DYNASTIES**

Jurisdiction	*Party*	*Majorities*	*Elections*	*Years*
ONTARIO	PC	9	12	1943-85
ALBERTA	Social Credit	9	9	1935-71
	PC	8	8	1971-98
P.E.I.	Liberal	6	6	1935-59
NOVA SCOTIA	Liberal	6	6	1933-56
NEWFOUNDLAND	Liberal	6	6	1949-71
CANADA	Liberal	5	5	1935-57
SASKATCHEWAN	CCF	5	5	1944-64
B.C.	Social Credit	6	6	1953-72
NEWFOUNDLAND	PC	5	6	1972-89

election of Harris in 1999. The Quebec Union Nationale majority government of 1966, followed in turn by two Liberal majorities and then by two Parti Québécois majority governments is the only similar period of electoral instability to be found. The transition from remarkable stability to continual turnover in the governing party ran from about 1975 to 1987, a period of two Conservative minority governments, a final Tory majority in 1981, followed by a Liberal minority government that was a short-lived informal coalition between the NDP and Liberals based on a reform programme hammered out between the two. The transition period covers the Conservative minority governments of 1975 and 1977, when on both occasions the Tory vote slipped below 40 per cent, followed by a recovery to 44 per cent and a final majority government in 1981. It was to be Tories' last hurrah before the party, at least in Mike Harris's thinking, entered the wilderness for the subsequent ten years to be born once again as a very different party of the New Right.

In the pages that follow, we do not attempt to detail the shifting class politics of Ontario but rather defend two general claims: first, that the end of the postwar economic development model is being followed by economic integration, labour market instability, and flexible accumulation; second, that the class compromises that provided the political cohesion of postwar Ontario have eroded into a period of political instability, party repositioning and new forms of more open class conflict. These two themes underscore a final point. Neo-liberalism in Ontario is a deeply contradictory political project that runs against the grain of Ontario's historical politics of a deeply stratified but consensus-building, one-province toryism. Its economic policies are likely—indeed are intended—to widen social inequalities as they deepen integration with the U.S., the fragile context in which the current Ontario economic recovery must be set. There is every reason to assume that Ontario politics will remain polarized and, out of necessity, more combative and more resourceful.

FROM PROSPERITY TO IMPASSE: TORY ONTARIO IN DECLINE?

By some measures Ontario can make a claim to be the most prosperous region of the world. The origins of this prosperity date back to the legacies of colonial occupation and settlement of agricultural lands that allowed capitalism to emerge slowly in the mid-nineteenth century as an extension of the European economic space. The agro-industrial complex that began to form in the major centres around Lake Ontario, as a result of the demand linkages from the agricultural export surpluses being earned and immigrant workers being drawn into the towns, was further bolstered by the import-substitution industrialization policies that were implicit in the National Policies of the Conservative Party of Sir John A. Macdonald. The tariff, settlement, and railway policies encouraged an Ontario-based domestic machinery and consumer goods industry to substitute for imports, with its products being purchased by income earned on resource exports, especially from western Canada, and the economic surpluses being increasingly controlled and re-allocated by the emergent financial centre of Toronto. By the turn of the century, Ontario was indisputably Canada's manufacturing heartland, rivalling—and directly connected to—the booming American midwest on the southern shores of the Great Lakes. By 1911 Toronto had as much as 35 per cent of its employment in manufacturing, and by 1940 almost half of Ontario's annual output was also from this sector.[1]

The "postwar golden age of capitalism" produced sustained economic growth in all regions of Canada and further consolidated Ontario's prosperity and its position as Canada's manufacturing centre (as well as the political grip of toryism over the province). In Ontario, the postwar period was one of exceptional accumulation, with an average real growth in Gross Provincial Product (GPP) of just under 5 per cent. It also marked a decisive break in the Ontario economy from what was still partially an agrarian economy rooted in the family farm to an urbanized manufacturing and service economy in the south, and a resource extraction economy that exploited Ontario's mineral and forest wealth of its northern hinterland.[2] Just under a quarter of the Ontario population was gainfully employed in agriculture in 1941, roughly equal to that in manufacturing; but by 1975 under 5 per cent of the population was employed in the primary sector as a whole. Following the war, manufacturing expanded its output and employment levels (although slowly diminishing its share of overall economic activity), in good part being led by the main Fordist mass production industries of autos, appliances, and consumer goods. In Ontario, as in Canada as a whole, the postwar boom also meant a boom in resource and processing industries such as mining, forestry, hydro-electricity, and steel that fed into the manufacturing sector and spread small towns across the north. Services grew even more impressively: their share of output more than doubled from about 25 per cent in 1940 to just over 56 per cent in 1975 (and accounting for about 65 per cent of employment), transforming cities like Ottawa, London, and Toronto into major government and financial networks of control. The strong pace of accumulation benefitted wage earners by creating hundreds of thousands of blue-collar semi-skilled jobs that produced household incomes, through the strong influence of the Ontario labour movement that was also formed in these processes, beyond the dreams of the previous "depression generation." These, of course, were the workers who laboured at Bell Telephone, Ontario Hydro, Inglis, Massey Ferguson,

Stelco, INCO, GM or in the growing federal and provincial civil services. Real per capita incomes tripled between 1939 and 1975, even while average annual hours worked showed a continual decline. The electorate, swelled by at first a trickle and later a river of immigrants to prosperous Ontario, translated economic stability and advancement into resounding majority after majority for successive and extraordinarily cautious Progressive Conservative governments.

There were aspects to the structure of Ontario industry through the boom, however, that alluded to problems of relative economic under-performance. The tariffs built up during the Depression and war mobilization, and the pent-up demand fuelling further investment in the mass production industries, implicitly reproduced the import-substitution industrialization model supporting Ontario manufacturing. This "intensive accumulation" often came in the form of American companies establishing branch plants in Canada. Given U.S. industrial leadership, the direct investment brought to Ontario leading technologies, but in plants that were "second-best" to the scale economies and innovation processes in the "home country." Ontario productivity levels could partly catch up to the U.S., but never forge ahead and were, moreover, always in danger of falling behind gains that were being posted by the rival economies that were developing new innovation systems, as in Germany and Japan. This was indeed what occurred through the boom. Productivity gains in Ontario industry contributed about half the increase in real GPP over the postwar period, much less than in Europe and Japan who were also growing faster, and declined sharply in the 1970s. It has stayed flat since, recovering only modestly in the late 1990s, setting up the "productivity puzzle" that has preoccupied Ontario industry analysts. It is necessary to underline, then, that Ontario postwar growth was equally spurred by extensive accumulation from new resources, land and imported capital being brought into capitalist sector production, and especially from the sheer growth in the stock of the labour force, at over 2.5 per cent per year on average.[3] The reliance on extensive growth made for a perpetual race for employment growth to keep up with labour force pressures, and in fact the reserve army of unemployed in Ontario showed a consistent long-term tendency to increase over the entire postwar period.

The concern with Ontario's competitive capacity had been raised at Queen's Park in the early 1960s with the formation of the Department of Economics and Development and the Ontario Economic Council (astonishingly before then the province did not even gather systematic information on the sectoral composition of the economy).[4] As Canada's industrial centre benefitting from national policies, the Ontario state never forwarded an industrial strategy beyond resource exploitation and the "extensive accumulation" of laying infrastructure supportive of urban growth, and indeed sprawl, that eventually created the 200-kilometre city around Toronto. It could rely on national tariffs protecting its branch plant manufacturing sector, or on policies such as the 1966 Auto Pact agreement with the U.S. which, in guaranteeing a quota of auto production in Canada, also guaranteed Ontario jobs. Even the giant Ontario Hydro had a guiding federal hand through its nuclear policy. Similarly, Ontario benefitted from federal tax centralization and income transfers as postwar inter-provincial trade patterns meant that the transfers in part came back as final demand for Ontario production. Industrial policy tended to be limited to trade promotion, until the establishment of the Ontario Development Councils in the mid-1970s made modest efforts to stimulate high-technology sectors. Indeed, the Ontario state had only the most limited economic planning capacities for its own activities, as the slapdash expansion of the post-secondary education sector in the 1960s and the chaos of municipal planning indicated, let alone a capacity to alter the path of capitalist sector accumulation. Despite being a region clearly at the core of the world economy, and in contrast to the Quebec or B.C. states of the 1960s and 1970s, Ontario maintained a painfully cautious market-oriented economic policy regime ill-prepared for economic crisis.[5]

With the turmoil and restructuring that gripped the world economy in the 1970s, some of the underlying weaknesses of the Ontario development model began to emerge immediately as more serious problems. As tariff protection wound down from the GATT process and international economic competition intensified, the Ontario branch-plant manufacturing sector went through a devastating phase of closures. The limited statistics gathered by the Ontario Ministry of Labour indicated just under 100 thousand layoffs across 700 establishments from 1974-79.[6] The de-industrialization fears emerging in Ontario working-class communities, that these layoffs foretold of the replacement of stable unionized jobs with decent pay by low-waged unstable jobs and higher unemployment, proved far more prescient about Ontario's future than the econometric modelling coming out of Ontario's establishment universities. Ontario's economy weakened relative to the commodity-producing regions of the west and kept Ontario growth rates below the national average throughout the 1970s. As economic growth began to slow, interest rates to rise, and inflation to sky-rocket, the take-home pay of workers eroded and mortgage rates rose to a point by the early 1980s where the pervasive dream of home ownership began to slip away from an increasing portion of the middle and working classes.

The Ontario mini-boom from 1983-89 was, from one perspective, remarkably strong. Real annual growth, for instance, exceeded 4 per cent and almost 900,000 jobs were added (almost half the new jobs in Canada), bringing the unemployment rate down to 5 per cent by 1988 from over 10 per cent after the "Reagan recession" of 1981-82.[7] Yet, from another vantage point, the growth was almost entirely "extensive" in form: productivity levels remained flat and what drove the Ontario economy ahead were longer hours of work and absolute increases in the volume of capital and labour employed in the capitalist sector.[8] There were other prominent signs of Ontario's "new economy." A competitive exchange rate from the strengthening of the U.S. dollar, which also spurred new plant investment by American auto companies and Japanese transplants, shifted the composition of the Ontario economy and increased dependence on exports to the U.S. and away from internal trade with the rest of Canada. As well, the employment recovery tended to be predominantly in the service sector, about one-third of new jobs occurring in business and financial services, about 25 per cent each in consumer services and goods production, and the rest in the broad public sector.[9] Indeed, although hidden by the arrogance of the "Bay Street boom" and the dispute over free trade, the 1980s recovery was re-positioning the Ontario economy: as a cheaper albeit efficient production zone within the North American auto complex through a low dollar (and via certain socialized wage costs not covered for U.S. plants); and as a financial and corporate control centre linking the Ontario and Canadian economy to the processes of internationalization. But these were the signs of widening societal polarization, not economic strength.

The sharpness of the 1990-91 recession starkly revealed Ontario's economic vulnerability to any general price shock, and the subsequent stagnation through the 1990s demonstrated Ontario's relative economic weakness and declining capacity to provide high employment for a growing portion of its population. The confluence of free trade, a zero-inflation policy strategy by the Bank of Canada that boosted interest rates and the dollar, and a global recession triggered an astonishing decline in output of 8 per cent in Ontario with almost 300,000 people thrown out of work.[10] Total output and employment levels only recovered by 1997. The Ontario manufacturing sector has suffered quite severe rationalization, with the alarming rise in permanent layoffs since 1990 indicating plant shutdowns. Yet, despite the rationalization of industry, in part prompted by the decade long adjustment to free trade and the neo-liberal policies of the 1990s, aggregate productivity performance remains sluggish and the source of long-term structural weakness in Ontario. As a portion of total output, manufacturing still remains significant at over one-fifth, but as a source of employment manufacturing fell from supplying one in four jobs in 1981 to about one in six jobs by 1993. The composition of capitalist sector service growth, with its sharp split between business and producer services versus clerical and a wide range of "servant" industries and occupations, is now key to employment growth and quality in Ontario (unless there is new growth in the state sector). The importance of the auto sector to Ontario cannot be underestimated: car and parts exports are approaching $50 billion annually and half of Ontario exports. Ontario trade figures suggest other problems: export trade is more concentrated in resources and the auto sectors to the U.S. than previously; high-tech industries apart from autos remain a minor employer and a small component of exports; and is potentially forming a persistent pattern of a net trade deficit with the U.S. and the rest of the world, but a surplus in trade with the rest of Canada. In other words, the Ontario economy through the 1990s was essentially stagnant except for trade, with the majority of new activity simply being a redistribution between sectors and between the social classes along the path of societal polarization set by the 1980s "boom." The higher growth levels and lower unemployment of 1999-2000 need to be set against the economic under-performance of the Ontario economy of the 1980s and 1990s. Moreover, this Ontario recovery has, more than any other, been driven by exports to the U.S. (whose own recovery has been worryingly fuelled by debt-led consumption) rather than by internal economic transformation of its value-creation capacity.

This polarization is vividly recorded in the labour market of the 1990s "recovery." Unemployment levels recently dropped to just under 6 per cent, but participation rates plummeted from over 70 per cent in 1989 to below 66 per cent in 1998, where it remains stuck, thereby removing 400,000 workers from the labour market.[11] From other evidence as well it is certainly appropriate to raise the spectre of a "jobless recovery": the proportion of long-term unemployed dramatically increased to almost 30 per cent after having fallen to about 13 per cent in the 1980s; the proportion of the population employed fell by over 6 per cent from 1989 to 1998; job loss per capita in Ontario over the last decade has been the largest of any province; and there has been a large growth of both self-employment and involuntary part-time work. This all suggests an extremely grim labour market, the improvement in the narrow measured unemployment rate masking the enormous growth in stagnant labour reserves as people have withdrawn from the active labour force. So in total there was in the 1990s a "jobs disaster" roughly parallel in dimensions to the "jobs miracle" of the 1980s. While areas of northern and eastern Ontario have large and increasing levels of unemployment and poverty that have grown steadily since the 1970s, in the 1990s mass unemployment and "pauperization" in the form of the homeless also characterized the core centre of Toronto.[12] One-half of all job losses in the wake of free trade and recession occurred in Metro Toronto alone; and estimates of productivity advance over time indicate that Toronto's rate has been only 40 per cent of the rest of Canada's since the 1970s, suggestive of the overall switch to service activity in Toronto and the movement of new plants to "greenfield" sites in the surrounding regions.[13]

The failure of the Ontario economy to provide adequate capitalist sector growth—public-sector employment having fallen as a portion of total employment consistently since the early 1970s and declining in absolute terms by 8.5 per cent from 1992-96[14]—is compellingly seen in the devastating increase in poverty. Real hourly wages in Ontario, a basic index of working-class incomes, fell by 0.1 per cent per year on average from 1979-89 and fell even more sharply during the recession of 1990-91 and barely increased during the subsequent recovery.[15] Through most of the 1990s about one in eight Ontarians (one in five children) were directly on social assistance. This is the largest provincial portion (after usually being the lowest) in Canada and about 45 per cent of the total number in Canada. The numbers of working poor are higher still and are estimated at between 20-25 per cent of the population (a figure, it should be noted, that showed growth through the "booming 80s").[16] Even neo-liberals have had to concede that the increased welfare caseloads reflect "that job losses in the 1990s might well have been permanent."[17] Economic dependency ratios, the measure of the economic burden of social transfers to the marginalized unable to obtain a market income, showed a sharp increase in the 1990s to over a quarter of the population (and above the Canadian average). Northern Ontario communities such as Elliot Lake, Sault Ste. Marie and even Premier Harris's home town of North Bay have dependency ratios from just below 40 per cent to an astonishing 70 per cent (poverty comparable to that of many Aboriginal reserves in Ontario).[18] These figures are consistent with reports across the province, from major centres like Ottawa and Toronto to smaller ones like Rainy River and Belleville (and even York University), that foodbank usage at the "peak" of the recovery in 2000 is often more than double what it used to be. The problems of hunger and housing are especially desperate in Toronto, the richest of Canada's major cities, with over 5,000 homeless living on the streets, causing even the conservative mayor to declare housing a national emergency.[19]

An optimistic view of these trends would attribute them to temporary and necessary adjustments of the Ontario economy to the "new realities" of the competitive environment from unsustainable government spending, globalization, and free trade. Ontario is now, it would be argued, positioned to re-establish its prosperity as a component of a larger North American economic bloc. There is, however, a more pessimistic, and more plausible, reading of the competitive austerity gripping the Ontario economy. A longer-term weakness in its development model has made Ontario susceptible to economic dislocation from the processes of economic internationalization. The rationalization of the branch-plant structure of the Ontario manufacturing sector, which is now one of the weakest in the advanced countries and would be ravaged without the auto sector, suggests this has already been the case. A number of other features point to an evolving export-oriented flexible accumulation model. Anaemic income growth and domestic demand have meant that capitalist sector growth is increasingly pulled, out of provincial economic weakness and not strength, by net exports. Export competitiveness is, moreover, increasingly premised on a cheap currency, low wages, and low taxes. The poor productivity performance means that a low dollar is pivotal to keep unit labour costs competitive for exports (and this holds even for the technologically advanced auto sector).[20] High unemployment, lax labour standards, and the spread of contingent work are extending wage austerity and flexibility through the labour market. And, in contrast to much popular rhetoric, corporate income tax rates and payroll taxes are lower than in neighbouring U.S. states and Québec.[21] Indeed, Ontario's budgetary crisis over the last decade is vividly illustrative of the economic impasse. The Ontario Government budgetary deficit more than anything else is linked to the rise in expenditures as a result of poor labour market performance (and the disproportionate decline in federal transfers at the very same time) and the subsequent burden of interest payments. Misguided tax cuts have disproportionately benefitted the wealthy (especially as the waged classes have been hit by rising user fees) and have added to the fiscal problem. But as a consequence of postwar prosperity and conservatism (and no government has yet altered it), the state sector in Ontario, in terms of budgetary revenues and expenditures at about 20 per cent of GPP, remains small and below the provincial average. Moreover, program spending at about 14 per cent of GPP is similar to what it was in the early 1970s despite the enormous growth in the marginalized from capitalist sector restructuring.[22] Competitive bargaining down of taxes has added to the revenue problems and social austerity. The end of Ontario's postwar prosperity has left, therefore, a crisis of redistribution in the state sector, and instability and reduced capacity in capitalist sector production. These impasses are intertwined with the profound instabilities and growing divisions of modern Ontario politics.

THE END OF THE TRUE BLUE TORIES: THE TRANSITION YEARS OF 1975-1985

The decline of one-party dominance in Ontario politics was a halting process that had several forces at work. The slowest of these might be simple generational replacement in the electorate. Those who voted the Conservatives to eight successive majorities had built up an habitual regularity in their support for the party and the local candidate. Many must have come to identify strongly with a Progressive Conservative government that had, if not brought about, at least presided over the longest boom economy in Ontario history. Over several majority governments local MPPs developed a network of contacts and a history within communities that boosted their re-election possibilities. While incumbency was an important cause and consequence of the string of Tory victories, after 1981 it began to decline. Hale notes that while "89.8 per cent of incumbents seeking re-election were successful in the four provincial elections between 1971 and 1981, ... elections since 1985 have seen a sharp drop in the re-election rate of incumbents from 81.2 per cent in 1985 to 58.4 per cent in 1990 and 44.8 per cent in 1995."[23]

Equally important in the decline in Conservative dominance were internal changes in the Conservative party. These changes in operation were not unique to that party but were the result of technological changes, the rise of polling, campaign advertising, media consultants, and all of the new ideas in campaign and party structures. These changes brought different ideas about how parties should be managed, who political leaders should turn to for advice, and the importance of party members in governing the province. In the Progressive Conservative party, these changes were exemplified in the emergence of the Big Blue Machine prior to the 1971 election and its subsequent importance in the inner councils of the party. The Big Blue Machine was a group of conservative activists who brought unique campaigning skills to the Davis administration: Norm Atkins was an advertising executive; Paul Weed ran a collection agency (no better training for a campaign fund-raiser); William Kelly, a corporate executive, became the bagman; and Robert Teetor, the pollster. Planning for the 1971 election reflected this change in the structure of the party. Atkins devised a campaign plan "with massive use of television and advertising [costing] about $4.5 million. It was an astounding figure to all concerned. The most expensive provincial campaign to that time had been Robarts' last election in 1967 which cost $1.7 million."[24] The significance of the Big Blue Machine was not really the success it brought; a majority government followed by two minorities and another majority was modest in comparison to the previous Tory run of success. Its success was partly in the lead it temporarily created over other parties in the political public relations game, but here the advantages were short-lived. More important still was the effect it had on the culture of the Conservative party. Throughout the Drew, Frost, and Robarts years, the Tories had successfully operated a network of patronage based on modest rewards for those who served the party:

> ... scrupulous attention was paid to the network's maintenance: no one who worked within it was supposed to labour without recognition, even if that involved only some small honour or a personal letter of thanks from the leader. One of the great strengths of the dynasty, which perhaps as much as anything accounts for its longevity, was that in every community there were respected citizens who were connected to it, spoke well of it, and who expected in return to have its ear on matters of local concern. After about 1980, however, there were increasing signs that the norm of reciprocity was falling into abeyance. It is possible that the norm itself was weakening, but it is equally likely that a party too long in power was becoming careless and out of touch with its grass roots. Patronage was being awarded to those who had performed no appreciable service, for reasons that were not readily discernible; local elites were being ignored, to their puzzlement and annoyance, even on issues directly affecting their communities; and for many, Queen's Park was beginning to feel much farther away.[25]

Changes to campaigning added significantly to costs. The party became more pre-occupied with fund-raising than grass-roots cultivating. Not only did this create a gradual distancing from the party membership but it also increased the party's reliance on large campaign donors. The Davis administration experienced a number of scandals that had their roots in the centralization of campaigning techniques. In the first administration, it was revealed that the company chosen to construct a government building had given $50,000 to the Tory party just prior to the awarding of the contract. The government's response to these scandals was to introduce the Election Finances Reform Act, which placed limits on campaign contributions and expenditures and forced the disclosure of all contributions. While this put a cap on the escalating race for campaign funds, it did not do away with campaign financing scandals.

While these political developments were important to the longevity of the Tories, it was the economic instability after 1974 that pre-occupied the government as the questions of Ontario's competitive capacity and growing social deficit could no longer be so easily evaded as in the long reign of Tory complacency. In the pre-neo-liberal world, even a market-oriented regime like Ontario's allowed some, albeit a modest, role for government in guiding the economy even to the point of participating in it to aid capitalist-sector production. The Davis government of 1971 to 1985 was, in this sense, every bit as interventionist, possibly even more so, than the NDP government elected in 1990. All of these efforts were needed in a period of rising unemployment and labour restiveness in the face of wage settlements that were quickly consumed by inflation, and in particular by the pressing need to modernize Ontario industry as economic internationalization intensified competitive pressures.

Throughout this period the successive Davis governments continued to expand social government spending: before the 1975 election the government brought in a guaranteed income program for the elderly as well as a free drug prescription program. The pre-1981 campaign BILD program (Board of Industrial Leadership and Development) was touted as a massive $1.5-billion expenditure designed to "do something about unemployment and industrial restructuring" and promising "advanced technology centres to be located in different communities." While the policy made good pre-election material, as Speirs pointed out, "most of BILD was a repackaging of highway and other projects which the ministries would have undertaken in the normal order of business. A few ideas were genuinely new, such as the technology sparking IDEA (Innovation Development for Employment Advancement) Corporation. IDEA later foundered in a morass of mismanagement caused by the confusion surrounding its original mandate."[26] While BILD may have been first and foremost an election strategy, it still affirmed the Conservative party's belief that government needed to aid industrial modernization. Bill Davis was no neo-liberal Margaret Thatcher or Ronald Reagan. He distanced himself even further from the two free marketers when shortly after the election Davis bought Ontario a "window on the petroleum industry" with a 25-per-cent purchase of Suncor Oil Company. (The purchase was, however, unpopular with the party and the cabinet and was in part driven by what Hugh Segal of the Big Blue Machine saw in the popularity of Petro-Canada, at that time the federal government-owned petroleum company.)

While the Suncor purchase surprised many in and outside the Conservative party, Davis saved his biggest policy bombshell to the end of his mandate, when he announced full funding for Roman Catholic schools in the province. The policy had more symbolic than financial importance (although more reactionary symbolism in the move away from a universal, non-denominational school system than of retrospective recognition of the historical marginality of Catholicism in Ontario). The government already funded education in Roman Catholic schools through grade 10, although grades 9 and 10 received less funding than the public system. The policy that Davis announced extended full funding to grades 9 through 13, bringing the separate school system onto the same funding basis as the public system. From some perspectives, Davis's action in the face of some chauvinistic party opposition was courageous, but it really was a case of political opportunism from a party in eclipse-like postwar prosperity. (Some say Davis was forced to keep a commitment made to the Archbishop of Toronto, who threatened opposition from the pulpits in the next election.)[27] Davis had been goaded to do something by the growing numbers of Catholic voters and because of the difficulty the Tory party was having in relating to non-Protestant and non-Anglo-Saxon communities. But many in the Tory party were shocked at Davis's program. Norman Sterling, who would surface ten years later on the Mike Harris team, had his objections noted in the Cabinet minutes. At heart, the party was a small-c conservative collection of views that was very Protestant and more than a little reluctant to provide a leg up to the Catholics. On this and other issues, the party began to split along lines that polarized the red-Tory leadership of the party and backroom advisors and the more right-wing traditional conservative views of the party and some of its MPPs. The Liberals and NDP could have opposed the policy and defended universalism, but they too worried about losing Catholic voters and opted for short-term opportunism.

Throughout his last term, Davis seemed to develop policy within a small circle of political confidants and the results often surprised party members and the public. He toyed with the idea of running against Brian Mulroney for the leadership of the federal Conservative party, but decided against it. To both party members and the public it seemed as though he was thinking of leaving. When he finally announced his retirement from office in late 1984, jockeying for the leadership, which had been going on quietly for some time, broke into an unseemly clamour that was unusual in party leadership races. The right-wing inclinations of the party members and delegates began to show in strong support for Frank Miller. But amongst voters, Miller was thought to be less popular than the other three candidates, Larry Grossman, Dennis Timbrell, and Roy McMurtry, who were thought of as red Tories and less enamoured of the market solutions favoured by the party's right wing. The final ballot secured a 77-vote victory for Miller over Grossman.

Frank Miller had several drawbacks as a marketable political leader. One thing the Tory dynasty had always done well was to recharge the youthfulness of the party with every successive new leader. But Frank Miller was two years older than the retiring Davis. His political views were decidedly right-wing and neo-liberal, something that the party delegates may have liked, but that the electorate was not yet ready to embrace. Miller had almost resigned from cabinet over the Suncor purchase and as health minister had tried to trim health-care expenditures by closing hospitals. He had established solid right-wing credentials within the party, opposing the involvement of government in business and supporting cutbacks in social spending. Miller came from a working-class background and had lived a creed of hard work and accomplishment including a scholarship to complete a Chemical Engineering degree at McGill. On the other hand, he had tried a lot of different careers: a teacher at a private school, a chemical engineer, and a Muskoka resort and car dealership owner. The media simplified the man into the car salesman from Bracebridge, an image that Miller did not successfully contest. But it was an image so at odds with the succession of Tory leaders that had preceded him that it gave voters a reason to think very hard about supporting the party. Miller also had the habit of speaking his mind, something Davis never could have been accused of, and the media was seldom short of compromising quotes. Before his strategists toned him down, Miller was also given to wearing loud checked suits and clothing that reporters took to be an indication of being out of style and out of touch.

Mike Harris supported Miller's leadership bid, they were both from the north, both from entrepreneurial backgrounds, and both opposed to the red-Tory policies of intervention in the economy and the continued expansion of the welfare state. The reward for Harris was to be made Minister of Natural Resources and Energy, but he hardly had time to move offices before an election was called. With what seemed to be opportunistic haste (the Tories were leading in the polls), Miller presented a traditional Tory package called Enterprise Ontario that concentrated on job retraining for women and young people, more money for daycare and a reduction in rent control ceilings. Many of the right-wingers in the party must have wondered at the new leader's direction, but the package secured their support by promising a reduction in business taxes.

Miller's capturing of the party leadership was a victory for the more conservative membership over what had come to be seen as the red-Tory, tax-and-spend big government party elite that were the operators of the Big Blue Machine. But the victory was a pyrrhic one. When the ballots had been counted, the Tories had won 52 seats with 37 per cent of the vote, while the Peterson Liberals had won 48 and 37.9 per cent of the vote. Bob Rae and the NDP held the balance of power with 25 seats. Miller had won the election with fewer votes but more seats than the Liberals. Both could claim a right to govern but the Lieutenant-Governor was obligated to ignore the verdict in the popular vote and favour that of the electoral system that had translated fewer votes into more seats for the Tories. He asked Miller to form the government. Miller knew his government would not last long without the support of either the Liberals or the NDP. Neither was likely to support the dying days of the 42-year-long Tory regime. Rae announced that the NDP was open to offers and the courting began. What emerged was a pact with the Liberals that committed the parties to a common legislative agenda in return for NDP support in the Legislature for a two-year period. Rae apparently suggested a formal coalition with NDP ministers in the cabinet, but this was rejected. There was opposition within the NDP to a formal agreement to support the unknown Liberals, but the desire to defeat the Conservatives overcame this caution. Despite the announcement of the agreement, Miller carried on and introduced a throne speech but was defeated in the debate that followed. He submitted his resignation without requesting that the Lieutenant Governor call an election, thus bringing to an end one of the longest unbroken stretches of one party government in Canadian history.

The Tory defeat swept Mike Harris out of a minister's office and onto the opposition benches. Frank Miller resigned as leader in August, defeated by the continuing infighting from the unfinished leadership campaign and the recriminations that followed from being the first Tory leader in memory to lose an election. The party's right-wing ascendency had been short lived, for the delegates gave the leadership to Larry Grossman, who in turn resigned after the disastrous 1987 election, paving the way for Mike Harris and the right wing to reclaim the leadership and begin to lay the ground for the Common Sense Revolution that brought the party out of the wilderness and back into government less than a decade later.

MODERNIZATION OR LIBERALIZATION? THE ONTARIO LIBERAL MOMENT 1985-1990

The Liberals' 1985 election platform was the product of years in opposition and never having had the responsibility of turning a promise into a policy. In this they were like the NDP of 1990 who similarly promised what they subsequently found they could not or did not want to deliver. Peterson was a sharp contrast to Frank Miller, a young, successful businessman who was to all appearances the personification of urban yuppie values. After "renovation" by the image consultants, he made an energetic and articulate leader.[28] The Liberal campaign, in keeping with its populist inclinations, promised something for everyone: "job creation, an end to extra billing [by doctors], the abolishment of medicare premiums, the introduction of a denticare program, sales tax breaks, rent controls, equal pay for work of equal value, daycare, increased job skills training in high schools, selling beer and wine in corner stores."[29] To this platform, the Accord with the NDP added policy on freedom of information, an environmental spills bill, reforms that opened up the operation of the legislature and introduced television coverage, election financing reforms that further limited campaign spending, separate school funding, low interest loans for farmers, workplace protection for workers and reforms to the unionization procedure, more strict environmental regulation, and affordable housing.[30] It was a needed agenda of modernization given the backwardness into which Queen's Park had fallen under the long Tory reign, and the optimism of change and assurance of majority support in the Legislature carried the government forward on a wave of energy. Some things did get done, others (such as denticare and corner store liquor sales) fell to the side, and the more ambitious plans for finding a new location for Ontario in the global economy were intensively mooted but little else.[31]

The two years of Liberal government under the Accord were a tremendous success for the Liberals. As NDP supporters who had opposed the Accord feared, the Liberals gathered virtually all of the credit for the reforms. Peterson, with the assistance of a knowledgeable team of advisors that included Hershell Ezrin, Gordon Ashworth, pollsters Martin Goldfarb and Michael Marzollini, and media specialist Gabor Apor, built an image of media-wise youthful energy. Peterson was open and accessible and his trademark red tie had a kind of muted flamboyancy that spoke to the values of those who were part of the rising economy. Peterson extensively reformed the cabinet and bureaucracy and created independent advisory bodies such as the Premier's Councils to provide advice to supplement that of the Ontario Public Service. The notion of stakeholder became pervasive as the party's particular brand of "one-province, one society" populism that marked its ideological underpinnings and was worked out in day-to-day policy. Peterson's openness, his cultivated image of being in touch, an ordinary guy, a jogger and boxer, who had kids and a working spouse, who loved to listen (the television campaign ads of 1985, 1987, and 1990 are filled with these images)—all of these things molded the sense of the Liberal government being with and for the people. This was, of course, a false and constructed image. By and large, the Ontario working classes did not share in the prosperity of the 1980s "mini-boom" that was partly driven by sky-rocketing real estate values and the fattening wallets of Bay Street stockbrokers. The poor had little to be thankful for as taxes rose and real wages stagnated and most of the policies that would have benefitted working-class people such as daycare, denticare and a fairer distribution of the tax load did not make progress, while public moneys went to luxury playpens like the SkyDome money pit. The government dialogue with stakeholders did not include the less well-off.

Once the NDP two-year guarantee of support expired, Peterson lost no time in calling an election, despite the unredeemed campaign pledges. He was riding a wave of public support that no politician or campaign strategist could resist. The August election was almost a forgone conclusion: the Liberals captured 47 per cent of the vote and 95 of 125 seats, the Grossman-led Conservatives fell to third place with only 16 seats and 25 per cent of the vote. The NDP gained about 2 per cent in popular vote to 26 per cent, but fell from 25 to 19 seats. The Tories had hit rock bottom, losing 36 seats since 1985 and winning 54 fewer than their last majority in 1981. The party had accumulated an enormous debt to finance the election and now seemed hopelessly out of touch with all but its core supporters. Grossman announced that he would retire and Andy Brandt became the interim leader. The time was ripe for reconstructing their image and populist message. The NDP could only reflect on the injustice of a Liberal government rewarded for policies that owed much to the NDP. Those who had argued against the Accord with the Liberals now were certain that Rae and his advisors had taken a wrong turn.

The Liberal government, buoyed by the resurgence of the economy, continued its mildly stimulative economic policies despite the lowering of its credit rating. The Northern Ontario Heritage Fund was established to assist the economy of the hinterland. There was some attempt to restrain health-care expenses by controlling doctors' fees. A tax-supported home ownership savings plan was introduced. The government also eliminated the share of health care paid for by taxpayers and replaced it with a payroll tax. Environmental measures were strengthened, the regulation of resource industries improved, and the government introduced recycling programs. On other issues the government was less progressive. At the behest of employers it watered down workplace safety legislation that gave workers the right to shut down hazardous workplaces and it reduced the coverage of workers' compensation. Over the opposition of labour groups, the government brought in a Sunday shopping law that was soon defeated in the courts, and the provincial government withdrew from legislating on the matter (the courts later settling in favour).

The Liberal government had tried to construct a spotless reputation by introducing conflict-of-interest guidelines for members and cabinet ministers. While these proved to be largely toothless, they enhanced the image of a government that was immune to even the class interests of the wealthy. Part of the success of the Liberal government was the image of efficient and modern management that it presented. Reforms to governmental structures that appeared to open the government to closer accounting and to seek out greater citizen input were an important part of the creation of this modern impartial governing image. This was a key part of the practical moralism that grounded the Peterson populist appeal. This was a government that could never yield to class favouritism. The weakness of this moralism was the impossibility of a party of business like the Liberals living up to it. Not long after the election and almost throughout the duration of the government, Peterson spent considerable time dealing with political scandals: the housing minister was accused of accepting campaign donations from developers, the Solicitor General tried to intercede with the OPP on behalf of a friend, the citizenship minister was accused by the Commission on Election Finances of having made personal use of campaign donations, a key advisor was found to have accepted a refrigerator and a new coat of house paint from land development interests. Some of these scandals were connected to what became known as the Patti Starr Affair. Patti Starr was a Liberal fundraiser who had connections to a number of very wealthy land and housing development companies. The president of one of these companies, Tridel, became president of the Ontario wing of the federal Liberal party. Starr channelled contributions from the industry into party and candidate bank accounts without following the proper procedures.[32]

From the point of view of preserving the party's spotless image, Peterson handled the affair badly. Campaign donation-related stories continued to appear in the press, linking the Liberals to the development industry at a time when house and land prices were escalating by as much as 50 per cent per year. Enormous fortunes were made between 1984 and 1989 in the land and housing bonanza of suburban Toronto; there were even suggestions that Peterson had benefitted from these connections. But what emerged from the stories were the outlines of a series of links between senior people in the party and developers that gave the latter favoured access to government contracts, preferential treatment in obtaining development permits and sewer rights, and protection from inquiries that might reveal potentially criminal activities. For example, Peterson refused calls from citizen groups who requested an inquiry into development practices in York region where one developer had given $112,000 to the 1987 Liberal campaign. Another company linked to the same development interests had a private audience with Peterson to learn about bidding on a $1-billion garbage disposal contract. Peterson's father-in-law was a London developer who had been offered the opportunity to purchase a piece of the disposal company. One of the developers was connected to the company that purchased the Peterson family business for $9.6 million. The Premier's share of the business had been placed in a blind trust, but the link between the development industry and the gain for Peterson was an easy one for most reporters and electors to make. The more the press dug into the connections, the more they found. Many of the allegations were not proven, and many others were not illegal, or as much as was revealed did not appear to be illegal. But the whole issue began to gather speed as it rolled on and finally Peterson was forced to call a public inquiry that was mandated to discover "whether a benefit, advantage or reward of any kind was conferred upon any elected or unelected public official or any member of his or her family" as a result of relationships with Starr or Tridel. The terms of the inquiry seemed narrow enough to minimize the damage to the Liberal party, but in April 1990 the Commission was terminated by a Supreme Court decision that ruled the terms of the inquiry to be invalid. The impression of a network of favours granted to business and of their special access to government decision-makers continued to grow. This affected the ability of the Liberal party to defend and expand its version of populism. While many issues seemed small stuff, they grew like a cancer on the party's credibility, suggesting that public office was being used for private gain. As Attorney General Ian Scott said: "I don't know whether Ashworth received a refrigerator, but assuming he did, the interesting thing was the number of people that thought I got a fridge, if not better."[33]

The Liberals' ambitious social spending, coupled with the failure to reform the tax system, led inevitably to tax increases (although in a province with historically low government expenditures and taxes this was in part just catch-up). Personal income taxes were raised in the 1985, 1988 and 1989 budgets, payroll taxes were increased, high income surtaxes appeared ("high" turned out to be quite low), there was an increase in the provincial sales tax, and almost every budget contained higher taxes on all or some of alcohol, cigarettes, and gasoline.[34] In 1990, the federal government worsened the situation dramatically by capping transfer payments to Ontario. The federal finance minister justified this downloading in the interests of federal budget balancing by suggesting that the Peterson government's reform of the social assistance policies would lead to exploding growth in the federal government's 50-per-cent share of the program. The cap on CAP and the "fed bashing" that provincial governments have often found useful at election time were to become common themes in the next two governments. The cost to Ontario's treasury as a result of the federal government cap has been estimated at "$400 million in 1990-91 and roughly two billion dollars annually for the rest of the mandate."[35]

As the Liberals headed into the election only three years into their five-year mandate, the unfavourable news had begun to accumulate. The economy was slowing down and taxes kept going up, but services seemed to stay the same or decline. The government's reputation was in question, and the leader was looking like a loser on the Meech Lake constitutional reforms and in his confusing opposition to the Free Trade Agreement. Indeed, the Liberals were moving in two directions at once on trade and industrial policy: on the one hand, they had established a number of studies, such as the *Transitions* report on welfare reform, and some modest policies that favoured more interventionist strategies to target high-technology sectors and high-skills training; on the other, they had been moving toward policies that favoured freer markets and internationalization of financial markets. Yet Liberal support in the polls remained high. Peterson and his close advisors must have thought a re-election bid was worth the gamble against the growing likelihood that all of the bad news would coalesce into an assured defeat two years later.

Indeed, the defeat of the Liberal government in 1990 was one of the most unexpected results in Ontario history. The party entered the campaign at over 50 per cent in the public opinion polls, but a combination of factors very quickly whittled down that lead. Editorialists and opposition leaders made much of the opportunism and unjustified cost in the early election call. Peterson talked about needing a renewed mandate to continue his reforms, but there was little substance to the platform. The slowing economy was a second area of concern. Martin Goldfarb, the Liberal pollster, found that "people with families, especially the middle class, are extremely concerned about the erosion of their prosperity. We have to be seen to be protecting the interests of the middle class and that means we have to reassure them."[36] The average family income had been stagnant or in decline for some time, and the feeling of falling behind had only been masked by the addition of extra incomes or longer working hours. The Liberal tax increases were adding further burdens to household incomes and there had been no significant new program such as daycare to show for those increases. On top of these and other anxieties, such as retirement income and the cost of educating children, was the noisy dialogue of the debt and how high interest charges were consuming an ever larger share of government spending. There may even have been a sense that the wealthy were not sharing these anxieties. There should also have been concern about Peterson's image and performance. Under the cloud of scandals, he began to appear like any other "lying politician." Since his image and credibility had been a central part of the party's populist appeal, any threat to them could have serious electoral consequences. In an understandable wish to avoid the scandals, Peterson immersed himself in the Meech Lake process and the "saving of Canada," and tended to talk more about this than a reform program for a divided province that was again reeling from a recession and fears about what free trade—a policy that a majority were against—would bring.

A PROGRESSIVE COMPETITIVENESS AGENDA: SOCIAL DEMOCRACY IN ONTARIO 1990-1995

The 1990 campaign was as much lost by the Liberals as won by the NDP. For the Conservatives, it was a trial run for their new and relatively unknown leader, Mike Harris, and the tax fighter campaign that would find rebirth and support in the 1995 Common Sense Revolution. But for the most part, the Tories were not a factor: their vote dropped by just over 1 per cent and they gained four seats but were still mired in third place. Mike Harris's performance did not seem to hold great promise for the future. The Liberal and NDP campaigns were, in some ways, amazingly inept. The NDP entered the campaign without a platform, content to attack the government's credibility and offer little in the way of alternatives. As their support grew, strategists began to see the need for a plan to lay before the media and the electorate. The *Agenda for the People* was cobbled together by campaign strategists over two or three days. The document showed a budget including $4-billion worth of campaign promises and a projected surplus for the coming year. The NDP policy book included promises for a minimum corporate tax of 8 per cent that would raise a billion dollars, succession duties on the super rich, the dropping of the poor from the tax rolls, increased funding for education, small amounts for reduced interest rate loans to farmers and small businesses, reduced rate mortgages for home owners, public automobile insurance, improved worker protection, better job training, increased minimum wages, pay equity and employment equity, funding for daycare spaces, increased social assistance rates, more non-profit housing units, stricter rent controls, tougher environmental regulations, and highways and economic development funds for northern Ontario.[37] While the *Agenda* may have been nothing but an election ploy, the promises it contained came back to haunt the party over its term in office.

The populist content of the NDP campaign was a departure from the Liberal and Conservative messages of past elections. The NDP, partly intentionally, partly by accident, and partly by history, constructed a populist image that for the first time replaced a dialogue about Ontario that was universal with a class and social justice edge. The message was not the familiar one that promised all Ontario moving forward to meet the challenges of a prosperous future, a theme that featured prominently in the Liberal campaign advertising, but of a coalition of those who had not got ahead, indeed who were slipping backwards, while others were prospering. The *Agenda* built a sense that the NDP was bringing together a coalition of labour, environmentalists, the less well-off, and the victims of the late-1980s boom economy. There was an "us" and "them" in the populist appeal of the NDP that had never been present in former populist constructions promising a government for all. The image was reinforced by controversial election campaign ads that introduced the harder edge of negative campaign advertising into Ontario elections. The party's ads were based on fictional newscasts that related partly fictional stories about Liberal graft.

The euphoria of election night, September 6, 1990, was something most NDP activists and supporters had never experienced nor since equalled. The party had captured government for the first time in Canada's most populous province. The electoral system gave the party a solid majority, translating 37.6 per cent of the vote into 57 per cent or 74 of the legislature's 130 seats. Perhaps the party did not reflect enough on how the election hinged on the votes of a very few number of voters in a handful of ridings that made the difference between a majority, minority and even the continued exile of opposition. This was not a landslide victory, even though seat totals gave that impression. The new government's project from the outset might best have been thought of as building a base to ensure another term in office. Rae and others around him seemed aware of this long-term project but saw the answer in moving the party to the right where they perceived that most voters placed themselves ideologically. The choice of Convocation Hall, Rae's *alma mater*, to host the swearing-in ceremony seemed to be saying that nothing revolutionary was afoot: despite being the first left-wing government in the province's history it could still cuddle up symbolically to the history of wealth and privilege that the University of Toronto represents. Rae verbalized this symbolism in saying that the government intended, even amidst the economic instability of Ontario since the 1970s and the societal polarization that had emerged through the 1980s, to be "a government for all people." In effect, Rae was attempting to reconstruct the "one-province" strategy of prosperous Ontario through a "social partnership" that incorporated the labour movement. Those who had paid for Ontario's economic crisis already through falling wages and growing poverty would soon be asked to pay again so that those who had benefitted through higher profits and income might offer a "partnership" to re-establish the prosperity of the old Ontario for the "new times" of a global economy.

The NDP caucus was the most representative of any party caucus in Ontario history. It included 19 women MPPs, one fewer than all the parties had elected in the previous election and three more than the Liberals had elected in 1987. When Bob Rae introduced his first cabinet, 11 of the 25 members were women, a proportion far in excess of any other cabinet in Canadian political history. The caucus also included a number of minority representatives as well as a number of union members and workers who had left the shop floor for a Queen's Park office. But such broad representation had a cost in lack of experience in government. Only 17 of the 74-member caucus had been previously elected, and many of the newly appointed cabinet ministers were learning how to be ministers and members at the same time.

The NDP Government inherited a deteriorating financial situation that the Liberals had kept secret with their optimistic budget projections of a slight surplus for 1990. As the recession began to bite, the Rae government was faced with rising welfare costs and declining tax revenues as unemployment rose and companies left Ontario for the U.S. and later Mexico. In addition, they had to deal with federal government cutbacks and the cap on transfer payments. When the deficit turned out to be more like $2 billion without any increased program spending, the reality of what could be accomplished without major tax increases began to be apparent. Furthermore, neo-liberal arguments against government deficits had gained significant ground, making normal counter-cyclical deficits an unpopular strategy for the government:

> For years, the deficit had played an iconic role in discussions of fiscal policy in the legislature and the provincial media. The much-prized AAA rating bestowed on Ontario debt by the bond-rating agencies symbolized for many the fiscal rectitude of Canada's wealthiest province. It frequently was invoked by Premier Bill Davis and his supporters to justify both the slow pace of change under Conservative governments and their concern about deficit finance.[38]

It quickly became apparent to Rae and his key ministers that a ballooning deficit would cause political and fiscal problems.

While Finance Minister Floyd Laughren now considered a large stimulative deficit to be out of the question, the government could still move ahead on other items from the *Agenda*. But on almost all of the issues they encountered organized and well-financed opposition from the business community. The legislation on rent controls stirred up vigorous protest from the landlord community. Bill 40, the labour legislation that banned the use of replacement workers in strikes and set up a wage protection fund that secured termination wages and benefits when companies closed, was popular with organized labour but was opposed by employer groups who, uncharacteristically, turned out to picket the legislature. Increases to the minimum wage and pay and employment equity legislation also stirred up business opposition to the government. Perhaps a combination of the inexperience of the government and the apparent lack of active support from unions resulted in the labour reforms dragging out over an energy-sapping eighteen months.

Public auto insurance had been a touchstone of NDP policy for many years, but the experience of opposition to other parts of the *Agenda* and the fiscal situation caused the government to rethink the issue. Rae claimed that a publicly run program would mean job losses in the private insurance industry and would cost the treasury too much. He backed away from the reforms. The party faithful felt badly betrayed by the reversal, but it was the first of several such reversals to come. NDP positions opposing Sunday shopping and casino gambling were reversed with the same apparent ease. The *Agenda* promise to reform the tax system led to the Fair Tax Commission, radical in its organization, progressive in some of its recommendations but confused in how to implement them. As a result, the pressing issue of fairer taxes in a province of growing income inequalities came to nought. These and other examples sent a message to many NDP supporters that the government's commitment to its traditional redistributional agenda was weak at best, being abandoned at worst, in the idealistic—and in many respects hopelessly moderate—objective of forging a partnership accord with the business community. Many of those who had entered the government from social groups, eager to help with the implementation of what they thought would be progressive policies, began to drift away from party and government positions to take up, once again, more familiar roles as government critics. This time, they had a feeling of being lied to; the disillusionment, even if often stemming from the naïveté of the capitalist forces that had to be confronted in an economy increasingly internationalized and in relative decline, was palpable.

The government's concern about the mounting deficit led to an expenditure control plan that culminated in the Social Contract, a collection of cuts that totalled $4 billion. In light of the fiscal situation, the government viewed the cuts to public-sector wages as progressive because they saved jobs and exempted the lowest paid workers from cuts. The hopes of the early days for a "progressive competitiveness" revitalization of an Ontario of partnerships had become a strategy of "shared austerity" amongst Ontario workers. Public-sector workers and unions viewed the measures as betrayals of the NDP's most basic commitment to the sanctity of collectively bargained contracts. The Social Contract split the labour movement, its key allies, and badly weakened support for the party.

In its last months, the NDP seemed to move increasingly towards neoliberal and socially conservative positions. Welfare recipients were vilified in a highly publicized crackdown on welfare fraud that mistakenly suggested that fraud was at an all-time high. While the government had increased welfare payments, at the height of the recession they appeared to be laying the groundwork for future cutbacks. The caucus and party were further divided on the issue of same-sex spousal pension benefits. In allowing a rare free vote on an issue that many in the party thought to be far more than a matter of personal conscience, the government seemed to be moving towards socially conservative positions.

TABLE 7.2 **ONTARIO ELECTIONS 1971-1995**

		ELECTION YEAR								
		1971	*1975*	*1977*	*1981*	*1985*	*1987*	*1990*	*1995*	*1999*
PC	*seats*	78	51	58	70	52	16	20	82	59
	% vote	44.5	36.1	39.7	44.4	37.0	24.7	23.5	44.8	45.1
	% seats	66.7	40.8	46.4	56.0	41.6	12.3	15.4	63.1	57.3
LIBERAL	*seats*	20	35	34	34	48	95	36	30	35
	% vote	27.8	34.3	31.5	33.7	37.9	47.3	32.4	31.1	39.9
	% seats	17.1	28.0	27.2	27.2	38.4	73.1	27.7	23.1	33.9
NDP	*seats*	19	38	33	21	25	19	74	17	9
	% vote	27.1	28.9	28.0	21.1	23.8	25.7	37.6	20.6	12.6
	% seats	16.2	30.4	26.4	16.8	20.0	14.6	56.9	13.1	8.7
OTHER	*seats*	0	1	0	0	0	0	0	1	0
	% vote	0.6	0.7	0.8	0.8	1.4	2.3	6.5	3.4	2.5
	% seats	0.0	0.8	0.0	0.0	0.0	0.0	0.0	0.8	0
	TURNOUT	73.1	67.5	65.2	57.7	61.1	62.3	63.6	62.4	62

HARRIS AND THE NEO-LIBERAL REVOLUTION AFTER 1995

The disappointment of the 1990 election seemed to make Mike Harris more determined to rebuild the party around neo-liberal principles. But before that could begin, the party finances had to be rebuilt. Part of the rebuilding required a reintegration of the party faithful into party policy creation. The party was restructured with policy advisory councils, and held policy conferences and policy tours with the leader front and centre.[39] As one party pamphlet described the process, it was intended "to avoid the pitfalls of 'vacuum-created' or solely 'poll-inspired' policy pronouncements."[40] The process led, in part, to the creation of the 1995 platform, *The Common Sense Revolution* (CSR), but it was equally important in building up the party membership and funds and advocating a more neo-liberal direction that was popular with portions of the party. Harris also met with the business community with the help of Bill Farlinger, a party insider who was later to become the head of Ontario Hydro, and a key figure in its proposed privatization. He sold his neo-liberal message and gathered funds for the party with such success that by 1993 the party debt had been lowered from five to three million dollars.

Throughout the period of the NDP government, the party prepared and released a number of policy documents that became parts of the CSR and later policy under the new government.[41] Harris and his young right-wing advisors, Tom Long, Leslie Noble, Alister Campbell, Mitch Patten, and Tony Clement, were convinced that a platform that included tax cuts, deficit reduction, a balanced budget, an end to the state's efforts to re-engineer society with programs such as pay and employment equity and what they saw as initiative-sapping welfare benefits, would respond to the concerns of a significant number of voters. The CSR emerged out of the policy process, Harris's advisors, and the close attention of Mark Mullins, a young private-sector financial analyst from the Bay Street offices that had been profiting even through the province's economic stagnation. The election strategy group gambled not only on the new policies but also on the strategy of releasing the detailed promises of the CSR almost a year before the election. The party need not have worried about the CSR receiving close scrutiny, since they were far behind the Liberals in the polls and the media largely ignored it despite the print run of one million copies and the catchy 1-800 free phone number.

The content of the CSR was far less uniquely revolutionary than the Conservatives pretended. It was in fact a collection of neo-liberal policies that had been slowly adopted since 1975 by the federal government with the turn to monetarism by the Bank of Canada, in many other provinces and in other countries. Many of the ideas were not even particularly new to the Ontario state: the two governments before Harris had already adopted proposals of fiscal austerity and de-regulation, and a longer lineage could be traced back to the Davis cabinet. The basic CSR strategy was a mixture of personal income tax cuts benefitting the wealthy and financed by expenditure cuts, assistance to business in the form of deregulation, and a weakening of labour protections to increase downward wage flexibility. Entrepreneurial opportunities were to be created through downsizing of government and contracting-out the provision of whatever services remained. A balanced budget, the holy grail of neo-liberal discourse, would follow within four years. All this was promised while "protecting" health care funding and "maintaining classroom spending"—slogans that have proven politically slippery. There were also commitments to cut welfare payments and introduce a requirement to work, to cut the number of MPPs, to amalgamate school boards, to cut funding to universities and allow tuition fees to rise, to scrap job training programs, to cut and download highway building costs, to end subsidies to non-profit public housing, to reduce worker injury benefits, and more. The CSR added up to a brazen attack on the social welfare state, and, to the surprise of the poll-leading Liberals, it worked.

The CSR was the most effective campaign document in recent Ontario history. But it was joined to the Conservatives' other asset, Mike Harris. Almost all mention of the Progressive Conservative party and its unpopular connections to the defeated national Progressive Conservative government of Brian Mulroney were expunged from the CSR document and campaign material and replaced by the Mike Harris Team or the Mike Harris Government. Harris was an effective salesperson, the opposite of Bob Rae's cleverness and David Peterson's superficiality, and blunt in a way that could be equated with common sense. And more, he appealed to the sense of shared values and "consensus" that harked back to the petty-bourgeois image of Ontario prosperity: the faith of getting ahead with hard work, entrepreneurship and pulling together to get through adversity—the mythical values of small-town Ontario and the "suburban dream" in the sprouting edge cities of the Toronto metropolis. But here was also a message of division and "coercion": he praised the work ethic against those on welfare and in unions; warned that people of colour and women should not be given a head start on employment against hardworking and worthy white males; said that anyone who gets welfare should have to work for it and make a contribution like other Ontarians; observed that you cannot spend more than you have without mortgaging the future of youth; argued that entrepreneurs create jobs and that the public-sector employees, from civil servants to teachers, are overpaid, inefficient and overly protected while private-sector workers face insecurity. Harris's demeanour both before and after the election was stern, morally certain, often scolding, always unbending, and imbued with the conviction of being there to do a job and not to listen. In this sense he was very much like Margaret Thatcher, the leader of the British Conservative party and long time prime minister, dividing the public between worthy Ontarians and those who needed to be whipped into shape.[42] The "one-province, one-society" politics of postwar prosperous Ontario had become the divisive "two-province, divided-society" strategy setting morally upright Ontarians of individualistic and entrepreneurial values against the morally corrupted Ontarians of collectivist and egalitarian values. Clearly embedded in this was "class struggle from above" as it explicitly meant that the Harris government would seek to strengthen business interests and to directly challenge unions and roll back other gains of the labour movement in social legislation.

The 1995 campaign was brilliantly scripted by Harris's advisors. The campaign ads were a replay of the "consent and coercion" message, slickly mixing sharp "attack ads" on welfare recipients and employment equity interspersed with Mike Harris "on the road ads" that featured him listening to every demographic group imaginable. The Harris ads strategically dominated key geographic regions, and the media buy strategy far outdistanced the poorly prepared NDP and Liberal campaigns.[43] While they entered the campaign trailing the Liberals, the Conservatives quickly made up the ground. The Lyn McLeod-led Liberals floundered with a relatively unknown leader, a confusing campaign strategy, and a vague platform. The NDP, inexplicably, focused their campaign on Bob Rae despite his low standing in the polls. Their campaign was short on promises; there was to be no last minute platform of the *Agenda* type from 1990. If there was a message, it was an appeal to voters to recognize the humane face of the government's spending reductions—its message of "shared austerity" in a "province for all." Beyond that, the appeal was based solely on a call to trust the party to do what was right and fair. In the end, this appeal depended on credibility, and given the NDP's string of broken promises while in office, it was hardly a winning strategy.

Mike Harris emerged from the election and the Conservative wilderness with a solid majority government. He wasted little time in implementing the promises of the CSR. In the longest legislative session in Ontario history, the Harris government introduced legislation that reshaped politics and policy in Ontario. Reform bills were introduced in such volume that in some instances they had to be combined into massive omnibus bills that included legislation on many unrelated topics, a practice that breached the most basic liberal democratic practice of adequate notice and parliamentary debate before the people's representatives. The agenda left little or no room for public consultation and many groups were shut out of hearings on the bills. One of the first things the government did was repeal the NDP's labour legislation and followed that up with reforms of the Worker's Compensation Board and workplace safety legislation. All these initiatives were considered by labour to be hostile. As promised in campaign ads and the CSR, the government quickly scuttled employment equity. Welfare recipients, who had been demonized by the Harris campaign, saw rates cut drastically followed by the introduction of a workfare program that requires recipients to do community work. The government moved to reorganize health care, freezing costs, increasing and initiating user fees, and appointing an arm's length commission to chart and implement the reforms. Hospitals closed and staff jobs were lost. The speed of change produced a growing sense of disorder in the health-care system, and changes only began to slow when Elizabeth Witmer replaced Jim Wilson as minister in 1997. The Ontario Public Service was drastically pared. The government projected that over 10,000 public-sector jobs would be cut by 1997-98. Ministries were required to act as businesses, contracting out of service provision increased, and services were simply cut. The regulatory capacity of the government was savaged by removing staff, in some instances to the point where a judge could find that the Ministry of Natural Resources was not fulfilling its mandate to manage timber resources.

A major plank of neo-liberal economics was implemented in the first budget, where provincial income tax rates were cut by 30 per cent in the hope of stimulating the economy out of its increasingly dire stagnation. As critics pointed out, the wealthy gained more from the tax cuts than did average and low-income earners. The government reformed primary and secondary education by amalgamating and reducing the authority of school boards, cutting spending and rearranging the education taxing responsibilities of local government. They introduced more standardized testing and began revisions to the curriculum that had a back-to-basics theme. Primary and secondary teachers walked off the job for two weeks, joined by lively community-based education groups sprouting up, in political protest to the reforms in Bill 160. University and college funding was cut by $400 million, tuition fees were permitted to rise, and some programs were freed of all tuition fee regulation. In one of its most contentious acts, the government reorganized municipal government in the greater Toronto area, amalgamating several cities and reorganizing taxing and spending responsibilities. At the same time the government grasped the very thorny problem of changing a property tax system that had glaring inequities. Changes to property tax will likely fall most heavily on those living in the former city of Toronto and most favour those in the suburban belt who returned Tories as MPPs. The government also cut transfers to municipalities by $650 million and downloaded responsibilities. Many of the reforms affected democratic representation on school boards and local government, and the Tories also moved to reduce the number of MPPs from 130 to 103, with ridings identical to the number of federal seats in the province. While introducing a bill to allow referenda made them appear more democratic, the government also ignored the results of an informal referendum of Metro Toronto residents that opposed municipal amalgamation.[44] On privatization, a project closest to the government's ideological heart, some progress was made through the downloading of services to municipalities and contracting out, especially in areas such as waste water treatment, drinking water provision, parks and highway maintenance. The quality of service provision declined in step even though user fees were most often added. The big "prizes," those that business interest most cherished—Ontario Hydro, TVO and the Liquor Control Board—remained in government hands. The role of Ontario Hydro was radically altered, paving the way for private competition in the energy market and, just prior to the election, the government sold, for a mere $3.2 billion, the rights to 99 years of tolls on Highway 407. It could not be doubted that the CSR had profoundly altered and deeply divided the Ontario political landscape.

CONTINUING THE REVOLUTION: THE 1999 RE-ELECTION OF THE HARRIS GOVERNMENT

The re-election of Harris on June 3, 1999 cemented the radical reforms of the 1995-99 PC government and ensured that Ontario would continue down the neo-liberal policy path that the first administration had blazed. In a reduced legislature, the Tories won 59 of 103 seats with 45.7 per cent of the vote. The Liberals gained a few seats to 35 and 38 per cent of the vote, while the NDP crashed to 13 per cent of the vote and 9 seats, 3 below the minimum for official party status in the legislature. As in 1995, the Tory campaign was a well-executed, generously funded and probably the most undemocratic electoral campaign that postwar Ontario had witnessed. The Tories went into the campaign with at least a three-to-one edge in fund-raising over the other two parties, and they probably spent all of the greatly increased central party spending limit of $4.2 million.[45] This spending was over and above the tens of millions of public monies spent on government advertising in the months prior to the election. Moreover, the Harris government changed the election financing rules and the elections act to their own advantage and fundamentally changed the nature of election campaigns in Ontario: they reduced the number of seats in the legislature and increased the size of ridings; they shortened the election period from about 40 days to just 28 days; they drastically increased the limits on contributions to the parties and increased the spending limits. In a shortened campaign, television advertising becomes an even more important way of communicating with voters. With almost two weeks less to campaign, there is less time to organize volunteers and do door-to-door canvasses in ridings that have increased in size by almost 35 per cent. This meant that less-well funded parties that rely on non-monetary forms of political mobilization, such as volunteers, are at a disadvantage, and parties with money, like the Tories, can purchase enough television spots to "out-advertise" the other parties by a wide margin.

The other remarkable feature of the election campaign was the extent of third-party or advocacy advertising. It is difficult to get precise figures on what groups spent on advertising campaigns for and against the Harris government, but the figure was probably between 5 and 10 million dollars. That is far more than advocacy groups admitted to spending in the 1988 federal Free Trade election, which featured a similar rash of non-party advertising. Teachers' and nurses' unions and the Canadian Autoworkers ran anti-Harris television ads or produced videos that were widely distributed. Two pro-Harris groups were equally involved: Ontarians for Responsible Government, an off-shoot of the National Citizens Coalition, ran radio ads targeting 14 Liberal candidates, while the Coalition for a Better Ontario, backed by a number of wealthy Tory party supporters, ran television ads and placed ads in major newspapers. Here, too, business resources outweighed the funds of community and union groups. All democratic theory links procedural and substantive democracy to just rules and equal capacity to forward ideas and organize. On both these grounds the Ontario election failed miserably: democracy in Ontario now sings with a distinctly upper-class voice.

The heavily skewed electoral funding solidly outflanked all other electoral strategies. A coalition of unions, as well as a number of separate unions, citizen groups, and even the *Toronto Star*, recommended strategic voting to defeat the Harris Tories. Several lists of candidates, a mixture of NDP and Liberal, were proposed as the strongest alternative to defeat the Tory candidates. Strategic voting worked to defeat some prominent cabinet ministers, yet there was no cooperation between the campaigns of the Liberals or the NDP, as each sought out its own advantage. The NDP nosedive in the last days of the campaign probably reflected this swing to defeat Harris at all costs, since the NDP and its leader Howard Hampton were generally thought to have run a strong campaign. Seventy-five of the party's candidates failed to get even 15 per cent of the vote, costing the party hundreds of thousands of dollars in lost public funding. The marriage between unions and the NDP that had been shaky ever since the Rae government's Social Contract, and the shift to the right of social democracy, edged even closer to a separation if not yet an outright divorce.

The 1999 Harris campaign document, *Blueprint*, was less revolutionary in its rhetoric than the CSR of 1995, but just as clear in its direction. It again called for more personal income tax cuts and residential property tax cuts as its central plank. It also promised to cut the small business tax rate, to establish an independent tax system, and enact a law making any tax increases subject to referenda. It also continued the populist message of division and coercion so apparent in the CSR and repeated in *Blueprint*'s proposals that welfare recipients be subjected to drug testing and that the work-for-welfare program be expanded. The *Blueprint* also promised more standardized testing and extending the testing regime to students and teachers alike. The government's goals on continued privatization, after the sale of Highway 407 and the parts of Ontario Hydro, remain unclear, but rumours about privatization of the Liquor Control Board, parts of the prison system, as well as TVO continue to circulate. But to offset criticism, the *Blueprint* suggested increased health care and education funding (both areas where the government was thought to be vulnerable), and a giant public works fund, although none of these measures restored real levels of expenditure prior to the previous cuts. Quite clearly, the government's intention is to consolidate and build upon the theme of liberal reforms and to continue to exploit deepening regional and class divisions in Ontario.

There is still strong support for the government's aggressive attack on those segments of society that had previously been supported by the welfare state: single mothers, the unemployed, those on welfare, the mentally ill, the unskilled, and, to a greater extent, those in unions and public servants more generally. And even more widely, Harris is judged to be undertaking the necessary re-positioning of a weakened Ontario economy toward development based on flexible accumulation in an internationalizing North American market. The long-term instability and problems of Ontario capitalism make it a closed question that societal polarizations within Ontario will continue.

CONCLUSIONS: DIVIDED PROVINCE, GROWING PROTESTS

There are two key aspects, we have argued, to analyzing contemporary Ontario politics: a longer-term weakness in the capacity of the Ontario economy to provide high employment and rising incomes for an increasing portion of its population, and new—and probably growing—strains within the political system. The first feature is often masked by the continued relative economic strength of Ontario within Canada and, to a degree at least for southern Ontario, intensified economic integration with the U.S. over the last decade through financial and trade flows. The prominent financial and entertainment sectors dominating the core city centre of Toronto and the booming auto sector rimming the southern Great Lakes are its powerful symbols. These often-cited indices of a new dynamic "region-state" of Ontario, however, do not compensate for the growing polarizations between the regions and social classes of Ontario.

The persistent trends of economic dislocation provide some much-needed perspective on a certain conception of Ontario that has become fashionable amongst the business and academic elites of the province. There is all too much hubris in Thomas Courchene's recent claims that Ontario is now evolving into its natural historic niche as a region-state of North America through fiscal restraint and off-loading of social programs to municipalities to create "untraded interdependencies and positive locational externalities," and that Ontario's problems primarily lie in overcoming the late 1980s "high-tax, high-debt, and high-transfer economy." The Harris government's neo-liberal CSR is simply, in Courchene's view, a necessary re-positioning of Ontario in response to the inevitable, irreversible, and completely just processes of competitiveness and globalization: "Queen's Park has been transformed ... to a pro-active, competitive-driven, coordinator and innovator designed to privilege the province and its citizens in the new global order."[46] This diagnosis at least is really a case of political assertion masquerading as social analysis. The problems that Ontario faces have much earlier origins than the 1980s, and they have hardly been unique in kind from the difficulties facing other jurisdictions in Canada and the U.S. Moreover, the case is becoming unassailable that the neo-liberal prescriptions of government restraint and economic internationalization, which after all have been the general policy direction of Canada and Ontario for well over a decade now, have not resolved underlying economic problems and have been directly adding to social inequalities. The lost decade of the 1990s in Ontario for employment and incomes is only now being eased by the force of the export boom to the U.S. But the boom may be coming to an end. Whether the neo-liberal changes wrought by the CSR will be reversed in the short term is moot; that a growing portion of Ontario's waged classes will suffer increased hardship and further anti-democratic restraints from neo-liberal policies, unless they are reversed in the long term, is not.

The Fordist pattern of accumulation that produced stable "one-province" Toryism over the postwar period has given way to the competitive austerity of low wages and government cuts of flexible accumulation. The economic dislocation no doubt explains the quite remarkable break from Ontario having one of the most stable political regimes in Canada to one of the most volatile in alternating governing parties. This volatility, too, is often masked by the three parties that have dominated postwar Ontario remaining intact although clearly realigned in terms of policy agendas. Much of the opposition political rhetoric over the electoral period nostalgically called for the old "one-province," with the Liberals being rewarded with a dominant standing in opinion polls. Indeed, Opposition leader Dalton McGuinty's policy statements were noteworthy mainly for what will be restored—pre-kindergarten classes, health-care cuts, central funding of welfare, and so on. But contradictorily, the Liberal policies were as fiscally conservative as those that the government offered. The NDP's campaign was more credible, if just as nostalgic in calling for the restoration of government services and directly linking them to reversing the Harris tax cut (an honesty all too rare in Ontario public discourse these days).

The re-election of the Harris neo-liberal regime with its clearly divisive "two-provinces, two-societies" strategy seems to return a basic stability to Ontario politics. However, this would be a seriously misleading register of the political conjuncture: the political spectrum has clearly shifted to the Right, and all three Ontario parties have adopted neo-liberal policies and austerity over the course of their government mandate.[47] The real chasm and source of strain to the Ontario political system has come from outside the political parties for some time. It is seen in the unprecedented size and diversity of extra-parliamentary mobilizations that have spread across the province in the 1990s: from Days of Action in Thunder Bay and Hamilton and other cities, to wildcat strikes by hospital and auto workers, to gay liberation marches through the streets of Sudbury, to student occupations of the Bay Street banks, to general strikes and political actions by teachers and parents. Who would have ever thought that Ontario—the staid political home of Frost and Davis—would be the foremost place in North America leading the battle against neo-liberalism, fitting comfortably alongside the protests in Paris, Athens, and Chiapas? The Days of Action, work stoppages, have ended—but the protests and unrest continue in other forms across the province.

Yet as impressive as these political protests have been, as both potent politically transformative events and as the real opposition to the anti-democratic and anti-egalitarian policies of neo-liberalism, there is still a sharp division to be accounted for. The Ontario Federation of Labour, as the dispute over strategic voting vividly illustrated, has been split in how opposition to the Tories should proceed (although there is also some parallel division among community groups). On the one side, the so-called "Pink Paper Group" of private-sector unions, largely centred around the United Steelworkers, favoured unquestioned political support of the NDP and a return to the "progressive competitiveness" strategy of "one-province, social-partnership" Ontario.[48] The obstacle here, and it is as obvious today as it was during the NDP's term in office, is that as long as capital is allowed the present degree of internationalization and mobility, nowhere has the political ground proven fertile to strike a "partnership" with the capitalist classes, either on a national or regional basis, that would prevent the processes of competitive austerity from taking hold.[49] For all the discussion of the Third Way by Tony Blair's British Labour government, to cite the example that is increasingly influential in the NDP nationally and in Ontario, it has proven quite accommodating to the policy legacy of Thatcherism.

On the other side, the Canadian Auto Workers and public sector unions like CUPE, the so-called "Alliance," along with significant community coalitions like the Metro Toronto Network for Social Justice, have questioned whether the NDP would provide any serious alternative to the "class struggle from above" being waged by the capitalist classes and government elites (and thus voting for the NDP was strategically secondary to defeating the Tories). Moreover, the economic strategy centred on competitiveness and social partnerships that this alternative presumes is likely, in this view, to sharpen social divisions and the instabilities of globalization. The political challenges of the day can only be met by "class struggle from below" that builds new solidarities and institutions, and that brings a distinct class interest into social bargaining. As a recent CAW convention put it:

> We've had two decades of the corporate revolution. They've had the chance to implement key pieces of their agenda, promising each time that this particular piece will do the trick.... At the end of all this we can assert, loudly and with justifiable anger, that the solutions of our economic elite have failed us miserably, though their own privileges remain solidly intact. It's time to hold them accountable for the mess we're in, and challenge their leadership role in our economy and society.... At all times resistance represents a crucial step in keeping certain ideas alive and creating the possibility of building more developed strategies in the future.[50]

In Ontario, this is also a direct political challenge to the "finance capital" power bloc that dominates Canada.[51] Its success will depend equally upon political developments across Canada, and internationally, as socialist movements find new ways to struggle together in support of political and economic strategies that would allow social development outside the withering competitive uniformity of globalization and neo-liberalism. Any move toward a more egalitarian participatory democracy in Ontario, or indeed just the reversal of existing trends of social polarization and political authoritarianism, will likely emerge out of the imagination, boldness, and political consolidation of this movement for an alternative social and economic order.

NOTES

1 See D. McCalla, *Planting the Province: The Economic History of Upper Canada, 1784-1870* (Toronto: University of Toronto Press, 1993); I. Drummond, *Progress without Planning: The Economic History of Ontario from Confederation to the Second World War* (Toronto: University of Toronto Press, 1987); and G. Kealey, *Toronto Workers Respond to Industrial Capitalism, 1867-1892* (Toronto: University of Toronto Press, 1980).

2 This section draws upon K. Rea, *The Prosperous Years: The Economic History of Ontario, 1939-75* (Toronto: University of Toronto Press, 1985), Chs. 5 and 11; and D. Richmond, *The Economic Transformation of Ontario, 1945-1973* (Toronto: Ontario Economic Council, 1974).

3 Rea, *Prosperous Years*, Ch. 2.

4 Rea, *Prosperous Years*, 219.

5 R. Finbow, "The State Agenda in Quebec and Ontario, 1960-1980," *Journal of Canadian Studies* 18:1 (1983); and M. Jenkin, *The Challenge of Diversity: Industrial Policy in the Canadian Federation* (Ottawa: Science Council of Canada, 1983).

6 M. Gunderson, "Alternative Mechanisms for Dealing with Permanent Layoffs, Dismissals and Plant Closings," *Adapting to Change: Labour Market Adjustment in Canada*, ed. C. Riddell (Toronto: University of Toronto Press, 1986), 116.

7 M. Gertler, "Groping Towards Reflexivity: Responding to Industrial Change in Ontario," *The Rise of the Rustbelt* ed. P. Cooke (London: UCL Press, 1995), 105; and A. Diem, "Ontario and the World Region," in *Ontario: Geographical Perspectives on Economy and Environment* ed. B. Mitchell (Waterloo: University of Waterloo, 1991).

8 T. Courchene with C. Telmer, *From Heartland to North American Region State: The Social, Fiscal and Federal Evolution of Ontario* (Toronto: University of Toronto, Faculty of Management, 1998), 34.

9 Government of Ontario, *Ontario Economic Outlook 1993* (Toronto: Ministry of Finance, 1993), 70.

10 Government of Ontario, *Ontario Economic Outlook 1994-1998* (Toronto: Ministry of Finance, 1994).

11 This section draws on the OFL, *The Ontario Alternate Budget Papers* (Toronto: Lorimer, 1997), and the 1999 and 2000 Alternate Budget Papers, a provincial-level counterpart to the Alternate Federal Budget project.

12 There are many dimensions to the social polarization within Toronto as it interacts with ethnic composition. See R. Murdie, "Economic Restructuring and Social Polarization in Toronto," *Social Polarization in Post-Industrial Metropolises*, J. O'Loughlan and J. Friedrichs, eds. (Berlin: De Gruyter, 1996).

13 See M. Gertler, *Toronto: The State of the Regional Economy* (Toronto: Working Papers of the Waterfront Resource Centre, N. 6, 1991); and J. Britton, "A Regional Industrial Perspective on Canada under Free Trade," *International Journal of Urban and Regional Research* 17:4 (1993): 564-65.

14 CCSD, *Public Sector Downsizing: The Impact on Job Quality in Canada* (Ottawa: CCSD, 1997). This general deterioration can be seen from a slightly different and broader angle in the decline in the quality of life index for Ontario from 1990 to 1997: Ontario Social Development Council, *Quality of Life Index for Ontario* (Toronto: OSCD, 1997).

15 Government of Ontario, *Ontario Budget 1991* (Toronto: Treasurer of Ontario, 1991), 97; P. Dungan, "Ontario's Economic Outlook," *Revolution at Queen's Park*, ed. S. Noel (Toronto: Lorimer, 1997), 130; and *Alternate Budget Papers*, 60-61. The horrific $9-an-hour cut in what were already modest wages by meatpackers at Maple Leaf Foods at Burlington, agreed to by the UFCW after a bitter strike in March 1998, is an example of the wage deflation affecting "old" Ontario industries, while the "new" Ontario has seen record and obscene salaries on Bay Street. See "Maple Leaf Strikers Vote for Contract," *Globe and Mail*, 7 March 1998.

16 A. Moscovitch, "Social Assistance in the New Ontario," *Open for Business, Closed to People: Mike Harris's Ontario* D. Ralph, A. Regimbaud and N. St-Amand, eds. (Halifax: Fernwood, 1997); and Government of Canada, A New Framework for Economic Policy (Ottawa: Department of Finance, 1994).

17 Courchene, *From Heartland*, 85.

18 D. Leadbeater, *Increased Transfer Dependency in the Elliot Lake and North Shore Communities* (Sudbury: Laurentian University, INORD, Elliot Lake Tracking and Adjustment Study, 1997).

19 Ontario Social Safety Network, *Ontario's Welfare Rate Cuts: An Anniversary Report* (Toronto: OSSN, 1996); and United Way of Greater Toronto, *Toronto at a Turning Point* (Toronto: United Way, 1999).

20 See "Ontario's Economic Future is the Sum of its Auto Parts," *Globe and Mail*, 2 March 1996; and Greater Toronto Area Task Force, Greater Toronto (Toronto: Queen's Printer, 1996), 54-56. It should be noted that the auto sector is also vulnerable from world overcapacity, especially as the Asian crisis has undercut the market for producers there, such as Korea.

21 Drache finds (before the Harris cuts) that corporate income tax rates in Ontario at 35.3 per cent but averaging 40 per cent in bordering U.S. states, and similar results for payroll taxes. See *Governance and Public Policy in a Global Economy*, 53.

22 *Alternate Budget Papers*, 23-25; and R. Drummond, "Ontario Revenue Budgets, 1960-1980," *Journal of Canadian Studies* 18:1 (1983).

23 G. Hale, "Changing Patterns of Party Support in Ontario," *Revolution at Queen's Park*, ed. Noel, 111.

24 Manthorpe, *The Power and the Tories*, 133.

25 S. Noel, "The Ontario Political Culture: An Interpretation," *The Government and Politics of Ontario*, 5th ed., G. White, ed. (Toronto: University of Toronto Press, 1997), 62.

26 R. Speirs, *Out of the Blue: The Fall of the Tory Dynasty in Ontario* (Toronto: Macmillan, 1986), 9-10.

27 Speirs, *Out of the Blue*, 22-23.

28 G. Gagnon. and D. Rath, *Not Without Cause: David Peterson's Fall from Grace* (Toronto: Harper Collins, 1991), 21-22.

29 R. Dyck, *Provincial Politics in Canada*, 2nd ed. (Toronto: Prentice Hall, 1991), 328.

30 Courchene, *From Heartland*, 116-19.

31 The Liberal view is best seen in the study from its second term: Premier's Council Report, *People and Skills in the New Global Economy* (Toronto: Queen's Printer, 1990). There were other significant reports on training and on the community college system as part of an effort to forge a new competitiveness strategy for Ontario industry. The NDP would also take this up.

32 Gagnon and Rath, *Not Without Cause*, 59-73.

33 Gagnon and Rath, *Not Without Cause*, 73.

34 See the list of Liberal Government tax increases in Courchene, *From Heartland*, 92-94.

35 Courchene, *From Heartland*, 78.

36 Courchene, *From Heartland*, 4.

37 A complete list of the promises can be found in G. Ehring and W. Roberts, *Giving Away a Miracle: Lost Dreams and Broken Promises and the Ontario NDP* (Oakville: Mosaic Press, 1993), 277-79. Also see the discussion in J. Jenson and R. Mahon, "From 'Premier Bob' to 'Rae Days': The Impasse of Ontario New Democrats," *La Social-Démocratie en cette Fin de Siècle* J. Beaud and J. Prevost, eds. (Sainte-Foy: Presses de l'Université du Québec, 1996).

38 C. Rachlis and D. Wolfe, "An Insiders' View of the NDP Government of Ontario," *Government and Politics of Ontario*, White, ed., 336; see also N. Bradford "Prospects for Associative Governance: Lessons from Ontario," *Politics and Society* 26: 4 (1998).

39 The process of creating the CSR is described in Ibbitson, *Promised Land*, 43-74.

40 Progressive Conservative Party of Ontario, *Make Your Common Sense Count* (Toronto: Party Pamphlet, undated).

41 A good example is *A Blueprint for Learning in Ontario* (Toronto: Ontario Progressive Conservative Caucus, 1992).

42 For a fuller comparison of the Harris- and Thatcher-led revolutions see P. Browne, "Déjà Vu: Thatcherism in Ontario," *Open for Business*, Ralph, *et al.*, eds., 37-44.

43 For a more detailed account of the campaign and media advertising see R. MacDermid, "TV Advertising Campaigns in the 1995 Ontario Election," *Revolution at Queen's Park*, Noel, ed., 74-106; and R. Drummond and R. MacDermid, "Elections and Campaigning: They Blew our Doors off with the Buy," *The Government and Politics of Ontario*, White, ed., 189-215.

44 For a fuller description of the Harris policies see *Open for Business*, Ralph, *et al.*, eds.

45 Robert MacDermid, Funding the Common Sense Revolutionaries: Contributions to the Progressive Conservative Party of Ontario, 1995-97 (Toronto: Centre for Social Justice, 1999).

46 Courchene, *From Heartland*, 284, 197, and 213. In comparison see D. Cameron, "Post-Modern Ontario and the Laurentian Theses," *Canada: The State of the Federation 1994* D. Brown and J. Hebert, eds. (Kingston: Queen's Institute of Intergovernmental Relations, 1994).

47 In this regard, the political divisions on the left over strategic voting to defeat the Tories seem badly misplaced, as the political repositioning of social democracy in general needs to be accounted for over and above specific electoral allegiances.

48 The most powerful statement of this position has been the election of an NDP backroom link to the labour movement, Wayne Samuelson, as new head of the OFL. For the basis for this view see D. Drache, ed., *Getting on Track: Social Democratic Strategies for Ontario* (Montreal: McGill-Queen's University Press, 1992).

49 For an analysis of these strategies see G. Albo, "A World Market of Opportunities? Capitalist Obstacles and Left Economic Policy," *Socialist Register 1997: Ruthless Criticism of All that Exists* L. Panitch, ed. (London: Merlin, 1997).

50 CAW, *False Solutions, Growing Protests: Recapturing the Agenda* (Toronto: CAW Convention, 1996), 8, 11, and 23; CAW, *Working Class Politics in the 21st Century* (Toronto: CAW, 2000).

51 W. Carroll, "Neoliberalism and the Re-composition of Finance Capital in Canada," *Capital and Class* 38 (1989).

8 MANITOBA

Paradigm and Shift: A Sketch of Manitoba Politics[1]

ALEX NETHERTON

PARADIGM, CHANGE, AND CHOICE

How do we define the role of the state and then imagine the process of change?[2] For some change occurs every time a new political party takes power—such as when Premier Gary Doer's recent electoral victory returned the NDP to power after 11 years in opposition. Yet not every electoral turnover can bring significant change. For others, such change is limited because effective power is concentrated in the hands of a few key élites and institutions. For others, politics is about the mediation of the structured inequality of class relations, and change, therefore, stems primarily from social structure and the effects of class struggle on political power. Yet not all politics and policies can be reduced to class relations, and the class nature of politics, while important and insightful, may not tell us what we want to know.[3]

If one holds that states or governments have to strategize, analyse, and make difficult and complex decisions for which they need political support, then it is worthwhile to consider state intervention as a paradigm and then to think of change as a paradigm shift. Building from the work of Peter A. Hall, we can define a paradigm as the dominant sets of ideas that govern state intervention.[4] A paradigm defines the most important problems to be addressed by the state and identifies a set of preferred policies to solve them. Over time, governments institutionalize paradigms through state structures. The longer those institutions are working and in place, the more the political regime, paradigm and administration become intermeshed. Thus, a paradigm can establish the parameters of political debate, and have lasting legacies.[5] They are "path dependent" in that a decision taken at one point of time can structure later alternatives. At root, they link what the state does with real world events and highlight the proactive, strategizing, and "social learning" role of states in the political economy. Envisaged this way, this chapter reduces the question of change in Manitoba politics over the past 150 years to five distinct paradigms sketched out in the table below.

Why does paradigm shift occur? Ostensibly, paradigms develop anomalies—problems that can not be managed or resolved within the confines of the paradigm. New problem issues arise which make older thinking redundant. Also, newer ideas can surface that broaden or change political objectives. Such ideas, like many innovations, are then "sold" to the public. Given the entrenched position of regimes, change becomes a difficult task. Paradigms, after all, are not consumer items purchased online or at the mart. Nor are they simply bureaucratic or academic constructions. Rather, they are constructed and implemented over time by intellectual, administrative and political processes and rest on solid bases of social support.[6] Governments can substantially differ in the way that they implement a common paradigm. Securing support from a coalition of some, but not all, key socio-political actors is essential to implementing a paradigm. For the most part, according to Peter Gourevitch, these coalitions are constant over time, but small shifts can have large significance—just as a small shift in the earth's tectonic plates along well-known fault lines can produce a major earthquake.[7]

How does paradigm shift occur? Anomalies lead to a fragmentation of authority and the articulation of a wider range of possible alternatives. These ideas are picked up by parties and key socio-economic actors. Major shifts take place as these players contest political power, and thus the process of change involves a discursive struggle conditioned by the major cleavages and conventions of political life.[8] This is not always a clinically or conceptually tidy electoral process; outcomes are uncertain and there is no guarantee that political leadership can successfully institutionalize a new paradigm. As popular media likes to emphasize, one of the most difficult tasks of all is for a politician to keep a promise.

If paradigm shifts are linked to contests for political power, then they are also closely related to the major political cleavages that have shaped any polity's development. In the case of the province of Manitoba, there are five interrelated cleavages: the relationships of Manitoba to the broader Canadian and international political economies; the profound cultural conflicts between First Nations, French, "multicultural," and "mainstream" society; the endurance of a set of political class conflicts; the urban-rural tensions, primarily between Winnipeg and the rest of the province; and the uneven development between the relatively prosperous southern and central wheat-growing area, a less prosperous Interlake, and a large North.

The analysis of paradigms and paradigm shifts allows us to understand what sets of ideas have animated state intervention and helped manage the province's primary cleavages, the reasons for periodic and abrupt changes which have occurred in the role of the state, and the extent to which Manitoba's development is dependent on decisions taken at various points in the province's past.

FORMATIVE CONTESTS: MANITOBA AND THE NATIONAL POLICY

It is curious to think that a place with "Friendly Manitoba" stamped on every licence place was born of rebellion, mass migration, and class revolts. Why? Manitoba became the stage upon which domestic and external forces contested the shape of the development of the Prairies within Confederation. Canada's National Policy, what political economist Vernon Fowke refers to as a mixture of constitutional development, immigration, land settlement and economic policies, was oriented after 1867 towards developing an integrated east-west transcontinental economy based upon the export of prairie wheat.[9] Present-day Manitoba was a part of "Rupert's Land," the territory literally sold to Canada by the Hudson's Bay Company.

When Canada bought "Rupert's Land," the Indian and Métis peoples, whose livelihoods were tied to land and furs, apparently came with the package. But these were not voiceless, subservient peoples. Certainly the political regime under merchant capitalism was marked by the paternalistic authority of the company, but this paternalism was not fully accepted by Indian and Métis. They had struggled to fundamentally change their governance regime and, by mid-century, had achieved some success. The Métis, in particular, became the dominant force in the territory and considered themselves to be a "new nation." Gerald Friesen states that the Métis were granted representation on the Council of the Assiniboia, the governance structure of the Hudson's Bay Company, and laws were published in English and French.[10] The Métis, however, had no such recognition or voice in the circle of power in the Dominion. They were not consulted about the sale of their lands, nor did they figure largely in plans for the wheat economy. In this sense, the National Policy, broadly defined as the complex of policies that focussed on the West, threatened their very existence.

The Métis Province

In what has to be recognized as a brilliant strategic defence, Louis Riel, leader of the Métis, seized the moment to proclaim a provisional government. Riel then bargained for entry into Confederation as a province, and was successful, not because the Canadian Government supported the idea of a Métis province, but largely because the Métis had allies in French Canada and their military power and organization was superior to all else

TABLE 8.1 **A SKETCH OF SUCCESSIVE PARADIGMS**

PARADIGM/GEOPOLITICAL DEFINITION	SUBSTANTIVE CHARACTERISTICS
MERCHANT CAPITALISM AND THE FUR TRADE, 1850-69 *(Rupert's Land tied to Imperial Markets)*	» Autonomous native/"half breed" settlement under the paternalistic authority of the Hudson's Bay Company » Export fur trade, subsistence agriculture (Selkirk), and the buffalo hunt » Emergence of Métis provisional government led by Louis Riel and the negotiation of terms of entry into Confederation
NATIONAL POLICY, 1870-1922 *(Manitoba and the international wheat boom)* *Rapid economic development through railway building, immigration and homesteading, and expansive wheat export, regional manufacturing service and wholesale trade.*	» Province is subservient to and part of Dominion National Policy » Development of intensely partisan, autonomous provincial political parties and attempts to manage heightened class conflict such as the Winnipeg General Strike and the Farmers' revolt. » Marginalization of Métis and aboriginal peoples. » Prairie resettlement and rise of Winnipeg as a sub-metropolitan centre redefines political economy.
NEOCLASSICAL RENTIER REDISTRIBUTIVE, 1922-58 *(Manitoba as a "Prairie Province")* *(contraction of the wheat economy and limited expansion of new industrial staples in northern Manitoba)*	» Manitoba politics redefined by Liberal-Progressive image of state and society » Rural/urban (the city vs. the province) cleavages dominate provincial political life while class-based cleavages dominate Winnipeg politics » Redefinition of provincial politics through conventions "non-partisanship" and limited "business-like" government » 1920s—Province successfully bargains with external resource capital to facilitate economic linkages to Winnipeg and redistribution to rural Manitoba » 1930-45—Preoccupied by staggering debt, province looks to changes in constitution and federalism to solve economic and fiscal problems

	» 1945-58—Conventions of limited government and non-partisan anti-CCF "coalition" governments stifle economic and political development
KEYNESIAN MODERNIZATION, 1958-88 *(Manitoba and the New West)* *(promoted continental resource and hydro industrialisation but did not develop long-term and sustainable industrial growth)*	» Provincial state becomes catalyst to modernize infrastructure, induce economic development, and implement welfare state » Capacity of provincial state is conditioned by fiscal federalism, national leadership, and levels of economic growth » Re-emergence of intense partisanship and multi-party system dominated by the NDP and conservative parties » Political discourse is dominated by competition between alternative versions of Keynesian modernization and then between neo-conservatism and NDP Keynesianism » Keynesianism discredited by changes in trade, fiscal, and economic conditions » Hydro strategy discredited by financial failure and significant unresolved social and environmental impacts affecting aboriginal peoples
GLOBALIZATION/NEO-LIBERALISM, 1988- *(Manitoba as part of the mid-continent region of NAFTA)* *Conservatives restructure state and engineer a competitive repositioning of Manitoba economy within the mid-continent*	» Province becomes agent to impose greater market and fiscal discipline upon society, politics, and the economy through privatization, deregulation, and fiscal restraint » Province's policy thrust is clearly pushed by national trade and fiscal policies as well as older Manitoba political conventions » Period begins with three-party system (rise of Liberals) but then returns to competition between Conservatives and NDP » Conservatives embed neo-liberal conventions in all major policy areas—yet fail to fully legitimise paradigm due to its social cost and opposition, political scandal, and policy contradiction » NDP given opportunity of re-establishing social democratic image of society within neo-liberal constraints

on the plains.[11] The new province, called Manitoba, took the form of a small postage stamp encompassing the territory stretching from the American border to the area surrounding Fort Garry (present-day Winnipeg). The new constitution borrowed from the innovations developed in Canada's 1841 Constitution by providing that English and French had equal legislative representation and that the courts and legislature were to function in both languages.

Métis efforts to breath life into these new structures, however, failed. First, the Manitoba Métis were without effective leadership. Riel made enemies, particularly when his government summarily executed an Ontario Orangeman (an anti-Catholic Protestant) for insurrection. For this, the leader was charged with treason, popularly demonized in Protestant Ontario, and (though elected to Parliament) banished from the Queen's Dominions. The original boundaries of Manitoba enclosed but a fraction of the Northwest Territories, and the Métis, willingly or unwillingly, began to disperse, leaving the tiny province. The vast majority went further west, finally settling in present-day Saskatchewan. There a second Métis rebellion failed to gain the support of First Nations and was met by more capable Canadian military forces. The rebellion was crushed, Louis Riel was hanged for treason, and Macdonald refused to recognize the Métis identity, leaving a bitter legacy and ongoing controversy.[12]

Between "Old Ontario" and New Society

The tectonic plates of the Prairie political economy shifted ground as the National Policy took off. Ottawa maintained ownership of the majority of prairie lands, controlled all the key levers of economic and fiscal policy, immigration, and homesteading, and maintained separate jurisdiction over Indians. Political life was dominated by federal parties and marked by boosterism, partisanship, and corruption. In Manitoba, within ten years, the society based upon subsistence agriculture, furs, and the buffalo hunt had all but disappeared as 150,000 new immigrants from Ontario began to shape the new province in their own image. Within five years, another wave of immigration, primarily European, would begin that would define the architecture of Prairie re-settlement.

The Manitoban political community changed to reflect the new reality. Founded in 1873, Winnipeg arose as an aspiring metropolitan centre for the Prairie region, tied on one side as a client to British and central-Canadian financial, economic, and political interests and, on the other side to the booming pioneer wheat economy. These ambitions were cut short for a series of reasons, perhaps the most important being that Winnipeg's geopolitical status as the primary "Gateway to the West" ended when the completion of the Panama Canal in 1914 allowed Port of Vancouver, British Columbia, to emerge as the Pacific "Gateway to the West." Still, within Manitoba, economic and political power shifted to the emerging Winnipeg élite and the complex institutional structures of the transcontinental wheat economy.[13]

The Manitoba government attempted to define its autonomy within the context of the National Policy and to fashion its constitution and political conventions to new social exigencies. In a series of controversial initiatives, the Government of Manitoba dropped the bilingual provisions of its constitution in 1890, and incrementally implemented a general policy of assimilation towards the French and all the new "strangers in our midst." Indians, as well, were marginalized and then set apart from provincial society by the Dominion Government's treaty, reserve, and assimilative Indian Administration. By the time resettlement was complete, everyone, from Aboriginals to Ukrainians, met in public institutions such as schools, the judiciary, and Legislature that outlawed all languages save English. The net result was that Métis and Aboriginal interests on the Prairies were pushed aside—as was Cartier's idea of a West defined by the duality of central-Canadian society.[14]

The Winnipeg General Strike and Its Legacy

The National Policy did not produce a stable society or economy. Clearly the boosterism of Winnipeg business and political leadership foresaw limitless horizons. For the majority, however, economic conditions on the frontier, despite the label of "wheat boom," were volatile and rough. Immigrants came to create equity on land with their labour, yet also incurred debt and experienced the uncertainties of weather and international markets. Until 1914, international peace, the investment boom, and immigration kept the economic ball in the air. Then war stopped the flow of capital and people to the West and disrupted patterns of trade. The war economy brought a series of political and economic crises marked by high inflation and agricultural labour shortages. At the end of hostilities the two major pillars of the Manitoba economy, manufacturing and agriculture, sank into a depression. Winnipeg was the regional centre of the Prairie labour market—and the depression, therefore, left the City with large numbers of unemployed concentrated in the relatively impoverished "north end." At this time employers neither automatically recognized unions nor negotiated and implemented wide-ranging collective agreements without a show of force from unions. In 1919 organized labour experimented with a novel organizational form, the One Big Union (OBU), and a new political tool—the general strike—to accomplish collective bargaining objectives.

For six weeks strikers wrestled with authorities for control over Canada's third-largest city. Given the "red scare" produced by the Bolshevik Revolution, the confrontation at Winnipeg emerged as a major national political crisis, eventually crushed by a business-led "citizens' committee" with the help of the Canadian armed forces and all levels of government.

Although the General Strike was not a purposefully revolutionary struggle, its legacy cannot be isolated to immediate place and time.[15] For one, the strike and its political legacy weakened the power of the city, particularly its business and financial interests. Second, the strike brought class-based political discourse to the forefront of Winnipeg politics, transforming civic discourse for the next three decades into an ideological struggle between agents of business and labour. Third, the strike helped drive a wedge between farmers and labour in provincial politics. The majority of farmers did not demonstrate support for the General Strike, and as a result an enduring political gulf developed between urban working-class and rural farmers' politics.[16] This would translate into the exclusion of labour interests from the provincial affairs when the United Farmers of Manitoba took power.

The Farmers' Revolt

Manitoba politics was profoundly marked by this urban/rural cleavage. Winnipeg, "the city," had the wealth, power, and prestige of a regional metropolitan centre. Its institutions and leadership guarded their wealth and autonomy while rural Manitoba, "the province," was left the rest. Most of "the province," however, was composed of farmers and small communities that centred on the wheat economy. By the second decade of the century Canadian farmers had developed a broad moral critique of the political system and unregulated capitalist development, a critique that would take them to Parliament as Progressives during the 1920s.[17] The largest farmers' organization, the United Farmers of Manitoba (UFM), then decided to enter into provincial politics to have the policies of the provincial government meet the needs of agriculture.[18] The decision of the UFM to participate in political life was also based upon the assumption that the existing parties and politicians were unable to represent the interests of agriculture or indeed the interests of society generally. The farmers were to usher in a period of progressive reform.

Electoral considerations led farm leaders to quickly realize that they would need a political alliance with Winnipeg in order to take power. The UFM was close to the Liberals and sought out the support of business in an alliance that promised to give Manitobans a new form of government. It would be strictly provincial in its orientation and would be "business-like" in its approach to decision making and public accounts. Sound administration would replace the corrupt patronage system and "group government" would allegedly replace the partisan distortion of legislative affairs.[19] The UFM won the 1922 election, and under different names—"United Farmers," "Progressives," and then "Liberal-Progressives"—this group held power until 1958.

THE LIBERAL-PROGRESSIVE IMAGE OF STATE AND SOCIETY

The Liberal-Progressives were able to institutionalize the first "made in Manitoba" conventions of governance, initially termed "Brackenism" after John Bracken, the leading agricultural economist who became Manitoba's long-serving premier (1922-42). These conventions, and the paradigm of state intervention which they represented, were responses to turbulence in the international political economy and continued to be so through the Depression and World War II. The paradigm can be termed neoclassical rentier-redistributive. It was neoclassical in that it respected the primacy of markets and the importance of fiscal orthodoxy—balancing the books. Stated another way, both farmers and business could agree on a very limited government.

Business and farmers saw Manitoba's economic development in terms of an expanded capitalist development of agriculture, manufacturing, and the new resource staples from the Canadian shield (minerals, timber, pulp and paper, and hydro). Their faith in markets implied a rejection of the doctrines of public ownership and planning found in other agrarian populist movements and in labour circles, but they did not embrace a laissez-faire view of market society. Liberal-Progressives were ideologically critical of monopoly power and supported state intervention that would offset or control concentrated market power.[20] Practically speaking, however, they were bent on creating industrial development by inducing external capital to open up the north and invest in new industrial staples. Governments promoted public resources and investment possibilities then negotiated with interested capital the terms of private resource entitlements and the public returns to be gained from them, hence the rentier-redistributive elements of the paradigm.[21]

By the 1930 transfer of resources, these policies proved highly successful. The UFM cleaned up public finances and moved the tax burden from land to income, meaning that Winnipeg and industrial Manitoba emerged as the central sources of public revenues.[22] Not only did Manitoba lead the Prairies in hydro development, it also had the region's first pulp and paper complex, hard rock mines, and a railway to the Port of Churchill on

Hudson's Bay—all initiatives that set high expectations about the terms of redistribution to be had from northern resource industrialization. Some decisions were controversial. For example, although both farmers' and workers' movements advocated the public ownership of utilities, the UFM government decided, in 1928, to give a private central-Canadian-controlled utility, the Winnipeg Electric Company (WEC), a 30-year lease for one site, Seven Sisters, that contained about 50 per cent of the province's accessible hydro power. Why? WEC offered a long-term contract to supply cheap power to the Manitoba Power Commission (MPC), the rural or "provincial" utility, responsible for rural electrification.

Redefining Provincial Politics through Depression and War

The dominant paradigm encountered a great deal of stress and difficulty attempting to manage the Depression and war-related exigencies. The idea of using rents from resource industrialization for the development of the "province" was dashed when WEC and the pulp and paper sector were forced into "financial reorganization" and Winnipeg business declined with the value of agricultural economy. In response, the Manitoba government did all the "right" things according to its neoclassical thinking. Expenditures were cut and taxes increased, but the economy did not bounce back and the fiscal situation worsened.

Urban and industrial unemployment ruptured the assumptions underpinning fiscal orthodoxy. Constitutional and fiscal responsibility for poverty and unemployment was still considered a matter for local government. However, local governments were without income and incurring the burden of providing relief to those in need. The province then bailed out the municipalities, including Winnipeg, by borrowing from Ottawa. By 1932 the province itself was on the verge of bankruptcy and help from Prime Minister Bennett's Conservative federal government was only forthcoming on condition that the province balance its books or else surrender control of its finances to a federally appointed controller.[23] With balanced budgets, increasing "dead weight" debt and an unbearable tax burden, Manitoba was on a race to the bottom.

With seemingly important anomalies one would expect that something new was needed. Liberal-Progressives centred their analysis upon the Constitution, fiscal policy, and markets. Stuart Garson, first as minister of finance and then as premier (1942-48) steered Liberal-Progressive thinking into the direction of the reform Liberalism then prevalent in English-Canadian Liberal Party circles. *Manitoba's Case*, the multiple-volume provincial submission to the Royal Commission on Dominion-Provincial

Economic Relations (Rowell-Sirois Commission), for example, defined the 1930s crisis in terms of the unfortunate and wasteful closure of trade as well as the imbalance of fiscal capacity and jurisdiction found within the British North America Act.[24] The Liberal-Progressives argued that constitutional responsibility had to be matched by capacity. Hence there ought to be a centralization of power over social policy because only the central government had the capacity to fulfill these responsibilities. The switch from capital to the federal government as a source of redistribution coincided with the change in Manitoba's place within Confederation. The province fell from the strongest Prairie political economy to an impoverished "have-not" province—a transformation that also reflected the fall of Winnipeg business.

The first international response to the depression was trade protection—anathema to an agricultural export economy. John Bracken, as the senior Prairie first minister and an acknowledged expert agricultural economist, feared that the Prairie wheat economy could not survive without secure long-term access to international markets. Bracken did not think federal trade policy reflected agriculture's interests and was so convinced that Ottawa had to do more that in the summer of 1939, just months before the declaration of war, Bracken and his minister of finance, Stuart Garson, were in Berlin promoting barter exchange (Manitoba agricultural produce for German electrical equipment) with the Nazi political leadership.[25]

The Liberal-Progressives competed with the Conservatives as well as the newly-formed CCF and Social Credit to offer their paradigmatic solutions to the new exigencies of depression and war. Indeed, the political scene was increasingly fragmented. The Conservatives were thoroughly handicapped on the Prairies because of the federal government's harsh enforcement of the status quo. For socialists the essential problem was capitalism—and the emergence of the CCF reflected a growing belief in centralization, redistribution, state ownership and planning, and the necessity of replacing capitalism with an alternative economic system. For Social Credit, the problems were financial and related to underconsumption and, on the Prairies, to a lack of capital.

Premiers Bracken and Garson then became masters at selling "non-partisanship" as a political virtue, a strategy that brought the Liberals, Conservatives, for a brief period the CCF and, informally, Social Credit, into various coalitions oriented towards creating a united front for the Rowell-Sirois Report and the war effort.[26] Harkening to their roots in the critique of "partyism" within the farmers' movement, these non-partisan coalitions appeared to place policy commitment above partisan interest. All significant political interests had to agree on principles of governance: debt repayment and fiscal orthodoxy, neoclassical faith in markets, and a restructured and centralized redistributive federalism. What they did, in fact, was to absorb all of the fragmented political forces within the province—even briefly the CCF (1940-42)—into a large coalition.

The crucial contest came in the first post-World War II election when Garson tried to place the Liberal-Progressive coalition as an alternative between "socialism" and the "status quo." Accordingly, Garson found a way to finance a massive program of rural electrification and placed a set of mega-projects on the table that would be built as economic conditions warranted.[27] The Farm Electrification Programme, the most ambitious of its kind in the post-war period, beat off a CCF challenge and rekindled the bonds between rural Manitoba and the farmers' party. In Winnipeg, however, the Liberal-Progressives were routed by the CCF in the 1945 election, but electoral distribution under Liberal-Progressive Manitoba ensured that this was of little political consequence. Winnipeg had 36 per cent of registered voters but only 18 per cent of the seats in the Legislature. The CCF ended up in opposition, though it gained more votes than any other party!

Douglas Campbell, the last Liberal-Progressive premier, held on to older traditions of nonpartisanship, but dropped the early emphasis on promotion, rentier bargaining, and redistribution to concentrate on fiscal orthodoxy and almost laissez-faire liberalism. Yet, by the late 1950s, the whole Liberal-Progressive image of state and politics had become irrelevant and an impediment to meet the challenges of the postwar period. Manitoba was no longer overshadowed by a crushing public debt; rather, it had one of the lowest per capita debts in the country.[28] Similarly, Manitobans had moved from being oppressed by the heaviest tax burden in the country to that of shouldering fewer taxes than most provinces.[29] Ottawa had also established a public wheat board and, to secure access to international markets, had taken responsibility for relief (unemployment insurance) and other expensive programs of income redistribution. At the same time the postwar rationalization of agriculture reduced rural labour requirements and fostered a process of urbanization and out-of-province migration. The economy had declined relative to the other Prairie provinces and in relation to the national economy. As a result, the major challenge facing Manitoba was to foster sufficient economic growth to employ its own population.

Decades of non-partisanship and the habit of looking at politics as administration had not only stifled public debate and provincial political life, but they had also, according to historian W.L. Morton (whose father had been a cabinet minister in several farmers' governments) made the Liberal-Progressives an established and unaccountable political elite.[30] They simply did not face any meaningful opposition. Certainly, Winnipeg politics retained the older, intensely partisan traditions of class politics, but the 1950s cold-war climate and the electoral system effectively inoculated the province from the CCF and urban social democracy. Yet the Liberal-Progressives never regained political or popular support in Winnipeg—as was evidenced by the failure of the Campbell government to win a symbolically important referendum on the public takeover of WEC and a reorganization of transportation and utility services in the Greater Winnipeg region.[31]

KEYNESIAN MODERNIZATION: CONSERVATIVE AND SOCIAL DEMOCRATIC ALTERNATIVES

The 1958 election signalled the beginning of a "quiet revolution" in Manitoba politics because it marked the end of the political and economic conventions that had crystalized and defined Manitoba government and politics for 36 years. The new Keynesian modernization paradigm would govern Manitoba politics for another three decades. It was also defined by meaningful partisan competition and alternative governments. During the first twenty years the Progressive Conservative and New Democratic Parties offered competing visions of modernization. For the third decade the NDP's Keynesianism contested with the Conservatives' neo-conservatism.

Manitoba's modernization was closely tied to fortunate circumstances: the embedded liberalism of the new post-war international system, a western economy that provided three decades of economic growth, and Ottawa's efforts to modernize the federation's fiscal structure and orchestrate the institutionalization of a national welfare state. The importance of a central role for Ottawa should not, however, obscure the fact that the same factors also increased the administrative, fiscal, and financial capacity of the provincial state. The emerging paradigm was Keynesian in that the full weight of the provincial public power was used to foster economic growth and full employment and establish a provincial welfare state. Emphasis turned from agriculture and rural Manitoba to manufacturing and large-scale resource investment and to the social services demanded by urban life. Above all, what distinguishes this period is the new role played by the public sector in reshaping or modernizing the older Prairie society.[32]

Manitoba's Quiet Revolution: Roblin's Conservative Modernization

The tone of the general modernization program, the new script for government, and some of the new political conventions were set by the Conservative Party under Duff Roblin during the 1958-67 period. In order to start the modernization process Roblin had to exorcise the province of the ideology and conventions of the Liberal-Progressives, not an easy task considering the degree to which the former paradigm had been institutionalized.[33] The exorcism was conducted by a myriad of special planning processes and royal commissions on education, northern development, and municipal reform whose recommendations were translated into legislation and institutions.[34]

Business, for Roblin, was ultimately the key agent of modernization—and his reforms were oriented towards stimulating its development. Accordingly the Conservatives began a process in which business and government worked in a sort of partnership or process of indicative planning to map out a new role for the provincial state in economic development. The first initiative was conducted under the auspices of a Committee on Manitoba's Economic Future (COMEF). A second, more detailed policy-oriented process was conducted in a Targets for Economic Development Commission (TED). The Manitoba government invested a great deal of time and research in these planning processes, making them as important to paradigmatic thinking as previous Liberal-Progressive efforts for the Rowell-Sirois Commission.

New and powerful agencies emerged to implement the Roblin economic strategy. The Department of Industry and Commerce took a leading coordinating role.[35] The Manitoba Development Fund (MDF) became a vehicle to induce investment by new firms by offering loans and financial subsidies to expand or locate in Manitoba.[36] Though the strategy started off with a focus on small business, the Conservative economic strategy increasingly turned to providing subsidies and incentives for the promotion of resource industrialization or "mega-projects." By 1967 the Development Fund had attracted investors for a large-scale integrated forest complex, Churchill Forest Industries, at The Pas in Northern Manitoba. The Roblin government also amalgamated the two provincially owned electrical utilities, one that had been the Liberal-Progressives' instrument for rural electrification and the one that emerged from the 1950s takeover of the Winnipeg Electric Company, into one large utility, Manitoba Hydro. Manitoba Hydro then emerged as the central author of provincial energy policy and embarked on a massive river-diversion project in Northern Manitoba on the Churchill and Nelson rivers.

Roblin's modernization placed fiscal pressures on the provincial government that translated into the introduction of a new comprehensive sales tax and produced a backlash within business and party circles.[37] When Duff Roblin resigned to run for the leadership of the national Progressive Conservative Party, the party chose Walter Weir, an older rural Conservative, to become premier. The party thought that "Roblinism" was spent. Weir represented a move back to older Liberal-Progressive conventions concerning the fiscal limitations of government activities and much was made of his opposition to big government, Medicare, and welfare state initiatives.

The Conservatives were not alone in rethinking the "quiet revolution." The provincial Liberal-Progressives, renamed the "Liberal Party," after being torn between newer national influences and their older conventions, finally chose the latter.[38] Only the apparently weak and internally divided NDP remained consistent in its support of a broad-based Keynesian modernization programme.[39] In mid-1969 Walter Weir decided to take advantage of the situation by dissolving the Legislature, which had been paralysed by a conflict over hydro development, and called a surprise general election.[40]

The 1969 election polarized the fragmented political system and thus redefined Manitoba's political landscape. A new east-west fault line divided the provincial political society in two. The NDP gained its first election victory by building on its North Winnipeg base and taking the North and Interlake regions—formally Liberal-Progressive strongholds. The more prosperous south Winnipeg and agricultural south were held by the Conservatives. Premier Edward Schreyer's NDP had only the most tenuous hold on power—one that was solidified only when some urban Liberals joined the NDP caucus and cabinet.[41]

Social Democratic Continuity and Crisis Management

During the 1969-73 period Manitoba's first NDP government maintained the pace of the earlier Roblin governments, though the second term was marked by crisis management. The "social democratic" version of Keynesian modernization reflected slightly different assumptions concerning the role of government than did its Conservative predecessor.[42] Generally, where Conservatives placed emphasis on promoting economic growth, the NDP placed emphasis on steering and managing growth to meet social and regional objectives. NDP planning differed from the Conservative model of business-government collaboration by drawing more on a national network of social democrats, party notables, and academics organized around central and coordinating agencies of government.

The Schreyer government's Resource and Economic Development Secretariat, for example, authored *Guidelines for the Seventies*, a set of criteria used by central agencies to frame, coordinate, and evaluate the policy of line departments. Other Crown Corporations, such as Manitoba Hydro, operated under different policy parameters. Coordination would be difficult and it would take time to leave a social democratic stamp on Manitoban public policy.[43]

Premier Schreyer's NDP practised a mild form of social democracy—leading to two different assessments of his government. James McAllister presents the argument that it did not perform much differently than any other provincial government, an argument that implies that parties do not matter.[44] From an opposite position, Cy Gonick argues that Schreyer, unlike Duff Roblin, did not push his party far enough.[45] To the extent that all governments are subject to paradigmatic constraints, McAllister is correct. However, all governments exert choice. The Schreyer NDP government may have been comparable to other provincial regimes–but still made a much different set of decisions than Walter Weir. Similarly, Schreyer may or may not have been able to push his party further left—but any considered analysis of the government has to reflect its ideological mixture and tenuous hold on political power.

Schreyer and the Manitoba NDP rejected the left nationalist "Waffle" programme put forward by the Ontario wing of the party and with it the idea of bringing major mineral companies, such as INCO, under public ownership or of pricing the cost of electricity at a level that would draw substantial economic rents from water resources.[46] Neither was this form of radicalism really expected by the electorate. For example, the government came close to defeat in the legislature during its first year when it fulfilled an election promise to bring private automobile insurance under a public monopoly.

Many key areas of policy were path-dependent on previous decisions. Using financial incentives to attract foreign capital was a highlight of the Conservative economic strategy. Accordingly, the Conservatives authorized the MDF to award foreign interests over $100 million in loans and subsidies to establish an integrated forest complex at The Pas.[47] It turned out, however, that the principals simply took the money and ran. The swindle left the Manitoba government a partially completed forest complex which was quickly put under public ownership by the NDP. The name of the MDF was changed to become the Manitoba Development Corporation (MDC), and its new mandate was to become a public holding and investment corporation. Similarly, the NDP's hydro policy, a key modernization portfolio, was structured by an earlier decision of the Roblin Government, which had committed and partially built the infrastructure for a massive river diversion in northern Manitoba. The NDP continued with a version of the Nelson

River hydro strategy—one that they hoped would produce less social and environmental impact than the plans of the predecessors.

During the NDP's first term the Greater Winnipeg Region was completely overhauled to create one large "Unicity" and its political structures changed to include a form of urban participatory democracy. A Department of Northern Affairs was established in conjunction with a planning and policy process oriented towards northern community development. In contrast to the Weir administration, the NDP embraced Medicare and also extended the provincial welfare state and social services, reformed the tax regime to include redistributive objectives, reformed provincial labour legislation, embarked upon programmes of regional development and, as mentioned previously, brought the automobile insurance industry under public ownership.[48]

During the Schreyer government's second term of office, 1973-77, the economic assumptions underpinning the Keynesian paradigm began to unravel. The 1973 "oil crisis," stagflation, and decreasing levels of fiscal resources produced new sets of constraints upon governments and, in the Manitoba case, threatened the viability of the provincial economic strategy. The pace of reform slowed down and more attention was paid to managing the economic and political problems of existing policies. For example, there was no overall plan or strategy which informed MDC activities. Rather, given the economic turbulence, it ended up as the collector of bad debts. The NDP hydro policy was subject to massive cost overruns as well as ongoing political and environmental problems. Also, in 1977, declining federal transfers contributed to the NDP government's fiscal problems.

The NDP continued with the province's traditional approach to federalism, strongly defending Ottawa's leadership in redistribution, fiscal matters, and federal leadership in addressing the decade's new problems stemming from the "energy crisis" and inflation. The NDP also accepted the federal consensus on the new definition of Canada as a bilingual and multicultural nation as well as changes in the federation's symbolic order to reflect the new definition. The implicit assumption was that the changes only concerned the federal government and would not change the definition of Manitoba as a unilingual province. The concept of multiculturalism, however, became important to the NDP. As Thomas Peterson indicates, the NDP administration was the first in provincial history to reflect, by its cabinet and caucus, Manitoba's non-French and non-English multicultural heritage.[49] Nevertheless, intergovernmental tensions did develop when Winnipeg resented Ottawa's push to negotiate with Aboriginal peoples over the unforeseen environmental impact of the hydro mega-projects.

By the time the 1977 election was called it appeared that the Keynesian party was over. The period of high rates of economic growth and healthy government finances, the continued secular development of public social services, the use of governments to modernize and develop society, the excitement of reform, and the uniqueness of Manitoba's own "quiet revolution" were finished. New economic and fiscal conditions placed the NDP on the defensive.[50] The NDP did not propose any new paradigmatic script to address changes in circumstances; the Conservative Party under Sterling Lyon, however, had started campaigning long before the election had been called. The new Conservative leader had completely distanced the party from Roblin. Lyon promised to rid Manitoba of the "socialist" (read "Keynesian") influences and to implement his own form of neo-conservatism. His 1977 victory gave him the mandate to do so.[51]

Keynesianism Contested: Sterling Lyon's Failed Thatcher Revolution

The rise of Lyon's neo-conservatism marked the end of the period of consensus on the essentials of the paradigm of state intervention and the rise of a decade of intense political contestation between the Conservatives and NDP. Premier Lyon's neo-conservative alternative failed after one term, although it became a harbinger of things to come. Politics pivoted on paradigmatic contestation.

The neo-conservatism of the Lyon government drew upon the earlier Liberal-Progressive image of state and society. Its stated objectives were to balance the budget and to attain "economy and efficiency" in the administration of government. It was to be five years of "acute protracted restraint" of public-sector activities intended to curb the excesses of welfare state dependence and to put the private sector back in full control of provincial economic development.[52] As in previous paradigm changes, the Manitoba government attempted to define a new script for itself. The counter to the NDP *Guidelines for the 1970s* was the Lyon government's *The Report of the Task Force on the Organization and Economy of Government* and *The Report of the Commission of Inquiry into Manitoba Hydro*.[53] The exorcisms could discredit specific activities of previous governments and get the skeletons out of the closet, but they had neither the intellectual nor the analytical power to legitimize new rules of the game. They were more than anything else ideological statements and helped produce a political discourse that polarized the electorate along class lines.[54]

Surprisingly enough, economic policy proved to be the central weakness of Lyon's neo-conservatism. The basic problem facing the government was that once the public spigot had been turned off, private investment did not jump in to take its place. During 1978-80, the government's finances improved and private investment increased, but the provincial economy did not bounce back from the curtailment of public sector investment.[55] The Lyon government then focussed on a mega-project strategy, much like that of the previous Conservative governments. Throughout 1981 the government concentrated on three projects: a hydro project called Limestone, an aluminum smelter, and a potash mine.[56] The mega-projects, however, did not materialize. Indeed, the Manitoba economy was doing poorly relative to the sister Prairie provinces which were experiencing resource booms.[57] As in the late 1950s, low rates of economic growth, unemployment and population loss returned to the public agenda.[58] The recession left the Lyon government with greater fiscal and economic problems than its predecessor.

Unlike the NDP, the Lyon administration was, in many ways, in opposing ideological quarters to the last Trudeau federal government. Lyon became a part of the "group of eight" premiers opposed to Trudeau's unilateral constitutional initiative. As Nelson Wiseman indicates, as a Conservative Lyon strongly objected to the Charter of Rights and Liberties because it would limit the sovereignty of Parliament.[59] Premier Lyon ended up as the only premier outside of Quebec to object to the proposal, though he eventually bent under pressure from the federal and other provincial governments to sign the deal.

Political life in Manitoba changed significantly during the short term of the Lyon government. Lyon's legacy was to foster political polarization and to structure the party system around two poles representing paradigmatic alternatives. The December 1981 election saw the popular vote of the Conservatives drop about 5 per cent, the collapse of Liberal Party support, and an increase of nearly 10 per cent for the NDP.[60] Sterling Lyon's neo-conservative revolution failed because political polarization benefitted social democrats more than neo-conservatives, a lesson not to be forgotten by future party strategists. Nevertheless, the Conservative Party's share of the popular vote remained comparable to that of the 1960s when it formed a series of majority governments. The NDP, now headed by another moderate, Howard Pawley, won a majority government.

The Last Hurrah for Keynesian Politics: Howard Pawley and the Crisis of Social Democracy

The NDP's Keynesianism proved to be a relative economic success, yet a political failure. After gaining a narrow re-election victory in 1986, the government's two-seat legislative majority disintegrated with resignations and betrayal.[61] The government fell in 1988 and the party was routed in subsequent elections. Fundamentally, the government could not manage or resolve the anomalies of the Keynesian paradigm and, as a result, it fell to the "crisis of social democracy": where traditional NDP patterns of state intervention eroded social and political support from its own core constituencies.[62]

The paradigmatic thinking of the Pawley government represented both continuity and change from the Schreyer years. The government was not in the lineage of Roblin and Schreyer as modernizers. Rather, the party became the focal point of political opposition to the Lyon government's neo-conservatism. The party stood for the use of the state to foster economic development, to promote social justice by means of securing the welfare state, to meet the legitimate objectives of key social movements, and to ensure full employment. These objectives were rooted primarily in 1960s Keynesian-welfare-state social democracy. The problem facing the New Democrats was that the capacity of the provincial government to deliver on these objectives was diminishing while the political attacks on Keynesianism were becoming more powerful. For example, during the Lyon years the language of Keynesianism's anomalies—debt and deficit, cutbacks and restraint, inflation and stagflation—had permeated national and provincial political discourse. Indeed, the Canadian government would launch the Macdonald Commission to address the anomalies of Keynesianism at the same time that the Manitoba NDP would be implementing its last and best Keynesian programme.[63] Bucking trends, it was the Keynesians' "last hurrah."

Initially, thinking on economic strategy was highly influenced by the Saskatchewan NDP government's resource policies. This form of social democracy promised that economic growth could be achieved when governments took an entrepreneurial and redistributive role in the resource sector.[64] Instead of waiting to induce private capital to invest in mega-projects, the NDP would use Crown Corporations to make the investments themselves and thus use the state to redistribute economic rents to foster economic development, pay for the welfare state or serve as a substitute for taxation. As in the days of the Liberal-Progressives, the trick was to negotiate a deal that would secure good prices and secure access to markets for Manitoba resources.

Economic conditions made the implementation of this strategy difficult. However, by 1984, the Pawley government had negotiated a long-term export contract that provided the financial basis for the construction of the next hydro mega-project at Limestone on the Nelson River.[65] In learning lessons from the 1970s, the Pawley government purposefully linked the project to special employment and training programs for Aboriginal and Northern peoples and used its influence to negotiate industrial benefits for Winnipeg.[66] The economic climate gave the provincial government greater leverage when dealing with suppliers; as a result, the project eventually came in under cost, certainly a major accomplishment of the Pawley government.

Over the decade it also became clear that it would take a long time before rents could be redistributed from the northern Hydro strategy. The Manitoba public sector was still digesting the costs of the 1970s projects, particularly the exchange rate losses on hydro debt held by U.S. creditors. Also, in the north, there were still great uncertainty about how to mitigate and compensate those affected by the 1970s water diversion. One unexpected problem was that periodic drought weakened the utility's water and revenue potential. Rent redistribution became a distant possibility.

The Pawley government faced a choice between belt tightening in a recession or using fiscal resources in a counter-cyclical economic policy. It chose the latter, pouring money into a Jobs Fund and undertaking other initiatives to maintain employment and social services. These interventions consistently moderated and ameliorated the business cycle. Manitoba's level of economic growth surpassed the national and regional average and the levels of unemployment were lower until 1987, when mega-project construction entered its final phase. Key public investments and a more diversified economic structure enabled Manitoba to weather the recession which devastated the economies of its sister provinces. These successes helped the NDP win the 1986 election, albeit with a majority of only two seats.

Given these successes, why and how did the NDP fall into a "crisis of social democracy"? The purposefully counter-cyclical economic policy had exacted high financial and political costs. Confidence in the government's ability to manage the economy was eroded by increasing debt and a highly politicized series of rate and fee increases in the major Crown Corporations. By 1988 the general purpose debt had risen 200 per cent over the 1982 level, making it the largest single component of the public debt. New taxes, including an unpopular poll tax, were also implemented to cover these costs and to compensate for declining federal transfers. Given these circumstances, the 1987 NDP budget turned towards reducing deficits and restraining public sector expenditures. Ostensibly, the long-term political strategy was to get the fiscal situation under control in time to put tax reductions on the agenda before the next election. However, the NDP's two-seat majority dwindled with one resignation, and the government fell when one of its own backbenchers voted against the 1988 budget, one that contained a highly unpopular restraint program.[67]

Federalism and Fragmentation

Substantial change in national policies and federal-provincial relations increasingly constrained and isolated the Pawley government. First, bilingualism came back to Manitoba politics.[68] Following litigation, the Supreme Court of Canada ruled that the suspension of French-language rights in the legislature and courts was unconstitutional. The language provisions of the original Manitoba Act had to be restored, and Manitoba faced the prospect of translating all of its legislation. The Pawley government then negotiated a program with leadership by the Franco-Manitoban minority that lessened the burden of translation, yet increased the level of French-language services beyond that mentioned in the original Manitoba Act. However, the NDP's restoration of French-language rights met with broad opposition. The Conservative Party, under Lyon's leadership, walked out of the legislature and then helped organize a series of municipal referendums on the issue, all of which rejected the negotiated settlement. The *de facto* non-confidence motions weakened the government and effectively defended the definition of Manitoba as a unilingual and multicultural society. Moreover, the notion that constitutional changes needed popular approval as opposed to any form of élite accommodation also emerged as an integral part of the province's political conventions.[69]

The Pawley NDP was increasingly isolated and at odds with the Mulroney Conservative government's economic policy. The federal strategy of fiscal restraint, high interest rates, privatization, deregulation, and free trade prioritized markets—and as a result stood fundamentally opposed to the social democratic idea of controlling and managing business cycles.[70] Without powerful allies in Parliament or in other provincial capitals, the NDP could not stop obvious federal discrimination, such as when the Mulroney government decided to award a key military service contract to service CF-18s to a Québec company, despite an acknowledged superior bid from a Winnipeg company.

Without any doubt the April 1988 elections buried Keynesianism in Manitoba. The Conservatives, led by Gary Filmon, were able to form a minority government, with their principal source of electoral support remaining in rural Manitoba. The real change was that the Liberals, under Sharon Carstairs, had picked up enough NDP support in Winnipeg and the Interlake to be just a few seats short of forming the government. The NDP, under a new leader, Gary Doer, fell to a level of political representation and popular support reminiscent of the 1950s.

NEO-CONSERVATIVE GLOBALIZATION: THE FILMON YEARS

The 1988 election marked the shift to the contemporary globalization-neoliberal policy paradigm marked by fiscal orthodoxy, attention to market competitiveness, deregulation, and privatization. The paradigm is termed "globalization" because it is characterized by economic restructuring that has followed the North Americanization of the Canadian economy through the FTA and NAFTA. It is "neo-liberal" in that both the emerging international regimes and Canadian federal economic policy moved away from the redistributive embedded liberalism of the postwar period to focus on issues relating to competitiveness; opening up domestic goods and services to GATT-comparable and -enforceable trading rules; securing international trade, location, investment, and intellectual property rights; and systematically constraining domestic governments from interference in trade-related markets.[71]

Clearly, this is a complex and unfolding process that has changed the nature of the provincial state. Robert Campbell argues that unlike the Keynesian period where shared jurisdiction placed emphasis on joint federal-provincial responsibility and action, the new trade and monetary priorities have given Ottawa, not the provinces, a greater role in shaping policy.[72] Ronald D. Kneebone argues similarly that Ottawa has been able to bend most provinces into line towards greater fiscal orthodoxy.[73] The new international regimes have clearly privileged the interests of transnational capital. Ian Robinson goes so far as to use the term "residual federalism" to describe the effects of the loss of jurisdiction and relative autonomy in this new paradigm.[74]

Neo-liberalism often becomes conflated to neo-conservatism largely because "conservative" parties have extolled its virtues and come to power to implement it. Manitoba is no exception to this rule. The Filmon Conservatives rose to power prescribing the necessity of implementing a form of neo-conservatism—and lost power only when this had been politically and economically discredited. The recently elected NDP, in this sense, has the opportunity to establish a social democratic version of neo-liberalism—just as the Schreyer NDP had an opportunity to give a social democratic image to Manitoba's modernization.

Reshaping the State: Filmon's Neo-conservatism

Although the Manitoba Conservatives had been poised to forcefully implement radical changes, the 1988, 1990 and to a lesser extent the 1995 elections did not give the Conservatives a mandate to do so. The implosion of the NDP had translated into the rise of the Liberal party and a functioning, but unstable, three-party system. Manitoba Conservatives responded to this fragmentation by placing conventions of governance—particularly fiscal orthodoxy—above party politics. Accordingly, the implementation of the new paradigm became interpreted more as a matter of necessity than of choice. Given that the NDP economic thinking had been thoroughly discredited and that the Liberals were divided, Manitoba politics was in fact thoroughly dominated by the Conservative Party and its evolving program. The Conservatives moved slowly, but steadily, to implement a moderate paradigm. At mid-decade, however, the Filmon government, drawing lessons from the more radical Klein and Harris revolutions, began to implement a Manitoba equivalent. This initiative reshaped the state in Manitoba. And yet the government had embarked on policies for which it had no popular mandate. By 1998 the Filmon program had polarized Manitoba politics and the government was embroiled in political scandal. By the 1999 election its program had lost credibility—and the Filmon government lost political power.

The new neo-conservative policy paradigm began with pragmatic incrementalism. The Conservatives continued with the expenditure control model of governance created in the last years of the Pawley administration and extended it to major portfolios such as education and health. The Conservatives then restructured the delivery of social services, particularly health services, to conform more to a centralized model of expenditure control.[75] Similar changes in the public school system simultaneously centralized control over education in the hands of the provincial government and established a process of consumer selection among schools for parents. Additionally, in keeping with its ideology, the provincial government established a stricter curriculum for students in the public school system.

Given an all-party consensus on the limitations of fiscal policy, the restructuring of social service delivery became the key point of contestation. Popular opposition then set limits on administrative restructuring. For example, an attempt to privatize home health-care services was met by a nurses' strike and sufficient popular support to force the government to eventually withdraw the initiative.[76] In a similar vein, financial exigency was the excuse used by the administration of the University of Manitoba to erode the tenure system and unilaterally decide upon academic policy, a move that was met with a bitter and eventually successful strike. Industrial relations were also restructured. The Conservative government replaced the NDP pattern of negotiated restraint in the public sector with legislated rollbacks.[77] Until 1995 it did not radically alter private-sector collective bargaining.[78] However, after the 1995 election it brought in legislation that weakened the autonomous collective bargaining power of trade-union leadership, increased the financial and political accountability of unions to members and the general public, and introduced measures to deal harshly with any union militancy.[79]

After 22 years of budget deficits, the provincial budget ran its first surplus by the 1995 election. Then, in a reverse of the 1970s "contagion from the left," the Manitoba government drew lessons from other neo-conservative regimes.[80] For example, the Filmon government capped its fiscal policy with a mandatory balanced budget law tougher and more comprehensive than those on the books in Alberta or New Brunswick.[81] According to this law, cabinet ministers are responsible (on pain of losing up to 40 per cent of their salaries) to ensure that the provincial books are balanced. Capital as well as operating costs of governments are included. The legislation also holds that the Legislature has no right to increase or introduce new taxes until majority consent has been gained in a province-wide plebiscite. Regardless of whether all this legislation would stand up to judicial review, the fact of the matter is that it has become a major symbol of the neo-conservative conventions of governance institutionalized during the Filmon years—and as such will likely structure fiscal politics for over time. The success of the fiscal policy, discussed below, led the Filmon government to establish a Lower Tax Commission just before the 1999 election.[82]

Like previous Conservative regimes, the Filmon government institutionalized governance partnerships with business and used them to manage public-sector restructuring.[83] Neo-conservatives typically offer privatization as a means to accomplish public-sector restructuring. This was the case for the Manitoba Telephone System (MTS). The MTS was one of the older Manitoba institutions which served to protect the local population from external monopoly capital (Bell Telephone) and to redistribute wealth from the city to the province.[84] Soon after the 1995 election, however, the Filmon government announced plans to privatize the company on the grounds that it did not have the financial capacity to make the transition from telephone utility to telecommunications services company.[85] Privatization, it was claimed, would give the company needed capital, relieve it of historic debt and, therefore, give it a chance to survive in the new competitive market.

The MTS privatization decision was politically charged and its legitimacy was called into question. No commitment had been made to privatize it during the election, no other restructuring alternatives were publicly considered, the legislation was rammed through the legislature, and the stock option was undervalued, thus providing a nice public subsidy for the new share subscribers.[86] Advocates of privatization assumed that the rightness of the decision made an authoritative resolution necessary.[87] Political opposition also feared that the privatization of Manitoba Hydro would be justified by the necessity of restructuring the energy sector. Instead, the Filmon government later adopted a convergence policy by authorizing Manitoba Hydro to buy equity in the province's largest natural gas company (a long-term NDP policy objective), suggesting that there were significant political and economic limits to the Filmon government's neo-conservatism.

In contrast to the NDP's rent-seeking/redistribution economic strategy, the Filmon Conservatives emphasized the business climate and market issues.[88] At issue was the repositioning of Manitoba within the mid-continental region of the North American economy after the FTA and NAFTA trade agreements changed the structural position of Manitoba from a small but "average" province in a national economy to a much smaller jurisdiction with a larger continental region. Indeed, Manitoba's share of national capital formation has steadily declined as has the relative position of Winnipeg compared to other Canadian cities.[89]

In order to maintain a competitive position and attract investment, the tax and regulatory frameworks were changed. Smaller communities found some success in attracting telemarketing investment and decentralized provincial government services. The combinations of cutbacks and the pursuit of business climate policies worked to foster above-average levels of investment and employment growth. Manitoba's resource strategy similarly focussed on providing incentives for investment and a regulatory climate that supports rapid development of production facilities. Several small mines were developed and Inco undertook significant reinvestment in the Thompson area. The 1999 budget and Lower Tax Commission linked tax policy changes to regional competition.

Within Manitoba, the population is moving from west to south-east, although Winnipeg continues to be the regional centre. Winnipeg's post-war growth was based, in part, on the logic of rural staples production; greater efficiency gains in rural Manitoba agriculture produced urbanization and the need for economic development and diversification. Part of that diversification has come from the provision of local services and public administration. The promise of the hydro mega-projects and other resource investment was a set of development linkages to the city. Yet diversification into exportable services and manufacturing has been slow.

Previous governments used northern hydro mega-projects to provide new staples linkages for Winnipeg and the north. By the 1990s, however, the older modernization strategy proved unworkable.[90] The 1992 U.S. Energy Policy Act (EPA) then changed the dynamics of Manitoba hydro policy because it organized the North American continent into a set of regional energy trading pools. Manitoba's participation in one of these pools allowed it for the first time, in alliance with a U.S. partner, to market hydro-generated energy throughout the continent.[91] This market restructuring occurred as Limestone came on-line—a combination that has meant that for the first time in modern Manitoba history the hydro strategy promises to pay off.[92] The not insignificant cost is that the Manitoba energy policy regime is as much regulated by Washington as by Winnipeg. The Manitoba government will struggle to keep control over the provincial hydro as it adjusts to regulatory pressure fostering a profound Americanization and regionalization of the energy sector.[93]

The Manitoba Conservatives also dominated provincial politics after 1988 by adapting older conventions of non-partisanship to handle volatile questions. In this sense it was much more skilled than previous governments at insulating itself from storms emanating from federal politics, such as those presented by the Meech Lake and Charlottetown Accords, the fiscal policy of successive federal governments, policies concerning funding compensation for the 1997 Red River Flood victims and even the competition between Reform and the rump Conservatives.

As the Filmon government approached the 1999 election, a decade of protracted restraint had left a residue of profound and simmering social tensions. Indeed, what the NDP eventually termed "hallway medicine" to sum up the effects of underfunding and overcrowding eventually became a key symbol of the problem with the Filmon government's restraint programme. Clearly, the generalized acknowledgement that the status quo was not acceptable placed greater demands on the provincial government. Yet the problems in health care had federal as well as provincial origins because declining federal transfers caused much of the fiscal misery. Given this, only a collaborative reworking of social policy, euphemistically termed the social union, provided the path for the restoration of integrity for both social and fiscal policy.[94]

A collaborative resolution to fiscal and social policy presumed, however, agreement on the real limits of provincial finances. But, during the election, the Filmon Conservatives fundamentally contradicted their own fiscal policy. Following their emphasis on competitive repositioning, the Conservatives promised to reduce taxes by $500 million in order to make Manitoba's tax rates comparable to other jurisdictions in the region. To ensure that this did not exacerbate restraint problems, the Conservatives also promised to restore $500 million in spending to social programs. Needless to say, a government that had been dishing out restraint for a decade by embedding an orthodox zero-sum view of public finances in Manitoba politics could not credibly state that it could find one billion dollars to get re-elected. Gary Doer's NDP campaign, on the other hand, promised to respect the fiscal policy legislation set by the Conservatives and did not promise much more than ending "hallway medicine."

The politicization of Conservative policy anomalies did not necessarily translate into an NDP victory. Two other factors helped. The Conservative Party lost political integrity and credibility when an inquiry revealed that it had illicitly funded "independent" First Nations candidates in Northern Manitoba in order to fragment NDP support during the 1995 election.[95] Although the Liberal Party had risen to be a significant force in Manitoba politics, it didn't develop a cohesive base of support or program. Its vote collapsed, meaning that the cumulative effect of the decade of restraint was to polarize the electorate. As in previous cases, a polarized electorate translated into an NDP victory in which the 1969 fault lines defined political power. The Conservatives remained strong in their traditional rural agricultural bases, but were unable to branch out to gain substantial support in north Winnipeg or the less privileged regions of the province.

An NDP Alternative?

If this analysis is correct, the 1990s solidified support around different neoliberal alternatives. Accordingly, one would expect the Manitoba NDP, like other social democratic movements, to maintain certain continuities, particularly the adherence to orthodox fiscal policies and acceptance of market constraints.[96] Certainly, within these limits, if Doer's government is in line with its NDP predecessors, the image of the provincial state will be one of redistributive social justice rather than market individualism. It may also more viscerally represent a different social base than its Conservative predecessors: urban Winnipeg, urban and northern First Nations peoples, northerners, and the union movement. Difference may also be seen in the social democratic emphasis on a rent-seeking resource policy rather than the competitive repositioning of the Filmon government.

CONCLUSIONS

This chapter began with the question of how we can define the role of the state and then imagine the process of change. A model of paradigm and paradigm shift was outlined and then applied to Manitoba. These paradigms have been the means by which Manitoba governments have mediated between domestic and external forces and attempted to shape state intervention in their interests. Louis Riel's provisional government and negotiated constitution of the Métis province was a means of accommodating First Nations, French, and Catholic interests with the emerging National Policy. The National Policy, in turn, completely redefined Manitoba. Not all subordinate classes were successful. Labour was defeated and isolated by the Winnipeg General Strike. Farmers, on the other hand, rejected alliances with labour; instead, they formed a political alliance with business that produced an enduring image of the provincial state and society.

Built into the Liberal-Progressive image of state and society was the idea that the primary role of government was to provide stability while navigating turbulence and crises. Like the last of the great windjammers, the idea was that the ship of state would trim sails and batten down hatches when times got tough. Great licence was given to private capital on the condition that proceeds were shared by the state. This passive neo-classical rentier-redistributive paradigm became the set of ideas that shaped the development of Manitoba as a province. During the 1920s it provided the base for the industrialization and reorganization of the province. The Depression experience entrenched it as a form of restrained governance which feared and managed great debts, balanced its books, and subscribed more to rural values of self-reliance than to the welfare state. By the 1950s the more limited role given to government could not deal with the problems at hand.

Peace, postwar reconstruction, and growth produced a revolution in expectations and the apparent capacity to reach them; Keynesian modernization marked a real rupture with the past. Keynesian modernizers, both Conservative and NDP, used the state to bring about what was considered long-term economic and social development, purposely departing from the short-term fiscal perspective of the previous neo-classical paradigm. The architecture of the contemporary welfare state originates from this period: Manitoba's university and college, public school, and health care systems, as well as its modern economic infrastructure—transportation, hydro systems, and water control mechanisms including the now celebrated Red River Floodway. It was a highly politicized paradigm and during its last phases it was marked by contestation between neo-liberal and Keynesian alternatives.

During the 1970s the Keynesian bubble began to burst particularly as the internationalization of Western economies produced competitive trade, economic, and fiscal stresses. Technological changes also heralded the so-called third wave. Since the 1980s the secular trend has been to institutionalize neo-liberal trade regimes, from the FTA and NAFTA to the World Trade Organization. Manitoba's neo-conservatism returned to a more disciplined state which focussed on fiscal prudence, competitiveness and business climate objectives, assuming that achieving these objectives would translate into the fulfilment of other goals, such as fiscal security, a minimum standard of social services, and sustainable employment. Clearly, that limited view of state and democratic life could not sustain majority support. Now the NDP has a new opportunity to forge a "post-Keynesian" social democratic alternative to replace the discredited neo-conservative orthodoxy. In doing so, however, it will have to respect many of the same paradigmatic limitations. In this sense governments are more path-dependent if they are operating within a well-established regime than if they themselves are making the shift.

NOTES

1 An earlier draft of this chapter benefitted from the thoughtful comments and suggestions of Jim Silver, University of Winnipeg. Thanks also for the suggestions from Winnipeg writer Doug Smith; Paul Thomas and Geoff Lambert, both from the University of Manitoba; and Allan Seager, Simon Fraser University.

2 See Robert R. Alford and Roger Friedland, *Powers of Theory: Capitalism, the State and Democracy* (Cambridge: Cambridge University Press, 1985).

3 Peter A. Hall "Patterns of Economic Policy: An Organizational Approach," *The State in Capitalist Europe: A Casebook*, ed. Stephen Bornstein, David Held, and Joel Krieger (London: George Allen and Unwin, 1984), 21-53.

4 Peter A. Hall, *Governing the Economy: The Politics of State Intervention in Britain and France* (New York: Oxford University Press, 1986); Peter A. Hall, "Policy Paradigms, Social Learning and the State: The Case of Economic Policy-making in Great Britain," *Comparative Politics* (April 1993): 275-97; Jane Jenson, "'Different' but not 'exceptional': Canada's permeable fordism," *Canadian Review of Sociology and Anthropology* 26:1 (1989): 69-94.

5 Jane Jenson, "Representation in Crisis: The Roots of Canada's Permeable Fordism," *Canadian Journal of Political Science* 23:4 (December 1990): 653-83, especially 675-83.

6 Peter A. Hall, ed., *The Political Power of Economic Ideas: Keynesianism Across Nations* (Princeton: Princeton University Press, 1989), 370-86.

7 Peter Gourevitch, *Politics in Hard Times* (Ithaca: Cornell University Press, 1986).

8 Jenson, "Representation in Crisis," 653-83, especially 675-83.

9 V.C. Fowke, "The National Policy, Old and New," *Approaches to Canadian Economic History*, ed. W.T. Easterbrook and M.H. Watkins (Toronto: McClelland and Stewart, 1967), 237-58.

10 Gerald Friesen, "Bilingualism in Manitoba: The Historical Context," *River Road: Essays on Manitoba and Prairie History* (Winnipeg: The University of Manitoba Press, 1996), 23.

11 W.L. Morton, *Manitoba, A History*, rev. ed. (Toronto: University of Toronto Press, 1967), 121-50.

12 For an overview see Gerald Friesen, "The Collective Writings of Louis Riel," in *River Road*, 17-22. The major defence of the Macdonald government and argument for assimilation is contained in G.F.G. Stanley, *The Birth of Western Canada* (Toronto, 1960); Thomas Flanagan, *Louis David Riel: Prophet of the New World* (Toronto : University of Toronto Press, 1979); Thomas Flanagan, *Riel and the Rebellion: 1885 Reconsidered* (Saskatoon: Western Producer Prairie Books, 1983); Thomas Flanagan, *Metis Lands in Manitoba* (Calgary: University of Calgary Press, 1991). The Métis position is contained works of D.N. Sprague: "The Manitoba Land Question," *Journal of Canadian Studies* 15:3 (Autumn 1980): 74-84; *Canada and the Métis, 1869-1885* (Waterloo: Wilfrid Laurier University Press, 1988); "Government Lawlessness and the in the Administration of Manitoba Land Claims, 1876-1887," *Manitoba Law Journal* 10 (1980): 415-41; and "Dispossession vs. Accommodation in Plaintiff vs. Defendant Accounts of Métis Dispersal from Manitoba, 1870-1881," *Prairie Forum* (1991): 137-55.

13 Paul Phillips, "The Hinterland Perspective: The Political Economy of Vernon Fowke," *Canadian Journal of Social and Political Thought* (Spring, 1978).

14 Nelson Wiseman, "Provincial Political Cultures," *Provinces: Canadian Provincial Politics*, ed. Christopher Dunn (Peterborough: Broadview, 1996).

15 See the discussion in the last chapter of David Jay Bercuson, *Confrontation at Winnipeg: Labour, Industrial Relations and the General Strike*, 2nd ed. (Montreal and Kingston: McGill-Queen's University Press, 1990).

16 Jeffery Taylor, *Fashioning Farmers: Ideology, Agricultural Knowledge and the Manitoba Farm Movement, 1890-1925* (Regina: Canadian Plains Research Centre, 1994).

17 See David Laycock's discussion of "Crypto-Liberalism" in his *Populism and Democratic Thought in the Canadian Prairies, 1910-1945* (Toronto: University of Toronto Press, 1990), 23-68; and John English, *The Decline of Politics: The Conservatives and the Party System, 1901-1920* (Toronto: University of Toronto Press, 1977).

18 John Bracken, *John Bracken Says* (Toronto: Oxford University Press, 1944).

19 Morton, *Manitoba*; and John Kendle's discussion of "Brackenism" in his *John Bracken: A Political Biography* (Toronto: University of Toronto Press, 1979), 37-67.

20 For example, cooperative wheat pools as opposed to public marketing boards to offset the power of the private grain exchange, competitive hydro companies to serve Winnipeg instead of forming one large monopoly, and a whole series of publicly supported agricultural credit institutions, including a provincial savings office as well as a provincial telephone system to offset the power of established Eastern capital. See Morton, *Manitoba*, 385; H.V. Nelles, "Public Ownership of Utilities in Manitoba and Ontario, 1906-1930," *Canadian Historical Review* VII:4 (December 1976): 461-84; R.M. Pearson, *Provincial Finance in Manitoba* (Winnipeg: Economic Survey Board, 1938), 15-16; and Alex Netherton, "From Rentiership to Continental Modernization: Shifting Paradigms of State Intervention in Hydro in Manitoba, 1922-1977" (Ph.D. diss. Carleton University, 1993), 51-110.

21 Like other jurisdictions Manitoba offered incentives for private sector investment—railway subsidies, loan guarantees, hydro and timber rights. In return, revenues from resources in terms of licences, water power rentals or royalties were to be used by the government of Manitoba to aid in its overall objective of redistribution to farmers and "the province." See Kendle, *John Bracken*, 52-63.

22 Manitoba. Provincial Treasurer, *Budget Speech and Economic Review* (Winnipeg: Department of the Treasury, 1923, 1925, 1927).

23 See Morton, *Manitoba*, 424-26.

24 Manitoba, *Manitoba's Case: A Submission Presented to the Royal Commission on Dominion—Provincial Relations by the Government of the Province of Manitoba* (Winnipeg: King's Printer, 1937); Nelson Wiseman, *Social Democracy in Manitoba: A History of the CCF/NDP* (Winnipeg: University of Manitoba Press, 1983), 24-36; Morton, *Manitoba*, 421-39; Manitoba, Provincial Treasurer, *Budget Speech* (Winnipeg: Department of the Treasury, 1937).

25 "Bracken to Call Special Session," *Free Press* 22 June 1939; "Bracken Seeks Barter Deal Despite Protests: Says Ottawa Objection Won't Halt Plan to send Produce to Germany," *Tribune*, 13 July 1939; "Barter Deal Terms," *Free Press*, 17 July 1939; Bracken Still Hopes for Barter," *Free Press*, 20 July 1939; "No Barter Deal Says Council," *Free Press*, 25 July 1939; "City Council Opposes Bracken Barter Deal," *Tribune*, 25 July 1939; "Bracken Responds to City Council," *Free Press*, 27 July 1939; "Brandon Hopes: Bracken Denies Plan is Pro-German," *Free Press*,

1 August 1939; "Bracken's Nazi Deal," *Brandon Sun*, 3 August 1939; "Discuss Manitoba's Barter Project," *Free Press*, 8 August 1939; "Major Praises Trade Deal," *Free Press*, 9 August 1939; "These Barter Deals," *Free Press*, 11 August 1939; "Barter Deal Not Necessary," *The Financial Times*, 18 August 1939.

26 Netherton, "From Rentiership to Continental Modernization," 504.

27 There were two major Liberal-Progressive initiatives in postwar planning. Emerson P. Schmidt, Chairman, *A Farm Electrification Programme: Report of the Manitoba Electrification Enquiry Commission 1942* (Winnipeg: King's Printer, 1943); W.J. Parker, Chairman, *Final Report of the Advisory Committee on Coordination of Post-War Planning* (Winnipeg: King's Printer, 21 January 1946).

28 Manitoba, Provincial Treasurer, *Budget Speech and Economic Review* (Winnipeg: Department of the Treasury, 1955), 13-14.

29 Manitoba, *Budget Speech* (1955), 17.

30 Murray S. Donnelly, *The Government of Manitoba* (Toronto: University of Toronto Press), 96, 105-07.

31 Netherton, "From Rentiership to Continental Modernization," chap. 4 and 5.

32 Gonick, "The Manitoba Economy," 28-32.

33 *Financial Post*, 6 April 1960, 50-51.

34 Sean McCaffrey, "Policy Continuity Between the Roblin and Schreyer Governments, 1958-1977" (M.A. thesis, University of Manitoba, 1986).

35 Harold Chorney, "The Political Economy of Provincial Economic Development Policy: A Case Study of Manitoba" (M.A. thesis, University of Manitoba, 1970).

36 Chorney, "The Political Economy," 80-119; Harold Chorney and Phillip Hansen, "The Falling Rate of Legitimation," *Toward a Humanist Political Economy* (Montreal: Black Rose Books, 1992), 72-100.

37 Manitoba, Provincial Treasurer, *Budget Speech* (Winnipeg, Queen's Printer, 1967), 13-16.

38 Thomas Peterson, "Manitoba," *Canadian Annual Review 1967*, ed. John Saywell (Toronto: University of Toronto Press, 1967), 155; and Peterson, "Manitoba," *Canadian Annual Review 1968* (Toronto: University of Toronto Press, 1968), 167-68.

39 Wiseman, *Social Democracy*, 117-24.

40 Paul Barber and Thomas Peterson, "Some Factors Affecting the 1969 NDP Victory in Manitoba," *Lakehead University Review* III:2 (1970): 120-33.

41 Tom Peterson, "Manitoba Ethnic and Class Politics," *Canadian Provincial Politics*, 2nd ed., ed. Martin Robin (Scarborough: Prentice Hall, 1978).

42 Manitoba, *Guidelines for the Seventies*, Vols. 1-3 (Winnipeg: Queen's Printer, 1973).

43 John Loxley, "The Great Northern Plan," *Studies in Political Economy* 6 (Autumn 1981): 151-82; John Loxley, "Economic Planning Under Social Democracy," *The Political Economy of Manitoba*, ed. Jim Silver and Jeremy Hull (Regina: Canadian Plains Research Centre, 1991), 318-30.

44 James McAllister, *The Government of Edward Schreyer: Democratic Socialism in Manitoba* (Kingston and Montreal: McGill-Queen's University Press, 1984).

45 Cy Gonick, "The Manitoba Economy Since World War II," *The Political Economy of Manitoba*, Silver and Hull, eds. 25-48.

46 The rent-seeking resource strategy was defined in the following documents: Eric Kierans, *Report on Natural Resources Policy in Manitoba*, Prepared for the Secretariat for Planning and Priorities Committee of Cabinet (Winnipeg: Government of Manitoba, 1973); Eric Kierans, "Addendum," in Manitoba Hydro, Manitoba Hydro Task Force, *Report on Examination of a Proposal for Long Term Exports of 1000MW to Northern States Power Company, 1973* (1976 Sessional Paper No. 94). The NDP's rejection of these ideas is documented in McAllister, 138-39; Wiseman, *Social Democracy*, 143-44; and Netherton, "From Rentiership to Continental Modernization," 388-97.

47 Rhodes Smith, Chairman, *Report of the Commission of Inquiry into the Pas Forestry and Industrial Complex* (Winnipeg: Queen's Printer, 1974).

48 Peterson, "Manitoba," *Canadian Annual Review 1969*, 130-33; Peterson, "Manitoba," *Canadian Annual Review 1970*, 256-60; Peterson, "Manitoba," *Canadian Annual Review 1971*, 164-66; Peterson, "Manitoba," *Canadian Annual Review 1972*, 181-83; Peterson, "Manitoba," *Canadian Annual Review 1973*, 151-58.

49 Peterson, "Manitoba Ethnic and Class Politics."

50 Wiseman, *Social Democracy*, 128-30; Donnelly, "Manitoba," *Canadian Annual Review 1977*, 182-85.

51 George Janosik and Robert Voline (pseudonyms), "Blood-bath in the Red River Valley," *This Magazine* 12:2 (August 1978): 28-34.

52 Janosik and Voline, "Blood-bath"; Geoff Lambert, "Manitoba," *Canadian Annual Review 1978*; Gonick, "The Manitoba Economy," 36-37.

53 Janosik and Voline, "Blood-bath."

54 Harold Chorney and Phillip Hansen, "Neo-conservatism, social democracy and 'province building': the experience of Manitoba," *Canadian Review of Sociology and Anthropology* 22:1 (1985): 1-29.

55 Manitoba, Minister of Finance, *Budget Address* (1981), 77-79.

56 Lambert, "Manitoba," *Canadian Annual Review 1981*; *Financial Post* 23 May 1981, 9; *Winnipeg Free Press*, 2 May 1981, 9.

57 John Richards and Larry Pratt, *Prairie Capitalism: Power and Influence in the New West* (Toronto: McClelland and Stewart, 1979); *Financial Post*, 14 April 1979, 4; Lambert, "Manitoba," *Canadian Annual Review 1980*, 287-89; Lambert, "Manitoba," *Canadian Annual Review 1981*, 400-01.

58 Chorney and Hansen, "Neo-conservatism," 10-11.

59 Nelson Wiseman, "In Search of Manitoba's Constitutional Position," *Journal of Canadian Studies* 29:3 (1994).

60 Chorney and Hansen, "Neo-conservatism," 14.

61 *Western Report*, 21 March 1988, 5-8.

62 Gosta Esping Andersen, *Politics Against Markets: The Social Democratic Road to Power* (Princeton: Princeton University Press, 1985), 289-324.

63 Canada, Donald Macdonald, Chairman, *Report of the Royal Commission on the Economic Union and Development Prospects for Canada* (Ottawa: Minister of Supply and Services, 1985). The Macdonald Commission defined a neo-liberal policy paradigm broadly influential in shaping the market-based economic strategy that followed.

64 Richards and Pratt, *Prairie Capitalism*, 250-78, 304-30; Thomas Gunton and John Richards, "Mineral Policy in Western Canada," *Prairie Forum* 14 (Fall 1989): 195-208.

65 The actual contract was controversial because it directly tied the export revenues of Manitoba electricity to the long term cost of coal. The underlying assumption was that the value of coal would continue its above average rate of increase and, therefore, generate large economic rents. See Canada, National Energy Board, *Reasons for Decisions* (Ottawa: National Energy Board, 1985); *Winnipeg Free Press*, 12 January 1984, 6; *Winnipeg Free Press*, 19 April 1984, 6; *Winnipeg Free Press*, 21 April 1984, 7; *Winnipeg Free Press*, 26 June 1984, 6; *Winnipeg Free Press*, 29 June 1984, 6; *Winnipeg Free Press*, 14 November 1984, 6; Manitoba Hydro, *Annual Report 1985*, 10.

66 The procurement budget for Limestone was used to foster local sourcing, technology transfer and other economic spin-offs, even when it placed the utility's credibility in jeopardy with out-of-province bidders. Finally, the investment was closely integrated with the NDP job and social policy. The NDP Minister of Northern Affairs, Elijah Harper, signed contracts with the native organizations and provincial trade unions which gave employment priority first to native peoples (in conjunction with training programs), second to northerners, third to other residents of the province, and fourth to out-of-province workers. Though the program fell somewhat short of its targets, the reality was that it made an important impact on the aboriginal labour market and labour force skills. See: *Winnipeg Free Press*, 27 June 1986, 6; *Winnipeg Free Press*, 7 July 1986, 6; *Winnipeg Free Press*, 18 December 1986, 7; Lambert, "Manitoba," *Canadian Annual Review 1985*, 36-37; Jeremy Hull, "Aboriginal Peoples and the Labour Market," *Hard Bargains: The Manitoba Labour Movement Confronts the 1990s*, ed. Errol Black and Jim Silver (Winnipeg: Manitoba Labour History Series, 1990), 93-96.

67 Gonick "Manitoba Economy," 38; *Winnipeg Free Press*, 28 February 1987, 7; Minister of Finance, *Budget Address* (Winnipeg: Ministry of Finance, 1988), 30-33.

68 Russell Doern, *The Battle Over Bilingualism: the Manitoba Language Question 1983-1985* (Winnipeg: Cambridge Publishers, 1985).

69 Nelson Wiseman, "In Search of Manitoba's Constitutional Position," *Journal of Canadian Studies* 29:3 (1994).

70 Andersen, *Politics Against Markets.*

71 Lorraine Eden and Maureen Appel Molot, "Canada's National Policies: Reflections on 125 Years," *Canadian Public Policy* 19:3 (1993): 232-51.

72 Robert M. Campbell, "Federalism and Economic Policy," *New Trends in Canadian Federalism*, ed. François Rocher and Miriam Smith (Peterborough: Broadview Press, 1995), 187-210.

73 Ronald D. Kneebone, "Four Decades of Deficits and Debt," *Unnecessary Debts*, ed. Lars Osberg and Pierre Fortin (Toronto: Lorimer, 1996): 39-70.

74 Ian Robinson, "Trade Policy, Globalization and the Future of Canadian Federalism," *New Trends*, ed. Rocher and Smith, 234-69.

75 Bill 49, The Regional Health Authorities and Consequential Amendments Act.

76 Doug Smith, *We Are Workers Just Like You: the 1996 Manitoba Horne Lake Strike* (Winnipeg: Manitoba Environment Employees Union, 1996).

77 Gene Swimmer, "Provincial Policies Concerning Collective Bargaining," *Provinces*, ed. Dunn, 370-71. Professional Institute of the Public Service of Canada, "Filmon Fridays are back, and boy, do people hate them," *Canadian Press Newswire*, 5 August 1997.

78 Errol Black and Jim Silver, "Final Offer Selection: The Manitoba Experience," *Hard Bargains*, ed. Black and Silver, 237-60.

79 Francis Russell, "Tories strike anti-labour pose," *Winnipeg Free Press*, 10 April 1996, A12; *Two Manitobas: Widening the Gap : An Analysis of the Conservative Government's 1996 Legislative Package* (Winnipeg: Choices, 1996); Errol Black, "The Manitoba Government Declares War on Workers and Trade Unions," *Canadian Dimension* 30:5 (September/October, 1996); "President Olfert: Manitoba Government Employees' Union head has seen many changes in decade," Interview, *Winnipeg Free Press*, 20 October 1996, B4; McKie, "Unions seek to alter Tory labour bill," *Winnipeg Free Press*, 22 October 1996, B4, A5; Francis Russell, "Unions fight for civilized values," *Winnipeg Free Press*, 4 September 1996, A10; Francis Russell, "Tories with a vengeance," *Winnipeg Free Press*, 24 May 1996, A10.

80 Canadian Press, "Political message on Prairies one of tough love in 1995," *Canadian Press Newswire*, 14 December 1995.

81 Manitoba, *Balanced Budget, Debt Repayment and Taxpayer's Protection and Consequential Amendments Act* (3 November 1997); Robin Richardson, "Manitoba Leads on Balance Budgets: Proposed Law Would Be Strongest in Canada," *Financial Post* 31 August 1995, 9.

82 Manitoba, *1999 Annual Budget*.

83 Howard Pawley, "In the Public Interest," *Provinces*, ed. Dunn, 314-17; Jeanne Kirk Laux and Maureen Appel Molot, *State Capitalism: Public Enterprise in Canada* (Ithaca: Cornell University Press, 1988); and Errol Black and Jim Silver, "In Defence of Public Ownership: The Case of Manitoba," *Prairie Forum* 15 (Spring 1990): 123-25.

84 See the discussion of MTS in Carl Goldenberg, *Report of the Government Commercial Enterprises Survey* (Winnipeg: King's Printer, 1940).

85 "Manitoba Tel on block in $750m share issue," *Financial Post Daily*, 9:52, 3 May 1996, 1; "Debt pushes MTS onto selling block," *Computing Canada* 22:13 (20 June 1996): 33,36; Fred Cleverley, "Should Tories sell Manitoba Telephone System? We can't afford MTS anymore," *Winnipeg Free Press*, 3 November 1966, B2; "Tories win battle but war is just starting?," *Winnipeg Free Press*, 29 November 1996, A3, Q1.

86 Francis Russell, "Privatizing MTS by stealth," *Winnipeg Free Press*, 29 January 1996, A6; Errol Black and Paula Mallea, "The Privatization of Manitoba Telephone System," *Canadian Dimension* 31:2 (March/April, 1997): 11-13.

87 "Telephone company's value rises after privatization," *Canadian Press Newswire*, 30 May 1997; "Privatized phone company all set to lead economy," *Financial Post Daily*, 10:34, 3 April 1997.

88 Department of Industry and Commerce, Manitoba Development Board, *Framework for Growth: Policy Implications for Manitoba* (Winnipeg: Industry and Commerce, n.d.).

89 Jim Silver, *Thin Ice: Money, Politics and the Demise of the NHL Franchise* (Halifax: Fernwood, 1996): 12-13.

90 The government did try to float another Nelson River mega-project ostensibly to be built at Ontario Hydro's request as a substitute for more expensive and environmentally damaging nuclear and coal generated energy. Ontario Hydro, however, dropped the project when its real energy problems—an escalating debt and overabundance of expensive capacity—brought the utility into the centre of a privatization and reorganization debate. See Ronald J. Daniels, ed., *Ontario Hydro at the Millennium*

(Montreal and Kingston: University of Toronto Faculty of Law and McGill-Queen's University Press, 1996), 120-21.

91 U.S. Energy Information Administration, *The Changing Structure of the Electric Power Industry: An Update* (Washington, DC: Department of Energy, December 1996).

92 Manitoba Hydro, Annual Report (Winnipeg, 1998).

93 Joseph Diamond and Jon Edwards, *Mergers, Aquisitions, and Market Power in the Electric Power Industry* (California Energy Commission, 4 April 1997).

94 Harvey Lazar, "The Federal Role in a New Social Union: Ottawa at a Crossroads," *Canada: The State of the Federation*, ed. H. Lazar (Kingston: Queen's University Institute of Intergovernmental Relations, 1997), 105-36.

95 Scott Edmonds, "Manitoba Premier Hopes for Better Times as Election Call Nears," *Canadian Press Newswire*, 17 December 1998; Scott Edmonds, "Elections Manitoba Knocked for Failure to Uncover Vote- Rigging Plan," *Canadian Press Newswire*, 3 November 1998; Adam Killick, "Manitoba Tories Financed Bid to Split Vote, Inquiry Told: Premier's Former Chief of Staff Details Failed Campaign Plan," *National Post*, 12 January 1999, A1, A2; David Roberts, "Manitoba Inquiry Raises Possibility of Criminal Charges: Former Chief of Staff to Filmon Says Actions Were Clearly Overzealous and Crossed the Line," *Globe & Mail*, 13 January 1999, A3; Adam Killick, "Tories in Scandal Will Be Ousted, Filmon Promises," *National Post*, 14 January 1999, A6; "Manitoba Premier Hopes to Survive Scandals—Martin," *Calgary Herald*, 8 January 1999; "Scandal Besmirches Manitoba's Once Clean, Bland Leader: Gary Filmon's Long Tenure in Office May Be Threatened by Findings of Vote-Rigging in the Last Election—Martin," *Vancouver Sun*, 28 January 1999, A19.

96 Herbert Ketshelt, *The Transformation of European Social Democracy* (Cambridge: Cambridge University Press, 1994).

9 SASKATCHEWAN

From Entrepreneurial State to Embedded State

KEN RASMUSSEN

Few provinces have seen their fortunes rise and decline as much as Saskatchewan's have over the past two decades. From a peak of power and influence in the mid-1970s when it helped define the "entrepreneurial state," to the point of near bankruptcy in the early 1990s, the province of Saskatchewan has been on the kind of roller-coaster ride long associated with resource-dependent economies. The overriding objective of every Saskatchewan government in the postwar era has been to end this unstable dependency on international commodity markets and bring stability to the province through economic diversification. Yet their obvious inability to find long-term solutions to the problem says something important about the provincial state in Saskatchewan. In particular it indicates the relative weakness of the provincial state in the face of the much stronger international trading system on which Saskatchewan depends.

At one point during the 1970s it appeared that the provincial state in Saskatchewan was well on its way to becoming an aggressive entrepreneurial actor in staple-led economic development. Indeed, the province was considered by many to be a leading practitioner of what was known as "state capitalism," or less grandly, "province-building."[1] During the 1970s Saskatchewan displayed many of the signs of a strong and autonomous provincial state: it had a pattern of decision-making which displayed a high degree of bureaucratic centralization, the quality of its bureaucratic elite was high, it established powerful, autonomous economic institutions, and it displayed a willingness to stand up to the strongest elements in the province—both capital and labour. There is little question that the state in Saskatchewan during this period acted with considerable autonomy in relation to domestic politics, federal/provincial relations, and even internationally, aggressively pursuing Saskatchewan's strategic interests in the face of hostile and powerful opponents on all sides.

However, just as quickly as it was being defined as a strong entrepreneurial actor the provincial state suffered a number of setbacks which appear to have re-established it in its original pattern as a fragmented, open political structure, easily penetrated by the most influential elements of Saskatchewan society. The Saskatchewan state now appears much less autonomous from domestic pressures, federal initiatives, and international market forces than it was during the 1970s. This diminished autonomy can be seen as a consequence of a number of influences: the all-out assault by free-market ideology in the 1980s which explicitly tried to diminish state power through the process of privatization, deregulation, and decentralization; budget deficits and debts and reductions in federal transfers; the Charter of Rights and Freedoms and with it the rise of identity politics; the rapid erosion of political parties as a source of public policy; and perhaps most important of all, the various international trade agreements entered into by the federal government. The pressures associated with these constraints, particularly globalization, budget deficits, and federal transfer reductions, have simultaneously reduced the autonomy of the Saskatchewan state as an independent actor, but at the same time forced it to act decisively with regard to local interests in the name of restructuring.

This decline in state autonomy is a reflection of what Alan Cairns has called the "embedded state." Cairns focuses on the structural limitations faced by party governments stemming from the extent to which the national and provincial states in Canada are "embedded" in society, leaving little room for governments of any political stripe to manoeuvre. This analysis is particularly suggestive in Saskatchewan, where decades of aggressive, entrepreneurial government activity have extended the state into almost every sphere of daily life. We now have in Saskatchewan a highly politicized society that is "caught in the web of interdependence with the state." The provincial state, in turn, is "embedded" in society, "tied down by its multiple linkages with society, which restrain its maneuverability."[2] What this means in practical terms, for example, is that the retrenchment of expenditure becomes a very uneven process, even for the most committed of neo-conservative governments.[3] Equally, the inability of the New Democratic Party (NDP) in the 1990s to move forward with a new coherent vision of a vigorous entrepreneurial state in Saskatchewan is a reflection of the overwhelming, ongoing obligations for already existing social programs and the powerful interests that exist primarily to preserve these programs.

The impact of the embedded state on a new government is particularly sobering, since they obviously inherit massive program commitments. These programs are entrenched in bureaucracies, supported by clientele groups, protected within existing budgetary procedures, and preserved by their sheer numbers and by cabinet's inability to deal with more than a fraction of the government's overall business. Hence their existence is almost tantamount to their survival. As Cairns colourfully notes: "To turn around a huge loaded oil tanker steaming full speed ahead is child's play when contrasted with the difficulty of engineering a significant change of direction for the great ship of state. The latter task is beyond the capacity of particular governments between elections."[4]

What this image of the embedded state implies is that the choices of various former governments force the past onto the present. That is, "historical choices can lock in particular approaches, especially when major investments premised on chosen approaches have been made and when powerful interests have grown up around them."[5] This leads to a situation in which policy changes are most often incremental in nature, and when major policy changes are necessary they must be attempted with enormous political will while risking high levels of political opposition.[6] The domestic policy legacy, when combined with the influence of external constraints like the Charter of Rights and Freedoms and the North American Free Trade Agreement (NAFTA), reduces the room for party governments of any political persuasion to manoeuvre.

The paradox of the embedded state is that while external pressures are simultaneously weakening the Saskatchewan state, at the same time they force it to act more autonomously from local interests. As external constraints undermine the autonomy of the Saskatchewan state with regards to international and federal/provincial forces, the Saskatchewan state needs to be strong and reasonably autonomous from mass pressures if it is to respond effectively to these external challenges. The provincial state in Saskatchewan is faced with external constraints on its actions, but must respond to internal demands and pressures from the highly politicized societies that it has created over the past thirty years. Decisions within the embedded provincial state are consequently not guided by an overarching philosophy, but rather by the desire to maintain support from the broadest possible constituency of well-organized voters who are anxious about the prospect of reduced income or services. This chapter will explore the paradoxical dilemmas encountered by the embedded state in Saskatchewan which faces increasing external constraints along with a growing need to act autonomously from the society it governs.

Responding to external constraints is of course not new. Indeed, the political history of Saskatchewan is in essence the history of state responses to powerful outside forces, most often in conjunction with strong domestic support. What has changed recently in Saskatchewan, however, is the nature of external forces which limit provincial initiatives. Developments such as the Charter of Rights and Freedoms, debts and deficits, transfer payment reductions, and the various internal and external trade arrangements that have emerged over the past decade now often create coercive barriers to action. Equally important is the fact that these new constraints have been accompanied by changes in the domestic social structure of the province. No longer can a government rely on the kind of coherent or unambiguous support for entrepreneurial actions that was available in the past.

THE RISE AND FALL OF THE ENTREPRENEURIAL STATE IN SASKATCHEWAN

Saskatchewan has always been subject to external constraints. In its first years as a province the constraints were almost all external and included a hostile federal government, powerful railway and grain transportation monopolies, volatile international commodity markets, and indifferent banks. Yet these same constraints inspired governments to take action designed to address these forces. During the first period of Saskatchewan politics (1905-44), the Liberal government that dominated this era provided progressive legislation and institutional support that encouraged the development of co-operative organizations as a means to deal with the challenges faced by its overwhelmingly rural constituency. The Agricultural Co-operative Associations Act (1913), the Co-operative Marketing Act (1926), and the Credit Union Act (1937), not to mention many special acts such as those for the Saskatchewan Wheat Pool and Saskatchewan Federated Co-ops, were important in supporting and promoting the development of a strong co-op sector. The government also provided institutional support in the form of the Co-operative Organization Branch of the Department of Agriculture.

The key domestic factor in producing these responses by the provincial state was the effective alliance between the Liberal party and the Saskatchewan Grain Growers Association (SGGA). The period from 1905-29, in particular, was characterized by the close attention which the Saskatchewan Liberal government paid to the expressed wishes of the SGGA, and through which the Liberal party ensured itself of the support of the agrarian electorate.[7] This close connection is important in understanding actions of the provincial state which challenged both the federal government and the market. As David Laycock has pointed out, "From the moment they settled in the new land, prairie farmers perceived economic co-operation as an obvious alternative to exploitation especially when it became clear that the federal state could not be relied on for protection from private firms with political connections."[8] Co-ops emerged quickly as an important economic entity in the province and began to influence the politics of both the SGGA and the Liberal party. But it should also be noted

TABLE 9.1 **GOVERNMENTS OF SASKATCHEWAN**

PREMIER	PARTY	DURATION
Walter Scott	Liberal	1905-16
William Martin	Liberal	1916-22
Charles A. Dunning	Liberal	1922-26
J.G. (Jimmy) Gardiner	Liberal	1926-29
J.T.M. Anderson	Co-operative Conservative/Progressive	1929-34
J.G. (Jimmy) Gardiner	Liberal	1934-35
William J. Patterson	Liberal	1935-44
T.C. (Tommy) Douglas	CCF	1944-61
Woodrow S. Lloyd	CCF	1961-64
Ross Thatcher	Liberal	1964-71
Allan E. Blakeney	NDP	1971-82
Grant Devine	Progressive Conservative	1982-91
Roy Romanow	NDP	1991-99
Roy Romanow	NDP/Liberal Coalition	1999-

that Liberal party support of co-operation and the co-operatives "implied few major departures from prevailing economic and political practise."[9]

The ability of the Liberal government to contain farmer unrest reached its limit during the Great Depression. The election of 1929 brought about the first defeat for the Liberals, but more importantly provided an opening for a new and powerful coalition of voters. In rural Saskatchewan, with the Liberal party out of office, farmers took the opportunity to enter politics directly through the United Farmers of Canada-Saskatchewan Section. In the cities, the Independent Labour Party, lead by M.J. Coldwell, emerged at roughly the same time. These two organizations eventually came together to form a farmer/labour alliance within the structure of the Co-operative Commonwealth Federation-Saskatchewan Section (CCF) in 1934. From these origins in the early 1930s until its victory in 1944, the new organization "acted as a true political party. Its two principal tasks were to attract as much support as it could from the Liberals and to prevent the rise of a challenger to its monopoly of the opposition."[10]

After winning the election in 1944, the CCF proceeded to displace the Liberals as the governing party in Saskatchewan. The provincial state now began slowly and tentatively to engage in more entrepreneurial or province-building policies due, as always, to the constraints of international commodity markets, but with the strong support of the dispersed rural population. Yet even with wheat remaining king and farmers exercising a dominant influence on provincial politics, the CCF quickly found the limits of the provincial state. During its first two years in office the government attempted to implement many of its most radical entrepreneurial initiatives, directly intervening in competitive sectors of the economy, most notably with the legendary box and shoe factories. However, after a string of serious setbacks due to a lack of sufficient capital, managerial expertise, and downstream distribution, the government changed direction and offered a much more moderate approach to governing Saskatchewan.[11]

This decision to slow down, or abandon, the most radical reforms was an important decision given that the urban middle class had consistently opposed the CCF. While the CCF could get elected without their support during much of this period this could not be sustained, and in the future policies that appealed to the increasing urban middle class would need to be contemplated. As Lipset noted at the time, "The elections statistics cited tend to confirm the interpretation that the CCF has been primarily a farmer-labor [sic] party. In every election that it has contested, the party received more support from these two groups than it did from the urban middle classes."[12] For the time being, however, when the CCF tried to make overtures to the small business community it consistently ran headlong into opposition by farmers who were still in the process of building complementary organizations in the form of co-operative stores, credit unions and insurance companies. For the farmers, small-business people represented the "profit system" and "economic oppression." Of course small-business people were equally hostile to the CCF which they saw as wanting to take over retail distribution, medicine, banking, and insurance under either co-operative or government control, both of which were antithetical to the middle-class businessperson and professional.

In the end, most of the government's major successes during this era were in the social policy and service provision domains, which began the slow process of embedding the state within society. With a solid base of support in rural Saskatchewan, and with the direction of reform already mapped out by British social democrats, the CCF government made a host of substantial achievements during its two decades in office. It introduced hospital insurance, government auto insurance, rural electrification, it expanded rural telephone services, renovated the province's educational system, provided progressive labour legislation, increased minimum wages, and so on. The critics of this period were left to point out what did not happen. The biggest criticism was that the socialists scared off investment which instead flowed to Manitoba and Alberta. The CCF was seen to be too heavy-handed and dictatorial in its activities. And even if many of the things that the CCF provided the people of Saskatchewan were good, the critics argued that the price in terms of high taxes and lost revenues was too high to pay.[13] A typical complaint was that "one of the pathological symptoms of seventeen years of Socialist economic and welfare practices in Saskatchewan is the incidence of high taxation. Direct and hidden taxes imposed by the government have multiplied like rabbits."[14] This, curiously enough, is the same criticism levelled at the current NDP government by its opponents on the right.

It is reasonably clear that the CCF government desperately wanted to bring about economic diversification. However, while initially committed to undertaking this activity through public enterprise, the government's lack of capital, expertise, and knowledge of markets meant that this effort was doomed to failure. The government became convinced that private capital needed to be invested in the province if it was to develop, and thus the enduring notion of an economy with three pillars was born: co-operatives, public enterprise, and private enterprise would all be encouraged, with the government taking a lead in economic planning. "To the extent that the provincial government could contribute to indigenously controlled, large-scale economic activity, it was primarily in the fields of Crown control of various utilities and consumer services (like insurance) active support for co-operative entrepreneurship in the areas of retail and wholesale trading, financial services (credit unions) and polices designed to subsidize farmers and protect the viability of rural centres."[15] While there was a tremendous debate within the CCF party and cabinet about the issue of economic policies surrounding resource development, the decision was eventually made to proceed through private-sector initiative, much to the consternation of party radicals like Joe Phelps. Of course, significant local pressure from the business community did help convince "party leaders to abandon this significant attempt at regional entrepreneurship by a provincial government."[16]

The next party to govern Saskatchewan was even more reluctant to engage in entrepreneurial activity. The election of the Liberal government of Ross Thatcher in 1964, as with any provincial election, can be attributed to a number of factors: a result of a slight shift in voting behaviour in certain centres; the departure of T.C. Douglas to federal politics; CCF support of religious school funding for high schools; and an exhausted party leadership tired from the divisive fight over Medicare.[17] The Liberal party that emerged from two decades of opposition, however, was one that had reoriented itself, consolidating its support among the business community and becoming the party of "free enterprise," even though the long standing tradition of the Liberal party had been one of reform. Much of the farm leadership had abandoned the Liberal party and headed for the CCF, so the

Liberals quickly become the preserve of the business and professional class in the province. Thus it is not surprising that during this period in opposition the Liberal party had committed itself to individual liberty and a rejection of the CCF collectivist view of society.[18] The Liberals had opposed many CCF experiments with public enterprise, public auto insurance, and state-run health insurance, yet they had made no major attacks on these programs largely because of their overwhelming popular support in Saskatchewan.

The most important aspect of the Liberal return to power was that it coincided with the period in which market conditions were becoming favourable for the development of many of the province's natural resources, including potash and pulp and paper. Like the CCF, this development was to take place largely though the use of private capital. The political battles then tended to focus on the CCF's claim that the Liberals were giving the province's resource away to foreign capitalists, and the Liberals' claim that the CCF was simply the mouthpiece for the international labour organizations. The question in the debate at this time was the nature of the resource deals as opposed to having private capital invest in the province.

Despite the highly-charged rhetoric surrounding resource development, the Liberals eventually came face-to-face with Saskatchewan's market constraints and began to take a leadership role in the area of resource development. The idea of building a pulp mill had been one that Saskatchewan politicians had longed for, and conditions finally resulted in the development of the Prince Albert Pulp Company 1968—which would ultimately be purchased in its entirety by the NDP in 1980. To get this company off the ground the government made numerous concessions, including a loan guarantee, cutting rights to 18,000 square miles of timber, and the establishment of a Crown corporation, Saskatchewan Forest Products, which would supply wood for the first four years.[19] The Liberal party was willing to act as an entrepreneur in the name of development, even though it had long championed the use of the private sector.

The pulp mill was the centre of the Liberals' industrial strategy, and this mill was quickly followed by another in Meadow Lake. Once again this was a partnership of private and public ownership, but along with loan guarantees and infrastructure, the government was granting the company cutting rights to huge tracts of northern bushland. The government was to be a minority shareholder in the project.[20] These and similar projects demarcated the partisan battle-lines in the province. The NDP charged that this was a give-away of the province's resources to American capitalists and involved unwarranted concessions to wealthy American companies, a common opposition complaint no matter in what province such developments took place. For the NDP it was an example of a private corporation making the gains and the government taking the risk. Indeed, this was an accurate criticism as the province agreed to supply timber to the mill at a loss to encourage its success. It was also a resonant criticism because of growing concerns throughout Canada about foreign investment.[21] As a result of this mood, the government's second deal in Meadow Lake received much more scrutiny in terms of whether it was in the best interest of the province to strike such favourable deals with foreign capitalists.[22]

At the same time as these sorts of questions were being raised, economic conditions began to deteriorate, resulting in the start of the strained relations between the province and the resource sector. In 1969 the government intervened in the potash industry with production controls and a floor price, leading to the first of many challenges from the potash companies that the government was exceeding its constitutional jurisdiction by interfering with inter-provincial trade and commerce. The Liberal government also introduced the province's first deficit budget in over a decade, largely as a result of increased costs of health and education. To compound matters the wheat economy was suffering some rough patches toward the end of the 1960s when the effects of the green revolution began to be felt around the world, leading to increased yields and reduced prices for farmers.[23]

The autocratic style of leadership of Ross Thatcher and the problems in the economy were troubling signs for the Liberals as they headed into the 1971 election. The Liberals campaigned on their record and tried to instil fears that if the NDP won the election, the development of the province would cease. But the NDP under Allan Blakeney campaigned on its strengths in building health care and education, and it developed one of the most detailed and notable election platforms in Canadian political history, the "New Deal for People," which proved to be a remarkable blueprint for most government actions.[24] The NDP suggested it would end the give-away of the province's resources to American business and provide strong fiscal leadership. The Liberals countered with aggressive anti-socialist rhetoric which proved to be ineffective; even dire warnings that the NDP was under the influence of the radical Waffle movement caused little concern among voters.

The NDP victory in 1971 was due, in part, to the unpopularity of Ross Thatcher and failed Liberal policies. But it was also due to the shifting distribution of population in the province that was leading to increased growth in urban areas. The NDP succeeded in attracting this growing young and left-leaning urban middle class and the increasing ranks of professionals who were increasingly attracted to the promise of more active government, greater provincial control of resource development, and innovative programs like the land bank plan which helped young farmers remain on the land.

By the early 1970s a capable and effective entrepreneurial elite emerged within the Saskatchewan bureaucracy. This group, with the electoral support of the traditional "left-populist" coalition of farmers and labour, and the urban middle class, managed to successfully develop Crown-run enterprises that engaged in aggressive resource development. This effort began with the creation of a small exploration company called the Saskatchewan Oil and Gas Exploration Company (SaskOil) in 1973, followed by the Saskatchewan Mining Development Corporation (SMDC) in 1974, which was set up to tap into the potential of hard rock minerals in northern Saskatchewan, particularly uranium and gold. In 1976 the Potash Corporation of Saskatchewan was created, and it quickly purchased 50 per cent of the capacity of the provincial potash industry. This decision was inspired by a negative ruling by the Supreme Court of Canada, which found the province had exceeded its jurisdiction when it tried to tax potash exports.[25] By the end of the 1980s, Saskatchewan had created its so-called "family" of Crown corporations, which included some of the largest resource producers in the province, as well as all major utilities, and plans for aggressive expansion were well underway.

The provincial state had taken a major step and was now operating in the competitive sectors of the economy. This proved to be, for the most part, a pragmatic and well-managed endeavour that succeeded in reducing the province's dependence on wheat, promoted the social democratic goal of collective ownership, and responded to challenges by the federal government for revenues and by the industry for control of the pace of development. As a result of this activity Saskatchewan gained a reputation as a leader among provinces in the development of the local economy, although all provinces, including Alberta, were heavily engaged in similar province-building strategies.[26]

Yet at the very peak of this entrepreneurial activity in 1982 the Blakeney government was defeated. Once again many factors led to the government's defeat, not the least of which was the criticism that the NDP was too technocratic, always looking for a bureaucratic rather than a political solution. The party also lost the support of many of its core constituencies: trade unionists were unhappy with its support for federal price and wage controls, and with its ordering strikers back to work; feminists were dismayed at its refusal to ensure full access to abortion and failure to spend more money on child care; socialists were offended by the attempt to promote public ownership as a non-ideological issue; and environmentalists and peace activists felt betrayed by the eagerness to support uranium developments. On top of this the NDP failed to recognize that the middle class was more interested in relief from high interest rates and was less interested in new spending proposals, however worthy. The NDP's pre-election budget clearly had nothing to offer middle-income earners who were beginning to feel the pinch of the recession of the early 1980s. As Blakeney himself noted after the election, "It is very clear from the results, that we were not responding to the aspirations and expectation of the people of Saskatchewan."[27]

It might have been logical to assume that with the demise of the Blakeney NDP the entire state-led entrepreneurial tradition would have ended, but in fact one of the great surprises was that the long tradition of "province-building" in Saskatchewan was carried on during the decade of Tory government between 1982 and 1991. Despite a powerful commitment to free enterprise, Grant Devine and the Progressive Conservative Party came face-to-face with Saskatchewan's hinterland status and felt compelled to intervene in the economy of the province, although ideologically opposed to it.[28] They made aggressive use of joint ventures, loan guarantees, subsidies, tax concessions, and other ad hoc financing schemes to engage in a large number of well-publicized, but mainly flawed, investments in such activity as heavy oil upgrades, computer translation, fertilizer plants, shopping cart manufacturing, life insurance, and so on. They also privatized a number of the province's best-run and most profitable public enterprises in an attempt to generate a larger private-sector presence in the province and build a new private-enterprise culture. Like Ross Thatcher's Liberal government in the 1960s, the Devine Conservatives of the 1980s clearly saw themselves as the embodiment of the free-enterprise spirit in the province, and unquestionably rode the very wide coattails of Margaret Thatcher, Ronald Reagan, and Brian Mulroney, portraying themselves as committed neo-conservatives. But just like other free-enterprise governments in the past, they too eventually overcame their resistance to state-led development and acted aggressively in the hope of confronting the constraints that face a resource-dependent province.

As the PC government became more entrepreneurial, it also became more mired in scandal, bad investments, and rising debts. Initial enthusiasm for tax cuts resulted in little or no new economic activity and was quickly superseded by tax increases in an effort to control the deficit. The result was that the PCs compromised their free-market ideology and became a reluctant partner in development. However, unlike the NDP, who always wanted to be both an active partner in an enterprise or an outright owner, the Conservatives were content to be a silent partner and a temporary and reluctant owner. If the venture succeeded, the government pulled out, leaving the private partner to reap the profits. If the venture faltered, the government stayed in to prop it up. Thus, without the ability to generate new revenues, provincial deficits began to soar. By 1991, Grant Devine and the Conservative Party had lost whatever popularity they had through a combination of political scandals, personal foibles, arrogance, bad management, and guilt by association with Brian Mulroney's Tories. They were easily defeated in 1991 by the NDP, who promised little other than fiscal competence and personal integrity.

The return of the NDP in Saskatchewan was clearly as much about the popular distaste for the Conservatives as it was about the desire to move the province in a new direction. The NDP simply ran a classic front-runner campaign. It began with a substantial lead in the polls and maintained it throughout by refusing to offer details about their plans. Largely, it must be admitted, it refused to offer details because it didn't have any. While the NDP hurled barbs at the easy target of Grant Devine and his discredited Tories, it made no mistakes and rode a wave of voter hostility.

The fact that the NDP came to power with no clearly articulated agenda was itself an important indication of the changing nature of social democracy. The NDP was losing its traditional identification with labour and was making an appeal to a broader array of voters, many with disparate and often competing interests. In this sense, the NDP, if any questions remained, had moved from its former position as an ideological party towards the dominant brokerage party model. With a decline in voter identification with the issue of class, the NDP played it safe and tried to reassure voters that it would offer good, honest government.

Yet given its history of aggressive state action designed to confront the problems and constraints faced by a hinterland economy, few people in the province, particularly NDP partisans, were prepared for the extent to which the election of the Romanow government signalled the end of Saskatchewan's tradition of activist, entrepreneurial government. Since coming to power there has been no attempt to engage in any economic initiative akin to the Crown-sector development of the 1970s; nor has there been any attempt to use government capital to lever economic activity out of the private sector as in the 1980s. During the 1990s economic policies were secondary to the fiscal imperative of budget management, in particular deficit reduction. This movement away from entrepreneurialism was made explicit by Roy Romanow, who noted that while the Crown sector is important, "What we need now is to really put a concerted game plan in place for value-added production from those resources. And moving from there to identify entrepreneurial ideas, new products, new markets...." He went on to note that the biggest change in moving away from a reliance on the Crown sector "is that there just isn't any more money for major Crown corporation involvement."[29] In place of a strong philosophy of economic intervention and province-building, we now had the language of fiscal crisis, restraint and market-centred development, all of which would be needed to make business more competitive so that the surpluses could be transferred in the name of income equality—policies that resemble those of Tory Blair's New Labour.[30]

SOCIAL TRANSFORMATION IN SASKATCHEWAN

In order to understand this stunning transformation in the philosophy of the governing party, some understanding of the social transformation underway in Saskatchewan over the past two decades is needed. Indeed, the emergence of new political and economic barriers noted previously have combined with the overall policy legacy to produce an embedded provincial state, but they have also produced substantial transformation in the social structure of Saskatchewan and consequently the orientation of the party system and the nature of coalition-building in which the various parties engage. The most notable change in this regard has been the termination of the progressive farmer-labour alliance that used to be the backbone of support for the CCF and later the NDP governments. This coalition at one time provided the solid electoral constituency favouring the more aggressive use of state power aimed at redressing inequality and income insecurity in Saskatchewan. What has emerged are two new but very loose coalitions of "flexible partisans."[31] One consists of voters in rural Saskatchewan who are clear victims of the tremendous restructuring in the agricultural economy but who support the anti-government, free-market, low-taxation policies associated with the former Reform party. The other consists of urban voters made up of service-sector workers, teachers, professionals, trade unionists, and public-sector workers who have also struggled to maintain their position under difficult circumstances, but who still favour what might be termed activist government 1990s style.

The first coalition is based on support from farmers, small-business people, primary-sector workers, and seniors, mostly in rural areas and in smaller urban communities, who feel a strong sense of dislocation and anxiety about the future of rural Saskatchewan. Their concerns come about naturally and are directly related to a series of disturbing changes: rail line abandonment, grain elevator closures, hospital closures, deteriorating roads, declining job opportunities, and an eroding tax base are all sources of the sense of discomfort in rural Saskatchewan. Rural voters may still favour the "populism" so much a part of the prairie tradition, but they are now more enamoured with the right-wing, low-tax, anti-Quebec populism of the old Reform party rather than the "tax and spend" populism associated with the "socialist" NDP. The farmers who have managed to survive economic restructuring in the province have done so on the basis of viewing farming as a capital-intensive small business, and have abandoned romantic notions of farming as an ennobling way of life. No longer are they the "agrarian socialists" or the "independent commodity producers" who used to be the backbone of progressive social democracy in Saskatchewan. These small farmers of the past have been replaced by a new class of "agri-business" entrepreneurs who have hundreds of thousands, and in many cases millions, of dollars invested in land and equipment, and whose natural allies have increasingly come to be the small business community. Farm size has increased in Saskatchewan over the past two decades, and with it the number of individual farmers have decreased (Table 9.2). Between 1976 and 1996, 14,000 Saskatchewan farms have ceased to exist, creating insecurity and a high level of concern amongst farmers eager to maintain their economic position. Electorally, this voting block first asserted itself in 1986 when it gave Grant Devine his second term in office with a smaller percentage of the popular vote than the NDP received due to an electoral map which heavily favoured rural Saskatchewan. This coalition has strongly supported non-NDP parties in the 1991, 1995 and 1999 provincial elections in Saskatchewan and has been a strong presence in both federal elections in the 1990s, voting for the traditional prairie protest message, only this time selecting the Reform party as opposed to the NDP as the vehicle of their protest.

The other electoral coalition is urban and consists of professionals (lawyers, teachers, social workers), public-sector workers, trade unionists, and progressive farmers who have supported the NDP more or less consistently since the 1970s. As urbanization in the province has continued, and

TABLE 9.2 **AVERAGE SIZE OF FARMS IN SASKATCHEWAN**

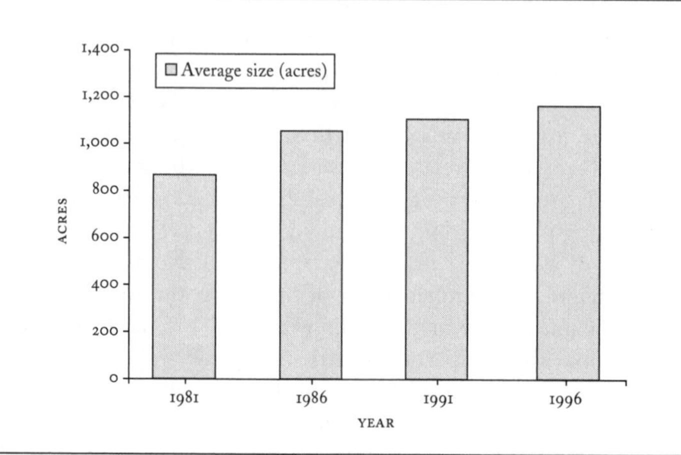

Source: Statistics Canada, Census of Canada

as the employment structures have increasingly come to reflect a service-oriented economy, a distinct urban voting block, often dependent on employment by some level of government, has begun to assert itself in Regina and Saskatoon and some of the smaller urban centres such as Moose Jaw and Prince Albert, which were NDP strongholds in the 1990s. This changing dynamic can be seen in any number of policy outputs of the NDP government which have tended to favour, or have been perceived to favour, urban areas, most notably redistribution within the Legislature from 66 to 58 seats and health-care reform which involved shutting down/conversion of 51 small rural hospitals. Both actions were viewed as anti-rural policies, the latter leading to sustained anti-government protests.

These changes are reflected within the NDP itself, which has become much more of an urban party in which middle-class professional politicians have taken over the leadership of the party, replacing the older farmer/labour alliance that was a key to the party's strength in the 1940s and 1950s. Labour has increasingly been marginalized, shunted aside in the party's quest to appeal to the centre of the spectrum. This marginalization of labour can be seen in the tremendous difficulty organized labour had in getting reforms to the Trade Union Act: reform legislation was tabled only in April 1994, three and a half years after the NDP came to power, and when it did come it contained none of the progressive measures, such as prohibition of replacement workers, that unions had demanded. In B.C. and Ontario, by way of contrast, reformed labour legislation was among the first policies enacted by new NDP governments in those provinces. The same is true of pay equity: Saskatchewan remains one of the few provinces without pay equity legislation, despite strong and persistent pressure from organized labour.

The changes to the social and class structure of Saskatchewan are, of course, a product of the changing rural economy and shifts in the nature of employment. Like all provinces Saskatchewan has witnessed a decline in employment in the primary sector, slow growth in secondary manufacturing, and steady growth in the so-called "human-oriented service sector"—health and social services, human relations, finance, marketing, research and development, public relations, entertainment, and communications (see Table 9.3). This "new" urban class in Saskatchewan has developed later than in most other provinces, but like their counterparts they are increasingly predisposed to place a premium on good public services, particularly health care and education, without sacrificing too much in terms of tax increases. This class has had to gain and maintain its position under difficult economic circumstances, and this has left it rather unwilling to share its portion of a dwindling economic pie in order to prop up expensive programs that can support only very dubious records of achievement. Yet all the same, there is little indication of a strong anti-tax sentiment in this group, nor is there

TABLE 9.3 **EMPLOYED BY INDUSTRY IN SASKATCHEWAN**

	THOUSANDS								
	1990	1991	1992	1993	1994	1995	1996	1997	1998
Agriculture	87	88	78	79	70	72	71	67	71
Non-Agriculture	372	371	372	376	387	388	390	407	407
Primary Industries	13	14	13	12	11	14	17	16	16
Manufacturing	26	26	26	26	28	31	31	34	31
Service	150	154	155	156	159	154	159	166	173
Public Sector	30	30	30	30	30	29	29	28	27

Source: Statistics Canada 71-220 Labour Force Annual Averages

much evidence that they would like to see cuts to government programs from which they would not likely benefit, such as welfare. At the same time, however, this new urban coalition has also promoted a wide range of progressive social policy priorities, many of which have long been associated with social democratic ideology, e.g., the expansion of the realm of individual autonomy, protection of women's and minorities' rights, and encouragement of self-expression and a diversity of lifestyles.

These new divisions, which have become more apparent over the last two decades, contrast sharply with earlier periods when rural Saskatchewan dominated provincial politics and was involved very directly in the governance of the province. The rural population was active in politics mainly because of the nature of Saskatchewan's extensive system of municipalities which necessitated that farmers be involved in their own local governance, often creating individuals with the skills necessary to perform well in provincial politics. The same was true of the network of co-operatives which, during the 1940s and 1950s, were almost exclusively governed by rural-based organization. Under such conditions a large portion of the rural population became accustomed to playing an active role in different organizations. In Saskatchewan it was the farmers who controlled most local organizations, compared to businesspeople and the professional middle class in the large urban areas. In rural Saskatchewan, hospital, YMCA, community and other organizations were dominated by farmers. The Wheat Pool itself was a strongly democratic organization in which one out of every six members was an elected member of the Wheat Pool committees in their localities.

The previous tendency in Saskatchewan had been to spread political responsibility among countless citizens boards; this brought about wider political participation and made politics more anonymous and less dependent on outstanding leadership. Lipset noted about this period, "Political participation of the ordinary citizen in Saskatchewan is not restricted to the intermediary recurring elections. Politics is organized to be a daily concern and responsibility of the common citizen."[32] Sharing in the government of their communities was a common experience, and Saskatchewan politics were more decentralized than it is today. Yet all of this activity was more of a functional requirement of the wheat economy than some grand plan to create a small-scale democracy on the prairies based upon the anti-statist and co-operative traditions of the CCF and its Fabian intellectuals. Thus, inevitably, with the coming of good roads, more reliable automobiles, the increase in farm size, elevator closures and rail-line abandonment, we have begun to witness the breakdown of smaller rural communities. The consensus within the farm community has also broken down, with many farmers now favouring a reduced role for such intermediary organizations as the Canada Wheat Board and a greater freedom for farmers to sell their grain on their own. Hence, divisions have begun to occur in rural Saskatchewan between those more prosperous farmers who now wish to see an end to government monopolies, and those mostly represented by the National Farmers Union, who wish to see a strong government presence in the rural economy.

Progressive grass-roots political activity, of course, still takes place in Saskatchewan, but it is now more likely to be a product of the new decentralized pluralism in urban areas. The previously fixed identities associated with economic class have been replaced by a flux of new identities that are often contextualized by gender, race, ethnicity, sexual preference, education, social role, and so on. For over a decade now, social commentators have emphasized the extent to which various "postmaterialist" values and policy priorities—e.g., ecology, women's rights, and multiculturalism—have displaced traditional, materialist concerns—e.g., jobs, economic stability, and pensions. This has furthered the process of social fragmentation and individualization, which had added considerably to the process of dealignment and realignment. In particular, Saskatchewan, along with all other provinces, has seen the rise of new social movements that share a conspicuous rejection of the old ideologies, including social democracy. This is reflected in their basis of identification, which no longer derives from traditionally established political and socio-economic codes (left/right or working class/capitalist class), but from a range of different issues (gender, race, age, locality, etc.).[33] All of this has naturally been observed by the NDP, which has shifted in response to the challenges noted above.

The confirmation of the division between rural and urban coalitions was vividly demonstrated during the 1999 provincial election in which the NDP won the majority of its 29 seats in the legislature in the cities of Regina (11/11) and Saskatoon (10/11), and the rest in larger regional centres like

Prince Albert (2/2) and Moose Jaw (2/2) and in Northern Saskatchewan (2/2). The Saskatchewan Party picked up all of its 26 seats in rural Saskatchewan and has no urban representation. Clearly the province is facing a divisive rural/urban split based on how the two coalitions view the primary issues facing the province. These divisions will likely be exacerbated by the nature of the party system in Saskatchewan, which will exploit this split for partisan advantage.

THE NDP AND THE PARTY SYSTEM

Given the institutional and intellectual constraints on social democracy, the shift in voting alliances and the decline in party identification, it is natural that in opposition the NDP would emphasize partisan competition over creative policy debate. Indeed, one of the truths about Saskatchewan politics is that party competition is fierce, resulting in such a highly partisan legislative atmosphere that it sometimes imperils the proper workings of parliamentary democracy in the province.[34] At no time was this more evident than during the Progressive Conservative government in the 1980s, especially during its second term, in which the government centralized power in the cabinet and increasingly ignored the legislative assembly.[35] As a consequence of this atmosphere, NDP MLAS in Saskatchewan have adopted an intensely partisan attitude and share a visceral dislike for their legislative opponents. They become so deeply immersed in the adversarial practices of their chamber that they cannot realistically see any alternative method of making decisions than the purely partisan one. The key explanations for government action, in this case, are more often to be found in the dialectic of government-opposition rivalry (the "ins" versus the "outs") rather than in the application of the principles of social democracy.

Of course, the advantages of maintaining this highly adversarial and competitive atmosphere accrue more to the NDP than any other party because of the fact that it is the "natural governing party." Within this interpretation, the party that has a greater chance of winning an election will have a greater chance of attracting and recruiting candidates of first-rate ability. Indeed, the party's previous success, even in the face of electoral defeats in 1982 and 1986, meant that it was able to maintain an extremely high degree of internal stability as well as attracting candidates with broadly popular appeal. While electoral defeats in minority or opposition parties contribute to conflict and the conflict contributes to electoral defeats, this vicious cycle is avoided in a party like the NDP, with its status as the natural governing party. As George Perlin has noted, "A party with expectations of governing will select candidates with the skills, abilities and resources to win and to govern. The party will calculate more strategically about winning and will attract more of the politically ambitious, who will seek the party as an avenue to political advancement."[36]

In contrast, the opposition parties in Saskatchewan are often in disarray, no more so than in the face of their defeats in the 1991 and 1995 provincial elections, both of which the NDP easily won. An amazing display of this thesis is to be found in the virtual disintegration of the Conservative party, and the ongoing strife, leadership controversies, and desertion of half the legislative caucus of the provincial Liberal party to the newly formed Saskatchewan Party. The result of all this activity is that the provincial Conservative party has taken a 10-year hiatus from all political activity in the province, with the blessing of the national leader. In its place has emerged a new "free enterprise" coalition called the Saskatchewan Party, composed of disaffected Liberal MLAs and the remaining Tory caucus, all with the vocal and highly visible support by a handful of Reform party MPs from rural Saskatchewan. The total disintegration of the Conservatives was a consequence of both the party's political legacy of debts and deficits and the province's most serious political scandal. This scandal involved a total of 20 former Conservative cabinet ministers and MLAs, all of whom were charged with defrauding the Saskatchewan Legislature: 15 have been convicted, including Conservative senator and former deputy premier Eric Bernston; three have been acquitted and two are pending hearings. Added to all this activity were persistent rumours that the Reform party would jump into this vacuum on the right with its first foray into provincial politics. The result was the seemingly frantic efforts to create a new right-wing coalition.

The party system in Saskatchewan has, since 1944, been increasingly polarized between something known as the "free-enterprise" vote that has an ideological predisposition not to vote for the NDP, leaning toward the Liberals and the Tories, and now the Saskatchewan Party, depending on who appears to have the greatest chance of victory (Table 9.4). These opposition parties will raid the other's base of support and often present themselves as the only credible alternative to the NDP.[37] The NDP usually has only one legitimate opponent on the right, although the Liberals and the Tories have often competed in any election, allowing the NDP to gain office with 40 per cent or less of the popular vote. This occurred most recently in the 1999 election when the NDP managed to form a minority government while receiving less of the popular vote than the Saskatchewan Party. The NDP, of course, is only too happy to see this situation continue and will do what it can to engage in the politics of "divide and conquer" at election time, preferring to see at least two or maybe three "right-wing" parties competing for the "free enterprise" anti-NDP vote.

As the dominant party, therefore, the NDP remains capable of attracting both a broad membership and attractive candidates. Yet this fact has also led to a structure which has become increasingly controlled from the top. This is a phenomenon noticed very early in the history of democratic par-

TABLE 9.4 **SASKATCHEWAN PROVINCIAL ELECTION RESULTS SINCE 1921**

	LIBERAL		CCF/NDP		CONSERVATIVES	
	Popular vote (%)	*seats*	*Popular vote (%)*	*seats*	*Popular vote (%)*	*seats*
1921	51	46	8*	6	7	3
1925	52	50	23*	6	18	3
1929	46	28	7**	5	36	24
1934	48	50	24†	5	27	—
1938	45	38	19	10	12	—
1944	35	5	53	47	11	—
1948	31	19	48	31	8	—
1952	39	11	54	42	2	—
1956	30	14	45	36	2	—
1960	33	17	41	37	14	—
1964	40	32	40	25	19	1
1967	46	35	44	24	10	—
1971	43	15	55	45	2	—
1975	32	15	40	39	28	7
1978	14	—	48	44	38	17
1982	5	—	38	9	54	55
1986	10	1	45	25	45	38
1991	23	1	51	55	26	10
1995	35	11	47	42	18	5
1999	20.2	4	38.7	29	39.6††	25

* Progressives † Farmer-Labour Party ** Mostly Independents †† Saskatchewan Party

Source: Adapted from Rand Dyck, *Provincial Politics in Canada*, 3rd ed. (Scarborough: Prentice Hall Canada Inc, 1996).

ties, most notably in the pioneering work of Robert Michels.[38] The ability of the NDP leadership to control the party was given its most forceful expression in their ability to have a resolution opposing uranium mining reversed in the face of tremendous grass-roots resistance.[39]

Despite elite control and a lack of intellectual vigour, the NDP remains a popular coalition of progressive farmers, urban unions, middle-class professionals, and public-sector workers and is probably the most successful membership-based party in the country. The broad composition of its support has helped the party avoid the decline that many social democratic parties experienced in the 1980s. The decline of other parties of the left is generally seen to be based on the dual shock to organized labour of deindustrialization and globalization which were destroying the working-class foundation on which Western social democratic parties were based. In Saskatchewan there was no industrial workforce to disorganize through globalization, and local businesses threatening to go "global" was never a realistic possibility. Indeed, some support for "globalilzation" or free trade has always been a feature of the Saskatchewan state because of the need to find stable and reliable export markets for its natural resources.

The NDP in Saskatchewan, because of its history of governing, managed to weather the 1980s as a government-in-exile, and did not concern itself with a debate on a new policy agenda for the 1990s. It maintained its popularity, its support, and its structure, and is still very much a mass-based political party. And while the party machine has remained strong, it has become, as with other parties, largely a machine for running elections, nominating candidates, and reviewing leadership. Like other political parties, the NDP is not a structure for making policy. The point to emphasize is that the NDP in Saskatchewan during the 1980s increasingly focused on electoral positioning and failed to articulate a new economic or social vision. Indeed the 1991 campaign chair, Jack Messer, noted at an NDP convention shortly after the election: "I know a lot of you were showing a little bit of concern [about the lack of a platform] but the discipline and the strategy and the logic of that contributed largely to us winning the election."[40] The admission that a weak platform was part of the strategy, however, did not imply that the party had a clearly articulated vision for economic development waiting to be announced—it did not. This is a far cry from the NDP's election 20 years earlier, when they came to power with their famous Waffle-inspired "New Deal for People" which provided a clear framework from which most of the government's economic and social policy innovations came. In contrast, the party in 1991 appeared to have abandoned whatever class affiliations it had as well as its ideological presuppositions, appearing to many to be the advanced wing of reforming market liberalism.

When campaigning in 1991 the Saskatchewan NDP had the advantage of being a party that had an experienced and highly credible leader and a veteran core of MLAs, many of whom had cabinet experience. They were running against an unpopular premier and an equally despised government. Thus they had no need to run a positive campaign with a clearly defined social democratic agenda. The NDP had a large lead in the polls before the election and it ran a classic front-runner campaign. Even the NDP slogan "The Saskatchewan Way" captured the moderate, common-sense approach, compared to the Tory slogan with its Wagnerian overtones, "The Courage and the Will," which merely reflected the excesses of the decade of conservative ideological rule in the province.

In subsequent election campaigns the NDP continued to concentrate on the contrast between the Tories' fiscal irresponsibility and their successful elimination of the budget deficit. Even in the 1999 campaign the NDP was still making allusions to Grant Devine, and the major prop Roy Romanow routinely pointed to was a graph that showed the years of Tory deficits and the turnaround in public finances orchestrated by his government. The NDP made it clear that they represented the party of professionalism and fiscal conservatism. The NDP's campaigns during the 1990s were waged in a very cautious style that underpromised, and played on the fears that voters should have about the opposition, which in 1999 was the Saskatchewan Party, but which the NDP dubbed throughout the campaign the "Saskatories." Caution, however, is as much a product of the constraints associated with governing the embedded state as it is about the preferred style of the premier. As less cautious NDP premiers have discovered, bold action from an ideologically committed party government sitting atop an embedded provincial state can produce unwelcome reactions, both from enemies as well as from friends, quickly eroding any government's limited political capital.

THE NDP IN SASKATCHEWAN: STEERING THE EMBEDDED STATE

With few new ideas of how to proceed with economic development, with formidable new barriers to interventionist economic activity, with continued economic stagnation due to low commodity prices, and with no coherent constituency that would support aggressive state-led entrepreneurialism, the NDP in Saskatchewan, almost by default, made the debt and deficit the major issue during their last years in opposition. In the run-up to the 1991 election, the NDP endlessly discussed the issue of provincial finances, pledging to "open the books" if elected. The party also managed to successfully appropriate the anti-tax sentiment that began with the introduction of the

Goods and Services Tax (GST) by the federal Conservative party in 1991, and which was fuelled by the provincial decision to harmonize the provincial sales tax with it. When this was coupled with the mushrooming debt crisis (apparent since 1986, when the Conservative government announced immediately after the election that year that it had miscalculated the deficit, noting that it was $1.1 billion instead of the $200 million originally forecast) the NDP had an issue that they carried through their final two years in opposition, coasting to an easy return to office. By helping to unleash the hysteria over the deficit while in opposition, the NDP was bound to live with it when they came to office.

There was some speculation that the Saskatchewan NDP had seen the hysterical reaction of the business community to the Ontario NDP's first budget and was chased out of a high deficit strategy while in opposition. However, this misses a key point about the Saskatchewan NDP. Voters in the province accept that the NDP is the voice of fiscal responsibility, even fiscal conservatism. The NDP built up an enviable reputation for professional public administration during both the years of CCF government and the Blakeney government of the 1970s. There was a strong bureaucratic tradition that had been inherited from the old Fabian elements of the CCF that accepted the necessity of living within one's means.[41] It was a part of the small-town, small-"c" conservative values that have been a major part of Saskatchewan and continue to be a strong presence in the province.[42] Yet this natural tendency towards fiscal responsibility is enhanced by the constraints associated with the embedded state.

The key word in the government's lexicon of economic activity, as well as in most other areas of government policy, has been caution. Implicit in this is the recognition, lost in the pro-business hype and mega-project mania of the Devine years, that the province of Saskatchewan has a cyclical economy based on a few primary resources. While the Romanow government has not said that it has given up on economic development and diversification, it is clear that it holds out little hope for a significant diversification of the provincial economy away from a limited array of commodities that it produces and exports. The Premier confirmed this with a series of speeches he gave around the province shortly after coming to office in which he noted that "[t]en years of wasteful spending, careless management, and a lack of public accountability have brought Saskatchewan to the point of financial disaster."[43] The plan was to reign in spending, encourage thoughtful management, and create a strong sense of public accountability.

The first step in the articulation of the government's limited strategy for the provincial economy was to convince the people of the province that there was indeed a financial crisis, but that this crisis was manageable if people were willing to make the necessary sacrifices. During the election, the NDP had let it be known that they would establish a panel to examine the province's financial situation before the government made any decisions about what direction it would take. The Financial Management Review Commission, headed by a former associate of the Premier, Donald Gass, was to be the vehicle for this activity. It was established on November 19, 1991 and made its report early in 1992.

While the remaining Tory MLAs accused the government of using the Commission to conduct a political witch-hunt, there was considerable support for such an inquiry in the province as a whole. The final document that emerged, while critical of some past practices, avoided a major partisan attack on the previous administration and provided a number of sound recommendations for the improvement of public administration and increased public accountability, which the government quickly accepted.[44]

The message of the Gass Commission, which set the tone for subsequent government statements on the economy, was that "[w]e need to review our expectations and determine what we can realistically support with the income generated by Saskatchewan's economy and resources."[45] The need to review "our expectations" was based on the fact that the debt, upon critical examination, was much higher than had been reported. Using procedures established by the Public Sector Accounting and Auditing Committee (PSACC) of the Canadian Institute of Chartered Accountants, the government debt rose from $3.31 billion to $7.53 billion as of 31 March 1991. Added to this were a number of one-time write offs of bad loans which the government added to its 1991 deficit bringing the total accumulated debt to $8.865 billion. The Gass Commission and the Government both asked: What should the people of Saskatchewan expect, given this debt? The answer was they should expect less than they had in the past.

The government used the Commission as the first step in its attempt to foster a reduction of expectations. But the Commission was also to be valuable in helping increase the public's sense that the government was operating in their best interests. It is not surprising, therefore, that the government acted on many of the recommendations that concentrated on improving the accounting practices of government, which would help ensure a greater degree of accountability. In particular, the government moved quickly to avoid all the off-budget financial manipulation that had been used by the Conservatives to make the debt and deficit seem smaller. The NDP were also happy to give the Auditor-General, who had had a long-standing battle with the previous government over access to the financial records of Crown corporations, more authority to audit them. Many similar recommendations were acted on, including increasing control over Crown agencies and their reporting requirements; directing Crown agency revenues to general government revenues; establishing one easy-to-read financial statement for all government spending and revenues; tightening management control over government operations; tightening control over Crown agency reporting requirements; reviewing government contract tendering to dispel the perception of patronage; limiting the amount of funds that can be committed to any project without legislative approval; re-establishing the Crown Management Board as a Cabinet committee; and abolishing the Heritage Fund, to name the most prominent.

All of this was rather bloodless, but it did enhance accountability along with encouraging the belief that the NDP was not using state power in an aggressive manner because of the nature of the financial situation. As Gass noted, "Our economy can no longer support the public sector infrastructure that we have built to serve the quality of life and the standard of living we have come to expect."[46] This would become the theme not only of the government's first budget, released two months after the Commission reported, but of all subsequent budgets as well.

With the release of the Gass Commission report, many NDP supporters were quick to see the writing on the wall. In particular, the public-sector unions saw the momentum building for major budget cuts and quickly commissioned a counter-report by University of Prince Edward Island economics professor Jim Sentence. This report argued that the doom and gloom contained in the Gass report was not justified. Problems in Saskatchewan were related to the cyclical nature of the economy. As Sentence noted, "Overall the Province's current finances demonstrate no alarming tendencies, no evidence that debt financing will soon push expenditures to the point where infrastructure would have to be cut further to match available revenues."[47]

The unions used this to argue that the crisis was exaggerated and that spending levels should be maintained or even increased. None of the critics of the Gass Commission had much influence on the government, however. Romanow was firmly committed to a policy of deficit reduction, supported by the voting public. For the government, this was a policy that was intellectually correct, politically expedient, and an accurate reflection of the new embedded state's limited mobility.

The Gass Commission did, however, make one recommendation that led to the government's major economic policy statement. It suggested "that the government should review the mandate and role of the various agencies which are currently involved in economic development and diversification initiatives."[48] Out of this recommendation the government produced what has turned out to be its blueprint for the economy, "Partnership for Renewal: A Strategy for the Saskatchewan Economy." This was followed in 1996 by the government's "Partnership for Growth" strategy, which continued the same strategic focus. These documents confirm, if any confirmation is necessary, the government's retreat from entrepreneurial economic intervention and its desire to create the conditions that would allow "clusters" of private-sector enterprises to flourish. In fact, if anything can be said to have inspired the government economic development strategy it would probably be Michael Porter's work for the Business Council on National Issues (BCNI) and the Government of Canada.[49]

ECONOMIC POLICY IN SASKATCHEWAN: A PARTNERSHIP FOR RENEWAL

In between the government's first and second budgets, both of which included cuts in public spending between of 4 and 6 per cent, it released its major economic policy statement, the "Partnership for Renewal."[50] This was a small-"c" conservative document concerned with reducing government red tape, balancing the budget, streamlining regulation, and encouraging investment through taxation policy. It certainly had none of the flare or raised few of the expectations of the Ontario NDP's flirtation with European-style industrial strategy.[51] Nor was it a bold statement about the use of the Crown sector to gain control of the economy. While the NDP was committing itself to full employment by the year 2000, a positive climate for investment, and building on existing strengths, there was no concrete plan on how to achieve these goals, particularly in light of the government's firm stand on deficit reduction.

The document was filled with the now compulsory language about establishing partnerships, ensuring a competitive tax system, developing a strong educational system, maximizing trade opportunities, and streamlining the delivery of service for business. However, the document was revealing for what it said about the government's view of the Saskatchewan economy. The provincial state should have a more limited role in economic development: "In practical terms, the vision contained in our strategy is based on a mixed economy with a strong private sector and a continuing and expanding role for the co-operative sector which has always played a critical role in our economy. The vision also incorporates a strong role for the public sector as a legislative innovator, steward and advocate as well as a full partner with the private and co-operative sector."[52] There is no significant role for the state independent of the private sector. This new, limited role was to be guided by the following five principles:

1. working with economic development partners; (business, labour, communities, aboriginal groups, co-operatives, and farmers)
2. encouraging regional and community-led solutions to economic renewal;

3. working in partnership with business on market-led projects;
4. focusing support to maximize employment opportunities; and
5. establishing clear investment criteria to guide provincial economic development.

These were extremely modest principles, guaranteed not to offend—or to excite—anyone. They were a far cry from previous NDP calls for increased public ownership and central planning, but the government was operating in what it regarded as an era of diminishing expectations. The economic document really was, at best, a "rolling plan with a five-to-ten year time horizon [that would] be adapted to meet changing needs and conditions."[53]

The government also indicated in this document that it had lost faith in the state's ability to successfully engage in economic development activity. In this regard, the report noted that "approaches by governments in the past have not succeeded.... Several generic solutions aimed at stimulating economic growth have not been viewed as successful.... Governments have also been reluctant to share decision-making power with community economic development organizations and representatives of business...."[54] This is a government wary of venturing into the area of economic development, given the sad state of previous attempts.

The report also included acceptance of the fact that the Saskatchewan economy, rather than being able to diversify, must build on the limited strengths that exist in the province. Thus, the strategy aimed to "focus on identifying opportunities to sustain, improve and build around existing industries and businesses."[55] Gone was any belief in box and shoe factories, but equally absent were the Conservative party beliefs that a wide variety of manufacturing ventures, such as aircraft manufacturing, could be attracted to the province simply by providing generous financing or outright subsidies. Instead the government would concentrate on six strategic sectors: Mining/Minerals; Agri-Value; Forestry; Tourism; Energy; and Information and Communications Technology. Within each of these sectors the government would encourage a forging of "alliances between large in-province and out-of province companies and Saskatchewan's small to medium sized fast-growing firms.... The government plans to refocus its business support programs to nurture such firms as they strive to compete in global markets."[56]

The report did recommend the establishment of the Provincial Action Committee on the Economy (PACE) which would cost the government very little and create the appearance of activity. PACE, which was limited to an advisory role, quickly became one of the main links between the government and business. As one local newspaper columnist noted, "Romanow uses it as a primary window on the business world."[57] This body was dominated by private business figures: 20 of the 24 were either senior private-sector managers, co-op executives or public-sector managers with close ties to the NDP. PACE, however, did reflect the NDP's long held view that government, along with business and the co-ops, are the three main engines of the Saskatchewan economy. The committee was to meet regularly to review and advise the government on economic strategy, come up with new ideas on economic development, help implement the economic strategy, build consensus around specific initiatives, and develop co-operative partnerships in key sectors.

The other major initiative that emerged out of the Partnership for Renewal was the establishment of the so-called Regional Economic Development Authorities (REDA).[58] REDAs were an attempt to deal with the large-scale transformation taking place in rural Saskatchewan as well as to decentralize some economic decision-making. It was expected that 20,000 people were going to leave rural Saskatchewan in the 1990s. The rural population was in such a precipitous decline that much of the municipal and provincial infrastructure was not properly used and there was an excess of organizations involved in community, business, and economic development. In the past the provincial government, like its federal counterpart, had not been willing to share decision-making power with community economic development organizations, leading to frustration and delays on the part of local communities. In the 1990s, it was beginning to welcome the idea of sharing responsibility for economic development.

A final example of the movement away from a proactive role in economic development was the decision to eliminate the Saskatchewan Economic Development Corporation (SEDCO). SEDCO had been created by the NDP in 1963, with a mandate to diversify the province's economy by supplying manufacturing firms with loans and building industrial parks. However, even generous loans and the offer of subsidized space were not enough to attract much serious manufacturing to the province. The reason is simply that in market economies, hinterland regions do not normally become the site of secondary processing.[59] Equally important, however, is the fact that most other provinces are in the business of offering loans and other similar opportunities to business. Therefore, in the last decade of its existence, SEDCO ended up not subsidizing manufacturing firms, but rather was loaning money to restaurants, golf courses, flower shops, ice cream parlours, sporting goods stores—businesses which essentially add nothing to the economy but simply take market share from existing firms, something that always annoyed business advocacy groups like the Canadian Federation of Independent Business. And while the corporation had been profitable in 15 of its first 19 years, since 1982 (the year the Progressive

Conservative government came to power) it began to lose money as it became more politically oriented in its decision-making. SEDCO losses were eventually written off by the NDP and added on to the provincial debt. The organization was slowly dismantled, to be replaced by the Saskatchewan Opportunities Corporation (SOCO) in 1994. SOCO was to be more diligent and operate according to a more market-oriented approach, although given the manner in which it is structured it could become another SEDCO some time in the future.

At the very least these are extremely modest attempts at economic development, hardly different from similar plans in Alberta and Manitoba. When compared to the hundreds of millions of dollars that went into purchasing potash mines, uranium mines, pulp mills, and so on during the 1970s, or the millions that went to finance fertilizer plants and loan guarantees for insurance companies in the 1980s, this is a definite change in direction. The government's economic agenda is clearly one in which it wishes to see an attractive investment climate for business, but it has little interest in spending money to attract business. In general, the government indicates a profound suspicion about the ability of the state to generate economic activity on its own. In this regard the NDP government wants to create an economy that is attractive to investment, but it is wary of making investments of its own.

Much of this new reluctance to act entrepreneurially is a direct result of the numerous constraints outlined earlier, all of which have combined to produce in Saskatchewan an economic policy-making environment that is inhospitable to any direct government intervention in the economy. However, while this may be a break with provincial practice of the previous twenty years, it should not necessarily be seen as a departure from CCF-NDP tradition. The NDP in Saskatchewan has always been a party of fiscal conservatives, and there has been a constant recognition that the state of the province's finances were, and should always be, of primary importance in economic decision-making. When examined in relation to previous CCF-NDP budgets and policy statements, the current government is heir to that NDP tradition which emphasized Fabian bureaucratic management and fiscal responsibility. Thus, the criticism that "sound finance and fiscal conservatism are fundamentally incompatible with a just and equitable society and therefore with social democracy itself"[60] is obviously dismissed by the current government and many faithful NDP supporters. Typically, the government noted in a recent Throne Speech that they consider themselves to be the inheritors of Tommy Douglas's legacy in which fiscal responsibility is to be achieved "by sharing the burden equitably and protecting those least able to sacrifice."[61]

However, the NDP government's fiscal prudence and its success in battling deficits inevitably meant that there were decisions that negatively affected various interests in the province. As a consequence, no matter how happy citizens in general might have been with the NDP government's record on fiscal management, there were also citizens, often the same ones, who wanted increased spending. Concerns ranged from rural roads, schools, the farm crisis, social services, aboriginal poverty, post-secondary education, and of course health care. Nurses engaged in a frontal assault on the NDP in the summer of 1999 when they staged an illegal strike and defied back-to-work legislation, and farmers organized some of the most intense protests seen in Saskatchewan for decades. So no matter how "balanced" the NDP government felt it was with regards to its management of the economy, it slowly eroded its political capital, particularly in rural Saskatchewan. The re-election of a minority NDP government in 1999 with virtually no representation from rural Saskatchewan clearly indicates that steering the embedded provincial state during a period of retrenchment inevitably results in decisions that favour some interests over others. While the perception of the NDP government had been that it was "sharing the pain" equally, rural Saskatchewan was simmering with a resentment that spilled over in the months leading up to the election and finally produced the most polarized electoral outcome in Saskatchewan history. While the NDP did manage to form a coalition government with the small Liberal caucus giving the government political stability, it is also a strategy that may bring about what the "free-enterprise" coalition that now clusters around the Saskatchewan Party has always hoped and prayed for: a single place for the anti-NDP vote to reside.

CONCLUSION: THE END OF THE ENTREPRENEURIAL PROVINCIAL STATE?

It would appear that the era of aggressive expansion and entrepreneurial province-building in Saskatchewan has come to an end. The reasons for this are varied and complex, but would doubtless include the lack of faith in traditional state-led solutions; an intellectual barrenness on the Canadian left; changing employment and settlement patterns; free-trade agreements, including those emerging between provinces; constitutional amendments; declining provincial revenues; debts and deficits; and the Canadian Health and Social Transfer Act (CHST). All these new constraints have led to a retreat of the entrepreneurial state and its replacement by the embedded state, continually struggling to maintain its existing programs and unable to risk innovation, all the while trying to manage the process of fiscal retrenchment. This situation is reflected in the extremely modest policy agenda in Saskatchewan, no more so than in the area of economic development, where the dominant ideas include a belief that whatever growth occurs in the Saskatchewan economy will be in the area of primary resource production and export, with some very limited movement into secondary processing.

Critics of the current provincial government have seen these outputs as a failure of imagination on the part of the NDP, which has become a willing participant in a "global corporate agenda" lacking the will to challenge global capital.[62] Yet not considered is the possible role of the new constraints limiting the ability of a provincial government to control economic activity within its own jurisdiction, no matter how much imagination or will it displays. Most of the really useful levers of economic activity are controlled by federal governments, who have their own ideas about monetary policy, interest rates, currency exchange rates, tax incentives, job training, and trade laws. To make matters worse, there is a huge discrepancy between a provincial government's limited constitutional ability to raise revenue and its constitutional responsibilities over expensive areas of jurisdiction such as health care, welfare, and education. To be sure, provinces do have access to certain direct measures that influence industrial activity within their boundaries—spending powers, use of regulations, procurement policies, Crown corporations and agencies, and control of labour legislation. But these measures can be used only within very circumscribed policy areas and only within provincial borders. Moreover, there is no guarantee that governments in other provinces—not to mention at the federal level—will establish corresponding or complementary policies. Thus, to expect any sub-national government to create an economic policy that runs counter to the established policies of other provinces and the federal government in Canada is dangerous and foolhardy. The expectation that the NDP government in Saskatchewan could establish a sort of visionary social democratic industrial strategy is unrealistic, especially at a time when the federal government is fixated, above all else, on liberalized trade and deficit and debt control.

Overall, politicians in Saskatchewan today must face a variety of pressures and limitations not experienced by previous generations of provincial political actors. In socio-cultural terms, Saskatchewan is now a more diverse and fragmented society in which a variety of new and often vocal organized interests—women, ethnic minorities, aboriginal people, persons with disabilities, gays and lesbians, and environmentalists—make demands on the government from perspectives that do not fit neatly into pre-conceived notions of what is left, right or centre. And in a political-economic sense, Saskatchewan in the 1990s evokes the image of a society of diminished expectations and stalled economic growth (with emphasis being shifted to service sectors), in which rising budget deficits are no longer effectively handled by the classic economic remedies of capitalists or socialists.

On top of this, the NDP government came to office in Saskatchewan when the historic fortunes of social democratic economic policy were receiving harsh criticism. The rightward movement of the debate changed the nature of thinking about economic policy and required the NDP to alter some of its economic thinking, not entirely because it was flawed, but because this shift in public mood was not conducive to the kind of Keynesian economic policy that characterized the party in the past. The rightward slide of political rhetoric also resulted in some major policies that embody such preferences and limit the options available to others. Of course the major impediment was the movement towards comprehensive free trade with the United States and Mexico, through the FTA and NAFTA, as well as comprehensive trade with the rest of the world, embodied in GATT. This was part of the drift in the 1980s towards "globalization," which has been loudly proclaimed by all advanced industrial nations as the precondition of economic growth, and which the NDP government in Saskatchewan has embraced.

While constraints on the provincial state have always existed, they are more palpable now in Saskatchewan than perhaps anytime in the postwar era. Domestically, the Saskatchewan state is both autonomous from social forces within the province but is also constrained by the numerous different policies that it administers and from which people in the province benefit. Thus the province can still act autonomously, as it did when it restructured health care and closed or converted 51 rural hospitals. But when it acts now it faces a highly politicized society which guards and protects its programs with particular vigilance. This requires careful actions designed to maintain the support of the broadest possible constituency of well-organized voters anxious about the prospect of reduced income or services. Thus the NDP government has abandoned the doctrinaire remedies of the past which it feels would lead it to a morally redeeming failure, but it has failed to move beyond cautious and incremental actions on most policy fronts. As a consequence, the government has neither inspired optimism nor held out the possibility of a new vision of social democracy for the future. Yet, in the end, this limited approach might well define governance in the era of the embedded provincial state.

NOTES

1 Jeanne Kirk Laux and Maureen Appel Molot, *State Capitalism, Public Enterprise in Canada* (Ithaca: Cornell University Press, 1988); John Richards and Larry Pratt, *Prairie Capitalism: Power and Influence in the New West* (Toronto: McClelland and Stewart, 1979).

2 Alan Cairns, "The Embedded State: State-Society Relations in Canada," *State and Society: Canada in Comparative Perspective*, ed. Keith Banting (Toronto: University of Toronto Press, 1986), 55.

3 Paul Pierson, *Dismantling the Welfare State: Reagan, Thatcher and the Politics of Retrenchment* (Cambridge: Cambridge University Press, 1994).

4 Cairns, "The Embedded State," 57.

5 Keith Banting, George Hoberg and Richard Simion, *Degrees of Freedom: Canada and the United States in a Changing World* (Toronto: University of Toronto Press, 1996), 14.

6 Banting, *et al.*, 18.

7 Evelyn Eager, "The Conservatism of the Saskatchewan Electorate," *Politics in Saskatchewan*, ed. Norman Ward and Duff Spafford (Don Mills: Longmans Canada Ltd, 1968), 1-19, 6.

8 David Laycock, *Populism and Democratic Thought in the Canadian Prairies, 1910-1945* (Toronto: University of Toronto Press, 1990), 8-9.

9 Laycock, *Populism*, 285.

10 J.C. Courtney and David E. Smith, "Saskatchewan, Parties in a Politically Competitive Province," *Canadian Provincial Politics*, ed. Martin Robin (Scarborough: Prentice Hall Canada, 1972), 303.

11 See Richards and Pratt, *Prairie Capitalism*, Ch.6.

12 Seymour Martin Lipset, *Agrarian Socialism* (Berkeley: University of California Press, 1971), 200.

13 Robert Tyre, *Douglas in Saskatchewan: The Story of A Socialist Experiment* (Vancouver: Mitchell Press, 1962), 12.

14 Tyre, *Douglas in Saskatchewan*, 18.

15 Christopher Dunn and David Laycock, "Innovation and Competition in the Agricultural Heartland," *The Provincial State: Politics in Canada's Provinces and Territories*, ed. Keith Brownsey and Michael Howlett (Toronto: Copp Clark Pitman, 1992), 212.

16 Pratt and Richards, *Prairie Capitalism*, 10.

17 John Archer, *Saskatchewan: A History* (Saskatoon: Western Producer Prairie Books, 1980), 312.

18 Archer, *Saskatchewan: A History*, 276.

19 Barry Wilson, *Politics of Defeat: The Decline of the Liberal Party in Saskatchewan* (Saskatoon: Western Producer Prairie Books, 1980), 19.

20 Wilson, *Politics of Defeat*, 20.

21 See Kari Levitt, *Silent Surrender: The Multinational Corporation in Canada* (Toronto: Macmillan, 1970); Andrew Axline, *et al.*, eds., *Continental Community? Independence and Integration in North America* (Toronto: McClelland and Stewart, 1974).

22 Archer, *Saskatchewan: A History*, 329.

23 Archer, *Saskatchewan: A History*, 326.

24 Eleanor D. Glor, ed., *Policy Innovation in the Saskatchewan Public Sector, 1971-82* (Toronto: Captus Press, 1997).

25 Maureen Appel Molot and Jeanne Kirk Laux, "The Politics of Nationalization," *Canadian Journal of Political Science* 12 (June 1979): 227-58.

26 Michael Jenkins, *The Challenge of Diversity: Industrial Policy in the Canadian Federation* (Ottawa: Science Council of Canada, 1983).

27 *Regina Leader-Post*, 27 April 1982, A1.

28 James Pitsula and Ken Rasmussen, *Privatizing a Province: The New Right in Saskatchewan* (Vancouver: New Star Books, 1990), 56-70.

29 Dale Eisler, "NDP Immediately Face a Number of Tough Issues," *Saskatoon Star Phoenix*, 28 October 1991, A6.

30 Tony Blair, *New Britain: My Vision of a Young Country* (London: Westview Press, 1996).

31 Jon Pammett, "Elections," *Canadian Politics in the 1990s*, 3rd ed., ed. M.S. Whittington and G. Williams (Scarborough: Nelson Canada, 1990).

32 Lipset, *Agrarian Socialism*, 265.

33 Richard Sigurdson, "Preston Manning and the Politics of Postmodernism in Canada," *Canadian Journal of Political Science* 17 (June 1994): 254.

34 David E. Smith, "Saskatachewan: Approximating the Ideal," *Provincial and Territorial Legislatures in Canada*, ed. Gary Levy and Graham White (Toronto: University of Toronto Press, 1989).

35 Pitsula and Rasmussen, *Privatizing a Province*, 249-61.

36 George Perlin, *The Tory Syndrome: Leadership Politics and the Progressive Conservative Party* (Montreal: McGill-Queen's University Press, 1980), 198.

37 R.K. Carty and David Stewart, "Parties and Party System," *Provinces: Canadian Provincial Politics*, ed. Christopher Dunn (Peterborough: Broadview Press, 1996), 84.

38 Robert Michels, *Political Parties* (New York: Dover Publications Inc., 1959).

39 Clair Powell, "The Fall-Out From the NDP Convention," *Briarpatch* 22 (February 1993): 4-5.

40 *Regina Leader Post*, 8 January 1992, A2.

41 Meyer Brownstone, "The Douglas-Lloyd Governments: Innovation and Bureaucratic Adaptation," *Essays on the Left*, ed. Laurier LaPierre, *et al.* (Toronto: McClelland and Stewart, Ltd. 1971).

42 Scott Steele, "A National Mirror," *Maclean's*, 3 January 1994.

43 Roy Romanow, "Rebuilding Saskatchewan Together: Notes for an Address," Urban Municipalities Association Convention, Regina, 26 January 1992, 2.

44 Saskatchewan, *Report of the Saskatchewan Financial Management Review Commission*, Regina, 1992.

45 Saskatchewan, *Report of the Saskatchewan Financial Management Review Commission*, 5.

46 *Star-Phoenix*, 19 February 1992.

47 Jim Sentence, *Saskatchewan Fiscal Position: An Analysis and Evaluation*, study prepared for the Saskatchewan Government Employees Union, Regina, 1992.

48 Saskatchewan, *Partnership for Renewal: A Strategy for the Saskatchewan Economy*, Regina, 1992.

49 Michael Porter, *Canada at the Crossroads: The Reality of a New Competitive Environment* (Ottawa: BCNI and Supply and Services, 1991).

50 Saskatchewan, *Partnership for Renewal.*

51 Ontario, Ministry of Industry, Trade and Technology, *An Industrial Policy Framework for Ontario* (Toronto: Queen's Printer for Ontario, 1992).

52 Saskatchewan, *Partnership for Renewal*, 10.

53 Saskatchewan, *Partnership for Renewal*, 7.

54 Saskatchewan, *Partnership for Renewal*, 8.

55 Saskatchewan, *Partnership for Renewal*, 11.

56 Saskatchewan, *Partnership for Progress: A Report from Saskatchewan Economic Development*, 2 January 1994, 5.

57 Dale Eisler, "Divers Opinions Guide Government," *Regina Leader Post*, 30 March 1994, c6.

58 Saskatchewan, *Regional Economic Development Authorities: A Framework for Regional Community-Based Economic Development* (Regina: Saskatchewan Economic Development, June 1993).

59 Kenneth Norrie, "Some Comments on Prairie Economic Alienation," *Canadian Public Policy* 2 (Spring 1976): 211-24.

60 Harold Chorney, "Deficits—Fact or Fiction? Ontario's Public Finances and the Challenge of Full Employment," *Getting on Track: Social Democratic Strategies for Ontario*, ed. Daniel Drache (Montreal: McGill-Queen's University Press, 1992), 186.

61 Saskatchewan, "Speech From the Throne," *Hansard*, 7 February 1994.

62 Phillip Hansen, "Saskatchewan: The Failure of Political Imagination," *Studies in Political Economy* 43 (Spring, 1994): 161-67.

10 ALBERTA

Experiments in Governance—From Social Credit to the Klein Revolution

PETER J. SMITH

In February 1994 the Progressive Conservative government of Alberta headed by Premier Ralph Klein declared war on the provincial deficit. In this war, as in all wars, there were casualties and a call to common sacrifice. Every Albertan was expected to share the burden of the struggle against the common foe—the deficit. According to Klein, this was a battle that had to be fought and won. Government spending was out of control and drastic measures were necessary.[1] Soon after becoming premier, Klein opined that the source of the government's fiscal problem was "spending; and the cause of that spending is a public that expects and demands more government than is needed." If the public demand for government services was not curbed soon, "there would be no money to pave roads, to protect the environment, to run our court system...."[2] It was the type of statement that Klein had made several times before and would make many times again.

Indeed, there was a case to be made. Alberta's deficit and debt had been mounting throughout the 1980s and 1990s to a point that for the 1992-93 fiscal year the provincial deficit had risen to $3.4 billion. In other words, borrowing to cover the deficit comprised more than 20 per cent of total expenditures.[3] The cost for servicing the accumulated provincial debt had been steadily rising and now amounted to $1.4 billion or nearly 10 per cent of all provincial spending. In Klein's opinion, Alberta had "not a debt and deficit problem, not a debt and deficit situation; we face ... a debt and deficit crisis."[4] In addition, this was not a crisis of revenues, but one of expenditures. Alberta had to make drastic cuts in the provincial budget. Klein was so successful in convincing Albertans of the necessity of immediate action that his party was re-elected in June 1993 even though the Progressive Conservatives were the architects of the mess so now decried. How Klein and his party accomplished this remarkable feat is a fascinating story.

However, it is necessary to place what occurred in Alberta in the 1990s within a larger context, for what was occurring there was not unique.

Deficits, debt, and government cutbacks and restructuring were very much a Canadian and global phenomenon. The changes that the Klein government introduced must be seen as an attempt to adapt to changes in the global economy. Alberta has historically depended on exports of staples—wheat, oil, and natural gas—and has been very much aware of how international markets have affected its political and economic agenda. The 1990s were no different.

By the early 1990s the phenomenon of globalization was strongly affecting public policy. Most analysts would agree that the process of capitalist development and expansion is at the heart of globalization. This is hardly a new insight, for as the noted Canadian political economist Harold Innis observed sixty years ago in writing about the history of European trade, "external trade was an extension of internal trade."[5] In other words, capitalism has a quest for expanding markets which compels nation-based capitalist economies to push against and go beyond national boundaries. Driving this sudden surge of globalization was the slowdown of economic growth in advanced capitalist countries. Henry Magdoff notes, for example, that while the gross domestic product of the industrialized nations grew at the rate of 3.6 per cent per year between 1950 and 1973, between 1973 and 1989 it grew at a rate of only 2 per cent. Magdoff argues that this great slowdown in economic growth "spurred capital to seek and create new market opportunities."[6] In effect, the advanced industrial countries hoped that by unleashing the forces of the market internationally, their domestic economies would be put back on track. Domestic growth from now on would be export driven.

This was very much the story in the rest of Canada and Alberta. Indeed, the situation in Alberta was worse than in Canada and other countries. In 1982, after a decade of very strong economic growth, the output of the Alberta economy dropped by nearly 5 per cent (compared to a 3-per-cent decline nationally).[7] Moreover, Alberta's economy did not really begin to recover until 1985, but in 1986 oil and grain prices collapsed, driving home the vulnerability of the Alberta economy to international markets. The provincial government responded by becoming in effect "the midwife" of globalization, transforming the provincial spending and administrative apparatus as part of an effort to conform to the perceived demands of a global economy. These demands, according to Brodie and Friedman, form part of the new governing ideology, "the neoliberal consensus," which requires all governments to:

- maximize exports
- reduce social spending
- curtail state economic regulation

» enable market forces to restructure national economies as part of transnational or regional trading blocks.[8]

Economic decline in the 1980s and early 1990s in Alberta meant that the provincial government had to choose who its friends really were: a coalition of large capital in the form of multinational corporations in the resource sector; small businesses; farmers; and corporate lawyers and accountants. Abandoned were the public-sector middle and working classes, along with large elements of the private-sector working classes. In effect, Albertans were to witness in the 1980s and 1990s a transformation from the politics of plenty and consensus to the politics of scarcity and conflict. Social divisions became starker as the government began its program of restructuring.

The changes that occurred in the 1990s are only some of the changes that have transformed Alberta government and society since World War II. This chapter examines these changes and their consequences for public policy. It begins with an assessment of the Social Credit years, critically examining the thesis of C.B. Macpherson, which states that Alberta's political economy and party system were shaped by small independent commodity producers, mainly farmers, with a right-wing agenda of challenging the power of Eastern financiers and railroads.[9] It then moves to an analysis of the societal changes that undermined the ruling rural-based Social Credit party, in particular urbanization and the growth of an urban middle class, and that led to the victory of the Progressive Conservatives headed by Peter Lougheed in 1971.

The chapter then discusses the interventionist provincial state of the Lougheed years, and next, the fiscally troubled administration of Don Getty, who succeeded Lougheed as leader of the Progressive Conservatives and as premier in 1985. In 1992, facing the spectre of defeat, the Progressive Conservatives pushed Getty aside as premier, replacing him with Ralph Klein, former mayor of Calgary and, then, minister of the environment. Donning the mask of fiscal probity the party reinvented itself, adeptly distanced itself from the Getty years, and convinced Albertans that it, not the opposition Liberal and New Democratic parties, was the party of change, and won re-election in 1993.

INTERPRETING ALBERTA'S PARTY SYSTEM

For decades Alberta's politics have been characterized as distinct from other provinces. Extended periods of one-party domination of the legislature have been the most notable feature of the provincial party system; and the leading explanation for this phenomenon was provided by C.B. Macpherson nearly four decades ago.

In Macpherson's opinion, the longevity of a one-party system in Alberta was due to two factors: first, the fact that Alberta was a society of small independent commodity producers; and second, the fact that Alberta was a quasi-colonial economy. As a society of small independent commodity producers, the class composition of Alberta was relatively homogeneous. Reinforcing the homogeneity of the province's class composition was its quasi-colonial status. By this Macpherson meant that Alberta was a creation of the federal government and its independent producers were subordinate to the dictates of a fluctuating world market, bankers, and railroads. Combined, these two features reinforced the uniformity and solidarity of the political behaviour of Albertans and led to a rejection of the competitive party system. The result, according to Macpherson, was a "quasi-party" system with one party dominating for a long period only to be eventually replaced by another equally dominant party. With a weak or non-existent political opposition, the party system in Alberta under Social Credit (1935-71) became a plebiscitary system "in which the people give up their right of decision, criticism, and proposal, in return for the promise that everything will be done to implement the general will."[10]

According to Macpherson, the rank and file acquiesced to the authoritarian rule of Premier William Aberhart and his government, resulting in a political system in which ordinary people were peripheral to the policy process, and the power of the legislature and influence of political party organizations were debased.[11] Alberta to this day, many argue, has remained a quasi-party system governed by a small coterie of party elites in the cabinet. This and other portions of the chapter shall address the accuracy of this portrait of the Alberta party system from Social Credit to the present. In particular, it will consider the following questions:

- How homogeneous was Alberta society during the early Social Credit years?
- How conservative was Social Credit?
- Did Albertans overwhelmingly endorse and acquiesce to Social Credit policies during its years in office?
- How did Alberta society change in the 1950s and 1960s, and why was Social Credit able to remain in office?

» How can the victory of the Progressive Conservatives in 1971 be explained?
» How were the Progressive Conservatives able to reinvent themselves in 1993 and win re-election? What are the consequences for Alberta government and society?

THE TWO FACES OF SOCIAL CREDIT: 1935-1971

The traditional image of Social Credit is of a party pursuing a narrow range of monetary policies directed against the financial institutions believed to be responsible for the unjust monetary system which had caused the Depression.[12] Once this system was disallowed by the courts, the cutting edge of the Social Credit program was blunted; the party resorted to promising "good and honest government," eventually becoming just another conservative party championing free enterprise and crusading against socialism.

Recent scholarship, however, disputes the view that Social Credit was ever as homogeneous as Macpherson claimed, or that its policies were solely directed against the "henchmen of the financial interests."[13] Alvin Finkel, for example, posits the thesis that "the early Social Credit is best understood as a loose coalition of reformers rather than as a single minded ... movement to tame the financiers."[14] Included in this broad coalition were farmers, workers, the unemployed, struggling small-business people, and some middle-class professionals. Moreover, early Social Credit was not calling for a re-invigorated capitalist system cleansed by monetary reforms, but was delivering a broad indictment of capitalism itself.[15]

Once elected in 1935, Social Credit passed a wide range of progressive labour, health, and educational reforms, many of which horrified the business community.[16] While these measures were popular with the rank and file, many felt that the government had not gone far enough. Social Credit members challenged the party leadership and called for more generous relief policies and the nationalization of banks and resource industries.

Not until the second term of Aberhart and his succession by Ernest Manning in 1943 did Social Credit begin to move to the right. Manning was never as hostile to big business as Aberhart. He increasingly viewed the principal enemy of Social Credit as socialism, not big finance, particularly as the Cooperative Commonwealth Federation (CCF) rose in popularity, both nationally and provincially.[17] Alberta businesspeople, who in 1940 had been Social Credit's primary opposition, now saw the Social Credit as the best means of keeping the CCF out of power. This alliance with business was cemented during the 1940s and 1950s and lasted for twenty-five years. It was strengthened after 1947 when oil was discovered near Leduc. The American multinational oil companies were seen as the goose that laid the golden egg by the provincial government, whose revenues were already starting to rise as a result of increased wartime prosperity. During its period in office, the Social Credit government reached an understanding with the oil industry whereby the government was "content to sit back and collect royalties from energy companies small enough to leave the companies with huge profits but big enough to allow the government to provide the social services and build the roads that ensured Social Credit's continuous reelection with huge majorities."[18]

From the late 1940s until the present, natural resource revenues provided the largest percentage of provincial revenues and kept overall individual and corporate taxation low until the late 1980s. Increased revenues permitted the Manning government to spend far more generously than the national average for social services—education, health, public welfare—and highways, which allowed the government to develop a broad base of social support.

In brief, the prolonged period of economic growth, which lasted until 1982, substantially reduced the appeal for radical economic reform in Alberta. Social Credit now promoted itself as a good, honest government responsible for prosperity. At the same time, however, the discovery of oil and natural gas radically transformed the province's economic and social structure, bringing changes that would ultimately undermine support for Social Credit.

The most noticeable aspect of the transformation of Alberta was its change from a predominantly rural society of farmers to an urban society with a greatly increased service sector. In 1941, the last census before the Leduc discovery, the population of Alberta was 796,000. By 1951 it was 940,000, rising to 1,332,000 in 1961 and 1,628,000 in 1971.[19] Most of the growth in the non-agricultural sector was propelled by the development of the oil industry. As previously noted, it provided the provincial government with its primary source of revenues, reaching over 50 per cent of provincial revenues during the 1950s. The bulk of this revenue went towards social spending. From 1946 to 1971 social spending rose from 46 to 75 per cent of provincial expenditures.[20] By 1967, Alberta was spending $446 per capita for public services, compared to a national average of $333 per capita. Between 1946 and 1971, provincial expenditures grew astronomically from $29 million to $1 billion.[21] Even in an era of rapid government growth this was extraordinary.

With such bounty being provided primarily by a single revenue source, it should come as no surprise that the Manning government proved to be very accommodating to an American-controlled oil and natural gas industry. Central Canadian and British capital had earlier displayed little investment interest in the province, leaving the door open to American multinationals who, by 1963, controlled 62 per cent of Canada's oil and natural gas industries.[22] Perceiving its bargaining position as weak, Social Credit was content with regulation, not ownership, of the industry, and in getting a fair return on the extracted resource.

The approximately $10 billion that poured into the provincial economy between 1947 and 1971 transformed Alberta's labour force.[23] The largest growth occurred in the service industries, public and private. From 1941 to 1966, for example, the service sector grew from 36.4 per cent of the labour force to 59.2 per cent.[24] From 1946 to 1971 the provincial public service in particular grew from 3,431 to 18,648—over a fivefold increase. Of equal significance was the increase in non-commercial services such as hospitals, education, and welfare, which were provided largely by the public sector but not classified as part of the public service. Employment in these activities rose from 42,423 in 1941 to 168,485 in 1971, a fourfold increase.[25] Likewise, the private service sector—retail trade, finance, insurance, real estate—demonstrated correspondingly large increases. The pattern followed by Alberta during these years closely follows that of other Canadian provinces.[26]

While the growth of the service sector led to growth in the ranks of the middle class, its most significant impact was the creation of a vastly enlarged working class composed increasingly of women. Women are poorly represented in traditional working-class occupations, but the growth of the service sector provided many opportunities for female employment. The participation rate of women in the Alberta labour force leapt from 15.7 per cent for women in 1941 to 39.4 per cent in 1971.[27] The increase tended to be in clerical, sales, and service occupations, which are characterized by poor promotion opportunities, non-unionization, and low wages. The exceptions tended to be in the education and health-care professions.

These changes in demographics and class structure had a long-term impact on the evolution of provincial party politics. C.B. Macpherson's portrayal of Alberta politics dominated by farmers was never entirely accurate, but by the 1960s it was totally out of date. Nevertheless, the Social Credit party stayed in power from 1935 until 1971, winning elections under Ernest Manning, usually with lopsided legislative majorities. How can this be explained?

There are a variety of factors—economic, political, and social—that serve to explain Social Credit's longevity. Probably the most important factor was the long period of provincial prosperity, which permitted high per capita expenditures on social services and highways. Prosperity also took the hard edge off the 1930s radicalism and marginalized the urban poor and small farmers. Workers in many industries, while not happy with the anti-labour legislation of Social Credit, enjoyed wages sufficiently high to mollify discontent. Unsuccessful farmers now had the option of finding work in the rapidly expanding cities. The farmers that remained, though not prospering as much as their urban counterparts, nevertheless enjoyed higher incomes from good crops and the massive wheat sales to China and the USSR which began in the 1960s. Government assistance in the form of income supports, improved telephone service, and electrification schemes also pleased farmers. In the cities, the newly enlarged traditional and public-sector middle classes tolerated a party whose membership was predominantly rural.

However, while prosperity was a necessary factor to Social Credit's electoral strength, it was not sufficient in itself to keep Social Credit in office. Politically, Social Credit benefitted immensely from the peculiarities of Canada's first-past-the-post electoral system, which distorts the transformation of votes into legislative seats in multi-party races.

On the surface it would appear that the Alberta electorate overwhelmingly endorsed Social Credit with little or no dissent. In seven of its nine elections, for example, Social Credit won with at least 85 per cent of the seats, seemingly confirming the quasi-party nature of Alberta politics.[28] Yet in terms of popular vote the party averaged only 52 per cent in these elections. Put another way, virtually as many Albertans voted against the Social Credit party as ever voted for it. The fact is that the Canadian "electoral system superimposes on top of partisan division and diversity a facade of cohesion and consensus."[29] For example, in the 1940 election, Social Credit was bitterly opposed by business people and the professional classes who organized a coalition of Independents composed of Conservatives, Liberals, and remaining United Farmers of Alberta supporters. Social Credit won 63 per cent of the seats, seemingly an overwhelming endorsement, but in terms of votes, Social Credit and the Independents each won 43 per cent. The inability of business people to beat Social Credit meant that they were only too glad to join them when Ernest Manning extended an olive branch upon becoming party leader.[30]

Businesspeople particularly feared the Cooperative Commonwealth Federation, whose popular support was growing in the mid-1940s. Yet this growing support was never translated into legislative seats. In 1944 the CCF captured 25 per cent of the vote but won only two out of 57 legislative seats. Social Credit, on the other hand, received 52 per cent of the vote but won 52 out of 57 seats. The failure of the CCF to win more seats proved devastating and led to a feeling of political inefficacy on the part of many members of the working class and a growing depoliticization of public life throughout Alberta.[31] By 1955 the Liberals, with strong support from urban middle-class professionals who felt Social Credit was not sufficiently assisting the rapidly growing cities, had become the primary opposition to the government. In the 1955 election the Liberals won 31 per cent of the vote and 15 seats, while Social Credit won 46 per cent of the vote and 37 out of 61 seats. After 1955, however, Social Credit recovered and lopsided legislative majorities continued until the party's ultimate defeat in 1971.

The 1955 election demonstrated another aspect of the electoral system that kept the Social Credit party in power: the heavily rural bias in the apportionment of legislative seats. For example, in 1955 Calgary and Edmonton had an average of 17,768 and 18,153 electors per MLA respectively versus 7,411 electors per MLA in the rest of the province. In the 1955 election, Social Credit support dropped to 39 per cent in Edmonton and Calgary. If the seats had been more evenly distributed Social Credit may well have been reduced to a minority government. While there was a gradual improvement in the number of urban representatives by 1967, 28 per cent of the electorate, principally rural, could still elect one-half of the province's MLAs—a bias that has since been attenuated but not eliminated.[32]

In another sense, the 1955 election was a harbinger of things to come. It served notice that the urban centres would be the eventual locus of resistance to Social Credit. The cities represented the new social forces that wanted to play a more vital role in the political life of the province. By the 1960s Social Credit was increasingly out of step with the changed provincial realities. The party was overwhelmingly rural and dominated by farmers, small-business people, and rural teachers. Only 18 per cent of its members came from Edmonton and Calgary where half of all Albertans lived.[33] The transformation of Alberta's political economy, which brought prosperity and abundant revenues to the government, had proven to be a double-edged sword. The secular, affluent, urban middle classes increasingly distanced themselves from the Social Credit administration, which was viewed as old, tired, and rural-biased.

THE PROGRESSIVE CONSERVATIVE ERA: THE LOUGHEED AND GETTY YEARS

In 1967, the revived Progressive Conservatives under the leadership of Peter Lougheed made a breakthrough, winning six seats, five of them urban. Then in 1971 the Progressive Conservatives swept to power, capturing 46.4 per cent of the vote and 49 seats, compared to 41 per cent and 25 seats for Social Credit.[34] The Progressive Conservative breakthrough came in the cities, which had received an additional seven seats in an electoral redistribution. In Edmonton and Calgary they won 25 of 29 races, but outside of Edmonton and Calgary they earned only 22 out of 46 seats, and none at all south of Calgary. The new Tory cabinet reflected the passing of power from a rural petite bourgeoisie to the new urban middle classes. Of the 75

Tory candidates, 15 were businessmen, and 28 were professionals, including 11 lawyers.[35]

The first ten years of the Lougheed era were remarkable for the changes that occurred in Alberta's political economy. The Lougheed government demonstrated a much greater willingness than Social Credit to use the powers of the state to obtain its policy objectives. The Progressive Conservatives reorganized government departments and agencies and created new ones, they installed a new budgeting process, and greatly increased and refocused government spending from social development to economic development. They added a number of quasi-public corporations, and created the Alberta Heritage Savings Trust Fund (AHSTF). Many of these changes were funded by revenues from the booming oil and natural gas industry which attracted thousands of immigrants to the province.

According to Larry Pratt and John Richards, the activities of the Lougheed government represented nothing less than the use of the provincial state by a new bourgeoisie of indigenous businesspeople, urban professionals, and state administrators to "transfer wealth, industries, and decision making from central Canada to the western periphery."[36] However, while the Conservatives were willing to use the powers of the state to challenge external capital, particularly eastern Canadian capital and the federal government, their development strategy lacked coherence and, with some notable exceptions, was largely blocked. Always sceptical of Lougheed's economic development plans, which fostered urban growth, the resilient rural petite bourgeoisie began to reassert themselves within the party once the boom ended in 1982.

The transition from Social Credit to the Progressive Conservatives can be seen clearly in the spending priorities of the Lougheed government. While Social Credit emphasized social development, the Lougheed government emphasized economic development with the state as a strong actor.[37] Indeed, by 1981-82 "Alberta was devoting a much larger share of its budget to economic development spending than any of the provinces."[38] In pursuit of its goals, the government provided assistance to small businesses, family farms, northern regions, and municipalities through a variety of loan, subsidy, and grant programs. Emphasis was also put on the expansion of infrastructure—highways, communication, irrigation works, airports, container ports, and grain-hopper cars—to improve land-locked Alberta's ability to deliver its products to foreign markets while simultaneously aiding the development of a larger agricultural and manufacturing sector. These efforts also helped the Lougheed government to expand and solidify its political base. Farmers and rural small-business people who had initially resisted the Conservatives in 1971 responded to government subsidies, loan programs, and high spending on highways by voting overwhelmingly for the party in the 1975 election.

In the early 1970s, as part of its efforts to insure a healthy provincial oil industry, the government also undertook a variety of other measures that aided business. In 1973, it set up the Alberta Energy Company (AEC), a quasi-public company that had as one of its objectives the institution of a form of people's capitalism. The AEC was a unique mixed-stock venture in which Albertans and other Canadians (primarily the middle classes with disposable income) could buy shares and thus assist the strengthening of "the industrial and resource bases of the Canadian economy, particularly in Alberta."[39] In 1975, the provincial government, along with the federal government, provided equity investment in the giant Syncrude oil sands project. In an effort to stimulate the petrochemical industry, the government subsidized feedstock prices well below the going export price.[40] Finally, in order to provide the necessary infrastructure to expand the northern part of the province and control transportation links with the Northwest Territories, the government purchased Pacific Western Airlines in 1974.

As part of its "province-building" strategy the Lougheed government also greatly expanded the provincial bureaucracy. It added a number of departments including Federal and Intergovernmental Affairs (FIGA), Energy and Natural Resources, Treasury, and the Premier's Office. The government also placed much greater emphasis on vocational and technical training in a newly created Department of Advanced Education, and in 1979 added the Department of Economic Development. Full-time public service employment grew from 18,648 in 1971 to 32,729 in 1982.[41] More importantly, non-commercial service employment grew from 168,485 in 1971 to 336,740 by 1981.[42] Public spending increased from $1.4 billion in 1971-72 to $8.8 billion in 1981-82. Per capita spending in Alberta continued throughout this period to be the highest among the Canadian provinces.

Increased oil prices and higher royalty rates instituted by the Tories also made possible the creation of the Alberta Heritage Savings Trust Fund in 1976, into which billions of dollars of surplus revenue flowed. The fund was intended to be used to diversify the economy and as a rainy day fund, that is, as insurance against potential declines in provincial revenue. It was also seen as a symbol of provincial fiscal independence, that is, as an alternative source of provincial borrowing, and finally, as a means of improving the quality of life for Albertans. Greater prosperity led to a rapid growth in population, which increased from 1.6 million in 1971 to 2.2 million in 1981, putting increased pressure on government to expand services. By 1981 the labour force consisted of a greatly expanded public- and private-service sector with an enlarged middle and working class. The striking aspect of the growth of the service-sector working class was the degree to which the jobs were performed by women. By 1982 female labour force participation stood at 59 per cent, the highest in Canada.[43]

During the 1975 and 1979 election campaigns the governing Progressive Conservatives found themselves in an unassailable position. The prosperity of the province permitted the government to spend generously, assisting large and small capital by means of subsidized loans and tax incentives, building infrastructure, providing subsidies for new homeowners, increasing the public service, and maintaining the highest per capita rate of government spending in Canada. At the same time it reduced personal income taxes by 28 per cent in 1975 and kept corporate income taxes among the lowest in Canada.[44] The government was also strengthened by its spirited defence of provincial interests against those of eastern Canadian capital and against the efforts of the federal government to appropriate Alberta's surplus revenues through increased oil and gas taxes. As a result, the Tories won massive majorities, 69 seats in 1975 and 74 seats in 1979, earning 63 and 57 per cent of the popular vote, respectively, in these two elections.

By the early 1980s, however, performance was not matching promise and the government began to back away from its rhetoric of economic diversification. Although there were some successes, notably in the growth of the petrochemical industry, the provincial economy did not diversify in any significant manner in the 1970s and early 1980s. The government's adherence to a market ideology, in which the economic process had to take place "as much as possible through the private sector," limited the government's ability to provide or carry out an effective industrial strategy.[45] By 1984 the government was arguing that economic diversification had never really been a policy goal at all.

In 1982, the province suffered when the steam went out of the oil boom. A glutted oil market with falling oil prices, an economic recession throughout the industrialized world, high interest rates, and a protracted battle with Ottawa and the oil industry over economic rents (following the imposition of the National Energy Policy in 1980) spelled trouble for the Alberta government. The end of the boom meant hardships for the first time for many Albertans, particularly middle-class supporters of the Progressive Conservatives.

In February 1982, a loss in a rural by-election to a candidate from the right-wing separatist Western Canada Concept Party startled the Tories, and the government began to search for some means to quiet the growing unrest. Attempting to emulate its successes of the 1970s, the government responded with a counter-cyclical budget that increased provincial expenditures by 25 per cent. In the lead-up to the November 1982 election, the Tories used money from the AHSTF to subsidize homeowners, farmers, and small businesses hit by high interest rates. The hard-hit oil and natural gas industry also received royalty reductions and a variety of other tax breaks and grants.[46] With assurance that recovery was just around the corner, and a warning that a vote against the Tories could mean a "socialist" New Democratic Party government, the voters responded to Lougheed's call for the last time, giving the Progressive Conservatives 75 out of 79 seats and 62 per cent of the vote.

The election, however, marked a turning point in provincial economic policy. The government, stung by comments from large and small capital and from farmers that the public sector enjoyed a privileged position while they suffered, began to cut back the size of the public sector, a trend that has continued until this day. The signals that the government sent out were conflicting, however. While government restraint and the privatization of Pacific Western Airlines appeared to spell an end to interventionism, the creation of a venture capital company, Vencap, in 1983 and the release of a government White Paper on medium-term industrial policy in 1984 continued to stress the need for "positive," "pro-business" interventions. In the end, however, Vencap proved to be ineffectual and, with the vital exception of forestry, the White Paper was quietly shelved.

In 1985, Lougheed resigned and was replaced by Don Getty, a former provincial energy minister who had left the government in 1979 to go into the oil business. Getty, with his close ties to the oil industry, was the candidate of choice for the party establishment. Getty's debut, however, came at a most inauspicious time. Oil and natural gas prices, which had recovered in 1984 and 1985, plummeted drastically from U.S.$27 a barrel in the fall of 1985 to as low as $8 in April 1986. The resulting economic dislocation meant that more than 45,000 oil workers lost their jobs, including many professional engineers.[47] The other pillar of the provincial economy, agriculture, was similarly hard hit by falling grain prices. These difficulties in the private sector could not be offset by the public sector as the public service was in the midst of downsizing, declining from 32,729 employees in 1982 to 25,759 in 1986. By March of 1986 provincial unemployment stood at 10.2 per cent.

It was in these circumstances that the May 1986 election was held. In an effort to maintain its petit bourgeois base of support, the government promised $2 billion in twenty-year low-interest loans to farmers, equity financing and tax holidays to small-business people, and $400 million in reduced royalties and drilling incentives for the oil patch.[48] Unlike 1982, however, these efforts fell flat. By 1986 Albertans were clearly anxious about their future. The New Democrats capitalized on this discontent and argued for more government intervention to revive the economy. This message was particularly well received in Edmonton, with its large numbers of public servants and predominantly working-class population. New Democratic support in Edmonton jumped from 30.7 per cent of the popular vote in 1982 to 41.1 per cent and 11 seats in 1986, while the Liberals increased from 1.6 to 15.3 per cent and two seats. Progressive Conservative strength in Edmonton was reduced to four affluent middle-class ridings. Altogether, Progressive Conservative support throughout the province dropped from 62.2 per cent and 75 seats in 1982 to 51.1 per cent and 61 seats in 1986. The New Democrats won 16 seats with 29.1 per cent of the popular vote and the Liberals took four seats and 12.2 per cent of the vote. Progressive Conservative support was strongest in rural Alberta, particularly in the former Social Credit bastion south of Calgary.

Elsewhere in Canada such numbers for the governing party would have been considered an endorsement and triumph, but in Alberta they were considered a setback. For the first time in many years the province had a sizeable opposition. More ominous for the Tories was the continued weakened state of the province's economic base in the oil and natural gas, and agricultural sectors. The Getty government realized that as vital as their links to these industries were, they were weakening, and so economic alternatives had to be found. In 1986 the government seized upon the development of a pulp and paper industry in northern Alberta. Using the powers of the state including loans, loan guarantees, grants, and infrastructure—roads and bridges—the government facilitated spectacular growth in the province's pulp and paper industry. The total cost of the financial package was $1.3 billion.[49]

The Getty government also intensified the policy of public-sector restraint begun under Lougheed. Unlike British Columbia, where the restraint policies introduced in 1983 were direct and harsh, in Alberta under Getty, a less confrontational approach was adopted. Rather than exact sudden, deep cuts, the Getty Tories opted for a more gradual approach. Using a policy of attrition, the government continued to reduce the number of full-time employees in the public service, the number dropping below 25,000 by 1988. Spending on social programs especially was curtailed, although these cuts were often masked by inflation. As a matter of fact, during the very period that the Klein government claimed spending was out of control, Alberta had the tightest controls on spending of any government in Canada. Between 1986 and 1992 Alberta's spending on public programs grew at easily the lowest rate of all governments in Canada, 2.3 per cent, not adjusting for inflation or population growth.[50] Despite these efforts, government deficits had become a regular feature of Progressive Conservative budgets in the late 1980s and early 1990s.

Non-renewable oil and gas revenues, which had provided largesse to successive Alberta governments, dropped from about 55 per cent to 25 per cent of total public revenues between 1980 and 1990.[51] Forced to find alternative sources of revenue, the government began increasing personal income taxes and premiums for health-care insurance, and instituting user-pay fees for a variety of government services. Personal income taxes, for example, constituted 24.4 per cent of total government revenues in 1990, versus 11 per cent in 1980.[52] The squeeze was being put on both the middle and working classes as the percentage of revenues from corporate income taxes remained at approximately 6 per cent of total revenue. In addition, other programs to assist the working class and the poor, such as rental credits, were cut. In essence, the new politics of scarcity and conflict were replacing the old politics of plenty and consensus, which had been a feature of Alberta politics throughout the 1970s and 1980s. In a situation of declining revenues, the government was now having to make political choices about who its friends were in deciding where to allocate its scarce resources.

Now that Edmonton no longer supported the Tories, one choice that the government made was to retain its support in rural Alberta. Throughout the latter part of the 1980s the amount of subsidized low-interest loans to farmers rose to $1.8 billion. The amount of guaranteed loans to farmers had also increased dramatically, from $63 million in 1987 to $1.4 billion by December 1990.[53] To maintain their support among small-business people the government began a new program of low-interest loans and loan guarantees in 1986. By March 1990 these stood at $293 and $285 million respectively.[54] Overall, guaranteed loans to small and large capital increased from $637 million in 1987 to $3.2 billion in December 1990.[55]

The economic hard times in 1986-87 also led to confrontations between capital and labour. Striking or locked-out private-sector workers engaged police in a number of locations, the most severe being the bitter, and at times bloody, strike at the Gainer's meatpacking plant in Edmonton in 1986. The third week of June saw one of the largest union demonstrations in Edmonton as over 10,000 public- and private-sector workers, including meat-plant workers, carpenters, teachers, nurses, and other government workers marched on the legislature calling for reform of Alberta's restrictive labour laws. After 1986, labour strife continued in both the public and private sectors. No longer could social differences be papered over by government surpluses. Not only did economic hard times lead to confrontation between capital and labour, they also led to problems with many of the staunchest supporters of the Getty government. In 1987, one of the dreams of Alberta's indigenous bourgeoisie—their own financial institutions that would help diversify Alberta's economy—was shattered when two investment firms owned by the Principal Group of Companies collapsed. Gone with the dreams of Alberta's bourgeoisie were the savings of thousands of middle-class investors. In the investigation that ensued, the Alberta government was cited for its failure to properly regulate and oversee the failed companies. The collapse of Principal Group followed on the heels of the collapse of the Commercial and Northlands banks in 1985. The loss of these banks was of great symbolic importance in Alberta which, as a province, had struggled to free itself from outside finance capital, particularly from eastern Canada. Once again, Albertans felt vulnerable to external economic forces.

By 1987, in this climate of growing provincial unrest and economic hardship, the Getty government was desperate to provide Albertans with evidence that it was capable of diversifying the provincial economy. One of the most promising sectors for new investment was the forest industry. The development of new pulping processes in the 1980s—along with high pulp prices—now permitted Alberta's forest industry to utilize large strands of hardwoods previously considered uneconomical. In 1986, with the assistance of hundreds of millions in loan guarantees, many of them given to the largest and most profitable Japanese and American multinationals, forest companies began to invest heavily in Alberta's northern timber. Aggressive government promotion, including loan guarantees, infrastructure provision, generous royalty rates, and the promise of no public hearings, touched off a forestry boom in 1988-89. The boom included over $4.5 billion in proposed forestry projects underwritten by $600 million in provincial loan guarantees, $520 million in loans, and $160 million in promised infrastructure.[56]

By the spring of 1989, the Getty government considered itself secure enough to call an early election. The provincial economy had improved, spending on health and education had been increased to alleviate middle-class discontent, and hundreds of millions of dollars in loans and guaranteed loans were being handed out to capital, large and small. Nevertheless, despite the best efforts of the Getty government to highlight its agenda—economic diversification, the strengthening of the family, the protection of Alberta's interests against Ottawa—the campaign fell flat.

Efforts to revive it with promises to pave every highway in the province and establish a mortgage interest-shielding program for homeowners led to debate over the government's tax and expenditure policies, the provincial deficit and the government's (in)ability to manage its finances or the economy. In terms of popular vote, the result of the 1989 election was another setback for the government, but also, surprisingly, for the NDP. The Conservative share of the popular vote declined to 44.4 per cent while the New Democrats' support dropped to 26.4 per cent. The big winner in terms of popular votes, if not seats, was the Liberal Party, whose share of the popular vote rose to 28.6 per cent. Nevertheless, given the vagaries of the provincial electoral system, the Conservatives still won 59 out of 83 seats. The opposition in the legislature was now larger, with the New Democrats—thanks largely to a high concentration of votes in a number of Edmonton ridings—winning 16 seats and the Liberals 8.

The Tories suffered a large setback in the cities, garnering only 33 per cent of the vote in Edmonton (almost precisely the same as the New Democrats and Liberals) and only 43 per cent in Calgary. In what must be considered the ultimate irony in contemporary provincial politics, the Tories now had their strongest support in former Social Credit country—rural Alberta. The urban working and middle classes were now deserting the Tories in droves. In Edmonton the abandonment of the Tories by the public service was virtually complete.

The electoral setback in Edmonton led the Tories to drop Edmonton and the public sector from their future election plans. The remainder of 1989 and 1990 were marked by continued cutbacks in the size of the public service—including, for the first time actually occupied as opposed to budgeted positions—and the decentralization of parts of government departments to the new Tory bases of support in rural Alberta. In addition, the government privatized a number of selected government organizations, the largest of which was the $900-million privatization of Alberta Government Telephones. In his 1991 budget, the provincial treasurer announced further plans to privatize the public service.

At the same time government cutbacks in the public service were occurring, assistance to capital, principally in the form of loan guarantees, began to mount at an increasing rate. The rise in loan guarantees to over $3 billion in 1990-91 led the provincial auditor general to warn that "the government's increasing use of guarantees and indemnities without improved legislative control and appropriate accounting is cause for concern."[57] The words were uncannily accurate, for just as the auditor general's annual report was being released, the government was reporting hundreds of millions of dollars in annual losses as more and more private and public companies that had received loan guarantees ran into trouble or went into receivership.

The result was a sharp drop in popularity for the government. By 1992 the provincial Tories were desperate for Getty to leave office. They succeeded in their efforts, and in December 1992 Ralph Klein became the new leader of the Progressive Conservatives, and the new premier.

THE KLEIN REVOLUTION

Not long after becoming premier, Klein began to reveal the political acumen and personality that would propel him and his party to victory in the 1993 provincial election. In the 1980s and 1990s Canadians in general had become frustrated with politicians and their political institutions, feeling they were ignored.[58] Canadians were losing their customary deference to authority. What was true of Canadians in general was true of Albertans in particular. Albertans too wanted a greater say in the political process and were fed up with provincial politics, politicians, and the way government with its large deficits and mounting debt had been managed. They wanted a more responsive government.

Klein, more than any other politician in the province, had his hand on the public pulse and knew the time was ripe for large-scale governmental change. He proceeded, first, to "reinvent" the governing Progressive Conservative party and government itself. Klein started by remaking the provincial cabinet, reducing its numbers from 26 to 17, removing most ministers who had not supported him, or who were too closely associated with Getty, from cabinet and the inner cabinet (Priorities, Finance, and Coordination Committee). Very much aware that he had been propelled to leadership by the support of the party's rural backbenchers, Klein consolidated their support and symbolically acknowledged the desire for broader input into decision-making by introducing a new legislative committee system in which the government party backbench was more involved in government decision-making.[59]

From the changes in the cabinet and legislative committee system Klein turned his attention to wooing the public, enlisting their support for the upcoming election and the changes that were to follow. At the heart of the new era in government was a promise to balance the provincial budget even if massive cuts were made necessary. Again, Klein laid the blame for the deficits on the departed Getty and asserted that he now represented a party of change. However, shifting the blame onto Getty's shoulders and getting Albertans to accept his government's portrayal of the deficit and debt was no easy matter.

Klein did not move immediately in cutting the deficit. Rather, he put considerable effort into gaining trust and preparing Albertans for what was to come. It was here that Klein the populist was particularly adroit. He was aware of the democratic temper of the times. Drawing upon his earlier experience as environment minister, where he frequently employed a variety of means such as "multi-stakeholder consultations," Klein instituted a broad range of public forums and "independent" commissions with the stated intent of ascertaining public opinion on numerous subjects such as the state of provincial finances, the budget, tax reform, health, education, and welfare policy.

One of Klein's first moves was to have his treasurer appoint an "independent financial review commission" which would give Albertans the straight goods on the province's finances. Next he announced a roundtable on the provincial budget in which "ordinary" Albertans would provide guidance to the government on what should be done about the deficit and the debt. While this was a deft gesture of political symbolism, the participants were hardly ordinary. They were, in fact, corporate executives, cabinet ministers, and prominent bureaucrats. The roundtable was held March 29 and 30, 1993, and the independent financial review commission reported March 31. Together, they drove home the message the government wanted delivered to Albertans. Albertans had a structural deficit, expenditures exceeded revenues, and drastic cuts to government spending and the size of government were in order.[60]

Klein insisted that higher taxes were not the answer, and most Albertans agreed even though they did not want to cut key services in education and health. Klein solidified his government's support by abolishing the highly unpopular MLA pension scheme which had been criticized by the opposition Liberals. In doing so Klein demonstrated two critical points: first, that he could listen and act upon public concerns; and second, that this was a Klein, not a Getty, government.[61]

Soon after, in May 1993, Klein called a provincial election. The New Democratic Party, the Official Opposition, led by the earnest but stolid Ray Martin, with a platform of raising corporate income taxes, was never in the game. The Liberals, led by the stern Lawrence Decore, promised brutal cuts to government expenditures. The Progressive Conservatives led by the folksy Klein promised much the same thing, massive cuts. Corporate dollars returned to the Tories and combined with the more personable Klein, the Liberals found themselves outspent and saddled with a leader with a poor public image. These made the difference. The Conservative party regained its rural and Calgary support and was re-elected, taking 51 seats to the Liberals' 32. The NDP was shut out of the legislature. In terms of the popular vote the difference was much closer, the Progressive Conservatives capturing 44.3 per cent, the Liberals 40, and the NDP, 11.

With a new majority in hand the Klein government set out to remake the face of Alberta government. Klein acknowledged in the Speech from the Throne in the summer of 1993 that politicians were held in low esteem and that action was required:

> My government recognizes that these are extremely challenging times to be an MLA. Widespread discontent among voters has fuelled a cyni-

> cism about governments all over the world. Changing times require a fundamental change in the way government conducts the people's business. Positive change is what this government stands for, and positive change is what it will deliver.

The government had its own particular answer to what fuelled public discontent. It stated that "a perceived lack of fiscal responsibility is perhaps the greatest reason for the cynicism people have towards governments today."[62] In brief, by the summer of 1993 the politics of deficit and debt held centre stage in Alberta politics as they were to do shortly across Canada. Virtually every other issue was crowded out by the government's neo-liberal agenda of budget cutting and restructuring, an agenda that was fully revealed in the February 24, 1994 budget.

The strategy adopted by the government had, however, taken shape much earlier. It was a strategy in which the government and public sector in Canada conformed to the perceived dictates of a global economy. This strategy was first propounded in the federal Macdonald Commission report in 1985 (officially, the Royal Commission on the Economic Union and Development Prospects for Canada) and later adopted by the Mulroney and Chrétien governments.

Alberta had its equivalent to the Macdonald Commission report, called *Toward 2000 Together*, a major economic initiative launched by Premier Don Getty in August 1991. (The Klein government was not as original as it has claimed to be.) The purpose of the initiative, which culminated in a conference from May 27-29, 1992 of 550 well-connected participants, was to develop a "new economic strategy that will take Alberta into the twenty-first century as a strong competitor in the global market place."[63] Reports subsequent to the conference called for measures that very much match the neo-liberal ideological agenda, including the elimination of the deficit, the reduction of provincial debt, less government, the creation of a competitive tax system, new strategies to design, deliver, and finance social programs, and the "aggressive" marketing of Alberta products and of Alberta as a location for business and industrial expansion.[64]

The *Toward 2000* initiative was used by Ralph Klein in his drive to become party leader. In October 1992, Klein sent a letter to the Canadian Manufacturers' Association responding to questions posed to the Progressive Conservative leadership candidates. Attached to the letter was a six-page statement drafted by Economic Development and Trade, whose minister, Peter Elzinga, was a Klein supporter, echoing the economic strategy being advanced by *Toward 2000*. As Marc Lisac of the Edmonton *Journal* claims, what was particularly remarkable about Klein's response was that "it set out the map which the Alberta government followed.

Virtually everything came about and became the centre of the government's public strategies."[65]

The 1994 budget represented a radical attack on the province's deficit and government structure, and a redefinition of the role of government in society. The stated intent of the government was to eliminate the provincial deficit in four years. The budget adhered in most respects to the movement to globalization. First, government spending was cut by an average of 20 per cent. Some departments such as Alberta Environmental Protection were cut by 30 per cent. Second, the size of government itself was reduced, the number of employees dropping markedly. Third, the way government delivered its services was sharply altered. Fourth, it argued that government regulations had to be reduced. Fifth, increases in income and corporate taxes were not included, although fees for certain government services were. Finally, keeping with the ideological prescriptions of neo-liberalism, the role of government in society changed as well.[66]

The 1994 budget represented, above all, an attack on the welfare state and the programs it provides: education, health, and social services. Together they comprised 64 per cent of provincial expenditures in the 1994-95 budget.[67] Particularly hard-hit were welfare programs for the poor and marginalized members of society, one of the more popular decisions made by the government. Cutting programs also meant cutting the number of people delivering them. The government announced that public-service employment would be cut by another 1,800 positions, this following a cut of 8.4 per cent in 1993-94 which, in turn, had followed cuts in previous years. Indeed, between March 31, 1994 and March 31, 1996, government departments had cut, on average, 20 per cent of their departmental employees.[68] Non-departmental employees in the public sector such as nurses and support staff members, from clerks to cleaners, were reduced as well. While the cuts were devastating to all those affected, the charge has been made that women bore the brunt of the cuts to the welfare state, not only as workers (for example, nurses), but as clients, in particular the poor. Finally, as workers in the home and community, it was predominantly women who were expected to step in and take up the slack, whether it be raising funds for school libraries or computer equipment or in taking care of elderly or ailing relatives.[69]

Most of all the government changed the way it conducted its affairs. Government was to be run along the strict lines of a corporatist market model. Henceforth, the market would provide the criteria from which to model government and judge government's performance. Government in Alberta was being reinvented in the image of the market. However, rather than just a separation of public and private spheres occurring, market forces began penetrating the structure and operation of the Alberta state. According to Jon Pierre, "There appears to be a significant shift ... towards a 'marketization of the state' namely to employ market criteria for allocating public resources and also to measure the efficiency of public service producers and suppliers according to market criteria."[70]

The ultimate effect of the market penetration of the state is that the line between the public and the private becomes increasingly blurred. During the Klein years numerous government services have been privatized, for example liquor and motor vehicle licensing, with the services in most cases being heavily regulated and controlled by the Alberta government. Foremost among the actions of the government was the passage of the *Government Reorganization Act* in 1994, which gave the cabinet and individual ministers the power "to create programs and services, change regulations, make loans, sell government property, or transfer programs and services to the private sector which in turn could set fees—all without legislative approval."[71] In the wake of this legislation Alberta Environmental Protection permitted industries to monitor themselves, subject to government supervision and audit. One of the most interesting variants of this approach was the decision of the Department of Labour to allow private-sector organizations to create their own organizations to regulate themselves. Described as delegated administrative organizations, these entities have the following roles and characteristics:

- » enforce regulations established by the Minister;
- » are administered by user groups in the industry affected;
- » are non-profit;
- » receive no government funding; and
- » are audited by Alberta Labour.[72]

An example is the regulation of boilers, principally in the petrochemical industry, by the Alberta Boilers Safety Association. In the first year well over half the tens of thousands of pressure vessels in the province were uninspected.[73] Beyond this, the government instituted a broad system of contracting out services to the private sector, partnerships between government organizations and the private sector, and the requirement that all departments develop business plans detailing how they were going to deliver services to their customers.

With Albertans being transformed from citizens to customers, the relationship between the individual and the state was being radically changed. The difference between a citizen and a customer is profound. A citizen is both an individual and a member of a collectivity. As citizens we are politically empowered, that is, we have the right to participate, to a voice in the making of the decisions that affect us. Customers, on the other hand, are "bundles of preferences waiting to be satisfied."[74] As customers we are judged to be self-interested, atomized, private units, not members of a community. As customers we are economically empowered and have the power of "exit," not "voice," such that if we do not like what services are being provided we can (in theory) choose another.[75]

The role of Albertans as active, participatory citizens has been a doubtful notion since the period of the Social Credit government. According to C.B. MacPherson and David Laycock, Social Credit left a legacy of plebiscitary democracy in which Albertans had been relegated to voting for a government that enacted the general will of "the people."[76] In sum, for decades Albertans have never adhered to a strong, vibrant, active notion of citizenship in which they participated in the making of public policy. While Social Credit was never as hegemonic as MacPherson claims (Albertans have always been divided politically with, on average, half of the population voting for a government and half against it), there is no doubt that the Social Credit emphasis on the need for government and its experts to make decisions on behalf of the population left its mark on Alberta's political culture.

However, in the 1980s and 1990s, if the public uproar over the building of the Oldman River dam in southern Alberta and pulp mills in northern Alberta is any indication, a more active notion of citizenship began to emerge as Albertans vigorously contested the actions of the provincial government. How much this has been cut short with the triumph of customers over citizens in the rhetoric and actions of the Klein administration is still not known.

Performance indicators, especially in areas of education, are an excellent example of the transformation of individuals into consumers and customers. Performance indicators are intended to provide accountability to "taxpayers" and their "customers." Notice the absence of citizens. These indicators are expected to provide quantitative measures of performance, the establishment of clear standards against which public services can be assessed by users and taxpayers. Performance indicators have recently established a high profile in post-secondary education in Alberta and the rest of Canada. Every department of the Alberta government is expected to develop and publish its own set of performance indicators.

The rhetoric of the customer in neo-liberalism represents a de-politicization of the state. According to Janine Brodie,

> This discourse marks the ascendancy of the market *over* the state and *inside* the state and, thereby, atrophies the public, closes political spaces, and further marginalizes the already marginalized ... those very groups most likely to challenge the growing social inequalities that restructuring is creating.[77]

While the process of downsizing may have given the appearance that the government was relinquishing important powers, in many instances the opposite was occurring. For example, the use of performance indicators permits the government to have more supervision of a university's affairs than it did previously. In elementary and secondary education, the government took control of more than $1 billion in education property taxes away from local school boards. In doing so the government opened the door to new tax shifts away from corporations and onto homeowners and small business.[78]

In health, the government created another level of government altogether, eliminating hospital management boards and consolidating them into 17 new Regional Health Authorities run by government-appointed boards. In the summer of 1997 plans were afoot to create a new regional system to deliver children's services. The creation of regional authorities reflects a desire by government to deflect accountability over the tough tasks of making cuts from the government itself to these entities, thereby escaping political repercussions.

While the Klein government came under bitter attack from a variety of quarters, it persevered, insisting it would not blink on deficit cutting and dismissing its opponents as "special interests." The government insisted that it spoke for all Albertans. Such a claim is consistent with the populist tradition of plebiscitary democracy in Alberta, discussed previously, in which government enacts the general will of an undifferentiated people. In Alberta, during the Social Credit and Lougheed and Getty years the opponents of the people had been external—finance capital, the federal government and others. Today those opposing the general will of the people are "special interests," a variety of groups who, in recent decades, were able to secure some form of state funding and recognition.[79] These included social movements such as the women's, environmental, and aboriginal groups along with others, including welfare recipients, the sick, the elderly, the working poor, children, and certain elements of the middle classes such as teachers, professors, doctors, and public-sector employees, who are dependent on state spending. Labour, too, was a special interest. This is a broad spectrum of the population which transcends any narrowly class-based version of conflict, although a class interpretation indicates that the private-sector middle and business classes are the prime beneficiaries and the working poor and dispossessed the principal "losers" of the attack upon the state.

The strategy of denouncing their opponents as special interests proved to be politically effective for the Klein Tories. While the provincial cabinet still occasionally identifies Ottawa as a threat on such issues as the environment and greenhouse gases, for example, it is worth emphasizing that for the Klein Tories the threat to the general will of the people can now be found within the province. This, ironically, could lead to a much more polarized political culture than has previously existed in Alberta as the province divides into categories of them ("special interests") or us.

In February 1997, sporting a $3-billion surplus (approximately the same size as the deficit in 1994) the government called an election. The campaign, by all accounts, was low key and uneventful, the type of campaign Klein preferred. The Progressive Conservatives pointed to their record of successfully tackling the deficit, and made a few modest promises to relieve "pressure points," that is, critical program problems in such areas as health and education. The Liberals tried to focus voters' attention on the gravity of the cuts in health care and education, but their leader, Grant Mitchell, was handicapped by a poor image and three years of a fractious caucus. The New Democratic Party also focussed on health and education but made no pretense of trying to form the next government. Rather, they tried to achieve a more modest objective, simply to have one or two candidates elected. Besides incumbency, the Tories had one other advantage, the fact that there are no campaign expenditure limits in Alberta. This permitted the Tories to mount a costly media campaign with which the other parties could not compete. The only real surprise of the election was that opinion polls showing the Progressive Conservatives heading for a crushing victory, with over 65 per cent of the vote, and virtually all seats, were wildly inaccurate. While they won handily in terms of legislative seats, 63 seats to 18 for the Liberals and 2 for the New Democratic Party, in terms of the popular vote the government won 51 per cent, the historical average in Alberta. The Liberals won 33 per cent of support, the New Democratic Party, 8 per cent. Voter turnout was 57 per cent, down from 60 in 1993. Most of the Progressive Conservative support came from rural Alberta and Calgary, while Edmonton gave the Tories just one seat.

Moreover, it is not clear whether the legislative victory represented an endorsement of all the changes that were made. Throughout the campaign the government stressed its fiscal record, and public endorsement does not seem to go beyond that. Rather, the public exhibited little enthusiasm for the campaign, demonstrating, instead, a mixture of acceptance, apathy, and anger. Politically, however, Klein must be given credit as an adept politician. He correctly read the public distrust and cynicism about government and was able to convert it twice into election victories. While acknowledging the desire for greater participation in government he was able to sublimate this desire to his party's goal of remaking government in the image of the market.

The careful reader at this point might ask this: if the government ran a budget surplus of $3 billion were the cuts really necessary? After all, in 1992-93 the deficit was $3.4 billion. Indeed, there are those who contend that the drastic cuts were not necessary at all. Kevin Taft, in the highest selling nonfiction book ever published in Alberta, rebuts Klein's claims that government spending was out of control. Indeed, the evidence cited earlier in the chapter seems to substantiate Taft's claim. Taft traces the root of the provincial deficit to two problems: low energy prices and subsidies to the corporate sector. When Getty was premier, oil was as low as $8 a barrel, down from over $40 a barrel in 1981. Oil and gas revenues fell from $6 billion in 1985 to $2.7 billion in 1987.[80] By 1996 oil prices were averaging U.S. $22 a barrel. The government forecast $2.6 billion in revenue from non-renewable resources but took in $4 billion.[81]

The other source of the deficit, claims Taft, stems from massive public subsidies to free enterprise in Alberta:

> From 1986 to 1995, the period when the Alberta government faced its toughest economic constraints, its spending on economic development (grants, tax breaks, loan guarantees, programs, and so on) exceeded $20 *billion*, a sum unrivalled by any other province. In fact, far more was spent on this "corporate welfare" than on income support for the poor.[82]

Moreover, from 1986-87 to 1992-93 subsidies for industrial development in Alberta exceeded corporate taxes collected by $5.3 billion.[83] Taft's conclusions are similar to another controversial analysis of Alberta's deficit by Cooper and Neu. They argue that a phobia about deficits and debt was created in Alberta, that in fact Alberta had a deficit problem, but not a deficit crisis. They argue that "the rhetoric of debt and deficit currently serves as a convenient political rationale for restructuring Alberta's social and economic landscape."[84] That is, the attack upon the deficit was part of a thinly veiled ideological attack upon the role of the state in society, one element of the neo-liberal consensus discussed at the beginning of the chapter.

The Klein government's embrace of the neo-liberal consensus with its emphasis on globalization and markets represents a *volte-face* of the long-held view in Alberta that government had a role in protecting Albertans from the capriciousness of external capital and markets. Both Social Credit and the Progressive Conservatives under Lougheed shared the perspective that Alberta was an exploited hinterland of central Canada. Social Credit had fought eastern capital and Ottawa, and the Lougheed Tories had strongly defended provincial interests against the federal government and sought to create a more independent capitalist class and diversified economy. By the early 1980s the Progressive Conservatives had begun to recognize that their economic diversification strategy was not working and began acknowledging their dependence on external economic forces, whether it be on Japanese investment in its forest industry or American investment in the energy industry. Endorsements of free trade with the United States and

Mexico followed suit. The Klein Tories followed by acting as enthusiastic champions of globalization. The message was clear: Albertans had to sink or swim in a highly competitive global market economy and public policy had to be sublimated to this goal.

CONCLUSION

The result of the changes that were then undertaken by the Klein government is that in Alberta, a rich province, public programs have become the most poorly supported in Canada, whereas at one time they were the most highly supported. In large part this is by design. As Claude Denis notes, and as Klein himself has admitted in other words, one of the primary objectives of the Klein Tories has been to have Albertans change their expectations of government. For nearly 50 years, from the end of World War II, Albertans, like people elsewhere in Canada, expected government to ensure security and prosperity. The welfare state was expected to provide a social safety net and an array of educational and health services. It was also the government's responsibility to ensure the continuation of high living standards. One of the objectives of the Klein government has been to encourage Albertans to alter their expectations of government, to wake up and get used to the new realities of a competitive global economy and demand less of government. Albertans have had to become more self-disciplined, more self-reliant, and willing to conform to the demands of the global market.[85]

In sum, what is commonly described as the Klein revolution has represented an attack not only upon the deficit, and now the debt, but also upon government itself—what it does, how it is organized, how it delivers its programs and services, what citizens should expect from government, and how they should relate to government, as citizens or customers. The scope of the changes is startling, but how deeply set these changes are in the population is debatable. Albertans may have made sacrifices when the deficit loomed large, but now with huge surpluses the sense of self-discipline and sacrifice may well disappear. In fact, a poll conducted by the Alberta government in the summer of 1997 indicated that Albertans still see government playing an active part in their lives, a view at odds with the current administration. When asked what the most important issue facing the province was, 49 per cent said health care but only 9 per cent said taxes, an issue pushed by the corporate elite.[86] In the spring of 2000, when the Klein government pressed ahead with legislation to increase the role of the private sector in the delivery of health care by permitting overnight stays in private surgery clinics, Albertans demonstrated their strong disapproval in opinion polls, rallies, and a month of demonstrations at the provincial legislature, all to no avail.

In brief, Albertans are more concerned than ever about educational issues, health care, job creation, and the environment. This presents a dilemma for the government. Their battle over the deficit pushed other issues off the political agenda, but now with the battle over, and won in the opinion of most Albertans, Alberta's political space appears to be opening up again. Albertans once again expect government to play a more active role in their lives. If this assessment is accurate, the attempts of the government to discipline the population to expect less of government may not have been successful. If so, can the ruling Progressive Conservatives transform themselves once more or will Albertans begin looking for a political alternative?

NOTES

1 For an analysis of the rhetoric employed by Klein see Kevin Taft, *Shredding the Public Interest* (Edmonton: University of Alberta Press, 1997).

2 Ralph Klein, Speech to the Rotary Club, Edmonton, January, 1997 as quoted in Taft, *Shredding the Public Interest*, 62.

3 Alberta Provincial Budget, "Consolidated Fiscal Summary," 1995.

4 Ralph Klein, "Speech to the Fraser Institute," *Fraser Forum* (March 1995), 5.

5 Harold A. Innis, "The Penetrative Powers of the Price System," *Canadian Journal of Economics and Political Science* IV (1938): 299-319. Reprinted in Harold A. Innis, *Essays in Canadian Economic History*, ed. Mary Q. Innis (Toronto: University of Toronto Press, 1962), 255.

6 Harry Magdoff, "Globalization—To What End?", *Socialist Register—1992*, ed. Ralph Miliband and Leo Panitch (London: Merlin Press, 1992), 48, 50, 53.

7 Robert L. Mansell and Michael B. Percy, *Strength in Adversity: A Study of the Alberta Economy* (Edmonton: University of Alberta Press, 1990), 1.

8 See Janine Brodie, "Canadian Women, Changing State Forms, and Public Policy," *Women and Canadian Policy* (Toronto: Harcourt, Brace and Company, 1996), 4; and Harriet Friedman, "New Wine, new bottles: the regulation of capital on a world scale," *Studies in Political Economy* 36 (1991): 35.

9 C.B. Macpherson, *Democracy in Alberta: Social Credit and the Party System* (Toronto: University of Toronto Press, 1953).

10 Macpherson, *Democracy in Alberta*, 233.

11 Alvin Finkel, *The Social Credit Phenomenon in Alberta* (Toronto: University of Toronto Press, 1989), 60.

12 Carlo Caldarola, "The Social Credit in Alberta, 1935-1971," *Society and Politics in Alberta*, ed. Carlo Caldarola (Toronto: Methuen, 1979), 42.

13 William Aberhart, as quoted in Caldarola, "The Social Credit in Alberta," 42.

14 Alvin Finkel, *The Social Credit Phenomenon*, 4.

15 In 1934, Aberhart, for example promised to eliminate the "present vicious profit system." William Aberhart, *Arberta Social Credit Chronicle*, 16 November 1934, as quoted in Robert Hesketh (Paper presented at University of Alberta, Department of History, Fall 1990), 8.

16 Howard Palmer and Tamara Palmer, *Alberta, A New History* (Edmonton: Hurtig Publishers, 1990), 269; Finkel, *The Social Credit Phenomenon*, 42.

17 The argument that there was a disjuncture between an earlier, more left-wing and later, more conservative Social Credit party has been challenged in a recent book by Bob Hesketh. According to Hesketh, "there was no dramatic transition to the extreme right in the late 1930s and early 1940s." Moreover, Hesketh argues, the party continued to adhere to the social credit principles of Major Douglas in the making of public policy. Bob Hesketh, *Major Douglas and Alberta Social Credit* (Toronto: University of Toronto Press, 1997), 14, 15, 239.

18 Finkel, *The Social Credit Phenomenon*, 116.

19 Leszek Kosinski, "Population Characteristics and Trends," *Environment and Economy*, ed. B.M. Barr and P.J. Smith (Edmonton: Pica Pica Press, 1984), 38.

20 *Public Accounts of Alberta*, various years.

21 Caldarola, "The Social Credit in Alberta," 44.

22 Palmer and Palmer, *Alberta: A New History*, 314.

23 Caldarola, "The Social Credit in Alberta," 44.

24 R.E. Armit, *Measurement and Analysis of Employment and Income in Alberta: A Starting Point* (Edmonton: Human Resources Council, 1971), 49.

25 Armit, *Measurement and Analysis of Employment and Income in Alberta*; and Census of Canada, *Catalogue*, 94-736.

26 Michael Howlett, "De-Mythologizing Provincial Political Economies: The Development of the Service Sectors in the Provinces, 1911-1991," *Provinces: Canadian Provincial Politics*, ed. Christopher Dunn (Peterborough: Broadview Press, 1996), 423-49.

27 Department of Manpower and Labour, *Women in the Labour Force, Alberta* (Edmonton, April 1972).

28 In two other elections they won 62 per cent of the seats with 45 per cent of the vote.

29 Roger Gibbins, *et al.*, "The Party System," *Canadian Political Life, An Alberta Perspective,* ed. Roger Gibbins, *et al.* (Dubuque: Kendall/Hunt, 1990), 191.

30 For more on this point see John Richards and Larry Pratt, *Prairie Capitalism* (Toronto: McClelland and Stewart, 1979), 81, 82.

31 Finkel, *The Social Credit Phenomenon*, 125.

32 Bob Hesketh, "The Abolition of Preferential Voting in Alberta," *Prairie Forum* 12:1 (Spring 1987): 123-25.

33 Finkel, *The Social Credit Phenomenon*, 174.

34 Alberta Provincial Election Returns, 1971. The NDP won 11.1 per cent and one seat.

35 Palmer and Palmer, *Alberta: A New History*, 324.

36 Pratt and Richards, *Prairie Capitalism*, 20.

37 *Public Accounts of Alberta*. Economic development includes the areas of natural resources, agriculture, trade, industry, tourism, transportation, communications, labour, employment, and immigration.

38 Allan Maslove, ed., *Budgeting in the Provinces: Leadership and the Premiers* (Toronto: Institute of Public Administration of Canada, 1989), 3.

39 Ed Shaffer, "The Political Economy of Oil in Alberta," *Essays on the Political Economy of Alberta,* ed. David Leadbeater (Toronto: New Hogtown Press, 1984), 187.

40 Wayne Kondro, "The Broken Promise," *Running on Empty*, ed. Andrew Nikiforuk, *et al.* (Edmonton: NeWest Press, 1987), 155.

41 These figures are taken from *Turnover Analysis Systems* (Personnel Administration Office, 1986). They differ from the annual reports prior to 1982 in that they are calculated on an average monthly basis and they include only permanent full-time employees.

42 Statistics Canada, *Catalogue*, 95-941.

43 Jo-Ann Schwartzenberger, "Women in the Alberta Labour Force, A Statistical Overview, 1976-1986" (Alberta Legislative Assembly, 1987).

44 Budget Address, 1975.

45 Larry Pratt, "The Political Economy of Province-Building: Alberta's Development Strategy, 1971-1981," *Essays on the Political Economy of Alberta*, ed. Leadbeater, 207.

46 Budget Speech, 1983.

47 Kevin Cox, "The Bust," *Running On Empty*, ed. Andrew Nikiforuk, *et al.* (Edmonton: NeWest Press, 1987), 148.

48 Throne Speech, 3 April 1986; Budget Address, 1987.

49 For more on Alberta's forestry development see Larry Pratt and Ian Urquhart, *The Last Great Forest* (Edmonton: NeWest Press, 1994).

50 Taft, *Shredding the Public Interest*, 15, 16, 24.

51 Mark Dickerson and Stan Drabek, "Provincial Revenues and Expenditures in Alberta: The Boom and Bust Cycle," *Canadian Political Life*, ed. Gibbins, *et al.*, 140, 141.

52 Budget Address, 1980 and 1990.

53 *Public Accounts of Alberta* and Budget Address, 1991.

54 From Budget Address, March 1991, and *Public Accounts of Alberta.*

55 From Budget Address, March 1991.

56 Calculated from Edmonton *Journal*, 21 December 1990, A1.

57 Annual Report of the Auditor General, 31 March 1991, 10.

58 See, for example, Canada, Royal Commission on Electoral Reform and Party Financing [RCERPF], *Reforming Electoral Democracy*, Vol 1 (1991), 223.

59 David Stewart, "Klein's Makeover of the Alberta Conservatives," *The Trojan Horse*, ed. Trevor Harrison and Gordon Laxer (Montreal: Black Rose Books, 1995), 34-47.

60 On this point see Mark Lisac, *The Klein Revolution* (Edmonton: NeWest Press, 1995), Chap. 6, *passim.*

61 See Stewart, "Klein's Makeover," 43-45.

62 *Alberta Hansard*, 31 August 1993, 7-8.

63 Government of Alberta, *Toward 2000 Together: Program Overview*, 1992. The moderator of the conference, Hal Wyatt, commented on the absence of women and other minorities at the conference. "The leaders of our government, our businesses and other organizations must recognize one failure of the conference. While more minorities and women were in attendance than at many other similar venues, the group was definitely male-dominated, with too few representatives of our ethnic mosaic, and even fewer from environmental interest groups and also from the less privileged sectors of our society." Hal Wyatt, *Toward 2000 Together, Moderator's Report on Conference Proceedings* (August 1992), 2.

64 Wyatt, *Toward 2000 Together, Moderator's Report*; and *Toward 2000 Together: An Economic Strategy by Albertans for Albertans*, 1993.

65 Lisac, *The Klein Revolution*, 66.

66 Government of Alberta, *Budget '94: Securing Alberta's Future, The Financial Plan in Action*, 24 February 1994.

67 Alberta, *Budget '94*.

68 Personnel Administration Office, *Public Service Commissioner's Annual Report*, 12.

69 Gurston Dacks, Joyce Green, and Linda Trimble, "Road Kill: Women in Alberta's Drive Toward Deficit Reduction," *The Trojan Horse*, ed. Harrison and Laxer, 270-86.

70 Jon Pierre, "The Marketization of the State; Citizens, Consumers, and the Emergence of the Public Market," *Governance in a Changing Environment*, ed. B. Guy Peters and Donald J. Savoie (Montreal: McGill-Queen's University Press, 1995), 56.

71 Harrison, *Trojan Horse*, 126.

72 Christopher Bruce and Don Woytowich, "Delegated Administrative Organizations: Alberta's 'Third Option,'" *Alternative Service Delivery: Sharing Governance in Canada*, ed. Robin Ford and David Zussman (Toronto: KPMG Centre for Government Foundation and Institute of Public Administration of Canada, 1997), 220-33.

73 Mark Lisac, Edmonton *Journal*, 26 July 1997, A12.

74 Susan D. Phillips, "A More Democratic Canada?," *How Ottawa Spends, 1993-1994: A More Democratic Canada?* (Ottawa: Carleton University Press, 1993), 13.

75 For more on this notion see Pierre, "The Marketization of the State," and Albert O. Hirschman, *Exit, Voice, and Loyalty* (Cambridge, MA: Harvard University, 1970).

76 C.B. Macpherson, *Democracy in Alberta,* and David Laycock, *Populism and Democratic Thought in the Canadian Prairies, 1910-1945* (Toronto: University of Toronto Press, 1990), especially Chap. 5, "Social Credit and Plebiscitarian Populism."

77 Janine Brodie, "Meso-Discourse, State Forms and the Gendering of Liberal-Democratic Citizenship," *Citizenship Studies* 1:2 (1997): 223.

78 Lisac, *The Klein Revolution*, 191.

79 For an insightful analysis of "special interests" in Alberta see Trevor Harrison, Bill Johnston, and Harvey Krahn, "Special Interests and/or New Right Economics? The Ideological Bases of Reform Party Support in Alberta in the 1993 Federal Election," *Canadian Review of Sociology and Anthropology* 33:2 (1996): 159-79. Although the authors analyze the Reform Party, they acknowledge that "in many ways, Ralph Klein's Conservatives are the closest thing to a Reform government in Canada" (175).

80 Taft, *Shredding the Public Interest*, 19.

81 Budget 1997, Post-Election Update.

82 Taft, *Shredding the Public Interest*, 41.

83 Taft, *Shredding the Public Interest*, 48.

84 David Cooper and Dean Neu, "The Politics of Debt and Deficit in Alberta," *The Trojan Horse*, ed. Harrison and Laxer, 164.

85 Claude Denis, "The New Normal: Capitalist Discipline in Alberta in the 1990s," *The Trojan Horse*, ed. Harrison and Laxer, 86-101.

86 Alberta Growth Summit, "Albertans Respond: Questions that look to the year 2005," 24 July 1997. The poll, conducted by Environics West of Calgary, is based on a sample of 800 adults and has a margin of error of plus or minus 3.5 per cent in 95 out of 100 samples.

11 BRITISH COLUMBIA

Politics in a Post-Staples Political Economy

MICHAEL HOWLETT AND KEITH BROWNSEY

APPROACHES TO BRITISH COLUMBIA POLITICS

British Columbia is a complex polity, yet many academic and popular interpretations of the political life of the province deny this complexity, proffering instead simplistic explanations for the disarray in which provincial politics often finds itself.[1] This is true of both of the explanations that have dominated popular readings of the province: the analysis of the "politics of populist protest," and that of the "politics of class exploitation."[2]

The "politics of populist protest"[3] provides a good example of the problems caused by the over-simplification of the province's history, social structure, and political life. In this analysis, until recently the province was dominated by a relatively small elite that had been the primary beneficiary of the early exploitation of the province's immense timber and mineral resources. This economic and political elite was able to cement its control over the social and cultural life of the province through its domination of the provincial political system until it was unseated by a popular protest movement in the 1930s and 1940s under the reform Liberal government of T.D. Pattullo. In this view the elite has managed to retain control over the economy of the province, but it has lost control of the traditional party system and the government to a coalition of groups—including both small business and labour—that had failed to benefit from the exploitation of the province's resources.[4]

In the popular version of the politics of populism that dominates media coverage of the province, the links between the political realm and the provincial economy and social structure have been almost completely severed. Without these linkages, the focus of analysis shifts from populist protest to "popularity politics" in which the central feature of political life in the province becomes the personality of the premier. These individuals are seen to have the single-handed ability to mold and reflect the ideals and passions of the province. In this analysis the premiers are elevated in stature until they assume near heroic, or villainous, proportions.[5]

Although widely accepted and repeated in the media and in popular political discourse by a wide range of other opinion-leaders, this analysis focuses on only a narrow selection of political variables. It ignores, for example, the fact that provincial political leaders are often narrowly elected and can in no way claim to represent more than the "general will" of a slight plurality of the population. Other significant political variables such as the structure and nature of provincial party, electoral, and legislative systems, or the nature of provincial voting behaviour are also neglected.[6]

The attribution of a great deal of autonomy to political leaders found in populist accounts contrasts sharply with the second general approach to B.C. politics, which focuses on the "politics of class." In the latter view, politics is often reduced to economics, and the actions of individual leaders, party officials, and voters are construed as being determined by the functional pre-requisites of the provincial economy and social structure.[7]

Unlike the populist analysis which is based on an elite-mass model of social stratification,[8] analyses of the "politics of class" are based upon the assumption that the driving force behind provincial politics is a bitter, dichotomous class struggle. That is, politics is not viewed simply as the result of an ongoing elite-mass conflict, but as the outcome of a very specific struggle between those who own the means of production and control the economic base of social life—capitalists and their supporters—and those who do not—workers and supporters of the working class.[9]

In this view, B.C. politics is, and has been, the politics of right versus left. An established capitalist class has utilized the party system to control the state and has used the state to control the working class through the enactment of various pieces of repressive legislation. Working-class organizations have been penalized by anti-labour legislation and the manipulation of electoral boundaries. Workers have been fragmented and divided through give-aways of shares of provincial companies, provision of state-sponsored social welfare schemes and minimum employment standards. At the same time business has been rewarded through generous tax treatment of both small and large business, the provision of low-interest loans, and preferential financing. In this view, the fact that capitalists have supported different governing political parties does not disguise the fact that they are capitalist parties or that their opposition over the past sixty years has come from parties supported by and sympathetic to labour. This tradition of political analysis, however, suffers from difficulties in linking the concept of class analysis with democratic politics. That is, it fails to explain how the state remains an instrument of a minority of the population—capitalists—in a polity organized around the universal adult franchise in which "workers" are in the majority. More academic analyses do attempt to deal with this question and suggest that overlapping cleavages such as region, ethnicity, or gender obscure class cleavages and fragment workers' votes. Others suggest that trade-union leadership has either failed to organize significant numbers of workers or has compromised with capitalists by agreeing to forsake demands for radical change in exchange for union recognition. This, in turn, has undermined the development of a working-class consciousness and, therefore, class voting on the part of workers. With respect to British Columbia, however, convincing evidence of either of these two factors is lacking.[10]

Problems with both of these traditional approaches to understanding B.C. politics led to new models which emerged in the early 1980s. In attempting to grapple with what appeared to be a major shift in provincial government policy characterized by public-sector cutbacks, privatization, and "restraint," for example, some analysts suggested that these initiatives could be best explained by shifting the level of analysis from the provincial to the global. They argued that these actions on the part of the provincial government were caused by shifts in the nature of the global economy and the inability of domestic economic policies to deal with sudden changes in international flows of capital and commodities. The thesis put forward was that the "new" direction in government policy could be attributed to the importation of British and American-style neo-conservative or new-liberal thought into the province as the provincial government attempted to restructure the provincial economy in the response to the new global "realities" of increased competition and rapid movements of capital and technologies across national boundaries.[11] Although the exact mechanisms through which international and domestic ideologies co-mingle remains unclear, this analysis highlights the manner in which the international and domestic provincial political economies are inextricably linked and mutually reinforcing.[12] It should be noted, however, that while the nature of the provincial economy has a significant impact on the provincial state, so too do the activities of the provincial state have a significant impact on the nature of provincial society and the provincial economy.[13] The activities of provincial political leaders and the timing of their actions, therefore, can be understood to originate in their own need to construct and retain successful electoral coalitions in the context of a provincial society shifting from a staples or resource base to a post-staples or service-sector-based economy.[14]

THE ORIGINS OF THE BRITISH COLUMBIA POLITICAL ECONOMY: FRONTIER STAPLES EXPLOITATION

British Columbia began its history as a settler colony based on resource exploitation. The first permanent European settlements in B.C. were in the northeastern corner of the province, established as outposts of the fur-trading empires of the Hudson's Bay Company and its rivals. Spanish explorers charted the southern coast and inland waters on expeditions mounted from Mexico and Peru while Russian fur traders visited the coast from their stations in Alaska, Hawaii, and California. By the late eighteenth and early nineteenth centuries, most of these early explorers were replaced by British and American traders who wanted control of the Oregon Territory surrounding the Columbia river and the access to the interior of the continent that it provided.[15]

Together these various adventurers created a small fur-based economy that succeeded in disrupting long-established aboriginal hunting, trapping, and fishing methods, drawing the existing population into a primitive market economy.[16] Rudimentary institutions of government were established in this era and changed very little with the colony's entrance into Confederation in 1871. In 1885, however, the character of the province changed completely with the completion of the Canadian Pacific Railway (CPR) linking the province to the growing Canadian domestic market—and especially to the demand for large supplies of timber required to construct settlements in the prairie region.[17] The completion of the Panama Canal in 1917 further opened up European markets to B.C. fish, timber, and mineral exports and contributed to the creation of the staples resource economy characteristic of the first half of the twentieth century in the province.

Dominated by local business elites, the provincial government granted large tracts of land to consortia who were planning to build railways. As a result of this policy large amounts of timber and other resources fell into private hands.[18] Immediately upon completion of the CPR, eastern lumber interests, both Canadian and American, began to display an interest in largely untouched West Coast timber supplies. Local mills grew as the demand for timber in the expanding terminus city of Vancouver increased, and new mills were established by eastern interests to supply markets in B.C., the Canadian Prairies, and the mid-western U.S.[19] Although its impact was great, this era of pure exploitation of the province's resources for company profits and government revenues was much shorter-lived in British Columbia than in central or eastern Canada. This was due to the late period in which the industry developed, and to the large size and relatively sophisticated nature of the companies that entered the province between 1888 and 1910.[20]

In the nineteenth and early twentieth centuries political life in British Columbia was focused on one issue: economic expansion through resource development. As governments collapsed and re-formed with great regularity the one constant was an emphasis on the promotion of greater and greater resource exploitation. As the population increased, political parties began to take a recognizable form, and party government was introduced in 1903.[21] At the same time, the amounts of capital needed in mining and forestry increased due to economies of scale in producing for an expanding global market. In response, the Conservative government of Richard McBride sought to create a stable climate for resource investment and modified resource regulations to ensure that investors received a large return on their investments through guaranteed access to cheap resources.[22]

By 1908, however, the provincial government discovered that, in the face of large, well-organized and experienced private operators, a policy of *laissez-faire* in the lumber industry quickly led to a crisis in which development of much of the timber on Crown lands threatened to elude government control entirely, with no guarantee of any significant reinvestment in the resource base.[23] This resulted in the establishment of the Royal Commission of Inquiry on Timber and Forestry (the Fulton Commission) in 1910 and an end to unregulated resource exploitation.[24] The Fulton Commission ushered in the beginnings of a new era in the province as the provincial government began to take the first steps towards the administration of timber resources. This was the beginning of the modern administrative state in British Columbia.[25]

THE CONSOLIDATION OF THE STAPLES POLITICAL ECONOMY: THE GROWTH OF THE PUBLIC SECTOR AND THE CONCENTRATION OF CAPITAL

As the frontier staples-based political economy moved from the era of relatively unfettered resource exploitation to one of resource management, the provincial government and public sector slowly came to take on most of the form of a modern state. As it did, the traditional political party system broke down and a new one centred on the politics of class took shape. The "new politics" of the old political economy solidified during World War II as the democratic socialist Co-operative Commonwealth Federation (CCF) emerged as the electoral voice of the provincial labour movement and became a serious rival for political power at the polls. The emergence of the CCF forced a series of coalitions on the part of the supporters and leaders of traditional political parties in order to keep the CCF out of office.[26]

The provincial election of October 21, 1941 signalled this change in British Columbia political life. The governing Liberals under Premier T.D.

Patullo dropped from 31 to 21 seats in the legislature while the CCF won 14 seats and status as the official opposition. The Liberals and Conservatives formed a coalition government led by former Liberal finance minister John Hart. With World War II as a catalyst, this first anti- CCF coalition government oversaw a massive expansion in the primary exploitation and secondary processing of the province's natural resources—notably in pulp and paper, and aluminum smelting—and a parallel expansion in social services provided by the state. In the ten years from 1939 to 1949, the provincial population increased by more than 40 per cent, while the gross value of forestry production tripled from $102.8 million in 1940 to $360 million in 1949. Mineral production almost doubled over the same period, growing from $75.7 million to $133 million. The gross value of total provincial production jumped from $311 million to $960 million by 1949.[27]

The period from 1941 to 1952 also witnessed the consolidation of many provincial resource companies into larger units, and the entrance into British Columbia of large multinational resource companies such as Crown-Zellerbach, Anaconda, Bethlehem, Kaiser, and Alcan. In the forest sector the Sloan Commission of 1945 set the tone for the future development of provincial forests by large capital. The Commission recommended, and the government implemented, a modified tenure arrangement and imposed land-management costs on forest companies. These two changes served as barriers to entry into the industry for small non-integrated producers and gave substantial cost advantages to vertically integrated firms.[28]

Significantly, during this period government expenditure as a percentage of Gross Provincial Product (GPP) also nearly doubled. Provincial spending on roads and bridges rose 500 per cent between 1940 and 1950, from $2.9 million to $14.4 million. Outlays for education jumped as dramatically. In 1940 the province spent $4.5 million on schools and universities; by 1950 the figure was closer to $14.3 million. The government also introduced hospital insurance in 1948, providing coverage for all provincial residents and a ready method of financing massive hospital construction.[29]

Prior to the war, the provincial economy was dominated by transportation and resource exploitation activities which employed significant numbers of manual workers in a combination of small and large companies. The transportation sector was dominated by large, integrated corporate concerns, principally railroads. In the three critical resource industries of forestry, mining, and fishing, however, competitive markets existed with a plethora of small firms. However, spurred on by the growth in the scale of production that occurred during World War II, and by the introduction of new technological processes in the postwar period, there was an increasing concentration of activities in the resource sector. As these industries became more capital intensive, a decline in the number of manual workers in this sector also occurred.[30] While employment declined in the resource sector, it grew in the service sector. Almost all of this growth was non-manual in nature and was centred in the managerial, scientific, technical, and clerical duties associated with the substantial rise in government expenditures and employment,[31] as well as with the bureaucratization of large corporate capital.

This development led to the creation of a large, non-manual labour force. Traditionally, many persons engaged in non-manual occupations were engaged in professional activities—such as medicine, law, or accountancy—or in very small-scale retail trade. Both of these service sector occupational groups formed the backbone of the so-called "old" middle class or traditional petite bourgeoisie.[32] However, these groups were never very large and while they certainly did not disappear, it was not growth in these occupations that led to changes in the provincial workforce. Rather, most of the changes occurred in two other classes. First, a very large rate of growth can be found in managerial, technical, and scientific occupations in both the public and the private sector. These occupations fall into the professional-managerial or the "new" middle class associated with modern industrial states.[33] However, the most significant growth occurred among the "public" sector working class, so called to distinguish it from its private-sector neighbour.[34]

The increases in the percentage of the workforce employed in managerial and proprietary, and professional and technical occupations in B.C. after 1941 are readily apparent. Broadly defined to include teachers, health care, municipal government and public enterprise workers as well as traditional civil service personnel, employment in the public sector alone grew by 542 per cent between 1947 and 1975, from 35,851 workers to 229,855. The rate of growth in this sector was double that of the labour force as a whole over the same period, so that by the mid-1970s members of the public-sector working class alone accounted for over 15 per cent of employees in the province.[35] These workers were dependent on the provincial state for their livelihoods and appear to have voted in favour of an expansionist, statist government during the period of the Liberal-Conservative coalition.

Due to internal rivalries, the anti-CCF coalition of Liberals and Conservatives collapsed in 1952. Thanks to an experiment with a preferential ballot, it re-emerged in the form of a provincial Social Credit Party.[36] Committed to a policy of continuing statist expansion, W.A.C. Bennett's Social Credit government also continued the old coalition policy of consolidating large corporate control of the resource sector while increasing public services.[37] Both large and small capital and the public-sector workforce supported this new "coalition," and Bennett used the provincial state to provide infrastructure to business while at the same time increasing

TABLE 11.1 **RISE OF NON-MANUAL LABOUR IN BRITISH COLUMBIA 1941-1971**

Year	*% labour force*	*# non-manual jobs*	*% increase*
1951	47	437,688	40
1961	55	560,462	28
1971	60	824,489	47

Source: Rennie Warburton and David Coburn, "The Rise of Non-Manual Work in British Columbia," *BC Studies* 59 (1983): 5-27.

public-sector employment. Extensions of the provincially-owned railway system were announced annually in budget speeches, as were major highway developments and other improvements to the provincial economic infrastructure. While professing the importance of small business, Bennett assisted the expansion of large corporations and fostered the creation of a small business sector dependent on either the transnational corporation or state expenditures for its existence. In the forest sector, for example, by the mid-1970s over 70 per cent of all timber leases were held by the ten largest forest companies in the province. The same companies owned 35 per cent of provincial lumber mills, 74 per cent of plywood plants, 90 per cent of provincial pulp capacity, and 100 per cent of provincial paper production.[38] Tax concessions, royalty holidays, low stumpage rates, and inexpensive hydroelectricity for large resource companies were all features of Bennett's economic policy.[39] Bennett also continued the coalition's policy of countering CCF demands for "provincialization" of the resource sector by providing a variety of social services through the state. Employment in the public sector continued to expand as new schools, hospitals, and universities were built to serve the needs of the increased population. The number of highway and transportation workers also increased in order to construct and administer this new physical infrastructure.[40]

With the consolidation of the resource sector by large capital and the creation of a large public sector, the composition of the provincial workforce changed substantially between 1952 and 1972. As Table 11.1 shows, employment in the service, or non-manual, sector of the economy grew rapidly from 437,688 in 1951 to 824,489 in 1971, an increase of almost 100 per cent in absolute terms and an increase of 13 per cent of the provincial labour force. Many of the newly-emerging technical and managerial jobs created during this period were directly dependent on public-sector spending, as was a substantial proportion of the overall provincial labour force. From 1952 until 1972, when the Bennett Socreds were finally removed from office by the NDP, government expenditures doubled again, rising from 6.5 to over 13 per cent of GPP.[41] This increase occurred despite Social Credit's manipulation of provincial debt loads in 1955 by transferring many debts and debt-related expenditures to various Crown corporations.

By the mid-1960s, the provincial economy had changed dramatically from one characteristic of an early frontier resource staples economy to one that exhibited all the features of a mature, advanced staple economy, including:

- substantial depletion of resource endowments;
- well established export markets for principle staple commodities;
- increasingly capital- and technology-intensive resource extraction processes;
- increasing competition from lower-cost staple regions;
- evolution of development from "pure" extraction to increased refining and secondary processing of resource commodities;
- increasing diversification of the industrial structure, with manufacturing, tourism, and local administration and services;
- evolution of settlements both within and outside the metropolis; and
- increasing pressure from "environmental" groups to inhibit traditional modes of resource extraction and stimulate development alternatives.[42]

While the province in this period could still be characterized as resource dependent, its economy had become more diffused and diversified than in the past. This change had also resulted in a significant change in the province's social formation. The earlier frontier staples economy had been composed of elements of large capital in the transportation sector, small capital in the resource sector, a traditional commercial or professional middle class, and a large private-sector working class engaged for the most part in manual occupations. By the early 1960s, the new middle class and the public-sector working class had grown substantially while small capital had declined as large capital moved into the provincial resource sector. This had important political implications. Teachers, public servants, and health-care workers no longer saw their interests furthered by an aging government dedicated to maintaining high levels of private-sector accumulation. With its coalition of often contradictory class divisions, the Social Credit government could no longer be sustained.

In 1972, the Social Credit coalition broke down and the New Democratic Party (NDP)—the old CCF Party that had been reconstituted in 1961 with clear links to organized labour—gained power under the leadership of David Barrett as some voters fled Social Credit for the Liberals and

Progressive Conservatives. The NDP government of 1972–1975 came to power promising reforms in education, health care, and social services—precisely those elements that had been supported by the expansionist policies of various provincial governments since the 1930s. Although the NDP was criticized for its lack of commitment to socialist principles,[43] and for its evident lack of managerial skills in putting its policies into operation,[44] it did manage to augment government control over the resource sector and to consolidate many social elements of the new political economy into the party's electoral coalition. In its attempts to control profits and capture economic rents, for example, the government created a state-owned monopoly over the marketing of natural gas and oil through the British Columbia Petroleum Corporation (BCPC). It also took public control of the automobile insurance industry under the direction of the Insurance Corporation of British Columbia (ICBC), and implemented an accelerated mineral royalty tax in the mining sector. The mineral tax in particular provoked a major anti-government public-relations blitz on the part of the mining industry and the threat of a province-wide capital strike by mining interests.[45] The party cemented its support among the new middle class and the public-sector working class by extending collective bargaining rights to the British Columbia Government Employee's Union (BCGEU).[46] On the other hand, the Barrett government legislated striking lumber, ferry, and pulp and paper unions back to work, alienating some of its traditional working-class support just prior to the 1975 election.[47]

The worst problem faced by the NDP, however, was that by 1975 the Social Credit Party had re-emerged as a coalition of anti-NDP forces[48] under W.R. (Bill) Bennett—W.A.C. Bennett's son. In the new circumstances caused by the evolution of the provincial social structure, the new coalition proved only just powerful enough in 1979, 1983, and 1986 to narrowly defeat the New Democratic Party. Supported by both public- and private-sector labour, the NDP was capable of securing over 40 per cent of the popular vote in each election while losing the elections decisively because of the first-past-the-post electoral system, which over-rewards the first-place party with seats.

TOWARDS A POST-STAPLES, SERVICE-SECTOR POLITICS: THE CONTEMPORARY BRITISH COLUMBIA POLITICAL ECONOMY

Economic development continued apace under the Bennett government, and by the early 1980s the British Columbia political economy had developed all the hallmarks of a "post-staples," "service-sector" society.[49] A number of structural shifts may be identified in this transition, including:

- severe pressures on the province's critical resource sector;
- the prospect of even more substantial contractions in resource industries over the 1990s and beyond, reflecting structural supply and demand conditions, as well as increasing public concerns about resource depletion and environmental degradation;
- rapid sector shifts in the economy, including:
  - a) a shift to services in the provincial economy;
  - b) rapid tertiarization; and
  - c) significant industrial expansion, in regional centres;
- an *internal* "reconfiguration" of growth and development, with a significant increase in metropolitan shares of population and employment, the emergence of regional economic centres, but the decline of smaller resource-dependent communities; and
- an *external* reorientation of key international relationships, characterized not merely by increasing trade and global markets, but also by a rapid integration within new markets, networks, and societies.[50]

The declining significance of the resource sector to the contemporary provincial economy can be seen in Table 11.2, which groups together resource-related primary extraction and secondary manufacturing activities in order to provide a better picture of the place of resources in the provincial economy of the early 1990s.

As these figures indicate, by the early 1990s only about $12.5 billion of B.C.'s total annual output of over $87 billion was directly accounted for by primary and secondary resource-sector production. Even assuming that each dollar produced in these two sectors was linked to as many as two additional service-sector dollars, resource activities accounted for only about one-third of British Columbia's annual production. Although substantial, this represents a significant decline from earlier historical periods. Nevertheless, resource-based economic activity remains important to specific aspects of the provincial economy. Much of the province's external trade, for example, remains resource-related, and traditional staples exports are the most important in these markets. About two-thirds of B.C.'s $22 billion in exports in 1994, for example, originated in the forest sector, with

TABLE 11.2
BRITISH COLUMBIA GDP–1994

	millions of $
Agriculture and related	2,158
Fishing and trapping	361
Forestry and related manufacturing	7,364
Mining and related manufacturing	3,108
Other manufacturing	3,292
Construction	6,509
Utilities	2,213
Transportation, storage, communication	7,793
Retail and wholesale trade	11,246
FIRE	18,527
Education	4,204
Health services	5,255
Other services	10,373
Public administration and defence	4,795
GDP at factor cost	87,198

Source: BC Stats, Industry Accounts: Special Aggregations (Victoria: Electronic Document Available at URL:http://www.bcstats.gov.bc.ca/data/bus_stat/bcea/tab07.htm).

approximately one-third resulting from softwood lumber sales.[51] Although it is true that "soft products" are having an increasing impact, the province's international trade remained very much oriented towards the export of bulk resource commodities to the U.S.[52]

While the role of the resource sector remains significant in terms of overall production and is particularly important in specific areas of the province, in terms of employment, its significance paled in comparison to that of the service sector. Table 11.3 shows the net absolute change in jobs by industry in the province between 1981 and 1991. As the table illustrates, a very large component of British Columbia's labour force was employed in the retail, wholesale, financial, transportation, communications, and public-service occupations which collectively comprise the service sector. Overall, B.C.'s development is in keeping with that of other provinces which also shifted from an economy and social structure dominated by high primary-sector employment in agricultural and/or resource-related pursuits to very high service-sector employment over the same time period. While not all the provinces have experienced the same rate of change, by 1991 the ten provinces differed by just over 5 per cent in terms of their dependence on service-sector activities, ranging from a "low" of about 68 per cent in Prince Edward Island and Saskatchewan to a "high" of almost 74 per cent in Nova Scotia and British Columbia.[53]

Three factors account for most of these changes in provincial occupational structures. First, the economic and social changes at the provincial level have led to the large-scale expansion of the provincial public sector and the creation of a mini-welfare state at the provincial level. By the late 1980s the provincial governments spent on average 45 percent of provincial GDP. That is, on average, almost one out of every two dollars generated in a province in a calendar year was spent by the public sector.[54]

The second major factor has been the practice of contracting out various activities by resource firms. Increased specialization and division of labour in private companies is not new, but it has progressed to the point where, for example, many forestry companies in British Columbia now contract out virtually all of their financial and harvesting activities, essentially remaining as contractors and product producers.[55] In most cases the contracting firms are much smaller than their predecessors, resulting in small-business employment growth as an aspect of service-sector development. The third factor contributing to the growth of the service sector has a more dramatic day-to-day impact on the life of families and communities. This is growth in service-sector employment due to the commercialization of former household tasks such as daycare, cleaning, and food preparation. These activities have gradually come to be performed in the private small-business sector. Although this transition may have had a positive effect on many households in that this work, traditionally undertaken by women, has been removed from the sphere of the family, these jobs tend to be low-paid and remain predominantly female.[56]

These three activities—growth in the public sector, contracting out, and commercialization of personal services—account for much of the growth in service-sector employment noted above. These changes in the basic occu-

TABLE 11.3

EMPLOYMENT GROWTH BY INDUSTRY 1981-1991

	net absolute change
Total Mining and Forestry	(19,600)
Total Resource Manufacturing	(20,100)
Other Manufacturing	7,000
Construction	9,600
Total Transportation	600
Finance, Transportation and Real Estate	17,200
Total Retail and Wholesale Trade	38,200
Total Business Services	37,800
Total Health and Services	46,100
Accommodation and Food	32,300
Education	22,000
TOTAL ECONOMY	219,300

Source: R. Kunin and J. Knauf, *Skill Shifts in Our Economy: A Decade in the Life of British Columbia* (Vancouver: Canadian Employment and Immigration Commission, 1992).

pational structure of the province have had a significant impact on provincial politics, as political parties have formed, fused, and failed in their effort to reflect changing public concerns originating in the changing day-to-day life of a majority of the provincial public. Not surprisingly, these activities have generated several issues related to public- and private-sector employment and working conditions that have come, in one form or another, to dominate British Columbia's political agenda in the contemporary "post-staples" period.[57]

This became apparent after 1983 when the new service-sector workforce flexed its political muscle for the first time in response to a Social Credit "austerity" budget. In addition to introducing a package of budget cuts, the government had proposed 23 bills which, among other things, would have limited the powers of municipalities and regional districts, extended compulsory review of wage levels of organized workers, expanded management rights in the workplace, abolished rent controls, and dissolved the provincial Human Rights Board.[58] Soon after the introduction of this legislation, opposition groups—labour, teachers, civil servants, senior citizens, the disabled, environmentalists, and others—coalesced in the labour-led Operation Solidarity and the Solidarity Coalition, an alliance of many new social movements. Led by the large public-sector unions and associations like the B.C. Government Employees Union (BCGEU), the Hospital Employees Union (HEU), and the B.C. Teachers' Federation (BCTF), and the private-sector International Woodworkers of America (IWA), a series of marches, rallies, and strikes were held throughout the province. A province-wide general strike was averted only at the last moment when the government agreed to withdraw and reconsider elements of its legislative package.

From 1983 to 1991, however, the major thrust of Social Credit policy initiatives was to attempt to limit the growth of this opposition coalition.[59] This was done through the privatization and deregulation of various government services and programs. Successive Social Credit governments argued that the elimination of rent controls, the privatization of a number of social agencies, the abolition of the provincial human rights commission, and overall cuts to the public sector of 25 per cent were said to be necessary because "the size and scope of the state had exceeded its proper role in society." While government workers' unions such as the Canadian Union of Public Employees (CUPE) and the BCGEU fought a losing battle against these program changes, the government of Bill Bennett understood that key segments of its electoral support in the private-sector business and labour communities favoured such policies. Simply put, the restraint program of 1983–84 was not only ideologically motivated, it was also good politics.[60]

The Social Credit government continued on the same course of privatization and restraint after the succession of William (Bill) Vander Zalm as party leader and premier in 1986 after Bennett's resignation from office. In 1991, however, after several major cabinet resignations and scandals, and following Vander Zalm's own resignation over allegations of conflict of interest related to the sale of his theme park to Taiwanese businessmen interested in obtaining a bank charter,[61] the Social Credit coalition again broke down. The NDP won control of the provincial government as Social Credit votes fled to a surprised provincial Liberal Party. Under the NDP's new leader Michael Harcourt, a former Vancouver mayor, the party moved quickly to consolidate its support. It renegotiated previously frozen teachers' salaries, eliminated public-sector wage freezes and restrictive labour legislation, and provided tax breaks and incentives for trade-union members.[62]

These moves helped the NDP to gain a second consecutive term in office in 1996 under its new leader, Glen Clark, when Harcourt stepped down in the wake of a minor scandal related to party finances from charity bingo which had occurred prior to his coming to power. Ominously for Clark, the anti-NDP coalition regrouped under the banner of the provincial Liberal Party, which selected another Vancouver ex-mayor, Gordon Campbell, as its head. With close ties to the trade-union movement, Clark and the New Democrats won a majority government with less than 40 per cent of the popular vote, one of the lowest vote totals for the NDP in several decades and almost two percentage points lower than the opposition Liberals. Clark's appeals to organized labour in both the public and private sector ensured their support for his party, but only the very fortuitous distribution of that vote across several ridings and the spoiler role played by a new provincial Reform Party in many northern ridings allowed the NDP to earn a razor-thin three-seat majority.[63]

Despite this evident lack of popular support, Clark led his government into several controversial policy areas. Consciously seeking to emulate W.A.C. Bennett's province-building style, Clark alienated many voters and members of his own party by eschewing the careful consensus-building of the Harcourt period in favour of attempting to exercise direct control from the Premier's Office over many areas of provincial life. Decisions on major and controversial items such as provincial wage guidelines, ICBC rate freezes, tuition fees, light rapid transit routes, and B.C. Ferry construction were made by the Premier with little consultation with the administration, affected parties, cabinet ministers or the legislative caucus.

While this style may have worked for W.A.C. Bennett in an earlier era of provincial government, Clark, like Vander Zalm before him, was to pay the price for such efforts in an era of complex administrative arrangements and enhanced citizen awareness. Opposition to Clark's personalistic style mounted with every problem encountered by any of the projects in which he had personally intervened. Media coverage of large-scale budget overruns associated with the construction of high-speed ferry catamarans to link the Lower Mainland and Vancouver Island, for example, embarrassed the government daily, and Clark was unable to avoid responsibility for this or any other issue in which he became personally involved.

In late 1999, Clark was finally brought down by a police investigation into his involvement with bidders for gambling casinos to be built under government licence. Although the nature of his involvement appeared to be minor, this controversy lost him the support of his caucus, and, like Vander Zalm, he was forced to resign rather than see his government fall. He was replaced temporarily by cabinet minister Dan Miller, who returned to Harcourt-style quiet government until a new leader could be selected in early 2000. Former attorney general Ujjal Dosanjh ran for the leadership on a law, order, and good government platform and easily won on the first ballot. When he was sworn in as premier, Dosanjh became Canada's first Indo-Canadian government leader.

Hence, despite their apparent success over two elections, the New Democrats face several very significant problems. First, with the collapse of the provincial Reform Party after the 1996 election, opposition groups in British Columbia, led by large and small capital, are now united behind the provincial Liberals. Without a divided opposition the NDP cannot maintain control of the government unless there is a significant improvement in its popularity. Second, under Clark, the NDP alienated certain elements within the new middle class and public-sector working class. This occurred as a result of the scandals and mismanagement that dogged the Clark government, but also involved longer-term factors such as concessions to the forestry industry and the traditional resource industries. This development represents a dramatic shift away from the pro-environmental stance of the Harcourt government, and many of the NDP's supporters within the large provincial environmental movement have questioned their support for the party as a result.[64] Due to these difficulties, the chances of the New Democrats retaining control of the provincial government appear highly unlikely.

CONCLUSION: UNDERSTANDING B.C. POLITICS

Most analyses of British Columbia politics have proceeded without an accurate picture of the provincial social structure or social formation. This has resulted, not surprisingly, in many observers jumping to conclusions that lack a firm grounding in empirical evidence concerning the province's political life. This is most apparent, for example, in works within the "politics of class" approach which have alleged that conflicts between workers and owners of the provincial resource industries have been a fundamental and determining characteristic in the evolution of provincial politics. Interpretations based on this notion of resource-based class struggles must be examined with care. Since at least 1911, British Columbia has consistently had a primary-sector labour force which was much smaller than the national average. Therefore, if this hypothesis is to explain B.C. politics, it must also explain politics in other provinces with higher levels of working-class membership, a suggestion that has never been seriously entertained in any of the existing literature on provincial politics.

Another predominant political myth centres on the notion that British Columbia remains a resource hinterland whose politics revolve around the exploitation of natural resources. Although this view had a basis in fact in the early years of the province and is perpetuated by every headline setting out the latest conflict between provincial loggers and environmentalists, it has much less basis in present-day British Columbia.[65] Rather than face a set of political problems arising out of the old staples political economy, politicians in B.C. must now grapple with issues which owe their origins to the new "post-staples" political economy which has emerged over the past half-century.[66]

Economic restructuring has involved the movement of capital offshore, global competition, and technological innovation, all of which have resulted in the downsizing of the provincial workforce and extensive manual-labour job loss. These shifts in the labour force have a number of implications for B.C. politics. The loss of existing jobs, and the inadequate creation of new jobs, or the creation of inadequate new jobs, for example, are increasingly problematic issues, as are mismatches between old and new economy skill requirements and endowments.[67]

The New Democrats, as the traditional party of labour in the province, have aligned themselves with the sectors that depend heavily on government spending, including both the re-vamped resource sector and the large post-World War II service sector. On the other hand, the former Social Credit governments and now the Liberal Party have allied themselves with large corporations as well as with elements of the traditional middle class of professionals and small businesses who prefer a regime of privatization, deregulation, and tax and deficit reduction. Elections in the province are now fought over marginal support loosely adhering to each coalition. Public-sector workers split off from the NDP when that party is forced to confront government spending issues,[68] and fragments of anti-NDP support move to third parties whenever the main anti-NDP party is forced to confront regulatory or taxation issues which business does not favour.[69]

This is not to say that the old strains and conflicts associated with a resource-based economy have completely vanished from the province. In fact, much of the service-sector growth and expansion has occurred in the heavily populated Lower Mainland and southern Vancouver Island regions, while other areas remain relatively more dependent on one or more of the traditional staple products such as fish, mining, or timber. As early as 1976, over 45 per cent of business services were "exported" from the Lower Mainland to the rest of the province, while between one-quarter and one-third of service-sector companies reported "exports" of greater than 25 per cent of their sales to locations in the province outside the Lower Mainland.[70] This situation reflects the metropolitan-hinterland linkages that continue to exist between the Lower Mainland and the rest of the province and underscores the overlaps that exist between continued rural staples resource production and urban, post-staples service-sector activities. However, although significant, this variation in regional political economies should not be exaggerated. While there remains a relatively greater dependence on primary-sector activities outside the Lower Mainland area—approximately 13 per cent of the labour force outside the Lower Mainland in the mid-1980s was employed in the primary sector compared to only 3 per cent in the Vancouver region—both regions were dominated by service-sector occupations. Fully 79 per cent of employment in the Lower Mainland was in this sector, while 69 per cent of employment in the rest of the province occurred in service-sector occupations.[71]

Over the course of its history, B.C. has moved from a frontier staples, to a mature staples, and now towards a post-staples political economy. These transitions have had significant implications for the provincial economy, society, and political life, and analyses of provincial politics must take these developments into account. Approaches that may have been useful for understanding provincial politics at previous points in the province's history no longer shed much light on the dynamics of contemporary British Columbia political life. However, an approach such as that developed in this chapter, which focuses on the effects of changes in the provincial economy on the composition of the provincial social structure and hence on partisan politics, helps to make sense out of long-term changes in the provincial party system and short-term electoral politics.

NOTES

1 For a review of the many contending approaches to studying B.C. political life see Patricia Marchak, "Class, Regional, and Institutional Sources of Social Conflict in B.C.," *B.C. Studies* 27 (1975): 30-49.

2 The feud between the two approaches has been ongoing and was particularly intense in the 1970s. See for example the debate surrounding Mark Sproule Jones, "Social Credit and the British Columbia Electorate," *B.C. Studies* 12 (1971-72): 34-62, with comments by Black, Robin, and Blake.

3 See D.V. Smiley, "Canada's Poujadists: A New Look at Social Credit," *Canadian Forum* 40 (1963); and E.R. Black, "British Columbia: The Politics of Exploitation," *Exploiting Our Economic Potential: Public Policy and the British Columbia Economy*, ed. R. Shearer (Toronto: Holt, Rinehart and Winston, 1968), 23-41.

4 Because of the absence of links to agrarian protest movements, this analysis is somewhat different from the analyses of populist protest which have been put forward in the case of the prairie provinces. On populism in Canada see David Laycock, *Populism and Democratic Thought in the Canadian Prairies, 1910-1945* (Toronto: University of Toronto Press, 1990). Nevertheless, analyses of British Columbia politics do share several more general similarities with considerations of prairie political life because of their common background in the Canadian tradition of "staples political economy." For a good summary of this approach to Canadian political economy see John Richards, "The Staple Debate," *Explorations in Canadian Economic History*, ed. Duncan Cameron (Ottawa: University of Ottawa Press, 1985) 45-72.

5 See Paddy Sherman, *Bennett* (Toronto: McClelland and Stewart, 1966); David Mitchell, *W.A.C. Bennett and the Rise of British Columbia* (Vancouver: Douglas and McIntyre, 1983); G.B. Nixon and L.T. Kavic, *The 1200 Days, A Shattered Dream: Dave Barrett and the NDP in BC 1972-75* (Coquitlam: Kaen, 1978); and David Mitchell, *Succession: The Political Re-Shaping of British Columbia* (Vancouver: Douglas and McIntyre, 1987). Academic works in the populist tradition are much more careful in their conclusions, and much more inclusive in their analyses. See Donald E. Blake, R.K. Carty, and Lynda Erickson, *Grassroots Politicians: Party Activists in British Columbia* (Vancouver: University of British Columbia Press, 1991), esp. Chapter 1; and Terry Morley, "Politics as Theatre: Paradox and Complexity in British Columbia," *Journal of Canadian Studies* 25:3 (1990): 19-37.

6 This is not always the case. See, for example, the critical works in this tradition such as those of Stan Persky. Stan Persky, *Fantasy Government* (Vancouver: New Star Books, 1989); Stan Persky, *Son of Socred* (Vancouver: New Star, 1979); Stan Persky, *Bennett II* (Vancouver: New Star, 1982).

7 See Martin Robin, "The Social Basis of Party Politics in British Columbia," *Queen's Quarterly* 72 (Winter 1965-66): 675-90; and Martin Robin, "British Columbia: The Politics of Class Conflict," *Canadian Provincial Politics*, ed. M. Robin (Scarborough: Prentice Hall, 1972).

8 See Leo Panitch, "Elites, Classes and Power in Canada," *Canadian Politics in the 1980's*, ed. M. Whittington and G. Williams (Toronto: Methuen, 1984), 229-51.

9 See P. Resnick, "The Political Economy of British Columbia: A Marxist Perspective," *Essays in B.C. Political Economy*, ed. Paul Knox and Philip Resnick (Vancouver: New Star, 1974); and articles by Art Kube, Rod Mickleburgh, and Meyer Brownstone in *Operation Solidarity: What Can We Learn?* (Ottawa: Centre for Policy Alternatives, 1984).

10 Goran Therborn, "The Rule of Capital and the Rise of Democracy," *New Left Review* 103 (1977): 3-41; Patricia Marchak, "Class, Regional, and Institutional Sources of Social Conflict in B.C.," *B.C. Studies* 27 (1975): 30-49; Bryan Palmer, *Solidarity: The Rise and Fall of an Opposition in British Columbia* (Vancouver: New Star, 1987).

11 Patricia Marchak, "The New Economic Reality: Substance and Rhetoric," *The New Reality: The Politics of Restraint in British Columbia*, ed. W. Carroll, W. Magnusson, C. Doyle, *et al.* (Vancouver: New Star, 1984); Patricia Marchak, *The New Right and the New Economic Reality* (Queen's University: Program of Studies in National and International Development Occasional Paper, 1985); and Philip Resnick, "Neo-Conservatism on the Periphery: The Lessons for B.C.," *B.C. Studies* 75, (1987): 3-23.

12 See Michael Howlett and Keith Brownsey, "The Old Reality and the New Reality: Party Politics and Public Policy in British Columbia 1941-1987," *Studies in Political Economy* 25 (Spring 1988): 141-76.

13 The reciprocal relationship existing between political and socio-economic variables in "statist" or "neo-institutional" studies is discussed in Margaret Weir and Theda Skocpol, "State Structures and the Possibilities for 'Keynesian' Responses to the Great Depression in Sweden, Britain and the United States," *Bringing the State Back In*, ed. P.B. Evans, D. Rueschemeyer, and T. Skocpol (Cambridge: Cambridge University Press, 1985), 107-168; and Peter Hall, "Policy Paradigms, Social Learning, and the State: The Case of Economic Policymaking in Britain," *Comparative Politics* 25:3 (April 1993): 275-96. In their analyses of voting patterns uncovered in the 1969, 1972, 1975 and 1979 provincial elections Blake, Johnston, and Elkins developed the thesis that political and economic variables have been linked together through the activities of the provincial state. That is, the growth of the provincial public sector and the provincial government's support for private sector-led resource megaprojects in the post World War II era have fundamentally altered the nature of both the provincial economy and electoral politics in the province. See Donald Blake, Richard Johnston, and David Elkins, "Sources of Change in the B.C. Party System," *B.C. Studies* 50 (1981): 3-28; Donald E. Blake, *Two Political Worlds: Parties and Voting in British Columbia* (Vancouver: University of British Columbia Press, 1985); and Donald E. Blake, "The Electoral Significance of Public Sector Bashing," *B.C. Studies* 62 (1984): 29-43.

14 Much of this analysis involves the application to British Columbia of models of political activity developed to explain the emergence of welfare states in Europe and to understand how capitalist democracies remain "capitalist." See G. Esping-Anderson, "Class Coalitions in the Making of West European Economies," *Political Power and Social Theory* 3 (1982); and G. Esping-Anderson and W. Korpi, "Social Policy as Class Politics in Postwar Capitalism," *Order and Conflict in Contemporary Capitalism*, ed. J. Goldthorpe (Oxford: Oxford University Press, 1984).

15 Margaret A. Ormsby, *British Columbia: A History* (Toronto: Macmillan, 1958) chap. 4.

16 Robin Fisher, *Contact and Conflict: Indian-European Relations in British Columbia, 1774-1890* (Vancouver: University of British Columbia Press, 1977).

17 On the history of the forest industry during and immediately after construction of the transcontinental railway see Joseph Collins Lawrence, *Markets and Capital: A History of the Lumber Industry of British Columbia (1778-1952)* (M.A. Thesis, University of British Columbia, 1957) 38-100.

18 W.A. Carrothers, "Forest Industries of British Columbia," *North American Assault on the Canadian Forest*, ed. A.R.M. Lower (New York: Greenwood Press, 1968).

19 Donald MacKay, *Empire of Wood: The MacMillan-Bloedel Story* (Vancouver: Douglas and McIntyre, 1981), 153-81.

20 See Michael Howlett, *Forest Policies in Canada: Resource Constraints and Political Conflicts in the Canadian Forest Sector* (Ph.D. dissertation, Queen's University, 1988).

21 Martin Robin, *The Rush For Spoils: The Company Province 1871-1933* (Toronto: McClelland and Stewart, 1974).

22 See Robert E. Cail, *Land, Man, and the Law: The Disposal of Crown Lands in British Columbia 1871-1913* (Vancouver: University of British Columbia Press, 1974).

23 See British Columbia, *Crown Charges for Early Timber Rights: Royalties and Other Levies for Harvesting Rights on Timber Leases, Licences and Berths in British Columbia—First Report of the Task Force on Crown Timber Disposal, February 1974* (Victoria: Ministry of Lands, Forests and Water Resources, 1974).

24 Peter Pearse, *Forest Policy in Canada* (Vancouver: U.B.C. Forest Economics and Policy Analysis Project Working Paper, 1985). Also see George Hoberg, "The Politics of Sustainability: Forestry Policy in British Columbia," *Politics, Policy, and Government in British Columbia*, ed. R.K. Carty (Vancouver: University of British Columbia Press, 1996).

25 Neil Swainson, "The Public Service," *The Reins of Power*, ed. R.T. Morley, *et al.* (Vancouver: Douglas and MacIntyre, 1983), 119-60.

26 On this era see Robin Fisher, *Duff Pattullo of British Columbia* (Toronto, Buffalo, London: University of Toronto Press, 1991); George M. Abbott, "Duff Pattullo and the Coalition Controversy of 1941," *B.C. Studies* 102 (1994): 30-53; and Dorothy G. Steeves, *The Compassionate Rebel. Ernest Winch and the Growth of Socialism in Western Canada* (Vancouver: J.J. Douglas, 1977), 160-61.

27 Canada, *Proceedings of the Conference of Federal and Provincial Governments*, Ottawa, 4-7 December 1950 (Ottawa: King's Printer, 1951) 117.

28 British Columbia, *Report of the Commissioner Relating to the Forest Resources of British Columbia 1945*, 2 vols. (Victoria: King's Printer 1945). See also Patricia Marchak, *Green Gold: The Forest Industry in British Columbia* (Vancouver: University of British Columbia Press, 1983), 29-54.

29 Canada, *Proceedings of the Conference of Federal and Provincial Governments*, 117.

30 On this process of concentration and labour displacement in the provincial forest sector see G.W. Taylor, *Timber: The History of the Forest Industry in British Columbia* (Vancouver: J.J. Douglas, 1975); MacKay, *Empire of Wood,* 153-81; and Marchak, *Green Gold*, 29-54. More generally see Rennie Warburton, "Conclusion: Capitalist Social Relations in British Columbia," *Workers, Capital and the State in British Columbia*, ed. R. Warburton and D. Coburn (Vancouver: University of British Columbia Press, 1988), 263-85.

31 On the pattern of public-sector growth in the province see Swainson, "The Public Service," 119-60.

32 On the old middle class or traditional petite bourgeoisie see Suzanne Berger, "The Uses of the Traditional Sectors in Italy: Why Declining Classes Survive," *The Petite Bourgeoisie: Comparative Studies of the Uneasy Stratum*, ed. Frank Bechhofer and Brian Elliot (London: Macmillan 1981) 71-89; and Nicos Poulantzas, *Classes in Contemporary Capitalism* (London: Verso, 1978).

33 Although the exact boundaries of this class are contested, at a minimum the new middle class or "new petty bourgeoisie" is composed of these new "professions." See G. Carchedi, "On the Economic Identification of the New Middle Class," *Economy and Society* 4 (1975): 1-86; Barbara and John Ehrenreich, "The Professional-Managerial Class," *Between Labour and Capital*, ed. P. Walker (Boston: South End Press, 1979), 5-45; N. Abercrombie and J. Urry, *Capital, Labour and the Middle Classes* (London: George Allen and Unwin, 1983); Erik Olin Wright, "Reflection on Classes," *The Debate on Classes*, ed. E.O. Wright, *et al.* (London: Verso, 1989), 49-77; and Val Burris, "The Discovery of the New Middle Class," *Theory and Society* 15 (1986): 317-49.

34 See Patrick Dunleavy, "The Political Implications of Sectoral Cleavages and the Growth in State Employment: Part I, The Analysis of Production Cleavages" and "Part II, Cleavage Structures and Political Alignments," *Political Studies* 28(3): 364-83 and 28(4): 527-49. See also P. Dunleavy, "The End of Class Politics," *Politics in Transition*, ed. A. Cochrane and J. Anderson (London: Sage, 1989), 172-223.

35 Rennie Warburton and David Coburn, "The Rise of Non-Manual Work in British Columbia," *B.C. Studies* 59 (1983).

36 See Donald Alper, "The Effects of Coalition Government on Party Structure: The Case of the Conservative Party in B.C.," *B.C. Studies* 33 (1977): 40-49.

37 Leonard B. Koffert, "'Reckoning with the Machine': The British Columbia Social Credit Movement as Social Criticism, 1932-52," *B.C. Studies* 124 (1999-2000): 9-39.

38 See Marchak, *Green Gold*, 30.

39 See the annual budget speeches presented by W.A.C. Bennett to the provincial legislature between 1955-72 for an overview of the various benefits and concessions given to large resource industries.

40 On this period generally see Stephen G. Tomblin, "W.A.C. Bennett and Province-Building in British Columbia," *B.C. Studies* 85 (1990): 45-61.

41 See British Columbia, *A Review of Resources, Production and Governmental Finances* (Victoria: Department of Finance, various issues, 1940-62).

42 Thomas A. Hutton, *Visions of a 'Post-Staples' Economy: Structural Change and Adjustment Issues in British Columbia.* PI #3 (Vancouver: Centre for Human Settlements, 1994), 4-5.

43 Persky, *Son of Socred.*

44 See Paul Tennant, "The NDP Government of British Columbia: Unaided Politicians in an Unaided Cabinet," *Canadian Public Policy* 3:4 (1977): 489-503; and Alan C. Cairns and Daniel Wong, "Socialism, Federalism, and the B.C. Party Systems 1933-1983," *Party Politics in Canada*, ed. Hugh G. Thorburn (Toronto: Prentice Hall, 1985).

45 Raymond W. Payne, "Corporate Power, Interest Groups, and the Development of Mining Policy in British Columbia 1972-1977," *B.C. Studies* 54 (1982): 3-37.

46 On the Higgins Commission and the unionization of the public service, see Norman Ruff, "Managing the Public Service," *The Reins of Power: Governing British Columbia*, ed. J.T. Morley, N.J. Ruff, *et al.* (Vancouver: Douglas and McIntyre, 1983), 172-77.

47 See P. Resnick, "Social Democracy in Power: The Case of British Columbia," *B.C. Studies* 34 (1977): 3-20.

48 Donald Blake, Richard Johnston, and David Elkins, "Sources of Change in the B.C. Party System," *B.C. Studies* 50 (1981): 3-28.

49 The transitions in social formation which accompany the development of a "post-industrial" service-sector economy are described in John Allen, "Towards a Post-Industrial Economy," *The Economy in Question*, ed. John Allen and Doreen Massey (London: Sage Publications, 1988), 91-135; J.I. Gershuny and I.D. Miles, *The New Service Economy: The Transformation of Employment in Industrial Societies* (London: Frances Pinter, 1983), 26-46; and Erik Olin Wright and Bill Martin, "The Transformation of the American Class Structure, 1960-1980," *American Journal of Sociology* 93:1 (1987): 1-29.

50 Adapted from Hutton, *Visions of a 'Post-Staples' Economy*, 1-2.

51 See B.C. Stats, *Quickfacts About British Columbia: Export Trade by Commodity* (Victoria: Electronic Document Available from URL: http://www.bcstats.gov.bc.ca/data/bus_stat/trade/netbwor.htm, 1996).

52 Roger Hayter and Trevor Barnes, "Innis' Staple Theory, Exports and Recession: British Columbia, 1981-86," *Economic Geography* 66 (1990): 150-73.

53 See Michael Howlett, "De-Mythologizing Provincial Political Economies: The Development of the Service Sectors in the Provinces 1911-1991," *Provinces*, ed. Christopher Dunn (Peterborough: Broadview Press, 1996).

54 See I.D. Horry and M. Walker, *Government Spending Facts* (Vancouver: Fraser Institute, 1991); and F. Petry, I.M. Imbeau, M. Clavet and J. Crete, *Measuring Government Growth in the Canadian Provinces: Decomposing Real Growth and Deflation Effects* (Montreal: Paper Presented to the Annual Meeting of the Canadian Political Science Association, 1995).

55 See Richard B. McKenzie, "The Emergence of the 'Service Economy': Fact or Artifact," *Conceptual Issues in Service Sector Research: A Symposium*, ed. Herbert G. Grubel (Vancouver: Fraser Institute, 1987), 73-97; Herbert G. Grubel and Michael A. Walker, *Service Industry Growth: Causes and Effects* (Vancouver: Fraser Institute, 1989); and James J. McRae, "Can Growth in the Service Sector Rescue Western Canada?," *Canadian Public Policy* 11 (Supplement) (1985): 351-53.

56 On gender divisions and segmentation in the contemporary provincial labour market see Trevor Barnes and Roger Hayter, "British Columbia's Private Sector in Recession, 1981-1986: Employment Flexibility without Trade Diversification?," *B.C. Studies* 98 (1993): 20-42.

57 See Marilyn Callahan and Chris McNiven, "British Columbia," *Privatization and Provincial Social Services in Canada: Policy, Administration and Service Delivery*, ed. J.S. Ismael and Y. Vaillancourt (Edmonton: University of Alberta Press, 1988), 13-40. On the similar situation found in other provinces see Keith Brownsey and Michael Howlett, eds., *The Provincial State: Politics in Canada's Provinces and Territories* (Toronto: Copp Clark Pitman, 1992) and Melville McMillan, ed., *Provincial Public Finances* (Toronto: Canadian Tax Foundation, 1991).

58 See W. Magnusson, W.K. Carroll, C. Doyle, *et al.*, *The New Reality: The Politics of Restraint in British Columbia* (Vancouver: New Star, 1984).

59 See Donald E. Blake, "The Electoral Significance of Public Sector Bashing," *B.C. Studies* 62 (1984): 29-43; Philip Resnick, "Neo-Conservatism on the Periphery: the Lessons from B.C.," *B.C. Studies* 75 (1987): 2-23; and Michael Howlett and Keith Brownsey, "The New Reality and the Old Reality: Party Politics and Public Policy in British Columbia 1941-1987," *Studies in Political Economy* 25 (Spring 1988).

60 See William K. Carroll and R.S. Ratner, "Social Democracy, Neo-Conservatism and Hegemonic Crisis in British Columbia," *Critical Sociology* 16:1 (1989): 29-53; and Robert C. Allen and Gideon Rosenbluth, eds., *Restraining the Economy: Social Credit Economic Policies for B.C. in the Eighties* (Vancouver: New Star Books, 1986).

61 On the decline of Social Credit during the Vander Zalm era see Graham Leslie, *Breach of Promise: Socred Ethics Under Vander Zalm* (Madeira Park: Harbour Publishing, 1991); Stan Persky, *Fantasy Government: Bill Vander Zalm and the Future of Social Credit* (Vancouver: New Star Books, 1989); and Gary Mason and Keith Baldrey, *Fantasyland: Inside the Reign of Bill Vander Zalm*, (Toronto: McGraw-Hill Ryerson, 1989). On the conflict of interest charges related to the sale of his theme park, see E.N. Hughes, *Report of the Honourable E. N. Hughes, Q.C. on the sale of Fantasy Garden World Inc.* (Victoria: Queen's Printer, 1991).

62 On the government's worker-based Working Opportunity Fund (WOF) see David Smith, "Harcourt Dangles Tax Break Investment Fund Carrot," *Vancouver Sun* 9 January 1992, D1.

63 On the general dynamics of the provincial party system see Donald E. Blake, R.K. Carty and L. Erickson, *Grassroots Politicians: Party Activists in British Columbia* (Vancouver: UBC Press, 1991); and Donald E. Blake, "The Politics of Polarization: Parties and Elections in British Columbia," *Politics, Policy and Government in British Columbia*, ed. Ken Carty (Vancouver: UBC Press, 1996), 67-84.

64 For a discussion of the differences between the various elements that support the New Democrats see Laurie E. Adkin, *Politics of Sustainable Development: Citizens, Unions and Corporations* (Montreal: Black Rose, 1995).

65 Michael Howlett and Keith Brownsey, "British Columbia: Public Sector Politics in a Rentier Resource Economy," *The Provincial State: Politics in Canada's Provinces and Territories*, ed. K. Brownsey and M. Howlett (Toronto: Copp Clark Pitman, 1992), 265-96.

66 See P.W. Daniels, K. O'Connor and T.A. Hutton, "The Planning Response to Urban Service Sector Growth: An International Comparison," *Growth and Change: A Journal of Urban and Regional Policy* 22:4 (1991): 3-26. More specifically see Trevor J. Barnes and Roger Hayter, "Economic Restructuring, Local Development and Resource Towns: Forest Communities in Coastal British Columbia," *Canadian Journal of Regional Science* 17:3 (1994): 289-310; and Trevor Barnes and Roger Hayter, "British Columbia's Private Sector in Recession, 1981-1986: Employment Flexibility without Trade Diversification?," *B.C. Studies* 98 (1993): 20-42.

67 See Craig Heron and Robert Storey, *On the Job: Confronting the Labour Process in Canada* (Montreal: McGill-Queen's University Press, 1986); and Stephen McBride, *Not Working* (Toronto: University of Toronto Press, 1992).

68 As occurred in Ontario under the Rae government. See Neil B. Freeman, *Budget Pink and Budget Blues: Fiscal Policy in the Ontario NDP Government, 1990-1994: A Preliminary Analysis* (Calgary: Paper Presented to the Annual General Meeting of the Canadian Political Science Association, 1994).

69 D.E. Blake and R.K. Carty, *Partisan Realignment in British Columbia: The Case of the Provincial Liberal Party* (Montreal: Paper Presented to the Annual General Meeting of the Canadian Political Science Association, 1995).

70 H. Craig David and Thomas A. Hutton, "Producer Services Exports from the Vancouver Metropolitan Region," *Canadian Journal of Regional Sciences* 14:3 (1991): 378-80; and D.F. Ley and T.A. Hutton, "Vancouver's Corporate Complex and Producer Services Sector: Linkages and Divergence Within a Provincial Staples Economy," *Regional Studies* 21 (1987): 413-24.

71 See H. Craig Davis, "Is the Metropolitan Vancouver Economy Uncoupling from the Rest of the Province?," *B.C. Studies* 98 (1993): 4.

12 THE NORTHWEST TERRITORIES

Old and New Class Politics on the Northern Frontier

PETER CLANCY

CLASSES, POLITICS, AND ACCUMULATION STRATEGIES

Traditionally the Northwest Territories has held a unique place in the Canadian consciousness as a region of vast distances and sparse human settlement. Its predominantly Aboriginal population was scattered across one-third of the land mass of Canada. The economic significance of the land and its resources was also part of this portrait. For millennia, Aboriginal society has been based on the harvest of wildlife. More recently, Arctic minerals, oil, and gas have been exploited by industrial Canada. Thomas Berger aptly captured the dual nature of this political economy in his phrase "northern homeland, northern frontier."

Since the 1999 political division between the western Northwest Territories and Nunavut, the national mindset requires adjustment. Picture the new boundary as a thread extending north at the Manitoba-Saskatchewan border, then angling northwest to Great Bear Lake before turning north again to the Arctic coast. From here it veers first east and then north, bisecting Victoria Island and points beyond. The effect of this geo-political division is to create a "new" Northwest Territories. Its 40,000 residents, living in more than 30 towns and settlements, include the Inuvialuit of the Beaufort region, the Dene and Métis of the Mackenzie Valley and south Slave regions, and the non-Natives centred in the larger commercial centres of Yellowknife, Inuvik, Hay River, and Fort Smith. Though Aboriginal northerners have become a central political force over the past generation, division has deprived them of a popular majority.

This chapter discusses the politics of the new Northwest Territories, by setting it against the historical backdrop of the shared territorial past. (Readers should bear in mind that the discussion of the period prior to April 1, 1999 covers the "old" Northwest Territories.) In particular, it examines the role of class in shaping postwar politics in the Northwest

Territories. It is an issue that has not been discussed extensively to date. Partly this follows from the way class politics is defined, since it is sometimes reserved for "pure" class expressions such as militant trade unions, socialist parties, or tightly organized employer groups. In such perspectives it is only where organized class vehicles drive the formal political agenda that class is accorded analytical primacy. Yet when more subtle formulations of class politics are recognized, its significance is readily uncovered. Here, for example, I will treat resource megaprojects, land-claim settlements, community co-operatives, and anti-trapping campaigns as both objects and agents of class politics in the North. Since a class structure forms an integral part of most societies, the mapping of class positions and their inter-relations and transformations over time provide an essential starting point. In a discerning set of studies begun almost forty years ago, Frank Vallee pioneered the analysis of class formation in the North.[1] Peter Usher's work on the class dynamics of hunter-trappers is equally seminal, and Marybelle Mitchell has offered an important recent treatment of class among the Inuit.[2]

In the opening section of this chapter, the class structure of the Northwest Territories will be contrasted at the two ends of the study period: the 1950s and the 1990s. The chapter is also concerned with the class structure of state policy in the Northwest Territories, including both the impact of social class on political institutions and the impact of political institutions on channelling class politics. This treatment highlights the essentially "political" character of economic growth processes. In frontier societies more than most, the core mechanisms of production and exchange are established and maintained only with state support. Utilizing the notion of an "accumulation strategy,"[3] I will identify and discuss the nature and consequences of those state policies most involved in social and economic development in the North.

The concept of an accumulation strategy is crucial in this regard as it identifies a set of market and state-secured relationships that confer decisive advantages on a beneficiary class or class fraction while constraining the actions and prospects of others. Politics emerges from an accumulation strategy because such strategies, given their differential class bases, are almost invariably contested. Once installed within a framework of state policy, however, a strategy may cease to be the target of explicit political challenge, and "normal politics" of a distinctly non-class character may proceed for relatively long periods of time. Nevertheless the most decisive political conflicts, and the ultimate measure of political dominance, will occur where fundamental class interests are at stake in transitional times. As the chapter unfolds, it will become apparent that northern development has involved the adoption and displacement of several different accumulation strategies that have had an impact on, and been influenced by, the changing class structure of northern society.

Throughout this discussion it will be evident that class power, in the North as elsewhere, does not derive automatically from economic position, but is politically mediated. It is in the political realm that class interests are organized, alliances, and coalitions are formed, and programs are forged. In the North, these interests have been pursued through many channels: electoral mobilization, associational lobbying, litigation in the courts, and negotiations at the Aboriginal claims table, to name the most prominent.

In all cases, the configuration of state institutions is a prime mediating variable in political and economic conflict. This is especially so in the North. Over the study period, no provincial jurisdiction has seen more dramatic transformations in state structure than the Government of the Northwest Territories (GNWT). The northern state has moved from administrative colonialism to liberal democracy, from a representational vacuum to a modified form of responsible government, from central jurisdictional dominance to provincial-style devolution. The result has been the opening up of a complex institutional grid, offering multiple points of access for class interests engaged in political struggles. In 1999 the state structure changed again, and it is on this field that accumulation strategies advanced by different classes and class coalitions compete for political dominance.

CLASSES IN THE NORTHERN SOCIAL FORMATION

The social formation of the Territories is composed of a complex set of classes that originated in quite distinct modes of production. Over time they have combined, as the productive relations of industrial capitalism have been grafted onto an historically earlier set of classes associated first with primitive communal production and later with petty (or small independent) commodity production aimed at the European fur trade.

The North has thus seen two major structural transformations. The first involved the encounter between the Aboriginal commune and merchant capitalism in the seventeenth to nineteenth centuries, while the second arrayed petty commodity capitalism against industrial capitalism throughout the twentieth. As a result of these combined processes, by 1945 the northern social formation included a large number of classes. There were subsistence-oriented hunter-gatherers, petty commodity producers of fur, wage labourers, and large and small capitalist employers. A brief overview of the historical roots of the contemporary social formation is set out below.

Aboriginal Communal Production

The earliest of the class elements found in the Territories today were the hunter-trapper-fishers devoted to subsistence production in what is often termed a "natural economy." Production units based on kinship ties generated material products for their *domestic* use, rather than for *exchange* or commercial sale. Such an economy existed for centuries and was built on an elaborate set of cultural and religious values, passed on between the generations. This form of production was found almost exclusively among Aboriginal northerners living "on the land." While exact proportions are difficult to quantify, subsistence production continued after 1945 among the Dene and Métis of the Mackenzie District, particularly in the distant bush areas. It was even more common among the Inuit living north of the treeline on the Arctic mainland and islands.

The Aboriginal commune was based on a number of key practices (sometimes described as "conditions of reproduction," since they were necessary if this communal enterprise was to continue from one generation to the next). First, mobility on the land was required to enable family units to reach a number of diverse resource pools when wildlife was available and prime. The Dene followed a seasonal round of hunting activities which typically would include a winter camp in the boreal or transitional forest devoted to fur trapping and caribou or moose-hunting, followed by a summer fishery, and a fall caribou hunt on the barrens.[4] Among the Inuit the round might entail a winter hunting seals on the sea ice, a spring bird hunt on land, a late summer caribou hunt in the interior, and a fall fishery at the coast.[5]

A second requirement was the recognition of, and respect for, rights over land and wildlife. These rights did not take the form of private ownership and exclusive property rights, but rather were rights of use which included the right of access for both group and individual producers. For example, fish camps were normally established at deep pools or river mouths where family or band groups worked together, year after year, to harvest, prepare, and share out the catch. Barren-ground caribou hunts were similarly organized, with the product redistributed to all participants. A third requirement was a pattern of group composition, often based on bilateral kin-relations, which allowed small groups of under a dozen families to combine and re-combine as dictated by the harvesting tasks, land base, and seasonal round. Only with such a strict set of rules and practices could an Aboriginal commune generate the material products necessary for its physical and social reproduction. However, given such conditions, it could be remarkably durable.

Petty Commodity Production

Historically, most Aboriginal communes were transformed into commercial or "petty commodity" enterprises by their contact with European and Canadian merchant capital. Typically this occurred in the form of the fur trade, although in some cases the first contacts were made by whaling companies. While the Athapaskan Dene were involved in the fur trade as early as 1680,[6] it was only after 1900 that direct commercial contact was made with most Inuit culture groups.[7] These contacts with merchants were rarely sudden and abrupt, but had a profound long-term impact on native society. The effect of trade was to create a new commodity production circuit within the Aboriginal commune, in which fur-bearing animals were trapped not for domestic needs but for exchange. It could take decades, generations, or even centuries before the imperatives of the fur trade actually interfered with the reproduction of Aboriginal communes. Yet wherever contacts occurred, the allocation of labour time between commodity and subsistence production changed within the commune, as did the continuing viability of the seasonal round of social, economic, and cultural activities.

The complete triumph of commodity production would preclude the fulfillment of domestic needs on the land. While Aboriginal people seldom went this far, the white, immigrant, grubstake trapper was the ultimate expression of this logic. Such enterprises, which expanded or contracted depending on the prevailing terms of exchange, required that total labour power be devoted, from fall to spring, to running an extensive trapline over hundreds of miles. Typically, the commercial trapper met his consumption needs of basic food, clothing, and equipment by buying an "outfit" from a merchant trader, usually as an advance against fur deliveries. Once domestic materials were obtained as commodities, the strictures of the natural economy no longer applied.[8]

Within Aboriginal society, there was a greater tendency to *combine* subsistence and commodity production, by grafting a limited period of commercial fur trapping onto the seasonal round. In this way two distinct logics of production could be serviced within the single hunting and trapping enterprise. Here the conditions of existence included both an outlet for commodity exchange, where goods such as guns and ammunition could be obtained, and access to subsistence resources to meet the majority of domestic needs. The compatibility or incompatibility of the two labour processes was determined by both ecological and social factors. Among the former, the availability of fur populations loomed large. Forest ecosystems could be rich in such wildlife, whereas barren land systems offered only a few species such as white fox. In addition, much depended on the physical proximity of fur grounds to subsistence harvesting sites. Among the socio-economic determinants were the accessibility of traders and the terms of exchange. During periods of Hudson's Bay Company monopoly, both price and credit conditions could be quite stable over time, whereas the competitive period after 1885 saw higher prices and a greater density of trade outlets.

The white commercial trapper and the Aboriginal hunter-trapper stand at opposite ends of the petty commodity spectrum. Business records on the volumes and values of fur production (per capita) indicate differing levels of market involvement by Aboriginal people,[9] meaning that there was considerable variation in class strengths over region, ethnic group, and time.[10] What is beyond doubt, however, is that by the early 1940s, the overwhelming proportion of native peoples had fallen into the petty commodity producer category.

In pursuing these activities, the Aboriginal population remained primarily rural, travelling to settlements or trading posts periodically. Most Aboriginal people lived within a relatively localized social setting involving a bush-camp and sub-tribal group.[11] Even with visits to trading posts, primary contact seldom extended to an entire tribal (i.e., language) group.[12] As subsistence and commodity production were combined in the social formation, two modes of production are articulated, or joined. Significantly, while a majority of native northerners followed similar economic practices, there was no regional, much less territory-wide, network through which they could mobilize politically to defend their common interests.

Today there are few if any subsistence hunter-trapper-fisher units of the classical type. Both the Dene and Métis in the Mackenzie District and the Inuit of the barrenlands have shifted their primary residence to settlements that offer commercial and government services. Yet neither the decline of the subsistence commune nor the intensive commercial trapline has meant the end of the native land-based economy. In fact, native participation in wildlife harvesting remains extremely important, particularly to the economy of isolated communities. Here once again the family serves as the enterprise unit, though in a structurally different form. It is sustained by a complex combination of wage income, transfer-payment income, and domestic subsistence production. In the native settlements, the supply of wage jobs is limited and often seasonal in nature, thus leaving extensive periods for hunting, trapping, and fishing.

The scarcity and highly seasonal character of wage income make the acquisition of the necessary harvesting instruments—ranging from guns, ammunition, and traps to boats, motors, and snowmobiles—quite difficult. Here the social wage provided by the welfare state has proved critical. The income injected by state transfer programs such as old age pensions, family allowances (formerly), unemployment insurance, and welfare significantly assists settlement residents in underwriting the commercial requirements of modern bush life. The final element in this equation is the value of the subsistence products, with country food constituting a major food source outside of the commercial marketplace.[13]

Industrial Capitalist Production

In virtually all parts of Canada, postwar society underwent powerful transformations, but nowhere was the pace and scope greater than in the North. Observers and analysts have been struck repeatedly by the dramatic transformation of northern society in little more than a generation. One significant result of this change has been the fact that while so many of today's political leaders—whether in the Aboriginal organizations or the Executive Council or the Legislative Assembly of the GNWT—were born on the land and raised in the social circumstances described above, today they are governing a much different type of society. While petty commodity production persists, it no longer prevails.

Even before 1945, another set of classes associated with industrial capitalist production had been established in the North. As elsewhere, this type of productive activity involved both wage labourers and corporate capitalists. In the North, these two new classes existed alongside communal producer, independent producer, and merchant interests in the rural areas but came to dominate social relations in the service and resource towns associated with industrial activities. These towns can be pictured as a series of commercial enclaves strung out across the North. In the Mackenzie District, Fort Smith served as the administrative centre and point of entry to the NWT, Hay River provided the hub for the Mackenzie River transport system, Yellowknife was a gold mining town, and Port Radium a company town for Eldorado Nuclear Ltd. The wage labour force was at first composed of miners and construction and transport workers (some of whom were unionized), together with assorted retail service workers. These seasonal and permanent jobs were filled almost exclusively by Euro-Canadian immigrants. In the resource sector, their employers were large, southern-based corporations (both private and state-owned), while resident small businesses shared the service sector with the ubiquitous Hudson's Bay Company.[14]

The figures presented in Table 12.1 attest to the growing importance of the wage-labour relationship in the Northwest Territories. Despite its limited penetration into many smaller native settlements, it is now the dominant component of the territorial economy and social formation. Particularly over the past 25 years, its growth has brought a progressive

TABLE 12.1 **NWT LABOUR FORCE BY SECTOR, 1971 AND 1997**

SECTOR	1971 Workers	1971 Percentage	1997 Workers	1997 Percentage
Goods Producing	2,430	22%	3,722	15%
Construction	445		1,045	
Service Producing	6,885	63%	21,049	85%
Transportation & Communication	1,115		2,256	
Trade	905		3,304	
Finance, Insurance & Real Estate	115		805	
Community, Business & Personal Services	2,270		8,811	
Public Administration	2,480		6,281	
Unspecified	1,635	15%	—	0
TOTAL	10,950		24,999	

Source: *Northwest Territories Statistical Abstract*, 1974 (Ottawa, 1974); *Statistics Quarterly* (June 1997).

broadening out of the wage-earning population. Yet this has not created a classic industrial society in the North. In fact, the service sector has far outpaced the manufacturing sector in the modern economy. This led Kenneth Rea to remark that the North "has displayed a tendency to develop like a 'post-industrial' region, having skipped the industrialization stage, except in some areas along the southern fringe."[15]

A number of trends should be noted here. First the service sector now dominates over primary and secondary employment. This pattern is certainly not unique to the Northwest Territories, as it has long prevailed in many provinces. However, the extent of service-sector dominance in the North is quite extreme. By 1997, it accounted for 87 per cent of gross territorial employment, while goods production accounted for only 13 per cent.[16] This rapid increase in service-sector employment conceals an equally striking growth in public-sector employment over the past generation. Such traits confound the popular image of a frontier resource economy.

Second, the seemingly inexorable expansion of the postwar administrative state was itself a class phenomenon. The first (federal government) phase, which occurred in the 1950s, represented the belated arrival of the welfare state together with an extensive modernization program targeted at land-based Aboriginal people. Next came the broadening out of the

Territorial administration following its transfer from Ottawa to Yellowknife in 1967. A third wave has seen the expansion of local government employment, particularly in the 1980s. As a result, by 1997 the 6281 full-time jobs in the "public administration" category exceeded the 3722 jobs in the *entire* goods-producing sector. With only a few sub-regional exceptions, the industrial resource sector has not provided the driving force in restructuring the northern social formation. In fact where it *has* boomed, the reliance on imported labour has dampened significantly its transformative impact on native life.

Third, the northern wage economy mirrors capitalism elsewhere by revealing both high-wage and low-wage segments. At one end are the skilled trade and resource jobs and the public service positions, which are often unionized. They offer above-average salaries and include generous "northern benefits." On the other are the unskilled, low security, low-wage positions in the personal service component of the service sector. In the North as elsewhere, women fill a disproportionately large number of the latter positions.

There is also a strong ethnic overlay to the northern class structure. Native people tend to be concentrated at the margin of the wage-labour market. They are far more likely than non-natives to hold short-term or seasonal jobs, or to be unemployed. As far back as 1971, Vallee noted the existence of a native *lumpenproletariat* in the Arctic.[17] In the 1990s, the contrast between native and non-native workers (reflected in both participation and duration of employment) remains striking, as Table 12.2 reveals.

Finally, it is important to note that the class contrast between town and rural society has not disappeared over our study period, though it assumes a more complex form today. Peter Usher distinguishes four types of populated centres: administrative and transport centres, resource towns, native

TABLE 12.2 **PERSONS WHO WORKED, NWT 1988**

	POPULATION *+15 years*	WORKED *1988*	*% working*	*+26 wks*	*%+26 wks*
Non-Aboriginal	15,039	13,785	92%	11,674	78%
Aboriginal	19,611	12,431	63%	6,122	31%
Inuit	9,662	5,770	62%	2,701	31%
Inuvialuit	1,797	1,279	71%	653	18%
Dene	5,715	3,295	58%	1,571	27%
Metis	2,437	1,887	77%	1,194	49%

Source: *Statistics Quarterly* (March 1990).

communities with more than 250 inhabitants, and native communities with less than 250. His comparison makes clear that the capitalist wage relationship is broadly stratified across the North. For the 19 centres in the first two categories, the 1981 mean income of tax filers exceeded $18,000, whereas for the 63 native centres the mean income was barely half that level. The contrast between full and seasonal wage employment is similarly stark: whereas 68 per cent of non-native earners worked more than eight months in 1981; only 28 per cent of native earners did so. Usher forecasted that:

> There will continue to be several dozen widely scattered communities that are predominantly native in composition and that will continue to be home to most native northerners ...These residents will continue to depend heavily on government and small business for wage employment and cash income, but such agencies will not provide full employment or sufficient cash income for anywhere near all the labour force. Consequently, renewable resources—fish and wildlife—will continue to play a very significant role in these local economies for both subsistence and commercial purposes.[18]

This combination of labour processes and income streams, which together consolidate this significant social category, is often described as a "mixed economy." While it reflects the three modes of production discussed above, it is best regarded as petit-bourgeois, given the still-central role of the household unit.

COMPETING ACCUMULATION STRATEGIES IN THE POSTWAR STATE

The following sections explore the role of the political apparatus in shaping changes in the northern class structure. They suggest that even in the absence of organized interests and open conflict, the state can implement policy measures that carry profound implications for class relations. The continued reproduction or expansion of a class category may hinge on the degree of policy support extended by the state. The concept of an accumulation strategy helps to illustrate how policy may, at critical moments, serve the advantages of designated classes while undermining others.

In the postwar period, a number of accumulation strategies have been articulated and addressed by the state in the North. In identifying them below, I will argue that the state has systematically advanced certain class programs while ignoring or retarding others. Such a political process acquires a dynamic quality over time, as the subordinate interests in one round may mount more authoritative challenges in the next. An important mediating factor in this ongoing contest for dominance is the institutional structure of the state in the North. Political channels for class expression are defined by the allocation of jurisdiction, legislative function, executive selection, bureaucratic design, and the composition of the political elite. Since the prospects for articulating, securing, and implementing a strategy are heavily politically determined in the North, special attention must be paid to the evolution of the territorial state.

RESOURCE CAPITAL AND THE ABORIGINAL PROLETARIAT

Equally dramatic as this social and economic transformation of the postwar North described above has been the change in its political institutions. In the 1940s the NWT remained a federal colony, still awaiting representative and responsible government. According to the *Northwest Territories Act*, executive power was vested in a commissioner who exercised legal powers conferred by a council. In practice, the commissioner was the deputy minister of the federal Department of Mines and Resources, whose mandate involved the management of Crown title to lands and resources north of the sixtieth parallel. For its part, the Northwest Territories Council was also made up of senior civil servants, appointed from the related departments doing business in the North (such as Indian Affairs, Health, National Defence, and External Affairs). Effectively constituted as an inter-departmental committee, the council met infrequently and passed such ordinances as required to empower the bureaucracy.[19]

In the absence of a territorial civil service, the Department of Mines and Resources handled general administrative matters.[20] As a cabinet portfolio, Mines and Resources was distinctly junior and was occupied by no fewer than five incumbents between 1947 and 1952. While the representative channels remained marginal, the state's capacity for administrative intervention rose markedly in the 1950s as a result of two major initiatives. The first occurred late in 1953, with the creation of the new Department of Northern Affairs and National Resources (DNANR). It was equipped with a strong mandate as Ottawa's lead department in the North, with broad authority to co-ordinate the overall federal presence. The second initiative followed at mid-decade, when the department announced a bold new economic development strategy in response to the perceived crisis in native society.

In the fullest sense, this constituted an accumulation strategy. The federal state would underwrite the investment costs of resource capital in an effort to transform the North into an industrial society and Aboriginal northerners into a working class. It represented a modernization program of vast proportions. Politically, this strategy was driven by concern that the petty commodity economy had collapsed structurally. First, the fur market entered one of its periodic slumps in the early 1950s, significantly reducing the credit terms and cash returns to trappers. Then senior Northern Affairs officials, already pessimistic for the eventual recovery of the fur market, concluded that the subsistence hunting side of rural production was even more imperilled. The most alarming evidence came in reports of Inuit starvation, particularly in the Keewatin interior. Here the closure of trading posts, coupled with a scarcity of caribou, resulted in deaths, emergency relief airlifts, and extensive publicity. Appraisals of the hunting economy were further diminished in administrative circles by the results of several caribou population surveys which reported precipitous declines in the great northern herds.[21] This prompted an urgent search for alternative livelihoods, which pointed toward settlement-based wage employment in the extractive industries.

In 1955 the new strategy was unveiled publicly, in a brief to the Gordon Royal Commission on Canada's Economic Prospects. Here the deputy minister outlined a comprehensive development program based on the massive provision of state-supported infrastructure to generate industrial investment and wage employment. The centrepiece was a railroad connecting the Mackenzie District to southern Canada, while a complementary network of resource roads and airports was extended across the North. Only an integrated program, it was argued, could meet a social challenge of this order:

> The people whose economy is disintegrating will not [wait]. A people who have been accustomed to supporting themselves by hard effort in a rigorous existence can be adjusted to a new way of life—to wage employment in mines or construction work, to lumbering or other activities ... the human problems of today and the economic development of tomorrow are inextricably intertwined in the Northwest Territories.[22]

Several years passed before the Department won political and bureaucratic approval for this program, but the Diefenbaker Government's endorsement of the Great Slave Lake Railway signalled its triumph. This infrastructure program, together with the federal management of Crown land rights in the North, remained the backbone of Ottawa's northern policy until the early 1980s.

The original emphasis on mining was broadened after 1968, when Atlantic Richfield struck oil at Prudhoe Bay on Alaska's North Slope. Indeed the federal government's resource branch was pre-occupied during the 1970s with oil and gas exploration and pipeline planning across the

Arctic, from the Mackenzie Delta to Lancaster Sound.[23] Even as Ottawa contemplated the transfer of provincial-type functions to the GNWT, it carefully guarded the resource jurisdiction. Firmly entrenched in federal administrative agencies, this accumulation strategy was vigorously pursued for more than 30 years, from the Gordon Commission (1956) to the National Energy Program (1980) and beyond.

In this case, the triumph of one class strategy entailed the abandonment of another. State agencies considered, then rejected, the possibility of public policy support for the wildlife economy. A policy review completed in 1950 noted several options, ranging from state-run trading outlets to fur price and income supports. It further argued that conditions in the rural economy varied widely by region, and that policy responses could be similarly tailored. While the Indian Affairs Branch supported such action, Northern Affairs systematically opposed all measures that might reinforce, much less aid the recovery of, the hunting-trapping economy.[24] Even though a majority of native northerners were rural petty producers in the 1950s, their class interests lacked sufficient weight to register at this time of crisis, when the most basic elements of northern economic policy were under review.

RESIDENT SMALL BUSINESS AND THE JUNIOR PARTNERSHIP STRATEGY

It is revealing that the strategy discussed above, which sought social restructuring by enlarging the wage economy, was formulated and maintained by federal administrative authorities, with minimal popular input from the North. Over time, however, representative political channels were opened up, mainly through changes to the NWT Council, with the result that resident interests found increasing expression. Over the quarter-century after 1950, the appointed Council was transformed slowly into a fully elected one.[25] During this period, the elected contingent reflected several dimensions of northern society. The Mackenzie District members of the 1950s were trappers, traders, and merchants who were sensitive to their rural and small-town constituents. Within the rather limited jurisdiction then exercised by the Council, they advocated support for petty commodity harvesting, through fur stabilization payments, trapper loans, positive game regulations, and income support payments.

However, as the elected contingent expanded in the 1960s, the pattern of advocacy changed. Through the life of the sixth, seventh, and eighth Councils (1966-79), the concerns of town-centred private businesses tended to predominate. It is in the committee work and resolutions of successive Councils that this perspective is most evident. They called for jurisdictional autonomy in the form of provincehood, declared categorical support for growth based on industrial mega-projects, and expressed frustration with and hostility toward both the size of the government sector and (after 1969) the land-claims politics of Aboriginal groups. While seldom expressed unanimously in Council, these policies were advanced by a coherent bloc of white businesspeople and professionals centred in the five largest urban areas where the commercial service economy was strongest.[26]

In this way the Council managed to articulate an accumulation strategy of its own, albeit one which could not stand entirely on its own. For the most part, the private-sector population was based economically in the service sector, engaged in transport, wholesale and retail trade, and professional activities. These small-sized enterprises faced a high-cost environment, small markets, and narrow margins of profitability at the best of times. Part of the social coherence of the private-sector population came from its opposition to the territorial public sector, which expanded rapidly after the 1967 transfer to Yellowknife. In general, civil servants enjoyed levels of job security, salary scales, and northern allowances (in the form of subsidized housing and assisted travel) that were unavailable to private employers and employees. These material affinities were fused with a liberal political ideology which presented northern society as a union of citizens with equal rights and common interests in the constitutional progress of territorial government toward provincehood. While it was voiced frequently in the Council, its most forceful exponent was Commissioner Stuart Hodgson. Resolutely resistant to political claims based on race or ethnicity, he challenged the "national" aspirations of Aboriginal groups with the counter-claim that "We are all Northerners." To this end the Commissioner promoted an evolution through southern political forms, including a structure of community politics based on the municipal model, encompassing all citizens.

In short, the private business sector defined its economic future in junior partnership with corporate business from the south, whether in the form of mines, oil and gas, or pipelines. Repeatedly the Council went on record in support of a Mackenzie Valley gas pipeline. Similarly it expressed alarm with the Dene, Métis, and Inuit proposals for Aboriginal claims settlement. Not only did these threaten a freeze on exploration and a delay in pipeline construction, but they also held out the prospect that large tracts of land might be permanently withdrawn from the "public" domain through the terms of settlement. Perhaps the Council reserved its greatest frustration for the Berger Inquiry of the mid-1970s. The Council view is aptly expressed by the title of its response: *You've Heard From the Radical Few About Canada's North ... Now Hear From the Moderate Many.*[27]

In retrospect it is apparent that the late 1970s witnessed a multi-dimensional transition in territorial political life. The Council increasingly found itself on the defensive, as the major policy decisions were being settled in areas beyond its control. Without question, the most dramatic political development was the emergence of Aboriginal associations as a counter-hegemonic force.[28] These organizations challenged the legitimacy of the territorial government while asserting the priority of native claims settlements over any other constitutional proposals. At the same time the content of the claims, contesting as they did the right to ownership and use of vast tracts of land, struck directly at the foundation of the mega-project strategy. Consequently, when the courts began to recognize a continuing Aboriginal title, the effect was cathartic.[29]

In 1977 this conflict was extended with Ottawa's acceptance of northern pipeline commissioner Thomas Berger's recommendation of a ten-year moratorium on pipeline routes across the northern Yukon. The result opened the way for native claims negotiations to proceed in a far less threatening atmosphere than before. Indeed, as the Aboriginal organizations submitted their claims proposals and began negotiations, the GNWT went to the table not as an independent party but as part of the federal team. Not long after, the federal government released a political development policy for the NWT that established separate tracks for native claims and constitutional development. Finally, 1980 saw the retirement of Commissioner Hodgson, which marked the end of appointed executive dominance in territorial politics. A collective Executive Committee had already emerged during the eighth Council, with three elected members joining Hodgson and his assistant commissioners. In this respect, the stage was set for the new Commissioner, John Parker, to lead a transition to an elected government leader (now premier), and an executive consisting of elected ministers alone.

THE PROGRESSIVE PETIT-BOURGEOIS ALLIANCE

The outcome of the 1979 territorial election signalled a changing political order. For one thing, the pattern of representation was unmistakably different.[30] In the enlarged Council (now Legislative Assembly) of twenty-two members, only eight came from urban ridings as opposed to multiple-settlement ridings. Moreover all fourteen of the "settlement" members were Aboriginal. Equally intriguing was the presence for the first time of experienced Aboriginal politicians from the Dene, Métis, Inuvialuit, and Inuit associations.[31] Not surprisingly, this Assembly spent much of its initial session reversing the flagship policy decisions of its predecessor. Strong resolutions were passed to endorse the prompt and fair settlement of native claims as a first priority, while the goal of provincial status was rescinded.

Over the ensuing decade, it became evident that control of the Territorial political agenda had passed from the resident white business bloc to a new coalition of petit-bourgeois elements within the assembly, allied with a new support network outside of the Assembly. The leadership element in the new coalition involved public- and para-public sector professionals in the "new" petit-bourgeoisie. Possessing varying degrees of formal education, they sold knowledge, skills, and services, generally involving administrative or technical expertise, either for general government or for specialty programs such as health, education, or welfare. While the greatest concentration is in federal and territorial headquarters staff ranks, this class is also widely spread across the North, through municipal governments and the community-based public services delivery structure. Significantly, this class also extends to the staff of Aboriginal organizations. Overall this category grew very rapidly after 1970 and was soon reflected in both electoral returns and labour patterns.

A second major element in this new bloc was the non-governmental native movement, including Dene, Métis, Inuit, and Inuvialuit living in predominantly native settlements. Here full-time employment is scarce, livelihoods are based on mixed sources of income, unemployment levels far exceed the territorial average, and people's attachment to government is largely as service consumers. This helps to explain the continuing tensions that surface between the political leadership of the bloc and the institutional civil service. Although occupational background reflects only one aspect of class position, the occupational profile of the legislative elite that emerges from Table 12.3 is indicative of the emerging alignments.

The new petit-bourgeois/native bloc was held together by a series of key policy commitments that proved to be quite durable over the 1980s. The first of these involved the defence of Territorial political autonomy against encroachments by Ottawa and the provinces. While it was initially forced on the Assembly from outside, this tactical unity engendered its own cohesive tendencies. During this same period of time there was a dramatic restructuring of executive authority, which was closely identified with the new northern leadership and which accentuated its legitimacy. However, the significance of this new politically dominant bloc was most clearly seen in the accumulation strategy that it sponsored. Since Aboriginal claims settlements were seen as major developmental institutions for native society, their fair and complete resolution became a strong priority. Settlements were expected to bring land rights, capital pools, and other entitlements into Aboriginal ownership, and create major new structures in the civil society of the North.

TABLE 12.3 **CLASS BACKGROUND OF LEGISLATIVE MEMBERS, 1975-2000**

	LEGISLATIVE ASSEMBLY						
	8th	*9th*	*10th*	*11th*	*12th*	*13th*	*14th*
New Petit-Bourgeoisie							
Civil Service	5	4	2	4	8	8	4
Para-Public	2	5	8	6	5	1	3
Aboriginal Associations	0	*4*	*4*	*4*	*6*	*6*	*1*
Hunter/Harvesters	0	1	2	0	0	0	0
SUB-TOTAL	7	14	16	14	19	15	8
Old Petit-Bourgeoisie							
Owner Manager	7	6	6	7	4	9	8
Lawyer	1	2	2	3	1	0	1
SUB-TOTAL	8	8	8	10	5	9	9
Working Class	0	0	0	0	0	0	2
TOTAL	15	22	24	24	24	24	19

Source: NWT *Legislative Assembly* (Yellowknife, 1980); *Ninth Legislative Assembly of the* NWT (Yellowknife, 1983); *The Eleventh Legislative Assembly of the* NWT (Yellowknife, n.d.); *Canadian Parlimentary Guide* (Toronto, 1991); *News/North Election Supplement* (October 1991); *Fourteenth Legislative Assembly: Official Voting Results* (Yellowknife, 2000).

A second distinguishing thread of the new accumulation strategy was the assertion of strategic state activity, as an economic motor in its own right. This contrasted with earlier views of the public service as a necessary evil whose expansionist appetite required constant check. In the new strategy, however, the public sector could only play this creative role after some major redesigns in terms of staffing, location, and control. In a series of proposals during the early 1980s, the GNWT explored the decentralization of service delivery and the devolution of program control to communities.[32] In a related initiative, regional and tribal authorities received support as an intermediate political level. After 1985 the focus shifted to indigenous staffing of the civil service, with an aggressive commitment to expand the number of Aboriginal civil servants. The third reflection of the new strategy was the NWT Economic Strategy of 1990. Here small business was identified as the prime vehicle, and settlement society the prime site, of economic development. The balance of this section expands upon these three key policy initiatives.

The ninth Assembly inaugurated a period of constitutional experiment that continues today. This was made possible in part by the widely shared view that the territorial government was an interim authority, which might give way to new designs. Among the proposals on the table were Aboriginal claims authorities, regional and tribal governments, the east-west division of the NWT, and the devolution of territorial programs to communities. To this end, the legislature created a Constitutional Alliance under whose auspices public debates and consultations were launched in search of a northern constitutional consensus.[33] In 1982 the Assembly also authorized the first plebiscite in territorial history, to decide the politically contentious question of east-west division.[34] At the same time, the Assembly mounted an extensive defence of territorial interests in the face of new national policy initiatives. First with Ottawa's proposed oil and gas lands regime, and later with the national constitutional proposals which culminated in the Patriation package, the legislature resisted all provisions which threatened the future of territorial and Aboriginal autonomy. This included the unprecedented visit of the entire Assembly (resolved into Committee of the Whole) to Ottawa in order to lobby Parliament and Cabinet.

Perhaps the most enduring legacy of this period was the revision of executive and legislative institutions. In the North this is most commonly described as the process of "consensus government."[35] This is a modified form of responsible government, in the absence of political parties, with a unique form of executive-legislative dynamic. In this system a members' caucus is convened immediately following an election, to select the government leader and executive council (cabinet) members. The executive committee was drawn increasingly from elected members, until 1986 when the government leader replaced the Commissioner as chair of the executive council. In this system, the government leader exercised the prerogative of assigning portfolios to ministers. Following the 1991 election, ministers were elected by the members' caucus for the first time.[36] Once in office, however, "It is the Minister's responsibility to take the general directions established by the Assembly, [and] develop policy which must be ratified by the Executive Council."[37]

The absence of parties has lent a distinctive quality to electoral and legislative politics. The fact that candidates run as independents confers significant autonomy on them while placing a premium on constituency representation.[38] Although this arrangement might result in constant fluctuations of government in other regimes, in the NWT it has not. Part of the reason for this stability has been the complex interweaving of the political and administrative branches of the state, as the dominant bloc in the Assembly has treated the public sector as a tool of economic development. Government in the Northwest Territories has become the largest single employer, as well as the largest purchaser and generator of products. This has opened up a number of strategic questions about the overall impact of the state. For the state as employer, this includes the location of jobs and the recruitment of personnel. For the state as purchaser, it highlights the role of a formal procurement policy. Many of these policy questions were either first articulated, or substantially revised, under the leadership of the new power bloc.

The staffing of the northern bureaucracy has been a continuing preoccupation since the postwar state began its growth. To take only one example, the arrangement of headquarters and field offices strongly affects the spatial distribution of job opportunities and income streams for northerners. The most lopsided version was seen in the federal Department of Northern Affairs, in which Ottawa positions significantly outnumbered field positions north of 60. With the expansion of a resident GNWT after 1967, four regional offices (later increased to five) were established as co-ordinating points for service delivery to the settlements, while the Yellowknife headquarters staff provided central control and direction. There have since been periodic attempts to re-calibrate the centre-field relationship: a 1977 de-centralization exercise, the 1981 proposal for internal devolution of control, the 1988 directive on building municipal units as "prime public authorities" in the settlements, and a 1991 "strength at two levels" initiative. The significant trend was displayed by a mounting concern to place program administration (though less often program control) wherever possible at the community level, thus maximizing the salaried positions in the field.

Personnel recruitment was similarly significant. The patterns of hiring, promotion, and retention defined class position and mobility patterns for northerners. Significantly, Ottawa's early industrial employment strategy failed to acknowledge the role of the public sector as an expanding avenue of wage employment. Moreover, for at least its first decade, the territorial civil service faced manpower shortages and skill deficits, due to the twin impacts of former federal employees reluctant to leave Ottawa for the North, and newly created programs in the GNWT. The solution was to concentrate on the "outside" recruitment of trained southern Canadians, attracted by favourable salary and benefit schemes. Even so there remained a problem of an extraordinarily high rate of circulation, as a full one-quarter of the civil service turned over in each year of the early 1970s. In response, an executive task force focused on organizational design and staff morale, through proposals for in-service training, review of job-classification, and a review of accommodation policies.[39]

The tenth Legislative Assembly redefined the recruitment issue in strategic terms, with the goal of maximizing northern employment. While this had figured nominally in GNWT policy for a long time, staffing profiles showed that indigenization remained a distant goal.[40] A reorientation was signalled by the executive council's formal announcement of its Native Employment Policy in 1985, backed up by an Equal Employment Directorate to monitor implementation.[41] Subsequently the affirmative action program was broadened to include women (1986) and long-time northern residents (1989). While the original native employment target of 52 per cent of staff positions by 1990 was not met, the long-term commitment was re-affirmed and coupled with a strong emphasis on education and training programs offered in the North.

These examples illustrated the new strategic economic approaches to public-sector development. The program both reflected and serviced the new middle-class component of the petit-bourgeois alliance at the core of the ascendant power bloc. Standing on its own, it bears intriguing similarities to the earlier wage-labour strategy, but using public- rather than private-sector industrial jobs. The more complicated nature of the new class compromise, however, was apparent in light of its other, more rural and market-oriented thrust.

This legislative coalition had to frame policies to satisfy all elements of its alliance. While many of these were urban- and public-sector oriented, others were not. The large and small native communities that send representatives to Yellowknife rest on a different class base than the larger commercial service centres. In addition to high levels of unemployment and seasonally fluctuating wage-labour demand, many families are sustained by a combination of wildlife harvesting (for domestic consumption), earned income, and public transfers. These individuals and communities also received attention from legislators, through a program of promoting small enterprise in the rural economy. The increased salience of wildlife management policies, together with heightened recognition of the economic significance of country food production, was a hallmark of the ninth Legislative Assembly. Consequently, the Department of Renewable Resources found itself under extremely close surveillance for several years, and it was during this time that the GNWT embarked on a number of pioneering policies in joint management authorities and harvester support programs.

It was shortly after the return of the eleventh Assembly in the fall of 1987 that a systematic economic policy review was launched. The Special Committee on the Northern Economy (SCONE) was charged with the task. Two years later it reported back to the Assembly, after an extensive set of public meetings and the receipt of special background studies.[42] There were several revealing features of the plan. First of all, it was clearly addressed to what the SCONE Report labelled the "underdeveloped communities" of the NWT. Furthermore, it proposed to target policy measures by community type. While the four mature service centres were deemed to be largely self-sustaining and best able to take up conventional business assistance, a second category of 16 "merging market communities" required support to attain that level. By contrast, the 41 smaller communities relied on land-based activities, with potential to specialize in such areas as tourism and crafts. The strategy proclaimed the centrality of private business enterprise, but insisted on the necessary role of state support, in providing infrastructure, training, and, where needed, capital.

Ultimately the class significance of this program turned on its implementation. However, as an expression of priorities, it suggested that small community enterprise in a variety of forms had acquired elevated importance. In the rural North, "private enterprise" was as likely to involve community co-operatives, land-claims authorities, municipal corporations, and wildlife harvesters as it was small independent proprietors. The prospect for local joint ventures, vertically integrated projects, and public-sector partnerships suggested the extent of this new state commitment to petit-bourgeois interests. In all of these forms, the aim was to make small capital far more accessible to resident, and particularly native, enterprise.

TERRITORIAL POLITICS IN THE 1990s

Territorial politics took another decisive turn in the 1990s, the full implications of which have yet to unfold. Since it is especially marked in the contrasting agendas of the eleventh and twelfth Legislative Assemblies, it is tempting to treat the intervening 1991 election as the fulcrum of political change. However, the true moment of transition was more diffuse.[43] Though the GNWT recorded the first in a string of fiscal deficits in 1989/90, it took several years before the severity of the structural squeeze was fully appreciated. Initially the small overruns could be absorbed by the GNWT's accumulated surplus, with little immediate impact upon expenditure profiles built up over decades of buoyant finance. But by 1991 the deepening economic recession and the curtailed federal transfers from the new federal Formula Financing Agreement combined to produce a four-fold increase in the deficit, and the fiscal crisis had arrived with a vengeance. Henceforth the finance minister came to dominate the government's overall outlook, the budget became the instrument of political control, and the severe fiscal discipline went a long way toward dampening the activist policy ethos that had characterized earlier administrations.

The year 1992 was equally critical for the shape of governing institutions. With the ratification of the Nunavut Final Agreement (NFA), the largest Aboriginal claim settlement passed from the negotiation phase to implementation.[44] Quite apart from the historic significance of the settlement to more than 17,000 Inuit beneficiaries, the NFA was linked to a Nunavut Political Accord which authorized a distinct Nunavut Territory before the close of the decade. Backed by a modest majority in a pan-territorial plebiscite, this launched the historic process of the constitutional division of the Northwest Territories. While the details of building Nunavut are the subject of another chapter, some comments on the politics of transition are in order, since this shaped both the twilight years of the NWT and the outlook for the new western territory.

The deepening fiscal crisis dominated the policy calculus of the twelfth Legislative Assembly (1991-95) and carried over into the thirteenth Legislative Assembly of the Northwest Territories (1995-99). Successive finance ministers have had little room to manoeuvre, since three-quarters of territorial revenues come from the annual federal transfer. Despite the appearance of a bilateral Formula Finance Agreement, the fact that Ottawa dictated its essential terms meant that the GNWT was forced to reconcile its shortfalls mainly on the expenditure side of its budget. The challenge was severe. Over the five-year period 1990/91 to 1994/95, the terms of the new formula (relative to the old) cost Yellowknife an estimated $540 million.[45] In the short term, the territorial government sought to reconcile this through a combination of administrative restructuring, salary and benefit cuts, and privatizations.

The twelfth Assembly inherited a systematic rationalization plan (*Strength at Two Levels*), which guided the first wave of change. Known also as the Beatty Report, it proposed to reduce the number of government departments (by merger) and redefine the allocation of central, regional, and local responsibilities in order to move program control closer to the community level. Beginning in 1992, the government won agreement for a series of salary freezes that were extended for more than five years. It also took an important and highly controversial decision to end the valuable staff accommodation benefits. For 25 years this had figured as part of the GNWT recruitment strategy, while at the same time creating a *de facto* dual housing market between public- and private-sector employees. The reduction of the benefit and privatization of government housing proved to be one of the most controversial aspects of fiscal restraint. Predictably, this was opposed by government employee associations, and it drew fire also from Nunavut interests fearing its inflationary impact on transition costs to the new government. By 1997 the cumulative legacy of employment restraint was evident in new headquarters-to-field-staff ratios. It also left hundreds of unfilled positions in the public service and raised serious questions about the effect this could have on program delivery. In the *Deficit Elimination Act* of 1995, the Legislative Assembly imposed formal limits on the finance minister's fiscal strategy by stipulating that the deficit not exceed 1 per cent of annual revenues in a given fiscal year and calling for an equivalent surplus in the following year. It also required a balanced budget by 1998/99 (the eve of division).[46]

In this context of shrinking expenditures, the GNWT opted for strategic choices. Here the terms of consensus government likely helped successive finance ministers to build legislative support for some extremely tough policy choices. In framing the budgets they could draw upon general advice from the Members' Caucus and specific advice from the Standing Committee on Finance. It was decided, for example, that the social envelope was to be protected as far as possible. As a result, spending on social programs actually expanded in relative terms over the period of restraint, from 58 to 61 per cent of overall expenditures. This priority acknowledged what one finance minister called the "staggering demographic factors" which made family and youth programs so important in northern society.[47] Accordingly, the budget tried to maintain a safety net with targeted income supports, social and health improvements, and training programs, even while the terms and delivery mechanisms of these policies were under review.

In this reorientation, the GNWT did not so much abandon its traditional responsibilities as scale down its level of commitment. As the then government leader Don Morin put it, with a budget of $1 billion "we can do a lot of good in the Northwest Territories."[48] But the guiding philosophy had tangibly shifted from the energetic activism of the prior decade to a more chastened awareness of limited state capacity. Henceforth the GNWT would stabilize rather than animate societal change. Finance Minister John Todd spelled out the implications, declaring in 1996 that "Government, by itself, can no longer sustain economic growth. The onus for future growth must be shifted to the private sector, to Aboriginal organizations and to communities where it belongs."[49] Significantly, this budget emphasized the need for "creative partnerships" for investment and employment, embracing "individuals, businesses, Aboriginal organizations, and all levels of government."

The new political priority was to support private capital in business and employment generation. Resource extraction projects formed an important part of this. As far back as 1991 the GNWT had talked optimistically about providing infrastructure to support an exploration boom which promised an extensive range of mines between Yellowknife and Coppermine. In the years that followed, the leading projects ebbed and flowed, and attention swung between base metals, gold, and diamonds. However, the GNWT expectation was couched in far more politically mature tones than had been the case in the 1970s. With partnership now came obligations, and socially responsible mega-projects were the order of the day. The GNWT intended to "reward companies that make genuine efforts to contribute to our economy, form real and lasting partnerships with northern and Aboriginal companies, and create jobs for our people."[50] In the mid-1990s, much attention centred on the BHP diamond property as a prototype for future ventures.[51] At the same time, the territorial government established an Investment Office to attract immigrant investment on favourable terms and to broaden the capital base available for the desired joint ventures.

To the extent that the multiple-interest joint venture becomes favoured in public policy and adopted in practice, this new accumulation strategy will need to reconcile some previously antagonistic interests. As indicated earlier, the emergence of a strong Aboriginal business ethic in the wake of land-claims settlements signalled an important reorientation, as the largest pools of indigenous northern capital tested their new potential. Mitchell aptly describes this as the birth of a native corporate elite.[52] The growing GNWT resolve to facilitate capitalist expansion can only intensify this trend. However, a strategy of capital partnerships will not come without complications, as a variety of distinct interests converge in joint enterprise. This is a politically controversial field, where northern business incentive policies will collide with Aboriginal investment preferences, and community-based corporations may find themselves uneasily allied with senior governments as well as private external capital. The ongoing disputes between NTI (Nunavut Tunngavik Inc., the Inuit claims authority) and the GNWT over government procurement contracting in the years leading up to division offers a prime example. At issue here was the degree of preference or exclusivity enjoyed by Nunavut claimant bodies under Article 24 of the Final Agreement. Intense disputes erupted over business tenders in Rankin Inlet and Iqualuit, as the NTI sought vigorously to extend its commercial reach.

To the tensions which will erupt among the constituent elements of the partner strategy must be added those between the new capitalist enterprise and local petit-bourgeoisie. It is to be expected that the latter class category, already amounting to an amalgam of small private business, small co-operative business, and independent domestic producers, will be stretched and even split by the new accumulation opportunities. Already local builders and contractors in NWT communities have had joint-venture experience with external firms, particularly in handling privatized government construction contracts in the 1990s. For this junior resident capital, the road to expansion may be through further integration in ever more elaborate commercial syndicates. At the other pole, the independent domestic producer segment of (predominantly Aboriginal) hunters, trappers, and fishers may find itself increasingly isolated. Despite the importance of domestic production, as demonstrated by the SCONE Report in 1989 and reaffirmed by the Royal

Commission on Aboriginal Peoples Report in 1996,[53] the extent of territorial state support has been decidedly modest and "hunter income support" is being deflected back for Aboriginal claim authorities to deal with.

Taking these tendencies together, the possibility cannot be discounted that the coalition of petit-bourgeois elements could collapse altogether. As we have seen, the progressive political orientations of the public-sector salariat have been undermined by recent retrenchment. At the same time, the horizons for indigenous and Aboriginal business have dramatically expanded. In such an event, the prime class cleavage may re-align along classically capitalist lines, with large and small corporate capital facing non-propertied elements including both independent domestic producers and wage workers.

POLITICS IN THE NEW NORTHWEST TERRITORIES

Since 1999, these class dynamics have been re-channelled through the separate state structures of the new Northwest Territories and Nunavut Territory. Inevitably, the year of division was one of multiple transitions. Most obviously, the eastern MLAs and ministers resigned from the GNWT, as the first Nunavut territorial election was held. A reconstituted NWT cabinet presided over the final nine months of the thirteenth Legislative Assembly (1995-99). The federal government appointed a new Commissioner for each territory, whose job was to exercise formal executive powers under the *Northwest Territories Act* and *Nunavut Act*. The re-allocation of government staff, physical facilities, and financial assets, which had been agreed upon during the Nunavut planning years, was implemented as well.

It should be noted that the closing sessions of the thirteenth Legislative Assembly were far from perfunctory, so far as the western region was concerned. In fact, several of the leading controversies pointed to the continuing political tensions that would beset the west. One of these involved the delineation of electoral constituencies and boundaries for the new NWT. Though the electoral boundaries commission had proposed that additional seats be created for both Yellowknife and Hay River—on the grounds that they contained the larger proportion of the new electorate—the Legislature chose not to accept this recommendation in the 1998 boundaries act. This prompted a citizens' group to mount a legal challenge on grounds of representational inequality. (Despite having 44 per cent of the population in the new NWT, Yellowknife was allotted only four of 14 proposed legislative seats.) NWT Supreme Court Justice de Weerdt held that rural areas could be "over-represented" to guarantee an effective democratic voice, but that this could not be achieved at the expense of other areas.[54] The Legislature solved this conundrum by expanding the assembly to 19 seats, allotting seven to the capital and two to Hay River. This struggle reflected an underlying difference in perspective about democratic practices, reflected in a political tension between the smaller, predominantly Aboriginal communities and the larger, predominantly non-Aboriginal towns. While division had resulted in Aboriginal northerners losing their majority electoral position in census terms, there was a willingness in the Legislature to tilt the representational balance in favour of rural ridings. Notably, the Aboriginal Summit (a group of association leaders) intervened in the court action to support the GNWT's (unsuccessful) defence of its boundaries legislation.

Another political controversy, which also came to a head during the period of division, involved a conflict-of-interest dispute centred on the then premier, Don Morin. In 1998, allegations had arisen over the premier's participation in certain land-use policy decisions that were of personal interest to him (on real-estate grounds). Eventually a formal inquiry was struck under the provisions of the conflict-of-interest statute. This concluded that the premier had failed to excuse himself from certain meetings, that he guided the decisions in directions which benefitted him, and that he provided the Legislature with documents that he knew contained untruths.[55] While Morin disputed the findings, the release of the inquiry report led to his resignation from the executive. In December 1998 he was succeeded as premier by Jim Antoine, an experienced Dene leader and minister from the Deh Cho region.

The Morin affair continued, first through a bias claim against the conflict-of-interest commissioner (which led to proposals for redefinition and procedural clarification).[56] In the longer perspective, this prolonged struggle raised certain questions about the efficacy of consensus-style government and its continued advantages for the NWT. For some, the affair highlighted the weakness of ministerial accountability in a collegial, non-party legislature where, it was noted, only one MLA had persistently sought to bring the conflict allegations to a public airing. (Not coincidentally, the New Democrats chose the 1999 campaign to mount a partial slate of candidates in six urban ridings. Though none won election, this was the first taste of partisan campaigning at the territorial level.) For others, it raised concerns about the extensive informal relations of executive decision-making that formed part of territorial government.[57] Part of the Morin case involved actions by several senior government officials. The review panel suggested that top bureaucrats should also be covered by the revised conflict rules.

The fourteenth NWT Legislative Assembly was chosen by general election in December 1999. Following the conventions of consensus government, the 19 members of the Legislative Caucus selected Stephen Kakfwi as premier, along with a five-member cabinet. A Dene leader from Deline, Kakfwi was the longest continuously serving MLA (since 1987) and a cabinet veteran who had held a wide range of portfolios. Most recently as minister of resources, wildlife, and economic development, he had been instrumental in the negotiations which saw the BHP agree to establish diamond processing (sorting and polishing) facilities in the North. In the spring of 2000, the Legislative Caucus unveiled its strategic framework document for the next four years. Titled *Towards a Better Tomorrow*, it set out a vision and a set of priorities to guide the government through its term.[58] This included a "unified and self-reliant territory," recognition of the "collective and individual rights of all Northerners," greater self-determination for Aboriginal people, balanced resource development, and a diversified economy.

In economic terms, territorial division has coincided with a striking renaissance of private investment prospects. This contrasts with the mid-1900s, which were years of economic doldrums and considerable anxiety. With the exception of the diamond-staking boom, the mining sector then appeared to be in retreat, while petroleum prices languished, and exploration seemed dormant. Yet beginning in the fall of 1998 the NWT's first commercial diamond mine, the Ekati venture, began production. Owned by Broken Hill Proprietary (BHP) of Australia and Dia Met of Kelowna, it almost doubled the annual value of NWT mineral output. A second project now under construction is Diavik Diamond Mines Inc., a partnership of Rio Tinto PLC of Britain and Aber Resources of Toronto. Significantly, the GNWT approached Ekati as a precedent-setting project, going to considerable lengths to negotiate northern commercial linkages at the construction, training, employment, sorting, and processing stages. Its success in this regard has cemented a network of commercial alliances between northern interests and external capital in the manner hypothesized earlier in the chapter. Of course this does not always ensure ready accord on regulatory policy questions. Both Ekati and Diavik have faced protracted negotiations over the terms of land-use permits and environmental undertakings. However, the underlying political alignments are notably more fluid than was the case 20 years ago. Then the southern exploration and pipeline consortia drew local support from non-native business alone, while the Aboriginal movement opposed any forms of commercial development prior to a comprehensive land-claims settlement. Today the list of sub-contractors linked to Diavik site development includes Aboriginal community firms, while on the other side several Dene Tribal Councils have joined conservation interests in calling for regulatory delays to allow for environmental impact reviews.

This picture is even more dramatic in the case of Arctic natural gas. A combination of commercial factors—including a downward trend in conventional supply estimates for Canada, rising international prices, and increased demand forecasts from gas-using industries—have brought the Alberta-based petroleum industry back to the NWT in a major way.[59] Massive new gas discoveries in the Fort Liard area in 1999-2000 are now being linked with the longstanding proven and potential reserves that were established in the Mackenzie Delta and Beaufort Sea in previous decades. As a result, in the spring of 2000 several production and transportation consortia outlined development scenarios that could cover the balance of the decade.

The critical political dimension that adds realism to these scenarios involves recent initiatives by both Aboriginal groups and the GNWT. For several years First Nations at Liard and in the Sahtu and Inuvialuit regions have been in negotiations with petroleum capital. This covered the formation of joint ventures in contracting and drilling, as well as the economic and environmental undertakings that would be part of petroleum development on Aboriginal settlement lands. Then, in November 1999, an all-chiefs conference voiced support for Mackenzie Valley petroleum development, subject to appropriate Aboriginal participation.[60] Principal among the necessary terms was majority Aboriginal ownership of the trunk pipeline project along the Valley route. The GNWT has also raised these issues to high priority. Premier Kakfwi visited Calgary oilmen in the spring of 2000 to endorse a $4-billion pipeline project, before moving on to Ottawa in search of parallel support. As the premier put it, "We think it's realistic to suggest that within ten years, with three diamond mines in operation and a natural gas pipeline down the valley, that we will be the first 'have' territory in the history of Canada."[61]

CONCLUSION

The fact that these newly emerging class dynamics intersect with a period of constitutional changes serves to heighten the political unpredictability of the moment. In effect, territorial division has altered the institutional avenues for class politics in the North. At the time of writing, it is difficult to predict with certainty the ultimate contours of this new state form. However, if recent trends hold, they are likely to shift the centre of political gravity toward local communities, although key public expenditure controls will likely remain, as now, at the territorial level. Initially at least the NWT seems destined to continue a version of "consensus government" by which the legislative members select a premier and a contingent of cabinet ministers from within their ranks in caucus. Beyond this, however, there is both the opportunity and the inclination to experiment with new forms. Debates on executive-legislative variations—such as the possibility of a directly elected premier, a two-chamber legislature, a party system, and dual-member constituencies electing male and female members—have already begun.

The future trajectories of politics in the new NWT may depend on the configurations of interests that are compressed into the new state system. Here there are some intriguing contrasts, many of them bearing class connotations. Three northerly Aboriginal peoples (the Inuvialuit, the Gwich'in, and Sahtu Dene and Métis) have implemented comprehensive claims agreements. Further south, the Dogrib Tribal Council concluded the first combined land claims and self-government agreement in the summer of 1999. In still more southerly districts, the Dene and Métis peoples are either in negotiation or have rejected the claims process.[62] These contrasting trends on the most fundamental political issue of Aboriginal rights is an apt reflection of the complex group interests and the contradictory trends that continue to drive the new NWT, making it one of the most socially pluralistic polities in the country.

If anything, the "residual" NWT suffers from a compounded crisis of identity and initiative, as the region that was, in a sense, left behind. The west showed its ambivalence in the 1992 referendum, lacking a strong affinity for either the territorial status quo or for east-west division. For Aboriginal residents, the significant political community has seldom been territorial in scope, but centred instead on either the tribal/band group or the locality. This explains why models of consociational democracy have periodically been proposed for the Mackenzie region, raising the possibility of a new territorial structure as an umbrella of constituent communities, with strong regional or local authorities in the lead. Such a vision was articulated by the Bourque Commission in 1992,[63] and many of its threads carry over to the constitutional discussions after 1996.

Yet it also seems possible that ready agreement on a "community of communities" model could be impaired by the widely contrasting projects being pursued by the constituent communities. Despite the recent endorsement of economic sovereignty through enterprise, a considerable distance still separates the Aboriginal settlement authorities now pursuing development strategies in the north Mackenzie and the Tribal Council bodies that have rejected available settlement options in the south. Since all of these regional communities, together with non-Aboriginal residents, enjoy organic representation in the Assembly, this considerably complicates the achievement and maintenance of consensus. This may be increasingly the case if the presently becalmed process of NWT constitutional development is rejuvenated. To illustrate, the detailed discussion paper released by the western Constitutional Working Group in 1996 proposed a new constitution, together with a companion agreement on Aboriginal self-government.[64] It outlined a single Legislative Assembly consisting of two parts: a General Assembly of 14 constituency-based representatives and an Aboriginal Peoples Assembly of eight representatives elected from designated First Nations. Enactment of public bills would occur through double majority approval, while the Aboriginal Peoples Assembly would constitute a separate legislative authority on matters of treaties, land claims agreements, and self-government. The fate of the *Partners* proposal, or any successor, will hinge upon the dual reactions of the northern public (at point of ratification) and the federal government (as the senior constitutional authority).

In sum, there is no shortage of pressing issues on the policy agenda of the new NWT. Nor is there any doubt that class politics will have a central bearing on their resolution.

NOTES

1 Frank G. Vallee, *Sociological Research in the Arctic* (Ottawa: Northern Coordination and Research Centre, 1962); Frank G. Vallee, *Kabloona and Eskimo in the Central Keewatin* (Ottawa: St. Paul's, 1967); and Frank G. Vallee, "The Emerging Northern Mosaic," *Canadian Society*, ed. Richard Ossenberg (Scarborough: Prentice Hall, 1971).

2 Peter J. Usher, *Fur Trade Posts of the Northwest Territories, 1870–1930* (Ottawa: Information Canada, 1971); Peter J. Usher, *The Bankslanders* (Ottawa: Information Canada, 1971); and Marybelle Mitchell, From *Talking Chiefs to Native Corporate Elite*, (Montreal: McGill-Queens, 1996).

3 Bob Jessop, *The Capitalist State* (Oxford: Martin Robertson, 1982).

4 James Van Stone, *The Changing Culture of the Snowdrift Chipewyan* (Ottawa: National Museum of Canada, 1965).

5 Keith J. Crowe, *A Cultural Geography of the Northern Foxe Basin* (Ottawa: Queen's Printer, 1980).

6 J.C. Yerbury, *The Sub-Arctic Indians and the Fur Trade, 1680–1860* (Vancouver: University of British Columbia Press, 1986); June Helm and David Damas, "The Contact-Traditional All Native Community of the Canadian North," *Anthropologica* 5 (1963): 9–21.

7 Usher, *Fur Trade Posts.*

8 Rene Fumeleau, *As Long As This Land Shall Last* (Toronto: McClelland and Stewart, 1975).

9 Arthur J. Ray, *The Canadian Fur Trade in the Industrial Age* (Toronto: University of Toronto Press, 1990).

10 For some revealing case studies, see June Helm, *The Lynx Point People* (Ottawa: National Museum of Canada, 1961); Van Stone, *The Changing Culture of the Snowdrift Chipewyan*; and Keith J. Crowe, *A History of the Original People of Northern Canada* (Montreal: McGill-Queen's Press, 1974).

11 Helm and Damas, "The Contact-Traditional All Native Community of the Canadian North," 9–21.

12 Within the Northwest Territories, at least seven tribes of Athapaskans are commonly recognized, including Chipewyan, Slave, Dogrib, Yellowknife, Mountain Hare and Kutchin. The corresponding Inuit language groups include the Mackenzie, Copper, Netsilik, Caribou, Igloolik, South Baffin, and Sadliq.

13 Hugh Brody, *The People's Land* (Harmondsworth: Penguin, 1979); Usher, *The Bankslanders.*

14 K.J. Rea, *The Political Economy of the Canadian North* (Toronto: University of Toronto Press, 1968).

15 K.J. Rea, *The Political Economy of Northern Development* (Ottawa: Science Council of Canada, 1976), 25.

16 Bureau of Statistics, Government of the Northwest Territories, *Statistics Quarterly* 19:2 (June 1997).

17 Vallee, "The Emerging Northern Mosaic."

18 Peter J. Usher, *The Devolution of Wildlife Management and the Prospects for Wildlife Conservation in the Northwest Territories* (Ottawa: Canadian Arctic Resources Committee, 1986), 31.

19 Morris Zaslow, "A Prelude to Self-Government in the Northwest Territories, 1905-1939," *The Canadian Northwest: Its Potentialities*, ed. Frank G. Underhill (Toronto: University of Toronto Press, 1958).

20 Shelagh D. Grant, *Sovereignty or Security?* (Vancouver: University of British Columbia Press, 1988).

21 Peter Clancy, "Working on the Railway," *Canadian Public Administration* 30 (1987): 450-71.

22 Canada, Department of Northern Affairs and National Resources, *The Northwest Territories: Its Economic Prospects* (Ottawa: Queen's Printer, 1955), 16-17.

23 François Bregha, *Bob Blair's Pipeline* (Toronto: Lorimer, 1979); Edgar J. Dosman, *The National Interest* (Toronto: McClelland and Stewart, 1975); and Douglas Pimlott, Dougald Brown, and Kenneth Sam, *Oil Under the Ice* (Ottawa: Canadian Arctic Resources Committee, 1976).

24 Peter Clancy, "State Policy and the Native Trapper: Post-war Policy Toward Fur in the Northwest Territories," *Aboriginal Resource Use in Canada*, ed. K. Abel and J. Friesen (Winnipeg: University of Manitoba Press, 1991).

25 This began with the establishment of three constituencies in the Mackenzie District in 1951. A fourth elected member joined the eight-person Council in 1954. Not until 1966 were three constituencies added for the Inuit of the central Arctic, eastern Arctic, and Keewatin. By 1971, only four appointees remained among the 14 members of the seventh Council, and the first fully elected Council of 15 members took office in 1975. The thirteenth Legislative Assembly of the Northwest Territories consisted of 24 members, with 14 elected from the west and 10 from the east of the Nunavut boundary. The post-division (fourteenth) Assembly includes 19 MLAS.

26 Peter Clancy, "Politics by Remote Control: Historical Perspectives on Devolution in Canada's North," *Devolution and Constitutional Development in the Canadian North*, ed. G. Dacks (Ottawa: Carleton University Press, 1990).

27 Government of the Northwest Territories, *You've Heard From the Radical Few About Canada's North ... Now Hear From the Moderate Many* (Yellowknife, 1977).

28 Francis Abele, "Dene-Government Relations: The Development of a New Political Minority," *Minorities and the Canadian State*, ed. N. Nevitte and A. Kornberg (Oakville: Mosaic Press, 1985); Peter Clancy, "Native Peoples and Politics in the Northwest Territories," *Canadian Politics: An Introduction to the Discipline*, ed. A. Gagnon and J. Bickerton (Peterborough: Broadview Press, 1990); and Gurston Dacks, *A Choice of Futures* (Toronto: Methuen, 1981).

29 Michael Asch, *Home and Native Land* (Toronto: Methuen, 1984).

30 Gurston Dacks, "The Aboriginal People and the Government of the Northwest Territories," *Governments in Conflict?*, ed. J.A. Long and M. Boldt (Toronto: University of Toronto Press, 1988); and M. Moore and G. Vanderhaden "Northern Problems or Canadian Opportunities," *Canadian Public Administration* 27 (1984): 182-87.

31 For brief biographies of territorial MLAs, see the profile documents published for the eighth, ninth, tenth, and eleventh assemblies. Government of the Northwest Territories, *Northwest Territories Legislative Assembly* (Yellowknife: Department of Information, 1980); Government of the Northwest Territories, *Ninth Legislative Assembly of the Northwest Territories* (Yellowknife: Department of Information, 1983); Government of the Northwest Territories, *Direction for the 1990s* (Yellowknife: 1988); Government of the Northwest Territories, *The Eleventh Legislative Assembly of the Northwest Territories* (Yellowknife: Culture and Communications, n.d.).

32 For a comprehensive treatment of devolution strategies, see Gurston Dacks, ed., *Evolution and Constitutional Development in the Canadian North* (Ottawa: Carleton University Press, 1990).

33 An extensive literature emerged from the work of the Constitutional Alliance, under the sponsorship of its two working groups. For the Western Constitutional Forum, see S. Iveson and A. Brockman, *Western Constitutional Forum, Chronology of Events* (Yellowknife: Western Constitutional Forum, 1987). Among the studies of the Nunavut Constitutional Forum is *Building Nunavut* (Yellowknife: Nunavut Constitutional Forum, 1983).

34 F. Abele and M. Dickerson, "The 1982 Plebiscite on Division of the Northwest Territories: Regional Government and Federal Policy," *Canadian Public Policy* 9 (1985): 1-15.

35 G. Dacks, "Politics on the Last Frontier: Consociationalism in the Northwest Territories," *Canadian Journal of Political Science* 19 (1986): 345-61; and G. White, "Westminster in the Arctic," *Canadian Journal of Political Science* 24 (1991): 499-524.

36 "Territorial Leadership Committee," Legislature of the Northwest Territories, *Debates*, 12-13 November 1991.

37 Government of the Northwest Territories, *The Eleventh Legislative Assembly*, 12.

38 Kevin O'Keefe, "Northwest Territories: Accommodating the Future," *Provincial and Territorial Legislatures in Canada*, ed. G. Levy and G. White (Toronto: University of Toronto Press, 1989).

39 Government of the Northwest Territories, *Report of the Task Force on Personnel Policy and Management* (Yellowknife, 1974).

40 C.E.S. Franks, "The Public Service in the North," *Canadian Public Administration* 27 (1984): 210-41.

41 Government of the Northwest Territories, *Working Together for Our Future* (Yellowknife: Equal Opportunities Directorate, 1985).

42 See Legislative Assembly of the Northwest Territories, *The SCONE Report: Building Our Economic Future* (Yellowknife, 1989). The background studies addressed the GNWT native employment policy, the banking system in the Territories, adult training programs, tourism programs, sustainable development policies, support for the domestic economy, and economic opportunities connected to native claims settlements.

43 For a detailed discussion of politics in the first half of the 1990s, see Kirk Cameron and Graham White, *Northern Governments in Transition* (Montreal: Institute for Research on Public Policy, 1995).

44 *Agreement Between the Inuit of the Nunavut Settlement Area and Her Majesty in Right of Canada*, (Ottawa: Tungavik Federation of Nunavut and Department of Indian and Northern Affairs, 1992).

45 *NWT Budget Address, 1995/96*, 20 February 1995 (Yellowknife).

46 Chapter 22, *Statutes of the Northwest Territories*, 1995.

47 *NWT Budget Address, 1996/97*, 2 May 1996 (Yellowknife).

48 *Debates*, Legislative Assembly of the Northwest Territories, 2nd Session, 18 February 1996, 2.

49 *Debates*, Legislative Assembly of the Northwest Territories, 2nd Session, 2 May 1996, 2.

50 *Debates*, 2 May 1996, 6.

51 See, for example, Kevin O'Reilly, "Diamond Mining and the Demise of Environmental Assessment in the North," *Northern Perspectives* 24:1-4 (Fall/Winter 1996); and Susan Wismer, "The Nasty Game," *Alternatives Journal* 22:4 (October/November 1996).

52 M. Mitchell, *From Talking Chiefs to a Native Corporate Elite* (Montreal and Kingston: McGill-Queen's University Press, 1996).

53 Royal Commission on Aboriginal Peoples, *Report*, vol.5 (Ottawa), 470.

54 Mark MacKinnon, "Parts of NWT electoral law declared unconstitutional," *Globe and Mail*, 8 March 1999, A4.

55 "Panel to Review Conflict of Interset Legislation that Led to Morin's Resignation," *Globe and Mail*, 23 January 1999, A11.

56 Jill Mahoney, "Give NWT Meatier Conflict Office, Review Panel Report Suggests," *Globe and Mail*, 9 April 1999, A12.

57 For one discussion, see Frances Widdowson and Albert Howard, "Corruption North of 60," *Policy Options* 20:1 (January-February 1999); Graham White, "The Tundra's Always Greener," *Policy Options* 20:4 (May 1999); and Frances Widdowson and Albert Howard, "Duplicity in the North," *Policy Options* 20:7 (September 1999).

58 Legislative Assembly of the Northwest Territories, *Towards a Better Tomorrow* (Yellowknife, 2000).

59 Roland George, "Arctic Exposure: Mackenzie Delta-Beaufort Sea Natural Gas–Is It Time?," *Oilweek*, 1 November 1999, <http://www.purvingertz.com>

60 Carol Howes, "Aboriginal groups stake out key role in Mackenzie Valley," *National Post*, 17 April 2000.

61 Carol Howes and Claudia Cattaneo, "Native support increases for Arctic pipelines," *National Post*, 17 April 2000.

62 For an overview of northern land claim developments, see Department of Indian and Northern Affairs, "Comprehensive Claims Policy and Status of Claims" (Ottawa, 2000).

63 Peter Clancy, "Political Autonomy in the North: Recent Developments," *The State of the Federation*, 1992, ed. D. Brown and R. Young, (Kingston: Institute of Intergovernmental Relations, 1992), 225-44.

64 Constitutional Working Group, *Partners in a New Beginning* (Yellowknife, 1996).

13 YUKON

Still Frontier, Always Homeland: Yukon Politics in the Year 2000

FLOYD McCORMICK

In 1977 Thomas Berger called Canada's north a frontier and a homeland. He also confronted Canadians with a choice: "whether the North is to be primarily a frontier for industry or a homeland for its peoples."[1] For the Yukon this description is as relevant today as it was then. The durability of the frontier/homeland dichotomy is significant; both the frontier and homeland economies require the control of land and natural resources. The struggle for the control of land continues to be at the root of political and economic relations in the Yukon. These relations are changing in important ways, and the catalysts for this change are two sets of negotiations that will alter the relationships among the Government of Canada, the Government of the Yukon, and Yukon First Nations (YFNs). The outcome of these negotiations will reduce federal government authority by transferring greater political and economic control to Yukoners. And as state structures evolve other important factors—the frontier/homeland dichotomy, and the Yukon's economic dependence on resource extraction—are also changing. There is, therefore, much uncertainty about both this emerging state structure and the future of the Yukon itself. And while intergovernmental relations are not the only important issue, the unprecedented nature of the current changes, and the simultaneous occurrence of these processes, makes such relations the most significant factor in the Yukon today.

This chapter will illustrate the nature of the emerging state structure in the Yukon, how it reached this point, and where it might end up. While there will be some historical focus, of primary importance are events since 1990.

THREE WAVES OF YUKON HISTORY

Three distinct "waves" mark the post-contact history of the Yukon. Each has had a profound effect on political and economic relations in the territory. The first two of these waves—the Klondike Gold Rush and the building of the Alaska Highway—crested quickly. The third, the resolution of YFN claims, is longer-lasting and on-going.

The story of the Klondike Gold Rush is well known. On August 16, 1896, two Tagish brothers, Skookum Jim and Dawson Charlie, their sister Kate, and Kate's husband George Carmack discovered gold in a small creek near Dawson City.[2] The gold rush ignited "when miners carrying thousands of dollars of gold disembarked from steamers in Seattle and San Francisco" in the summer of 1897. As many as 50,000 people trekked to the Klondike in the following year. At the height of the gold rush Dawson City was the largest Canadian city west of Winnipeg.[3] Not only did the gold rush establish mineral extraction as the foundation of the Yukon's economy, it also had a lasting effect on the territory's political future. The most important effect was the creation of the Yukon Territory in 1898. Until then the Yukon had been part of the Northwest Territories (NWT). The form of government created by the *Yukon Act* gave the federal government control of an area rich in mineral wealth and, not coincidentally, liquor revenues. The grip established by the federal government in 1898 has loosened only gradually since then.

The second wave occurred with the building of the Alaska Highway during World War II. Military planners decided to build the highway, airfields, an oil pipeline, and a refinery to stave off an anticipated Japanese invasion of the northwest coast. The Japanese invasion never occurred; instead, the Yukon was invaded by tens of thousands of military personnel (mostly American), engineers, and construction workers. One important political effect of this invasion was to allow Whitehorse to surpass Dawson City as the Yukon's centre of power. Whitehorse was a natural resting point for those headed to the Klondike. Located north of Miles Canyon and its then-imposing set of rapids, it was the last such obstacle along the Yukon River to Dawson City. Consequently it also became the natural point to locate the terminus of the White Pass and Yukon Route railway, completed in 1901. From there river boats transported goods to Dawson City. During the war the rail link made it possible to transport heavy equipment into the interior of the territory to build the highway. By the war's end Whitehorse had road, air and rail links to the outside world, and in 1953 the federal government moved the territorial capital from Dawson City to Whitehorse.[4]

The third wave—the negotiation of YFN claims—is happening because the Government of Canada never negotiated treaties with YFNs. This became a problem once non-aboriginal people arrived in large numbers and established permanent settlements. This historical wave rose in earnest in 1973 when the Yukon Native Brotherhood (YNB) presented its statement of claim, *Together Today for Our Children Tomorrow*, to the federal government. Submitted in the wake of the Supreme Court of Canada's decision in *Calder v. Attorney-General of British Columbia*, it was the first comprehensive land claim accepted for negotiation by the federal government.

The initial non-aboriginal reaction to the claim was "strongly negative." As Coates describes the situation,

> A number of non-Native Yukoners had clung to the belief that the Indians had accepted the developments of the past, and had developed a respect for the triumvirate of western civilization: religion, education, and government. The land claim had set that perception to rest.[5]

The politicians' response was also negative. The federal and territorial governments had envisioned the resolution of YFN claims as a glorified real-estate transaction: the transfer of cash and small parcels of land to aboriginal people in exchange for the extinguishment of aboriginal rights. *Together Today* proposed a different solution: an on-going set of political, economic, and social relationships based on the recognition of aboriginal rights. The difference between these two visions caused negotiations to became prolonged and, at times, acrimonious. In the end it was the YFN vision of aboriginal-state relations that prevailed. Attempts at changing political and economic relations in the Yukon are now inevitably enmeshed in a tripartite, not federal-territorial, political dynamic.

POLITICAL RELATIONS IN THE YUKON

Historically the Yukon's relationship with the federal government has been that of a colony. The territory's "constitution," the *Yukon Act*, is federal legislation that Parliament has unilaterally amended from time to time. The federal control over the composition and authority of the territorial council typifies this relationship. This, in turn, has meant federal government control over the land and resources in the territory. It should come as no surprise, therefore, that self-determination—for aboriginal and non-aboriginal Yukoners—has been the dominant political issue since 1898. For non-aboriginal Yukoners, greater self-determination has meant making the territorial government a representative and responsible democratic institution with the degree of legislative authority available to provincial governments. Over the years this movement has focused on two interrelated approaches: constitutional development (transforming the Yukon's status from a territory to a province) and political development (the transfer of greater responsibility to the territorial government commonly called devolution, and the establishment of representative and responsible government) without changing the Yukon's constitutional status.

YFNs were doubly colonized: by the inferior constitutional status of the Yukon, and by the *Indian Act*. There are, therefore, two approaches to enhanced YFN self-determination: the recognition of aboriginal rights through land claims and self-government negotiations, and the participation in negotiations regarding the evolution of the territorial government.

THE STRUGGLE FOR REPRESENTATIVE AND RESPONSIBLE GOVERNMENT

The federal government has often been an obstacle to Yukoners' desire for representative and responsible government. The government established in the *Yukon Act* consisted of "a commissioner with virtual dictatorial powers and a council of six members, all appointed by the governor-in-council...."[6] There was an immediate demand for an elected council but the federal government ruled this out because of the large number of non-British subjects living in the Dawson City area. However, democracy eventually prevailed, for a time. The *Yukon Act* was amended in 1899 to provide for two members elected by "natural-born and naturalized male British subjects." In 1902 the act was again amended to provide for five elected and five appointed members. A third amendment, in 1908, created a fully elected ten-member council.[7]

Since then the territorial council (later the Yukon Legislative Assembly) has remained a fully elected body. Yet as the post gold rush population declined, so did membership on the council. In 1919 the federal government reduced the council to three members. This reduction was drastic, yet the federal government's original intention was worse: to abolish the council entirely. Only intense opposition at the local level prevented this from happening. Still, until 1952 the federal government retained the right to abolish the council by way of an order-in-council.[8] The situation improved after that, but very gradually. Council membership increased to five in 1952, seven in 1961, twelve in 1974, and 16 in 1978. Membership reached its current complement of 17 in 1992.

However, securing representative government did not mean achieving responsible government. As the chief executive officer of the territory, the Commissioner answered to the federal cabinet, not the territorial council. The territory's executive did not include elected members until 1970. In that year the federal government formed an Executive Committee consisting of the Commissioner, two appointed assistant commissioners, and two elected council members.[9] Through the 1970s the composition of the Executive Committee changed until elected members gained a majority. Finally, in 1978 and 1979, letters of instruction from Hugh Faulkner and Jake Epp (successive ministers of the Department of Indian Affairs and Northern Development [DIAND]) reduced the role of the Commissioner and directed that the leader of the largest party in the legislative assembly[10] draw a cabinet (renamed Executive Council) from that assembly. Epp's letter instructed the Commissioner to "accept the advice of cabinet in all matters." In practice, responsible government had arrived.[11] In law, however, the DIAND minister retained the power to abolish responsible government by way of a subsequent letter of instruction.

Nevertheless, political development within the Yukon did not mean that the territory could play a role on the national stage. Over the past decade the Yukon government has participated in first ministers' and premiers' conferences, yet as a territory the Yukon has no vote in constitutional matters. This is a significant drawback because the land and resources of the territories have, at times, been at stake. The Meech Lake Accord, for example, dealt with the expansion of the provinces into the territories and the creation of new provinces in ways that challenged the interests of the territorial governments. Indeed, provincial expansionism has been a real threat in the past. In 1937, for example, British Columbia and the federal government began bilateral negotiations regarding the annexation of the Yukon to B.C.[12]

DEVOLUTION

The evolution of political institutions in the Yukon has not focused entirely on democratic issues. Also of concern is the range of jurisdiction that a representative and responsible government would exercise. For years Yukoners have petitioned the federal government to transfer to the territory areas of provincial-like jurisdiction exercised by DIAND. At times this has accompanied an expressed desire for provincehood.

Desires for constitutional development and devolution have occasionally clashed with YFN claims. This is hardly surprising given that the territorial government and YFNs were attempting to gain the same things—land, natural resources, jurisdictional authority, and money—from the federal government. Throughout the 1970s and early 1980s the territorial government insisted that Ottawa satisfy its demands as a "quid pro quo" for its acceptance of YFN claims.[13] The Yukon government's attempts to keep YFNs away from the constitutional development and devolution tables caused considerable friction, given the territorial government's insistence on its participation in land-claims negotiations.

Over the years, the Yukon government has expanded its range of jurisdiction, usually with some caveat attached. Sometimes this caveat is at the insistence of the territorial government, e.g., that the federal government guarantee it adequate financial resources to carry out new responsibilities. At other times, however, it is the federal government that limits the breadth of transfers. In 1971, for instance, the territorial government took control of the administration of justice,[14] yet this did not include the Crown attorney function, a role the territorial government has yet to acquire. Another example is territorial efforts to gain control over freshwater fisheries. Requests for control over this area of jurisdiction began in 1945, and by the end of the 1960s the federal government was ready to transfer authority. Later, however, the Department of Fisheries changed its position, and when the transfer took place in the fall of 1972 only control over freshwater sports fishing was devolved. As Janet Moodie Michael noted, "[w]ith this transfer the territory had to face that it was ultimately Ottawa that dictated the pace and scope of its increased powers...."[15]

Recent events offer hope that the devolution debate may soon end. In June 1996 the Government of Canada proposed to devolve "all remaining provincial-type powers and programs" of DIAND to the territorial government.[16] This proposal addressed authority for areas crucial to the territory's economy, including "the management and control of Crown lands, forestry, water, mines and minerals and the management of [the] environment."[17] The proposal received a mixed response. The Yukon government wanted these powers but objected to being treated like an interest group. Yukon Party government leader John Ostashek planned to negotiate the transfer of powers, not merely provide input to a DIAND decision-making process that was open to other parties. For their part, YFNs did not want devolution to proceed until all their claims were settled. Moreover, they expected to be a party to negotiations. These positions were a point of contention between YFNs and the Yukon government, with the latter wanting YFNs to participate in the process but not as a third, equal party. YFNs refused to cooperate with the government until it met their demands.

Prospects for the federal devolution proposal improved after the election of a New Democratic Party (NDP) government in September 1996. In November, the new government leader, Piers McDonald, met with DIAND minister Ron Irwin. Afterward they announced that there would be a negotiated transfer of authority and that YFNs would be at the devolution table.[18] Relations between YFNs and the Yukon government also improved. In January 1997 the Government of Yukon, the Council of Yukon First Nations (CYFN), the Kwanlin Dun First Nation, the Liard First Nation, and the Kaska Tribal Council signed a series of agreements, including one on devolution.[19] The parties agreed to establish a joint working group to present positions to the Government of Canada and respond to initiatives that come from Ottawa.[20]

In September 1999, with devolution negotiations ending, the Yukon government released a proposed new *Yukon Act*.[21] The proposed amendments to the existing *Yukon Act* fall into four categories. The first category contains those amendments needed to ensure that the territorial government has the legal authority to exercise the powers it will acquire through devolution. Amendments in the second category will modernize the language in the act. For example, the current *Yukon Act* refers to a "council" that governs the territory by passing "ordinances." The Yukon government wants this changed to say that the territory has a "legislature" that passes "laws." The third category of amendments is those that will enshrine in law the governing practices outlined in the letters of instruction from the federal cabinet to the Commissioner. Chief among these is the establishment of responsible government.[22] Amendments in the fourth category would enhance territorial status. One example is the proposal to change the Commissioner to a Lieutenant Governor.[23] This change would reflect the mostly ceremonial nature of the position since the establishment of responsible government. Another such change is the provision that the *Yukon Act* not be amended in future without the consent of the Yukon legislature.[24]

The federal government does not have to accept the proposed amendments, though it will surely accept those needed to implement the devolution agreement. Even if it did accept all the proposed amendments, enhanced territorial status will still fall short of provincial status. Unlike the provinces the Yukon will not own Crown land, exercise the Attorney General function, have its existence enshrined in the Constitution, or participate in the constitutional amendment process. The target date for the proclamation of the new *Yukon Act* is April 1, 2002.

PARTY POLITICS IN THE YUKON

Besides changes in government structure, another significant political change has been the introduction of party politics with the 1978 territorial election. Until recently territorial politics was highly polarized. Government power alternated from the right (Progressive Conservatives in 1978 and 1982) to the left (the NDP in 1985 and 1989), back to the right (the Yukon Party in 1992), and back to the left (NDP in 1996 and 1999). Yukoners finally found the political centre in April 2000 when they elected a Liberal party government under the leadership of Patricia Duncan.

Ideological considerations, especially the proper role and extent of government intervention in the economy, have played a role in territorial politics. Party positions on the crucial issue of YFN claims have also served to separate left from right. Historically, the NDP has been most sympathetic to YFN goals. In 1993 former NDP Government Leader Tony Penikett said that the Progressive Conservative governments that preceded his saw their role as

> represent[ing] the interests of the white people in the territory. I think they saw the CYI representing Indians, they saw themselves representing the whites, and the federal government representing itself. [The NDP's] approach was to argue that ... [t]he territorial government had to ... [represent] the broad public interest, including the interests of the aboriginal people, if [it] wanted to claim to govern for them, and on behalf of them which [it was] also claiming to do.[25]

Three indicators suggest that Yukon politics is becoming less polarized. The first is the emergence of the centrist Liberal Party. In the five general elections between 1985 and 2000 the Liberals' share of the vote increased from eight to 43 per cent. Over the same period the vote share of the Conservative Party (PC, later renamed the Yukon Party) decreased from 47 to 24 per cent. Another moderating factor is the resolution of YFN claims. With negotiations on the way to completion this issue has ceased to be a partisan one. In fact, during the 2000 territorial election the three parties tried to out-do one another in claiming that they could resolve the remaining claims most quickly. This consensus signals a change for the Yukon and contrasts sharply with the situation in British Columbia, where the provincial Liberal Party has launched a legal challenge to the Nisga'a Treaty. Third, during its term of office from 1996-2000 the NDP's fiscal and economic policies were less interventionist and more market-oriented. Its budgetary approach was been called "fiscally conservative, entrepreneurial socialism."[26] However, Piers McDonald resigned as party leader after his party's defeat in 2000. It remains to be seen if his successor will keep the NDP close to the centre of the political spectrum or move it back toward the left.

YFN CLAIMS

While constitutional development and devolution have proceeded gradually, the negotiation of land claims and self-government can be separated into two eras. The first ended in 1984 when YFNs held ratification votes on an agreement in principle (AIP) that had been in negotiation since 1973. Unfortunately for negotiators, YFNs rejected it. The reasons for this rejection were many: the agreement did not provide for enough land or self-government powers. Federal policy also required the extinguishment of aboriginal rights and title. In addition, YFNs had problems with the negotiations process vision of one settlement for the entire territory, since YFNs have differing interests and want to conclude their own agreements. Many people also considered the process too adversarial, secretive, and distant—most negotiations took place in Vancouver or Ottawa.

As indicated above, the NDP had a different approach to YFN claims, and its election in 1985 introduced a new dynamic as the parties attempted to restart negotiations. The NDP accorded greater legitimacy to YFN claims than had the PCs. It was the first government in Canada to recognize the right to self-government as an inherent right, not to require extinguishment of aboriginal title as a condition of settlement, and to accept that aboriginal title continue to exist on lands retained by YFNs.[27] It was also willing to go further concerning the amount of land ownership that first nations would retain and jurisdictions which YFN governments would exercise. It also fostered the adoption of an interest-based negotiations process, one that was more open, flexible and community based than the one that produced the AIP.[28] The NDP also dropped the "quid pro quo" approach to constitutional development, devolution, and YFN claims. The party did not abandon the territorial government's political development goals; instead, Penikett believed that once YFNs secured control of land and resources the position of the territorial government in securing similar control would improve.[29]

The claims process advanced despite the NDP's loss in the general election of October 1992. The newly-elected Yukon Party government made good on a campaign promise when on March 17, 1993, the Yukon Legislative Assembly passed the enabling legislation for final and self-government agreements. On May 29, 1993 the Government of Canada, the CYI, and the Yukon government signed the Umbrella Final Agreement (UFA).[30] On the same day four YFNs signed their final (land claim) and self-government agreements.[31]

As mentioned above *Together Today* proposed an on-going set of political, economic and social relationships based on the recognition of aboriginal rights. The UFA and the land-claim and self-government agreements reflect this vision. The agreements provide for land, economic benefits, and political rights. The land provisions address how much land YFNs will retain (individually and collectively) and the tenure provisions under which land will be retained. Economic provisions include compensation for the use and occupation of YFN lands in the absence of a treaty, arrangements for financial transfers to YFN governments and their citizens, guarantees of natural resource rents, guaranteed access to fish and wildlife, and economic development measures. There is also a buy-out of YFN citizens' exemption from income tax under section 87 of the *Indian Act*. Political rights fall into two broad categories: the first relates to the powers which YFN governments will exercise over their lands and citizens; the second guarantees representation on territorial and regional resource management boards. The degree of representation varies according to the board in question.

Seven YFNs have now signed final and self-government agreements.[32] In January 2000, however, the White River First Nation cancelled the ratification vote for the agreements it had negotiated. This cancellation signals an impasse in negotiations that has left the entire process stalled.

At issue are two financial aspects of the UFA. The first is the requirement that YFNs repay money they borrowed from the federal government to negotiate their agreements. The compensation amount for all YFNs is $242.673 million in 1989 dollars to be paid out over 15 years.[33] No precise figure is available for the entire outstanding loan amount. However, the seven YFNs that have signed agreements owe the federal government over $51 million against their compensation of $134 million.[34] YFNs are not asking the federal government to forgive all their loans. Council of Yukon First Nations Grand Chief Ed Schultz has said that those YFNs without agreements "are looking for … equitable treatment that the first group of first Nations got in terms of the loan compensation ration."[35] The first four YFNs to negotiate agreements must repay about 30 per cent of their compensation. The next three must repay about 50 per cent while the remaining seven YFNs say they must repay up to 60 per cent of their compensation.

The federal government has been immoveable on this issue. During a recent visit to the Yukon, Indian and Northern Affairs Minister Robert Nault said, "The federal government is not prepared at all to change our loans policy." He then suggested the federal government might suspend negotiations if this was unacceptable to YFNs.[36]

The second outstanding issue is the buy-out of the personal income tax exemption under Section 87 of the *Indian Act*. The problem, from the YFN perspective, is that all YFN citizens have had to pay income tax as of January 1, 1999 even if they belong to a YFN that has not yet signed its agreements. YFNs say their understanding of the UFA is that YFN citizens would not have to pay income tax until after their YFN signed its agreement.[37] Nault has also refused to renegotiate on this issue, or even to comment on it because the seven YFNs without agreements are suing the federal government over the issue.

The implementation of final and self-government agreements has a significant impact on YFN-federal government relations. Once a YFN's agreements become effective, the agreements, not the *Indian Act*, define the YFN's relationship with the federal government. When claims negotiations are complete the Indian Affairs program in the Yukon will shut down. If this doesn't happen there will be two classes of First Nations in the Yukon. Similarly, the devolution of powers to the Yukon government will eventually close the Northern Affairs program in the territory. If the state is a set "of organizations that have the ability to make binding decisions for people and organizations located within a territory,"[38] then the significance of these developments is clear. As the Yukon begins its second century the ability to make binding decisions for Yukoners will soon rest with Yukoners themselves to a greater degree than it has before. The YFN claims negotiations and the simultaneous evolution of the Yukon government add up to a unique process of state building in Canada. But given the current impasse one can't say when this process will end.

ECONOMIC RELATIONS IN THE YUKON[39]

The evolution of YFN self-government and the devolution of federal authority are changing the political context for economic relations. This context is changing as the Yukon is reaching "an economic crossroads."[40] Mining was the reason people flocked to the Klondike in 1898; since then, mining has been the cornerstone of the Yukon's economy. The health of other sectors—construction, service industries, real estate, wholesale and retail trade—has fluctuated with the boom and bust of the mining economy.

The latest bust started with the closure of the Anvil Range mine at Faro in February 1998. In full production the mine was the largest private sector employer in the territory, accounting for approximately 4 per cent of total Yukon employment. Historically Faro accounted for 70 to 85 per cent of total Yukon mineral production and 12 to 15 per cent of territorial Gross Domestic Product.[41] As the effects of the Faro closure rippled throughout the Yukon economy the population dropped from 33,390 in December 1997 to 31,070 in December 1999. Government is now the largest industry, accounting for 36 per cent of employment and 29 per cent of GDP.

With the decline in mining the Yukon government is devoting more resources to diversifying and strengthening the private sector. After its election in September 1996 the NDP struck a Yukon Forestry Commission "to prepare for the transfer of responsibility for lands and resources."[42] The economic potential of a Yukon forestry industry is uncertain. Trees cover just over half the Yukon, but the territory's climate and soil conditions make its forests less productive than those further south.[43] Another area of potential, and another directly related to devolution, is oil and gas. The territorial government developed the *Yukon Oil and Gas Act* in concert with YFNs. The act establishes a single regulatory regime for the territory. The territorial government estimates that the Yukon has reserves of 97 billion cubic metres of natural gas and six billion cubic metres of oil. The Yukon produced almost $18 million worth of natural gas in 1998, and the goal is to produce ten times as much by 2010.[44] Such optimistic forecasts have to contend with the fact that it costs ten times the national average to drill in the Yukon.[45]

One problem with forestry and oil and gas is that they keep the focus on resource extraction. These industries, like mining, are subject to boom and bust cycles. Tourism has also become increasingly important. Industry and government sources estimate that tourism directly employs 2,000 Yukoners and was responsible for $124 million in non-resident spending in 1996.[46] The territory has been successful in recent years in attracting tourists. Still, in the 1990s the Yukon celebrated the 50th or 100th anniversary of many significant events, and it remains to be seen if this momentum will carry into the new millennium.

In response to the situation, the NDP's 1998-99 budget introduced a "Trade and Investment Diversification Strategy." The trade aspect of this strategy is to promote the export of finished products and services through events like the federally sponsored Team Canada trade missions. The investment aspect has a double focus: making it easier for Yukon businesses to secure financing, and attracting investment to the Yukon.[47] This strategy was an example of the NDP's entrepreneurial approach to the economy. Rather than investing directly (such as attempting to reopen the Faro mine) the NDP chose to prime the private sector by introducing investment incentives (like the mining exploration tax credit) and marketing funds. It will take time to figure out how successful this approach will be. This is not only an economic problem but a political one, given that diversification is inevitably a long-term process while territorial governments must renew their mandates every four years. It suffices to say that the NDP's approach was not successful enough to ensure its re-election in 2000. The sluggish state of the economy was perhaps the main reason for the NDP's defeat.

It should be remembered, however, that while the Yukon may have limited potential for economic diversification, with a population of less than 35,000 the territory only needs limited success to turn around its economy.

YFN AGREEMENTS AND ECONOMIC RELATIONS

The extent and the nature of the economic provisions of the UFA attest to the importance that YFNs place on economic development and diversification. While the frontier/homeland distinction still applies, other generalities are gradually being replaced. The frontier/homeland dichotomy usually emphasizes the difference between exchange and harvesting economies. The exchange/harvesting dichotomy has in turn been generalized as non-aboriginal and aboriginal economies. The inference is that non-aboriginals, by treating the Yukon as a frontier, have modernized the territory's economy. Aboriginal people, on the other hand, have been content to harvest—hunting, fishing, trapping, and gathering—in their homeland. These different "choices" are meant to explain the difference in living standards between aboriginals and non-aboriginals.

This easy characterization was never true. Aboriginal peoples in the northwest traded before explorers came to the Yukon. Also, many aboriginal people, the most prominent being Skookum Jim, were integral players in the Klondike Gold Rush. Many aboriginal Yukoners used the exchange economy that emerged with the gold rush to augment their harvesting. This balance worked as long as aboriginal people could get jobs for cash that allowed them to purchase equipment and supplies. This pattern meant that their status rarely rose above that of labourer. Nevertheless, their cash demands were not large and the wage economy was a secondary economic pursuit.[48]

This balance did not last, however. Most of the prospectors who came north were too late to stake profitable claims. This created a pool of non-aboriginal workers who could provide full-time labour. Also, increased mechanization in the mining industry eventually reduced the need for manual labour. As riverboats disappeared with the building of highways, another source of income, as deck hand or woodcutter, also vanished. Successive influxes of non-aboriginals also wrested control of the harvesting economy from YFNs. Traditional food sources came under increased pressure during the gold rush and the building of the highway. When the North became more accessible after World War II, the Government of Canada took the opportunity to administer the area more closely. This meant, among other things, regulating the harvesting economy by, for example, requiring the registration of trap lines and charging license fees. By the 1950s aboriginal Yukoners were marginalized from both the exchange and harvesting economies.[49]

The UFA must be understood in this context. Land rights and the economic provisions address the need to reestablish YFN participation in the harvesting and exchange economies. Self-government is the institutional means of safeguarding this participation by ensuring that YFNS will not be the silent subjects of decision-making bodies they do not control.

Despite delays in finalizing and implementing their agreements YFNS have been active in the market economy. In June 1996 a consortium of six YFNS purchased the Yukon Inn, a Whitehorse hotel.[50] And in June 1997 the Little Salmon-Carmacks First Nation and the Carcross-Tagish First Nation formed a mineral exploration company in association with BYG Natural Resources Ltd. This company's mandate is to produce revenue for the first nations, but also to hire and train first nations citizens to enter the mining industry.[51] Unfortunately the general downturn in the mining economy has limited the effectiveness of this approach to economic development.

Unlike most Canadian governments, YFN governments intend to play a direct role in the economic development of their communities. In most communities they are the only entity with a large amount of capital. Therefore, YFN participation in the market economy is crucial, for the economic health of individuals and communities, and for the fiscal independence of YFN governments. Having lived as clients of DIAND for so long, YFNS are aware of the strong correlation between fiscal independence and political autonomy.

The legal standing given YFNS by their agreements, and their willingness to invest in commercial ventures, allows them to import their values and goals into economic development. In 1996 Kaska Dena Council chair Walter Carlick told mining industry representatives that "[t]he caution in our communities [concerning mining] should not be mistaken for opposition."[52] Turning that caution to support, however, requires that mining companies respect the rights and interests of first nations and involve them in decision-making processes. In other words they must respect the YFN view of the territory as a homeland, not a frontier to be abandoned once they have depleted its resources. Respecting YFN values will require reconciling the long-term lifestyle-oriented goals of first nations with the short-term profit-oriented goals of corporations. YFNS have expressed a similar ethic concerning forestry.[53]

However, the impasse over claims negotiations could adversely affect economic relations in the Yukon. Schultz has said that the foundation of claims negotiations is threatened by the federal government's position. Unresolved claims will lead to uncertainty over land tenure and impede investment in the territory. This, says Schultz, should concern all Yukoners.[54]

A recent controversy involving the Vuntut Gwitchin First Nation (VGFN) shows another kind of conflict that still occurs. At issue was a land-use permit for oil exploration issued by the federal government to Northern Cross Ltd. The VGFN wanted the permit revoked because it was not properly consulted. The permit pertained to an area near Eagle Plains that is within the traditional territory of the VGFN but is not land retained by it according to its final agreement. Still, the boards and committees created by the UFA give each YFN a say in the development of its traditional territory, not just the land it retains. The federal government refused to revoke the permit, so in June 1997 the VGFN took the Government of Canada to Federal Court. The court dismissed the case in October 1997. With the transfer of authority over oil and gas to the territory, the VGFN has continued the fight at the political level.

The dispute highlights the various aspects that can cause conflict between YFNs and government.[55] First there is the substantive aspect, the effects that exploration activity may have on the Porcupine Caribou herd. The VGFN relies on the herd as the basis of its harvesting economy. Second is the political aspect. The VGFN is attempting to secure protection of the herd's calving ground in the Arctic National Wildlife Refuge in Alaska. The area near Eagle Plains is the wintering ground for the herd. YFNs and environmentalists fear that allowing oil and gas activity in the wintering ground will compromise the effort to protect the calving ground by presenting a double standard. Finally, there is the procedural aspect. The Northern Cross application passed the criteria of the Canadian Environmental Assessment Act (CEAA). YFNs do not consider this act legitimate because it does not encompass their values and does not allow them sufficient authority in assessing applications. The UFA outlines a Development Assessment Process (DAP) that YFNs and the federal and territorial governments are to design and implement jointly. Yet since the parties have not completed the DAP negotiations, the CEAA still applies.

Other YFNs support the VGFN.[56] As a result the outcome of this conflict, or others like it, may hold consequences for YFN-state relations. Yukon government support for YFN claims may be tested if the potential for resource royalties increases substantially. Also, the legitimacy of agreements could be undermined if YFNs come to believe they cannot protect their cultures and ways of life.[57]

CONCLUSION

Political relations in the Yukon have undergone substantial change since 1898. The Yukon Government was once a small, federally appointed board of directors; today it is a fully representative and responsible body that employs more than 3,000 people and budgeted $512 million for fiscal 1999-2000. As the territorial government has evolved, the Yukon has attempted to divest itself of its colonial status. This process continues—assuming the claims negotiations impasse is solved, as it gains increased authority the territorial government will have to contend with the emergence of 14 YFN governments, each of which will possess varying resources and authority. In future, therefore, political relations in the Yukon will become an internally multilateral process. Institutional arrangements in the Yukon will continue to be unique.

It is not easy to predict the direction in which these relationships will proceed. The territorial government and YFNs have co-operated at times and been in conflict at times, depending on the issue and the interests at stake. That much will continue. Yet in the past both parties had something in common: they wanted money, land, and authority from the federal government. Their limited authority meant that direct conflicts were limited. Once current processes are complete, competition will occur on a wider front. The federal government will not be there to be labelled the scapegoat or play the mediator.

Institutions established by the UFA, such as resource management boards, will play a role in setting the tone of political relations. Evolving economic relations also will affect future political relations. YFN economic development will benefit the territory as a whole. The hegemony of neo-conservative economic doctrines among most governments in Canada seems to have sounded the death knell for direct government involvement in the economic life of the country. And like many hinterland regions the Yukon lacks large pools of local capital that could be used to develop the economy in ways that are sensitive and responsive to local needs. Yet YFN governments are taking an active role in developing their communities. Eventually they could provide important pools of capital for economic development across the territory. This pooling of resources should occur because in many ways the aboriginal and non-aboriginal populations are highly integrated and committed to living together. When the consortium of six YFNs purchased the Yukon Inn, Chief Joe Johnson of the Kluane First Nation said, "For the future of the next generation, we should get beyond our differences and start calling ourselves Yukoners instead of defining ourselves as native or non-native."[58] Good political relations between YFNs and the Yukon Government will foster this attitude.

Political and economic relations in the Yukon are changing, but the frontier/homeland dichotomy still exists and is not just a product of differing economic pursuits. The overriding demographic fact of Yukon society is the transience of the non-aboriginal population and the permanence of the aboriginal population. Reconciling the frontier and homeland world-views will not be easy, but the resolution of fundamental disagreements and the future of political, economic, and social relations depends on it.

NOTES

1 Mr Justice Thomas R. Berger, *Northern Frontier, Northern Homeland: The Report of the Mackenzie Valley Pipeline Inquiry* (Minister of Supply and Services Canada: Ottawa, 1977), 2.

2 Ken S. Coates and William R. Morrison, *Land of the Midnight Sun: A History of the Yukon* (Edmonton: Hurtig Publishers, 1988), 79.

3 Ken S. Coates, *Best Left as Indians: Native-White Relations in the Yukon Territory, 1840-1973* (Montreal and Kingston: McGill-Queen's University Press, 1991), 39.

4 Whitehorse's role as the Yukon's centre of power is the source of some tension. Approximately 70 per cent of Yukoners live in Whitehorse, but the city's population is overwhelmingly non-aboriginal, unlike the rest of the territory. And while the basis of the private-sector economy is resource extraction and tourism, Whitehorse is primarily a transportation, retail, service, political, and administrative centre. Not atypically, then, the centre of power is not demographically or economically representative of the whole. The result is a centre-periphery dynamic within the Yukon, one that favours Whitehorse even though only eight of the legislative assembly's 17 MLAs represent ridings entirely within the city's boundaries. Two of the ridings are partially within the boundaries of Whitehorse and are called "country-residential." The other seven ridings are completely rural. Tension between the centre and the periphery may be exacerbated by the 2000 election result. The Liberal Party won all eight Whitehorse seats and both country-residential seats, but none of the rural seats.

5 Coates, *Best Left As Indians*, 231.

6 Patrick L. Michael, "The Yukon: Parliamentary tradition in a small legislature," *Provincial and Territorial Legislatures in Canada*, ed. Gary Levy and Graham White (Toronto: University of Toronto Press, 1989), 190.

7 Michael, "The Yukon." 190.

8 Kirk Cameron and Graham Gomme, *The Yukon's Constitutional Foundations, Volume II: A Compendium of Documents Relating to the Constitutional Development of the Yukon Territory* (Whitehorse: Northern Directories Ltd., 1991), 5.

9 Michael, "The Yukon." 192.

10 With the introduction of party politics in 1978 the leader of the largest party in the assembly took the title "Government Leader." The Epp letter allowed the government leader to use the title "Premier." However, only Tony Penikett (1989-92) and Pat Duncan (2000-present) have done so.

11 Michael, "The Yukon." 192-93.

12 Richard Stuart, "Duff Pattulo and the Yukon Schools Question of 1937" *Canadian Historical Review* LXIV: 1 (March 1983): 25-44.

13 Interview with Arthur Pearson, Commissioner of the Yukon Territory (1976-78), July 29, 1993.

14 Janet Moodie Michael, "From Sissons to Meyer: The Administrative Development of the Yukon Government, 1948-1979", unpublished manuscript (Whitehorse: Yukon Archives, June 1987), 87-92.

15 Michael, "From Sissons to Meyer." 94.

16 Canada, *Devolution of the Northern Affairs Program to the Yukon Government: A Federal Proposal* (Ottawa: Indian and Northern Affairs Canada, 1996), ii.

17 Canada, *Devolution of the Northern Affairs Program to the Yukon Government: A Federal Proposal*, cover.

18 Karen Smith, "McDonald, Irwin stage 'agreeable' talk," *Whitehorse Star*, 18 November 1996, 4.

19 The CYFN is the successor organization to the Council for Yukon Indians (CYI). The latter three YFNs were members of the CYI but have not joined the CYFN.

20 Karen Smith, "Major devolution agreements signed," *Whitehorse Star*, 24 January 1997, 3.

21 Government of Yukon, *Proposed Yukon Act 1999*.

22 Government of Yukon, *Proposed Yukon Act 1999*, 5.

23 Government of Yukon, *Proposed Yukon Act 1999*, 4.

24 Government of Yukon, *Proposed Yukon Act 1999*, 17.

25 Interview with Tony Penikett, Premier of Yukon (1985-1992), 28 July 1993.

26 Floyd McCormick, "Fiscally conservative, entrepreneurial socialism is here!", *Yukon News*, 26 February 1999, 8.

27 Frank Cassidy, ed., *Aboriginal Self-Determination* (Lantzville, B.C., and Halifax: Oolichan Books and the Institute for Research on Public Policy, 1991), 143-50.

28 For a brief overview of the interest-based negotiations process see Chris Knight in Frank Cassidy, ed., *Reaching Just Settlements: Land Claims in British Columbia* (Lantzville, BC, and Halifax: Oolichan Books and the Institute for Research on Public Policy, 1991), 66-69.

29 Penikett interview.

30 The UFA is not a land claim or self-government agreement; it is an agreement among all 14 YFNs, the Government of Canada, and the Government of the Yukon that sets out the framework under which each YFN will negotiate its own land-claim and self-government agreements.

31 The four YFNs to sign on May 29, 1993 were the Vuntut Gwitchin First Nation, the Champagne-Aishihik First Nations, the First Nation of Nacho Nyak Dun, and the Teslin Tlingit Council.

32 In addition to the four YFNs mentioned above, the Selkirk First Nation (1997), the Little Salmon-Carmacks First Nation (1997), and the Tr'ondek Hwech'in (1998) have signed and are implementing agreements.

33 The Government of Canada, The Council for Yukon Indians, and the Government of the Yukon, *Umbrella Final Agreement: Council for Yukon Indians* (Ottawa: Minister of Supply and Services Canada, 1993), 215-16.

34 These figures are compiled from specific provision 19.5.5.1 in each of the YFN final agreements and Schedule A—Apportionment of the 1989 Aggregate Value in the UFA.

35 Nadine Petersen, "Ultimatum angers First Nations," *Yukon News*, 26 May 2000, 2.

36 Jason Small, "Stalemate reached on taxation, loans issues," *Whitehorse Star*, 23 May 2000, 2.

37 Petersen "Ultimatum angers First Nations."

38 Keith Brownsey and Michael Howlett, eds., "Introduction," *The Provincial State: Politics in Canada's Provinces and Territories* (Mississauga: Copp Clark, 1992), 1.

39 The following section does not discuss fiscal relations between governments. This is an important subject for investigation but beyond the scope of the current chapter. The history and future of federal-territorial fiscal relations is worthy of a chapter in itself. As for YFN-state fiscal relations there is little information to guide such an investigation, other than the UFA and the land-claim and self-government agreements.

40 The Conference Board of Canada, "Yukon Prospects: Outlook for the Yukon Economy" (The Conference Board of Canada, October 1999), 1.

41 Yukon Economic Development, Yukon Finance, "Economic and Fiscal Analysis of the Faro Mine Closure" (Whitehorse: Government of the Yukon, 28 November 1996), 1.

42 Honourable Piers McDonald, "1998-99 Budget Address" (Whitehorse: Yukon Finance, 1998), 11.

43 Conference Board of Canada, 38.

44 Conference Board of Canada, 38.

45 Adam Killick, "Harding gushing about oil act," *Yukon News*, 19 November 1997, 6; John McHutchoin, "Territory ready to tap into black gold," *Whitehorse Star*, 27 January 1998, 4.

46 "Economic Value of Yukon's Tourism Industry." Flyer published by the Tourism Industry Association of the Yukon and Tourism Yukon.

47 McDonald, "1998-99 Budget Address," 10-11.

48 Coates, *Best Left as Indians*, 32-46.

49 Coates, *Best Left as Indians*, 189-90.

50 Chuck Tobin, "Yukon Inn was bought for $4 million," *Whitehorse Star*, 4 June 1996, 5.

51 John Steinbachs, "First nations enter exploration business," *Whitehorse Star*, 19 June 1997, 5.

52 "Natives dig mining," *Yukon News*, 29 March 1996, 22.

53 John Steinbachs, "First nations will bring different ideas to forestry harvesting, meeting told," *Whitehorse Star*, 26 March 1997, 9.

54 Chuck Tobin, "Seething grand chief slams federal minister," *Whitehorse Star*, 26 May 2000, 6.

55 For a complete public statement of the VGFN position see "This repetition of history would hurt everyone," *Whitehorse Star*, 19 June 1997, 7.

56 Chuck Tobin, "First nations back anti-exploration bid," *Whitehorse Star*, 7 July 1997, 4.

57 D.P. Kassi [VGFN citizen], "Northern Cross decision a double cross," letter to the editor, *Yukon News*, 7 November 1997, 10.

58 Richard Mostyn, "First nations buy hotel," *Yukon News*, 5 June 1996, 4.

14 NUNAVUT

Inuit Self-Determination Through a Land Claim and Public Government?

JACK HICKS AND GRAHAM WHITE

Nunavut means "our land" in Inuktitut, the language of the Inuit, the aboriginal people of Canada's eastern and central Arctic.[1] It symbolizes how directly the creation of a new territory north of the tree-line emerged from Inuit political and cultural aspirations. Nunavut is an attempt by the large Inuit majority to regain control over their lives and to ensure their survival and development as a people.

Roughly 85 per cent of Nunavut's population are Inuit, so that although it has a "public government"—in which all residents, Inuit and non-Inuit, participate—Nunavut is primarily about Inuit needs and Inuit approaches to governance. As such, the political dynamics and the operation of government in Nunavut raise crucial questions about how state structures and political processes can better reflect the nature of society and economy. With its distinctive people, geography, economy, and government, Nunavut differs fundamentally from other Canadian provinces and territories. Accordingly, while Nunavut's population may be barely that of a small city in southern Canada, the emerging issues of politics and governance there are of wide interest and import.

Bringing a political economy approach to bear on Nunavut requires analysis of somewhat different issues and linkages than is usually the case. Political economy incorporates a range of approaches which view societies as structured by specific power relations, and economies as socially and politically embedded. The central linkage between the economic foundations of Nunavut society and its politics is ownership and control of the land itself, which is intimately tied to Inuit cultural values. If the standard analytical constructs of political economy, for example class structures and organizational entities such as labour unions and left-wing political parties, are less central in Nunavut than elsewhere in Canada (or perhaps more accurately, at this point assume quite different forms in Nunavut), the fundamental approach of political economy is nonetheless instructive. It is centrally concerned with linkages between politics and social structure, particularly ownership and control of economic institutions, and with the nature of the state and the state-society relationship. These are the questions which underlie this chapter. The politics of Nunavut are in essence about control over land and resources and, given the omnipresence of government, about the nature of the state and the influences on its activities.

Although it is clear that Nunavut is, in important respects, economically dependent on southern Canada, we do not root our analysis in the "dependency theory" which dominates the writings of many Canadian political economists. Given the tendency of Canadian analysts to focus on the degree to which Canada is allegedly "dependent" on the United States, it is not surprising that the Canadian North is often described simply as being "dependent" on southern Canada. But as Philip O'Brien has observed with regard to Latin America, "dependency can easily become a pseudo-concept which explains everything in general and hence nothing in particular."[2] Dependency approaches also tend to obscure the opportunity for agency. Any description of how dependent the Canadian Arctic is on fiscal transfers from the federal government should also recognize that—and be capable of explaining how—a highly "dependent" people managed to negotiate one of the most sweeping aboriginal rights and self-government packages in North America.[3]

In examining government and politics in Nunavut this chapter pursues two central issues: first, the prospects that the new regime in Nunavut will generate significant local control over the political and economic processes that affect its people's lives; second, the extent to which the design and operation of the state in Nunavut do in fact incorporate the values and perspectives of its people. These are, of course, universal themes but they are particularly highlighted in Nunavut because of the distinctiveness of Inuit culture and because no other Canadian attempt at aboriginal self-government has anything like the scope and magnitude of the Nunavut project. Our discussion and conclusions on these matters are necessarily preliminary, not least because as we write, Nunavut has existed for only a few months. Nonetheless, the opportunities and the problems confronting Nunavut and its people, as well as the need for Canadians outside the North to understand them, are sufficiently clear to warrant analysis.

The chapter begins with a brief sketch of Nunavut's geography, society, and economy; we then offer a summary of Nunavut's history, concentrating on changes to Inuit society, and a brief account of the principal features of the Inuit land claim, which in effect created Nunavut. Subsequent sections examine government and politics in Nunavut, with special emphasis on state-society linkages.

NUNAVUT: A PROFILE

Geography

Nunavut encompasses nearly a fifth of Canada's land mass. At more than 2.1 million square kilometres, Nunavut is substantially larger than Québec (the largest province), three times the size of Texas, and roughly the size of continental Europe. Were Nunavut independent, it would rank as the world's twelfth-largest country. Its western boundary, with the Northwest Territories (NWT), runs north from the intersection of the Manitoba-Saskatchewan border with the sixtieth parallel, roughly follows the tree-line (beyond which the climate is too harsh for trees) north-west to the Arctic Ocean, then cuts east and north through the western Arctic islands.[4] To the east, Nunavut's boundary is that of the pre-division NWT.

These boundaries illustrate that even as the creation of Nunavut represents increased Inuit control over their lives, it sets important limits on that control. Nunavut's boundaries derive from the 1993 land-claim settlement (described in greater detail below) in which Inuit agreed to surrender important aboriginal rights in exchange for (among other things) establishment of their long-sought-after homeland. Moreover, Nunavut's artificial boundaries attest to the practical compromises Inuit have had to make. First, Nunavut does not include all traditional Inuit territory, which extended into northern Manitoba and beyond Nunavut's western boundary.[5] Second, the Nunavut project is about enhancing the political autonomy of the Inuit in the eastern and central parts of the former NWT, so that the substantial numbers of Inuit in Nunavik (northern Québec) and Labrador, many of whom share close ties with Nunavut Inuit, are excluded by virtue of turn-of-the-century judicial and political decisions, imposed on Inuit without their knowledge, let alone consent. The Inuvialuit, the Inuit of the Mackenzie Delta, are also excluded from Nunavut.

Nunavut's physical features vary substantially, from the essentially flat "barrenlands" west of Hudson Bay to the soaring mountains and spectacular fiords of Baffin and Ellesmere Islands. Climatic variations also exist, though winters are long and severe; at best the ice in most of Nunavut's harbours and waterways does not break up until July, permitting only a limited period of shipping and navigation before fall freeze-up.

All Nunavut communities, with the single exception of Baker Lake, are located beside the sea, reflecting the importance of marine mammals in the traditional Inuit economy. By southern standards, communities are very isolated; Nunavut has virtually no roads, so transportation is primarily by air, which is extremely expensive. Bulk goods are usually shipped in from the south by "sea-lift" during the summer. The small local markets, the high cost of transportation, and the harsh conditions make for very high living costs. Residents in Nunavut may pay twice as much for groceries as people in the south, while construction costs are proportionately even higher.

Demography

Few parts of the globe are as sparsely populated as Nunavut, whose population was just 27,000 when it came into existence on April 1, 1999. The population is spread out among 25 communities: one "town" (the capital, Iqaluit)[6] and 24 "hamlets." Iqaluit, fast approaching 5,000, is by far the largest community; Rankin Inlet has 2,200 people and eight other communities have populations over 1,000. Eight Nunavut communities have populations between 500 and 1,000, and seven more have populations below 500. There are also two tiny settlements in the western part of the territory, and in the eastern part a few dozen people live in small "outpost camps," distant from the organized communities.[7]

Eighty-three per cent of Nunavut's people are Inuit. Non-Inuit are concentrated in the regional centres of Iqaluit, Rankin Inlet, and Cambridge Bay, and at the Nanisivik mine, so many of the smaller communities are more than 95 per cent Inuit. At 30 live births per 1,000 population, birth rates among Nunavut Inuit reflect a population undergoing a historic demographic transition. Nunavut's age structure differs dramatically from the Canadian norm: whereas roughly 20 per cent of the Canadian population is 15 years of age and under, in Nunavut the equivalent figure is roughly 40 per cent. Nunavut's birth rates have fallen considerably in recent years, and are now below the rate maintained by Canada as a whole during the "baby boom" years of the 1950s. Nonetheless, Nunavut's population growth rates are more than three times the national average. Both the rapid population growth and the unusual age structure have enormous social and economic consequences. Simply maintaining existing levels of social services, housing, education, and job creation in the face of such enormous population pressure is a mammoth challenge.

Economy

One of the most important aspects of Nunavut's wage economy is the limited degree to which, until recently, Inuit have participated in it. According to the Nunavut Bureau of Statistics' 1999 Community Labour Force Survey, Nunavut as a whole had a 66.6-per-cent labour force participation rate[8] and an unemployment rate of 20.7 per cent. (At that time Canada as a whole had a 64.5-per-cent labour force participation rate and an unemployment rate of 8.5 per cent.) However, Inuit had only a 60.1-per-cent labour force participation rate and a 28.0-per-cent unemployment rate, while the non-Inuit population had 91.3-per-cent participation and only 2.7-per-cent unemployment rates. Simply put, most non-Inuit are in Nunavut to work, and when their work ends, for whatever reason, they leave.

These unemployment rates are based on Canada-wide criteria which are not very appropriate to small Inuit communities. Using more appropriate criteria—adding "had not looked for work because they perceived no jobs to be available" to the standard "were without work and had actively looked for work in the previous four weeks"—raises the Inuit unemployment rate significantly but leaves the non-Inuit unemployment rate almost unchanged. Looking at these data from a different perspective, we can calculate that only 43.3 per cent of the adult Inuit population is employed in the wage economy—less than half the rate of adult non-aboriginal employment.

Nunavut's economy depends to an extraordinary degree on government. Well over half the territory's jobs are in the public sector and many others, in service and construction for example, are (directly or indirectly) dependent on government activity. (Public-sector employment involves far more than government bureaucrats; teachers and health care workers are important—and numerous—examples of para-public-sector employees.) In some communities, only a handful of private-sector jobs exist. Inuit hold a substantial number of public-sector jobs, but far fewer than their proportion of the overall population warrants. Moreover, the higher-paying and professional jobs tend to be occupied by non-Inuit. Not only, for example, are there no Inuit doctors, but none of the nurses in Nunavut is Inuit. A major goal of the Nunavut land claim and the creation of the Nunavut government is ensuring representative Inuit participation throughout the public sector.[9]

Government is a central economic force in another sense: the overall level of public subsidy of the economy. Precisely how this subsidy takes place is quite telling. The residents of Nunavut have the lowest economic dependency ratio—a common measure of dependence on government—of any provincial/territorial jurisdiction in Canada. Statistics Canada defines "economic dependency" as being total transfer payments to individuals divided by their total income. And while the overall level of social assistance payments has grown rapidly in recent years, especially in the Baffin region,[10] they are still a fraction of the region's wage income. In other words, people who don't have jobs in the wage economy exist on very limited amounts of cash. As individual economic actors, the people of Nunavut are very dependent on the wage income which they—and/or the other members of their families—earn.

The economy as a whole, however, relies on very high levels of cash transfers from the federal government. In the 2000-01 fiscal year, the Government of Nunavut will receive $21,327 per capita in federal funding, compared to $1,277 per capita for the provinces (with Newfoundland, at $2,751, receiving the highest per capita payment).[11] In the first Nunavut budget, 90.5 per cent of territorial revenue came from the federal government, most of it through a formula funding agreement. The basic grant from Canada amounted to $498.9 million, with another $53.7 flowing from Ottawa to Iqaluit through other federal programs. By fiscal 2003-04, Nunavut's fifth year, annual federal transfers to Nunavut are projected to reach $666 million.

Although federal funding is critical if the Government of Nunavut is to provide essential services to its residents, their magnitude renders Nunavut highly vulnerable to unilateral federal cutbacks in transfer payments. For example, in the final year before division, the Government of the Northwest Territories (GNWT) spent $1.25 billion on programs and services—a decrease, on a per capita basis, of roughly 11 per cent since 1995-96. Deep spending cuts were necessitated after the federal government, in the 1995 budget, announced changes to the formula funding agreement. These charges are estimated to have cost the GWNT $60 million annually. Subsequent forecasts of a key component of the funding formula, the Provincial-Local Government Spending Escalator, were revised downward, costing the GNWT a further $160 million over three years. The revised forecasts resulted primarily from provincial governments cutting their spending. (In other words, the policies of the Harris government in Ontario caused spending cuts in Nunavut communities by affecting components of the funding formula which reflect spending by the provincial governments.) The total impact of these cuts was that the GNWT received roughly $400 million less over the five-year life of the final pre-division formula financing agreement than was forecast when the agreement was concluded in December 1994—more than twice the amount expected by the federal government when it announced the cuts. This was is in addition to a $100-million reduction in federal funding for housing in the NWT.

Because the private sector is less developed in Nunavut than in the other territories and provinces, Nunavut is the most "fiscally dependent" jurisdiction in Canada, as measured by reliance on federal funding. Whereas over 90 per cent of the Government of Nunavut's revenue comes from Ottawa, in the NWT and the Yukon the figures are 81 and 71 per cent. Newfoundland, the province most dependent on federal transfers, receives 45 per cent of its revenue from Ottawa. The average among "have-not" provinces is 34 per cent; for all provinces it is 29 per cent.

Without the high level of federal transfers underwriting territorial government programs and services, few people could afford to live in the Arctic—at least not with a standard of living anywhere close to Canadian norms. For example, the elderly and the unemployed pay as little as $32 a month to live in public housing units which cost the government as much as $1,000 per month to build and maintain. At the same time, during the 1990s the GNWT dramatically raised rents for employed persons who live in government-owned housing to encourage them to build or purchase their own homes. Many Nunavut communities have very limited private housing markets, so that government-owned housing is essential. In the larger communities, limited amounts of expensive, privately owned rental housing are becoming available.

Private-sector economic activity is dominated by resource extraction. At present Nunavut's three mines produce lead and zinc, gold, and silver; extensive exploration and development work is underway for other precious and base metals as well as for uranium and diamonds. Vast reserves of oil and gas lie beneath the Arctic Ocean, but the tremendous logistical and environmental difficulties of extracting these resources and getting them to southern markets have thus far prevented sustained efforts at developing them. Mines in Nunavut—current and prospective—are owned and operated by large southern Canadian or foreign multinational firms. Tellingly, Inuit hold relatively few of the often very highly paid mining jobs in Nunavut. Indeed, many of the workers at these mines do not live in Nunavut in any real sense. They fly in from southern centres like Montreal or Edmonton for two or three weeks of intense work and then fly home for their time off.

Transportation, construction, and retail are the next most important sectors of the Nunavut economy. Since the mines are largely self-contained, in important ways it is in these sectors that southern capital is most evident and exerts its most direct influence on Nunavut society. Companies in these sectors, both the larger firms headquartered in southern Canada and smaller, locally owned enterprises, have long been predominantly owned and operated by non-Inuit. Inuit-owned companies are, however, becoming increasingly important players, as money from the land claim is channelled by Inuit organizations into long-term economic development projects. By way of illustration, a consortium of Inuit-owned firms is constructing the office buildings and other infrastructure needed for the Nunavut government.

The largest Inuit-owned companies are the "birthright development corporations" collectively owned by all Nunavut Inuit through their land claims organizations. While these firms are especially concerned about hiring and training Inuit, they must still be understood as essentially capitalist enterprises, not least for their role in fostering economic divisions in Inuit society that are strongly linked to political power: "although the development corporations are becoming increasingly important as employers of Inuit, their main significance is that they control the allocation of resources and wealth and that their economic control is combined with political control ... the native development corporation has enabled a small group of Inuit to become both powerful and wealthy."[12]

Only the three regional centres—Iqaluit, Rankin Inlet, and Cambridge Bay—have bank branches, although automated banking machines are starting to appear in the larger settlements. And while the banks are involved in large economic development projects (and are extremely interested in Inuit land-claim money), and Northern (formerly the Hudson's Bay Company) and Co-op stores partially fill the gap on a local basis, the historic role played by financial institutions has often been assumed by government. As Clancy has noted, "in frontier societies more than most, the core mechanisms of production and exchange are established and maintained only with state support."[13]

Tourism is a growing sector, but very high costs limit the number of visitors such that tourism remains a relatively minor component of the economy. Similarly, though many Nunavut residents earn money from arts and crafts (primarily stone carving), for the vast majority this represents only a small supplement to their income. (Reliable statistics on arts and crafts are notoriously difficult to collect.) Economic activity in arts and crafts has close ties to the extensive co-operative movement which is heavily involved in the production and marketing of Inuit art. Moreover, with most communities having only one or two large retail outlets, the community-owned Co-op stores are important economic institutions throughout Nunavut. As Marybelle Mitchell has observed, not only have the co-ops been the largest non-government employer of Inuit, "virtually all the Inuit population is involved in one way or another with a local co-operative."[14]

If the importance of the co-operative movement, with its local control and communal ethic, is noteworthy, the co-ops should not be seen as a fundamental challenge to capitalist values and economic processes in Nunavut. As Mitchell's exhaustive study of Inuit co-ops demonstrates, they are best understood as "the definitive link between the indigenous and capitalist modes of production ... [they are] communal in name but capitalist in effect."[15] Government played an unusual, indeed decisive, role in establishing co-ops in the north as a tool of economic development that would integrate aboriginal people into the capitalist wage economy.

In terms of dollar value, the traditional hunting, trapping, and fishing economy is of limited importance. Commercial fisheries off Baffin Island, harvesting of caribou for export, and similar endeavours hold some promise for development, but are ultimately limited in scale. Yet measuring hunting and fishing activities simply in terms of wages paid or sales generated is highly misleading. Particularly in the smaller communities, a significant proportion of food comes directly from the land. This "country food" is fresher and more nutritious than extremely expensive frozen meat flown in from Montreal or Winnipeg. The "replacement value" of country food harvested by Nunavummiut (Nunavut Inuit) has been estimated at between $30 and $35 million annually. Moreover, hunting and fishing have tremendous cultural importance both for individual Inuit, for whom going "on the land" is crucial to their identity, and for communities whose traditional values and ties are reinforced by the hunt itself and the sharing of the harvest.

INUIT AND THE STATE: FROM AUTONOMY TO SUBJUGATION (TO SELF-DETERMINATION?)

Contact and Colonization

The central theme in the recent history of the eastern and central Arctic has been the effect of Euro-Canadian contact on Inuit society and the resulting rapid social change within Inuit society. Accordingly, the creation of Nunavut, as well as the critical social, political, and economic problems it faces, must be understood in terms of Inuit society's evolution in a context of colonial domination by southern Canadian economic and political interests. In most fundamentals the Inuit experience replicates the history of other North American aboriginal peoples after contact with European society.[16] Overtaken by devastating social, economic, and cultural changes, their status as an autonomous, self-governing people disappeared as they lost control of their land and resources to governments imposed on them without their consent.

Prior to the advent of air travel, the eastern and central Arctic was far less accessible to Europeans (and later, Canadians) than the Mackenzie Valley or the Yukon and it offered few of the resources that drew Europeans and southerners north, such as fur, gold, and oil. Accordingly, Euro-Canadian contact with the Inuit of what we know today as Nunavut came much later and was much less extensive than for other aboriginal peoples of the Canadian north—or for other Inuit societies.[17] Significant interaction between Inuit and whalers from Europe and North America occurred in the nineteenth century, but most Inuit were not directly affected in fundamental ways by this contact. Only in the twentieth century did large-scale Euro-Canadian influence begin to dramatically affect Inuit society, as fur-traders, missionaries, and Royal Canadian Mounted Police (RCMP) officers spread throughout the North; unlike the whalers, they came to live permanently.

Economic integration preceded political integration as Hudson's Bay Company traders promoted the exploitation of local resources, most notably furs and skins. Traders offered Inuit strong material incentives—supplies, equipment, and other goods—for items such as white fox pelts. Many Inuit significantly altered their hunting practices (Inuit, for example, traditionally did not trap fox) and indeed their whole lifestyle, to meet the traders' demands, thereby tying themselves to the vagaries of the international commodity market as well as to specific companies, as the following extraordinary indenture document illustrates:

> I, ____, son of ____, do agree and promise on this ____ day of 1914, to serve the Hudson's Bay Company, faithfully, in the capacity of Hunter, and in such other capacity as the Hudson's Bay Company shall appoint, for the full term of five years, to be computed from the first day of June 1914. I do also hereby agree to obey all orders and commands given me by the said Company and that I will not be engaged in any other employment whatsoever, than that of the Hudson's Bay Company for the said term of five years, and that I will deliver my entire hunt of all foxes, bears, seals, walrus, wolf et cetera to the said company, for the said term of five years. In compensation for the above mentioned services, the Hudson's Bay Company agrees to pay me Thirty Netchik per year, and also pay me for my aforementioned entire hunt turned over to them at the usual prices allowed Eskimo Hunters by the said Company. In witness whereof, these presents have been executed at Lake Harbour on the ____ day of ____ 1914.[18]

When major downturns in those markets occurred, as exemplified when the price for white fox collapsed following World War II, the Inuit, who had come to depend on trade goods, were unable to return to traditional ways.[19] Economically, by the second half of the century Inuit had become subservient to outside forces and economic agents over whom they exercised no control. A similar dynamic reoccurred in the 1970s when animal rights activists destroyed the commercial market for sealskin, which had become a key pillar of the economy of the eastern and central Arctic.[20]

Incorporation and Social Change

Politically, Inuit were largely ignored by Canada until quite recently. Inuit never signed treaties or agreements with either British or Canadian authorities, nor were they conquered militarily. And yet Inuit ruefully discovered that whereas they had always governed themselves and exercised stewardship over their lands, a foreign, little understood entity called the Canadian Government had come, without their consent or agreement, to control their lives.

After World War II, the Canadian Government's minimalist northern presence gave way to activism, replete with extensive social engineering plans for aboriginal societies.[21] A variety of motives underlay this fundamental policy reversal: concern with the distress suffered by Inuit and other northern aboriginal peoples who, having become dependent on the capitalist economy, found themselves largely excluded from it; recognition of the Canadian state's obligations to aboriginal people, coupled with a strongly assimilationist agenda to eliminate the distinctive elements of aboriginal society; interest in fostering large-scale exploitation of the north's mineral and other resources; and desire to solidify Canada's disputed claim to sovereignty over the islands of the Arctic archipelago.

A key element in realizing these diverse goals was the creation of permanent settlements. Establishment of these communities symbolizes how, even very recently, the Canadian state controlled Inuit life in fundamental ways. Until well into the twentieth century Inuit did not live in permanent settlements, though they often gathered at traditional sites for hunting and fishing and for social purposes. Hence, all the communities in Nunavut are of recent origin (many dating only from the 1940s and 1950s), having grown where Europeans and southern Canadians located their institutions: Hudson's Bay Company trading posts, RCMP detachments, mission churches, military installations and the like. Even more tellingly, many Inuit did not settle in these communities willingly; they were coerced by the government to move into central locations to facilitate the delivery of public services such as health and education and also so that they could be assimilated into southern Canadian ways.[22] For the most part, this entailed bringing local Inuit into centralized communities. In some instances, however, Inuit were relocated great distances to serve the interests of the Canadian state; the most notorious example is that of the "High Arctic Exiles" of the 1950s who were moved thousands of kilometres from northern Québec to Ellesmere and Cornwallis islands in part to bolster Canadian claims to sovereignty over the far north.[23]

As was the case with First Nations across Canada, government officials sent children away to boarding schools (often run by the churches). As Hugh Brody has noted,

> the word *ilira* ... is used to refer to the fear of ghosts, the awe a strong father inspires in his children, and fear of the *Qadlunaat* [white man]. I often heard Inuit speak about their agreement to their children being taken away from their homes in camps, and being put in schools far away. This taking of children caused much heartache to Inuit parents, who are famous for their intense attachment to their children. Virtually every Inuit child embodies a much loved and respected older relative (in North Baffin, a recently deceased relative), the person who is the child's *atiq*. When a child is taken away, therefore, the families lose a loved (and potentially helpful) little person; the embodiment, almost the reincarnation, of an elder, the child's *atiq*, is also lost. Yet when this happened, Inuit seemed to accept the process. When older men and women told me about the grief the boarding school program caused them, I asked many times, "Why did you not complain? Why did you go along with it?" The answers repeatedly made use of *ilira*, fear, awe, a sense of intimidation. And when I explored these answers, asking more questions about the feelings and events that surrounded the taking of children out to school, I was told that all *Qadlunaat* made Inuit feel *ilira*. Often elders—both men and women—made the point in general terms: *iliranatualulautut*, "they were very *ilira*-making."[24]

It would be hard to underestimate the extent and the speed of social and cultural change experienced by the Inuit in recent decades. Most Inuit over the age of 40 were born on the land in snow houses or tents to nomadic families whose lives depended almost entirely on hunting, fishing, and trapping and who had almost no exposure to mainstream North American society. They now watch cable television in their living rooms while their children play video games or surf the internet. Life in permanent communities built upon the wage economy, the welfare state, and modern technology changed Inuit society fundamentally. Profound changes in economic activity were linked to other changes: traditional patterns of authority (for example, the respect accorded elders) were challenged by new forces, single-parent families (rare in traditional Inuit society) became common, and a range of traditional values and practices were weakened. The decline in the capacity of the Inuit to hunt was critical since hunting was not only the economic mainstay but also the cultural focus of traditional Inuit society.

For all this, Inuit were in, but not really of, Canadian society. Geographically, economically, and socially, they existed at the margins. State activism in the 1950s and 1960s brought Inuit important entitlements that other Canadians had long taken for granted, such as public health services, schooling, and social welfare. These benefits, however, came at enormous social cost. Not all Inuit could follow traditional economic pursuits. Increased pressure on the wildlife close to the settled communities (some of which were located far from good hunting areas) meant that hunters had to travel long distances, requiring mechanized equipment that was expensive to purchase and operate. Yet few paying jobs were available. Because of the cost of hunting, by the 1980s "only Inuit who do have a job, and hence an income, can afford to go hunting in the little spare time available. Inuit who do not have a job or a regular income cannot afford to go hunting, although they have plenty of time to do so."[25] (The Nunavut Harvester Support Program, created through the land claim, attempts to remedy this situation.)

The implicit presumption underpinning the government's reorganization of Inuit life was rejection of traditional economic activities in favour of integration into the North American wage economy, yet even when jobs were open to Inuit they were typically unskilled, low-paying, and often of only short duration. Unemployment and underemployment thus became chronic problems which combined with alienation from the land and from traditional culture to engender horrendous social problems: alcohol and substance abuse, family violence, youth suicide, and welfare dependency. In the words of one deeply pessimistic report about Inuit society, the "lords of the Arctic" had become "wards of the state."[26]

Although profoundly affected by government decisions, Inuit were permitted no role in politics or government. The NWT was ruled by Ottawa as a colony: for decades the Government of the Northwest Territories was in effect a committee of federal civil servants. Residents of Nunavut—both Inuit and non-Inuit—were unable to vote in federal elections until 1962 or in territorial elections until the 1960s.[27] When municipal governments were established in the settlements in the 1950s and 1960s they were allowed no significant powers. Until well into the 1980s, virtually no Inuk held a bureaucratic post of any influence in the territorial government.

Not only were Inuit systematically excluded from participating in it, but government persistently treated the Inuit in ways which in hindsight seem astoundingly patronizing and condescending. A booklet published by the Canadian Government for Inuit explained government in this way (with "Eskimo children" referring to all Inuit): "The King is helping all the children in his lands. He is giving aid to the Eskimo children also and has instructed His servants the Police in this way."[28] Perhaps the best illustration involves that most central element of identity: names. Government bureaucrats who had trouble understanding and keeping track of complex Inuit naming systems issued discs imprinted with identification numbers to all Inuit which were to be used in dealings with government in place of their names.[29] Inuit were told "Every Eskimo should have a disc bearing his identification number. Do not lose your disc. You will need it to obtain the King's help."[30]

Ethnic Mobilization and Class Differentiation

Inuit would never have survived as a people without enormous resilience, patience and determination. These qualities were critical in the Inuit struggle to regain control of their lives and their land. As well, compared to many other Canadian aboriginal peoples, the Inuit enjoy important advantages stemming from their relative isolation and the lack of readily exploitable resources in their lands. Their overwhelming numerical dominance may have only recently taken on political importance but it has facilitated retention of key elements of Inuit culture. Most notably, Inuktitut continues to rank among the healthiest aboriginal languages in Canada; the great majority of Nunavut Inuit continue to speak it[31] and in most Nunavut communities Inuktitut is heard far more often than English—except in some federal and territorial government offices.

Inuit differ from the other aboriginal peoples of Canada not just in history, language, and culture but in legal status as well. Inuit are not subject to the federal government's infamous *Indian Act* (though the 1939 Supreme Court ruling *Re: Eskimos* declared them in effect to be equivalent to Indians in that the federal government has a fiduciary responsibility to them).[32] This means that there have never been reserves established under the *Indian Act* for Inuit. It has also meant that some of the arbitrary, legalistic divisions that impede political action among other aboriginal peoples in Canada—between, for example, "status Indians," "non-status Indians," and Métis—do not exist among Inuit. In turn, this has made it easier to maintain Inuit unity, especially in terms of political direction.

One paradoxical result of Inuit contact with, and subsequent domination by, Euro-Canadian society has been the emergence of a group identity among Inuit. Prior to contact, Inuit identities and loyalties were rooted in local groups of extended families. The social and economic change wrought by contact served to differentiate Inuit from non-Inuit and to emphasize commonalities among Inuit, resulting in what has been termed "Inuit nationalism."[33] Thus, while regional divisions and antagonisms are certainly evident in contemporary Nunavut society and politics, they are generally subsumed into a larger Inuit identity and unity.

Life in the communities and (partial) integration into the wage economy also brought about economic differentiation among Inuit and development of a class system. Various forms and gradations of class groupings among Inuit can be discerned according to their role in productive practices, their participation in traditional or wage economies, their status as independent commodity producers, state workers, petty capitalists and the like.[34] While such class divisions do have relevance to social and political developments, they do not represent the defining socioeconomic dynamic within Nunavut society. In part this is because the Inuit economic elite remains small, as does the Inuit middle class, and in part it reflects disinclination among Inuit to think in terms of or identify themselves with standard class perspectives (while some Inuit belong to trade unions, for example, organized labour has only shallow roots in Inuit society).[35] Most critical, however, is the conjunction between class and ethnicity. The economic elite of Nunavut has long been primarily non-Inuit. Ownership and control of private capital—be it large firms based in the south or smaller, locally owned enterprises—is very much in the hands of non-Inuit. Similarly, non-Inuit predominate in high-paying, influential public-sector jobs, which carry unusual economic significance in a region as dependent on government as Nunavut.

Mitchell has described a process of dramatic and rapid social change among the Inuit, a "transformation of Inuit relationships from relatively egalitarian, apolitical family-based units to ethnoregional collectivities in which class distinctions are becoming an important line of affiliation."[36] Inuit are acutely aware of their subordinate economic status, but until recently they have seen the solution less in explicitly class terms than in enhanced political capacity as a people to run their own affairs. In short, culture, not class, has been the primary dynamic driving Inuit political activity. The rise of an Inuit economic elite, in large measure through the growth of the claims-funded development corporations, and the emergence of a strong Inuit political-administrative elite with the creation of Nunavut portend significant change in this dynamic.

As occurred in aboriginal societies elsewhere in Canada, an identifiable Inuit political elite emerged in the late 1960s and 1970s. Educated in non-Inuit ways yet rooted in a strong sense of Inuit identity, this political-administrative elite was not prepared to accept second-class status in their own land. Reflecting on this period, Tagak Curley—who was elected President of the Inuit Tapirisat of Canada (ITC) at its founding meeting in 1971—has noted that "The government's colonial system had a lot of power.... When I was growing up my parents were afraid of the white man. The government people were very intimidating to them. This was too much for me.... I knew I had a mission.... My mission was to create a voice for the Inuit people."[37] Though less aggressive and confrontational than other aboriginal leaders, and pragmatic as to the means of reaching their goal, the leadership of the Inuit organizations never wavered in their determination to establish an Inuit homeland. The principal vehicle the Inuit chose for pursuing their political goals was a sweeping land claim linked to a proposal for creation of an Inuit-dominated territory—Nunavut—in the eastern and central Arctic.

The pioneers of the land claim movement faced a degree of resistance from within Inuit society. Some Inuit thought that this might be the "communism" that the priests had warned them about and so the few who had been incorporated into the new elite in the NWT joined non-Inuit attacks on those in the land claim movement as radicals. Creating Nunavut would "really be quitting Canada because the principles of Canadian Confederation are against racial division," wrote one Inuit Member of the Yellowknife Assembly in Yellowknife, "with the territorial government's continuing plan to turn over more and more control for local matters to the local people, the Inuit have a bright political future and don't need their own territory."[38] Public education campaigns quickly resulted in overwhelming Inuit support for the proposal.

THE NUNAVUT LAND CLAIM

Negotiating the Claim

The first detailed proposal was put to the federal government by the Inuit Tapirisat of Canada in 1976. Through a decade and a half of protracted negotiations, which often seemed to have encountered insurmountable obstacles, the Inuit never wavered on their fundamental principles. Foremost among these were settlement of a comprehensive land claim which would set out and enshrine Inuit use of their lands, would compensate them for past and future use of Inuit lands by non-Inuit, and would create a new government in the eastern and central Arctic with capacity to protect and foster Inuit language, culture and social well-being.

A critical element in the Inuit position—which ultimately made it palatable to a reluctant federal government—was their willingness to accept in the new territory a "public government" rather than "aboriginal self-government." Under this public government approach all residents could vote, run for office, and otherwise participate in public affairs while the government's jurisdiction and activities would extend to all residents. In other words, Nunavut would in essence have a government like those of the provinces and territories, rather than following the aboriginal self-government model (proposed by many First Nations, including those in the

Mackenzie Valley) under which only aboriginal people would participate in government or be eligible for its programs and services.

If the Inuit were open—both philosophically and as a negotiating strategy—to the notion of a public government, they were insistent that they did not wish to be part of the existing Northwest Territories (which by the time the Nunavut negotiations were completed had attained very close to full responsible government and most of the important province-like powers). Inuit were never more than a large minority in the NWT (they constituted approximately 38 per cent of the population at the time of division) and the centres of economic and political power in the NWT were simply too remote, both geographically and culturally, from Inuit communities (Yellowknife, the NWT capital, is as far from Baffin Island communities as Vancouver is from Thunder Bay). Thus although Inuit were vitally concerned with decisions, programs, and funding from the NWT Government, their principal political focus was on creating Nunavut. (Inuit leader John Amagoalik once observed that the MLAs elected to the territorial legislature in Yellowknife were the Inuit "B Team"; the "A Team" was working on the land claim.)[39]

The political machinations and the events which culminated in the finalization of the Inuit land claim are far too complex to be reviewed here.[40] Moreover, for our purposes, the processes by which the land claim was realized are less important than its provisions. Suffice it to say that a slow, unspectacular process of negotiations unfolded throughout much of the 1980s. Bit by bit, sub-agreement by sub-agreement, a comprehensive land-claims settlement was put together. Progress was aided somewhat by the revision of federal land-claims policy in the wake of the 1985 Coolican Task Force Report. Revisions sanctioning decision-making powers for joint management boards, resource revenue sharing, and inclusion of offshore areas were particularly important for the Nunavut claim. Nunavut Inuit organizations played a significant part in the lobbying efforts needed to amend federal land claims policy to these ends.[41]

As one of the key players at the staff level for the Inuit organisations has noted,

> Moments of crisis and drama notwithstanding, the story of the twenty year old "Nunavut project" is best described as a process of consistent effort, endless negotiation, and detailed text. Unlike other negotiations involving aboriginal peoples that have sometimes captured intensive but fleeting attention, the "Nunavut project" ... followed a slow but comparatively steady course.[42]

By the early 1990s, most of the proprietary and resource management aspects of an agreement had been put together, and the moment of truth arrived: would Inuit accept the limitations of federal claims policy and drop the demand for a separate Nunavut territory and government in order to go forward, or would they put twenty years of efforts on the line by insisting "no Nunavut, no deal"?

Confident that the Inuit public would not accept a land-claims agreement without an accompanying commitment on a Nunavut territory and government, Inuit negotiators stood firm on the demand that the Nunavut Agreement contain—within its four corners, not in some collateral undertaking—a commitment to create Nunavut. Government of Canada representatives understood the depth of Inuit resolve on this point and, to the credit of those Ministers of the Crown and public servants working on the file, agreed to include the commitment to Nunavut as part of a land-claims agreement. The agreement was formalized in a document called the Nunavut Political Accord, signed by the Government of Canada, the GNWT, and the Inuit negotiating body Tungavik Federation of Nunavut (TFN).

The Conservative government of the day, under the increasingly unpopular prime minister Brian Mulroney, was badly in need of a "good news" story about its relationship with aboriginal peoples. The armed stand-off with the Mohawks at Oka, Québec, had made headlines and television newscasts around the world, and the country's political elites seemed unable to amend the Constitution to include (among other things) stronger guarantees of aboriginal peoples' self-government rights. In this context, even some politicians who had previously expressed reservations about Nunavut came to regard it as a positive, progressive initiative which the Canadian state could—and should—embrace.

The inclusion of a commitment to a Nunavut territory and government went well beyond the stated federal government land-claims policy of the time. This reality, no doubt, created certain political and bureaucratic risks for those involved in the negotiations. Calculated risks were also run by the Inuit, most notably in agreeing to territory-wide plebiscites in 1982 and 1992; the first was on the principle of dividing the NWT, the second on the specific boundary between the two new territories. In both, voters in the western part of the NWT opposed division while an overwhelming majority in Nunavut supported it—the overall result being a slim majority in favour.

Agreement on the precise boundary was a serious sticking point. Aside from Baker Lake, no permanent settlements are to be found in the vast tract of land between Great Slave Lake and the Inuit communities on Hudson Bay. However, both Inuit leaders and their Dene and Métis counterparts of the Mackenzie Valley sought control over these lands, with both groups pointing to eons of nomadic occupation, primarily for hunting. A boundary settlement was almost reached in the late 1980s, but ultimately negotiations proved unsuccessful. Yet without a definite boundary the Nunavut project could not proceed. In order to break the deadlock, the federal government appointed John Parker, the widely respected former commissioner, to consult those affected and propose a boundary. It was his compromise—a compromise generally acceptable to Inuit, but strongly opposed by certain Dene-Métis groups for whom it encroached too far into their traditional lands—that was put to a vote in 1992. (Shortly after the boundary was settled, the disputed territory turned out to be the focus of an intense diamond rush, but diamonds had not been a factor in the boundary conflict. Although promising sites exist in Nunavut, the first operating diamond mine is in the NWT just to the west of the boundary.)

The land claim itself was ratified in November of 1992: 69 per cent of eligible Inuit voters supported the settlement.[43] Inuit and government representatives signed the Nunavut Land Claims Agreement[44] in Iqaluit on May 25, 1993. Finally, in June 1993, Parliament enacted two separate pieces of legislation—the *Nunavut Land Claims Agreement Act* (ratifying the Nunavut land claim settlement), and the *Nunavut Act* (creating a Nunavut territory and government). Taken together, these two measures constitute the terms of a new social contract, or terms of confederation, between the Inuit of Nunavut and the people and government of Canada. The perspective of the Inuit leaders who first envisioned and articulated this new relationship and then negotiated it into reality is well expressed by one of their key legal counsel:

> ... it is remarkable to note how similar, in broad brush, the results of the "Nunavut project" are to the initial negotiating demands put forward in 1976. After almost two decades of hard work, concentration on the essential, willingness to take calculated risks, and refusal to take no for an answer, the Inuit of Nunavut have secured the Crown's agreement to a package that provides the Inuit of Nunavut with both an impressive array of land rights and responsibilities in their ancestral homeland and a new Nunavut Territory and Government that will, on account of an overwhelming Inuit majority, provide Inuit with political power in the contemporary legislative and administrative context of Canadian federalism.[45]

The Provisions of the Claim

As is the case with other comprehensive land-claim settlements, the Nunavut Land Claims Agreement (NLCA) is a "modern day treaty" which is entrenched under section 35 of the *Constitution Act, 1982*.

The Preamble to the NLCA states four basic objectives shared by the parties to the Agreement:

- » to provide for certainty and clarity of rights to ownership and use of lands and resources, and of rights for Inuit to participate in decision-making concerning the use, management and conservation of land, water and resources, including the offshore.
- » to provide Inuit with wildlife harvesting rights and rights to participate in decision making concerning wildlife harvesting.
- » to provide Inuit with financial compensation and means of participating in economic opportunities.
- » to encourage self-reliance and social well-being of Inuit.

At the heart of the NLCA is a fundamental exchange between the Inuit of Nunavut and the federal Crown. For their part, the Inuit agreed to surrender "any claims, rights, title and interests based on their assertion of an aboriginal title" anywhere in Canada (including the Nunavut Settlement Area). In return, the Agreement set out an array of constitutionally protected rights and benefits which the Inuit of Nunavut will exercise and enjoy in perpetuity. The most important of these provisions for the Inuit beneficiaries are:

- » $1.176 billion, to be paid over a 14-year period; these monies—administered by Nunavut Tunngavik Incorporated (NTI), the Inuit organization responsible for overseeing the claim—are not paid to individuals but are for the collective benefit of all Nunavut Inuit.
- » collective title to approximately 350,000 square kilometres of land, of which roughly 10 per cent include sub-surface mineral rights.
- » establishment of a series of co-management boards (often referred to as institutions of public government—or, in the acronym-laden North, IPGS) which will work alongside the Nunavut government but will not be a part of it. The Nunavut Wildlife Management Board (NWMB), for example, has equal numbers of Inuit-appointed and government-appointed members[46] to oversee wildlife harvesting and management, as well as specific wildlife harvesting rights and economic opportunities related to guiding, sports lodges, and commercial marketing of wildlife products. Other IPGS include the

Nunavut Planning Commission (NPC), with responsibility for land use planning; the Nunavut Impact Review Board (NIRB), which conducts environmental and socioeconomic reviews of development proposals; and the Nunavut Water Board (NWB).

» a series of other provisions, such as commitments to increase Inuit employment in government and to give preference to Inuit-owned businesses in government contracting, a share in royalties on non-renewable resources, a $13-million training trust fund, and a federal commitment to establish three national parks in Nunavut.

» last, but certainly not least: a commitment to create a Nunavut territory and a Nunavut government on April 1, 1999.

In effect, the Inuit of Nunavut surrendered their rights to lands and resources at common law—their "aboriginal title"—for the measures contained in the NLCA. This exchange did not involve any surrender of Inuit rights to self-government in existence at the time the land claim was agreed to, or which may be defined by future constitutional amendments.

Implementation of the NLCA is proceeding within the framework provided by a formal *Contract Relating to the Implementation of the Nunavut Final Agreement*, which was signed on May 25, 1993 in Iqaluit by TFN and by the federal and territorial governments. It contains extensive details on the responsibilities of many parties involved in the implementation of the NLCA, the activities this will require, time frames and guidelines for such activities, and the financial resources for implementation which will be allocated during the first ten-year period. A basic assumption running through the Implementation Contract is that successful implementation of the NLCA depends on the cooperation and commitment of many different parties, including Inuit organizations, departments of the federal and territorial governments, and the newly created IPGS.

The Implications of the Claim

A key objective of the NLCA is to implement a new land and resource management system in the Nunavut Settlement Area (NSA; the area to which the terms of the land claim apply) to replace an existing system which was perceived by Inuit negotiators to be "ad hoc, incremental, and fragmented...."[47] This system is intended to be comprehensive, exercising authority over the entire NSA including surface lands, waters, marine areas, and the maximum limit of land fast ice. It is also intended to achieve integration, linking a number of different institutions and processes together in one unified management system with jurisdiction over both Crown- and Inuit-owned lands in Nunavut.

Of central importance in this system will be the linkages established between land/habitat and wildlife management. At the centre of this new set of power-sharing arrangements between Inuit and non-Inuit are the four co-management bodies, or IPGs. In a strict legal sense, these institutions are "advisory" bodies who will make recommendations to federal and territorial government ministers, but in practice they are clearly intended to be decision-makers with sufficient resources and authority to function relatively independently from both government departments and Inuit organizations. The powers and authorities of existing federal and territorial departments are neither replaced nor superseded by those of the IPGs, but government departments are now required to share some of their powers and to include the co-management bodies in their decision-making processes. Depending on the issue, this power sharing will take various forms, ranging from structured consultations to a department's need to secure the "approval" of an IPG before proceeding with a decision or policy.

In the final analysis, the decisions of these institutions of public government are subject to ministerial authority and discretion. Even so, the NLCA spells out a number of conditions and circumstances under which this ministerial authority will be exercised. Beyond this, most of the traditional responsibilities of government departments will continue. Implementation of the NLCA is thus creating a new political and administrative regime in the eastern Arctic; a "regime" in the sense of "a method or system of government." Many types of important decisions are no longer made by unelected and/or unaccountable people in faraway board rooms; they are made in Nunavut, largely by residents of Nunavut. And "while the Nunavut Agreement provides for a wide range of constitutionally protected rights and benefits to Inuit, and to Inuit alone, it also reforms fundamentally the structures and processes for making decisions about the use of natural resources owned by the Crown."[48]

A good example of the magnitude of the changes brought about by the NLCA was the 1996 harvest of a bowhead whale near Repulse Bay. The fact that the federal Minister of Fisheries signed a permit authorizing the hunt made news in southern Canada. What was less clearly explained was that the authority to decide whether or not to harvest a bowhead now rests with the Nunavut Wildlife Management Board, and only the presentation of overwhelmingly contradictory data on the stocks—and the expenditure of significant political capital—could have prevented the federal minister from rubber-stamping the NWMB's decision.[49]

Similarly, the days are over of mining and other companies planning large projects in isolation from Inuit communities which would be affected. The NLCA requires that Inuit Impact and Benefit Agreements (IIBAs) be negotiated between the Inuit and the would-be developer. The first such

IIBA, between the Kitikmeot Inuit Association and Echo Bay Mines Ltd. for development of the Ulu gold deposit, covers the full range of "matters considered appropriate for Inuit benefits" under Schedule 26-1 of the NLCA. It is a legally binding agreement which aboriginal communities threatened by large non-renewable resource development elsewhere in the world would find mind-boggling.

One of the least recognized—yet farthest reaching—implications of the NLCA is that government departments must "consult" Inuit organizations and IPGs on most management decisions, policies, initiatives, and activities applicable in Nunavut. The fiduciary nature of government's obligation to undertake appropriate consultations was reinforced by a 1997 Federal Court decision on the "turbot dispute" between NTI and the Minister of Fisheries and Oceans. In his ruling, Justice Campbell remarked:

> I consider it very important to remember that the Agreement was struck within a context of acknowledgment of an Aboriginal right. The Agreement is, therefore, a solemn arrangement.... In particular, with respect to these provisions regarding "consultation" and "consideration," I find that they must be fully enforced.[50]

A subsequent court ruling overturned this particular decision, and the whole issue of consultation remains subject to legal action. Still, regardless of how consultation requirements are ultimately defined, their significance lies not in constituting an Inuit veto over governments, but in requiring governments to be acutely aware of, and sensitive to, Inuit concerns.

Finally, while many of the most talented Inuit managers have left the various levels of government to work for NTI, the regional Inuit associations, and the IPGs, implementation of the NLCA has also resulted in an important transformation of the ethnic framework: for the first time, there are now significant numbers of Euro-Canadians working for Inuit, reversing decades of subservience to Euro-Canadians in the wage economy.

THE NUNAVUT GOVERNMENT

Designing the Nunavut Government

To facilitate the creation of Nunavut, the *Nunavut Act* established a Nunavut Implementation Commission. The NIC was initially composed of nine commissioners and a chief commissioner—veteran Inuit leader John Amagoalik—appointed by the three signatories to the Nunavut Political Accord. Of the original ten commissioners, nine were Inuit, nine were resident in Nunavut, and eight were men.

The NIC's mandate was to advise the three signatories on the political and administrative design of the Nunavut government, including such diverse matters as the location of the capital, the development of human resources training programs, the organizational structure of the new government, the timetable for the assumption of the Nunavut government's responsibilities for the delivery of programs and services, and the division of assets and liabilities between Nunavut and the western territory.

Throughout the years from the passage of the *Nunavut Act* to the formal start-up of Nunavut in 1999, major policy decisions on governmental structure, implementation strategy, scheduling, and the like were made through a series of "Nunavut Leaders' Summits." These meetings took place two or three times a year in various Nunavut communities and brought together the elected leaders of the GNWT, NTI, and the Government of Canada, along with members of the NIC. The atmosphere of these meetings ranged from amicable and cooperative to bitter and confrontational, but they were crucial in giving political direction to the officials working towards setting up the new government. They also symbolized the genuine partnership, albeit at times a stormy one, between the signatories to the NCLA and the Nunavut Political Accord.

The NIC released its first comprehensive report, *Footprints in New Snow*, in March 1995. Over the following year and a half the NIC published eight specialized supplementary reports and then a second comprehensive report, *Footprints 2*, in October 1996. The NIC's political recommendations were contained in a supplementary report entitled *Nunavut's Legislature, Premier and First Election*, released in December 1996.

The GNWT did not respond in writing to *Footprints in New Snow*, but did issue a written response to *Footprints 2*. NTI responded in writing to both of the NIC's comprehensive reports, and their response to *Footprints 2* also contained a response to the NIC 's political recommendations. The NIC recommended the creation of what John Amagoalik termed "a public government with a democratically elected Legislative Assembly [which] will respect individual and collective rights as defined in the *Canadian Charter of Rights and Freedoms*. It will be a government that respects and reflects Canada's political traditions and institutions, and it will be a territory that remains firmly entrenched within the bounds of Canadian confederation."[51] As Amagoalik had promised years previously, "What we are proposing is not new; it will be a creature that Canadians will recognize."[52]

Initially, some thought it best for the Nunavut government to phase in over several years the active control over its full range of powers. On NIC's recommendation, however, the Nunavut government assumed responsibility for the full range of its jurisdictional powers on April 1, 1999. Since only about a third of a projected 640 headquarters staff were in place as of formal start-up,[53] a number of services and activities were contracted back to the government of the (post-division) NWT until the government of Nunavut was ready to deliver them. (In other words, for the first few years many programs and services which the people of Nunavut receive from the territorial level of government will be provided by GNWT staff—under contract to the Nunavut government.)[54] Examples include teacher certification and student records, health promotion services and tax collection. Even in areas contracted back to the GNWT, however, the government of Nunavut retains political control and policy direction.

The NIC recommended that the Nunavut government should be a streamlined government—leaner and more effective than the GNWT. *Footprints in New Snow* recommended a structure of just ten departments, no regional health boards, and a single, elected education board.[55] In addition to the community and regional-level staff already employed by the GNWT, the NIC projected that just over 600 new headquarters positions would be required—considerably fewer than previous estimates had assumed.

The Nunavut government will ultimately be highly decentralized. (All governments have networks of regional and local offices, but these are typically restricted to service delivery; the core functions of government administration, such as policy development, tend to be concentrated in the capital city.) For some it was important that the Nunavut government be decentralized so that as many communities as possible could share in the economic benefits arising from the stable, well-paid jobs that would come with the new government. Others believed that locating middle management and professional positions in communities would encourage Inuit participation in the bureaucracy. Still others saw a decentralized government as better suited to traditional Inuit political culture.

The NIC felt that modern communication technologies would allow extensive decentralization of the Nunavut government; however there was considerable debate both inside and outside the commission on the best way to achieve decentralization. One school of thought held that all the deputy ministers and their senior managers must be based in the capital, with decentralization to occur by placing some divisions (organizational subsets of departments) and many boards and agencies in smaller communities. (There was general agreement that "headquarters" jobs could not be spread across all of Nunavut's 25 communities, but that the ten largest communities—in addition to the capital—should have Nunavut government offices of some kind. All Nunavut communities have community-based territorial government workers such as teachers, nurses, etc.) Another school of thought held that the departments should be grouped by Executive/Central Agencies, Human Services, and Technical Services, with each "group" of departments (up to and including the deputy ministers) located in one of the three regional centres. The former school of thought won out, to the surprise and disappointment of those who had believed that popular support for the principle of "not recreating Yellowknife" (i.e., not centralizing government employment, economic benefits, and political power in the territorial capital of the NWT) would result in entire departments being located outside the capital.

The decentralization debate is reflective of two broader perspectives on the NIC's recommendations considered in their entirety. One holds that the NIC recommended an extremely conventional design, and thereby wasted an opportunity to radically rethink government from an Inuit perspective, while the other holds that the NIC's recommendations, while well intentioned, are optimistic to the point of naiveté about how cumbersome and expensive it will be to operate a decentralized government across a fifth of the land mass of Canada.

Given the need for extensive infrastructure construction (staff housing as well as office facilities) in the ten communities outside Iqaluit, and the complex implementation issues arising from large-scale transfer of jobs, it will be another 18 to 24 months before the decentralized model is completely in place. To take one example of what decentralization will mean, in the Department of Sustainable Development, the Policy, Planning and Payroll, Finance and Administration, and Parks, Protected Areas, and Tourism branches will be in Iqaluit, along with the deputy minister, but other headquarters units will be located outside the capital. The Fisheries, Wildlife and Environmental Protection branch will be in Igloolik; the Minerals, Oil and Gas branch will be in Arviat; and the Community Economic Development branch, along with the Nunavut Development Corporation and the Nunavut Business Development Corporation, will be in Cape Dorset. In addition, there are to be large regional offices in Pond Inlet and Kugluktuk and smaller regional offices in Arviat and Rankin Inlet.

The choice of a capital was one of the more "political" aspects of the NIC's mandate, and the commission therefore approached it with caution. The Commission developed a detailed analysis of how well the three leading contenders for the capital met the criteria it had established for the government as a whole—in particular, how well each of them fit in with the NIC's model of a decentralized government. After completing this analysis, the Commission acknowledged that Iqaluit was the best choice under the most important criteria, but stopped short of actually recommending that it be named the capital. The Nunavut leadership was unable to achieve consensus on the matter, and the delay in selecting a capital was threatening other aspects of the planning process, so Ron Irwin, the Minister of Indian and Northern Affairs, called for a public vote on the question. On December 11, 1995, 60 per cent of the voters chose Iqaluit over Rankin Inlet to be their capital.

Inuit rightly perceive that for the Nunavut government to serve their interests and to foster their culture, its staff must reflect the largely Inuit population and it must use Inuktitut as a working language. Article 23 of the land claim commits governments to "representative" levels of Inuit participation in the bureaucracy, but specifies no time frame. NIC recommended that 50 per cent of jobs at all levels of the Nunavut Government be filled by Inuit at start-up in 1999, with representative levels—i.e., 85 per cent Inuit—by 2008. Recruitment, training, and retention of Inuit for middle and senior management positions (which is closely tied to the use of Inuktitut, since few non-Inuit speak or write it) looms as one of the more problematic areas in developing the Nunavut government. The federal and territorial governments, NTI, NIC, and the Nunavut Implementation Training Committee developed a comprehensive Unified Human Resources Development Strategy, with short- and long-term responses to the problem. Ottawa allocated $40 million to fund this initiative, part of a $150-million allocation by the federal Cabinet to cover start-up costs associated with the creation of the new territory, including training costs, capital expenditures, operation and maintenance budgets, and the Office of the Interim Commissioner. This was substantially less than previous estimates.[56]

Designing the Nunavut Political System

The most controversial of the NIC's recommendations were those dealing with Nunavut's political system. Among the ironies of the creation of Nunavut was the federal government's establishment of the NIC to advise on a political system for Nunavut when only thirty years before it had offered to Inuit such simple-minded explanations of democracy as the following:

> Several men in the community will have been nominated to each position on the Council. In order to decide which of the men should have those positions, an election was held. Each person was probably asked

> to write, on a slip of paper, the name of the man he or she wished to have on the Council. When the voting was completed, the votes were counted and the man who received the highest number of votes was declared elected. It is unlikely that everyone voted for the man who was elected. People do not all think the same way so they are not likely at all to want the same man in office. The man who won the election was elected by the majority of the voters. The minority of the voters had to accept the decision of the majority. This is what democracy means.[57]

Prior to division the residents of Nunavut elected 10 of the 24 members of the Legislative Assembly of the Northwest Territories. The NWT legislature had no political parties; candidates presented themselves to the voters as individuals. In keeping with the Canadian norm, each electoral district elected a single Member of the Legislative Assembly (MLA). Despite the absence of parties, government followed the basic constitutional precepts of British-style "responsible government," with some uniquely northern modifications to the standard Westminster cabinet-parliamentary system. For example, the premier and the cabinet were elected by secret ballot of all 24 MLAs. The premier assigned ministers to portfolios and could discipline them, including firing them, as required. The premier could be disciplined—and, if necessary, replaced—by the MLAs.

The NIC recommended that Nunavut's first premier should be selected in the same manner as the premier of the Northwest Territories was chosen. There is considerable public support for strengthening the role of the premier by having that position directly elected by the voters, but the NIC concluded that there are so many complex and unresolved problems with this concept that it should be deferred to the first Nunavut Legislative Assembly. (Essentially, direct election of the premier involves grafting a new element onto the Westminster system of parliamentary government, an element which doesn't "fit" well with the internal logic of that system and may in fact be constitutionally incompatible with it. For example, if the premier is directly elected by the voters, how can he/she be disciplined by the MLAs? What is the relationship between the premier, the rest of the cabinet, and the rest of the MLAs? How would the premier be replaced if he/she were removed from office, resigned or died?) At a Nunavut Leaders' Summit in Cambridge Bay, the three parties to the Nunavut Political Accord agreed to an elected premiership for Nunavut "if practicable," but by the time of the January 1998 Nunavut Leaders' Summit in Iqaluit they had agreed that the issue should be decided after division. Nunavut's first premier was therefore selected in the same manner as the premier of the Northwest Territories.

Concerned that a very small legislature might prove unworkable, the NIC initially recommended that the Nunavut Legislative Assembly should consist of between 18 and 24 members and later narrowed its recommendation to either 20 or 22 members.[58] The three parties to the Nunavut Political Accord agreed with this recommendation. While the number of members may not have been surprising, the manner in which they might be selected was. The NIC recommended that the Nunavut Legislative Assembly should consist of equal numbers of men and women, using a system of 10 or 11 two-member constituencies each electing one male MLA and one female MLA.

Encouraged by the conviction of Chief Commissioner John Amagoalik, the Commission had expressed a desire to do whatever it could to encourage the full participation of women in Nunavut's political life. After spirited internal debate, in December 1994 the NIC released a discussion paper on the use of two-member constituencies with gender parity as a good way to achieve this. The Commission avoided making exaggerated claims for the merits of its proposal, and instead made a minimalist argument that the people of Nunavut would be best represented if the two abiding subsets of humanity were equally represented—especially in light of the disjunctive relations which exist between men and women in Nunavut today, and the scale of the social problems which the new government will face.[59]

Part of the beauty of such a proposal lies in its simplicity. When Nunavut's first election was called, the names of men wanting to run for MLA would have gone on one list and the names of women wanting to run for MLA would have gone on another list. On election day, each voter would be given two ballots—one for candidates on the list of male candidates and one for candidates on the list of female candidates. In each electoral district, both the man with the most votes and the woman with the most votes would be elected. Since each electoral district would be represented by one male MLA and one female MLA, the Nunavut Legislative Assembly would have been the first legislature in the world to have gender parity guaranteed by its very makeup. The proposal would also have functioned equally well with or without "party politics"—an important point since many people expect political parties to be formed in Nunavut in the future.

Despite its simplicity, there were two popular misconceptions about this proposal. The first was that men would vote for male candidates and women would vote for female candidates, the implication being that the NIC believed that only men can speak for men and only women can speak for women. In fact, each voter—male or female—would have cast two votes, one for a man and one for a woman. The second misconception was that gender parity would inflate the size of the legislature and increase the costs accordingly (*News/North*, a newspaper based in Yellowknife, erroneously estimated that the NIC's proposal would have cost the taxpayers an additional $1.8 to $2.2 million per year). In fact, since Canada, the GNWT, and NTI had agreed that there would be between 20 and 22 MLAS in the Nunavut Legislative Assembly, the question was only how those 20 to 22 MLAS would be selected, and there would have been no appreciable cost difference between electing 20 MLAS from 10 two-member constituencies and electing 20 MLAS from 20 single-member constituencies.

The release of the discussion paper ignited a vigorous public debate on the issue of women in politics in general, and on the proposal for gender parity in the Nunavut Legislative Assembly in particular. After receiving more positive than negative comment, the NIC formally recommended the proposal to the three parties to the Nunavut Political Accord in December 1996.[60] Nunavut Tunngavik Inc. also gave the proposal its strong endorsement, and despite some initial misgivings DIAND Minister Ron Irwin also came out in support. While some members of the Nunavut Caucus (the MLAS elected to represent Nunavut in the Legislative Assembly of the Northwest Territories) endorsed the proposal, most did not—with the most vociferous opponent being Manitok Thompson, the only female member of the Nunavut Caucus and the Minister Responsible for the Status of Women. At the Nunavut Leaders' Summit in Cambridge Bay, the GNWT surprised and angered the other parties around the table by peremptorily issuing a press release calling for a public vote on the matter. Since the three parties to the Nunavut Political Accord strove to reach agreement by consensus, and since the Nunavut Caucus refused to join the rest of the Nunavut leadership in support of the proposal, Minister Irwin agreed to hold a public vote on the question.

The campaign in the weeks leading up to the vote generated more heat than light. The "Yes" side was composed of NIC Chief Commissioner John Amagoalik, most of the NTI Board of Directors, the President of Pauktuutit (the national Inuit women's association), and youth and elder representatives. With $75,000 in financial support from NTI they produced and distributed pamphlets, posters and buttons, and—in the style of the "community tours" which had been used to inform Inuit of the contents of the land claim—chartered a small aircraft to visit a number of the communities for "town hall" style meetings.

The "No" side was less organized and largely unfunded. Manitok Thompson and other opponents of the proposal, the most vocal of whom resided in Rankin Inlet and Igloolik, joined the "Yes" side in making their arguments on phone-in shows on both community radio stations and Nunavut-wide CBC current affairs programs. The multiple lines of argument used by those opposing the proposal made it difficult for the "Yes" side to respond effectively. Some opponents clearly didn't understand the proposal, and argued that it would cost too much, or force men to be represented by men and women to be represented by women. Most opponents did understand the proposal, however, and argued that it would sow division between men and women where none currently existed, that women would be seen as "affirmative action" MLAs whose opinions would be taken less seriously than that of male MLAs, and that women need to "beat" men in order to be taken seriously in politics.

Where supporters saw a unique opportunity to implement a vision of a more balanced political system, opponents saw a plan which insulted women's abilities to get elected if they chose to run. Where supporters saw a way to recognize the differing perspectives that men and women tend to have on any given issue, opponents argued that disproportionate gender representation in politics is not important—that "people think with what's between their ears, not with what's between their legs." Where supporters saw a way to achieve a new partnership between men and women, opponents were insulted by a proposal that would "send women back to the stone age." Where supporters saw a gender-equal legislature as a return to the values of traditional Inuit society, in which families were built on an equal division of labour between men and women, opponents dismissed this view as a romanticized retelling of history. And where supporters saw the proposal as reflecting the "creative but within Canadian political norms" tone of the Nunavut project as a whole, opponents saw it as an unwelcome, unnecessary and unworkable scheme that the Nunavut leadership was trying to force on an unsuspecting electorate.

A vocal minority went so far as to suggest—often on Biblical grounds—that women have no business in politics, and widely held conservative religious beliefs appear to have been an important factor in the outcome. While many Christians, including some clergy, supported the proposal, the great majority of people commenting on it from a religious perspective were strongly opposed to it. (While most people think of shamanism when they think of Inuit religious beliefs, the population of Nunavut today tends to adhere to what anthropologist Robert Williamson has called "a quasi-fundamentalist, low-church Anglicanism," Roman Catholicism, or evangelical fundamentalism.)

The "damn the elites and their agreements" mindset which helped sink the Charlottetown Accord resonated in a side debate which came to dominate public discussion in the closing days of the campaign. The NTI Board of Directors had voted a modest amount of money to be used to publicize their support of the proposal, as they had done on other issues previously. Opponents of the proposal complained that NTI had no business "telling people how to vote," and that at the very least they should receive equal funding for pamphlets, posters, buttons, and community tours.

On May 26, 1997, the voters rejected the NIC's proposal for a Nunavut Legislature with gender parity by a margin of 57 to 43 per cent. In the absence of any polling data, one can only speculate on the reasons for this result. One explanation might be that while Nunavut residents expressed their desire for a government that is "different" from the GNWT, the GNWT remained the reference point for discussion of how the new government should be structured and how it should operate. The "one man, one vote" norm for electoral systems in Canada has been accepted and internalized as "the way elections are done," even though the results tend to be "one vote, one man"—indeed the Legislative Assembly of the NWT had the lowest proportion of female members of any provincial or territorial legislature in Canada. The NIC's suggestion to choose representatives in a slightly different manner was regarded by many people as just plain loopy.

Some may have voted against the proposal less because they objected to gender parity in the legislature than because they didn't wish to see dual-member ridings. A system with twice as many single-member districts would enhance the prospects of individual communities having their "own" MLAS. Another factor worth considering is the very low voter turn-out for the vote—just 39 per cent. Again, in the absence of polling data one can only speculate on the reasons for this. The date of the vote, in late spring when many families had already left town for spring camping, might have been a factor. But it might also be the case that while gender parity in decision-making structures is an issue that some people passionately support, and while other people are hotly opposed to measures intended to achieve gender parity, many people either didn't think the issue was worthy of all the attention it was receiving or were put off by the tone of the debate it had sparked.

While the debate was playing itself out, a three-person Nunavut Electoral Boundaries Commission (NEBC) was touring Nunavut communities. The NEBC had been established by the Legislative Assembly of the NWT to make recommendations on the area, boundaries, names and representation of Nunavut's electoral districts. As the public vote had not yet decided the question of gender parity and two-member constituencies, the NEBC was directed to include options for both 10 or 11 dual-member and 20 to 22 single-member electoral districts. The NEBC's report contained models for those options, but the Commission recommended a third option—a system of 17 single-member electoral districts in which Iqaluit would have two electoral districts and the 15 other electoral districts would contain between one and four communities each. The reason given in the report was that during community consultations "many citizens expressed a genuine concern about the expense of having 20-22 MLAS in the Nunavut legislature."[61] The NEBC did not address the NIC's rationale as to the need for at least 20 MLAS to ensure the effective operation of the legislature. The

Legislative Assembly later endorsed the NEBC's recommendations with minor modifications, but NTI continued to push for a larger legislature—and at the January 1998 Nunavut Leaders' Summit the three parties to the Nunavut Political Accord finally agreed that Nunavut's legislature would consist of 19 electoral districts.

Building Core Capacity

The *Nunavut Act* had established NIC to advise the parties (the federal and territorial governments and NTI) on crucial political and administrative design features for the territorial government. It also made provision for an Interim Commissioner of Nunavut, a federal public servant empowered to finalize the design for the government and to implement it. This key official was authorized to hire staff for the new government, enter into contracts and intergovernmental agreements on its behalf and generally take whatever administrative steps were required to ensure that the Nunavut government was fully up and running on April 1, 1999.

Initial expectations were that the Interim Commissioner would have to be in place no later than the end of 1995 if the necessary work was to be completed on time. For various political reasons, however, it was not until April 1997 that the federal government appointed Jack Anawak, the region's Liberal Member of Parliament, to serve as Interim Commissioner. In January 1998, the Office of the Interim Commissioner's detailed plans for the Nunavut government, based closely on the *Footprints 2* model, were approved by the three parties. Shortly thereafter, the first set of deputy ministers was appointed, following a Canada-wide competition. Only three of the eleven deputies were Inuit; six more were veteran GNWT bureaucrats, mostly based in Nunavut. Criticism of the low proportion of Inuit in this top management cadre was somewhat muted by the hiring of 14 assistant deputy ministers (the next level down in the administrative hierarchy), all of whom were Inuit. The new deputies began the task of staffing their departments, working up budgets, and sorting out myriad administrative matters.

With an enormous amount of work, facilitated by extensive give-and-take on the part of the three parties, the logistical details of creating the new government were addressed. Because of time pressures and other difficulties, a substantial number of operational and service delivery functions (such as electronic data processing and teacher certification) were contracted back to the GNWT, to be taken over by the Nunavut government as its capacity developed. Similarly, the commitment to a decentralized government remained, but construction of the necessary infrastructure and the actual transfer of jobs to the communities had not progressed very far by April 1. A very few important matters, such as the disposition of ownership of the critically important Northwest Territories Power Corporation between Nunavut and the NWT, remained to be resolved after division.

Early Days: Nunavut's First Election and Government

Nunavut's first election took place on February 15, 1999. Seventy-one candidates, including 11 Inuit women and 7 non-Inuit men, put their names forward for the 19 seats; all ran as independents, following the "consensus" model which had developed in the NWT. A very high proportion—88 per cent—of those eligible to vote cast ballots, electing one woman (Manitok Thompson, the former NWT minister who had campaigned against a gender-equal legislature), 14 Inuit men, and 4 non-Inuit men. The voters returned some MLAs with extensive political experience but rejected others, such as former NWT deputy premier Goo Arlooktoo, who had been widely tabbed in the southern media as a likely premier, in favour of candidates with minimal political seasoning. Similarly, the new legislature contained both very traditional Inuit, with limited facility in English, and Inuit with professional training.

When the MLAs gathered in Iqaluit in March, they chose as premier not Jack Anawak, the apparent front-runner, but 34-year-old Paul Okalik, who had won the riding of Iqaluit West. For many, Okalik symbolized their hopes for the new territory: overcoming brushes with the law in his youth, he had worked on the land claim and later became the first Inuk lawyer from Nunavut. After choosing Okalik as premier, the MLAs chose the balance of Nunavut's first cabinet. Both Anawak and Thompson were included, as was veteran Inuit politician James Arvaluk, two non-Inuit men who had served in the NWT legislature, and two Inuit newcomers to territorial politics.

The new government quickly got down to work. On the one hand they found themselves with little room to manoeuvre, given the relentless pressures for social spending: on education, health, housing and social services; yet on the other hand, they set themselves lofty, if often imprecise, goals in a comprehensive document they—MLAs and ministers alike—developed during the summer of 1999, entitled the "Bathurst Mandate."[62] By and large the first few months of the Nunavut Government were characterized by a "stay the course" approach. With some notable exceptions, such as an early decision to eliminate the regional health and education boards in 2000 and a controversial decision to establish a single time zone for Nunavut (in place of the three that had previously existed), the government's efforts were principally consumed with the difficult task of building governance capacity while maintaining and improving delivery of public services.

APRIL 1999 AND AFTER: CELEBRATION AND CRITICISM

It was quite a party. The celebrations marking the creation of Nunavut on April 1, 1999 were centred in the capital, Iqaluit, but community feasts and dances were held across the new territory. The formal ceremonies were attended by the Governor General and Prime Minister of Canada, and were broadcast live on television from sea to sea to sea and around the world. "The thrill of victory is quickly replaced by the awesome amount of work that must be done," Prime Minister Jean Chrétien, a former federal Minister of Indian Affairs and Northern Development, said at a legislative ceremony rich in Inuit tradition and music, "As Nunavut takes flight, you are dealing with immense challenges. Whether it is educating your fast-growing population, alleviating poverty and social breakdown, or building the capacity within your own government to address these challenges, you have your work cut out for you."

The long-awaited creation of Nunavut also focussed unprecedented media attention on the eastern and central Arctic. Not only did all major Canadian news organizations send reporters and camera crews to Nunavut in the days leading up to April 1, but so too did literally dozens of American, European, and even Asian newspapers and television networks. Most of the coverage was positive and supportive, albeit with references to the magnitude of the task ahead. For example, the *Manchester Guardian*, one of Britain's pre-eminent newspapers, observed:

> the emergence of Nunavut is unequivocally good news. While large tracts of the world are mired in war and insurgency, an ethnic minority has quietly negotiated an equitable deal with a central government that gives them the freedom to run their own affairs.[63]

The *Globe and Mail* proclaimed,

> Canada has done something of huge symbolic value.... Nunavut is a powerful and worthy experiment [which] deserves to succeed.[64]

Time magazine's correspondent wrote:

> Canada's first de facto experiment with native self-government—and only the second of its kind in the world. [It is] a socio-political experiment on an epic scale.[65]

The *Baltimore Sun* newspaper called Nunavut

> a bold and risky experiment in native self-government, one that has fired the hopes of aboriginal people around the world, from the Maori of New Zealand to the Mohawks of New York. Nunavut might be a symbol of hope, but it is also a stronghold of despair. On the instant of its birth, it becomes the poorest territory, by far, in Canada—a welfare basket case where desperate social conditions are made worse by physical isolation and a brutal climate.[66]

A small but vocal media contingent reacted very negatively to Nunavut. From the political right, especially commentators and publications openly hostile to aboriginal self-government aspirations, came volleys of condemnation and misinformation. A columnist in *Alberta Report* magazine wrote:

> The 25,000 people who live in the new territory ... mostly speak a foreign language ... the Inuit will [likely] have to put up with decades of corruption and political oppression from their own leaders.... Perhaps we should be toasting the birth of Nunavut with a chunk of raw seal meat (and) a glass of narwhal blood ... the day will live in infamy, as a huge step towards the race-based partitioning of Canada.[67]

A columnist in *Report Newsmagazine*, *Alberta Report*'s attempt to reach a national audience, suggested

> With little likelihood of solving Nunavut's problems any time soon, federal taxpayers could be forgiven for wondering if it might be wiser to ship its entire population south. Housing and feeding an Inuit family of four in Orlando, Florida, where a decent two-bedroom apartment rents for under $1,000 per month, would be far cheaper than the $100,000-plus in transfers the same family requires in Nunavut. Even if the family opted for a two-bedroom, two-bathroom air-conditioned suite with full kitchen facilities at the Sea World Ramada, the annual room charge of $62,800 and a $2,500 monthly allowance would still save Canadians almost $10,000 a year.[68]

The *National Post's* David Frum observed:

> The new territory of Nunavut is shaping up to be a mess of corruption and maladministration that will prove catastrophic both for the Inuit and the Canadian taxpayer.... Look at the system of government Nunavut is adopting ... it is carefully arranging to eliminate any orga-

> nized locus of opposition to the government. The Nunavut legislature will have no political parties. The leaders of Nunavut explain this with a lot of "Dancing [sic] With Wolves" hooey about confrontation and criticism being alien to native ways of life, etc.... But the real purpose of the exclusion of any mechanism for opposition is to ensure that nobody in the legislature will have the resources and incentive to scrutinize the doings of the Nunavut territorial government.[69]

According to Mel Smith, a British Columbia-based opponent of native land claims, "Nunavut is a case study in interest group liberalism run amok ... proposed by aggressive bureaucrats, prodded by the most powerful lobby in the country and acceded to by compliant politicians,"[70] while the *Ottawa Citizen* called Nunavut Canada's "first Bantustan, an apartheid-style ethnic homeland."[71] The *Wall Street Journal* paraphrased Owen Lippert, spokesperson for the Fraser Institute (a British Columbia-based right-wing think tank), as saying "They [Inuit] ... can't sell the land unless they want to sell it back to the Crown; and ... they can't build anything deemed offensive: no strip malls, no parking lots. In other words, they are not allowed to do the things that makes owning private property a worthwhile investment."[72]

While some of these attacks reflect general hostility to aboriginal peoples' aspirations, many were really targeted at another land claim altogether—that of the Nisga'a First Nation in British Columbia. Most of Nunavut's recent critics have no history of interest in Nunavut, and no track record of research and writing on Nunavut. Most have never even bothered to visit Nunavut. What they are interested in, however, is using Nunavut as a vehicle for scaremongering about what ratification of the Nisga'a land claim—described by a *National Post* columnist as "like a Visa card with no limit"[73]—would mean for British Columbia. When a director of the Canadian Taxpayers' Federation says that "southern Canadians should have been consulted before the Inuit-dominated territory split from the Northwest Territories in April,"[74] he really means that the non-native majority in British Columbia should have veto powers over First Nations land claims.

Not all the vociferous critics are journalists, politicians, and lobbyists. While the vast majority of informed academic commentary on Nunavut has been positive, the Toronto-based duo of Albert Howard and Frances Widdowson purport to bring academic analysis to northern issues, but their criticism seems no less driven by an odious sense of cultural superiority. Howard and Widdowson, who make much of the fact that they lived for several years in Yellowknife before returning to the south, argued in an article entitled "The Disaster of Nunavut" (published in the respected journal *Policy Options*) that Nunavut is "fundamentally unviable," and "will not enable the Inuit to assert more control over their lives and thereby improve social conditions in their communities."[75] They further assert that "Nunavut cannot be the answer to Inuit social problems because it is economically and culturally unviable.... The racially defined territory's existence will depend almost entirely on federal transfers, and attempting to artificially retain Inuit culture will isolate Inuit people further from the modern world."[76] Adopting a style that would have been extreme even in the assimilationist 1950s and 1960s, they urge Inuit to discard the "attitudes and values arising from a subsistence lifestyle [which] are a barrier to the social and political development of Inuit people."[77] They conclude, "the Inuit have as much capacity to become producers of economic value as anyone else,"[78] if only they would be like the rest of us (or as David Frum says, drop all the "'Dancing With Wolves' hooey").

Their certainty that Nunavut will prove to be an anthropological theme park where Inuit can (or must) forego the "disciplines of industrialization" in favour of an "artificial retention of Inuit culture"[79] could be dispelled by a visit to Greenland, Nunavut's neighbour across the Davis Strait. Far from being a polity determined to "warehouse the Inuit and ... [institutionalize] Inuit separation from the modern world," thereby maintaining Inuit culture "in the Neolithic period, preserving it as a museum piece for the rest of the world to observe,"[80] the development of Greenland's Home Rule Government has rapidly increased the speed of Greenlanders' integration into the world around them—including the world market for the products which Greenlanders produce. The Home Rule Government is, in effect, the vehicle through which Greenlanders have sought to negotiate the terms of their increased integration into the world.[81]

Widdowson and Howard have attracted media attention not because of the acuity of their "insights" nor for the power of their analyses—and certainly not because they offer any viable alternative strategies—but because so few other academics and policy analysts choose to write about Nunavut. The resulting intellectual (and publishing) vacuum is filled by people who, at the end of the day, find themselves in bed with the (former) Reform Party, columnists in the employ of Conrad Black, and others who really couldn't care less about Nunavut and whose real agenda is hostility to aboriginal self-government aspirations elsewhere.

To be sure, there are serious and valid criticisms to be made of the Nunavut project. As we await more knowledgeable and thoughtful critiques, it may be useful to summarize the weaknesses of the current crop of critics:

» they fall into and perpetuate major factual errors; for example, Nunavut is not a race-based government, but rather a public government in which all residents can participate;
» the fleeting and/or politically-motivated nature of their interest in

Nunavut tends to result in shallow coverage which offers little of substance to those involved in building Nunavut;

» they apparently wish to deny to the people of Nunavut what all other Canadians take for granted: the ability of people to run their own affairs as they wish, through local and regional democratically elected institutions;

» obsessed as they are with the magnitude of transfer payments from Ottawa, they rarely acknowledge facts well known to federal decision-makers: that having sovereignty over the eastern and central Arctic was costing Ottawa a bundle long before Nunavut came into being, and that the incremental cost of dividing the NWT in order to accommodate Inuit self-government interests is just a fraction of the overall cost of providing province-like programs and services to northern residents. As a public government, the Government of Nunavut is responsible for providing health, education, social services and so on to all who live within its boundaries. With a currently limited capacity to raise revenue through taxation, transfer payments from Ottawa are essential to sustain the same basic level of public services enjoyed by all Canadians, regardless of where they live;

» they fail to mention that other regions of the country were also highly dependent on the federal government before they achieved a level of economic development which allowed them to cover more of their own costs of government services;

» they tend to caricature the Inuit leaders who negotiated the Nunavut land claim as being rather naive and/or oblivious to the social problems in their communities, rather than recognizing them for what they were and are—pragmatic politicians who assessed the options which the Canadian political system offered them and their people, envisioned a new form of accommodating aboriginal self-government aspirations without threatening the territorial integrity of the state within which they found themselves, helped change the government policies which stood in their way, and earned the respect of their negotiating partners during the 20 long years it took to make their dream a reality;

» they offer no alternatives other than depopulating the Arctic and destroying Inuit as a distinct people—something that should never be seriously considered.

Problems, Politics, and Prospects

Robert Williamson, an anthropologist who was one of the first MLAS elected to represent an eastern Arctic constituency in the Legislative Assembly of the NWT, has written that Inuit must be understood as being

> a people within their habitat—interrelated socially, physically and metaphysically with their ancestral environment. The cosmology, pre-history and oral history give meaning, depth and predictability to the present and future. The language carries cultural meaning into the present and the future. The social organisation is integrated with the economy, the value system, and the acquisition, holding and deployment of power. The adaptability and learning capacity of the people in changing circumstances depend on confidence in themselves as bearers of a valued and respected contemporary identity, based on their own expression of culture. All of these are related to self-determination in the contemporary era.[82]

Indeed they are. What is less clear, however, is the degree to which the self-government and public government institutions created by the NLCA can sustain and foster that confidence and result in meaningful self-determination for the Inuit of Nunavut.

Inuit leaders such as John Amagoalik, Jose Kusugak (former President of NTI), Paul Quassa (the current NTI president), and Premier Paul Okalik are veterans of the struggle for Nunavut, and they take care to articulate a vision of a better future while they manage their enormous day-to-day responsibilities. Behind them is rising a layer of younger leaders, men and women who have worked their way up through government and elsewhere, acquiring the skills that effective self-government requires. Behind them is an even younger layer, often fresh out of school or not having gone as far in school as they might have, destined to be fast-tracked into management positions in the new structures.

This is one face of Nunavut, a new face of opportunity. The other face of Nunavut is one of mounting despair. "We live in the most violent jurisdiction in Canada," a woman writes in a weekly newspaper. "Ignoring the statistics is condoning violence. It is saying it is okay for our women to be beaten. Shelters don't cause the breakup of families or suicide; violence does."[83] As if in response, NTI First Vice-President James Eetoolook acknowledged:

> As in other societies, problems of domestic violence are a symptom of deeper economic and social problems in Inuit society that are aggravated by such things as: unemployment, underemployment, inade-

> quate and poorly designed government social policies and programs, and the rapid rate of technological change.[84]

Much of the responsibility for clear tangible actions that address these problems now rests with the Nunavut government. The challenges and contradictions inherent in the Nunavut project will make the initial years of the new government a critical time for all residents of the new territory. The actions of the new government will be monitored carefully by NTI, which became so frustrated with the GNWT that it formed an Inuit "shadow cabinet"—a "watchdog structure to safeguard Inuit rights."[85] And the actions of the entire Nunavut leadership—the public government, the IPGS, and the Inuit organizations themselves—are coming under increasing scrutiny at the community level. "We are hoping for action," women teacher trainees wrote the President of NTI after describing the social crisis in grim detail. "We are expecting to see a plan, with goals and a timetable. We are expecting our leaders to stand up and speak out continuously against violence, addiction and abuse in our communities."[86]

How will the leadership react should the population's demand for rapid, appropriate and effective changes in the public government policies not be adequately met by the fledgling Nunavut government? NTI's "shadow cabinet" certainly gives one food for thought. In addition to the politics of the relationships between NTI, the regional Inuit associations and the IPGS, 1999 saw the beginning of a complex relationship between a public government and an organization that can legitimately claim to represent the interests of 85 per cent of the public. Indeed, the presidents of NTI will almost certainly be elected by more voters than the premiers of Nunavut.

NTI, like the Makivik Corporation in Nunavik and the Inuvialuit Regional Corporation (IRC) in the Mackenzie Delta, wields a unique blend of political and economic power as it promotes the rights of, and manages the responsibilities of, its Inuit beneficiaries. NTI differs from Makivik and IRC in that whereas they represent a small minority of the total population of the province and territory in which they find themselves, NTI represents the overwhelming majority. Indeed, nowhere in Canada does a non-governmental organization exist with anything that even begins to approximate the clout and legitimacy that NTI carries in Nunavut. A high priority for both the Nunavut government and NTI was establishing principles to guide this unique and crucial relationship. In the fall of 1999, the premier of Nunavut and the president of NTI signed a political agreement, the *Clyde River Protocol*, outlining in broad terms the two organizations' understanding of their respective spheres of influence, the importance of respecting and consulting one another on areas of mutual concern, and the communications processes to achieve cooperation. (The agreement was named for the Baffin community in which it was to be signed, though in a typically northern turn of events, bad weather in Clyde River forced the signing ceremony to be relocated to Iqaluit.) NTI can be expected to give particular attention to how the territorial government addresses articles 23 ("Inuit employment within government") and 24 ("government contracts") of the land claim agreement as well as its progress incorporating "Inuit qaujimajatuqangit" (Inuit traditional knowledge; literally, "that which are long known by Inuit") into its modus operandi.

One of the key aspects of recent NWT political history is the gradual maturing of the GNWT as a territorial state, with its own political elite, its own bureaucratic hierarchy, and its own self-interests. How the Nunavut government may differ in this regard remains to be seen, but the fact that the creation of a new political regime is resulting in the formation of a new political elite is beyond dispute. And as Peter Clancy has noted in the most insightful discussion of class structures and accumulation strategies in the Northwest Territories to date,

> class power in the north as elsewhere does not derive automatically from economic position, but is politically mediated. It is in this political realm that class interests are organized, alliances and coalitions are formed, and programs are forged. In the north, these interests have been pursued through many channels: political parties and electoral mobilization, associational lobbying, litigation, or through negotiation at the aboriginal claims table.[87]

Successful negotiation at the aboriginal claims table is resulting in many profound changes in Nunavut society; a deepening of social differentiation—i.e., the more complete development of a class system among Nunavut Inuit—is one of them. The political and economic forces which have been set in motion will result in even more profound changes in the years to come.

One of those forces may be a growing realization among the Canadian body politic of the cost of maintaining Canadian sovereignty over the Arctic. Where the cost of maintaining and developing Nunavut has been hidden in a maze of federal and territorial funding agreements, the first budget of the Nunavut government—$610 million for a jurisdiction of 27,000 people—may come as a shock to many. Both the Nunavut and federal governments may find it necessary to arm Canadians with information about the cost of delivering government programs and services in the Arctic and with arguments as to why investments in Nunavut today will mean both healthier communities and reduced costs in the future—precisely the kind of argument which has gone out of favour during the lifetime of the current federal government. Similarly, Canadians will need to be reminded that in their early days many parts of the country enjoyed massive federal government infrastructure spending, on railways, canals and other facilities necessary for economic development. In contrast, the money Nunavut gets from Ottawa covers only costs of running the government; Nunavut has yet to see anything like the massive federal spending on economic development which many provinces enjoyed for decades.

Southern Canadians may be in for another kind of shock as living conditions in the new territorial jurisdiction become better publicized: the realization that living conditions in a region comprising a fifth of the country resemble those of Third World countries.[88] As a former Chief Medical Officer of the NWT noted before Nunavut came into existence,

> Division will consolidate not only the Inuit, but also their problems, [statistics on which] now are diluted by the presence of a substantial NWT non-aboriginal population, and to a lesser extent by the non-Inuit aboriginal population, whose health status is better than that of Inuit. Thus, the health status profile for Nunavut may come as a shock to many who may have become inured even to the depressing aspects of the overall NWT profile.[89]

These harsh realities come as no surprise to veteran politicians such as John Amagoalik, often called "the father of Nunavut." Nunavut "won't solve all of our problems overnight," he says, "but people will have a government they can relate to—a government that speaks and understands their language and understands their culture and priorities."[90] "We cannot expect miracles. Sitting over a hole in the ice for hours, not moving, waiting for a seal, takes patience. It took a lot of patience to get self-government. Now it will take more patience to solve our many problems."[91]

CONCLUSION

"The days of the Inuit are numbered," wrote American explorer Charles Francis Hall after visiting the Frobisher Bay area in 1861. "Fifty years may find them all passed away, without leaving one to tell that such a people ever lived." Hall's prediction proved far too bleak, and the Inuit of Nunavut survived both contact and colonization. While the last century has been tremendously difficult, they have endured. Looking to the future, it is possible to be both optimistic about the prospects for the creation of the Nunavut territory and government and alarmed about the future of Nunavut itself.

On the one hand, as Mary Simon—an Inuk from Nunavik who is a former member of the Nunavut Implementation Commission, and now Canada's ambassador to Denmark—said in a speech at Queen's University:

> the very scale of the Nunavut undertaking means it cannot be overlooked. Nunavut will constitute some 20 per cent of the land mass of Canada. Its boundaries will extend over a larger marine area than the boundaries of any Canadian province. For the first time in Canadian history, with the partial exception of the creation of Manitoba in 1870, a member of the federal-provincial-territorial club is being admitted for the precise purpose of supplying a specific aboriginal people with an enhanced opportunity for self-determination. This is ground-breaking stuff.

For a small, aboriginal society like the Inuit, the creation of Nunavut is an enormous achievement. Many federal officials express disbelief that the Inuit negotiators were able to "pull off" a dream that they thought far-fetched. Nunavut Tunngavik Inc. has had the ups and downs one expects from new institutions, but it would be hard to characterize it as anything other than realistically aggressive and competent in its promotion of Inuit interests—especially in regard to the creation of the Nunavut Government.

Nunavut follows Greenland as an example of a regional Inuit population equipping itself with political tools intended to counterbalance the power of the nation-states in which they reside. And their achievement may be of benefit to other aboriginal peoples who live in ethnically homogenous areas with a significant land base. Self-government by way of public government, which is the basis of both Greenlandic Home Rule and the Nunavut government, may be a way to meet the needs and aspirations of some other aboriginal peoples without threatening the territorial integrity of the states within which they exist. The degree of legislative and administrative autonomy which the Nunavut government will exercise may permit the development and implementation of a modern form of governance which reflects the customs and traditions of its citizens, with the flexibility to evolve at the pace they desire.

The Nunavut "package"—the provisions of the land claim and the resulting division of the NWT and the creation of the Nunavut territory and government—was designed to accommodate Inuit self-government aspirations yet also to fit comfortably within established traditions of mainstream Canadian governance. As we have demonstrated, it is not a radical departure. Another key lesson to be drawn from the Nunavut project is the extent to which major change in the situations of indigenous peoples can indeed occur if sufficient will exists—both political will and determination on the part of the indigenous people and good will and flexibility on the part of those in positions of political authority.

Still, the new territory and its government face enormous challenges: a young workforce with high levels of unemployment, low (but rising) educational levels, low average incomes with heavy and mounting dependence on social assistance, high costs for goods and public services, seriously inadequate public housing, high levels of substance abuse and other social problems (including suicide), and escalating rates of violence and incarceration. Indeed, a study commissioned by the federal government in 1988 predicted that Nunavut communities may become Arctic ghettos plagued by increasing rates of crime—with more in common with urban slums than with the independent, resourceful society that survived for thousands of years.[92]

Is it unrealistic to hope that the creation of Nunavut can prove this grim prediction wrong? The visionaries who gave birth to the Nunavut project and then negotiated it into existence did so in the belief that it would facilitate meaningful self-government, sustainable economic development, and healthy communities. However, the challenge of solving Nunavut's economic and social problems may well dwarf the considerable challenge of negotiating and implementing the aboriginal rights and "self-government through public government" arrangements which make up the Nunavut project.

NOTES

1 Nunavut is pronounced "NOO-na-voot." The language spoken by Inuit of Nunavut consists of seven dialects, which are essentially variations on a single language. Six of these dialects are collectively referred to as Inuktitut, and are written using a Syllabic writing system. The dialect spoken by the residents of the communities of Kugluktuk and Cambridge Bay, in the western part of the Kitikmeot region, is called Inuinnaqtun—and is written in Roman orthography. For further information see: Louis-Jacques Dorais, "The Canadian Inuit and their language," *Arctic Languages: An Awakening*, ed. Dirmid R.F. Collis (Paris: UNESCO, 1990), 185-289. (By contrast, the Dene of the Yukon and Northwest Territories comprise several different peoples each speaking a distinctive language.)

2 Philip O'Brien, "A critique of Latin American theories of dependency," *Beyond the Sociology of Development*, ed. Ivar Oxaal, *et al.* (London: Routledge & Kegan Paul, 1975), 12. For a critique of other social science concepts as they have been applied to aboriginal peoples, see: Tony Kaliss, "What was the 'other' that came on Columbus's ships? An interpretation of the writing about the interaction between northern native peoples in Canada and the United States and the 'other,'" *Journal of Indigenous Studies* 3:2 (1997): 27-42.

3 For a critique of dependency theory applied to aboriginal peoples in the current economic order, see Deborah Simmons, "After Chiapas: Aboriginal lands and resistance in the new North America," *Canadian Journal of Native Studies* 19:1 (1998). Simmons advocates an approach which accounts for the historical significance of aboriginal struggles within a global political economy, a method which allows for a material analysis of the linkages between such struggles on an international scale.

4 The curious route of the boundary, which bisects several large islands, reflects the boundaries established for the Inuvialuit land claim, settled in 1984.

5 Nunavut's boundaries also include areas that were historically used by Dene of northern Manitoba and Saskatchewan and the NWT.

6 Pronounced "ee-KAL-oo-eet."

7 The population of Nanisivik, a mine with an adjacent townsite, has no municipal government and is therefore not regarded as a "community"—although its resident population of just under 300 is usually included in territorial totals. Temporary residents at the Lupin and Polaris "fly-in/fly-out" mines are not counted as residents of the territory, nor are temporary residents at the Environment Canada meteorological station at Eureka or the Canadian Forces installation at Alert (both of which are on Ellesmere Island). Additional demographic, economic and other data can be obtained from the Nunavut Bureau of Statistics' web site (www.stats.gov.nu.ca).

8 "Labour force participation rate" is a measures of the extent to which residents of working age (age 15 and over) actually are in the work force—either working or seeking work.

9 See Article 23 ("Inuit Employment within Government") of the Nunavut Land Claims Agreement.

10 Between the 1990/91 and 1995/96 fiscal years, social assistance payments increased by 105 per cent in the Baffin region—compared to 52 per cent in the Keewatin region and 30 per cent in the Kitikmeot region. Data from GNWT Department of Education, Culture and Employment. A more encouraging note is that total social assistance payments across Nunavut declined—for the first time ever—between the 1997/98 and 1998/99 fiscal years, from $23.4 million to $21.6 million.

11 Budgetary data for this section from the GNWT Department of Finance, the Nunavut budget of May 1999 and the federal budget of February 2000.

12 Marybelle Mitchell, *From Talking Chiefs to a Native Corporate Élite* (Montréal and Kingston: McGill-Queen's University Press, 1996), 398 and 402.

13 Peter Clancy, "Northwest Territories: Class politics on the northern frontier," *The Provincial State: Politics in Canada's Provinces and Territories*, ed. Keith Brownsey and Michael Howlett (Mississauga: Copp Clark Pitman, 1992), 298.

14 Mitchell, *From Talking Chiefs*, 167.

15 Mitchell, *From Talking Chiefs*, 297 and 447.

16 For an authoritative survey of historical and modern Inuit societies, see David J. Damas, ed., *Arctic*, Handbook of North American Indians Vol. 5 (Washington, DC: Smithsonian Institution, 1984).

17 For a comprehensive review of Inuit groups and their differing interactions with European societies, see Hein van der Voort, "History of Eskimo interethnic contact and its linguistic consequences," *Atlas of Languages of Intercultural Communication in the Pacific, Asia, and the Americas*, ed. Stephen A. Wurm, *et al.* (Berlin: Mouton de Gruyter, 1996), 1043-94.

18 Text of a document found in the walls of a building in Kimmirut (Lake Harbour) in 1999.

19 It is important to note that while Inuit wage labour may have played a negligible role in the development of the Canadian economy, it was crucial to the viability of most Euro-Canadian ventures in the Arctic and it had a profound, transformative impact on Inuit society. For a theoretical overview of this understudied aspect of aboriginal history, see Martha Knack and Alice Littlefield, "Native American labor: Retrieving history, rethinking theory," *Native Americans and Wage Labor: Ethnohistorical Perspectives*, ed. Martha Knack and Alice Littlefield (Norman, Oklahoma: University of Oklahoma Press, 1996), 3-44. See also Steven High, "Native wage labour and independent production during the 'era of irrelevance,'" *Labour/Le Travail* 37 (1996): 243-64.

20 See George W. Wenzel, *Animal Rights, Human Rights: Ecology, Economy and Ideology in the Canadian Arctic* (Toronto: University of Toronto Press, 1991).

21 See Richard Diubaldo, *The Government of Canada and the Inuit, 1900-67* (Ottawa: Indian and Northern Affairs Canada, 1985).

22 See R. Quinn Duffy, *The Road to Nunavut: The Progress of the Eastern Arctic Inuit Since the Second World War* (Montreal and Kingston: McGill-Queen's University Press, 1988).

23 See Canada, Royal Commission on Aboriginal Peoples, *The High Arctic Relocation: A Report on the 1953-55 Relocation*, 3 vols. (Ottawa: Supply and Services Canada, 1994); Alan R. Marcus, *Relocating Eden: The Image and Politics of Inuit Exile in the Canadian Arctic* (Dartmouth, NH: University Press of New England, 1995); and Frank J. Tester and Peter Kulchyski, *Tammarniit (Mistakes): Inuit Relocation in the Eastern Arctic, 1939-63* (Vancouver: University of British Columbia Press, 1994).

24 Hugh Brody, "Some historical aspects of the High Arctic Exiles' experience," report prepared for the Royal Commission on Aboriginal Peoples (1993).

25 Colin Irwin, "Future imperfect: A controversial report on the prospects for Inuit society strikes a nerve in the NWT," *Northern Perspectives* 17:1 (1989): 4.

26 Irwin, "Future imperfect," 4.

27 Technically, barriers to Inuit voting in territorial elections were eliminated in 1954, but since no constituencies existed in the eastern or central Arctic until the 1960s, this was not much of an advance.

28 Canada, Department of Mines and Resources, Lands, Parks and Forest Branch, Bureau of Northwest Territories and Yukon Affairs, *The Book of Wisdom for Eskimo* (Ottawa, 1947), 19.

29 See Valerie Alia, *Names, Numbers and Northern Policy: Inuit, Project Surname and the Politics of Identity* (Halifax: Fernwood Publishing, 1994).

30 Canada, *The Book of Wisdom*, 20.

31 According to Statistics Canada's 1991 post-censal Aboriginal Peoples Survey, 96 per cent of adult (defined as age 15 and over) Inuit in Nunavut spoke Inuktitut.

32 See Richard J. Diubaldo, "The absurd little mouse: When Eskimos became Indians," *Journal of Canadian Studies* 16:2 (1981): 34-40.

33 See Mitchell, *From Talking Chiefs*, chapters 20-21.

34 Mitchell, *From Talking Chiefs*, chapters 6 and 16; and Clancy, "Northwest Territories."

35 It is worth noting, however, that in 1982—when the successful implementation of a Nunavut land claim and territorial government must have seemed like a distant dream—Inuit leader John Amagoalik (then president of the Inuit Tapirisat of Canada) wrote the ITC Board of Directors that he had been "thinking about trying to start some sort of labour movement in the North for about 10 years" (letter dated 22 February 1982). Charlie Peter, an aide to Amagoalik, wrote a memo to the Board which began by summing up the mounting socioeconomic woes in Inuit communities: "Universal lack of resistance by Inuit is also compounding this depressing situation," he concluded. "This lack of resistance is not due to lack of interest and concern, but it exists because of the lack of access to voicing these concerns in a manner which would be noticed and responded to adequately by the governments and business community. It is demoralizing and is eating away at the emotional and mental well-being of too many Inuit. In the minds of many Inuit the promisingly bright future painted for years by the territorial and federal governments has been a big illusion and instead have betrayed and used them. The planning and promotion of the likes of the Arctic Pilot Project, which are being pushed rudely at us, only confirm the growing pessimism which is depressing our spirits and fermenting anger inside us.... Inuit organizations in existence today are not geared towards meeting and taking real action on economic matters concerning

Inuit. The only recourse, then, is to start organizing Inuit labour so that the ordinary Inuit can renew their hopes and aspirations for the future" (memo dated 16 February 1982). Almost twenty years later we can see that while this initiative went nowhere, the frustration which fuelled it was channelled into successful enthopolitical activity.

36 Mitchell, *From Talking Chiefs*, ix.

37 Quoted in Jim Bell, "When Inuit Began to Talk Back to Government," *Nunatsiaq News*, 29 August 1997.

38 Quoted in "Nunavut: Inuit Tapirisat's proposal to split the NWT," *The Inuit North*, January 1980, 4.

39 Northwest Territories Electoral District Boundaries Commission, *Hearing Transcripts* II (hearing in Iqaluit, 10 October 1989), 12.

40 See John Merritt, Terry Fenge, Randy Ames and Peter Jull, *Nunavut: Political Choice and Manifest Destiny* (Ottawa: Canadian Arctic Resources Committee, 1989), especially chap. 4.

41 See Terry Fenge and Joanne Barnaby, "From recommendations to policy: Battling inertia to obtain a land claim policy," *Northern Perspectives* 15:1 (1987): 12-15.

42 John Merritt, "Nunavut: Canada turns a new page in the Arctic," *Canadian Parliamentary Review* (Summer 1993): 4.

43 Of those who actually cast votes, 85 per cent voted in favour. To guard against ratification of an agreement with such profound consequences by a small percentage of the population, the federal government's threshold for ratification of the claim was based on the number of eligible voters—so a non-vote was in effect a "no" vote.

44 Available on-line at the DIAND web site (www.inac.gc.ca/pubs/nunavut/).

45 Merritt, "Nunavut: Canada turns a new page," 5.

46 It should be noted that the members appointed by Inuit organizations need not be Inuit, and likewise the members appointed by government can be Inuit or non-Inuit.

47 John Merritt and Terry Fenge, "The Nunavut land claims settlement: Emerging issues in law and public administration," *Queen's Law Journal* 15:2 (1990): 270.

48 See Terry Fenge, "The Nunavut Agreement and sustainable development in the Canadian Arctic and the circumpolar world," *Becoming Visible: Indigenous Politics and Self-Government*, ed. Terje Brantenberg, *et al.* (Tromsø: Centre for Sámi Studies, University of Tromsø, 1995), 171-86.

49 A second bowhead was harvested near Pangnirtung in 1999.

50 Nunavut Tunngavik Inc. v. Canada, F.C.T.D., 1997

51 John Amagoalik, speech to Japanese parliamentarians visiting Iqaluit, 1 September 1995.

52 Quoted in Richard Hamilton, "TFN, feds reach final agreement: Boundary plebiscite March 16, Nunavut accord by April 1," *Nunatsiaq News*, 20 December 1991.

53 Most of the employees of the Nunavut government, especially those who delivered services directly to the public, were simply transferred from the Government of the Northwest Territories and continued to perform the same jobs in the same locations as they had prior to division. By contrast, the new government had to acquire virtually its entire "headquarters" staff, to perform central coordination, policy development and similar functions.

54 This represents a significant departure from what the NIC recommended: *Footprints 2* called for the new government to be fully staffed and operational by the end of its first year of operation. However, delays in the appointment of an Interim Commissioner to oversee actual implementation—and the pace of progress once that position was finally occupied—made a quick start-up impossible.

55 Under the GNWT, each region had an education board and a health board which administered programs on behalf of the territorial government.

56 Three studies by consulting firms Coopers & Lybrand and Price Waterhouse had put the one-time start-up costs at between $230 million and $500 million.

57 Canada, Northern Affairs and National Resources, Northern Administration Branch, Welfare Division, *Qaujivaallirutissat* (Ottawa, 1964), 38.

58 See Nunavut Implementation Commission, *Nunavut's Legislature, Premier and First Election* (Iqaluit, 1996), 13-16.

59 For an analysis of the principles of the proposal, see Lisa Young, "Gender equal legislatures: Evaluating the proposed Nunavut electoral system," *Canadian Public Policy* 23:2 (1997): 306-15.

60 See Nunavut Implementation Commission, *Nunavut's Legislature*, 31-65.

61 *Report of the Nunavut Electoral Boundary Commission*, 30 June 1997, 16.

62 Government of Nunavut, *Pinasuaqtavut: That which we've set out to do: Our hopes and plans for Nunavut ("The Bathurst Mandate")* (Iqaluit, 1999), available online at the Government of Nunavut's website, www.gov.nu.ca.

63 John Ryle, "What country are we in?" *Manchester Guardian*, 22 February 1999.

64 "Charting new territory" (editorial), *Globe and Mail*, 3 April 1999.

65 Andrew Purvis, "Nunavut gets ready," *Time*, 29 March 1999.

66 Colin Nickerson, "Inuit land born amid hope, fear: Nunavut: The New territory in Canada's Arctic will be the nation's poorest. But natives are overjoyed at the opportunity for self-rule," *Baltimore Sun*, 31 March 1999.

67 Paul Brunner, "Birth of Nunavut: The racial partitioning of Canada begins," *Alberta Report*, 12 April 1999.

68 Tom McFeely, "Move them to Florida," *Report Newsmagazine*, 22 November 1999.

69 "Nunavut needs protection from itself," *National Post*, 3 April 1999.

70 Quoted in Colin Levey, "Canada gives the Inuits a homeland, but no malls please," *Wall Street Journal*, 2 April 1999.

71 Dan Gardner, "It's just like South Africa, but without the beaches," *Ottawa Citizen*, 8 March 1999.

72 Levey, "Canada gives the Inuits a homeland...."

73 Mark Milke, "The treaty that keeps on giving: The Nisga'a treaty is like a Visa card with no limit," *National Post*, 28 October 1999.

74 Quoted in Shawn Ohler, "Nunavut to release first budget with 90% of it federal money," *National Post*, 14 May 1999.

75 Albert Howard and Frances Widdowson, "The Disaster of Nunavut," *Policy Options*, July/August 1999, 58.

76 Howard and Widdowson, "The Disaster of Nunavut."

77 Howard and Widdowson, "The Disaster of Nunavut," 60.

78 Howard and Widdowson, "The Disaster of Nunavut," 61.

79 Howard and Widdowson, "The Disaster of Nunavut," 60.

80 Howard and Widdowson, "The Disaster of Nunavut," 61.

81 On Home Rule in Greenland, see Jens Dahl, "Greenland: Political structure of self-government," *Arctic Anthropology* 23:1/2 (1986); Jack Hicks, "Greenland: Home Rule at the crossroads," *Arctic Circle* (Fall 1994); Finn Breinholt Larsen, "The quiet life of a revolution: Greenlandic Home Rule 1979-1992," *Études/Inuit/Studies* 16:1/2 (1992); Philip Lauritzen, *Highlights of an Arctic Revolution: The First 120 Months of Greenlandic Home Rule* (Nuuk: Atuakkiorfik, 1989); Birger Poppel, "Greenland's road to recovery and the pattern of settlement," *Nordic Journal of Regional Development and Territorial Policy* 8:2 (1997); and Axel Kjær Sørensen, "Greenland: From colony to Home Rule," *Ethnicity and Nation Building in the Nordic World*, ed. Sven Tagil (Carbondale, IL: Southern Illinois University Press, 1995).

82 Robert Williamson, "In the search for 'a people': The Inuit, their habitat, and economic politics," *Self-Determination: International Perspectives*, ed. Donald Clark and Robert Williamson (London: Macmillan, 1996), 322.

83 Rebecca Kudloo, Eastern Arctic Vice-President of the Status of Women Council of the NWT, "We are living in an epidemic of violence," letter to *Nunatsiaq News*, 11 February 1994. *Nunatsiaq News* is accessible on-line at www.nunatsiaq.com.

84 NTI press release issued 4 February 1994.

85 NTI press release issued 31 October 1997.

86 "State of health of the population of Nunavut," letter from Nunavut Arctic College Northern Teacher Education Program students to NTI President Jose Kusugak, dated 4 July 1995.

87 Clancy, "Northwest Territories," 298.

88 As T. Kue Young has pointed out, however, "the principal causes of death and disability are actually very different, as also is the nutritional status and the supply of health services." "The Canadian North and the Third World: Is the analogy appropriate?" *Canadian Journal of Public Health* 74 (1983).

89 David Kinloch, "Health and health services in the NWT: A review of policies and programs," unpublished report dated 21 March 1996, 72.

90 Quoted in Darcy Henton, "Inuit's Dream of Home Rule Coming True," *Toronto Star*, 5 March 1999.

91 Quoted in Philip Broughton, "Inuit look to a new homeland to solve old problems," *Daily Telegraph*, 23 February 1999.

92 Irwin, "Future imperfect."

15 REVIEW

Comparative Provincial Politics: A Review

CHRISTOPHER DUNN

If provinces are the laboratories of social experimentation, as Pierre Trudeau once contended, then their personnel, processes, structure, and outputs must be monitored and evaluated. Such is the job of comparative politics. In this review essay, I will examine the nature of the comparative politics exercise, offer a basic overview of comparative research done on provincial matters, and suggest the types of research that need to be undertaken.

One sub-theme runs through the piece, to appear and then occasionally disappear depending on the nature of the literature being reviewed. It is the theme of convergence and divergence: the question of increasing similarity/dissimilarity in provincial politics, a natural enough question for a comparative politics paper. I will argue—very tentatively—that provinces are becoming increasingly similar, at least to judge from the literature. However, I will also argue that it is time to ask more of the comparative provincial field. Canada went almost twenty years without a new comparative provincial textbook. The literature in some areas is now so dated that any generalizations are becoming hazardous.

In making this statement, of course, I take part in what may be called a "grand tradition" of comparative politics. It has become *pro forma* for analysts of review articles and books across the globe to bemoan the intermittent or sketchy nature of comparative exercises. Over a quarter century ago, for example, Alan Cairns complained about the centralist bias of Canadian political science textbooks and noted that even the provincial work done to date was the work of a small handful of scholars leading to "a monopoly situation in which the dominance of particular interpretations reflects the absence of alternatives."[1] While the charge about a "small handful" of scholars is manifestly not the case at present,[2] there has clearly been an ebb from the high tide of comparative provincial studies in the 1970s and early 1980s.

COMPARATIVE POLITICS: THE ENTERPRISE

The term "comparative provincial politics" is used here to mean the study of concepts or fields in more than one province in order to generate a range of micro-level and macro-level information. Clearly, it forms part of the larger enterprise of comparative politics, and so can benefit by whatever introspection has characterized that broader approach.

The approaches that have been adopted under the general rubric of comparative politics have been varied. They have included simpler and more complex approaches:

The Study of "Other" Polities

The traditional meaning of comparative politics has come to mean the study of a country other than one's own. This is the sense in which the Americans and British have used it in their literature, and it is the sense that continues to dominate, despite considerable efforts to introduce sophisticated comparativist perspectives. Somewhat exasperated, Sigelman and Gadbois noted in their early 1980s study of 565 articles in Comparative Politics and Comparative Political Studies, "we are hard pressed to say what they have in common except that almost all of them focus on politics outside the United States."[3] One imagines that similar findings would result today, in that and associated publications.

Single Polity, Universal Themes

Richard Rose calls extracting universal themes from the study of a single country a "comparable," if not "explicitly comparative" technique. He characterizes the approach as "extroverted case studies with generic concepts." He explains that "a study of a single country becomes an extroverted case study if it employs concepts that make it possible to derive generalizations that can be tested elsewhere."[4] Alexis de Tocqueville's *Democracy in America* is the stereotypical example. In it Tocqueville speculates that his study of American democracy may hold clues to "the image of democracy itself."[5] Arend Lijphart's seminal work on Dutch "consociationalism"—the elite accommodation that marked politics in the Netherlands—was a self-conscious attempt to generalize the concept to other fragmented democracies, and one which succeeded famously.[6]

TABLE 15.1 **APPROACHES TO THE STUDY OF COMPARATIVE POLITICS**

SIMPLER APPROACHES	COMPLEX APPROACHES
the study of "other" polities	typologies
single polity, universal themes	edited collections, multiple polities
case studies	systematic thematic comparisons, multiple polities
dichotomies	analysis

Case Studies

Dogan and Pelassy say that it may seem "paradoxical" to include case studies as a comparative technique, but if properly organized they can be of use. The case study author could ask the same question of the different countries considered, in order to lend consistency to the work; or an editor could sponsor collections in which experts study precise issues. Successful comparative case studies tend to focus on structural or systemic data, which allow translations of experiences in specific contexts to more general ones.[7] They are informed by theoretical perspectives, and the better ones aim to refine theory, either by extending its nuances, or by examining deviant cases.

Dichotomies

Dichotomies are an elementary division of reality. They amount to an "x" and a "non-x" classification. In other words, the political universe is seen as divided into two mutually exclusive categories, according to the criterion chosen. One uses this approach with the appropriate caution, since the classes amount to ideal types abstracted from reality; but much social science uses the dichotomy as an initial ordering. Observers split the world into developed/undeveloped, rural/urban, democratic/totalitarian, liberal/collectivist, federal/unitary, capitalist/socialist, small/large, rich/poor, meritocratic/ascriptive, and a number of others. The dichotomy can lead one to consider the idea of a continuum; alternatively, it can lead one away from it, if the poles are seen as "stringent alternatives."[8]

Typologies

Typologies are coherent and relatively broad inventories of data that allow for comparisons between political (or other) entities according to multiple gradations between poles, or cross-cutting axes of more than one set of poles. Typologies may be generated deductively or inductively, but the tendency is to use the inductive method based largely on the use of empirical data. Typologies may be borrowed from other national or international contexts and applied to the jurisdiction(s) being studied, or they may derive directly from the material under investigation. Examples of "imported" typologies widely used by many political scientists abound: Almond and Verba's participant, passive, and parochial cultures; Christopher Hood's categorization of instruments of government as falling under either nodality, authority, treasure or organization; and Maurice Duverger's categorization of parties according to their organization—mass, cadre or devotee.

Edited Collections Involving Multiple Polities

One technique of comparative politics is to arrange edited collections which provide their audiences with a review of multiple political systems or political concepts. Edward C. Page has used the term "juxtaposition" to summarize this approach, noting that it is "a collection of essays usually around a common theme but which lacks the coherence found in the thematic comparison—a coherence provided either through tight editing, through close collaboration between co-authors or through single authorship."[9] This may seem more pejorative a description than it really is: such collections have the advantage of being quick off the mark and providing the rough material for those who are interested in doing the more rigorous thematic comparisons.

Systematic Thematic Comparisons Across Polities

A systematic thematic comparison is one in which the author or authors begin with specific questions or objectives which are to be applied to multiple polities, apply consistent methodology throughout, gather comparable data, and provide generalizations based on such data. As Richard Rose notes, there is an inherent bias in this approach towards including a limited number of countries, since there is a decrease in the amount of detail the greater the number of countries studied, but conversely there is a need to include enough countries to allow representivity.[10] Harold L. Wilensky's *The Welfare State and Equality* (1975) is one example of the approach, as is Jean Blondel's *Government Ministers in the Contemporary World.*

Global Analysis

Statistical or indicator handbooks are global, not limited in scope, and provide an exhaustive listing and description of data arranged according to a standard listing of categories. Voting studies and analyses of public expenditure are the most common approaches taken in political science,[11] but there are other more ambitious attempts such as the *World Handbook of Political and Social Indicators* by Taylor and Jodice (1983).

COMPARATIVE PROVINCIAL POLITICS IN CANADA: A REVIEW

In light of the varied meanings that one can ascribe to comparative politics in the broad literature, it is interesting to contemplate the directions that the comparative thrust has taken in Canada's provinces. What this review will indicate is thin coverage in some areas and little in others. In short, students planning careers in political science will find they are needed in the comparative provincial area. In Table 15.2, I adopt, with appropriate modifications, the classification outlined above and summarize the research in each.

The Study of "Other" Provinces

This traditional approach has little apparent relevance to Canadian provincial politics. However, if one reflects on the preoccupation with the national question, the country's internal politics takes on the hue of a comparative politics exercise. A search of the Carleton University library under the subject heading "Québec Politics" reveals 1,124 entries. "Manitoba Politics" merits 105. So there is a sense in which Canadians investigate their significant others in the federation.

Still, academe mirrors the publishing world: most university political science departments do not usually have courses on provinces other than the one in which they are situated, or comparative, or Québec. The University of Toronto, as an example, has two comparative provincial politics courses and one on Ontario politics; the only "other" province to have its own course is Québec (Québec Politics and Social Change). The general pattern in Canadian universities is to have one provincial course, on comparative provincial politics.

Single Province, Universal Themes

Some studies of single provinces have not been notable for their tendency to generalize beyond the relevant borders. There are, however, some cases,

TABLE 15.2 **OVERVIEW OF APPROACHES TO COMPARATIVE PROVINCIAL POLITICS**

CATEGORY	AREA/AUTHOR/PUBLICATIONS
The study of "other" provinces	The study of Québec politics
Single province, universal themes	*Democracy in Alberta* (C.B. Macpherson, 1962); *Prairie Capitalism* (Pratt and Richards, 1979); *Populism and Democracy in the Canadian Prairies, 1910-1945* Laycock, 1990)
Case studies	Imbeau and Lachapelle, *Comparative Provincial Policy in Canada* (1996)
	CONVERGENCE/DIVERGENCE WRITERS: Poel (1976); McAllister (1984); Lutz (1989)
Dichotomies	Province-building vs. nation-building Large and small
Typologies	PROVINCIAL PARTY SYSTEMS: (Wilson, 1974; Jenson, 1976; McCormick, 1996; Dyck, 1996; Carty and Stewart, 1996)
	POLITICAL CULTURE: "The Canadian Political Cultures" (Wilson, 1974); "Party Systems" (Jenson, 1976); "Leadership and Clientelism" (Noel, 1976); "Provincial Political Cultures in Canada" (Simeon and Elkins, 1974, updated 1980); "Provincial Political Cultures" (Wiseman, 1996)
Edited collections involving multiple provinces	*The Provincial Political Systems* (Bellamy, Pammett and Rowat, 1976); *Canadian Provincial Politics* (Robin, 1978); *The Provincial State* (Brownsey and Howlett, 1992); *Politiques Provinciales Comparées* (Crete, Imbeau and Lachapelle, 1995); *Provinces: Comparative Provincial Politics* (Dunn, 1996)
Systematic thematic comparisons across provinces	GENERAL TEXTS: *Public Policy and Provincial Politics* (Chandler and Chandler, 1979); *Representative Bureaucracy in the Canadian Provinces* (Kornberg, Mishler and Clarke, 1982); *Ottawa and the Outer Provinces* (Tomblin, 1995)
	INSTITUTIONS: *Leaders and Parties in Canadian Politics: Experiences of the Provinces* (Carty, Erickson and Blake, 1992); *Planning and the Economy* (Thorburn, 1984); *In the Presence of Women* (Arscott and Trimble, 1997)
"Global" overviews of provinces	*Provincial Politics in Canada* (Dyck, 1996)

predominantly in the west, where intraprovincial experiences have been seen as significant for the larger national or international community. One example is C.B. Macpherson's *Democracy in Alberta*. Alvin Finkel says of the book that it is not only a lucid critique of the ideas of Major C.H. Douglas, the British engineer who fathered the basic theories of Social Credit, but "a brilliant work of political theory that places such ideas in the context of debates on the larger meaning of democracy in the western world."[12] Macpherson characterized Alberta by the 1950s and 1960s as having a "quasi-party system," a distinctive middle way between an "alternate-party system" (i.e., parties alternating in power), and a one-party state where there were no other operating parties, as in revolutionary or counter-revolutionary states: "The quasi-party system ... may be seen as a response to the problem of democratic government in a community mainly of independent commodity producers which forms a subordinate part of a more mature capitalist economy."[13] The community rejects the orthodox party system and supports a dominant local party to express its somewhat contradictory economic outlook. The community of independent producers, as a relatively homogenous small-propertied (petit bourgeois) class, resists the subordination of the capitalist economy but at the same time accepts the basic tenets of the capitalist system itself. The conundrum is solved by expressing class conflict in terms of local society resisting the forces of powerful outside capital. External forces are to blame; they must be fought, using the plebiscitarian state as the shield. Not only Alberta, but other prairie provinces had the same system in effect for several years; and Macpherson saw the possible future of Canadian federal politics lying in the quasi-party system. The general rule? "Our analysis has suggested that when these two attributes—quasi-colonial status and independent producer outlook—are combined in one society during a period of maturing or mature capitalism, we have the conditions for a quasiparty system."[14]

Sometimes the formula will join the search for universal themes with the investigation of more than one province. John Richards and Larry Pratt's *Prairie Capitalism*[15] reviews the development of resource policy in Alberta and Saskatchewan in the postwar period and draws some lessons for provincial policy options across the country. *Prairie Capitalism* is a study in the political economy tradition and one which avoids characterizing province-building as either inherently regressive or subject to the ineluctable laws of international economics. Canadian observers have, according to them, consistently underplayed the desirability or competency of provinces to undertake major entrepreneurial activities in pursuit of development goals. Provinces dependent on exploitation of staples are not, as commonly held, "the captive dependents or instruments of international capital"; some provinces are stronger than others and bargaining advantages may shift over time away from the foreign investor if political will and local entrepreneurship are powerful enough.

> Once the foreign investor has sunk his costs and has fixed assets in place and his monopoly of expertise has been eroded, under certain conditions there occurs a shift of power toward the province.... What begins as a relatively simple and highly unequal, often exploitative relationship evolves into a much more complex pattern of relations as the provincial government moves up a learning curve of skills and negotiating expertise and the foreign company faces the steady erosion of its monopoly power.[16]

Pratt and Richards end with a tentative generalization: "while we advance no claim of universality, our study of prairie oil, gas and potash suggests that the initial asymmetrics and disadvantages which are so often a feature of resources development can, given time and under certain circumstances, be overcome."[17]

Another work which stresses the universals embedded in particulars is *Populism and Democratic Thought in the Canadian Prairies, 1910 to 1945*. David Laycock's comparative study of Prairie populisms finds that there had been four variants of populist thought in early twentieth-century Prairie Canada: crypto-liberalism, radical democratic populism, social democratic populism, and plebiscitarian populism. Despite being a geographically-focused study of a particular era, Laycock finds lessons inherent in the material for all of Canada, even to the present day: "One of prairie populism's most valuable legacies to the jaded and alienated Canadians should have been a recognition of the value of participatory democracy and decentralized control over economic and political power."[18] However, this has not happened because of the technocratic impulse inherent in government, and because of the lack of a feeling of widespread class conflict—us and them—in the general population. Yet the most progressive examples of popular power—among the urban poor and the victims of government cutbacks, for example—will seek to integrate the two themes, participation and decentralization. The most regressive examples are those of conservative province-building politicians or Reform Party (as the Canadian Alliance was then called) advocates. Such individuals seek to deny this integration, and hence their claim to be the appropriate heirs to the populist tradition are mistaken.

Case Studies

One comparative technique is to "aggregate" case studies by asking the same question of them. Although the subject of "convergence" is not the major concern of Imbeau and Lachapelle's review of comparative provincial public policy in Canada[19]—they are primarily interested in identifying independent and dependent variables in the 33 comparative case studies (done between 1969-93) that they summarize—they do in fact consider whether or not the studies reveal convergence. The authors note that the convergence thesis is supported by some of the studies: economic factors explain at least 50 per cent of the variation in provincial welfare expenditures, the level of expenditures is fairly similar in all provinces, and federal transfers to provinces encourage similar economic growth. However, it is not supported by findings in other literature that they reviewed, which suggests that "politics matters." Public policy configurations differ between the provinces as a function of left-wing party strength and presence in government, the degree of party competition, and the degree of institutionalization of legislative assemblies. The authors conclude, however, that the state of research is too inconclusive and further studies are necessary.

Dichotomies

Dichotomies have been a fairly popular way of investigating comparative public policies in Canada. One prominent one counterpoises province-building and nation-building. Another traces the implications of large versus small provinces.

One dichotomy that has generated a varied body of literature is the distinction between nation-building and province-building. Representative authors in this stream are Alan Cairns and Edwin Black, and Garth Stevenson. Although the dichotomy in question concerns building the nation versus building the provinces, the authors devote most of their attention to the provincial side. The reason is contextual: at the time of the writing, most of the literature had been preoccupied with the federal state- and nation-building, and the authors felt justified in placing disproportionate emphasis on the provinces. Nonetheless, nation-building is mentioned, if obliquely.

Cairns and Black have been widely credited as having coined the term province-building, in a 1966 article. "Since 1867," they claim, "Canadians have been engaged not only in state-building but in province-building as well.... Perhaps the most important aspect of province-building concerns the growth of influential provincial elites in politics, administration and resource-based industries ... elite groups exist which flourish potent incentives and supports for the expansion of provincial power against that of the federal government."[20]

Provincial governments, they say, do not simply react to social economic and geographical forces but are creative forces in themselves. In other words, they create their own supports. Provincial cabinets have sole discretion in natural resource extraction, and frontier resource communities focus primarily on the provincial level for essential services and future development. Provincial jurisdictions are very nearly the only source of employment for new professional groups. Provincial identities are reinforced by the tendency for social institutions to be organized along provincial lines, even when there is no pressing functional need for them to be so structured.[21] Modern provincial planning, which Cairns and Black see as stressing long-term projections and priority-setting, is likely to lead to federal-provincial conflict when federal interventions hinder such provincial planning. A province wanting maximum leeway for legislative action and finances to allow this is likely to push for more tax room and federal withdrawal from provincial jurisdictions.[22]

Cairns's 1977 presidential address to the Canadian Political Science Association elaborates upon some of the themes of the earlier essay.[23] Cairns takes issue with two prevalent views of the role of governments in Canadian federalism, the anti-federalist school and sociological reductionism. He proposes an alternative which stresses the autonomy of governmental elites and the singular impact of government upon society. Cairns finds the dynamic of the system in the government and in the constitution, and not in society.

Provincial governments, he says, have not only met the minimum prerequisites for self-preservation but have gone further. Provincial political elites sit astride organizational pyramids, possessed of both protectionist and expansionist tendencies. The minimum prerequisites for provincial survival are protection of jurisdictional competence and of territorial integrity. The protectionist tendencies derive largely from history: each political office, especially those of prime ministers and premiers, has a history which constrains the succession of incumbents in it. However, expansionist tendencies also figure; premiers have also engaged in strategies that further their long-term institutional self-interest: "Governing elites view their task as the injection of federal or provincial meaning into society, giving it a degree of coherence and a pattern of dependence more suited to government than what would emerge from the unhindered working of social and market forces."[24]

One of the more powerful exponents of a political economy view of province-building is Garth Stevenson. For Stevenson, the growth of provincial bureaucracies is more a consequence than a cause of the growth of provincial power; neither has judicial interpretation been mainly responsible for the present division of functions between the national and provincial governments.[25] The increase in provincial power was, and is

> a reflection of the needs and preferences of dominant classes and class fractions within the provinces.... Both nation-building and province-building invariably are promoted by those class fractions that are dominant within the relevant territorial jurisdictions but are frustrated by having to share their power with external economic interests. In order to achieve their goals, these class fractions must gain some degree of wider popular support (or at least acquiescence) by identifying their own needs with those of the whole society. Depending on the circumstances, they may define their objectives as "catching up" with a more advanced economic unit ... or protecting some local economic advantage....[26]

The class fractions dominant in provinces have shifted over time.[27]

In another work, Stevenson elaborates upon provincial functions, borrowing the concepts of accumulation and legitimation from American Marxist scholar James O'Connor.[28] Stevenson suggests that the accumulation functions have increasingly been assumed by the provinces, whereas legitimation and coercion functions predominate at the federal level. He notes that with the possible exception of Québec, the provincial states appear generally much more vigorous in expanding their accumulation function. This reflects the fact that the Canadian bourgeoisie have more regionally specific and heterogeneous needs in regard to accumulation, as a result of the different types of economic activity that predominate in different regions, than they have in regard to legitimation.[29]

Dichotomies are sometimes used to show that the forces represented by the two poles can harm each other. A rather critical exposé of province-building versus nation-building is the monograph by Maxwell and Pestieau released in 1980.[30] Provinces have become competitive between themselves with regard to economic development and doubtful about the efficiency of federal efforts to reduce regional disparities, according to the authors. While every province uses somewhat different language to express its goals, in every case its principal goal is to provide creative earning opportunities for its people, and in some senses to counteract labour and capital mobility. Instead, each province seeks to maximize incomes, employment, and population growth in its own territory.[31] There will also be a drive to acquire provincial decision-making powers and influence on relevant federal powers. Specific policy instruments which are used somewhat resemble those of actors in international trade. "In summary, province-building has come into conflict with country-building for Canada as a whole. The provinces are attempting to achieve remarkably similar goals; in doing so, they become direct competitors for industrial location."[32] Young, Faucher and Blais have, for their part, disputed the contention that province-building conflicts with nation-building. There is no universal provincial pattern of resistance to federal incursions, aggressive actions or, for that matter, common interests. Political scientists focus on federal-provincial coordination failures, but tend to ignore examples of coordination successes, of which there are many.[33]

More recently, an imaginative dichotomy used in the literature features size: large versus small. Graham White says that when speaking of legislatures, cabinets, and bureaucracies, big is different than little.[34] The consequences of size for comparative analysis of Canadian institutions has been underappreciated. Both relative size and absolute size count here. The subliminal message of the piece is that convergence is possible only with provinces of matching scale. Legislatures are instructive in this regard. In small legislatures, roughly a third of the members will end up as the cabinet, while in larger legislatures, about a fifth of the legislature enters cabinet. This means that where a greater percentage of the governing caucus ends up in cabinet, cabinet mediocrity is more likely to result, and the role of caucus in controlling cabinet is lessened. And the smaller the legislature, the less chance of backbencher independence—both on the government and the opposition sides—since the structure of career incentives militate in favour of toeing the line. Smaller legislatures will have less effective committee systems; the number of opposition members available may be too small; but more especially the relative talent of the government backbenchers may be too low, with governments not enthusiastic about letting important initiatives be protected by second- and third-stringers. Larger legislatures feature greater specialization and role differentiation. Third-party health and minority governments are more possible in larger legislatures.

Cabinets have grown in the postwar period. Larger cabinets tend to have greater institutional complexity, weaker first ministers, more frequent and more extensive shuffles, and relatively less domination of the legislature. Larger cabinets become so unwieldy as to require an extensive cabinet committee system. The shift to the institutionalized, or structured, cabinet that coincided with the growth in cabinet size is often accompanied by a more constrained first minister who, like his or her ministers, must play by increasingly formal rules and who finds that knowledgeable groups of ministers pose more of a challenge when information is no longer the exclusive purview of the premier. However, provincial government is still premier's government. By this White means that in the smaller provinces it is easier, and probably more necessary, for the premier to become familiar with, and involved in, more issues than it is the federal case, where prime ministers tend to specialize.

Lastly, size of bureaucracies matters. White is more tentative in this area, offering hypotheses and statements of tendency. Large bureaucracies tend to add units vertically (i.e., levels of administration) first, and then horizontally; small bureaucracies tend to resist differentiation, adding on to existing units. Federal government departments tend to be more differentiated from their provincial counterparts. Tempering his statements with a proviso that organizational culture is also important, several Ottawa/Ontario government comparisons prevail: deputies and senior officials in Ottawa will know a significantly smaller proportion of departmental staff, will engage in more institutionalized and formal interaction with them, will decentralize decision making to a greater extent to regional offices, will interact with ministers (even in the case of deputy ministers) less than in Ontario, will communicate less with each other, and will face less interference from central agencies.

Typologies

Some of the richest writing in comparative provincial politics involves typologies. Subject areas like party systems and political cultures by their nature naturally lend themselves to an inventory process. Provincial differences are able to be nuanced appropriately; they also allow some initial responses to the question of whether provinces are converging, diverging, or just standing still.

Provincial political-party systems have been classified in numerous typologies. As the accompanying summary (Table 15.3) shows, authors differ in the specific categorizations they use and in the way they allocate provinces. John Wilson says that both the party system and the political culture of a province are a consequence of the stage of economic development that the provincial society has reached. As parties struggle to deal with the concerns of the new labouring class thrust up by industrialization, they go from a transitional phase of three parties to a two-party system where either the working class interest eliminates one of the older parties or is accommodated by one or both of them.[35] Chandler and Chandler note that provincial party systems vary and use a typology based on work by Douglas Rae (*The Political Consequences of Electoral Laws*, 1967) to explain how. There are four measures of competitiveness of use: bipartisan, fractionalization, one-party dominance, and party system instability.[36] Peter McCormick has a complex typology which melds together the concepts of a number of parties, the relative stability (lack of change) in the major competitors since World War II, and the competitive or non-competitive

TABLE 15.3 **TYPOLOGIES OF PARTY SYSTEMS**

AUTHOR	TYPES OF PARTY SYSTEM	PROVINCIAL EXAMPLES
Wilson (1974)	TYPE 1: *Two-party system* (found in "pre-industrial society"; landed gentry vs. industrialists)	NF, PEI, NB, NS
	Three-party system (found in industrializing society; a transitional system)	QC, ON, MB, BC
	TYPE 2: *Two-party system* (found in advanced industrial society; one of the Type 1 parties eliminated by labour party)	SK
	TYPE 3: *Two party-system* (found in advanced industrial society; one or both of the Type 1 parties accommodates or co-opts the labour interest)	AB
Chandler and Chandler (1979)	1. BIPARTISM. This means the extent to which two parties dominate the party system. It is estimated by measuring the combined share of votes or seats held by the two largest parties.	The examples of pure two-party systems are NF, PEI, and NB, with NS, QC, and SK as impure two-party systems. MB and ON are three-party; BC is an unstable three-party system.
	2. FRACTIONALIZATION. This term has a double meaning, referring to both the number of competing parties and their competitive positions.	BC, SK, and MB are the most competitive party systems at the level of seats.
	3. ONE-PARTY DOMINANCE. This term usually refers to the tendency of one party to remain in power over long periods, usually generations. One complication is that a new party with an	The classic examples of such dominance in a temporal sense are AB (1935-71) and ON (1943-85, the latter figure not available at the time, of course).

	overwhelming majority in seats can also qualify as one-party dominant. The term is ambiguous, however, because it can refer to both the dominance in seats and in votes. Dominance in seats and over time is the usual meaning attributed to the term.	
	4. PARTY SYSTEM INSTABILITY. This term refers to the degree of electoral or parliamentary instability of the party system, that is, whether or not the system is in flux or relatively unchanging.	The most unstable party systems—at the level of seats—are SK, QC, NB, and PEI.
McCormick (1988, 1996)	TYPE I: Two-Party/Stable/Very Competitive	All the Atlantic provinces; NB an exception?
	TYPE II: Two-Plus Party/Competitive/Unstable	BC, MB, SK
	TYPE IIa: Two-Plus Party/Stable/Competitive	ON
	TYPE IIb: Two-Party/Competitive/Unstable	QC
	TYPE III: One-Party/Unstable/Non-Competitive	AB
Dyck (1985, 1991, 1996)	One-party dominance	AB
	Two-party, little third-party support	PEI, NF, QC, NB
	"Middle position" on the presence of third parties	NS, BC
	Two-party with more evidence of third-party success	SK, MB, ON, AB
	Three-party system	ON, since 1960

cont'd. on page 456

TABLE 15.3 **TYPOLOGIES OF PARTY SYSTEMS (CONT'D.)**

AUTHOR	TYPES OF PARTY SYSTEM	PROVINCIAL EXAMPLES
Stewart (1994)	Stewart, by and large, depended on the same categories and definitions as Chandler and Chandler (1979).	1. BIPARTYISM is marked by an Ottawa River divide: strong east of it and weak west of it, at the level of votes (from 1945-90). At the level of seats (same years), the bipartyism pattern is more striking: in eight of the provinces the two largest parties held more than 90 per cent of the seats in the legislature. On average, third parties elected little more than 5 per cent of the provincial seats.
		2. ONE-PARTY DOMINANCE: If this condition is evidenced by one party winning an average of over 70 per cent of the seats, then this threshold was exceeded in five provinces from 1945 to 1990.
		3. PARTY SYSTEM INSTABILITY: The party systems of the Canadian provinces are far more unstable than those of Australian states, both in terms of votes and seats.
		4. FRACTIONALIZATION: In terms of seats, the most fractionalized provincial party systems are those of MB, BC, and ON. AB was the least competitive.
Carty and Stewart (1995)	1. One-party dominant system	AB
	2. Traditional two-party systems	PEI, NF, NS
	3. Three-party systems	MB, ON
	4. Polarized party systems	QC, BC, SK, NB

nature of election results over the years (that is, whether the popular vote received by the two major contenders was close or lopsided).[37] R.K. Carty and David Stewart base their classification system on the dynamics of party competition and relative party success since 1945.[38] David K. Stewart concludes his comparative examination of provincial party systems and Australian state party systems by attesting to the diversity revealed therein: the Atlantic provinces are unique in their bipartisanship and third-party weakness, the West demonstrates NDP and Social Credit successes and Liberal weakness, Québec is unique, and only Ontario and Manitoba are genuine multi-party systems.[39] Rand Dyck's categories are relatively similar to those of Carty and Stewart.[40]

However, the gist of the table is to suggest that the party systems differ markedly from one another, and have for some time. When a country has ten provinces and, according to some analysts like McCormick and Dyck, as many as five categories into which to slot party systems, there is not much homogenization taking place. As well, conflating the writers' works, one can see that many provinces are working at the same old pop stands they were a quarter-century ago. The Atlantic provinces' party systems are echoes of those of pre-industrialized Canada; having missed the manufacturing age, they seem destined to continue with the traditional, stable two-party systems. There is some consensus that Ontario and Manitoba are essentially three-party systems, in spite of occasional deviations. Alberta has not moved out of the one-party dominant category. Saskatchewan and British Columbia continue to exhibit polarized left-right politics. Third parties have a grip on legislative status, if not power, in the provinces west of the Ottawa River.

Analysts have also used typologies to categorize approaches to political culture. Table 15.4 summarizes the approaches used by the major national comparative political culture studies, and in a sense highlights the dated nature of the literature. However, recent studies of a regional nature suggest some movement towards convergence.

The earlier literature comprises a variety of snapshots demonstrating significant deviations between the provinces. John Wilson's article, cited earlier, deals not only with party systems but also with provincial political cultures. He teases the reader with musings about there being five or even ten different types of political culture before settling on three cultural stages: underdeveloped, transitional, and developed, such stages occurring as a function of the level of industrialization the provincial society has experienced.[41] Jane Jenson suggests a somewhat complementary approach. Using survey data from the 1974 National Election Study, she ranks provinces according to the strength of the relationship between partisanship and a number of variables such as religion, language, community size,

TABLE 15.4 **TYPOLOGIES OF PROVINCIAL POLITICAL CULTURES**

AUTHOR	TYPES OF POLITICAL CULTURE	PROVINCIAL EXAMPLES
Wilson (1974)	UNDERDEVELOPED: found in pre-industrial society or one beginning industrialization. Dominant cleavages are religious and ethnic origin, although Wilson examines only the former in the provinces.	NF, PEI, NB, NS
	TRANSITIONAL: found in industrializing provinces. Mix of cleavages from both the underdeveloped and developed cultures: religious, linguistic, class.	QC, ON, MB, BC
	DEVELOPED: class-oriented politics found in industrial provinces or those where the producing element feels dependent on the will of others whom they do not control.	AB, SK
Jenson (1976)	TRADITIONAL PARTY SYSTEMS: a stage of development of provincial society where the parties mobilize along the cleavages of language and religion.	NB, NS
	TRANSITIONAL PARTY SYSTEMS: a stage of development where the parties mobilize along the cleavages of urbanization (size of community) and age.	AB, NF, QC, ON, MB (the two latter have some traditional cleavages)
	MODERN PARTY SYSTEMS: a stage of development where the parties mobilize along class lines.	SK, BC, and (anomalously) PEI
Noel (1976)	STAGE I: *Patrons and Clients*: a relationship characteristic of rural, small producer societies. Consists of local patron owning land or capital assets and small number of clients dependent upon such. Dominant pattern in pre-Confederation Canada.	Now replaced in every province by Stages II and III.

	STAGE II: *Patrons, Brokers and Clients*: continues the Stage I relationship but interposes brokers (financial middlemen, promoters, lawyers and deal-makers) as crucial actors. Local patrons become dependent on brokers for benefits for themselves and clients. Dominant pattern around Confederation, with brokers crucial to large scale capital projects.	"Until well into the twentieth century," each premier presided over a network which incorporated residual Stage I aspects but which featured a wider network of patron-broker-client transactions, especially in the eastern provinces. In the more unsettled west, a purer Stage II prevailed, with a dominant premier surrounded by a coterie of brokers. Last exemplars were Bennett, Manning, Douglas, Garson.
	STAGE III: *Patrons, Brokers, Bureaucrats, and Clients*: sees the replacement of parties as instruments of clientelism by public bureaucracies, although small pockets of political patronage persist. Premiers depend on provincial bureaucracies, not parties, to distribute government benefits downwards. Bureaucrat-patrons and bureaucrat-brokers evolve, with power far exceeding that of any pre-Confederation actors. Dominant pattern since World War II.	Large, urban industrial societies tend towards Stage III. In no province does clientelism of one kind exist, but the degree to which III predominates is strongest in ON and weakest in NB and NF. Premiers (like Bourassa, Blackeney, Hatfield, Davis) live in dual worlds. They depend on bureaucracy *and* (less) on party patronage to win them electoral favour.
Simeon and Elkins (1980)	Contrast the provinces according to two aspects of political culture: POLITICAL EFFICACY: the sense of being personally politically influential and making one's voice heard; POLITICAL TRUST: the sense of popular support for and satisfaction with the political regime arising out of citizens' perception of politicians' competency and concern for their welfare.	

cont'd. on page 460

TABLE 15.4 **TYPOLOGIES OF PROVINCIAL POLITICAL CULTURES (CONT'D.)**

AUTHOR	TYPES OF POLITICAL CULTURE	PROVINCIAL EXAMPLES
Simeon and Elkins (1980) — cont'd.	Since these are analytically distinct they can be combined in the following typology:	Most in BC, MB, ON, QC (anglophone)—citizen society
	SUPPORTERS: display high sense of efficacy and trust DISAFFECTED: no trust in government and low efficacy	NF, NB, NS a majority—and fewest supporters
	DEFERENTIALS: trust regime, but do not feel efficacy	Low in all provinces; average a tenth of population
	CRITICS: distrust government but feel efficacy—mobilizable	Most common in BC and ON; least number in French Canada and the Maritimes
Wiseman (1996)	Says that the usually competing schools of thought in the area of political cultures (staples theory, formative events, fragment thesis) are in fact complementary when applied in the provincial context. However, much of the emphasis in the paper is devoted to the exposition of the fragment thesis, here applied for the first time to every province of Canada, in contrast to the partial coverage in past writings.	Among other things, Wiseman applies metaphorical images to each province: NEWFOUNDLAND: Canada's Ireland and west country England; MARITIMES: Canada's New England; QUÉBEC: New (Old) France; ONTARIO: America's Counter-Revolution; MANITOBA: the Prairies' Ontario; SASKATCHEWAN: the Prairies' Britain; ALBERTA: the Prairies' America; BRITISH COLUMBIA: Canada's Australia

age, and class. She then constructs a typology placing provincial political cultures along a continuum from traditional to transitional to modern, the determining factor in modernity being the extent to which the parties use class appeals.[42] Sid Noel sees the method of distribution of private, then government benefits as indicative of the stage of cultural development, the most complex stage of "clientelism" being found in large, urbanized, industrialized provinces that have experienced a growth in the role of government.[43] Simeon and Elkins, relying on data from the 1965, 1968, and 1974 National Election Studies, observe that feelings of trust and efficacy were highest among citizens of British Columbia, Manitoba, Ontario, and English Québec; lowest among Maritimers and French Québecers; Albertans and Saskatchewanites were midway between.[44] More recently, Nelson Wiseman both generalized his provincial fragment theory approach and showed its complementarity with what were previously perceived to be competing explanations, staples theory, and the "formative events" approach.[45] All point in the direction of provincial specificity.

If we conflate the information in Table 15.4, we find regional dissimilarities. The Atlantic provinces are alike: they are underdeveloped, pre-industrial societies with traditional cleavages relating to language and religion, more likely to be at Stage II clientelism with large-scale brokers as crucial actors, and more disaffected from the political system (low trust and efficacy patterns prevailing). Saskatchewan and British Columbia exhibit the greatest tendency to class-oriented politics; Manitoba, Ontario, and Québec tend to transitional-style politics which mix class and traditional-style cleavages. We also find a hint in the literature that the differences are to be long-lasting, that the provinces are to some extent prisoners of their pasts. They are made distinctive by their staple origins, their formative events, even the past economic development they have experienced—or, importantly, not experienced.

However, a newer thread in regional comparative literature offers the hypothesis that provincial cultures are converging. Roger Gibbons offers a nicely nuanced summary of Prairie development which combines socioeconomic homogenization with the vestigial elements of political particularity. Western Canada is being increasingly integrated into national society, he says: "The homogenization of economic, consumptive, cultural and recreational behaviour continues. It is part of a more global or at least continental trend in which regionally distinctive elements are being submerged by broader social and economic trends many of which emanate from the United States."[46] Yet federalism offers provincial governments as institutions a bulwark against national regimentation that the regional social order does not have, and so appeals to regional self-identification continue to be potent. As well, Ian Stewart has examined the more recent National

Election Studies up to 1984; his analysis shows that, contrary to Simeon and Elkins, interregional variations in trust and efficacy orientations are now quite small and that, in particular, the notion that Atlantic Canadians are a "uniquely disaffected lot" can be put to rest.[47]

Edited Collections Involving Multiple Provinces

Edited collections have been popular methods of studying provincial societies and their politics. In order to lend some coherence to the review of these collections—and one will recall that lack of coherence is the charge that is most often levelled at these collections—this review will focus on the idea of convergence and divergence. In other words, are provinces becoming more or less similar?

With earlier edited collections, convergence is difficult to discern, because their foci were narrower. Bellamy, Pammett and Rowat's (1976) collection, *The Provincial Political Systems*, is a case in point. Rather than seeking to master esoteric aspects, the collection instead is aimed at correcting a basic lacuna in Canadian politics, which arose from what was acknowledged to be its centralist orientation. "From a purely pragmatic viewpoint," say the authors, "it is now necessary to give recognition to the increasing stature of the provinces by attempting to provide a basic reservoir of resource material on provincial government and politics as a basis for offering more courses on the subject, and thus attracting more students and teachers into it as a field of scholarly study and research."[48] Given this basic aim, the question of convergence is not uppermost and is only obliquely tackled, by serendipity, in some essays. A. Paul Pross notes that there had been convergence of federal and provincial and professional pressure groups' perceptions on health policy and the directions it should take.[49] Anstett and Qualter notice convergence in the basically similar electoral procedures that all provinces adopted; there is a decline in partisanship and a rising concern for efficiency, and a growing concern to learn from each other.[50] Chandler and Chandler discuss, in terms of "policy trends," a greater share being spent by all provinces on health and education, a standing still of social welfare budgets, and relative decreases in transportation and natural resources spending, despite absolute increases in dollar amounts.[51] Ken Bryden notes that cabinet government has moved in a common direction, in most provinces, in terms of structured cabinets and support staffs, systematic policy evaluation and new techniques for expenditure control, and will not go back to more informal methods because of the new complexity of Canadian society.[52] These points of convergence are offset by the many articles which imply a static view of provincial institutional and cultural development, but this should not detract from the book's major contribution to the field.

Despite the obvious opening for comparative analysis implied in the subtitle to his 1978 edited collection *Canadian Provincial Politics: The Party Systems of the Ten Provinces*, Martin Robin offers no overview or generalizations about provincial party systems. Only one of the chapters, that by Courtney and Smith, places the party system being investigated—Saskatchewan—in a comparative context. They note that compared to the party systems of Manitoba and Alberta, Saskatchewan exhibits greater competitiveness and a higher rate of political participation, a fact they attribute, puzzlingly, to the effective management of dissent in the early twentieth century, early one-party dominance, and a pervasive need for cooperation in harsh pioneer conditions.[53]

By the time the edited collection *Provinces*[54] was published (1996), it was evident that the provinces had moved a fair distance into the convergence camp. True, there were distinct political cultures and party systems evident, but in many other areas the provinces had become increasingly similar. Perhaps the most striking article in this regard is by Michael Howlett,[55] who is critical of the literature's tendency to overemphasize interprovincial differences and underemphasize similarities and convergences, especially in the economic realm. Provincial myths are well known: Newfoundland's fishing economy, P.E.I.'s garden, Nova Scotia's golden age of wind and sail, New Brunswick's backwardness, Québec's defensive nationalism, Ontario's stability, Manitoba's farming, Saskatchewan's socialism with an agrarian base, the uniqueness of Alberta (first a homogenous class, then an oil economy susceptible to boom and bust), and lastly the resource hinterland that is said to be British Columbia. Yet they are just that—myths, notes Howlett. Some provinces (like Québec, Ontario, and B.C.) by mid-century may have developed relatively more activity and employment in secondary industry (manufacturing) and away from the reliance on staples production that originally characterized them. However, the reality today is that all provinces have highly developed tertiary (service-sector) economies wherein about 70 per cent of the gainfully employed are found. This also brings about a certain convergence in public policy issues: gender equality in the workplace, aid to small business, and family cohesion.

Certainly many institutional and process similarities have marked the provinces, the collection found. I note that a common pattern persisted for the last twenty years of hierarchical, institutionalized cabinets, with a clear tendency to position "coordinating" cabinet committees above the normal functional committees; that there is a common move towards fewer cabinet committees; and that a "PMO/PCO split"—a partisan/policy differentiation—occurred in almost all Executive Council Offices (Premier's Offices).

Provincial legislatures, over and above their essential commonalities (executive domination, imbalance of resources towards the cabinet, debilitating restrictions faced by legislative committees) are drawing even closer, White notes: "Although some provinces have made more progress than others, the general trend over the past decade or two has clearly been toward more effective legislatures. Members are better paid and have call on more extensive resources; procedural and administrative advances have enhanced provincial legislatures' independence from government and their overall capacity to influence public policy, to hold the government accountable, and to represent the people."[56] In his review of court systems in the provinces, Carl Baar finds that the merger, by 1992, of superior and county and district courts in all the provinces engendered a general lack of predictability about the type of sentences in section 96 courts and a general reduction in their criminal caseload.[57] Joan Boase estimates that with the drift in the 1990s toward cuts in federal fiscal transfers, provincial power-seeking, and a less communitarian Canadian public opinion, national standards and the social safety net were threatened in all provincial jurisdictions, which were now making use of market rhetoric.[58] Another article in the collection, a review of 33 articles on comparative provincial public policy conducted by Imbeau and Lachapelle, offers a more qualified view, as previously stated.[59]

Systematic Thematic Comparisons Across Provinces

Some sources take a more systematic comparative look at provinces in the sense of using one or more themes as a unifying element. This allows the authors to assemble a great deal of empirical data in the pursuit of limited aims. Parenthetically, it also allows many of them to address the question of convergence with more focus.

Some general textbooks have adopted a thematic approach. Kornberg, Mishler, and Clarke's *Representative Democracy in the Provinces* uses a hybrid theory of representative democracy as a standard for describing and evaluating the operation of provincial political systems[60] and finds them lacking. Canadians in all provinces demonstrate a minimum acceptable interest in the political process, but the authors feel that it could be enhanced by spreading the material and educational resources more evenly within and between provinces than at present. (The authors note that economic indicators have shown three classifications of province: the affluent, the moderately well-to-do, and the hard-pressed.) Parties' oligarchic nature and socio-economic selectivity are not conducive to long-term citizen participation in the electoral process. The ability of parties to perform representational functions is hindered by the single-member-plurality system which renders seat results incongruent with popular votes and fosters one-party dominance. This in turn freezes out the potential input into the system by opposition supporters and encourages long-term exclusive relationships between parties and interest groups. Bureaucracies have increased their influence in the era of the positive state, but are shielded from public accountability measures. There are institutional blockages to legislators enunciating and furthering the policy demands and needs of their constituents. Throughout the book, the authors note interprovincial differences—in party systems, socio-economic endowments, policy responsiveness (equitable sharing of resources)—but accord more importance to the common patterns of institutional and economic development. This allows them to posit a common need for improvement in representational democracy.

Steve Tomblin's *Ottawa and the Outer Provinces*, on the other hand, concentrates on the notion of regional integration and periphery provinces.[61] He is only partially optimistic about converging provincial policy. He reviews attempts at regional integration and finds that the only area of the country which is still considering the idea seriously is Atlantic Canada; but even here there is no "conservative monolith," and not much to support the popular view that economic and political development have been moving in a common direction. The Western provinces, and especially British Columbia and Alberta, have strongly resisted the idea of increased socio-economic or political union. The main reasons appear to be different province-building elite formations, the pull of larger North American economic regions, and the reluctance to share the comparative advantage of the provincial economy for no equivalent recompense.

Speaking of thematic reviews of institutions leads one to consider other contributions in the institutional vein. *Leaders and Parties in Canadian Politics: Experiences of the Provinces*, edited by Carty, Erickson, and Blake, focuses on the "hiring of new [political party] leaders and the firing of old ones." Similar to findings in the parties literature, the authors in the collection find a continued tendency to divergence; the leadership contests are different as a result of the distinctive provincial political cultures. Even some of the mechanics reveal continuing differences: in Québec and the Atlantic provinces, leadership votes in convention/membership reviews seldom go beyond one ballot, whereas most in Ontario take more than one ballot, with the Western provinces falling in between.[62]

A similarly focused thematic review is *In the Presence of Women: Representation in Canadian Governments*, edited by Arscott and Trimble.[63] The collection is a tightly-organized review by fourteen contributors who analyze women's participation and representation in the federal and provincial legislatures. It considers three levels of representation: getting elected, articulating issues and goals, and allocating resources between competing interests. The findings point away from convergence; the presence and impact of women vary widely between provinces. The opportunities for women to be elected hang on factors such as level of support for the NDP, increases in party competition, changes in party support, and electoral volatility. The success of women in articulating women's demands, and shifting resources towards causes like pay equity, maintenance support, and progressive labour standards depends on provincial political cultures, party ideologies affecting women, the location of representatives, and the belief systems of the women elected. The feminization of the legislatures appears to have gone furthest in B.C., Saskatchewan, Ontario (under Rae), Manitoba, and Québec, and been weakest in Alberta and the Atlantic provinces.[64]

"Global" Overviews of Provinces

Rand Dyck's reviews of provincial politics in Canada can be considered as a global, almost encyclopedic overview of the provincial scene.[65] His texts cover the full gamut of traditional political science concerns. Each chapter is devoted to coverage of a specific province and is done according to a standard template. Summarized are matters such as geography, economy, class, demographics, federal-provincial relations, political culture, party system, federal-provincial party links, party leadership, party ideology, electoral system, voting behaviour, pressure groups, the media, executive, legislature, bureaucracy, judiciary, municipal government, and the province's political evolution, covered decade by decade.

In his third edition, however, Dyck departs from what has largely been an emphasis on province-specific material and addresses the issue of convergence, of which he sees significant evidence. There is increasing similarity in governmental institutions, especially on a regional basis. Dyck reminds us that the Atlantic provinces have introduced a host of regional cooperation agreements in areas such as the economy, education, land registration, municipal training, geomatics, procurement, and environmental cooperation. Ontario and Québec, despite obvious differences, tend to stand as a cohesive entity on many fronts. The Prairie provinces have a penchant for direct democracy, cooperatives, progressive social policy, and polarized class politics, while eschewing formal intergovernmental ties, apart from the Prairie Economic Council.[66]

However, pan-Canadian provincial similarities started becoming even more pronounced than regional ones by the mid-1990s, Dyck says. On the institutional front, the provinces were reducing cabinet sizes, freezing legislative remuneration, reducing school board powers, and introducing the concept of regional health boards. In policy terms, the similarities were common obsessions with balanced budgets and expenditure reductions, public-sector wage freezes, health and social assistance cutbacks, training for welfare recipients, and exploitation of lottery revenues.[67]

CONCLUSION

One of the tasks of comparative politics is, of course, to compare, whether this be done explicitly or implicitly. This review has attempted to tease out some of the comparisons which are implicit in the literature or which, if explicit, tend to get buried in the multiple issues covered in a large and complex literature. We may note a tentative direction toward convergence revealed in the literature in a number of areas. Provinces are moving together in regards to their

- ability to rebalance relations with multinational corporations;
- citizens' concern for participation and democratization;
- level of expenditures;
- economic growth arising from federal transfers;
- province-building tendencies;
- institutional complexity, specialization, and decentralization (in the case of large provincial jurisdictions);
- political economies and policy issues arising from these; and
- tendencies toward a smaller state: smaller budgets, cabinets, legislative salaries, social assistance levels and school boards.

On the other hand, perhaps because federalism protects political careers and provides incentives to enhance the subjective elements of provincial identities, convergence has not been evident in the way provinces reflect their particular

- party systems;
- political cultures;
- opportunities for women in the political sphere; and
- orientations towards regional integration.

The preceding observations must be tinged with a heavy note of caution. The field has seen some major advances since Canadian political scientists awoke to the growing importance of provinces and to the need to understand them. Yet a quick review of literature will find many gaps and tentative steps. The experience to date is important not so much for concrete "lessons" as for a series of tentative hypotheses that have emerged and which beg further research. These hypotheses can be expressed in the following terms:

1. Provincial governments by themselves have the ability to overcome the asymmetries of power and knowledge in bargaining with multi-

national corporations in matters of large-scale economic development.

2. Citizen concern with decentralization and participation owes its origins to historical experiments in plebiscitarian democracy conducted in the provinces, and such concern acts as a counter to conservative province-building.
3. Province-building is a phenomenon unique to the postwar period.
4. Province-building grows from the self-interest of identifiable actors such as class fractions, provincial political elites, and senior bureaucrats.
5. Provincial party systems are relatively immune to convergence, and retain their basic patterns decade after decade.
6. Provincial political cultures differ or do not differ with regard to the indicators of trust and efficacy.
7. The nature of provincial political culture derives from the stage of economic development that the province has undergone.
8. The nature of the provincial political culture derives from the nature of its founding immigrant culture(s)/staple history/formative events.
9. The provincial political economies are all basically similar, dominated by the service sector, a factor which has homogenizing potential for policy agendas and policy outcomes.
10. Public policy configurations are not moving in the direction of convergence because "politics matters." That is, interprovincial policy differences exist and are due to the presence of left-wing parties, party competition, and governmental institutionalization.
11. Provincial institutions are becoming increasingly similar in their structure and operation.
12. Provincial public policies, in a functional sense, are becoming increasingly similar.
13. Regional intergovernmental agreements are resulting in a homogenization of the public policies to which they attend.
14. Provinces have systematically ignored improving the quality and extent of representational democracy.

Such is the present utility of the comparative provincial exercise: to pose some interesting questions. That many of the questions have yet to be answered is, in a sense, useful. It gives a new generation of political scientists a program of study. Let us hope they adopt it.

SELECTED BIBLIOGRAPHY: COMPARATIVE PROVINCIAL POLITICS

General

Brownsey, Keith, and Michael Howlett, eds., *The Provincial State: Politics in Canada's Provinces and Territories.* Toronto: Copp Clark Pitman, 1992.

Cairns, Alan C. "The Study of the Provinces: A Review Article." *B.C. Studies* 16 (1972): 73-82.

Dunn, Christopher. *Provinces: Canadian Provincial Politics.* Peterborough: Broadview Press, 1996.

Dyck, Rand. *Provincial Politics in Canada.* Toronto: Nelson, 1996.

Elkins, David J., and Richard Simeon, *Small Worlds: Provinces and Parties in Canadian Political Life.* Toronto: Methuen, 1980.

Gibbins, Roger. *Prairie Politics and Society.* Toronto: Butterworths, 1980.

Kornberg, Alan, William Mischler, and Harold D. Clarke. *Representative Democracy in the Canadian Provinces* (Scarborough: Prentice Hall Canada, 1982).

Pal, Leslie, and David Taras, eds. *Prime Ministers and Premiers: Political Leadership and Public Policy in Canada.* Scarborough, Ont.: Prentice Hall Canada, 1988.

Read, J.E. "The Early Provincial Constitutions." *Canadian Bar Review* XXVI:4 (April 1948). 621-37.

Robin, Martin. *Canadian Provincial Politics: The Party Systems of the Ten Provinces.* Scarborough: Prentice Hall, 1978.

Wiktor, Christian L., and Guy Tanguay. *Constitutions of Canada, Federal and Provincial = Les constitutions du Canada, fédérales et provinciales.* Dobbs Ferry, NY: Oceana Publications, 1978.

Comparative Provincial Political Cultures

Beck, J. Murray. "An Atlantic Region Political Culture: A Chimera." *Eastern and Western Perspectives.* Ed. D.J. Bercuson and P.A. Buckner. Toronto: University of Toronto Press, 1981. 147-68.

Bell, David V.J. "Political Culture in Canada." *Canadian Politics in the 1990s.* Ed. Michael Whittington and Glen Williams. 4th ed. Scarborough: Nelson, 1995. 115-74.

Bellamy, David. "The Atlantic Provinces." *The Provincial Political Systems: Comparative Essays.* Ed. David Bellamy, Jon Pammett, and Donald C. Rowat. Toronto: Methuen, 1976. 3-18.

Chandler, Marsha A., and William M. Chandler. *Public Policy and Provincial Politics.* Toronto: McGraw-Hill Ryerson, 1979.

Finbow, Robert, "Dependents or Dissidents? The Atlantic Provinces in Canada's Constitutional Reform Process, 1967-1992." *Canadian Journal of Political Science/Revue Canadienne de Science Politique* 27:3 (September 1991). 465-91.

Laycock, David. *Populism and Democratic Thought in the Prairies, 1910-1945.* Toronto: University of Toronto Press, 1989.

Morton, W.L. "The Bias of Prairie Politics." *Historical Essays on the Prairie Provinces.* Ed. Donald Swainson. Toronto: McClelland and Stewart, 1970.

Noel, S.J.R. "Leadership and Clientelism." Bellamy, *et al.* 197-213.

Simeon, Richard, and David Elkins. "Provincial Political Cultures in Canada." Simeon and Elkins 31-70.

Simeon, Richard, and David Elkins. "Regional Political Cultures in Canada." Elkins and Simeon 15-52.

Simeon, Richard, and David J. Elkins. "Regional Political Cultures in Canada." *Canadian Journal of Political Science* 7 (1974): 397-437.

Simpson, Jeffrey. *Spoils of Power*. Toronto: Collins, 1988.

Stewart, Ian. *Roasting Chestnuts: The Mythology of Maritime Political Culture*. Vancouver: University of British Columbia Press, 1994.

Stewart, Ian. "All the King's Horses: A The Study of Canadian Political Culture." *Canadian Politics: An Introduction*. Ed. Alain G. Gagnon and James P. Bickerton. Peterborough: Broadview, 1990. 75-92.

Stewart, Ian. "More than Just a Line on the Map: The Political Culture of the Nova Scotia-New Brunswick Boundary." *Publius* 20:1 (Winter 1990). 99-112

Wilson, John M. "The Canadian Political Cultures: Towards a Redefinition of the Nature of the Canadian Political Systems," *Canadian Journal of Political Science* 7:3 (September 1974). 438-83.

Wiseman, Nelson. "The Pattern of Prairie Leadership." *Prime Ministers and Premiers*. Ed. Leslie Pal and David Taras. Scarborough: Prentice Hall, 1988. 178-91.

Young, R.A. "Teaching and Research in Maritime Politics: Old Stereotypes and New Directions." *Journal of Canadian Studies* 21:2 (1986): 133-156.

Party and Electoral Systems

Brodie, M.J., and Jane Jenson, *Crisis, Challenge and Change: Party and Class in Canada*. Toronto: Methuen, 1980; 2nd ed. Ottawa: Carleton University Press, 1988.

Cross, Bill. "Direct Election of Party Leaders: Provincial Experiences and Lessons Learned." Canadian Political Science Association Annual General Meeting. University of Calgary. Calgary: 1994.

Dyck, Rand. "Relations Between Federal and Provincial Parties." *Canadian Parties in Transition*. Ed. A.C. Gagnon and A.B. Tanguay. Scarborough: Nelson Canada, 1989. 186-219.

Jenson, Jane. "Party Systems." Bellamy, *et al.* 57-72.

MacDonald, Donald C. "Election Finances Legislation in Canada." *Party Politics in Canada*. Ed. Hugh Thorburn. 6th ed. Scarborough: Prentice Hall, 1991. 68-79.

Jon Pammett. "Class Voting and Class Consciousness in Canada." *Canadian Review of Sociology and Anthropology* 24:2 (1987). 269-90.

Seidle, F. Leslie, ed. *Provincial Party and Election finance in Canada*. Royal Commission on Electoral Reform and Party Financing. Ottawa: Supply and Services Canada. 1991.

Smith, P.J., and M.W. Conley. "Empty Harbours, Empty Dreams: The Democratic Socialist Tradition in Atlantic Canada." *Building the Co-operative Commonwealth: Essays on the Democratic Socialist Tradition in Canada*. Ed. J.W. Brennan. Regina: Canadian Plains Research Centre, 1984. 227-51.

Executives

Carty, R. Kenneth, Lynda Erickson and Donald E. Blake, eds. *Leaders and Parties in Canadian Politics: Experiences of the Provinces*. Toronto: Harcourt Brace Jovanovich, 1992.

Dunn, Christopher. *The Institutionalized Cabinet: Governing the Western Provinces*. Montreal and Kingston: McGill-Queen's University Press, 1995.

—. "Changing the Design: Cabinet Decision-Making in Three Provincial Governments." *Canadian Public Administration* XXXIV (Winter, 1991): 621-40.

Elkins, David J. and Richard Simeon, ed. *Small Worlds: Provinces and Parties in Canadian Political Life*. Toronto: Methuen, 1980.

Latouche, Daniel. "From Premier to Prime Minister: Leadership, State and Society in Quebec." Pal and Taras. 137-57.

Loreto, Richard A. and Graham White, "The Premier and the Cabinet."*The Government and Politics of Ontario*. ed. G. White. 4th ed. Scarborough: Nelson, 1990. 79-102.

Pal, Leslie A. "The Political Executive and Political Leadership in Alberta." *Government and Politics in Alberta*. Ed. Allan Tupper and Roger Gibbins. Edmonton: University of Alberta Press, 1992. 1-30.

Savoie, Donald. ed. *Taking Power: Managing Government Transitions.* Toronto: Institute of Public Administration of Canada, 1993.

Smith, Jennifer. "Ruling Small Worlds: Political Leadership in Atlantic Canada." Pal and Taras 126-36.

White, Graham. "Big is Different than Little: On Taking Size Seriously in the Analysis of Canadian Governmental Institutions. *Canadian Public Administration* 33 (1990). 526-50.

Legislatures

Atkinson, Michael, and Graham White. "The Development of Provincial Legislatures." *Parliament, Policy and Representation*. Ed. H.D. Clarke, *et al.* Toronto: Methuen, 1980. 255-75.

Barnes, Emery. "The Size of Legislatures: Perspectives on Provincial Assemblies." *Canadian Parliamentary Review* 18:1 (1995): 2-8.

Englemann, Frederick. "The Legislature." Tupper and Gibbins 137-66.

Fleming, R.J. *Canadian Legislatures 1992*. Agincourt: Global Press, 1992.

Kitchin, G.W. "The Abolition of Upper Chambers." *Provincial Government and Politics*. Ed. D.C. Rowat. Ottawa: Carleton University, 1973. 74-79.

Levy, Gary, and Graham White. "Introduction: The Comparative Analysis of Canadian Provincial and Territorial Legislatures." *Provincial and Territorial Assemblies in Canada*. Ed. Gary Levy and Graham White. Toronto: University of Toronto Press, 1989. 1-12.

Moncrief, Gary. "Professionalism and Careerism in Canadian Provincial Assemblies: Comparisons to U.S. State Legislatures." *Legislative Studies Quarterly* 19:1 (1994): 33-48.

—. "Professionalization and Careerism in Canadian Provincial Assemblies." *Legislative Studies Quarterly* XIX (February 1994): 33-48.

Pasis, Harvey E. "The Inequality of Distribution in the Canadian Provincial Assemblies." *Canadian Journal of Political Science* 5:3 (1972): 433-36.

Smith, David. "Saskatchewan: Approximating the Ideal." Levy and White 47-67.

Stewart, Ian. "Prince Edward Island: 'A Damned Queer Parliament.' Levy and White 13-28.

White, Graham. "The Legislature: Influence Not Power." Levy and White 63-78.

Public Services

Dion, Stephane, J.I. Gow, and J. Bourgault. "Evolution of the Role of Central Agencies in the Quebec Government 1960-1990," *Quebec: State and Society*. Ed. Alain-G. Gagnon. 2nd ed. Toronto: Nelson, 1993. 224-42.

Hodgetts, J.E., and O.P. Dwivedi. *Provincial Governments as Employers.* Montreal: McGill-Queen's University Press, 1974.

—. "Administration and Personnel." Bellamy *et al.* 341-56.

Jamieson, E.G. "Provincial Employees." Rowat 210-26.

Lindquist, Evert A., and Karen B. Murray. "A Reconnaissance of Canadian Administrative Reform During the Early 1990s." *Canadian Public Administration* 37 (Fall, 1994): 468-89.

Lindquist, Evert, and Graham White. "Streams, Springs and Stones: Ontario Public Service Reform in the 1980s and 1990s." *Canadian Public Administration* 37 (Summer, 1994)" 267-301.

Love, J.D. "The Merit Principle in the Provincial Governments of Atlantic Canada." *Canadian Public Administration 31* (Fall, 1988): 335-51.

Stanbury, W.T. "Controlling the Growth of Provincial Governments: The Role of Privatization." *Provincial Public Finances: Plaudits, Problems and Prospects*. Vol 2. Ed. Melville McMillan. Toronto: Canadian Tax Foundation, 1991. 371-402.

Public Policy

Blais, A., J.M. Cousineau,and K. McRoberts. "The Determinants of Minimum Wage Rates." *Public Choice* 62 (1989): 15-24.

Boychuk, Gerald. "Comparative Provincial Assistance Regimes: Towards a Political Economy of the Canadian Welfare State." Canadian Political Science Association Annual General Meeting. University of Calgary. Calgary: June 1994.

Chandler, Marsha A. "The Politics of Provincial Resource Policy." *The Politics of Canadian Public Policy*. Ed. Michael Atkinson and Marsha Chandler. Toronto: University of Toronto Press, 1983.

—. "State Enterprise and Partisanship in Provincial Politics." *Canadian Journal of Political Science* (December 1982). 711-40.

Chandler, Marsha, and William Chandler. *Public Policy and Provincial Politics*. Toronto: McGraw-Hill Ryerson, 1979.

Chandler, William. "Canadian Socialism and Policy Impact: Contagion from the Left?" *Canadian Journal of Political Science* (December 1977): 755-80.

Falcone, D., and W. Mishler. "Legislative Determinants of Provincial Health Policy in Canada: A Diachronic Analysis." *Journal of Politics* 39 (1977): 345-67.

Gow, James Iain. *Learning from Others: Administrative Innovations Among Canadian Governments*. Toronto: Institute of Public Administration of Canada, 1994.

Hardin, Herschel. *The Privatization Putsch*. Halifax: Institute for Research on Public Policy, 1989.

Howe, Brian. "Human Rights in Hard Times: The Post-war Canadian Experience." *Canadian Public Administration* 35:4 (Winter 1992): 464-533.

Hurley, Jeremiah, Jonathan Lomas, and Vandna Bhatia. "When Tinkering is not Enough: Provincial Reform to Manage Health Care Resources." *Canadian Public Administration* 37 (Fall 1994): 490-514.

Jones, L.R. "Coping with Revenue and Expenditure Restraints in the Provincial Government Context." *Canadian Public Administration* 29:4 (Winter 1986): 525-41.

—."Financial Restraint Management and Budget Control in Canadian Provincial Governments." *Canadian Public Administration* 29:2 (Summer 1986): 259-81.

Kneebone, Ronald D. "Deficits and Debt in Canada: Some Lessons from Recent History." *Canadian Public Policy* 20:2 (1994): 152-64.

Liveo di Matteo. "Fiscal Centralization at the Provincial-Local Level in Canada, 1961-1991." *Canadian Tax Journal* 43:3 (1995): 639-59.

McAllister, J.A. "Fiscal Capacity and Tax Effort: Explaining Public Expenditures in the 10 Canadian Provinces." Canadian Political Science Association, Annual General Meeting, June 1984.

McCormick, Peter. *Canada's Courts*. Toronto: Lorimer, 1994.

Michas, N.A. "Variations in the Level of Provincial Municipal Expenditures in Canada: An Econometric Analysis." *Public Finance* 24 (1969): 597-613.

Mishler, W., and D.B. Campbell. "The Healthy State: Legislative Responsiveness to Public Health Care Needs in Canada, 1920-1970." *Comparative Politics* 10:4 (July 1978): 479-97.

Molot, M.A. "The Provinces and Privatization: Are the Provinces Really Getting Out of Business?" Canadian Political Science Association Annual General Meeting. McMaster University. Hamilton: June 1987.

Molot, M.A., and J.K. Laux. "The Politics of Nationalization." *Canadian Journal of Political Science* 12:2 (June 1979): 227-58.

Pitsula, J.M., and Ken Rasmussen. *Privatizing a Province*. Vancouver: New Star Books, 1990.

Poel, Dale. "The Diffusion of Legislation among the Canadian Provinces: A Statistical Analysis." *Canadian Journal of Political Science* 9:4 (December 1976): 605-26.

Richards, John, and Larry Pratt. *Prairie Capitalism: Power and Influence in the New West*. Toronto: McClelland and Stewart, 1979.

Thorburn, Hugh. *Planning and the Economy*. Toronto: Canadian Institute for Economic Policy, 1984.

Tupper, Allan, and G.B. Doern. eds. *Public Corporations and Public Policy in Canada*. Montreal: Institute for Research on Public Policy, 1981.

Vining, A.R. "Provincial Hydro-Utilities." Tupper and Doern 149-88.

Vining, A.R., and R. Botterell. "An Overview of the Origins, Growth, Size and Functions of Provincial Crown Corporations" *Crown Corporations in Canada: the Calculus of Instrument Choice*. Ed. J.R.S. Prichard. Toronto: Butterworths, 1983. 303-67.

Winfield, Mark. "The Ultimate Horizontal Issue: The Environmental Policy Experiences of Alberta and Ontario, 1971-1993." *Canadian Journal of Political Science* 27 (March 1994): 129-52.

Intergovernmental Relations

Bercuson, David, and Barry Cooper. *Deconfederation: Canada Without Quebec*. Toronto: Key Porter Books, 1991.

Boothe, Paul. *Closing the Books: Dividing Federal Assets and Debt If Canada Breaks Up*. Vancouver: Fraser Institute, 1991.

Dalhousie University, Halifax, Nova Scotia Institute of Public Affairs. *Interprovincial Relations in the Maritime Provinces*. Ed. Richard H. Leach. Fredricton, NB: Institute of Public Affairs, 1970.

Day, Douglas. "Marine Boundaries, Jurisdictional Disputes, and Offshore Hydrocarbon Exploration in Eastern Canada." *Journal of Canadian Studies* (Fall 1988): 60-89.

Gartner, Gerry J. "A Review of Cooperation Among Western Provinces." *Canadian Public Administration* 20 (1977): 174-87.

Lightbody, James. *Canadian Metropolitics: Governing Our Cities*. Toronto: Copp Clark, 1995.

Tindal, Richard C., and Susan Nobes Tindal. *Local Government in Canada*. 4th ed. Toronto: McGraw-Hill Ryerson, 1995.

Tomblin, Stephen G. "The Council of Maritime Premiers: Is It Promoting the Integration of Government Services in the Maritimes?" M.A. diss. Dalhousie University, 1979

Province-Building

Black, E.R.,and A.C. Cairns. "A Different Perspective on Canadian Federalism." *Canadian Public Administration* 9:1 (1966): 27-44.

McMillan, M.L., and Kenneth H. Norrie. "Province-Building versus a Rentier Society." *Canadian Public Policy* 6 Supplement (February 1980): 27-34.

Young, R.A., Philippe Faucher, and André Blais, "The Concept of Province-Building: A Critique." *Canadian Journal of Political Science* 17:4 (December 1984): 783-818.

NOTES

1 Alan Cairns, "The Study of the Provinces: A Review Article," *B.C. Studies* 14 (Summer 1972): 73-82 at 76.

2 If one reviews the number of political scientists listing "Canadian Politics" as their "subject specialization" in the 1996 CPSA *Directory of Political Scientists in Canada*, one finds about 550. By contrast, if one adds up all those listing "Western Canada" (around 150), "Ontario" (150), "Québec" (200), "Atlantic Canada" (50), "Northwest Territories" and "Yukon" (15), in the "List by Geographical Specialization," one sees that the numbers are essentially the same. Of course, not all the provincial scholars are comparativists, but the numbers indicate a certain passivity.

3 Lee Sigelman and George H. Gadbois, "Contemporary Comparative Politics: An Inventory and Assessment," *Contemporary Political Studies* 16:3 (1983): 301.

4 Richard Rose, "Comparing Forms of Comparative Analysis," *Political Studies* 39 (1991): 454.

5 Alexis de Tocqueville, Democracy in America, Vol. 1 (New York: Vintage Books, 1954), 14.

6 See for example Arend Lijphart, *Democracy in Plural Societies: A Comparative Exploration* (New Haven, CT: Yale UP, 1977); *Democracies: Patterns of Majoritarian and Consensus Government in Twenty-One Countries* (New Haven: Yale UP, 1984).

7 Mattei Dogan and Dominique Pelassy, *How to Compare Nations: Strategies in Comparative Politics*, 2nd ed. (Chatham, NJ: Chatham House Publishers, 1990), 120-21.

8 Dogan and Pelassy, *How to Compare Nations*, 163-67 at 167.

9 Edward C. Page, "Comparative Public Administration in Britain," *Public Administration* 73 (1995): 131.

10 Rose, "Comparing Forms of Comparative Analysis," 456.

11 Rose, "Comparing Forms of Comparative Analysis," 457.

12 Alvin Finkel, *The Social Credit Phenomenon in Alberta* (Toronto: University of Toronto Press, 1989), 6.

13 C.B. Macpherson, *Democracy in Alberta: Social Credit and the Party System*, 2nd ed. (Toronto: University of Toronto Press, 1962), 239.

14 Macpherson, *Democracy in Alberta*, 249.

15 John Richards and Larry Pratt, *Prairie Capitalism: Power and Influence in the New West* (Toronto: McClelland and Stewart, 1979).

16 Richards and Pratt, *Prairie Capitalism*, 9.

17 Richards and Pratt, *Prairie Capitalism*, 328.

18 David Laycock, *Populism and Democratic Thought on the Canadian Prairies, 1910 to 1945* (Toronto: University of Toronto Press, 1989), 297-98.

19 Louis M. Imbeau and Guy Lachapelle, "Comparative Public Policy in Canada," *Provinces: Canadian Provincial Politics*, ed. Christopher Dunn (Peterborough: Broadview Press, 1996), 401-22.

20 Edwin R. Black and Alan C. Cairns, "A Different Perspective on Canadian Federalism," *Canadian Federalism: Myth or Reality*, ed. Peter J. Meekison (Toronto: Methuen, 1971), 95.

21 Black and Cairns, "A Different Perspective," 93-98.

22 Black and Cairns, "A Different Perspective," 96-97.

23 Alan C. Cairns, "The Governments and Societies of Canadian Federalism," *Canadian Journal of Political Science* 10:4 (December 1977).

24 Cairns, "Governments and Societies," 706.

25 Garth Stevenson, *Unfulfilled Union: Canadian Federalism and National Unity* (Toronto: Gage, 1979), 82.

26 Stevenson, *Unfulfilled Union*, 103-04.

27 Stevenson, *Unfulfilled Union*, 96-101. Stevenson wrote that the political economy of Canadian provinces consisted of three dominant sectors. The resource sector predominated in Alberta, British Columbia, and Newfoundland; the manufacturing sector was American-based and concentrated in Ontario; and the agricultural sector, once significant, has declined in all provinces. The federal government was the protector of tariff-based Canadian-owned industries in Québec, Ontario, Manitoba, and the Maritimes, and of chartered banks and life-insurance companies.

28 Garth Stevenson, "Federalism and the Political Economy of the Provincial State," *The Canadian State: Political Economy and Political Power*, ed. Leo Panitch (Toronto: University of Toronto Press, 1977). The book by O'Connor upon which much of the analysis is based is *The Fiscal Crisis of the State* (New York, 1973). The accumulation concept refers to governmental aid of entrepreneurial activity, and the legitimation function to assurance of welfarestate social harmony.

29 Stevenson, "Federalism and the Political Economy," 89.

30 Judith Maxwell and Carole Pestieau, *Economic Realities of Contemporary Confederation* (Montreal: C.D. Howe Research Institute, 1980), chap. 6.

31 Maxwell and Pestieau, *Economic Realities*, 83-84.

32 Maxwell and Pestieau, *Economic Realities*, 91.

33 R.A. Young, Phillippe Faucher, and André Blais, "The Concept of Province-Building: A Critique," *Perspectives on Canadian Federalism*, ed. R.D. Olling and M.W. Westmacott (Scarborough: Prentice Hall, 1988), 136-63.

34 Graham White, "Big is Different than Little: on taking size seriously in the analysis of Canadian governmental institutions," *Canadian Public Administration* 33:4 (Winter 1990): 526-50. White does not ignore the possibility that factors other than size may affect the operation of institutions, only that size thresholds—big, small—are obviously important and need more attention.

35 John Wilson, "The Canadian Political Cultures: Towards a Redefinition of the Nature of the Canadian Political System," *Politics Canada*, 4th ed., ed. Paul Fox (Toronto: McGraw-Hill Ryerson, 1977), 316-37, at 318-20.

36 Marsha Chandler and William M. Chandler, *Public Policy and Provincial Politics* (Toronto: McGraw-Hill Ryerson, 1979), 54-66.

37 Peter McCormick, "Provincial Party System, 1945-1993," *Canadian Parties in Transition*, 2nd ed., ed. A. Brian Tanguay and Alain-G. Gagnon (Toronto: Nelson Canada, 1996), 349-71.

38 R.K. Carty and David Stewart, "Parties and Party Systems," *Provinces*, ed. Dunn, 63-94 at 78.

39 David K. Stewart, "Comparing Party Systems in the Canadian Provinces and the Australian States," *Parties and Federalism in Australia and Canada*, ed. Campbell Sharman (Canberra: ANU, 1994), 186-210.

40 Rand Dyck, *Provincial Politics in Canada: Towards the Turn of the Century* (Scarborough: Prentice Hall, 1996), 649-50.

41 John Wilson, "Canadian Political Cultures."

42 Jane Jenson, "Party Systems," *The Provincial Political Systems*, ed. David Bellamy, *et al.* (Toronto: Methuen, 1976), 118-31.

43 S.J.R. Noel, "Leadership and Clientelism," *Provincial Political Systems*, ed. Bellamy, *et al.*, 197-213.

44 Richard Simeon and David J. Elkins, "Provincial Political Cultures in Canada," *Small Worlds: Provinces and Parties in Canadian Political Life*, ed. David J. Elkins and Richard Simeon (Toronto: Methuen, 1980), 31-76.

45 Nelson Wiseman, "Provincial Political Cultures," *Provinces*, ed. Dunn, 21-62.

46 Roger Gibbons, *Prairie Politics and Society: Regionalism in Decline* (Toronto: Butterworths, 1980), 197.

47 Ian Stewart, *Roasting Chestnuts: The Mythology of Maritime Political Culture* (Vancouver: UBC Press, 1994), chap. 2.

48 David J. Bellamy, Jon H. Pammett and Donald C. Rowat, eds., *The Provincial Political Systems: Comparative Essays* (Toronto: Methuen, 1976), "Preface."

49 A. Paul Pross, "Pressure Groups," *Provincial Political Systems*, ed. Bellamy, *et al.*, 142-43.

50 Andrue Anstett and Terence Qualter, "Election Systems," *Provincial Political Systems*, ed. Bellamy, *et al.*, 147-60.

51 William M. Chandler and Marsha A. Chandler, "Policy Trends," Bellamy *et al.*, *Provincial Political Systems*, 237-54.

52 Ken Bryden, "Cabinets," *Provincial Political Systems*, ed. Bellamy, *et al.*, 310-22.

53 John C. Courtney and David E. Smith, "Saskatchewan: Parties in a Politically Competitive Province," *Canadian Provincial Politics: The Party Systems of the Ten Provinces*, ed. Martin Robin (Scarborough: Prentice Hall, 1978), 300-02.

54 Christopher Dunn, *Provinces: Canadian Provincial Politics* (Peterborough: Broadview Press, 1996).

55 Michael Howlett, "DeMythologizing Provincial Political Economies: The Development of the Service Sectors in the Provinces, 1911-1991," *Provinces*, ed. Dunn, 423-48.

56 Graham White, "Comparing Provincial Legislatures," *Provinces*, ed. Dunn, 225.

57 Carl Baar, "Court Systems of the Provinces," *Provinces*, ed. Dunn, 229-52.

58 Joan Boase, "Trends in Social Policy: Towards the Millennium," *Provinces*, ed. Dunn, 449-77.

59 Louis M. Imbeau and Guy Lachapelle, "Comparative Provincial Public Policy in Canada," *Provinces*, ed. Dunn, 401-22.

60 Allan Kornberg, William Mishler, and Harold D. Clarke, *Representative Democracy in the Canadian Provinces* (Scarborough: Prentice Hall 1982).

61 Stephen G. Tomblin, *Ottawa and the Outer Provinces: The Challenge of Regional Integration in the Provinces* (Toronto: Lorimer, 1995), 107.

62 R.K. Carty, Lynda Erickson, and Donald E. Blake, eds., *Leaders and Parties in Canadian Politics: Experiences of the Provinces* (Toronto: Harcourt Brace Jovanovich, 1992), "Introduction," 6.

63 Jane Arscott and Linda Trimble, eds., *In the Presence of Women: Representation in Canadian Governments* (Toronto: Harcourt Brace and Company, 1997).

64 Jane Arscott and Linda Trimble, "In the Presence of Women: Representation and Political Power," *In the Presence of Women*, 117.

65 Dyck, *Provincial Politics in Canada*.

66 Dyck, *Provincial Politics in Canada*, 653-55.

67 Dyck, *Provincial Politics in Canada*, 655.

CONTRIBUTORS

GREGORY ALBO is an associate professor of political science at York University. An editor of *Studies in Political Economy*, he has written on a wide range of issues in Canadian political economy, with a focus on issues of unions and work.

LUC BERNIER is professor of public policy at l'Ecole nationale d'administration publique (Université du Québec). He taught for two years at Concordia University after finishing his Ph.D. in political science at Northwestern University. He is the author of several articles and chapters on Quebec politics, public policies and public administration including *The Quebec Democracy* with Guy Lachapelle, Gerald Bernier and Daniel Salee, of *L'Administration publique* with Carolle Simard. In 1996, he published *De Paris à Washington: la politique internationale du Québec* (Sainte-Foy: PUQ). His research interests are administrative reform, privatization and the development of the Quebec state.

JAMES BICKERTON is professor of political science at St. Francis Xavier University. His recent publications have been in the areas of parties and elections, regional political economy and Nova Scotia politics. He is the author of *Nova Scotia, Ottawa and the Politics of Regional Development*, co-author of *The Almanac of Canadian Politics*, and co-editor of *Canadian Politics*.

KEITH BROWNSEY teaches political science at Mount Royal College in Calgary. He is the author of several articles on provincial politics and government. He is also the editor of *Reinventing Political Parties*.

PETER CLANCY is professor of political science at St. Francis Xavier University. His research and teaching interests include the Canadian North, the politics of resource management, and business-government relations. He is the author of a number of articles on the politics of Canada's North.

CHRISTOPHER DUNN is an associate professor of political science at Memorial University of Newfoundland, St. John's. His teaching and research interests include Canadian federal and provincial politics, the Constitution, public policy, and public administration. He is the author of *The Institutionalized Cabinet: Governing the Western Provinces* and *Canadian Political Debates: Opposing Views on Issues that Divide Canadians*, and the editor of *Provinces: Canadian Provincial Politics.*

JACK HICKS served as the Nunavut Implementation Commission's Director of Research. He lives in Iqaluit, where he works for the territorial government.

MICHAEL HOWLETT is professor in the department of political science, Simon Fraser University. He is the author of numerous articles and books focussing on public policy, Canadian resource and environmental policy, and Canadian political economy.

ROBERT MACDERMID is an associate professor of political science at York University. He writes on Canadian and Ontario politics with a focus on elections and campaigning.

FLOYD McCORMICK is an adjunct instructor in political science at Yukon College, Whitehorse. His research interests include government and politics in the Yukon, and aboriginal rights and self-government.

HUGH MELLON teaches at King's College, University of Western Ontario. He is the author of various articles focusing on public administration, federalism, and education policy. He is the co-editor of collections on Canadian federalism and Canadian public administration and public policy.

DAVID MILNE has recently retired from the University of Prince Edward island. Currently teaching abroad, he continues his interest in Canadian federalism. He is the author of *The Canadian Constitution* and *Tug of War: Ottawa and the Provinces under Trudeau and Mulroney.*

ALEX NETHERTON is a political scientist teaching in the department of political science and the Centre for Canadian Studies at Simon Fraser University. He is a research associate of the Institute of Governance Studies, Simon Fraser University. He has published several articles on electrical energy policy paradigms, Canada-U.S. relations, and comparative social democracy.

KEN RASMUSSEN is an associate professor of public administration at the University of Regina. He has a Ph.D. in political science from the University of Toronto and is the author of numerous articles on public administration. He is the co-author of *Privatizing a Province: The New Right in Saskatchewan* and *Social Democracy in the 1990s: The NDP in Saskatchewan.*

PETER JAY SMITH is professor and chair of the Centre for State and Legal Studies at Athabasca University. He has written a number of articles on Alberta public policy and political economy.

VALERIE SUMMERS is an associate professor in the department of political science at Memorial University of Newfoundland. Her areas of teaching and research include Newfoundland political economy, Canadian politics, and women and politics. She is the author of *Regime Change in a Resource Economy: the Politics of Underdevelopment in Newfoundland since 1825.*

GRAHAM WHITE is professor of political science at the University of Toronto at Mississauga. His most recent books are *Northern Government in Transition* and *Government and Politics of Ontario*, 5th ed.

INDEX